MASTERPIECES OF FRENCH PAINTING

LES CHEFS-D'ŒUVRE DE LA PEINTURE FRANÇAISE

MEISTERWERKE DER FRANZÖSISCHEN MALEREI

LAS OBRAS MAESTRAS DE LA PINTURA FRANCESA

I CAPOLAVORI DELLA PITTURA FRANCESE

MEESTERWERKEN UIT DE FRANSE SCHILDERKUNST

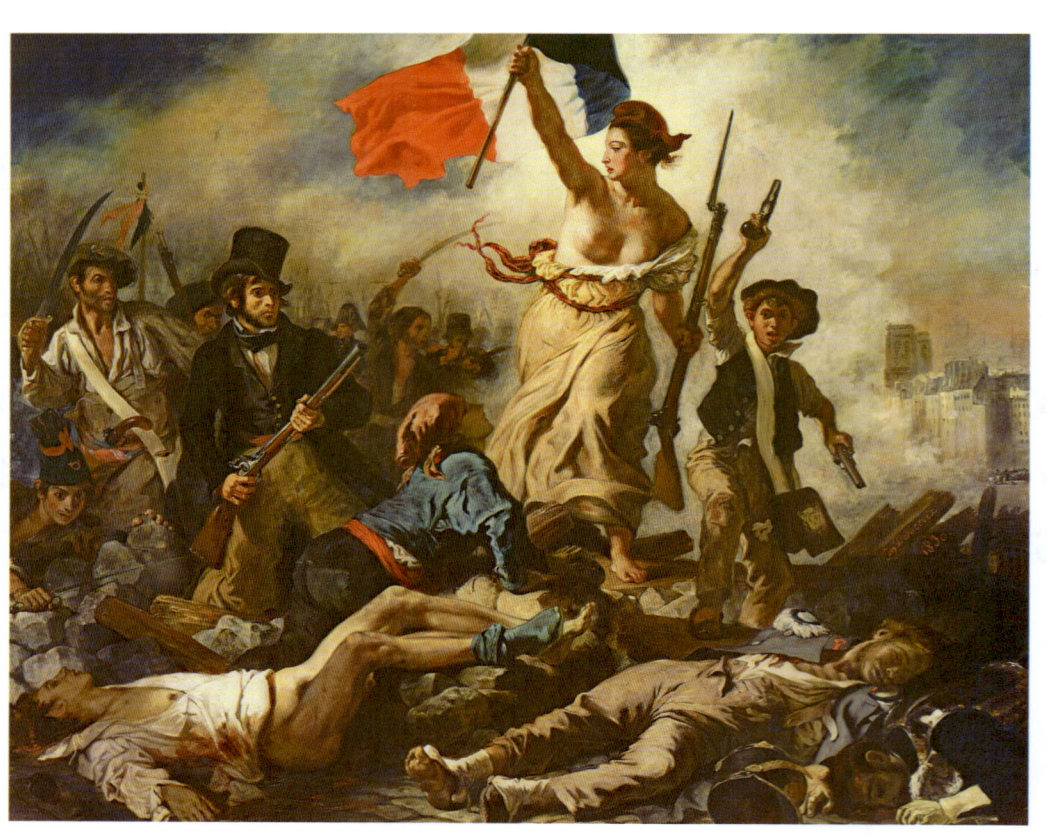

HAJO DÜCHTING

MASTERPIECES OF FRENCH PAINTING
LES CHEFS-D'ŒUVRE DE LA PEINTURE FRANÇAISE
MEISTERWERKE DER FRANZÖSISCHEN MALEREI
LAS OBRAS MAESTRAS DE LA PINTURA FRANCESA
I CAPOLAVORI DELLA PITTURA FRANCESE
MEESTERWERKEN UIT DE FRANSE SCHILDERKUNST

p. 2

Eugène Delacroix (1798–1863)

Liberty Leading the People (28 July 1830)

La Liberté guidant le peuple (28 juillet 1830)

Die Freiheit führt das Volk an (28. Juli 1830)

La Libertad guiando al pueblo (28 de julio de 1830)

La libertà che guida il popolo (28 luglio 1830)

De vrijheid voor het volk (28 juli 1830)

1830–1831, Oil on canvas/Huile sur toile, 260 × 325 cm, Musée du Louvre, Paris

KÖNEMANN
© 2016 koenemann.com GmbH
www.koenemann.com

ÉDITIONS
PLACE DES
VICTOIRES

© Éditions Place des Victoires
6, rue du Mail – 75002 Paris
www.victoires.com
Dépôt légal : 4ᵉ trimestre 2016
ISBN: 978-2-8099-1340-8

Concept, Project Management: koenemann.com GmbH
Text: Hajo Düchting

Translations: David Nash (English), Denis-Armand Canal (French text),
Virginie de Bermond-Gettle (French captions)

Spanish, Italian and Dutch translation:
✗ TEXTCASE Translation Agency
info@textcase.nl
textcase.de   textcase.eu

Art Direction: Oliver Hessmann
Layout: Christoph Eiden
Picture credits: Bridgeman Images, akg-images gmbh (pp. 30, 32, 41)

ISBN: 978-3-95588-080-4 (GB)
       978-3-7419-1836-0 (D)
       978-3-95588-079-8 (E)
       978-3-95588-525-0 (I)
       978-3-7419-0994-8 (NL)

Printed in Spain by Liberdúplex

Contents   Sommaire   Inhalt   Índice   Indice   Inhoud

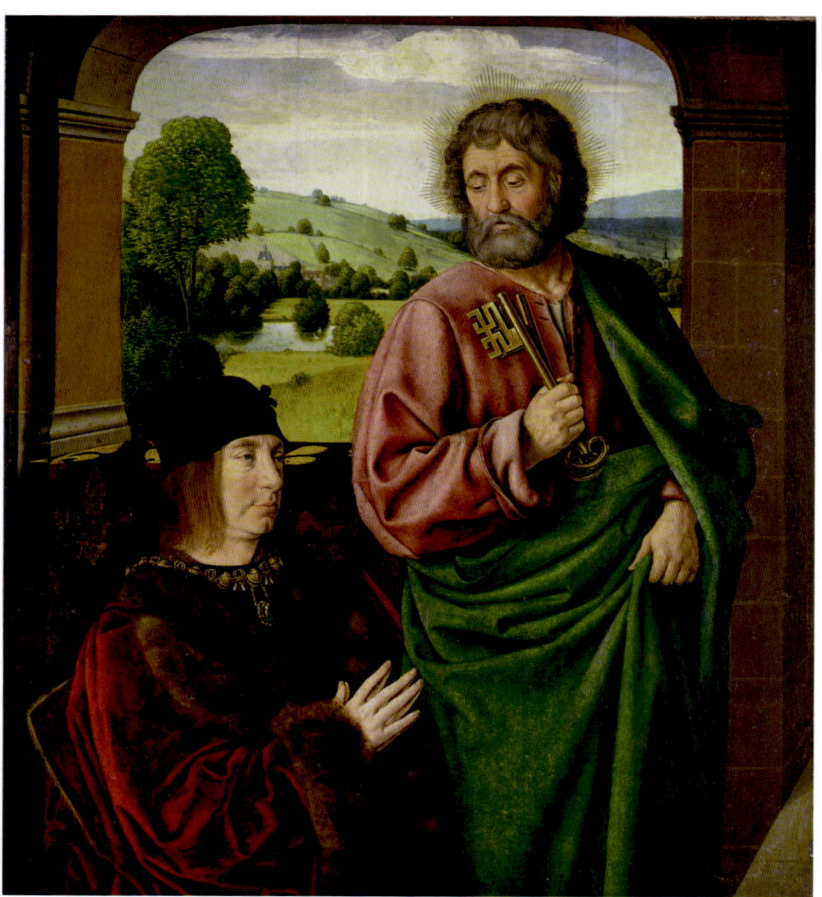

On the origins of French art

When term "French Art" is mentioned, the art connoisseur may immediately think of the images from the 19th century, particularly the paintings of the impressionists, with whom the beginning of modern art is linked and which are now among the incunabula of Western painting. Perhaps one may also be familiar with their forerunners, the painters of the Barbizon School, who were led by Jean-Baptiste-Camille Corot, with his dreamy landscapes which he would outline in situ and then complete in the studio, or the audacious romantic Eugène Delacroix, whose breast-baring *Liberty Leading the People* is today seen as an emblem of French art.

Naissance de l'art français

« L'art français » est un concept qui suggère aussitôt à l'amateur les tableaux du xixe siècle – avant tout ceux des impressionnistes auxquels se rattache le début de l'art moderne et qui comptent aujourd'hui parmi les incontournables de la peinture occidentale. On connaît peut-être aussi ceux des prédécesseurs des impressionnistes : les peintres de l'école de Barbizon – surtout Jean-Baptiste Camille Corot, avec ses paysages rêveurs esquissés « sur le motif », mais terminés en atelier – ou ceux de l'audacieux romantique Eugène Delacroix dont *La Liberté* aux seins nus figure aujourd'hui au nombre des emblèmes de l'art français.

Zur Entstehung der französischen Kunst

Beim Begriff „Französische Kunst" fallen dem Kunstkenner sofort die Bilder aus dem 19. Jahrhundert ein, vor allem die Gemälde der Impressionisten, mit denen der Beginn der Modernen Kunst verknüpft wird und die heute zu den Inkunabeln der westlichen Malerei zählen. Vielleicht kennt man auch die Vorläufer, die Maler der Schule von Barbizon, allen voran Jean-Baptiste Camille Corot mit seinen verträumten, bereits vor Ort skizzierten, aber im Atelier vollendeten Landschaften, oder den wagemutigen Romantiker Eugène Delacroix, dessen barbusige *Freiheit* heute zu den Insignien der französischen Kunst gehört.

Georges de La Tour (1593–1652)

The Fortune Teller

La Diseuse de bonne aventure

Die Wahrsagerin

La buenaventura

L'indovina

De waarzegster

c. 1630, Oil on canvas/Huile sur toile,
102 × 123,5 cm, Metropolitan Museum of Art,
New York

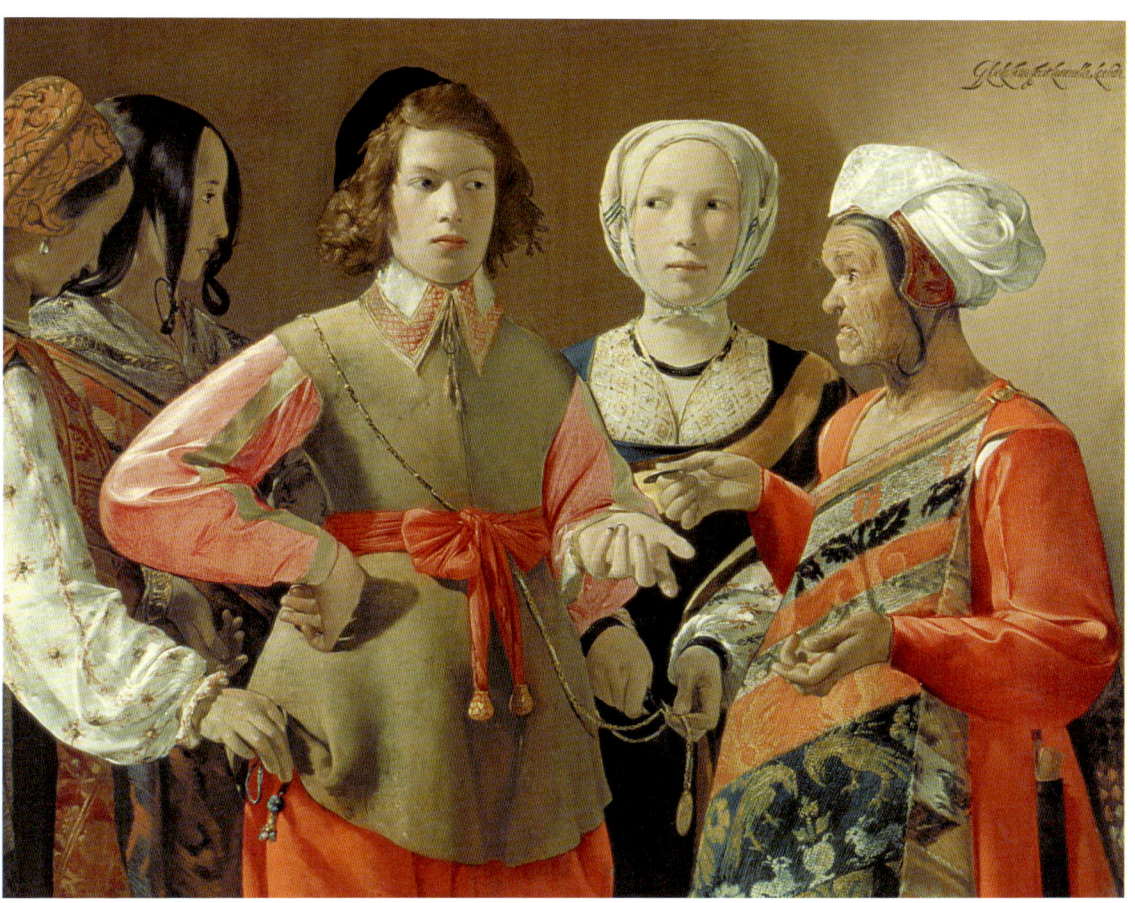

Sobre los orígenes del arte francés

El término "arte francés" evoca en el conocedor de arte inmediatamente las imágenes de pinturas del XIX, sobre todo las de los impresionistas, que se asocian con los inicios del arte moderno y se cuentan hoy en día entre los incunables de la pintura occidental. Tal vez sepa el conocedor también de sus predecesores, los pintores de la escuela de Barbizon, en especial Jean-Baptiste Camille Corot con sus paisajes ensoñadores, bocetados in situ pero terminados en el taller, o el audaz romántico Eugène Delacroix cuya *Libertad* descalza se considera hoy en día uno de los símbolos del arte francés.

La rinascita dell'antichità

Il concetto di "arte francese" porta subito alla mente degli intenditori d'arte i quadri del XIX secolo, in particolare i dipinti degli Impressionisti, ai quali si associa l'inizio dell'arte moderna e che oggi appartengono agli incunaboli della pittura occidentale. Magari si conoscono anche i precursori, i pittori della scuola di Barbizon, primo fra tutti Jean-Baptiste Camille Corot con i suoi paesaggi idillici abbozzati sul posto ma completati in studio, o l'audace romantico Eugène Delacroix, la cui *Libertà* a seno nudo oggi fa parte dei simboli dell'arte francese.

Het ontstaan van de Franse kunst

Bij het begrip 'Franse kunst' denkt de liefhebber meteen aan schilderijen uit de negentiende eeuw, vooral het werk van de impressionisten, die worden verbonden met de geboorte van de moderne kunst en nu tot de onbetwiste hoogtepunten van de westerse cultuur worden gerekend. Misschien weten we ook iets van hun directe voorlopers, de School van Barbizon en zijn voornaamste vertegenwoordiger, Jean-Baptiste Camille Corot, die zijn sfeervolle landschappen al in de vrije natuur schetste maar nog in het atelier uitwerkte, of van de stoutmoedig romantische schilder Eugène Delacroix, die de *Vrijheid* met ontblote borsten schilderde en haar tot een icoon van de Franse cultuur maakte.

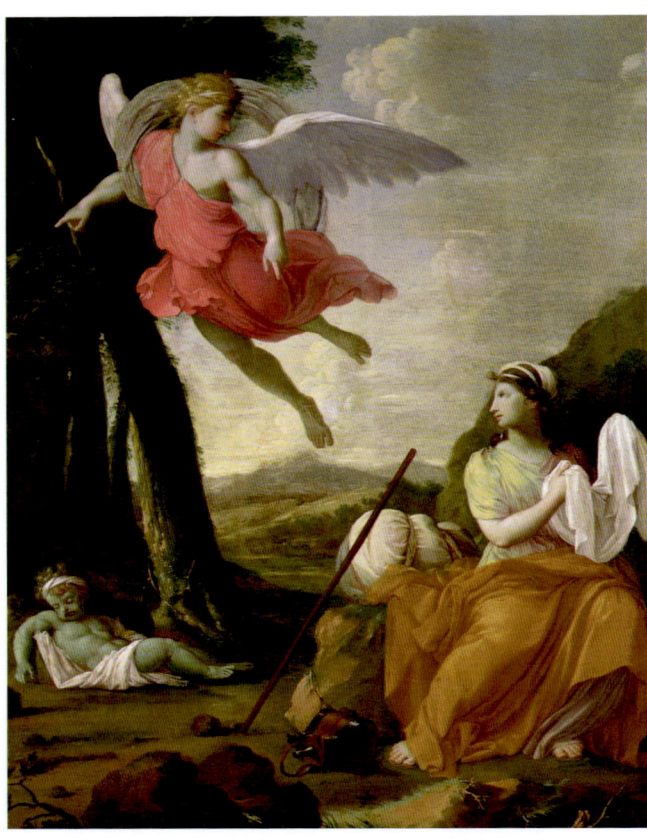

Eustache Le Sueur (1616–1655)

Hagar and Ishmael Rescued by the Angel

Agar et Ismaël secourus par l'ange

Hagar und Ishmael werden vom Engel gerettet

Agar e Ismael salvados por el ángel

Agar e Ismaele salvati dall'angelo

Hagar en Ismaël gered door engelen

c. 1648, Oil on canvas/Huile sur toile, 159 × 114 cm, Musée des Beaux-Arts de Rennes, Rennes

The history of French art begins, however, much earlier at about the turn of the millennium with the Carolingian and Ottonian art (Romanesque). This includes not only paintings and sculptures, but especially early on, buildings such as the famous Gothic cathedrals with their wonderful stained glass windows, and also many highly varied handicrafts of gold jewelry, tapestries, pottery and porcelain. This book focuses on the painting and presents a wealth of well-known and lesser-known works from the beginnings of the painting up until the late 19th century, from the School of Fontainebleau until late-impressionism and symbolism.

L'histoire de cet art commence pourtant beaucoup plus tôt, au tournant du millénaire de l'art carolingien et ottonien (art préroman). Elle englobe non seulement des peintures et des sculptures, mais aussi – avant tout dans les premiers temps – des édifices comme les célèbres cathédrales avec leurs merveilleux vitraux, et un artisanat extrêmement varié d'orfèvrerie, tapisserie, céramique et porcelaine. Le présent volume se concentre sur la peinture et présente un grand nombre de chefs-d'œuvre connus et moins connus, depuis les débuts de la peinture jusqu'à la fin du XIXᵉ siècle – de l'école de Fontainebleau à l'impressionnisme tardif et au symbolisme.

Die Geschichte der französischen Kunst beginnt aber viel früher, etwa um die Jahrtausendwende mit der karolingischen und ottonischen Kunst (Romanik) und umfasst nicht nur Gemälde und Plastiken, sondern vor allem in den Anfängen Bauwerke, wie die berühmten gotischen Kathedralen mit ihren wundervollen Glasfenstern und ein äußerst vielfältiges Kunsthandwerk von Goldschmuck, Gobelins, Keramik und Porzellan. Dieser Band konzentriert sich auf die Malerei und zeigt eine Fülle von bekannten und weniger bekannten Kunstwerken aus den Anfängen der Malerei bis ins späte 19. Jahrhundert, von der Schule von Fontainebleau bis zu Spätimpressionismus und Symbolismus.

Louise Moillon (1610–1696)
The Fruit and Vegetable Seller
La Marchande de fruits et légumes
Die Frucht- und Gemüseverkäuferin
La vendedora de frutas y verduras
La venditrice di frutta e verdura
De fruit- en groenteverkoopster
1630, Oil on wood/Huile sur bois,
120 × 165 cm, Musée du Louvre, Paris

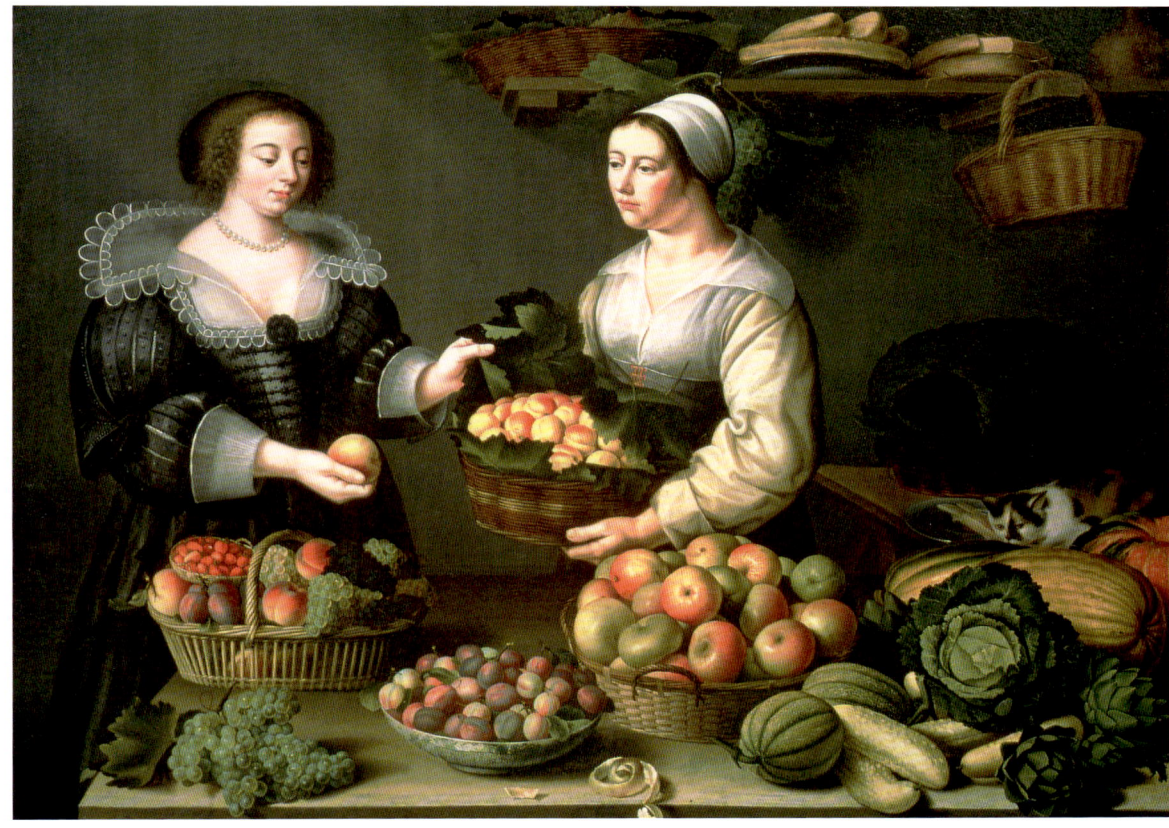

Pero la historia del arte francés comienza mucho antes, allá por el cambio de milenio, con el arte carolingio y otoniano (Románico) y abarca no solo pinturas y artes plásticas, sino también arquitectura (especialmente en los inicios) como las famosas catedrales góticas con sus fantásticas vidrieras y multitud de trabajos artesanales de orfebrería, tapices, cerámicas y porcelana. Este tomo se centra en la pintura, mostrando una amplia gama de obras de arte famosas y no tan famosas desde los inicios de la pintura hasta finales del XIX, desde la escuela de Fontainebleau hasta el impresionismo tardío y el simbolismo.

La storia dell'arte francese comincia però molto prima, più o meno durante il passaggio da un millennio all'altro con l'arte carolingia e ottoniana (il romanico) e comprende non solo dipinti e sculture, ma soprattutto agli inizi edifici come le famose cattedrali gotiche, con le loro meravigliose vetrate e un artigianato artistico estremamente vario composto da ornamenti dorati, arazzi, ceramica e porcellana. Questo gruppo si concentra sulla pittura e mostra una quantità di opere d'arte conosciute e meno conosciute dagli inizi della pittura fino al tardo XIX secolo, dalla scuola di Fontainebleau fino al tardo Impressionismo e al Simbolismo.

Maar de geschiedenis van de Franse kunst begint veel eerder, rond de millenniumwisseling van het jaar 1000, met de Karolingische en Ottoonse kunst (Romaanse kunst) en ze omvat niet alleen schilder- en beeldhouwkunst maar, vooral in het begin, de architectuur van de beroemde gotische kathedralen, met hun magnifieke glas-in-loodvensters, en een grote diversiteit aan creaties uit de goudsmeedkunst, naast schitterende tapijten (gobelins), keramiek en porselein. In dit boek richten we ons op de schilderkunst en tonen we een schat aan bekende en minder bekende werken, van de vroege Franse schilderkunst tot de late negentiende eeuw en van de School van Fontainebleau tot het late impressionisme en het symbolisme.

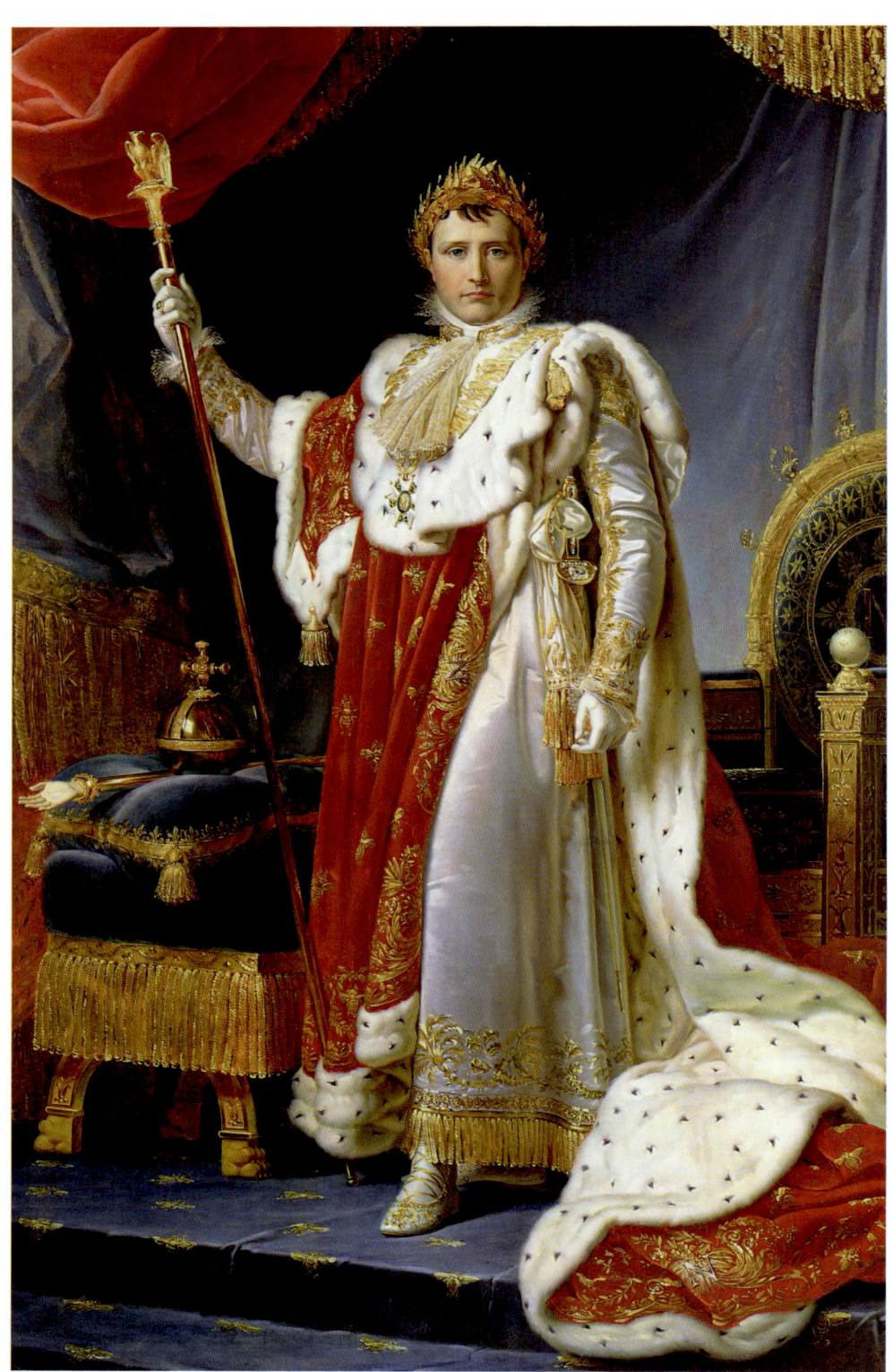

François Gérard (1770–1837)

Napoleon I in his Coronation Robe

Napoléon Ier en costume de sacre

Napoleon I. in seiner Krönungsrobe

Napoleón I con la túnica de su coronación

Napoleone I con le vesti dell'incoronazione

Napoleon I in zijn koningsmantel

c. 1805, Oil on canvas/Huile sur toile, 225,5 × 145,5 cm, Château de Versailles, Versailles

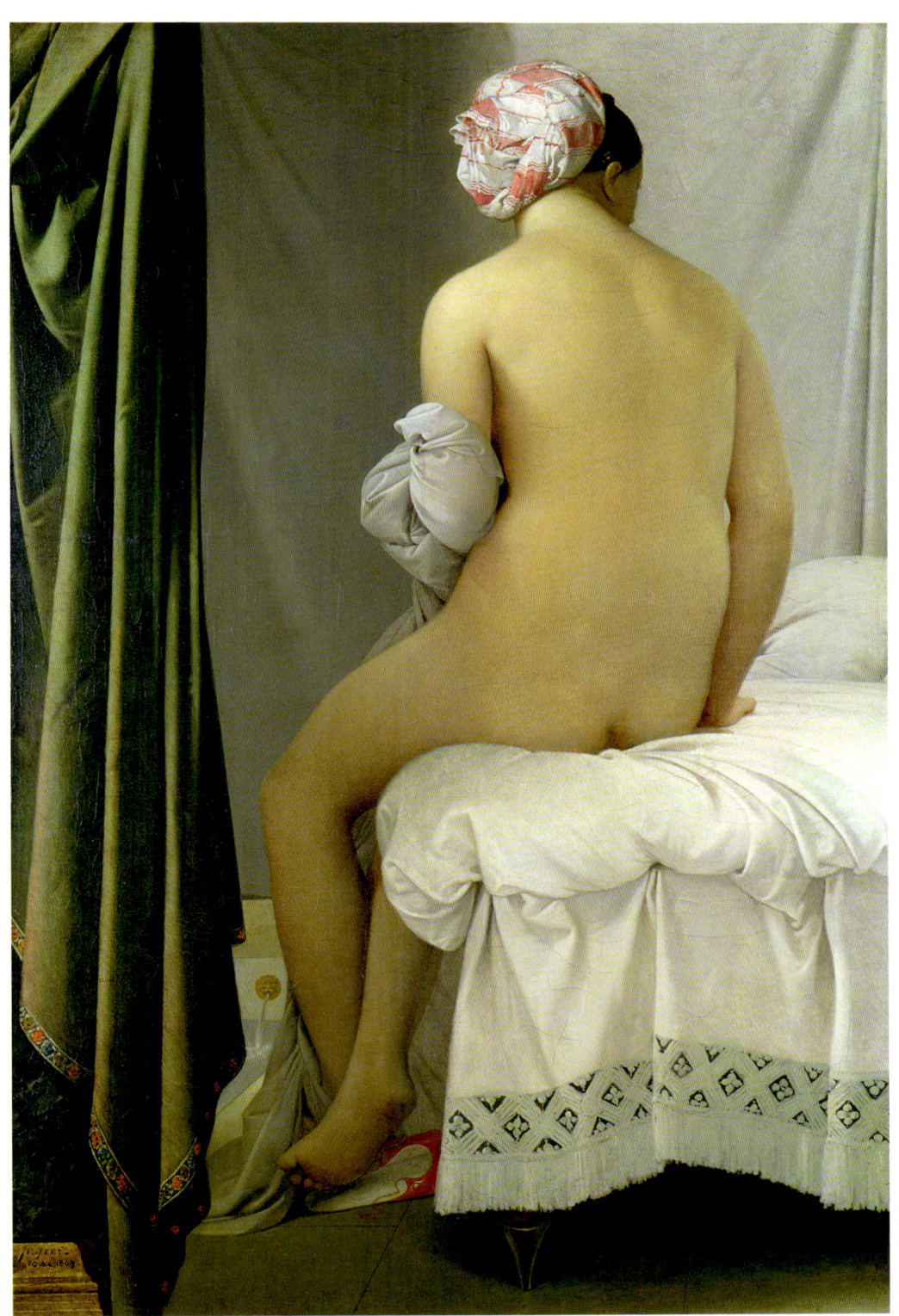

Jean-Auguste-Dominique Ingres (1780–1867)

The Bather, *called* Baigneuse Valpinçon

La Baigneuse Valpinçon

Die Badende von Valpinçon

La bañista de Valpinçon

La bagnante di Valpinçon

De Baadster van Valpinçon

1808, Oil on canvas/Huile sur toile, 146 × 97,5 cm,
Musée du Louvre, Paris

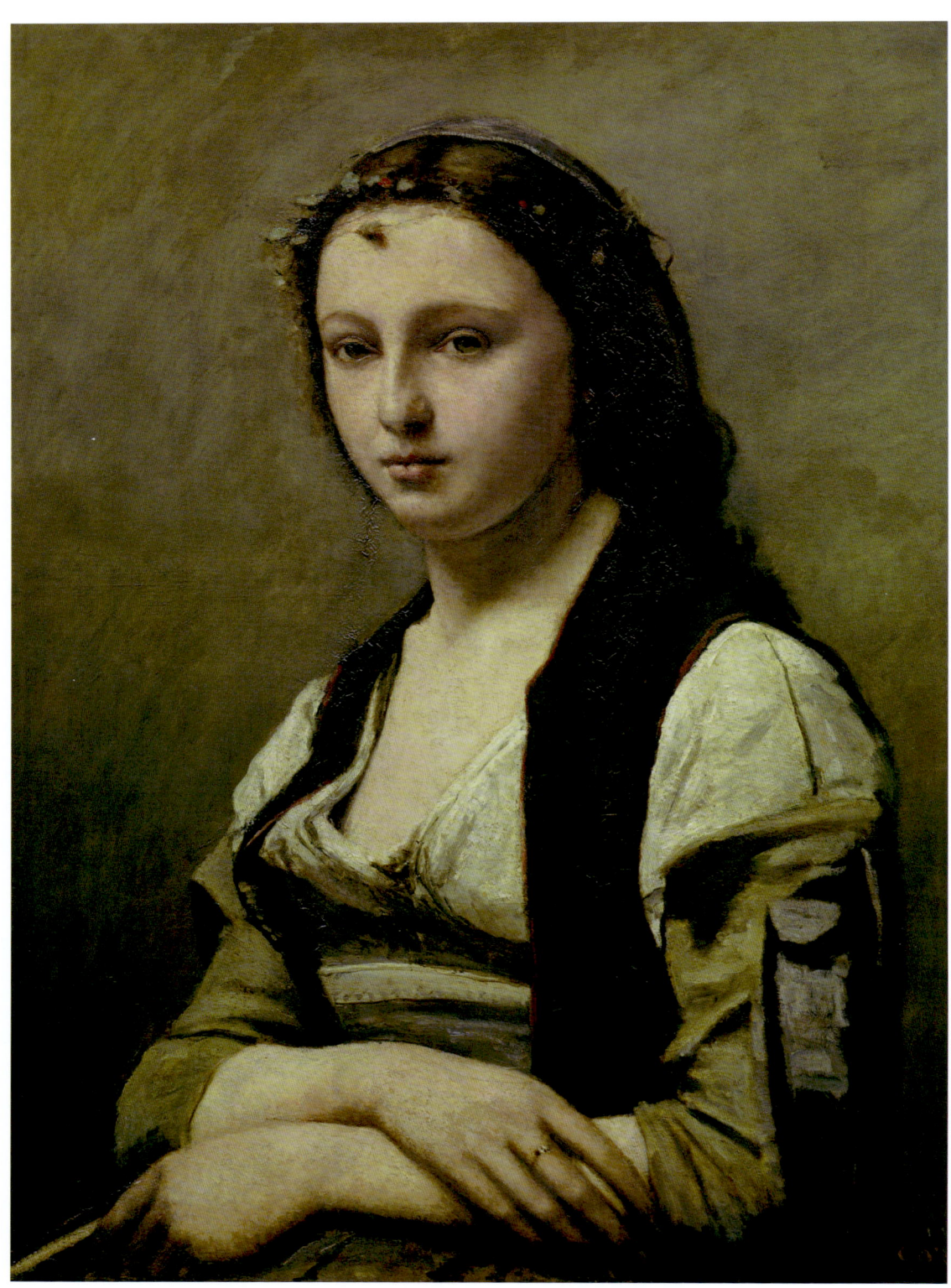

Camille Corot (1796–1875)

The Woman with the Pearl

La Femme à la perle

Die Frau mit der Perle

La mujer con la perla

La donna con la perla

De vrouw met de parel

c. 1868, Oil on canvas/Huile sur toile,
70 × 55 cm, Musée du Louvre, Paris

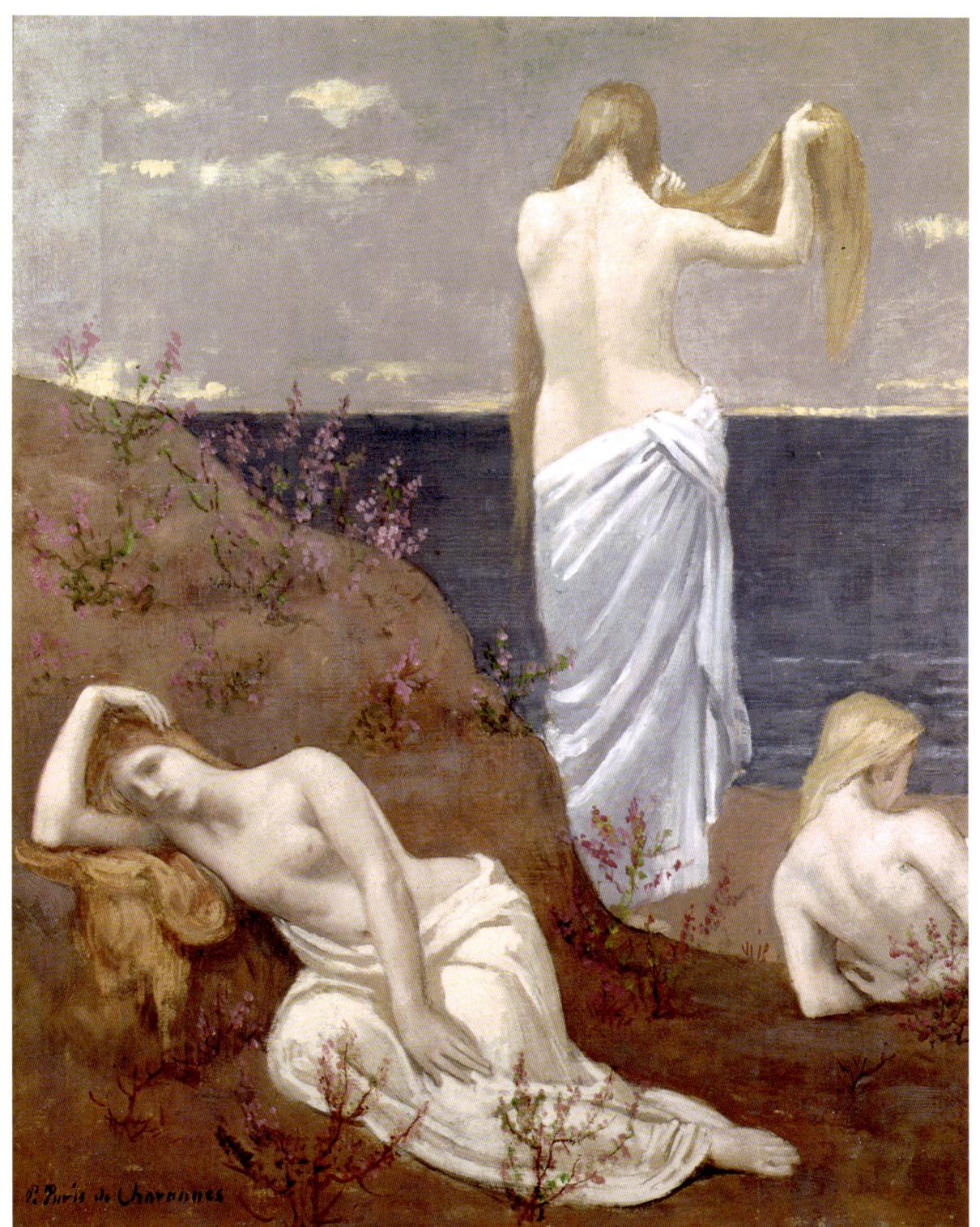

**Pierre Puvis de Chavannes
(1824–1898)**

Young Girls by the Sea

Jeunes Filles au bord de la mer

Junge Mädchen am Meer

Jovencitas en el mar

Ragazze in riva al mare

Jong meisje aan zee

1879, Oil on canvas/Huile sur toile,
205,4 × 156 cm, Musée d'Orsay, Paris

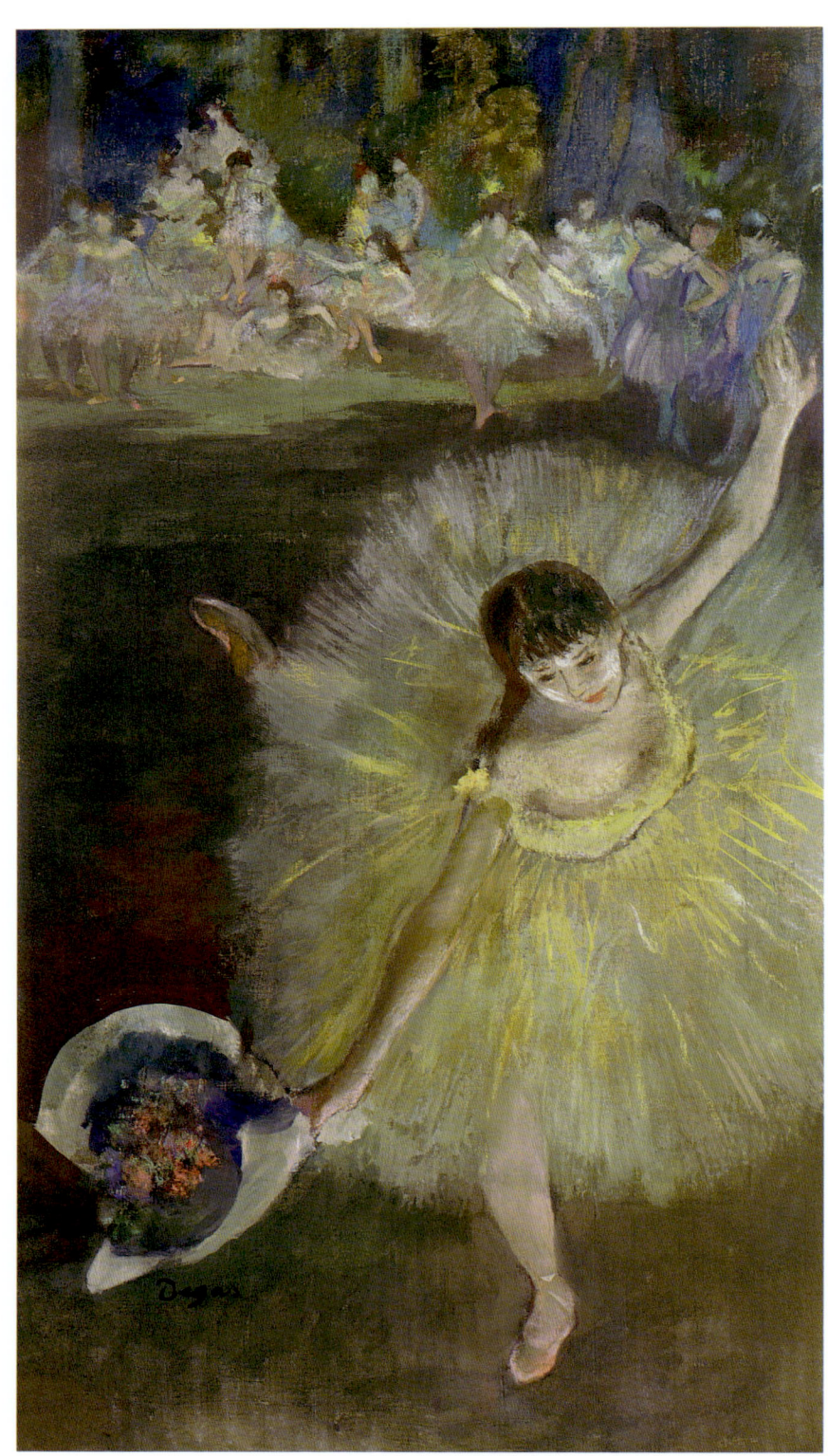

Edgar Degas (1834–1917)

End of an Arabesque

Fin d'arabesque

Ende einer Vorstellung

Final de un arabesco

Fine di un Arabesque

Einde van een voorstelling

1877, Oil and pastels on canvas/ Huile et pastel sur toile, 65,4 × 36,5 cm, Musée d'Orsay, Paris

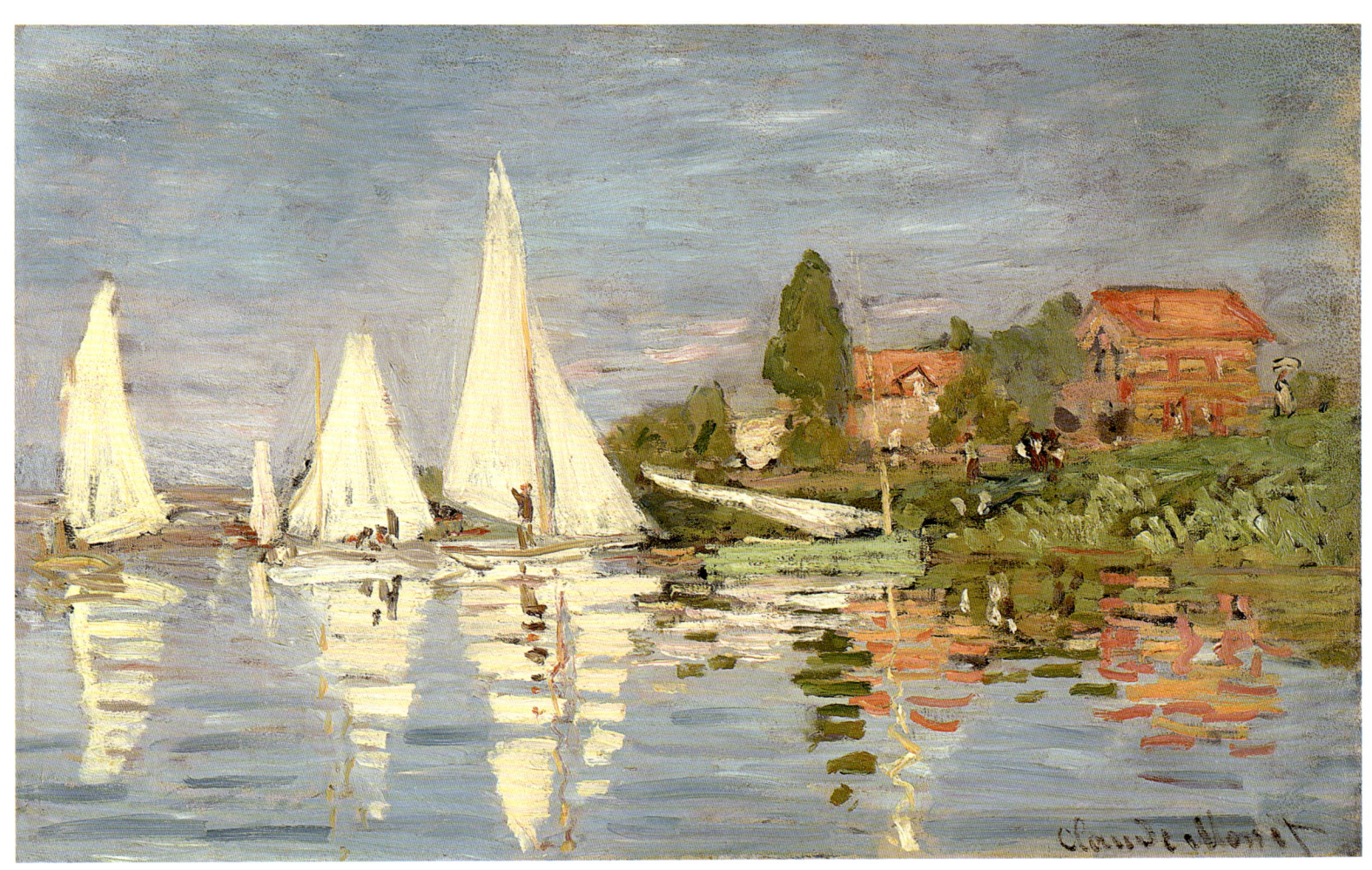

Claude Monet (1840–1926)

Regatta at Argenteuil

Régates à Argenteuil

Regatta in Argenteuil

Regata en Argenteuil

Regate ad Argenteuil

Regatta in Argenteuil

c. 1872, Oil on canvas/Huile sur toile, 48 × 75 cm, Musée d'Orsay, Paris

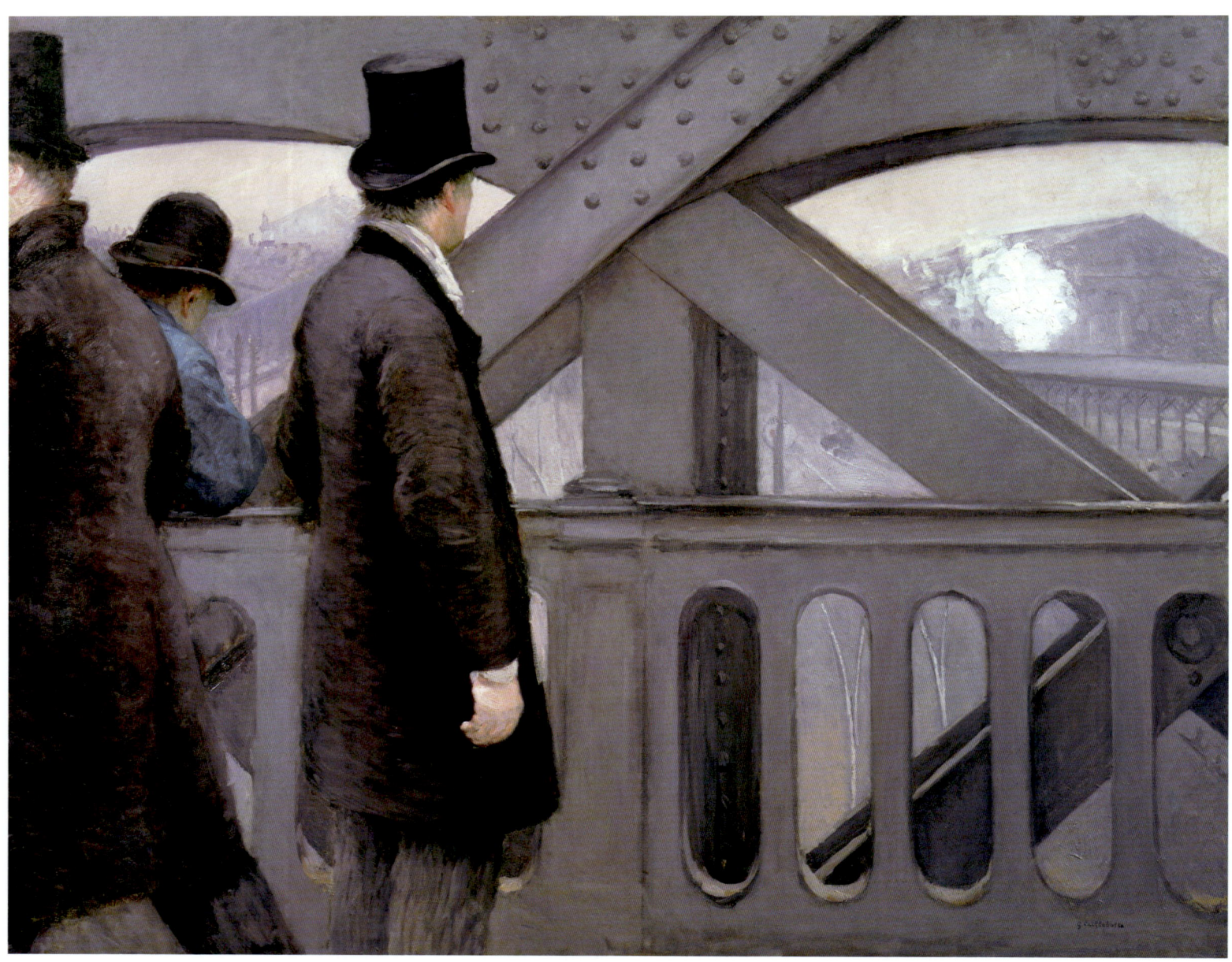

Gustave Caillebotte (1848–1894)

Le Pont de l'Europe   Die Europabrücke   Il ponte dell'Europa

Le Pont de l'Europe   El puente de Europa   De Europabrug

1877, Oil on canvas/Huile sur toile, 105,7 × 130,8 cm, Kimbell Art Museum, Fort Worth

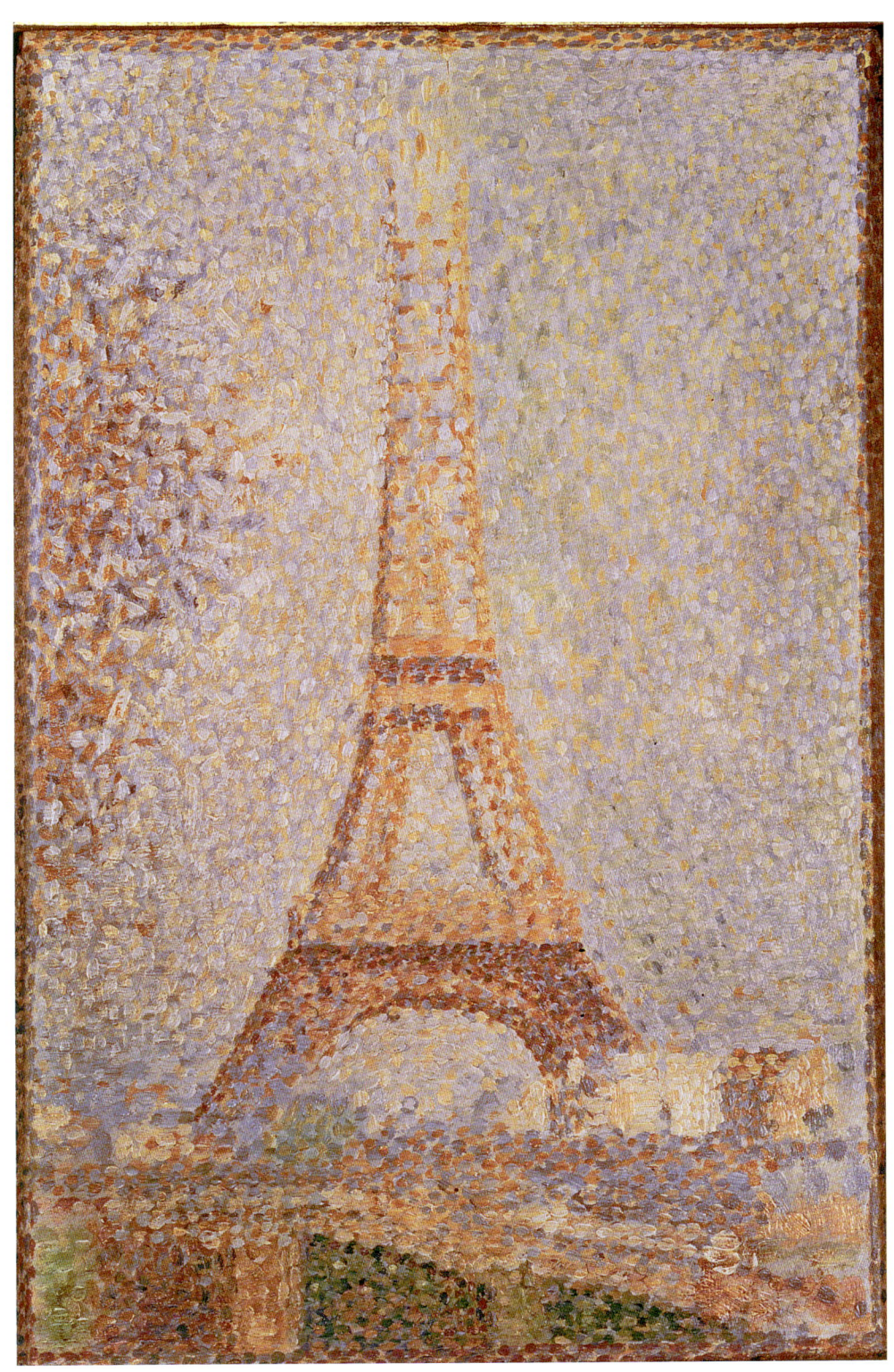

Georges Seurat (1859–1891)

The Eiffel Tower

La Tour Eiffel

Der Eiffelturm

La torre Eiffel

La Tour Eiffel

De Eiffeltoren

c. 1889, Oil on wood/Huile sur bois, 24 × 15 cm,
Legion of Honor, San Francisco

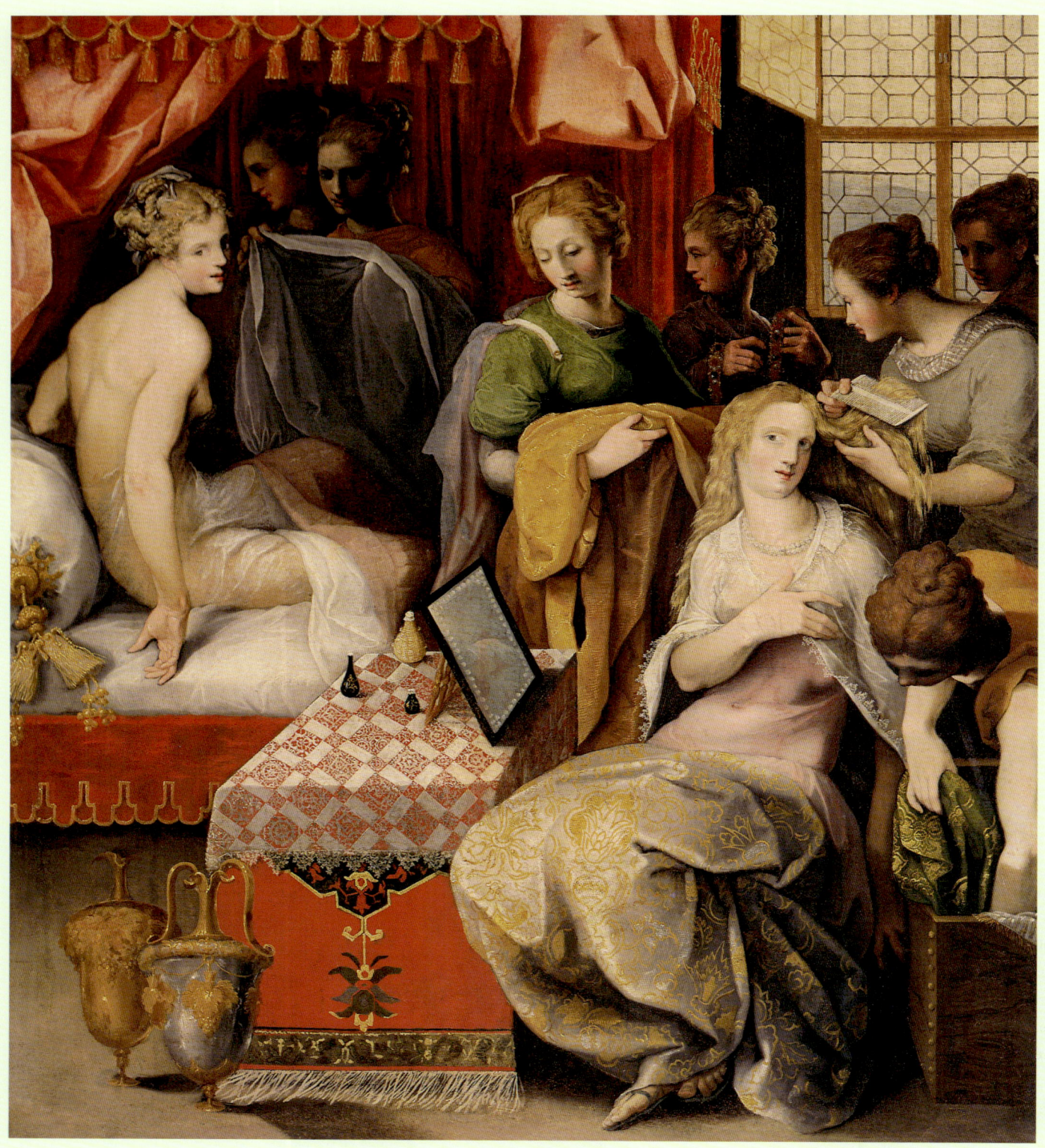

RENAISSANCE AND MANNERISM
RENAISSANCE ET MANIÉRISME
RENAISSANCE UND MANIERISMUS
RENACIMIENTO Y MANIERISMO
RINASCIMENTO E MANIERISMO
RENAISSANCE EN MANIËRISME

Toussaint Dubreuil (workshop of/atelier) (1561–1602)

Hyante and Climene at their Toilet

Hyante et Climène à leur toilette

Hyante und Climene bei der Toilette

Hiante y Climène en el baño

Hyante e Climene alla toeletta

Hyanthe en Clymene bij het toilet

n. d., Oil on canvas/Huile sur toile, 107 × 97 cm, Musée du Louvre, Paris

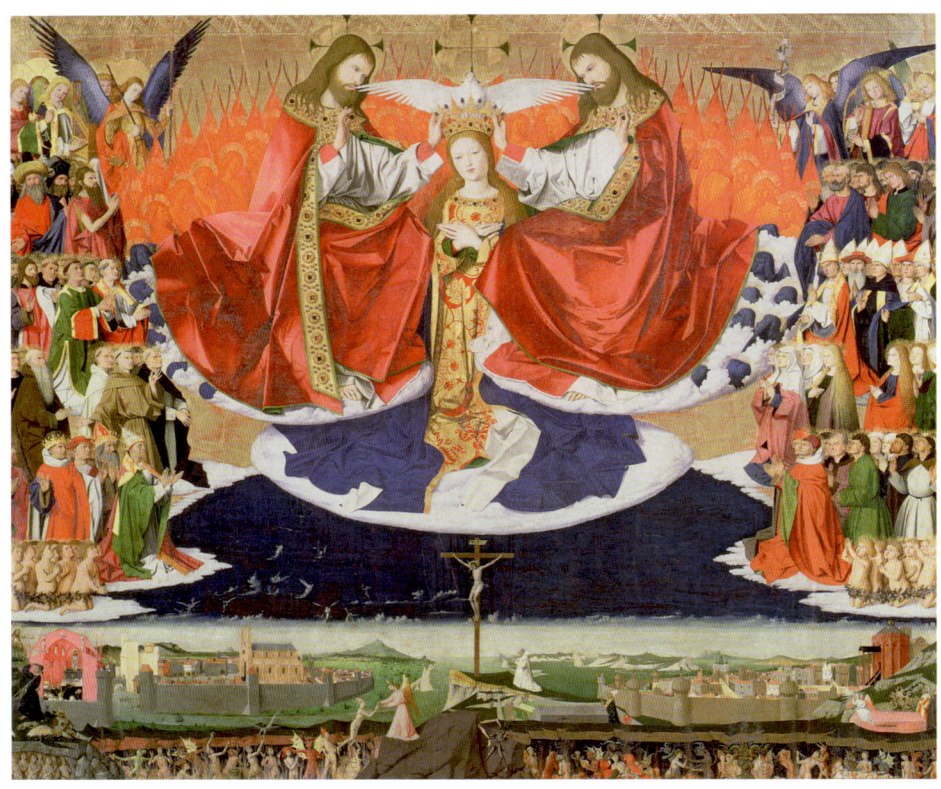

Enguerrand Quarton (c. 1410–1466)

The Coronation of the Virgin

Le Couronnement de la Vierge

Die Krönung der Jungfrau

La coronación de la Virgen

L'incoronazione della Vergine

De kroning van de Maagd Maria

c. 1454, Oil on wood/Huile sur bois, 183 × 220 cm,
Musée Pierre-de-Luxembourg, Villeneuve-lès-
Avignon

The rebirth of antiquity

One can place the beginning of the Renaissance, in general, with the flourishing of art in northern Italy, particularly in the city states of Florence and Siena with their outstanding painters such as Giotto, Duccio and Simone Martini. But in France during the 14th and 15th centuries, a great flowering of art also took place, which was certainly influenced by Italian painting. Since the reign of Louis IX (St. Louis, reigned from 1226 to 1270) France regarded itself as a model for a Christian, chivalrous way of life. This country was not only the mother country of the great monastic reforms of the 11th and 12th centuries, but also the seat of the highest schools of the collegiate and Episcopal churches and home to the first real university, in Paris. The Gothic

La résurrection de l'Antiquité

On considère généralement comme le début de la Renaissance l'épanouissement artistique en Italie du Nord, dans les cités-États de Florence et de Sienne, avec leurs peintres remarquables tels Giotto, Duccio ou Simone Martini. En France toutefois, dès les xive et xve siècles, se développe une grande floraison artistique (nourrie, il est vrai, de la peinture italienne). Depuis le règne de Louis IX (Saint Louis, 1226–1270), la France a valeur d'exemple pour les formes de vie chrétienne et chevaleresque. Le pays n'est pas seulement la patrie des grands ordres réformateurs des xie et xiie siècles, mais il est aussi le siège des hautes écoles auprès des monastères et des cathédrales, et celui de la première université véritable à Paris. Son architecture gothique

Die Wiedergeburt der Antike

Zwar setzt man den Beginn der Renaissance allgemein mit dem Aufblühen der Kunst in Oberitalien, in den Stadtstaaten Florenz und Siena mit ihren hervorragenden Malern, wie Giotto, Duccio oder Simone Martini an. Doch entfaltete sich gerade in Frankreich im 14. und 15. Jahrhundert eine große Blüte der Kunst, die allerdings auch von der italienischen Malerei zehrte. Frankreich galt seit der Herrschaft von Ludwig IX. (Ludwig der Heilige, 1226–1270) als vorbildlich für christliche, ritterliche Lebensformen. Dieses Land war nicht nur das Mutterland der großen Reformorden des 11. und 12. Jahrhunderts, sondern auch Sitz der hohen Schulen an den Stifts- und Bischofskirchen, die Heimat der ersten echten Universität in Paris. Die Architektur der Gotik

Master of Moulins/Le Maître de Moulins (Jean Hey) (fl. 1480–1500)

Anne of France Lady of Beaujeu, Duchess of Bourbon, Presented by St. John the Evangelist
(right hand wing of a triptych)

Anne de France, dame de Beaujeu, duchesse de Bourbon, présentée par saint Jean l'Évangéliste
(volet droit d'un triptyque)

Anne von Frankreich wird vom Hl. Johannes dem Täufer vorgestellt *(rechte Tafel eines Triptychons)*

Ana de Francia presentada por San Juan Bautista *(panel derecho de un tríptico)*

Anna di Francia presentata da San Giovanni Battista *(tavola di destra di un trittico)*

Anna van Frankrijk voorgesteld door de Heilige Johannes de Doper *(rechter paneel van een drieluik)*

c. 1492–1493, Oil on wood/Huile sur bois, 73 × 53 cm, Musée du Louvre, Paris

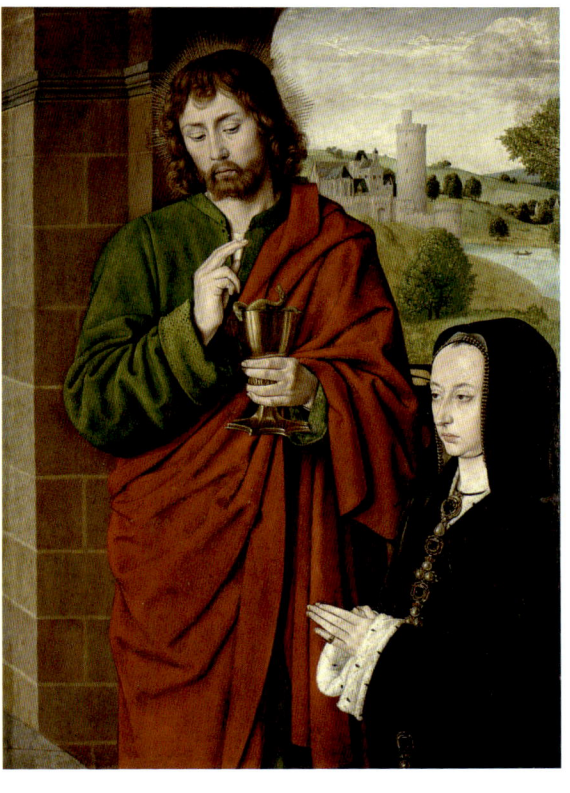

El renacer de la Antigüedad

Generalmente se sitúa el inicio del Renacimiento en la eclosión artística del norte de Italia que se da en las ciudades estado de Florencia y Siena, con sus extraordinarios pintores (como Giotto, Duccio o Simone Martini). Sin embargo en Francia también hubo en los siglos XIV y XV un brote artístico importante, espoleado también por la pintura italiana. Francia era considerada desde el reinado de Luis IX (Luis el Santo, 1226–1270) como un ejemplo del estilo de vida cristiano y caballeresco. Esta no era solo la patria de las grandes órdenes reformistas del XI y XII, sino que también albergaba las escuelas de colegiatas e iglesias episcopales, así como la sede de la primera universidad en París. La arquitectura del Gótico se propagó por toda Europa, las

La rinascita dell'antichità

Generalmente si stabilisce con precisione l'inizio del Rinascimento con lo sbocciare dell'arte nell'Italia settentrionale, nelle città-stato di Firenze e Siena con i loro eccezionali pittori come Giotto, Duccio o Simone Martini. Tuttavia già in Francia nei secoli XIV e XV si sviluppò una grande fioritura dell'arte, che però viveva anche della pittura italiana. A partire dalla dominazione di Luigi IX (Luigi il Santo, 1226–1270), la Francia era considerata un esempio di stili di vita cristiani e cavallereschi. Questo paese non era soltanto la madrepatria dei grandi ordini riformatori dei secoli XI e XII, ma anche la sede delle scuole superiori di collegiate e chiese vescovili, oltre che la patria della prima vera università di Parigi. L'architettura gotica si diffuse in tutta Europa,

De wedergeboorte van de klassieken

De renaissance begon met de bloei van de schilderkunst in Noord-Italië, waarbij vooral de stadstaten Florence en Siena met grote schilders als Giotto, Duccio en Simone Martini de toon aangaven. Maar tegelijkertijd maakte Frankrijk in de veertiende en vijftiende eeuw een grote bloeitijd in de schilderkunst door, waarbij ook uit Italiaanse voorbeelden werd geput. Frankrijk gaf sinds de heerschappij van Louis IX (Lodewijk 'de Heilige', 1226–1270) de toon aan in de christelijke, ridderlijke levensstijl. Niet alleen was het land in de elfde en twaalfde eeuw de bakermat geweest van de hervormingsbeweging van de nieuwe kloosterorden, het was ook het land van de hogere dom- en stiftsscholen en van de eerste echte universiteit, die van Parijs. De architectuur van de gotiek beïnvloedde

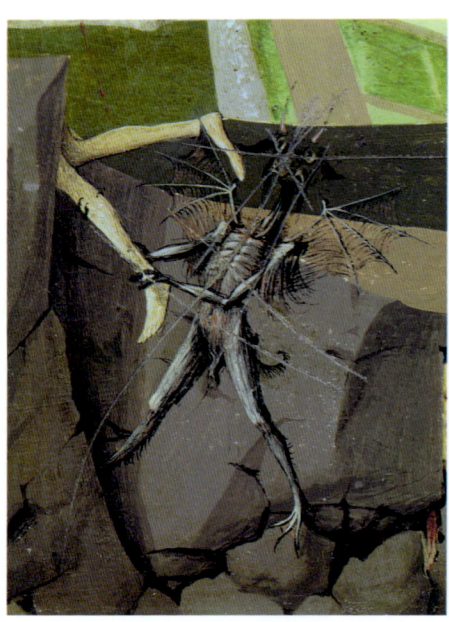

Enguerrand Quarton (c. 1410–1466)

A Demon, from the *Coronation of the Virgin* (detail)

Un démon du *Couronnement de la Vierge* (détail)

Ein Dämon aus *Die Krönung der Jungfrau* (Detail)

Un demonio de *La coronación de la Virgen* (detalle)

Un demone dalla *Incoronazione della Vergine* (dettaglio)

Een demon uit *De kroning van de Maagd* (detail)

c. 1454, Oil on wood/Huile sur bois, 183 × 220 cm, Musée Pierre-de-Luxembourg, Villeneuve-lès-Avignon

architectural style radiated throughout Europe, the churches and palaces were splendidly furnished and, with the advent of illuminated texts, there arose a collector class which searched more for aesthetic enjoyment than religious inspiration. It was only gradually that painting broke away from the great religiously inspired construction projects and the decorative wishes of the princes. Around 1430, painting was the leading artistic genre in Europe. The large altarpieces, along with the ecclesiastical frescoes, now carried the signatures of renowned painters whose allure reached into all of Europe's royal houses. Simone Martini became, in 1317, the first court painter and was primarily in the service of the French royal house of Anjou and their courtiers and partisans.

The time around 1400 was, however, overshadowed by gloomy crises: the papal schism of 1378 to 1414, strong economic and social shifts, the bloody wars and civil wars, along with general political confusion. These

rayonne dans toute l'Europe ; ses églises et ses palais sont somptueusement aménagés. L'apparition de la miniature fait naître un goût de la collection recherchant moins le recueillement religieux que la jouissance esthétique. Peu à peu la peinture se détache des grands programmes de construction et de décoration religieux des princes. Vers 1430, la peinture est désormais le genre artistique moteur en Europe. Les grands retables, mais aussi les cycles de fresques religieuses, portent à présent la signature de maîtres devenus célèbres et dont le rayonnement atteint toutes les maisons princières et royales d'Europe. En 1317, Simone Martini est le premier peintre de cour, principalement au service de la maison royale d'Anjou (d'origine française) à Naples, comme de ses courtisans et de ses partisans.

Le début du xvᵉ siècle est cependant assombri par des crises : le schisme pontifical depuis 1378, les grands bouleversements économiques et sociaux, les guerres extérieures et les guerres civiles sanglantes, la confusion

strahlte auf ganz Europa aus, die Kirchen und Paläste wurden prachtvoll ausgestattet, und mit dem Aufkommen der Buchmalerei entstand ein erstes Sammlertum, das weniger die religiöse Andacht suchte, als den ästhetische Genuss. Erst nach und nach löste sich die Malerei von den großen religiös motivierten Bauvorhaben und Dekorationswünschen der Fürsten. Um 1430 ist die Malerei die führende Kunstgattung Europas. Die großen Altarbilder, aber auch die kirchlichen Freskenzyklen tragen jetzt die Handschrift eines bekannt gewordenen Malers, dessen Ausstrahlung alle europäischen Fürsten- und Königshäuser erreicht. Simone Martini wird 1317 der erste Hofmaler und steht hauptsächlich im Dienst des aus Frankreich stammenden Königshauses von Anjou und für dessen Hofleute und Parteigänger.

Die Zeit um 1400 ist jedoch geprägt von düsteren Krisen: Das päpstliche Schisma seit 1378, die starken wirtschaftlichen und gesellschaftlichen Umschichtungen, die blutigen Kriege und Bürgerkriege, die

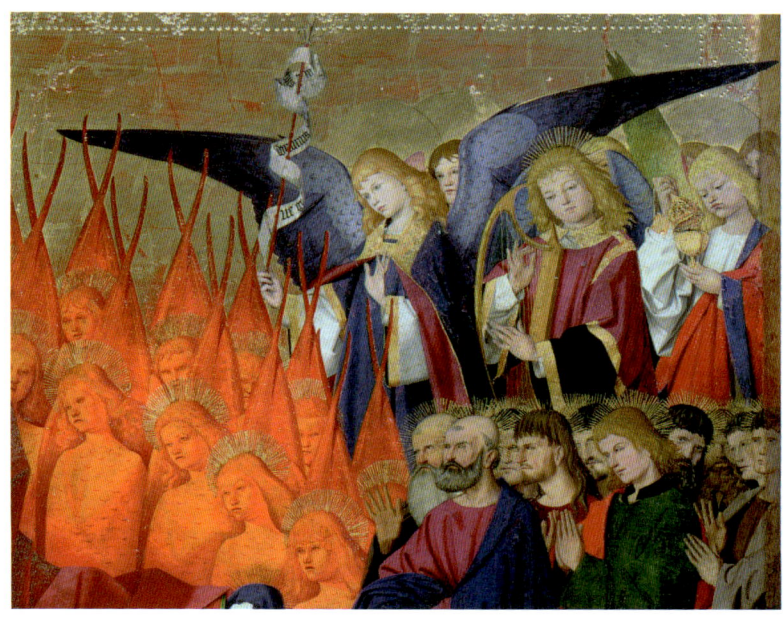

Enguerrand Quarton (c. 1410–1466)

An Angel, from the *Coronation of the Virgin* (detail)

Un ange du *Couronnement de la Vierge* (détail)

Ein Engel aus *Die Krönung der Jungfrau* (Detail)

Un ángel de *La coronación de la Virgen* (detalle)

Un angelo dalla *Incoronazione della Vergine* (dettaglio)

Een engel uit *De kroning van de Maagd* (detail)

c. 1454, Oil on wood/Huile sur bois, 183 × 220 cm, Musée
Pierre-de-Luxembourg, Villeneuve-lès-Avignon

iglesias y palacios se decoraron profusamente, y con la llegada de las ilustraciones de los libros se generó un espíritu de coleccionismo que buscaba más el placer estético que la devoción religiosa. Solo poco a poco la pintura fue separándose de los grandes proyectos arquitectónicos y deseos decorativos de los gobernantes. Alrededor de 1430 la pintura ya era la disciplina artística principal en Europa. Los grandes retablos, pero también los ciclos de pinturas al fresco en las iglesias, llevan entonces ya la firma de un pintor reconocido, cuya fama se propaga así al resto de casas reales y gobiernos europeos. Simone Martini se convierte en 1317 en el primer pintor de la corte, al servicio principalmente de la casa real de Anjou, procedente de Francia, y de sus cortesanos y partidarios.

Y sin embargo la época alrededor del 1400 está caracterizada por sombrías crisis: El cisma papal de 1378, los violentos movimientos redistributivos tanto sociales como económicos, las sangrientas guerras

le chiese e i palazzi furono sontuosamente arredati, e con l'avvento della miniatura ebbe origine il primo collezionismo, che non cercava tanto la devozione religiosa quanto il piacere estetico. Solo gradualmente la pittura si distaccò dai grandi progetti di costruzione motivati dalla religione e dai desideri decorativi dei principi. Verso il 1430 la pittura diventa il genere artistico dominante in Europa. Le grandi pale degli altari, ma anche i cicli di affreschi ecclesiastici portano ora la firma di un pittore diventato famoso, il cui carisma arriva in tutte le case principesche e reali d'Europa. Nel 1317 Simone Martini divenne il primo pittore di corte e fu a servizio principalmente nelle case reali di origine francese degli Angiò e dei loro cortigiani e seguaci.

L'epoca intorno al 1400 è tuttavia caratterizzata da fosche crisi: dopo lo scisma papale del 1378 i grandi riordinamenti economici e sociali, le sanguinose guerre anche civili, il disordine politico generale costituiscono un forte contrasto con la "bella"

heel Europa, kerken en paleizen werden weelderig ingericht en met de opkomst van de boekschilderkunst ontstond een vroege klasse van verzamelaars die veeleer op zoek waren naar esthetische verrukkingen dan naar religieuze aandachtigheid. Slechts geleidelijk maakte de schilderkunst zich los van de ambitieuze, door religie geïnspireerde architectuur en decoraties van de vorsten. Rond 1430 was de schilderkunst het voornaamste artistieke ambacht geworden in Europa. Grote altaarstukken maar ook kerkelijke frescocyclussen droegen nu de signatuur van een kunstenaar die naam had gemaakt en wiens invloed alle Europese vorstenhuizen bereikte. Simone Martini werd in 1317 de eerste hofschilder en hij werkte hoofdzakelijk voor het uit Frankrijk stammende koningshuis van Anjou en voor de hovelingen en volgelingen van dat huis.

Maar de tijd rond 1400 werd beheerst door diepe crises: sinds 1378 was de kerk gespleten door het Westerse Schisma, Europa maakte ingrijpende sociaal-economische

were all in stark contrast to the "beautiful" painting of the time, which consciously and deliberately presented a harmonious counterpart to the reality.

The Italian courts looked back to antiquity and its art forms, as well as to its philosophical and literary traditions, with their large cities experiencing a considerable economic upswing. The French court, however, remained more reserved towards antiquity and anyway, due to the "Hundred Years War" (1337–1453) with England, things had become financially constrained and the funds that had helped in the development of late Gothic courtly art were now needed for the war.

The center of the artistic renewal was Burgundy, which had detached itself from France to fight on the side of England, and in the Duke of Burgundy it had found a great patron of the arts. The appointment of Jan van Eyck to the court of Burgundy ushered in a new era of painting, especially concerning technique, with the consistent use of oils and glazing. New clients came from the mercantile class of the Flemish cities of Bruges and Ghent, leading to a great flourishing of painting.

In 1500, the great struggles between the powerful monarchies of Europe such as France, Spain, England and the Holy Roman Empire were played out on Italian soil. Although the Italian states could retain their independence, the centers of political power shifted significantly towards the countries north of the Alps. In the course of their campaigns, the rulers of these lands came into contact with the Renaissance culture in Italy and began to orient themselves towards these ideas, in order to display their own power and growing national consciousness.

Charles VIII (ruled 1483–1498), Louis XII (ruled 1498–1515) and Francis I (ruled 1515–1547) strengthened the strong royal

politique générale contrastent fortement avec la « belle peinture » de cette époque, qui montre une image d'harmonie consciemment opposée à la réalité. Tandis que dans les cours princières d'Italie, le retour à l'Antiquité et à ses formes artistiques, mais aussi à sa tradition philosophique et littéraire, entraîne un immense essor des grandes villes, la cour royale de France reste plus réservée vis-à-vis de cette même Antiquité. De toute façon, mobilisés économiquement par la guerre de Cent Ans contre l'Angleterre (1337–1453), les moyens financiers qui ont contribué à l'épanouissement de l'art de cour du gothique tardif sont tous utilisés pour les opérations militaires et diplomatiques. Le foyer du renouveau artistique est alors le duché de Bourgogne, indépendant de la France et allié des Anglais, dont les ducs sont de grands mécènes. Appelé à la cour de Bourgogne, Jan van Eyck ouvre une nouvelle époque de la peinture – avant tout dans la technique, avec un emploi systématique de la peinture à l'huile et des glacis. De nouveaux commanditaires, issus des élites marchandes des villes flamandes de Bruges et de Gand, contribuent à l'extraordinaire épanouissement de la peinture.

Au tout début du XVIᵉ siècle, c'est en Italie que se déroulent les grandes luttes de puissance entre les principales monarchies européennes telles que la France, l'Espagne, l'Angleterre et le Saint Empire romain. Les États italiens réussissent à préserver leur indépendance, mais les grands centres de décision politique se déplacent dans les pays situés au nord des Alpes. Lors de leurs campagnes militaires, les rois et les princes entrent en contact avec la culture italienne de la Renaissance et commencent à se tourner vers elle, afin de démontrer leur puissance personnelle et l'orgueil de la conscience nationale croissante.

allgemeine politische Wirrnis stehen im großen Kontrast zu der „schönen" Malerei dieser Zeit, die ein bewusst harmonisierendes Gegenbild zur Realität zeigt.

Während an den italienischen Höfen der Rückgriff auf die Antike, auf ihre Kunstformen, aber auch auf ihre philosophische und literarische Tradition, den großen Städten einen ungeheuren Aufschwung verschaffte, blieb der französische Hof zur Antike reservierter. Ohnehin durch den „Hundertjährigen Krieg" (1337–1453) mit England wirtschaftlich angespannt, wurden die finanziellen Mittel, die bei der Entwicklung der spätgotischen höfischen Kunst geholfen hatten, nun für den Krieg benötigt.

Zentrum der künstlerischen Erneuerung wurde das sich von Frankreich ablösende Burgund, das auf Seiten Englands kämpfte, und in Herzog von Burgund einen großen Kunstmäzen gefunden hatte. Mit dem an den Hof von Burgund berufenen Jan van Eyck begann ein neues Zeitalter der Malerei, vor allem in der Technik, mit der konsequenten Anwendung der Ölmalerei und der Lasurtechnik. Neue Auftraggeber kamen aus der Kaufmannsschicht der flämischen Städte Brügge und Gent und führten zu einer großen Blüte der Malerei.

Um 1500 spielten sich auf italienischem Boden die großen Machtkämpfe zwischen den mächtigeren europäischen Monarchien, wie Frankreich, Spanien, England und dem Heilige Römische Reich ab. Die italienischen Staaten konnten zwar ihre Unabhängigkeit bewahren, doch die politischen Machtzentren verlagerten sich deutlich in die Länder nördlich der Alpen. Auf ihren Kriegszügen kamen die Herrscher in Kontakt mit der Renaissance-Kultur Italiens und begannen sich daran zu orientieren, um ihre eigene Macht und ihr wachsendes nationales Selbstbewusstsein zur Schau zu stellen.

y guerras civiles y la confusión política general contrastan con la belleza de la pintura de la época, que muestra una imagen conscientemente contraria a la realidad.

Mientras que en la corte italiana la vuelta a la Antigüedad, con sus formas artísticas y su tradición literaria y filosófica, significó un gigantesco impulso para las grandes ciudades, la Antigüedad quedó reservada en Francia a la corte. Ya en dificultades económicas por la "Guerra de los 100 años" con Inglaterra (1337–1453), ahora los medios que se destinaban al desarrollo del arte gótico tardío de la corte se transfirieron a la guerra.

El centro de la renovación artística sería la región de Borgoña, que se había separado de Francia y luchaba del lado inglés, siendo el Duque de Borgoña un gran mecenas del arte. Con Jan van Eyck, contratado en la corte de Borgoña, se inició una nueva época en la pintura, sobre todo técnicamente, con la utilización del óleo y la técnica de veladuras. Nuevos encargos, provenientes de la clase mercantil de las ciudades flamencas de Brujas y Gante, contribuyeron también al gran desarrollo de la pintura.

Hacia 1500 las grandes luchas de poder entre las monarquías europeas (Francia, España, Inglaterra y el Sacro Imperio Romano Germánico) se lidiaban en suelo italiano. Los estados italianos pudieron mantener su independencia, si bien los centros de poder político se desplazaron claramente hacia los países al norte de los Alpes. Durante sus campañas militares los gobernantes entraron en contacto con la cultura del Renacimiento italiana y empezaron a adoptarla como muestra de su propio poder y su creciente consciencia nacional.

Carlos VIII (reinar 1483–1498), Luis XII (reinar 1498–1515) y Francisco I (reinar 1515–1547) cimentaron en Francia la supremacía de la

pittura di quest'epoca, che mostra un'antitesi della realtà armoniosamente consapevole.

Mentre nelle corti italiane il ricorso all'antichità, alle sue forme artistiche ma anche alla sua tradizione filosofica e letteraria creò un enorme entusiasmo nelle grandi città, la corte francese rimase più fredda nei confronti dell'antichità. In ogni caso a causa della onerosa "guerra dei cent'anni" (1337–1453) con l'Inghilterra, i mezzi finanziari che avevano aiutato lo sviluppo dell'arte cortigiana tardo gotica erano ora necessari per la guerra.

Il centro del rinnovamento artistico divenne la Borgogna, che si stava staccando dalla Francia e combatteva a fianco dell'Inghilterra, trovando nel duca di Borgogna un grande mecenate artistico. Con Jan van Eyck, nominato alla corte di Borgogna, iniziò una nuova età della pittura, soprattutto per quanto riguarda la tecnica, con il conseguente impiego della pittura ad olio e della tecnica della velatura. Nuovi committenti arrivarono dal ceto dei commercianti delle città fiamminghe di Bruges e Gand e portarono ad una grande fioritura della pittura.

Intorno al 1500 sul territorio italiano si svolsero le grandi lotte di potere tra le importanti monarchie europee, come Francia, Spagna, Inghilterra e il Sacro Romano impero. Gli stati italiani furono certamente in grado di mantenere la loro indipendenza, tuttavia i centri del potere politico si spostarono chiaramente nei paesi a nord delle Alpi. Durante le loro campagne militari, i sovrani vennero a contatto con la cultura rinascimentale italiana e iniziarono a ostentare la propria potenza e la crescente coscienza nazionale.

Carlo VIII (regnare 1483–1498), Luigi XII (regnare 1498–1515) e Francesco I (regnare 1515–1547) consolidarono in Francia la forte supremazia reale. Allo stesso tempo la

veranderingen door en kampte met bloedige oorlogen en burgeroorlogen. Dit was een tijd van grootscheepse politieke chaos die in schril contrast stond met de 'lieflijke' schilderkunst van deze periode, waarin de werkelijkheid bewust werd tegengesproken met een harmonieus ideaal.

Terwijl aan de Italiaanse hoven werd teruggegrepen op de klassieken en hun kunstuitingen en ook op hun filosofische en literaire tradities – een ontwikkeling die de grote Italiaanse steden tot ongekende bloei bracht –, werd de klassieke oudheid aan het Franse hof minder enthousiast omarmd. Frankrijk was door de Honderdjarige Oorlog (1337–1453) met Engeland in een economische crisis beland en de financiële middelen waarmee de laatgotische hofkunst nog zo was bevorderd, waren nu voor de oorlogvoering nodig.

Tot een centrum van artistieke vernieuwing ontpopte zich nu het van Frankrijk afgescheiden hertogdom Bourgondië, dat aan Engelse zijde vocht en in hertog Karel de Stoute een grote mecenas had gevonden. De schilder Jan van Eyck werd naar het Bourgondische hof ontboden en luidde een nieuw tijdperk in de schilderkunst in, met name in de schildertechniek: zijn consequente gebruik van olieverf en de glaceertechniek. Nieuwe opdrachtgevers kwamen uit de rijke koopmansfamilies van Brugge en Gent, en brachten de Vlaamse schilderkunst tot grote bloei.

Rond 1500 speelde zich op Italiaanse bodem een verbitterde strijd tussen de Europese grootmachten Frankrijk, Spanje, Engeland en het Heilige Roomse Rijk af. De Italiaanse staatjes wisten hun onafhankelijkheid te behouden, maar het politieke machtscentrum verplaatste zich duidelijk naar de landen ten noorden van de Alpen. Tijdens hun militaire campagnes in Italië kwamen de vorsten in contact met de Italiaanse renaissancecultuur en begonnen hun vorstelijke

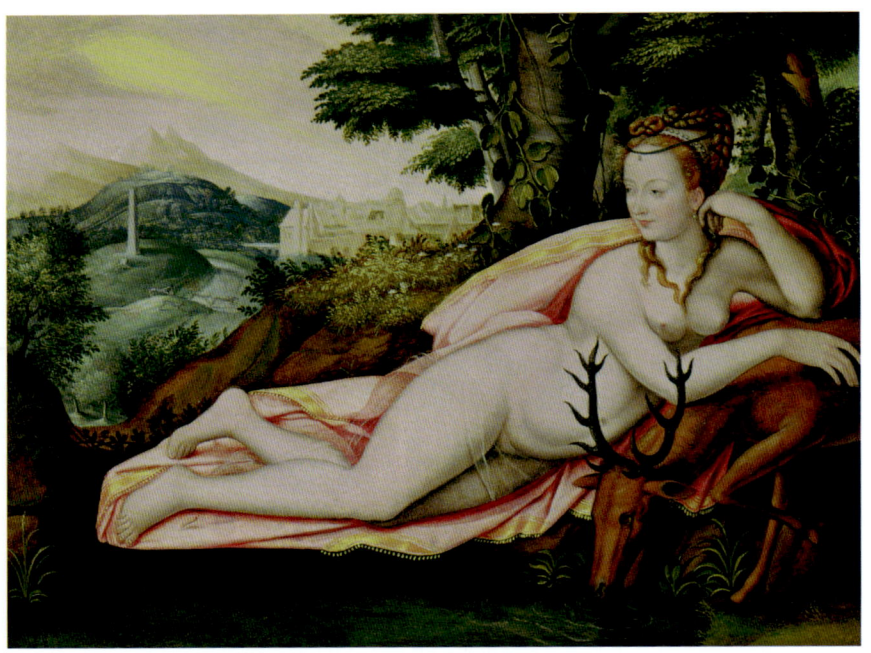

Fontainebleau School/École de Fontainebleau (fl. 1530–1570)

Diane de Poitiers as Diana the Huntress

Diane de Poitiers en Diane chasseresse

Diane von Poitiers als Diana die Jägerin

Diana de Poitiers como la Diana cazadora

Diane de Poitiers come Diana la cacciatrice

Diane de Poitiers als Diana de jaagster

n. d., Oil on canvas/Huile sur toile, 52 × 64 cm, Musée de la Vénerie, Senlis

supremacy in France. At the same time Italian culture became increasingly fashionable. This contemporary taste found considerable support from Francis I, who used the Italian design forms to create a representation of his authority with an ambitious architectural and artistic program. Following the example of the Italian Renaissance rulers, he enriched the royal library with classical and humanist texts. Many Italian artists gathered at his court, with Leonardo da Vinci, Andrea del Sarto, Rosso Fiorentino and Francesco Primaticcio amongst them. Francis I acquired numerous works by Italian painters, such as the *Mona Lisa* by Leonardo. He also had copies made of Michelangelo's sculptures, which were to adorn palaces and gardens. His sculpture collection also included bronze copies of famous antique statues such as the *Apollo Belvedere,* or the *Laocoön Group,* which were made from plaster casts of the originals. The rooms of his new chateau in Fontainebleau, near Paris, were

Les règnes de Charles VIII (1483–1498), Louis XII (1498–1515) et François Ier (1515–1547) renforcent en France la forte domination royale. Dans le même temps, la vogue de la culture italienne ne cesse de croître. François Ier favorise ce goût et, en utilisant les formes de représentation italienne, magnifie son autorité, par un programme artistique et architectural ambitieux. Sur le modèle des princes italiens de la Renaissance, il enrichit la bibliothèque royale de textes classiques et humanistes. À sa cour se retrouvent de nombreux artistes italiens dont Léonard de Vinci, Andrea del Sarto, Rosso Fiorentino et Francesco Primaticcio. François Ier acquiert en outre de nombreuses œuvres des peintres italiens comme, par exemple, la *Joconde* de Léonard. Il fait réaliser des copies de sculptures de Michel-Ange pour orner châteaux et jardins. La collection royale de sculptures comporte également des copies en bronze de statues célèbres telles que l'*Apollon du Belvédère* ou le groupe du *Laocoon,*

Karl VIII. (regiert 1483–1498), Ludwig XII. (regiert 1498–1515) und Franz I. (regiert 1515–1547) festigten in Frankreich die starke königliche Vormacht. Gleichzeitig kam die italienische Kultur immer mehr in Mode. Dieser Zeitgeschmack wurde ganz wesentlich durch Franz I. gefördert. Er bediente sich der italienischen Gestaltungsformen, um ein Bild seiner Autorität in einem ehrgeizigen Kunst- und Architekturprogramm zu schaffen. Nach dem Vorbild der italienischen Renaissance-Herrscher bereicherte er die königliche Bibliothek mit klassischen und humanistischen Texten. An seinem Hof versammelten sich italienische Künstler, unter ihnen Leonardo da Vinci, Andrea del Sarto, Rosso Fiorentino und Francesco Primaticcio. Franz I. erwarb zudem zahlreiche Werke italienischer Maler, wie beispielsweise die *Mona Lisa* von Leonardo. Von Michelangelos Skulpturen ließ er Kopien anfertigen, die Schlösser und Gärten schmücken sollten. Seine Skulpturensammlung

Allegory of Water *or* Allegory of Love
Allégorie mythologique
Allegorie des Wassers *oder* Allegorie der Liebe
Alegoría del agua *o* alegoría del amor
Allegoria dell'acqua *o* allegoria dell'amore
Allegorie van het Water, *of:* Allegorie van de Liefde

c. 1580, Oil on canvas/Huile sur toile, 130 × 96 cm, Musée du Louvre, Paris

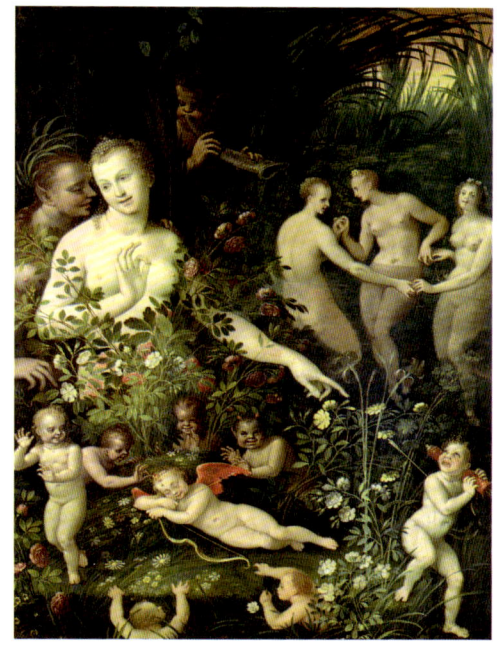

casa real. Al mismo tiempo la cultura italiana estaba cada vez más en boga; este gusto fue apoyado en especial por Francisco I. Se apropió de las formas de representación italianas para crear una imagen de su autoridad mediante un ambicioso programa artístico y arquitectónico. Siguiendo el ejemplo de los gobernantes del Renacimiento italiano enriqueció la biblioteca real con textos clásicos y humanistas. A su corte acudieron artistas italianos, entre otros Leonardo da Vinci, Andrea del Sarto, Rosso Fiorentino o Francesco Primaticcio. Francisco I adquirió además multitud de obras de pintores italianos, por ejemplo la *Mona Lisa* de Leonardo. Mandó realizar copias de las esculturas de Miguel Ángel, para decorar sus castillos y jardines. Su colección de esculturas incluía además copias en bronce de estatuas famosas de la Antigüedad, como el *Apolo de Belvedere* o el *Laocoonte,* realizadas a partir de moldes de escayola. Las estancias de su nuevo castillo en Fontainebleau, cerca de París,

cultura italiana diventò sempre più di moda. Questo gusto dell'epoca fu notevolmente favorito durante il regno di Francesco I. Egli si servì delle forme di espressione italiane per creare un'immagine della sua autorità in un ambizioso programma artistico e architettonico. Seguendo l'esempio dei sovrani del Rinascimento italiano, egli arricchì la biblioteca reale con testi classici e umanistici. Alla sua corte si riunirono artisti italiani, tra i quali Leonardo da Vinci, Andrea del Sarto, Rosso Fiorentino e Francesco Primaticcio. Francesco I acquistò inoltre numerose opere di pittori italiani, come ad esempio la *Mona Lisa* di Leonardo. Egli fece realizzare delle copie delle sculture di Michelangelo, che dovevano abbellire castelli e giardini. La sua collezione di sculture comprendeva inoltre copie in bronzo di famose statue dell'antichità come *Apollo del Belvedere,* o il *Gruppo del Laocoonte,* che fu creato da calchi in gesso. Le stanze del suo nuovo castello di Fontainebleau vicino a Parigi

macht in een groeiend nationaal bewustzijn ten toon te spreiden.

Karel VIII (1483–1498), Lodewijk XII (1498–1515) en Frans I (1515–1547) vestigden een zelfbewuste monarchie in Frankrijk, terwijl tegelijkertijd de Italiaanse cultuur steeds meer in de mode raakte. De smaak van de tijd werd in hoge mate bepaald door Frans I, die Italiaanse stijlen gebruikte om in een ambitieus programma van kunst- en bouwwerken een imago van autoriteit uit te stralen. Naar het voorbeeld van de Italiaanse renaissancevorsten verrijkte hij de koninklijke bibliotheek met klassieke en humanistische teksten. Aan zijn hof verzamelden zich Italiaanse kunstenaars als Leonardo da Vinci, Andrea del Sarto, Rosso Fiorentino en Francesco Primaticcio. Ook schafte Frans I talloze werken van Italiaanse kunstenaars aan, waaronder de *Mona Lisa* van Leonardo. Hij liet kopieën van Michelangelo's beeldhouwwerken vervaardigen, die zijn kastelen en tuinen moesten sieren. Zijn

decorated in Italian style with stucco and painted panels. The iconography of the School of Fontainebleau, developed by Francesco Primaticcio and Rosso Fiorentino, included historical, mythological and Christian themes in which the French king was glorified.

The increased power of the European royal houses was shaken by violent religious crises and schisms and their subsequent harsh and mercilessly conducted religious wars. The negative consequences of the Reformation were experienced by Martin Luther during the bloodily suppressed Peasants' Revolt. The Catholic Church had staged a counter-attack with the reforms of the Council of Trent in the mid-16th century, which restored the religious (Catholic) life in many parts of Europe, but the extraordinary religious tensions also affected the art, resulting in the destruction of the subtle balance between reality and idealism, between the sacred and the profane spheres in the diverse "mannerisms" of the late Renaissance. The crisis of the High Renaissance, however, was certainly also a result of a new world view, which was fuelled by the discoveries of Christopher Columbus and Amerigo Vespucci, the circumnavigation of Africa by Vasco da Gama and the first circumnavigation of the globe by Fernão de Magalhães (Ferdinand Magellan), placing Europe at the center of the world. In addition, Copernicus discovered the 'new planetary motion', in which the sun and not the earth was placed at the center of planetary orbits.

réalisées à partir de moulages en plâtre. Les salles de son nouveau château, à Fontainebleau, sont décorées de stucs et de panneaux peints dans le style italien. Sous l'impulsion de Francesco Primaticcio et de Rosso Fiorentino naît un courant artistique que les historiens d'art appellent l'« école de Fontainebleau », dont l'iconographie repose sur des sujets mythologiques, historiques et chrétiens dans lesquels le roi de France se trouve glorifié.

La puissance accrue des maisons royales européennes est toutefois ébranlée par des crises et scissions religieuses très violentes, suivies de guerres de religion acharnées et sans merci. Martin Luther a vécu lui-même les conséquences funestes de la Réforme avec l'écrasement sanglant de la guerre des Paysans. Au milieu du XVIᵉ siècle, l'Église catholique allume des contre-feux avec les réformes du concile de Trente et restaure la foi catholique dans de larges parties de l'Europe. Les tensions religieuses exacerbées ont toutefois aussi ébranlé l'art, entraînant la destruction de l'équilibre subtil entre réalité et idéalité comme entre le profane et le sacré, dans les divers « maniérismes » de la Renaissance tardive. La crise de la Haute Renaissance fut aussi la conséquence d'une nouvelle vision du monde apportée par les découvertes de Christophe Colomb et d'Amerigo Vespucci, le contournement de l'Afrique par Vasco de Gama et le premier tour du monde à la voile par Fernand de Magellan, qui relativisent la position de l'Europe comme centre du monde. Copernic découvre en outre le « nouveau » mouvement des planètes : ce n'est plus désormais la Terre mais le Soleil qui est au centre du système.

umfasste außerdem Bronzekopien berühmter antiker Statuen wie der *Apollo von Belvedere,* oder die *Laokoon-Gruppe,* die von Gipsabgüssen gemacht wurden. Die Räume seines neuen Schlosses in Fontainebleau bei Paris wurden im italienischen Stil mit Stuckarbeiten und gemalten Paneelen geschmückt. Die von Francesco Primaticcio und Rosso Fiorentino entwickelte Ikonographie der Schule von Fontainebleau umfasste historische, mythologische und christliche Themen, in denen der französische König verherrlicht wurde.

Die gesteigerte Macht der europäischen Königshäuser wurde aber durch heftige Glaubenskrisen und Abspaltungen mit in der Folge intensiv und erbarmungslos geführten Glaubenskriegen erschüttert. Diese negativen Folgen der Reformation hat Martin Luther mit den blutig niedergeschlagenen Bauernkriegen noch erlebt. Die katholische Kirche hat mit den Reformen des Tridentiner Konzils um die Mitte des 16. Jahrhunderts zum Gegenschlag ausgeholt und das religiöse (katholische) Leben in weiten Teilen Europas wiederhergestellt. Doch die außerordentlichen religiösen Spannungen erschüttern auch die Kunst, was zur Zerstörung der subtilen Balance zwischen Realität und Idealität, zwischen profaner und sakraler Sphäre in den mannigfaltigen „Manierismen" der Spätrenaissance führte. Die Krise der Hochrenaissance war allerdings auch Folge eines neuen Weltbildes, das durch die Entdeckungen von Christoph Kolumbus und Amerigo Vespucci, der Umseglung Afrikas durch Vasco da Gama und die erste Weltumseglung von Fernão de Magalhães gefördert wurde und Europa als Mittelpunkt der Welt relativierte. Kopernikus entdeckte zudem die neue Planetenbewegung: Nicht die Erde, sondern die Sonne steht im Zentrum der Planetenbahnen.

se decoraron en estilo italiano con paneles pintados y trabajos en estuco. La iconografía de la Escuela de Fontainebleau, desarrollada por Francesco Primaticcio y Rosso Fiorentino incluía temas históricos, mitológicos y cristianos, en los que se glorificaba al Rey de Francia.

El poder al alza de las casas reales europeas se vio sin embargo sacudido por violentas crisis de fe y escisiones, con consecuentes intensas y despiadadas guerras de religión. El propio Martín Lutero vivió estos efectos negativos de la Reforma, con las sangrientas guerras de los campesinos alemanes. La Iglesia católica presentó su contragolpe con las reformas del Concilio de Trento a mediados del XVI, consiguiendo volver a encauzar la vida religiosa (católica) en gran parte de Europa. Y sin embargo estas extraordinarias tensiones religiosas alcanzaron también al arte, lo que llevó a la disrupción del precario equilibrio entre realidad e identidad, entre las esferas sacra y profana, en los diversos "manierismos" del Renacimiento tardío. La crisis del Alto Renacimiento también era consecuencia de una nueva imagen global que relativizaba el rol de Europa como centro del mundo tras los descubrimientos de Cristóbal Colón, Américo Vespucio, la travesía por la costa africana de Vasco da Gama o la primera vuelta al mundo de Fernando de Magallanes. Copérnico descubrió además un nuevo movimiento planetario: no era la Tierra, sino el Sol, el que ocupaba el centro del sistema.

furono decorate in stile italiano con opere in stucco e pannelli dipinti. L'iconografia della Scuola di Fontainebleau sviluppata da Francesco Primaticcio e dal Rosso Fiorentino comprendeva temi storici, mitologici e cristiani, nei quali fu glorificato il re francese.

L'accresciuta potenza delle case reali europee fu però sconvolta da violente crisi di credo religioso e separazioni, che causarono guerre di religione condotte con intensità e crudeltà. Queste conseguenze negative della Riforma le aveva già vissute Martin Lutero con le guerre dei contadini represse nel sangue. La Chiesa Cattolica passò al contrattacco con le riforme del Concilio di Trento della metà del XVI secolo e ricostruì la vita religiosa (cattolica) in gran parte dell'Europa. Ma le straordinarie tensioni religiose scossero anche l'arte, causando la distruzione del sottile equilibrio tra realtà e idealità, e tra sfera profana e sacra negli svariati "manierismi" del tardo Rinascimento. La crisi dell'alto Rinascimento fu tuttavia anche la conseguenza di una nuova visione del mondo, che fu favorita dalle scoperte di Cristoforo Colombo e Amerigo Vespucci, dalla circumnavigazione dell'Africa di Vasco da Gama e dalla prima circumnavigazione del globo di Fernão de Magalhães, relativizzando l'Europa come centro del mondo. Copernico scoprì inoltre il nuovo movimento planetario: non era la terra a trovarsi al centro dell'orbita dei pianeti, bensì il sole.

collectie beeldhouwwerken omvatte daarnaast bronskopieën van beroemde klassieke werken als de *Apollo van Belvedère* en van de *Laocoöngroep* liet hij een gipsafgietsel maken. De zalen van zijn nieuwe slot in Fontainebleau bij Parijs werden in Italiaanse stijl met stucwerk en beschilderde wandpanelen gedecoreerd. De iconografie die daarbij door Francesco Primaticcio en Rosso Fiorentino werd ontwikkeld en die als de School van Fontainebleau werd aangeduid, omvatte historische, mythologische en christelijke motieven waarin de Franse koning werd verheerlijkt.

Maar de machtsbevestiging van de Europese vorstenhuizen werd verstoord door een ingrijpende geloofscrisis en kerkelijke afsplitsingen, die tot intense en meedogenloze godsdienstoorlogen leidden. Martin Luther zelf was nog getuige van de negatieve uitwerkingen van de protestantse Reformatie, toen de Boerenopstanden bloedig werden neergeslagen. Met de hervormingen van het Concilie van Trente, halverwege de zestiende eeuw, begon de katholieke kerk aan een tegenoffensief en werd het katholieke leven in grote delen van Europa in ere hersteld. De grote religieuze spanningen schokten ook de kunst, wat tot een verstoring van de subtiele balans tussen realiteit en ideaal leidde, tussen het profane en sacrale, en zich uitte in de vele 'maniëristische' stromingen van de late renaissance. Maar de crisis van de hoge renaissance was zeker ook het gevolg van het nieuwe wereldbeeld dat na de ontdekkingen van Cristoffel Columbus en Amerigo Vespucci, de zeilreis om de Kaap de Goede Hoop door Vasco da Gama en de eerste zeilreis rond de wereld door Ferdinand Magellaan was ontstaan en waarin de plaats van Europa als middelpunt van de wereld werd gerelativeerd. Bovendien bood Copernicus nieuw inzicht in de bewegingen van de planeten, waardoor niet de aarde maar de zon in het centrum van de kosmos kwam te staan.

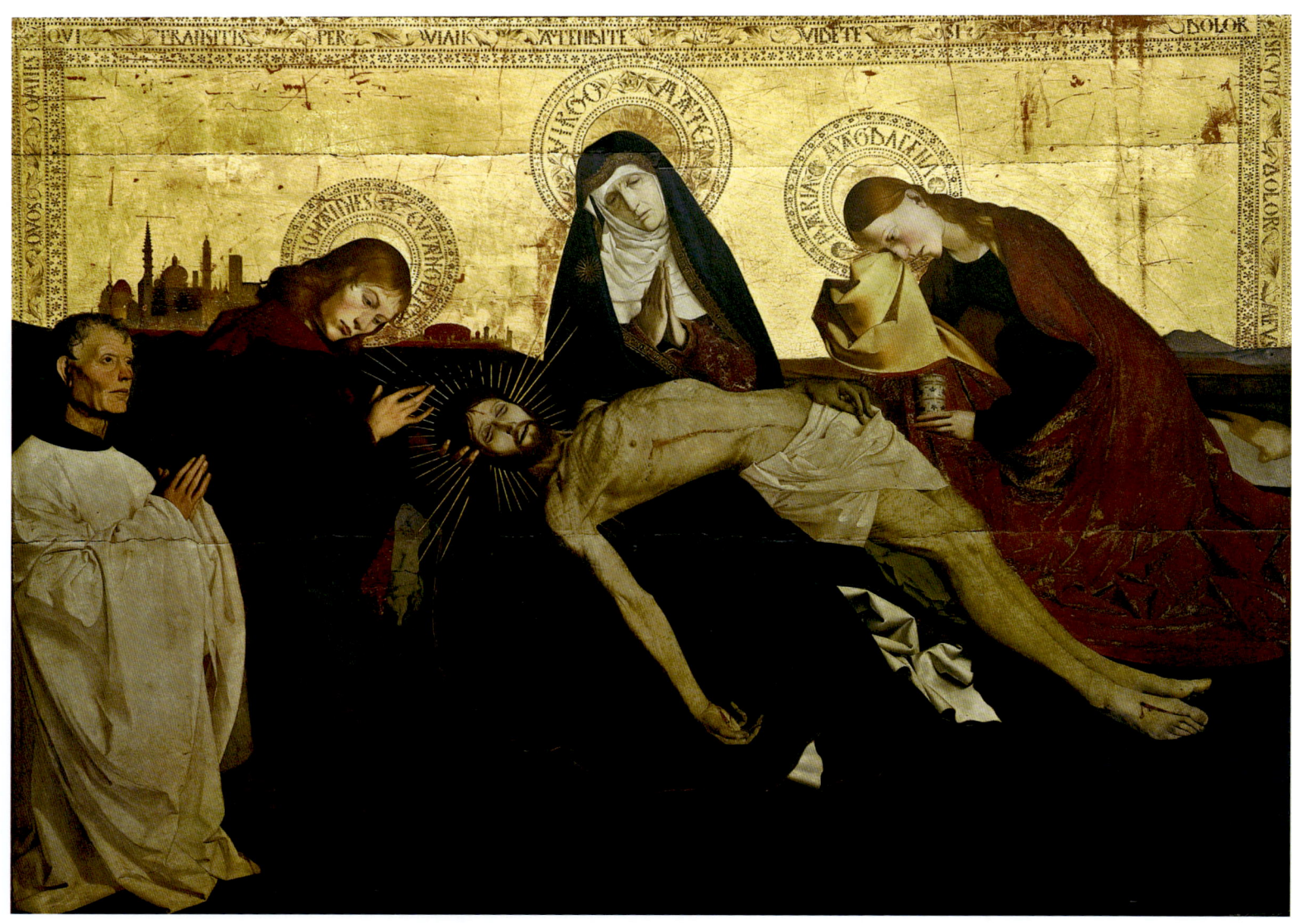

Enguerrand Quarton (c. 1410–1466)

The Pietà of Avignon

Pietà de Villeneuve-lès-Avignon

Pietà von Avignon

Pietá de Aviñón

Pietà di Avignone

Piëta van Avignon

c. 1455, Oil on wood/Huile sur bois, 163 × 218 cm, Musée du Louvre, Paris

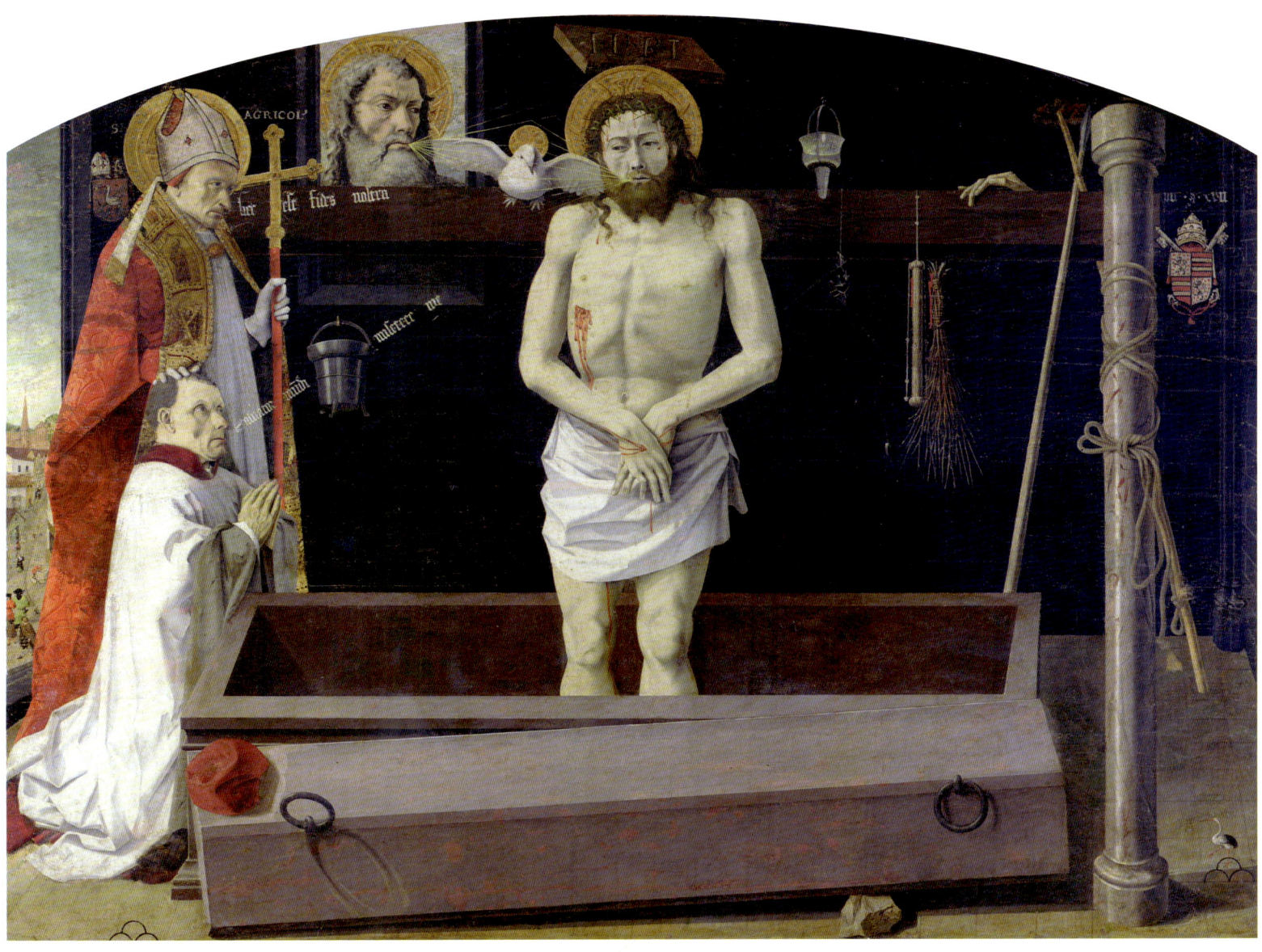

Provençal Painter/Peintre provençal

The Altarpiece of Boulbon

Le Retable de Boulbon

Altarretabel von Boulbon

El retablo de Boulbon

La Pala di Boulbon

Het retabel van Boulbon

c. 1450, Oil on wood/Huile sur bois, 172 × 228 cm, Musée du Louvre, Paris

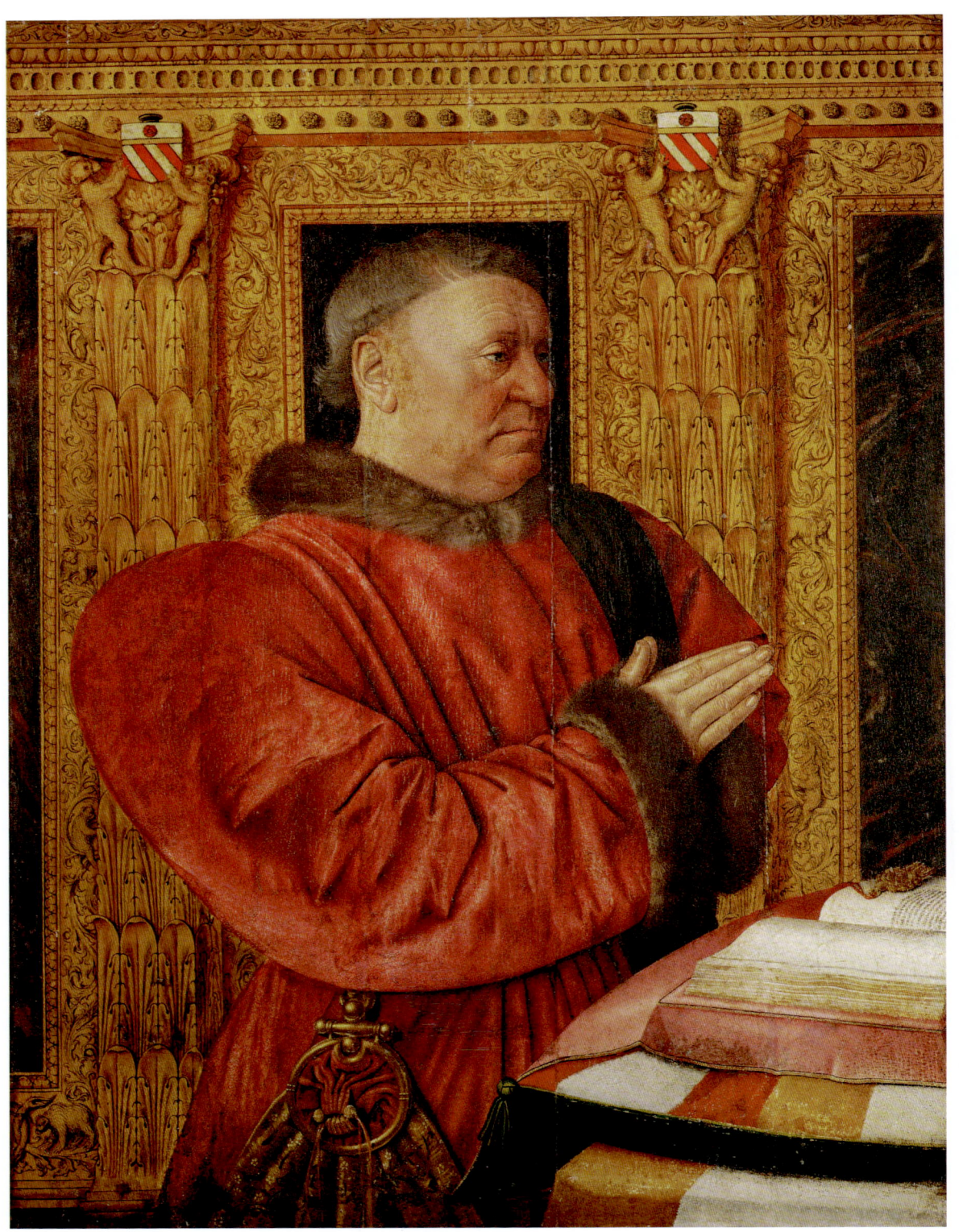

Jean Fouquet (c. 1420–c. 1480)

Portrait of Guillaume Jouvenel des Ursins

Guillaume Jouvenel des Ursins (1401–1472), chancelier de France

Bildnis des Guillaume Jouvenel des Ursins

Retrato de Guillaume Jouvenel des Ursins

Ritratto di Guillaume Jouvenel des Ursins

Portret van Guillaume Jouvenel des Ursins

c. 1465, Oil on wood/Huile sur bois, 93 × 73 cm, Musée du Louvre, Paris

Jean Fouquet (c. 1420–c. 1480)

Virgin and Child surrounded by cherubim and seraphim *(right wing af Melun diptych)*

La Vierge et l'Enfant entourés d'anges *(volet droit du diptyque de Melun)*

Die thronende Madonna mit dem Christuskind *(rechter Flügel des Diptychons von Melun)*

La Virgen de Melun/Virgen con Niño y ángeles *(ala derecha del díptico de Melun)*

Madonna del latte in trono col Bambino *(pannello destro del Dittico di Melun)*

De Maagd en het Kind, door engelen omringd *(rechtervleugel van de diptiek van Melun)*

c. 1452–1458, Oil on wood/Huile sur bois, 91,8 × 83,3 cm, Museum voor Schone Kunsten, Antwerpen

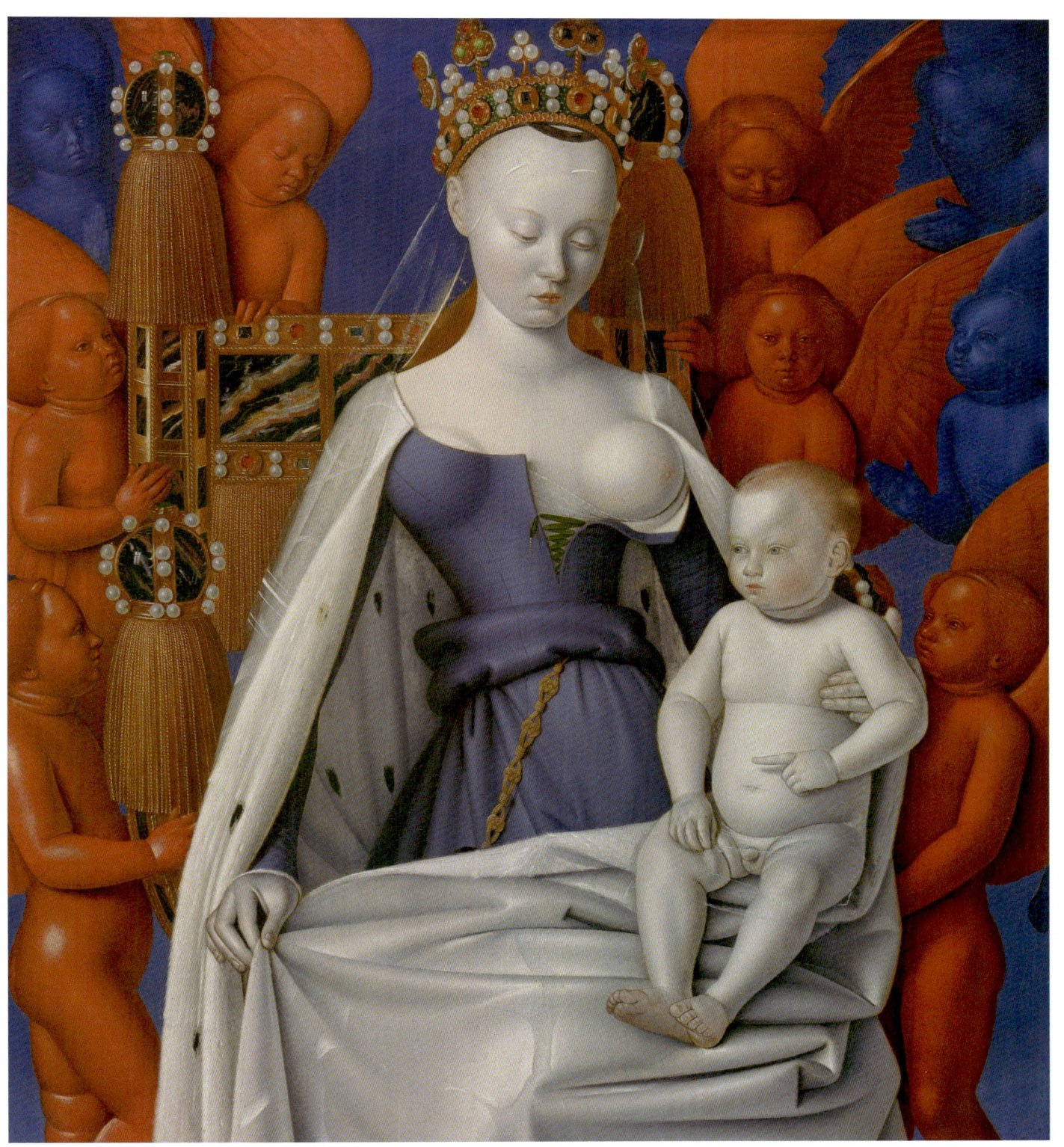

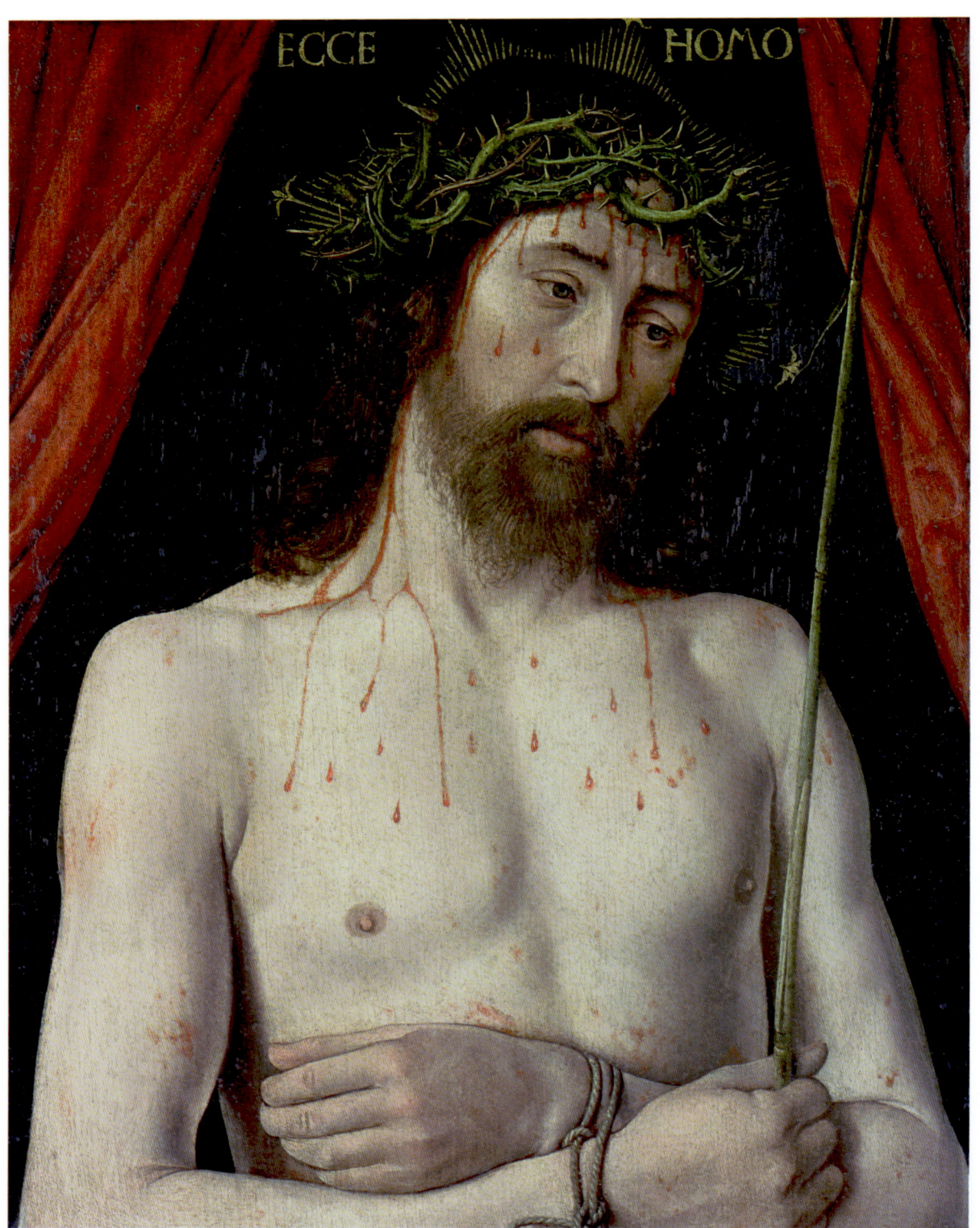

**Master of Moulins/
Le Maître de Moulins (Jean Hey)
(fl. 1480–1500)**

Ecce Homo

c. 1494, Oil on wood/Huile sur bois,
39 × 30 cm, Musées royaux des
Beaux-Arts de Belgique, Bruxelles

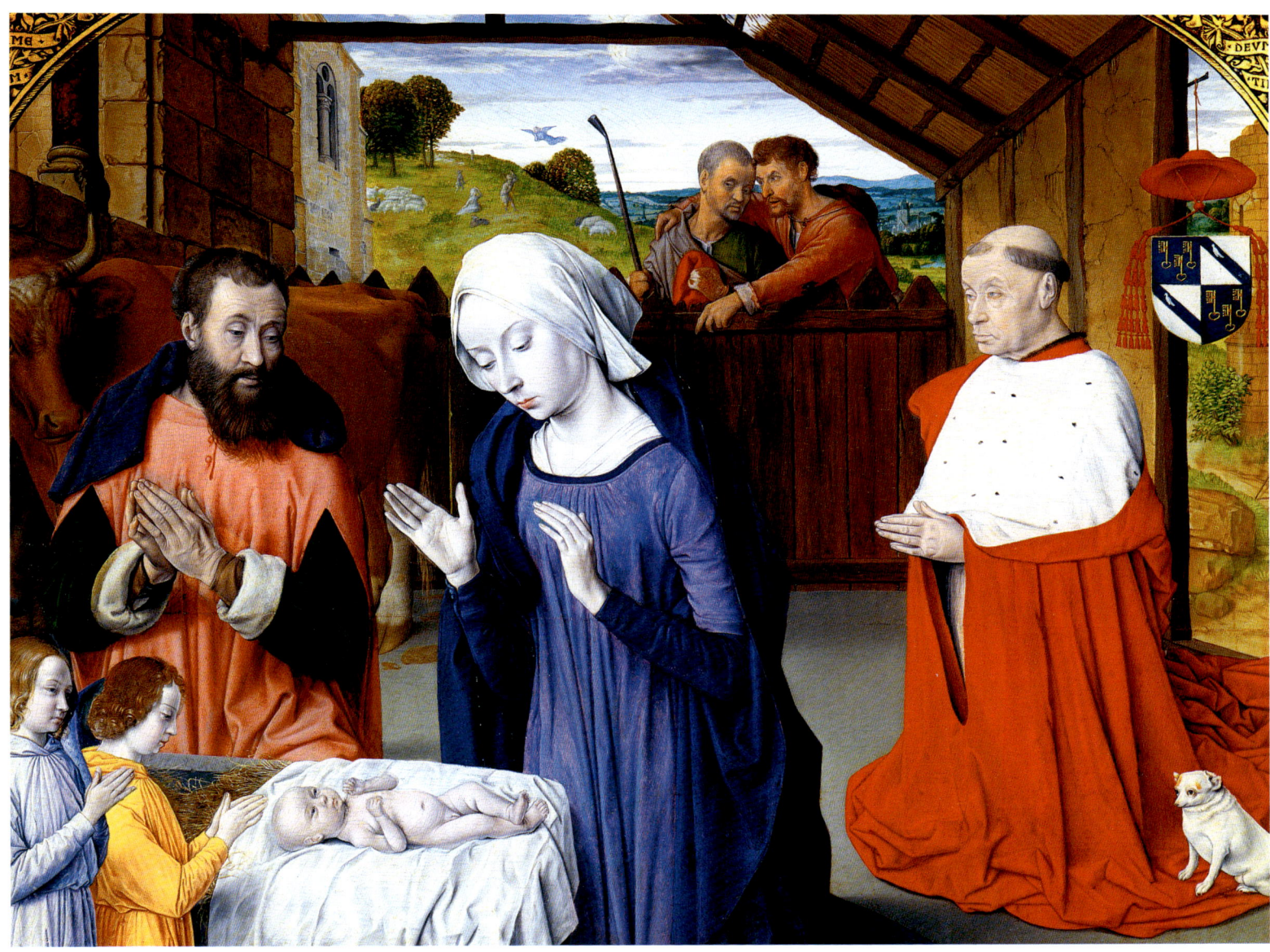

Master of Moulins/Le Maître de Moulins (Jean Hey) (fl. 1480–1500)

The Nativity

La Nativité

Die Geburt Jesu

La Natividad

Natività

De geboorte van Jezus

n. d., Oil on wood/Huile sur bois, 55 × 71 cm, Musée Rolin, Autun

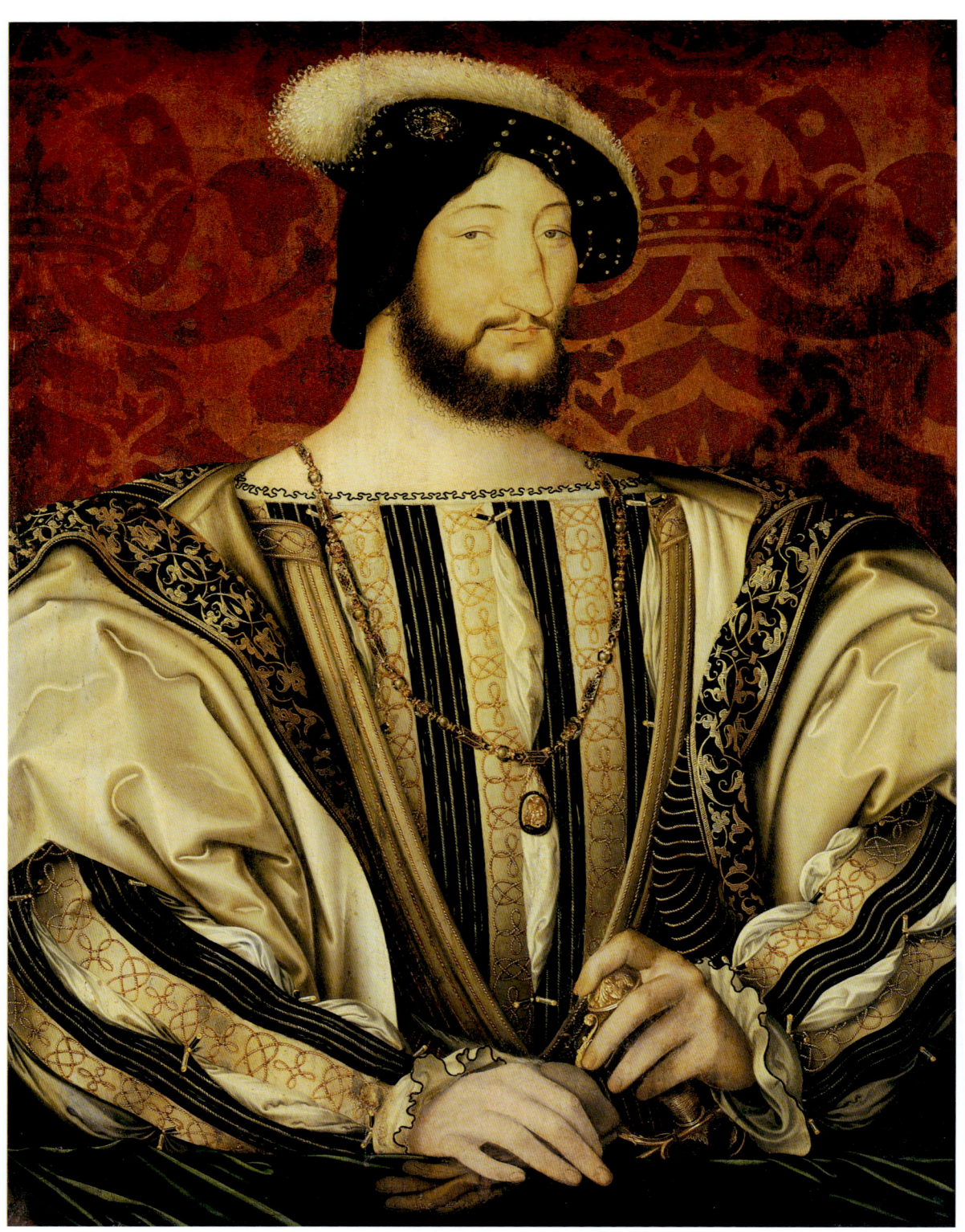

Jean Clouet (c. 1480–c. 1541)

King Francis I of France

Portrait de François Ier, roi de France

König Franz I. von Frankreich

Rey Francisco I de Francia

Francesco I di Francia

Koning Frans I van Frankrijk

c. 1530, Oil on wood/Huile sur bois, 96 × 74 cm, Musée du Louvre, Paris

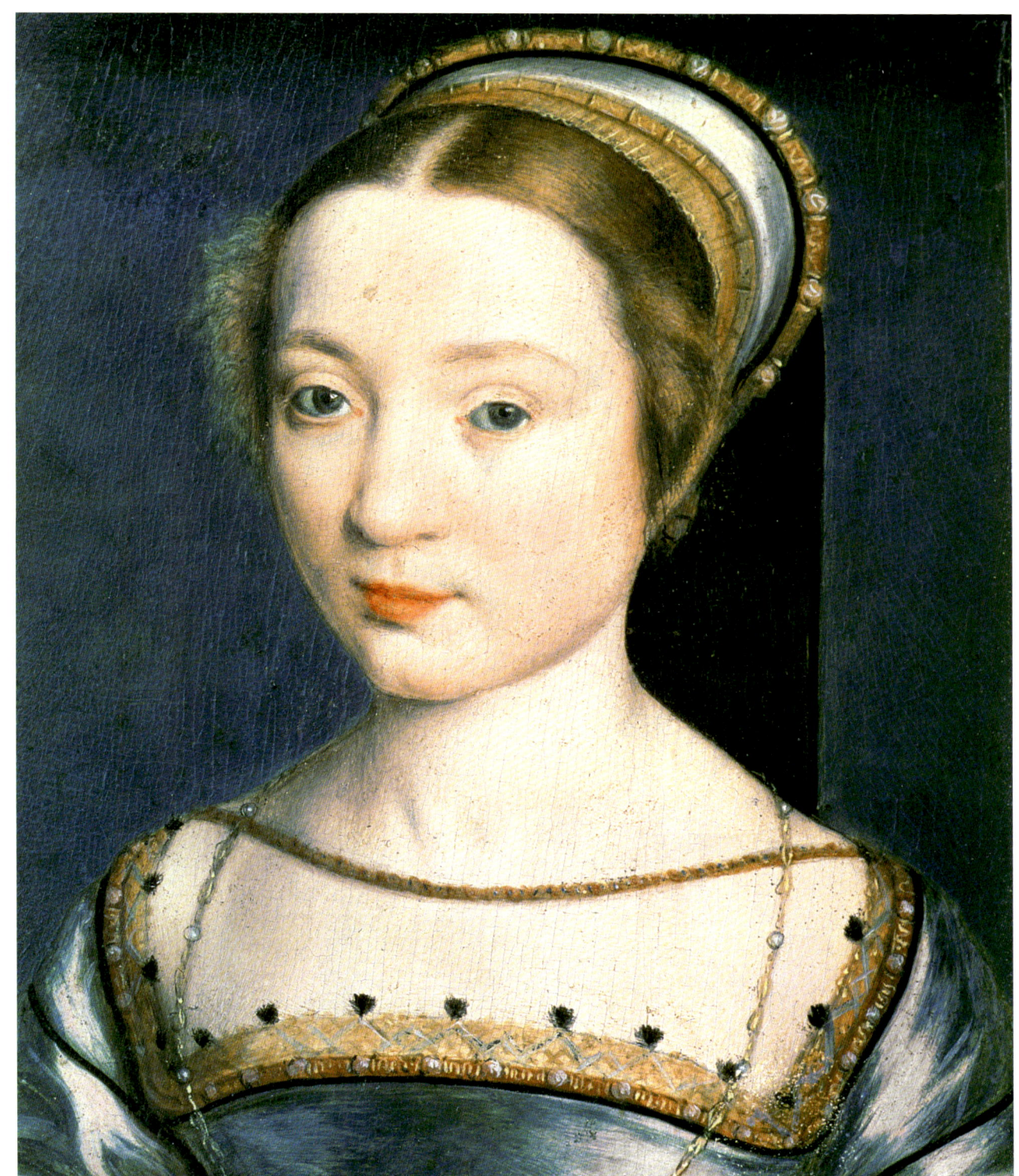

Corneille de Lyon
(c. 1500–c. 1574)

Portrait of Queen Claude

Portrait de Claude de
France

Porträt der Königin
Claude

Retrato de la reina
Claudia

Ritratto della regina
Claudia

Portret van koningin
Claude

n. d., Oil on wood/Huile sur
bois, 11,5 × 10 cm, Pushkin
State Museum of Fine Arts,
Moscow

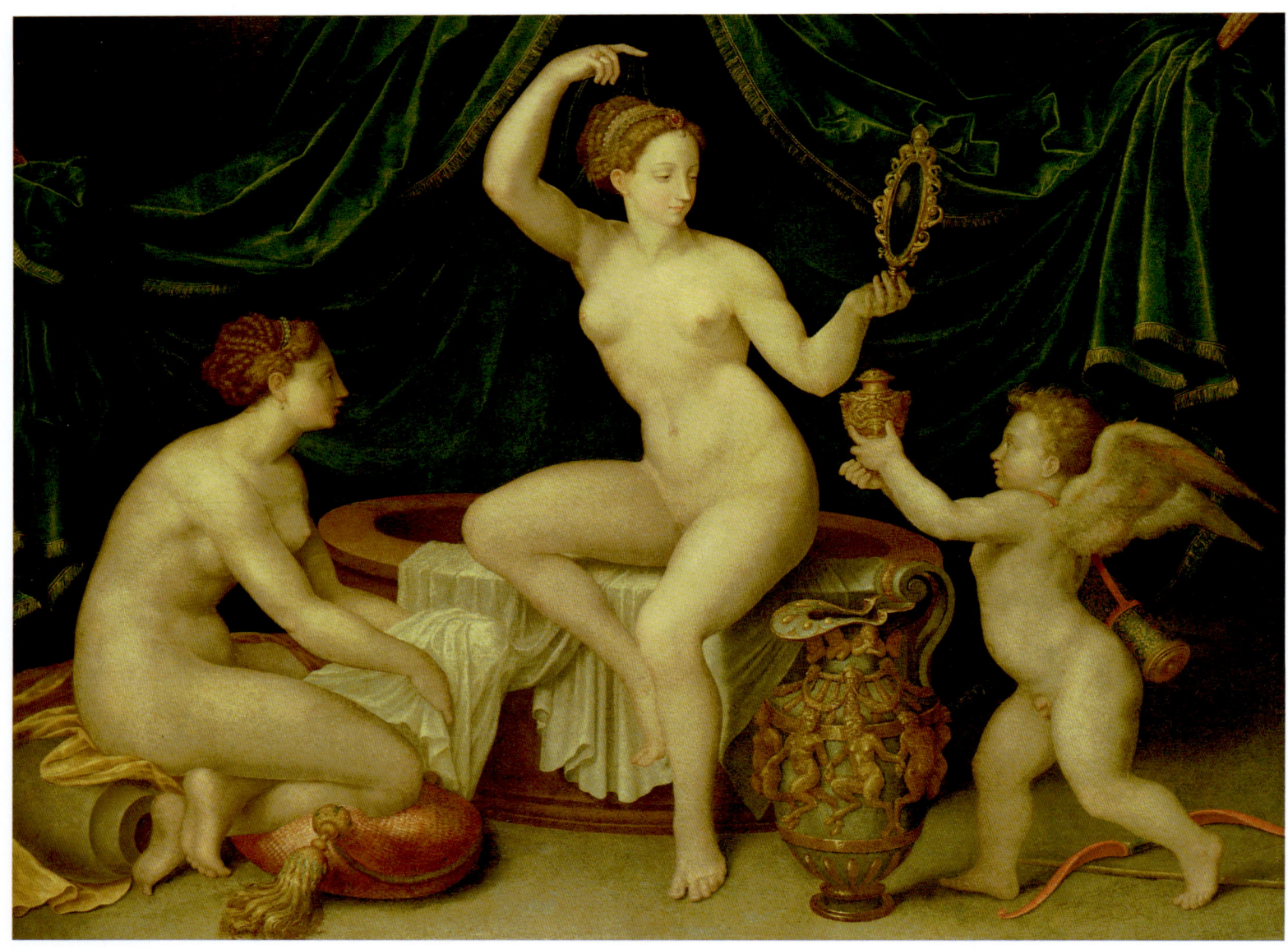

Fontainebleau School/École de Fontainebleau (fl. 1530–1570)

Venus at her Toilet

Vénus à sa toilette

Venus bei ihrer Toilette

Venus en su aseo

Venere nel suo bagno

Het toilet van Venus

c. 1550, Oil on canvas/Huile sur toile, 97 × 126 cm, Musée du Louvre, Paris

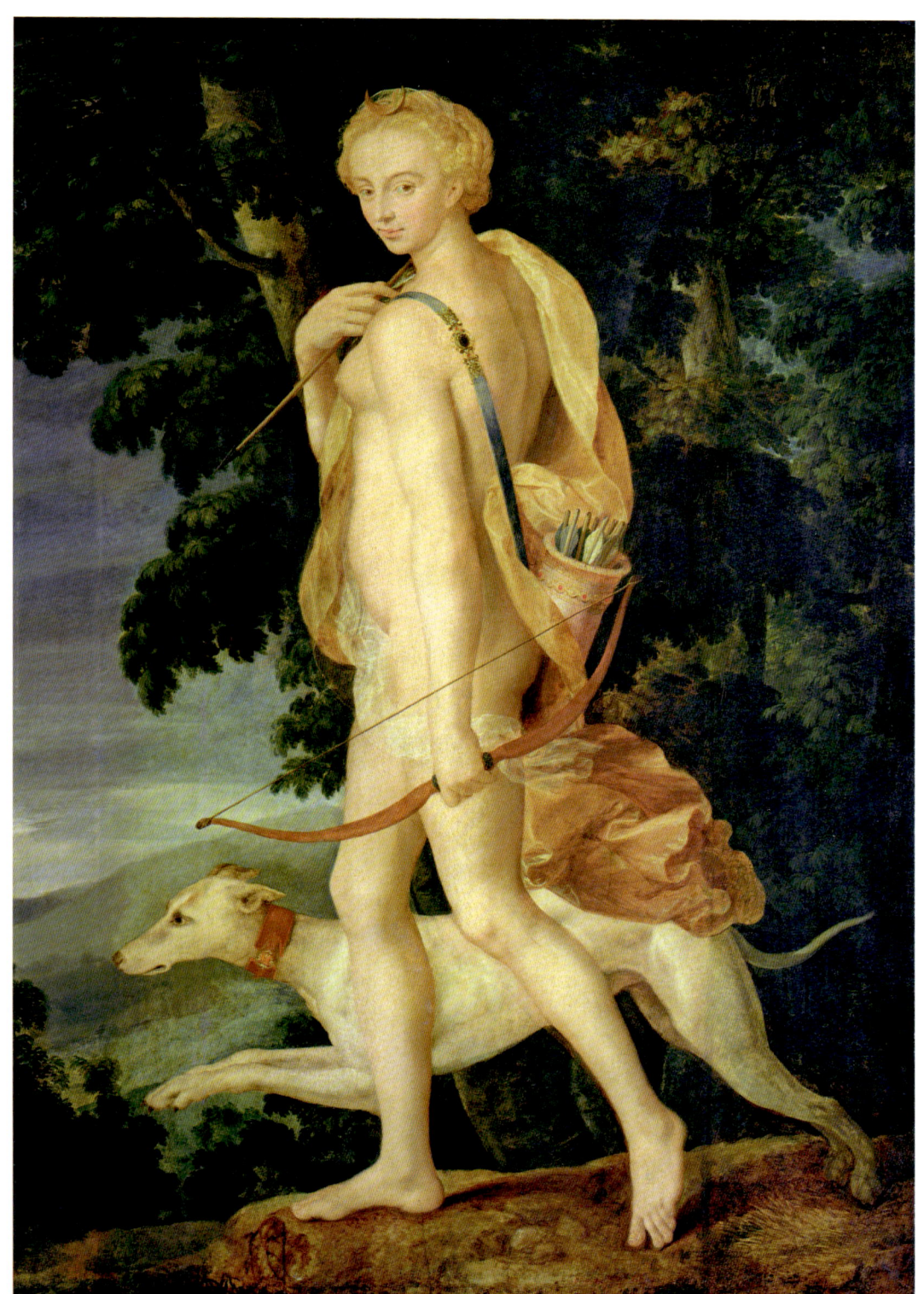

Fontainebleau School/École de Fontainebleau
(fl. 1530–1570)

Diana the Huntress

Diane chasseresse

Diana die Jägerin

Diana como cazadora

Diana la cacciatrice

Diana de Jaagster

c. 1550, Oil on wood/Huile sur bois, 191 × 132 cm,
Musée du Louvre, Paris

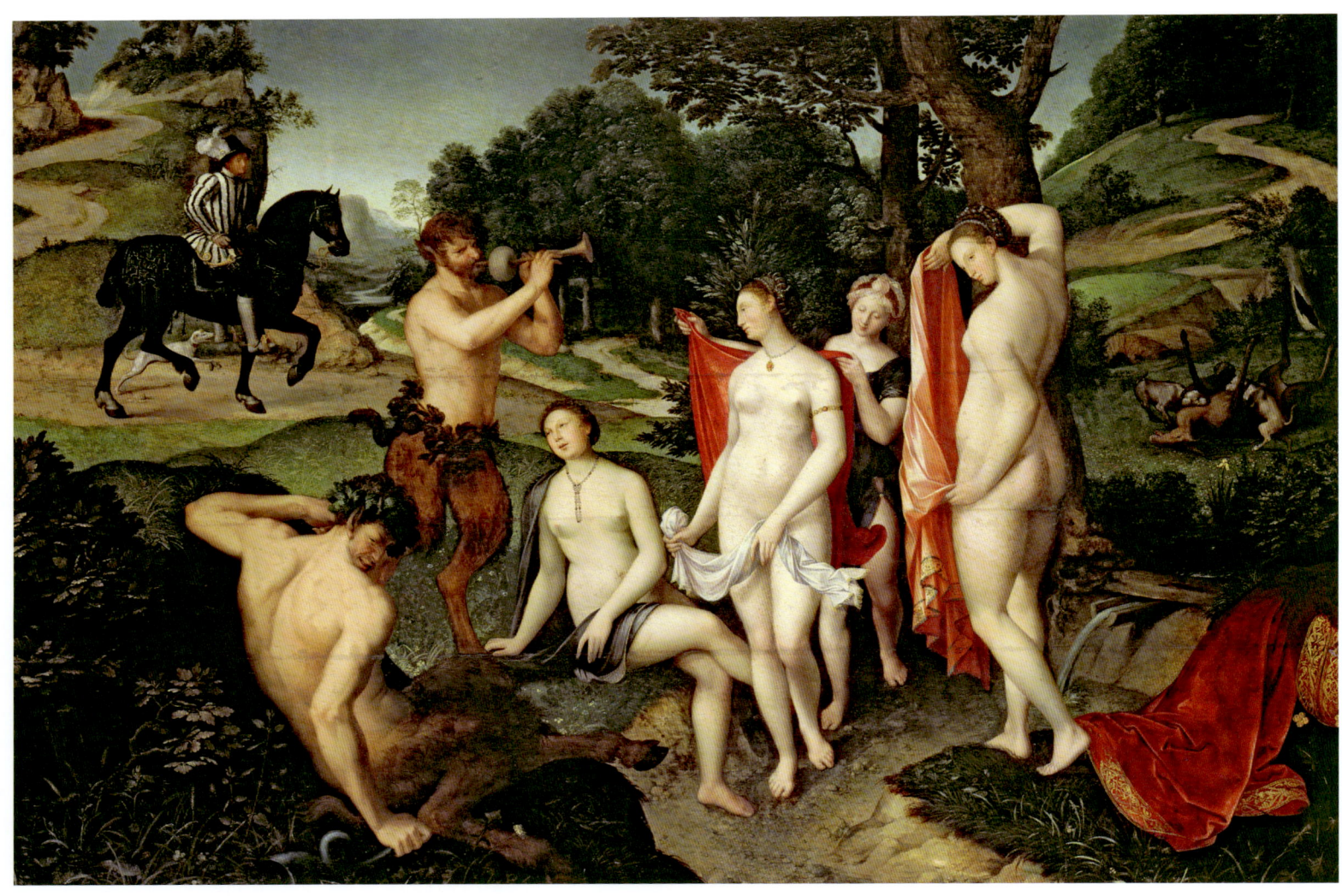

François Clouet (c. 1520–1572)

The Bath Of Diana

Le Bain de Diane

Das Bad der Diana

El baño de diana

Il bagno di Diana

Het bad van Diana

n. d., Oil on wood/Huile sur bois, 136 × 196,5 cm, Musée des Beaux-Arts, Rouen

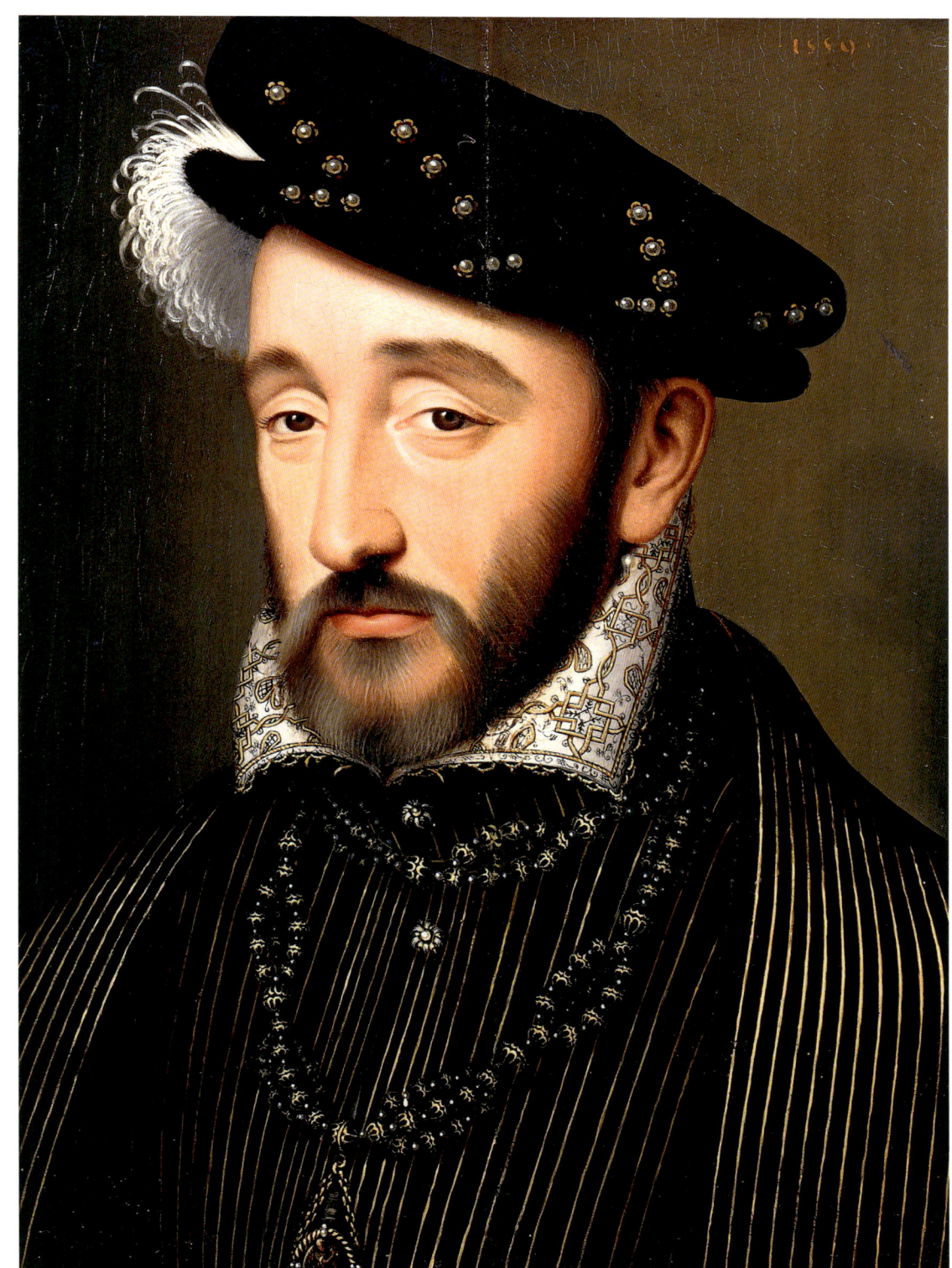

François Clouet (c. 1520–1572)

Portrait of Henry II

Portrait d'Henri II, roi de France

Bildnis von Henri II

Retrato de Enrique II

Ritratto di Enrico II, re di Francia

Portret van Henri II

n. d., Oil on wood/Huile sur bois, 30 × 22 cm,
Château de Versailles, Versailles

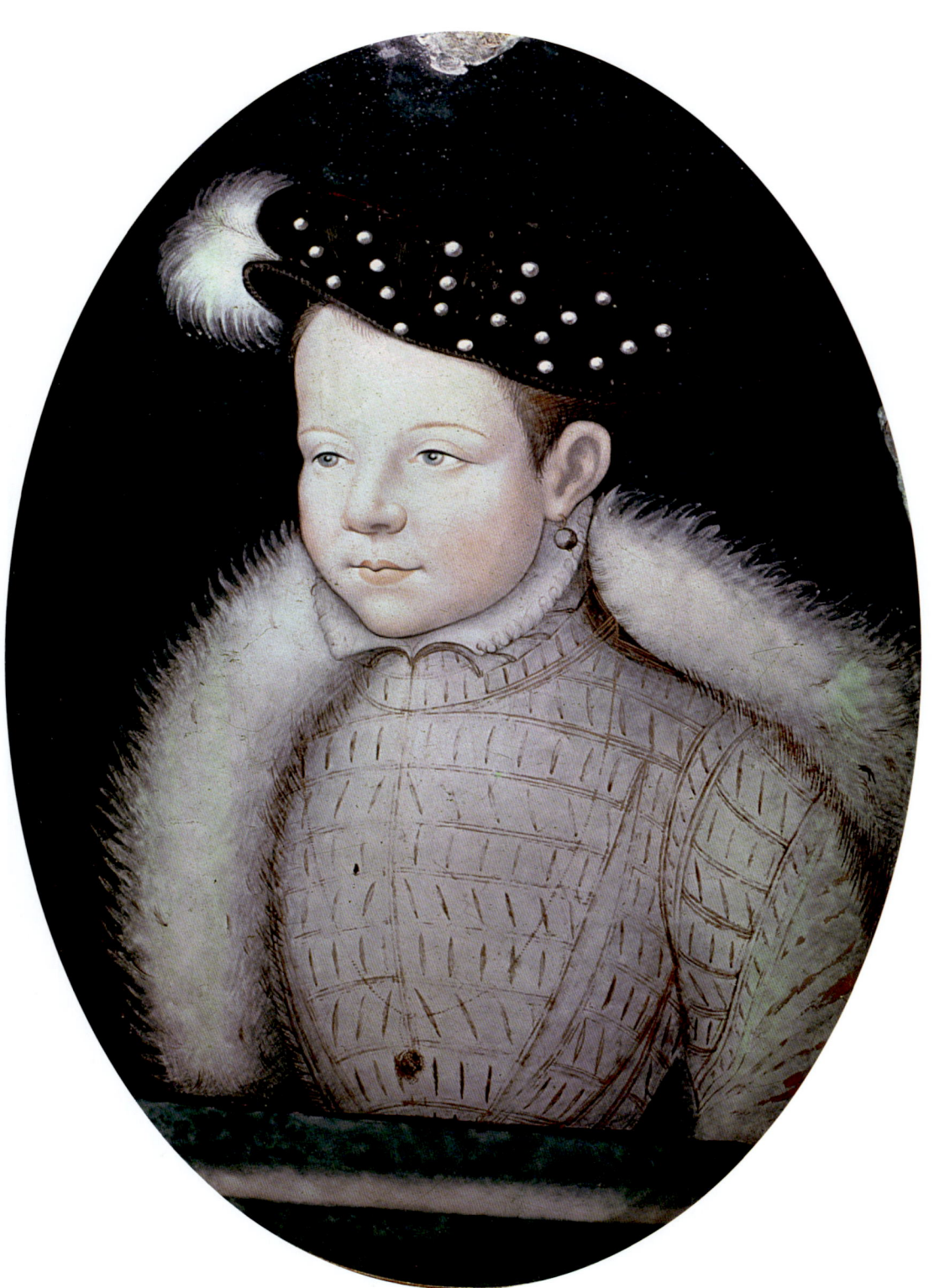

Léonard Limosin (attributed to/attribué à)
(c. 1505–c. 1577)

Portrait of Francis II as Dauphin of France

Portrait du futur François II

Porträt von Franz II.

Retrato de Francisco II

Ritratto di Francesco II

Portret van Frans II

c. 1553, Enamel on copper/Email sur cuivre,
44,8 × 31,9 cm, Musée du Louvre, Paris

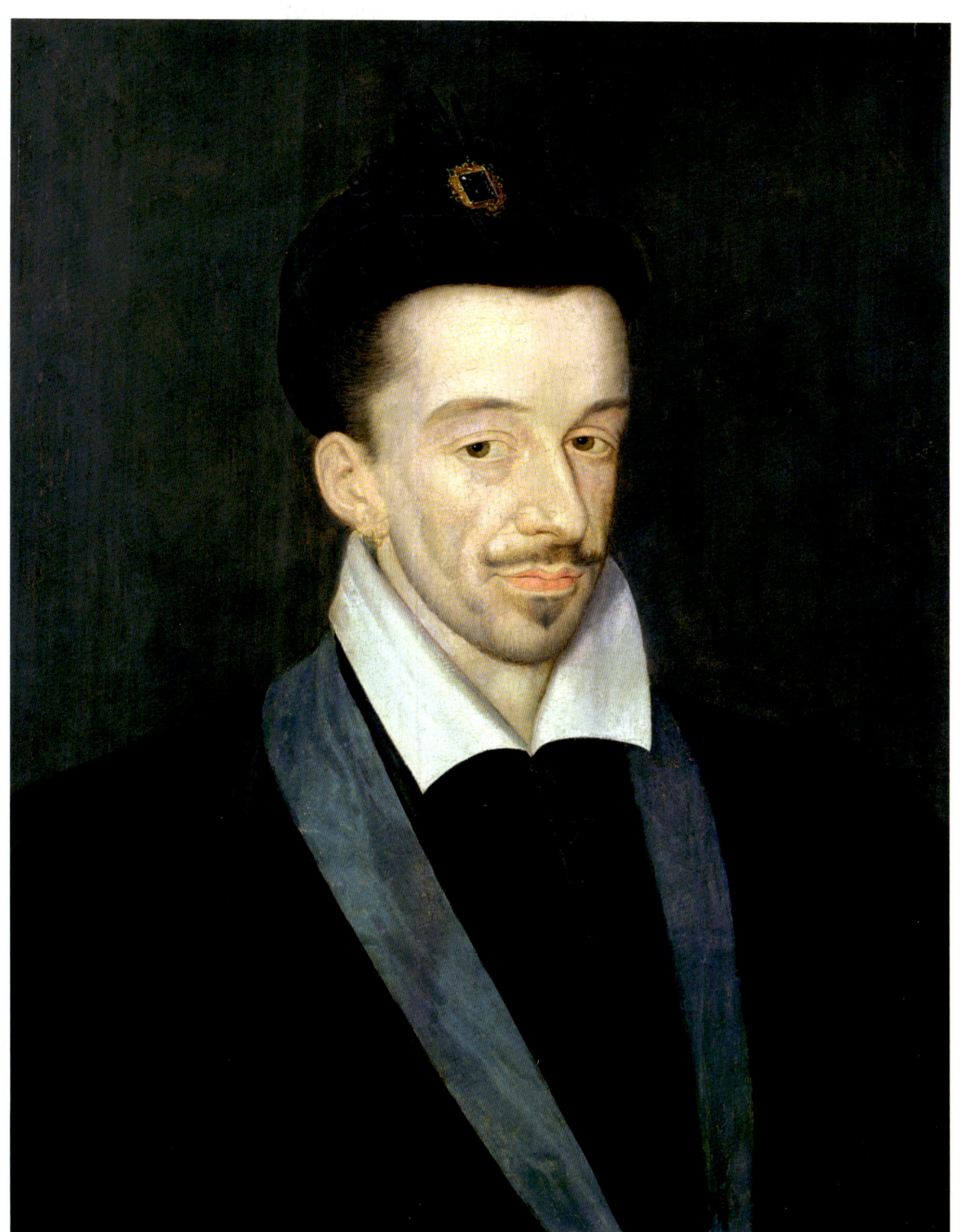

François Quesnel (attributed to/ attribué à) (c. 1545–1616)

Portrait of Henri III

Portrait d'Henri III

Porträt Henri III.

Retrato de Enrique III

Ritratto di Enrico III

Portret van Hendrik III

c. 1582, Oil on canvas/Huile sur toile, 66 × 52 cm, Musée du Louvre, Paris

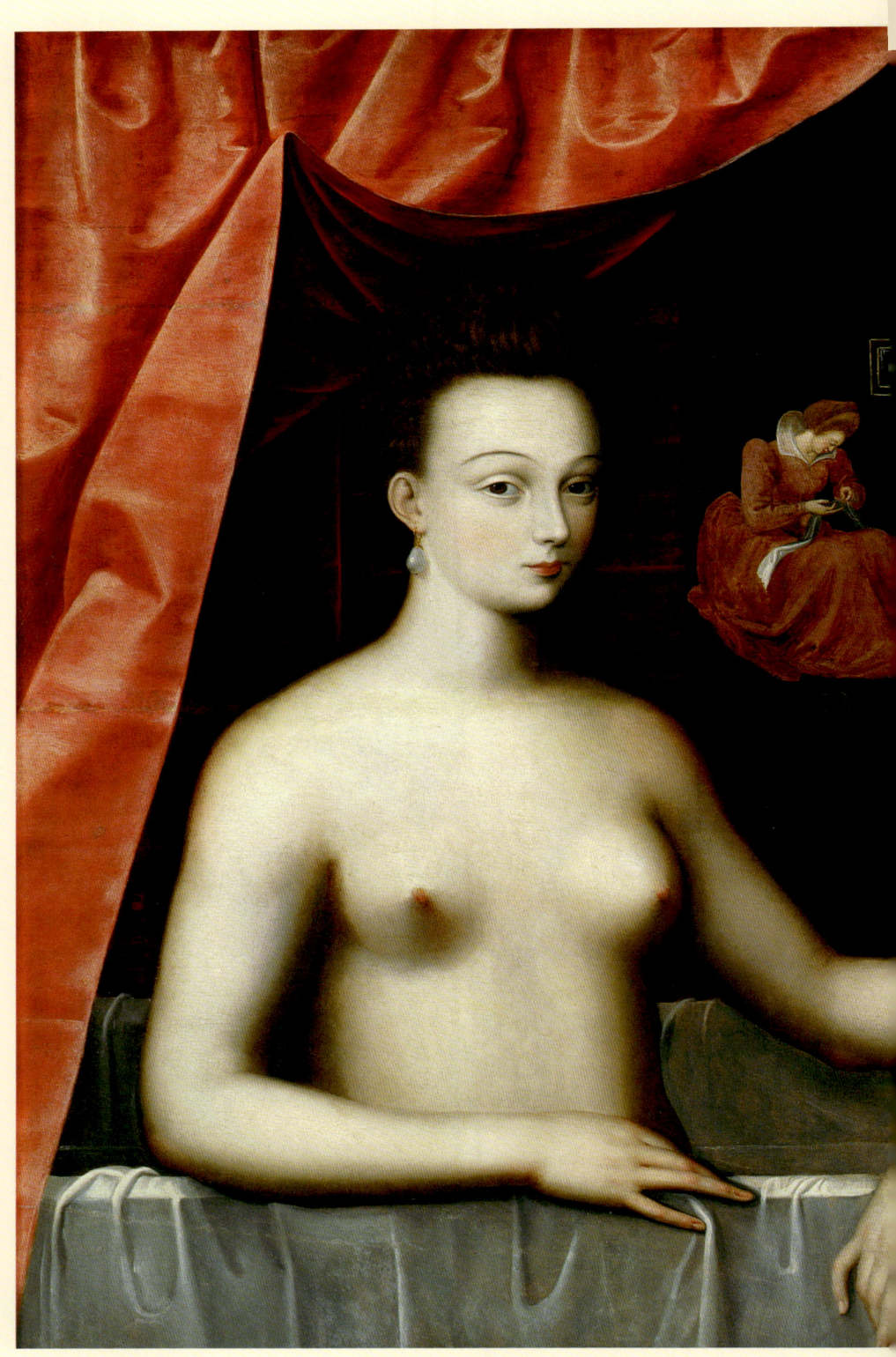

Fontainebleau School/École de Fontainebleau (fl. 1590–1620)

Gabrielle d'Estrees and her sister, the Duchess of Villars

Portrait présumé de Gabrielle d'Estrées et de sa sœur,
la duchesse de Villars

Gabrielle d'Estrees und ihre Schwester, die Herzogin von Villars

Gabrielle d'Estrees y su hermana la Condesa de Villars

Gabrielle d'Estrees e sua sorella, la duchessa di Villars

Gabrielle d'Estrées en haar zuster, de hertogin van Villars

c. 1594, Oil on wood/Huile sur bois, 96 × 125 cm, Musée du Louvre, Paris

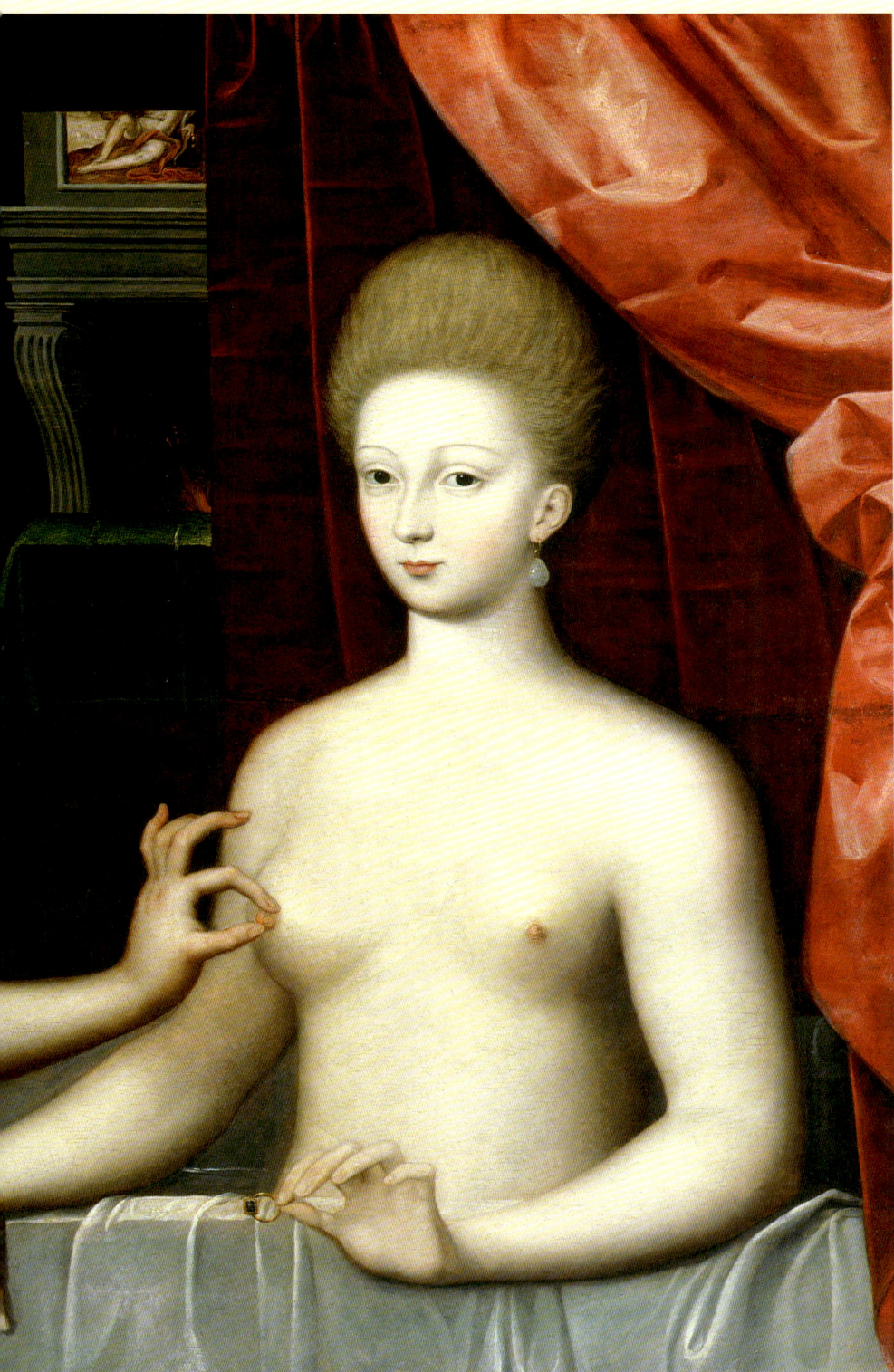

With sophisticated use of perspective, the viewer is drawn into the depths of the image. The open curtain reveals two nudes in a bathtub. The tweak on the nipple of Gabrielle d' Estrées is interpreted as an indication of her pregnancy. In fact, she gave birth in June 1594 to a boy who was said to be the bastard child of her and Henry IV. The servant in the background is thought to be sewing children's clothing. The reproduction of flesh tones is an example of the skillful, Italian-schooled, painting technique.

Des perspectives spatiales raffinées conduisent le regard du spectateur vers les profondeurs du tableau. Gabrielle d'Estrées et l'une de ses sœurs – la duchesse de Villars – sont assises dans leur bain, derrière une barrière recouverte d'un drap blanc. Cette dernière pince le téton de sa sœur, geste pouvant faire allusion à la grossesse de Gabrielle d'Estrées, qui donne naissance en 1594 à César de Vendôme, enfant illégitime de Henri IV. En arrière-plan, la servante est d'ailleurs peut-être en train de coudre des vêtements d'enfant. Le rendu de la peau est un exemple de l'appropriation des techniques de peinture de l'école italienne.

Mit raffinierten Raumeinblicken wird der Betrachter in die Tiefe des Bildes gelenkt. Der aufgeschlagene Vorhang enthüllt zwei Akte in einer Badewanne. Der Griff an die Brustwarze von Gabrielle d'Estrées wird als Hinweis auf ihre Schwangerschaft gedeutet. Tatsächlich gebar sie im Juni 1594 einen Jungen, der als gemeinsames Kind von ihr und Heinrich IV. ausgegeben wurde. Die Dienerin im Hintergrund soll Kinderkleidung nähen. Die Wiedergabe des Inkarnats zeigt die hohe, an italienischer Malerei geschulte Malkultur.

El espectador percibe aquí la profundidad de la imagen a través de las refinadas vistas de espacios. La cortina, entreabierta, enmarca dos desnudos en una bañera. La mano sobre el pezón de Gabrielle d'Estrées se interpreta como una prueba de su embarazo, y en efecto dio a luz a un varón en junio de 1594, que se consideró hijo de su unión con Enrique IV. La sirvienta al fondo estaría cosiendo ropa de niño. La precisión en la presentación de la piel muestra una cultura pictórica muy refinada, aprendida de la pintura italiana.

L'osservatore viene guidato nelle profondità del quadro grazie alle raffinate visioni dello spazio. La tenda sollevata rivela due nudi in una vasca da bagno. Il pizzicotto al capezzolo di Gabrielle d'Estrées si può interpretare come un'allusione alla sua gravidanza. In effetti nel giugno 1594 partorì un bambino, che fu cresciuto come figlio in comune da lei e Enrico IV. La serva sullo sfondo sta cucendo vestiti per bambini. L'esecuzione dell'incarnato indica la grande cultura pittorica che si è formata sulla pittura italiana.

Met geraffineerde inkijkjes in de ruimtelijkheid wordt de beschouwer tot diep in het schilderij meegenomen. Het terzijde geschoven gordijn onthult twee naakten in een bad. Het gebaar waarmee de tepel van Gabrielle d'Estrées wordt aangeraakt, wordt als een aanwijzing voor haar zwangerschap gezien. Ze schonk in juni 1594 inderdaad het leven aan een zoontje, dat als gemeenschappelijk kind van haar en Hendrik IV werd erkend. De hofdame op de achtergrond naait waarschijnlijk kinderkleding. De weergave van het incarnaat (de geschilderde naakte huid) getuigt van een verfijnde, op Italiaanse leest geschoeide schildercultuur.

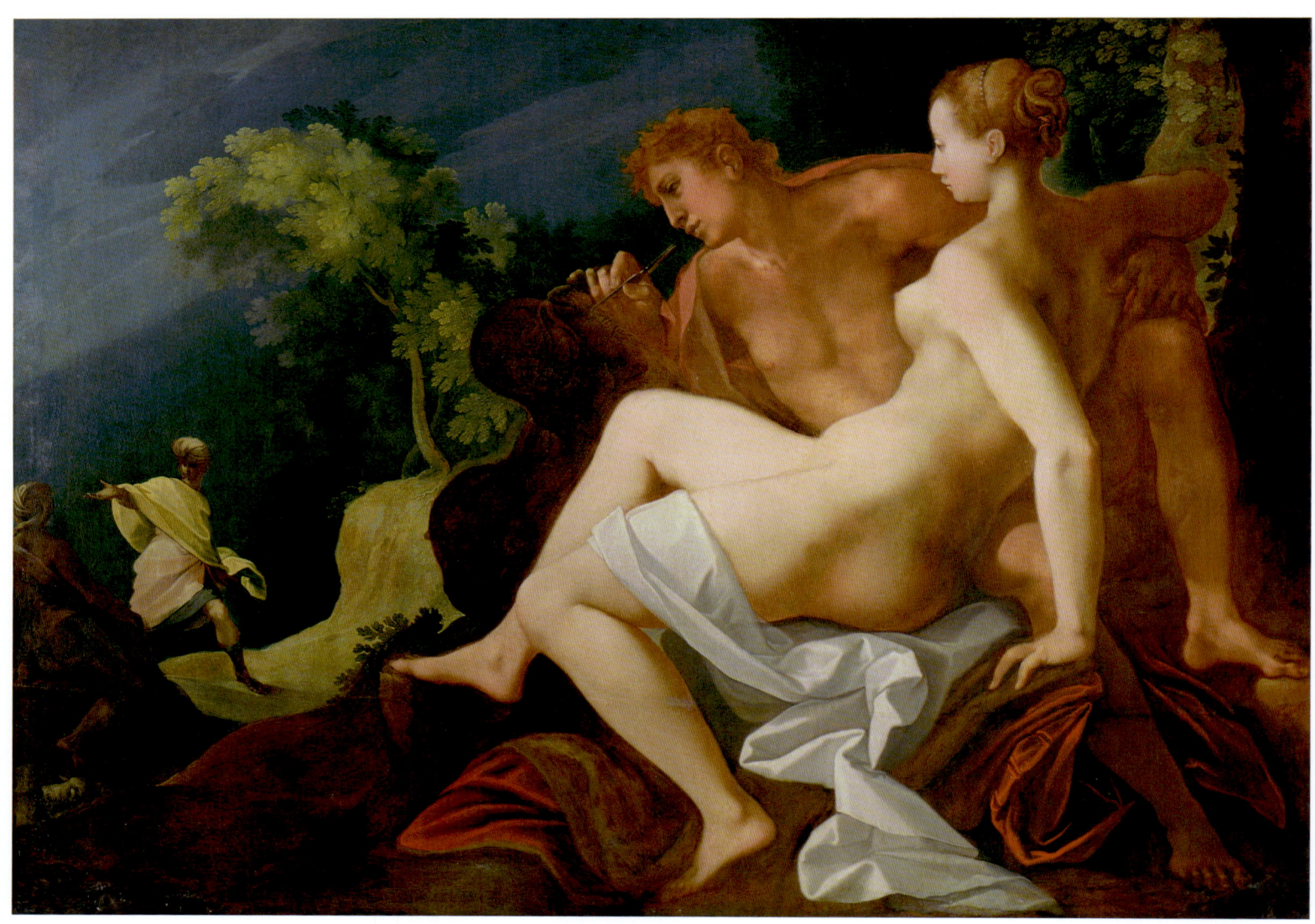

Toussaint Dubreuil (1561–1602)

Angelica and Medor

Angélique et Médor

Angelika und Medor

Angélica y Medoro

Angelica e Medoro

Angelica en Medoro

n. d., Oil on canvas/Huile sur toile, 144 × 200 cm, Musée du Louvre, Paris

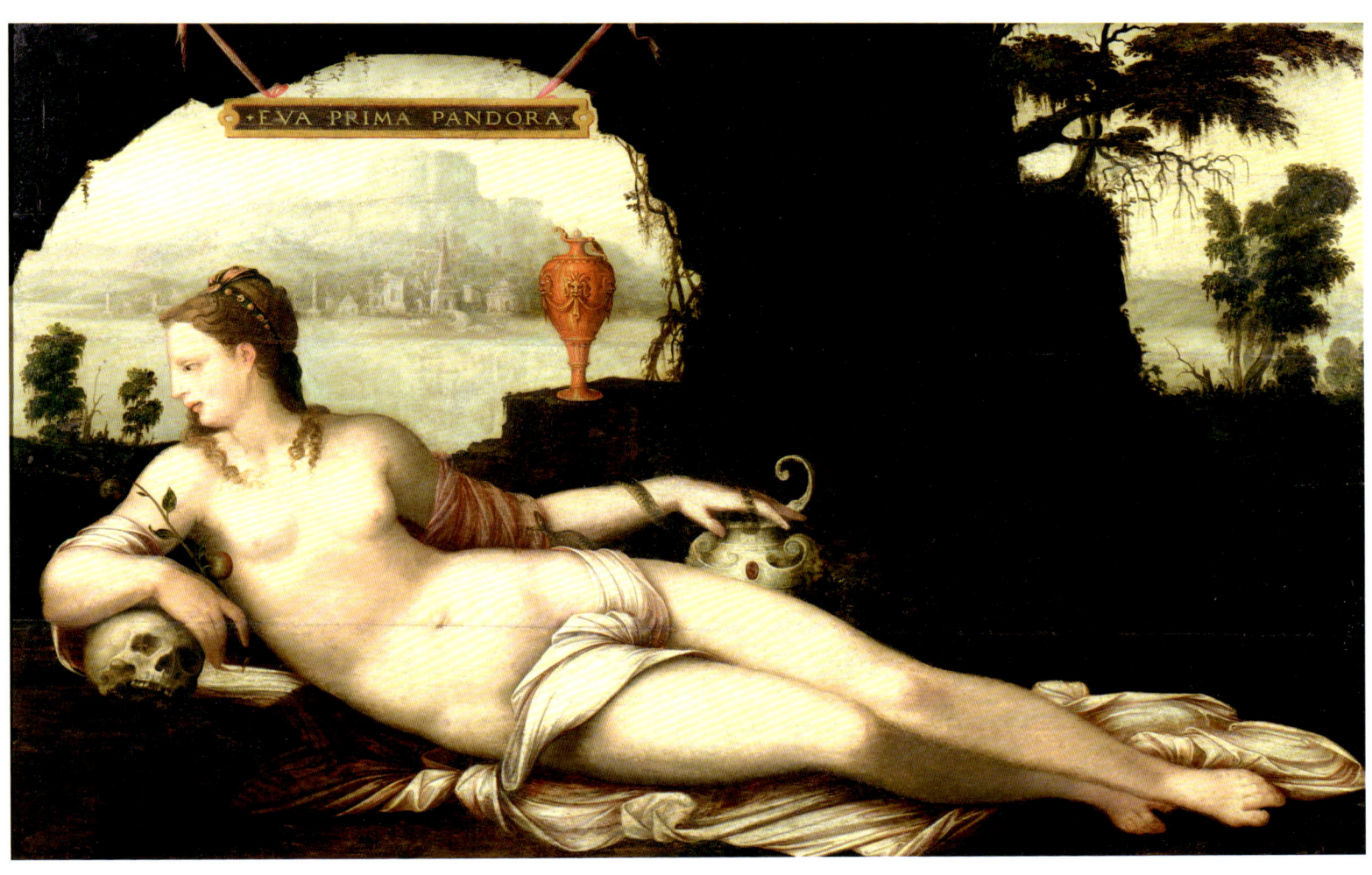

Jean Cousin le Vieux (c. 1490–c. 1560)

Eva Prima Pandora (Eve, the First Pandora)

c. 1550, Oil on canvas/Huile sur toile, 97 × 150 cm, Musée du Louvre, Paris

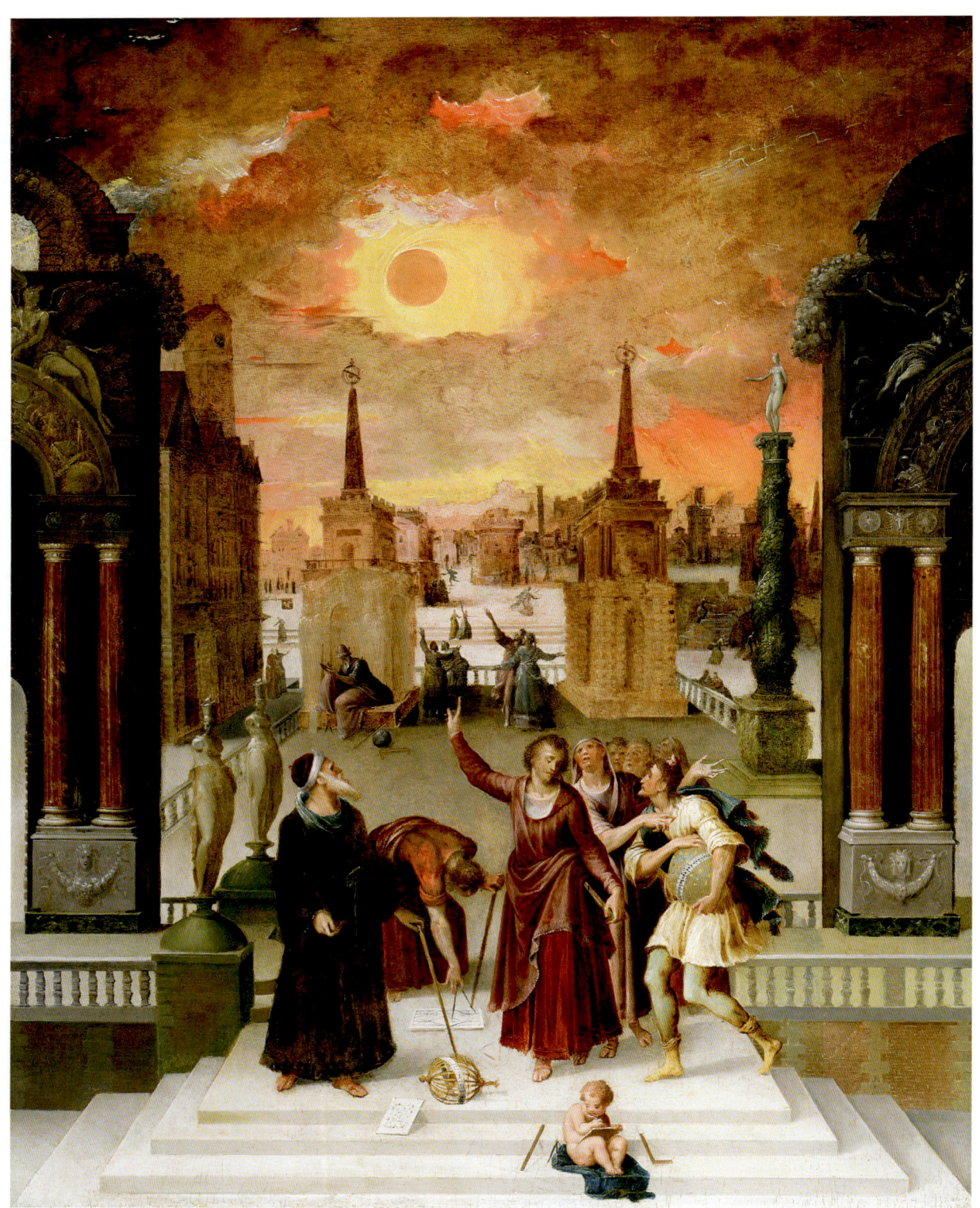

Antoine Caron (1521–1599)

Dionysius, the Aeropagite, Converting the Pagan Philosophers

Denys l'Aréopagite converstissant les philosophes païens

Dionysius Areopagita bekehrt die Pagan Philosophen

Dionisio Areopagita confirtiendo a los filósofos paganos

Dionigi l'Areopagita converte i filosofi pagani

Dionysius de Areopagiet die heidense filosofen bekeert

c. 1570, Oil on wood/Huile sur bois, 92,7 × 72,1 cm, The J. Paul Getty Museum, Los Angeles

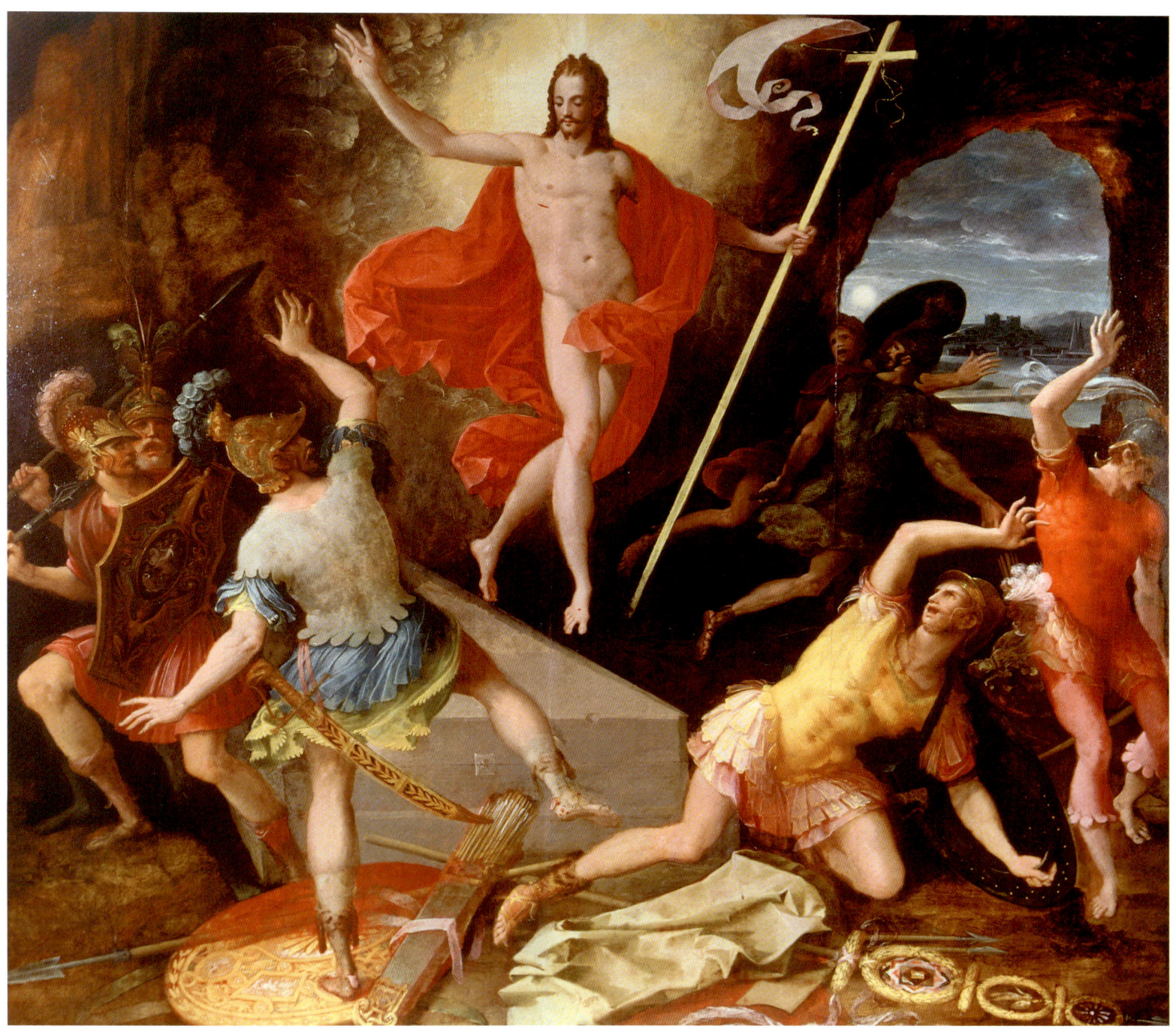

Antoine Caron (1521–1599)

The Resurrection   Die Auferstehung   La Risurrezione

La Résurrection   La Resurrección   De opstanding

c. 1589, Oil on wood/Huile sur bois, 124 × 138 cm, Musée de l'Oise, Beauvais

BAROQUE, CLASSICISM AND ROCOCO
BAROQUE, CLASSICISME ET ROCOCO
BAROCK, KLASSIZISMUS UND ROKOKO
BARROCO, CLASICISMO Y ROCOCÓ
BAROCCO, CLASSICISMO E ROCOCÒ
BAROK, CLASSICISME EN ROCOCO

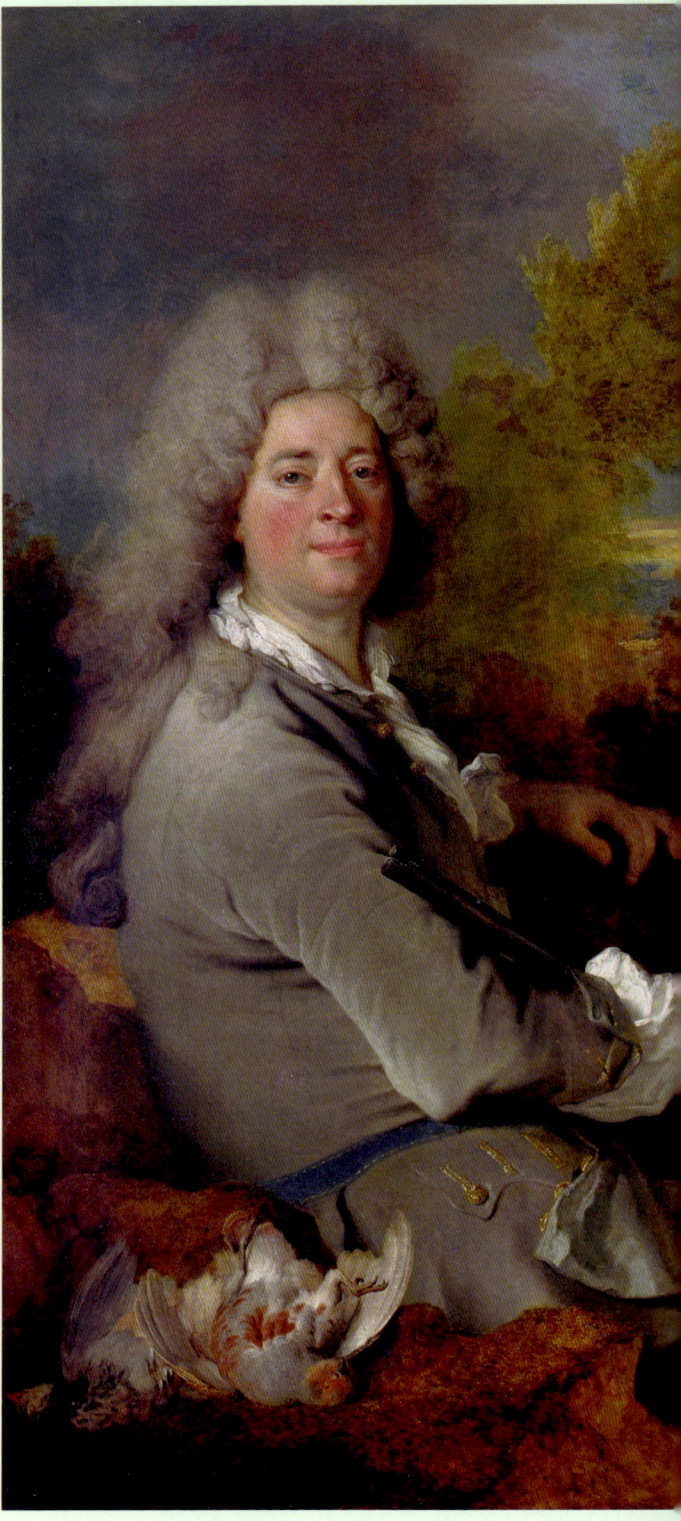

Nicolas de Largillière (1656–1746)

Family Portrait

Portrait de famille

Porträt der Familie

Retrato de familia

Ritratto di famiglia

Familieportret

c. 1730, Oil on canvas/Huile sur toile, 149 × 200 cm, Musée du Louvre, Paris

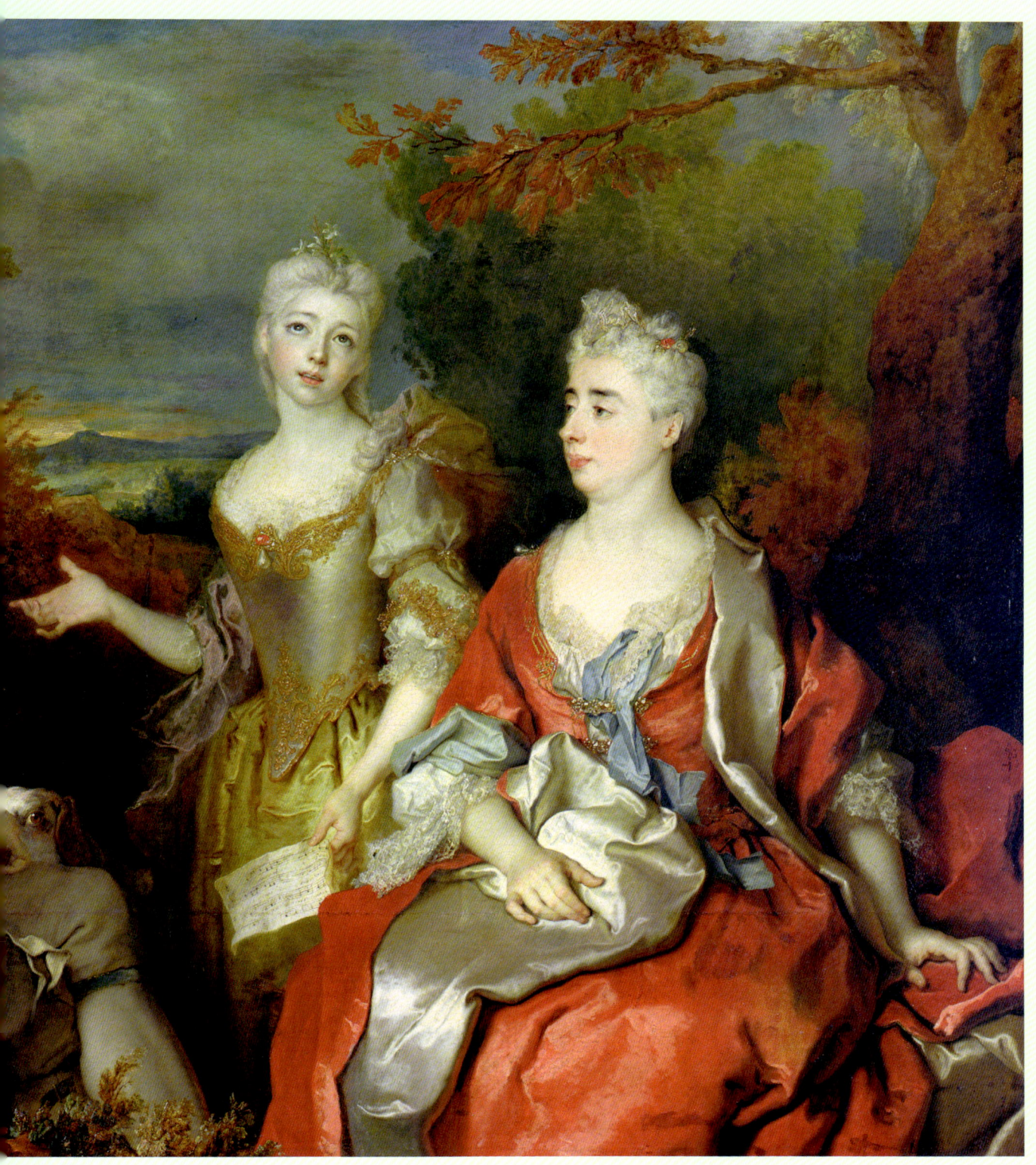

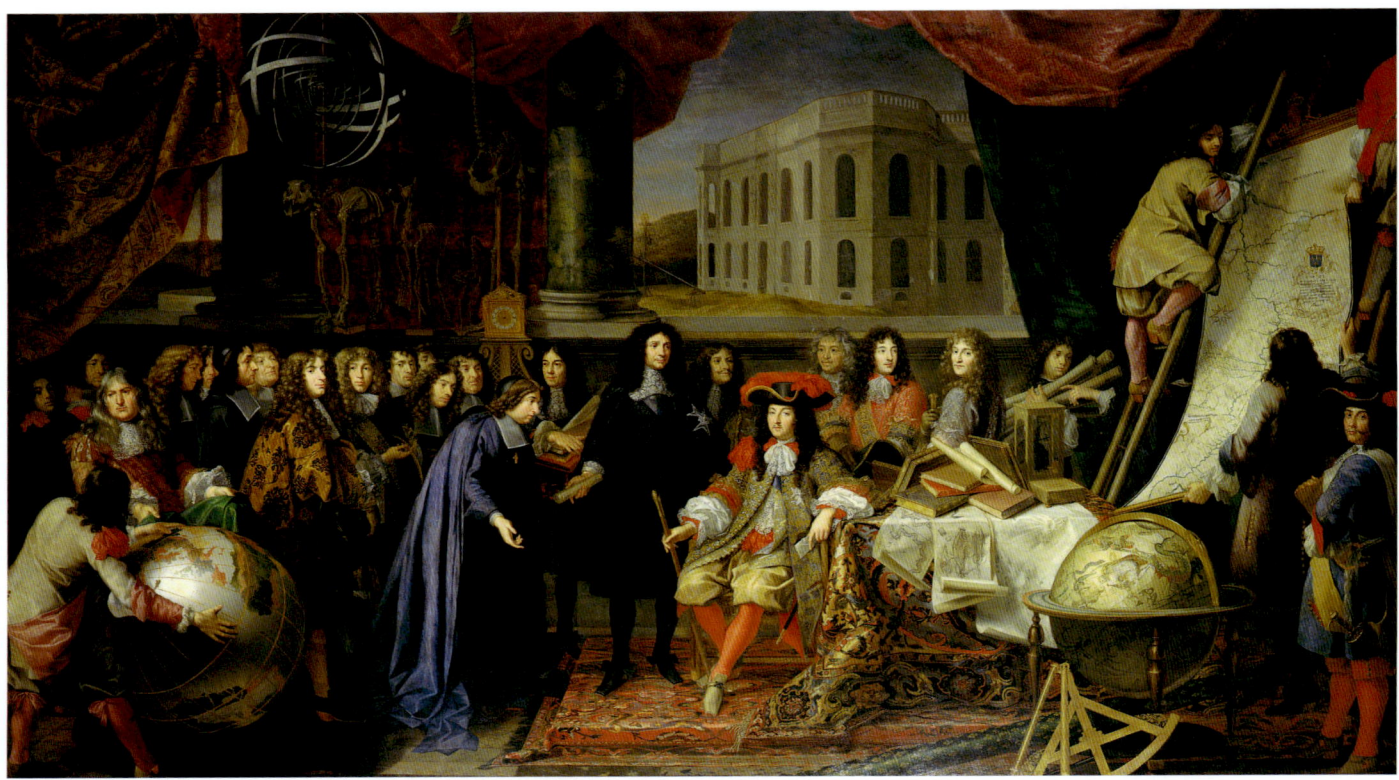

Reformation and Counter-Reformation

The Baroque—the era between absolutism and enlightenment—is considered to be the last pan-European style. Secular vitality and refined sensuality, religious intellectuality and rigorous asceticism, a wide variety of forms and strict adherence to rules stand in opposition to each other. At the same time, illusionism brought the stage-like and theatrical into art. Theater, ceremony and courtly celebration were not just expressions of baroque vitality, but also an elaborate way to control the masses.

In France, painting was primarily influenced by absolutism, for which Louis XIV stood as the best representative. Although the use of the arts to represent political power was not new, it had never before been

Réforme et Contre-Réforme

Le baroque – période comprise entre l'absolutisme et les Lumières – passe pour le dernier style propre à l'ensemble de l'Europe. Joie de vivre profane et sensualité revendiquée, spiritualité religieuse et ascèse rigoureuse, vaste variété des formes et respect sévère des règles s'y opposent en forts contrastes. Le trompe-l'œil fait également entrer dans l'art la scène et le théâtre. Conjointement à ce dernier, la cérémonie et la fête officielle ne sont plus seulement une expression de la vitalité baroque, mais aussi des formes artistiques propres à régir les masses. En France, la peinture est d'abord tout entière sous le signe de l'absolutisme dont Louis XIV est le meilleur représentant. L'engagement des arts dans la représentation de la puissance politique n'est

Reformation und Gegenreformation

Der Barock – das Zeitalter zwischen Absolutismus und Aufklärung – gilt als der letzte gesamteuropäische Stil. Weltliche Lebensfreude und vornehme Sinnlichkeit, religiöse Geistigkeit und strenge Askese, breite Formenvielfalt und strenge Regelhaftigkeit stehen sich gegenüber. Gleichzeitig dringt mit dem Illusionismus das Bühnenhafte und Theatralische in die Kunst ein. Theater, Zeremonie und höfisches Fest sind nicht nur Ausdruck barocker Vitalität, sondern auch kunstvoller Form zur Bewältigung von Massen. In Frankreich steht die Malerei zunächst ganz im Zeichen des Absolutismus, für den Ludwig XIV. ihr bester Repräsentant ist. Zwar ist der Einsatz der Künste zur Darstellung politischer Macht nicht neu, doch nie zuvor

Henri Testelin (1616–1695)

Jean-Baptiste Colbert Presenting the Members of the Royal Academy of Science to Louis XIV

Colbert présente les membres de l'Académie royale des sciences à Louis XIV

Jean-Baptiste Colbert stellt die Mitglieder der Académie Royale des Sciences Ludwig XIV. vor

Jean-Baptiste Colbert presenta a los miembros de la Academia Real de las Ciencias a Luis XIV

Jean-Baptiste Colbert presenta i membri dell'Accademia Reale delle Scienze a Luigi XIV

Jean-Baptiste Colbert stelt de leden van de Académie Royale des Sciences voor aan Lodewijk XIV

c. 1680, Oil on canvas/Huile sur toile, 348 × 590 cm, Château de Versailles, Versailles

Reforma y Contrarreforma

El Barroco –época entre el absolutismo y la Ilustración– se considera el último estilo conjunto europeo. Aquí se presentan, en oposición, la alegría vital y elegante sensualidad con el ascetismo severo y la espiritualidad religiosas, una gran variedad de formas con un rígido sistema de reglas. Al mismo tiempo el ilusionismo introduce la escenografía y teatralidad en el arte. El teatro, la ceremonia y las fiestas de la corte no son solo expresión de la vitalidad barroca, sino también una forma artística de dominar a las masas.

En Francia la pintura se encuentra en un principio bajo total dominio del absolutismo, con Luis XIV como su mejor representante. Si bien la utilización del arte para la presentación del poder político no es algo nuevo, nunca

Riforma e controriforma

Il Barocco, l'epoca tra l'assolutismo e l'illuminismo, è considerato l'ultimo stile comune all'Europa. Gioia di vivere laica e sensualità raffinata, spiritualità religiosa e severa ascesi, ampia varietà di forme e rigida regolarità si oppongono l'una all'altra. Contemporaneamente con l'illusionismo la scenografia e la teatralità penetrano nell'arte. Il teatro, le cerimonie e le feste di corte non sono solo l'espressione della vitalità barocca, ma anche una forma artistica di superiorità verso le masse.

In Francia la pittura all'inizio è all'insegna dell'assolutismo, del quale Luigi XIV è il miglior rappresentante. Certamente l'utilizzo delle arti per rappresentare la potenza politica non è nuovo, tuttavia mai prima d'ora questo

Reformatie en Contrareformatie

De barok – het tijdperk tussen absolutisme en Verlichting – wordt beschouwd als de laatste stijlperiode die heel Europa omvatte. In deze stijl streden wereldlijk levensplezier en verheven zinnelijkheid, religieuze verrukking en strenge ascese, een veelheid van vormentalen en strikte stijlregels om de voorrang. Tegelijkertijd drong aan de hand van illusionistische effecten het theatrale de kunst binnen. Voorstellingen, ceremonies en hoofse feesten getuigden niet alleen van de vitaliteit van de barok maar waren ook artistieke middelen waarmee de massa werd bespeeld.

In Frankrijk stond de schilderkunst aanvankelijk geheel in het teken van het absolutisme, met Lodewijk XIV als de belichaming daarvan. Het aanwenden van de

so well organized, through institutions and their directors, and with such power in the undertaking of great projects.

When Louis took over the government he chose Jean-Baptiste Colbert (1619–1683) as a consultant in matters of art who then reorganized the Gobelins Manufactory *(Manufacture Royale des Meubles de la Couronne),* which was equipped for all special undertakings of luxury furnishing and decoration. Simultaneously, Colbert was appointed as the director of the Royal Academy of Painting and Sculpture, which had been in existence since 1648, along with Charles Le Brun, resulting in this organisation becoming the instrument of the royal artistic policy. After Colbert was appointed in 1664 as *Surintendant des Bâtiments* (head of the state building authority), and with the founding in 1671 of the Academy of Architecture, he had supervision of all architectural projects and the training of architects in his hand. The culmination of this centralized power came in 1666 with the creation of the French Academy in Rome.

French Baroque is therefore inseparable from the ideas of the Academy, its academic theory and discussion. An example of this may be seen in the academic dispute between supporters of color, the Rubenists, and the followers of the line, the Poussinists which, although heatedly discussed, after some time had only theoretical value and was not taken seriously in practice. Whether the genius Antoine Watteau (1684–1721) was a real Rubenist cannot be answered with certainty, with his intensive and spiritualised use of colors. An alleged Rubenist such as Pierre Mignard (1612–1695) left it unclear, with his external adaptations. Paradoxically, it was Nicolas Poussin, the creator of mythological scenes and heroic landscapes

certes pas une nouveauté, mais jamais jusque-là cet objectif n'avait été aussi bien organisé par des institutions et des intendants dotés d'une telle plénitude de pouvoirs, et poursuivi par d'aussi grands projets.

Lorsque Louis XIV arrive au pouvoir (1661), il choisit Jean-Baptiste Colbert (1619–1683) comme conseiller, y compris dans le domaine des beaux-arts. Ce dernier réorganise dès 1663 la Manufacture royale des Meubles de la Couronne, chargée de toutes les commandes spéciales des aménagements et décorations de luxe, jusques aux tapisseries. Dans le même temps, Colbert est nommé – avec Charles Le Brun – directeur de l'Académie royale de peinture et de sculpture, fondée en 1648 et devenue ainsi l'instrument parfait de la politique artistique royale. Surintendant des Bâtiments en 1664, et contrôlant à partir de 1671 la totalité des projets architecturaux et la formation des architectes avec la fondation de l'Académie d'architecture, Colbert couronne le tout en créant l'Académie de France à Rome, en 1666.

L'art baroque français est donc inséparable de l'esprit académique, de sa formation théorique et de ses débats. En peinture, on en trouverait l'illustration dans la querelle entre tenants de la couleur (ou « rubénistes ») et tenants de la ligne (ou « poussinistes ») : passée la violence des premières controverses, le débat n'a plus rapidement qu'une valeur théorique à laquelle plus personne ne prête attention. Le génial Watteau (1684–1721) était-il un authentique rubéniste ? Impossible de l'affirmer avec certitude, malgré ses couleurs si intenses et approfondies. Un prétendu rubéniste comme Pierre Mignard (1612–1695) laisse l'affaire en suspens grâce à des solutions extérieures. Et c'est paradoxalement Nicolas Poussin, créateur de scènes mythologiques et de paysages héroïques, qui rentre déçu de Paris à

ist dieser Zweck so wohlorganisiert durch Institutionen und Intendanten und mit solcher Machtfülle und durch so große Projekte angestrebt worden.

Als Ludwig die Regierung übernahm, wählte er Jean-Baptiste Colbert (1619–1683) zum Berater auch in Fragen der Kunst. Dieser reorganisierte 1663 die *Manufacture Royale des Meubles de la Couronne,* die für alle Sonderaufgaben der Luxuseinrichtung und Dekoration bis hin zu Gobelins ausgerüstet wurde. Gleichzeitig wurde Colbert zusammen mit Le Brun Leiter der seit 1648 bestehenden *Académie Royale de Peinture et de Sculpture,* die damit ganz zum Instrument der königlichen Kunstpolitik wurde. Nachdem Colbert seit 1664 als *Surintendant des Bâtiments* (Leiter der staatlichen Bauaufsichtsbehörde) und 1671 mit der Gründung der Akademie der Baukunst auch die Aufsicht über alle architektonischen Projekte und die Ausbildung der Architekten in der Hand hatte, kam 1666 als Krönung dieser Zentralgewalt noch die Gründung der französischen Akademie in Rom hinzu.

Französische Barockkunst ist demnach von dem Gedanken der Akademie, der akademischen Theoriebildung und Diskussion nicht zu trennen. Ein Beispiel ist in dem akademische Streit zwischen Anhängern der Farbe, den Rubenisten und den Anhängern der Linie, den Poussinisten, zu sehen, der heftig ausgetragen nach einiger Zeit jedoch nur noch theoretischen Wert hatte und in der Praxis nicht mehr ernst genommen wurde. Ob der geniale Antoine Watteau (1684–1721) ein echter Rubenist war, lässt sich kaum mit Sicherheit beantworten, so farbstark und verinnerlicht seine Farben auch waren. Ein angeblicher Rubenist wie Pierre Mignard (1612–1695) beließ es hingen bei äußerlichen Adaptionen. Paradoxerweise ist es gerade Nicolas Poussin, der Schöpfer mythologischer Szenen und

antes había estado tan organizada mediante instituciones y programadores, ni contaba con tanto poder o se perseguía mediante proyectos tan ambiciosos.

Cuando Luis XIV se hizo con el gobierno escogió a Jean-Baptiste Colbert (1619–1683) como consejero en las cuestiones de arte. Este reorganizó en 1663 la *Manufacture Royale des Meubles de la Couronne,* que se preparó para todas las tareas especiales de decoración y mobiliario de lujo, incluyendo tapicería. Al mismo tiempo Colbert dirigió junto a Le Brun la *Académie Royale de Peinture et de Sculpture,* creada en 1648, convirtiéndola así completamente en un instrumento de la política artística del Rey. Sabiendo que Colbert ostentaba además desde 1664 el título de *Surintendant des Bâtiments* (Superintendente de los inspectores públicos de edificios) y supervisaba todos los proyectos arquitectónicos y la educación de los arquitectos desde 1671 con la fundación de la Academia de la arquitectura, en 1666 esta centralización de poder culminó en la creación de la Academia Francesa en Roma.

El arte barroco francés no puede consecuentemente separarse de los preceptos de la Academia, de sus discusiones y desarrollos de teorías. Un ejemplo de esto lo muestra la lucha académica entre los partidarios de Rubens (partidarios del color) y los de Poussin (partidarios de la línea). Esta dura batalla, librada durante un tiempo, terminó por tener un valor puramente teórico y no tomarse en serio en la práctica. No podemos contestar con certeza si el genial Antoine Watteau (1684–1721) era un verdadero partidario de Rubens, incluso si sus colores eran tan vivos e intensos. Un supuesto "rubenista" como Pierre Mignard (1612–1695) en realidad lo era solo en algunos aspectos más o menos superficiales. Paradójicamente fue justo Nicolas Poussin,

scopo è così ben organizzato tramite le istituzioni e gli intendenti e perseguito con così tanta potenza e grandi progetti.

Quando Luigi prese il potere, scelse Jean-Baptiste Colbert (1619–1683) come consigliere anche in materia di arte. Questi nel 1663 riorganizzò la *Manufacture Royale des Meubles de la Couronne,* che fu attrezzata per tutti gli incarichi speciali, dall'arredamento di lusso e la decorazione fino agli arazzi. Nel contempo Colbert, insieme a Le Brun, divenne direttore della *Académie Royale de Peinture et de Sculpture* fondata nel 1648, che divenne strumento della politica artistica reale. Dopo che nel 1664 fu nominato *Surintendant des Bâtiments* (direttore dell'ispettorato edile statale) e nel 1671 con la fondazione dell'Accademia di architettura assunse anche il controllo di tutti i progetti architettonici e della formazione degli architetti, nel 1666 Colbert aggiunse come coronamento di questo potere centrale anche la fondazione dell'Accademia francese a Roma.

L'arte barocca francese non va dunque separata dalle idee dell'Accademia, della creazione teorica e della discussione accademica. Un esempio si trova nel diverbio accademico tra i sostenitori del colore, i Rubenisti, e i sostenitori della linea, i Poussinisti, che diede luogo ad un'aspra discussione ma dopo un po' di tempo aveva solo valore teorico e in pratica non fu più preso sul serio. Se il geniale Antoine Watteau (1684–1721) fosse un vero rubenista non si può affermare con sicurezza, tanto intensi e interiorizzati erano i suoi colori. Un presunto rubenista come Pierre Mignard (1612–1695) lo lasciò in sospeso con adattamenti esterni. Paradossalmente fu proprio Nicolas Poussin, il creatore di scene mitologiche e paesaggi eroici, che ritornò all'Accademia francese di Roma deluso da Parigi. Il suo antipodo

kunsten voor het uitbeelden van politieke macht was natuurlijk niet nieuw, maar nog nooit eerder werd dit doel zo doelbewust en door instituties en functionarissen zo zelfbewust in grootse projecten nagestreefd.

Toen Lodewijk XIV de troon besteeg, koos hij Jean-Baptiste Colbert (1619–1683) ook als zijn adviseur op het gebied van de kunsten. Colbert reorganiseerde in 1663 de *Manufacture Royale des Meubles de la Couronne,* die voortaan verantwoordelijk was voor alle speciale opdrachten op het gebied van de inrichting en decoratie van de koninklijke paleizen, met inbegrip van de gobelins. Ook kreeg Colbert samen met Le Brun de leiding over de in 1648 opgerichte *Académie Royale de Peinture et de Sculpture,* die daarmee geheel tot instrument van de koninklijke kunstpolitiek werd gemaakt. In 1664 werd Colbert benoemd tot *surintendant des bâtiments* ('minister' van officiële bouwwerken) en in 1671 kreeg hij bij de oprichting van de Academie voor Bouwkunst ook de leiding over alle bouwprojecten en architectenopleidingen, waarna zijn carrière in 1666 werd bekroond met de oprichting van de Franse Academie in Rome.

De Franse barokkunst kan daardoor niet los worden gezien van het idee van de academie en van academische theorieën en debatten over kunst. Een voorbeeld is de strijd onder de academici tussen de pleitbezorgers van uitbundig kleurgebruik, de 'rubenisten' (naar Rubens), en die van de strikte lijncompositie, de 'poussenisten' (naar Poussin), die in alle hevigheid woedde maar uiteindelijk slechts van theoretisch belang was en in de kunstpraktijk niet serieus werd genomen. Of de geniale Antoine Watteau (1684–1721) een echte rubenist was, kan niet met zekerheid worden gezegd, hoe uitbundig en intens zijn kleurgebruik ook was. Bij de vermeende rubenist Pierre Mignard (1612–1695) bleef het bij uiterlijke aanpassingen. Vreemd genoeg was het juist Nicolas Poussin

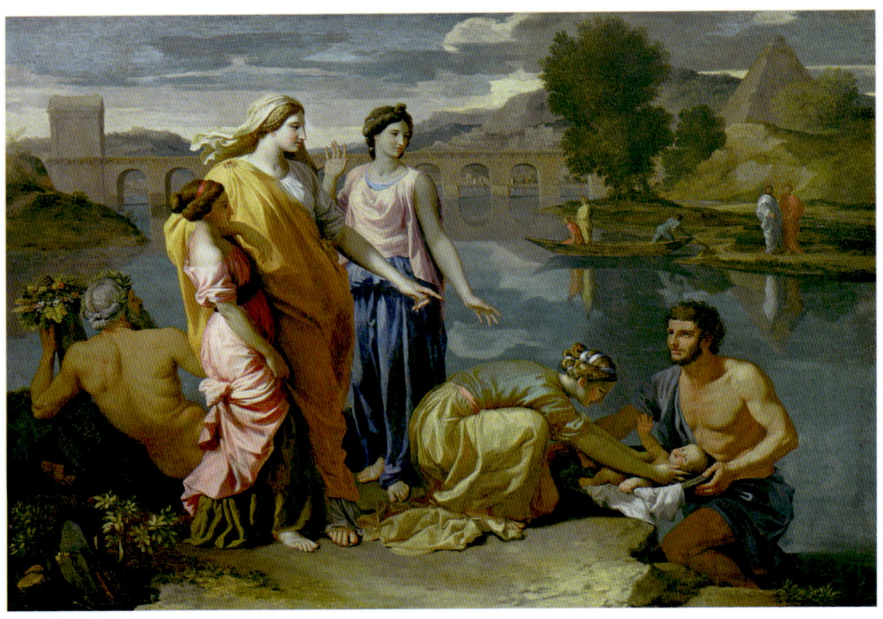

Nicolas Poussin (1594–1665)

The Finding of Moses

Moïse sauvé des eaux

Die Auffindung von Moses

El encuentro de Moisés

Mosè salvato dalle acque

De vinding van Mozes

1638, Oil on canvas/Huile sur toile, 94 × 121 cm, Musée du Louvre, Paris

who, disappointed by Paris, returned to the French Academy in Rome. His opposite, Claude Lorrain (1600–1682), lived for some time in Rome, where he created his best mythological landscapes with romantic atmospheres, staged in sight of the ancient remains bearing their melancholic aura. Flemish influenced painters like the brothers Antoine (around 1600–1648), Louis (around 1602–1648) and Mathieu Le Nain (around 1610–1677) turned against "petty" genre topics, declaring that also the everyday life of peasants was worthy of depiction. Although the Lorraine artist Georges de La Tour (1593–1652) took over Caravaggio's dramatic chiaroscuro contrasts, he did not assume that artist's subject choice, which was geared to everyday reality. His night scenes appear artificially staged, but are also heavy with religious spirituality. Even the great Florence-schooled etcher Jacques Callot (1592/1593–1635) contributed more to the greatness of French painting in the 17th century than all the Paris-based academic painters— Charles Le Brun not excluded.

l'Académie de Rome. Son exact opposé, Claude Lorrain (1600–1682) vit plus longtemps là-bas. Il y crée ses meilleurs paysages mythologiques à l'atmosphère romantique, face aux vestiges antiques rayonnants de mélancolie. Des peintres sous influence flamande comme les frères Antoine (vers 1600–1648), Louis (vers 1597–1648) et Matthieu (vers 1607–1677) Le Nain se consacrent en revanche à des scènes de genre plus « humbles », en élevant la vie quotidienne des paysans à la dignité du tableau. Le Lorrain Georges de la Tour (1593–1652) reprend les clairs-obscurs dramatiques de Caravage, mais sans le réalisme propre aux représentations de celui-ci, démarquées du quotidien. Ses scènes nocturnes donnent l'impression de mises en scène artificielles, mais aussi de spiritualisation religieuse. Formé à Florence, le grand graveur Jacques Callot (autre Lorrain, v. 1592–1635) contribue lui aussi à la grandeur de la peinture française du XVIIe siècle – bien davantage que tous les peintres académiques installés à Paris, Charles Le Brun compris.

heroischer Landschaften, der enttäuscht von Paris an die französische Akademie von Rom zurückkehrte. Sein Antipode Claude Lorrain (1600–1682) lebte schon länger in Rom, wo er seine besten mythologischen Landschaften mit ihrer romantischen Stimmung angesichts der antiken Überreste mit ihrer melancholischen Ausstrahlung schuf. Flämisch beinflusste Maler wie die Gebr. Antoine (um 1600–1648), Louis (um 1602–1648) und Mathieu Le Nain (um 1610–1677) wandten sich dagegen „niederen" Genrethemen zu und befanden auch den Alltag der Bauern als bildwürdig. Der Lothringer Georges de la Tour (1593–1652) übernahm zwar Caravaggios dramatische Hell-Dunkel-Kontraste, jedoch nicht dessen an der Alltagswirklichkeit orientierte Gegenstandsauffassung. Seine Nachtszenen wirken künstlich inszeniert, aber auch von religiöser Vergeistigung getragen. Auch der in Florenz geschulte großartige Radierer Jacques Callot (um 1592/93–1635) trug mehr zur Größe der französischen Malerei des 17. Jahrhunderts

Claude Lorrain (1600–1682)

Sea Port at Sunset

Port de mer au soleil couchant

Seehafen bei Sonnenuntergang

Puerto marítimo a la puesta del sol

Porto al tramonto

Zeehaven bij zonsondergang

1639, Oil on canvas/Huile sur toile, 103 × 137 cm, Musée du Louvre, Paris

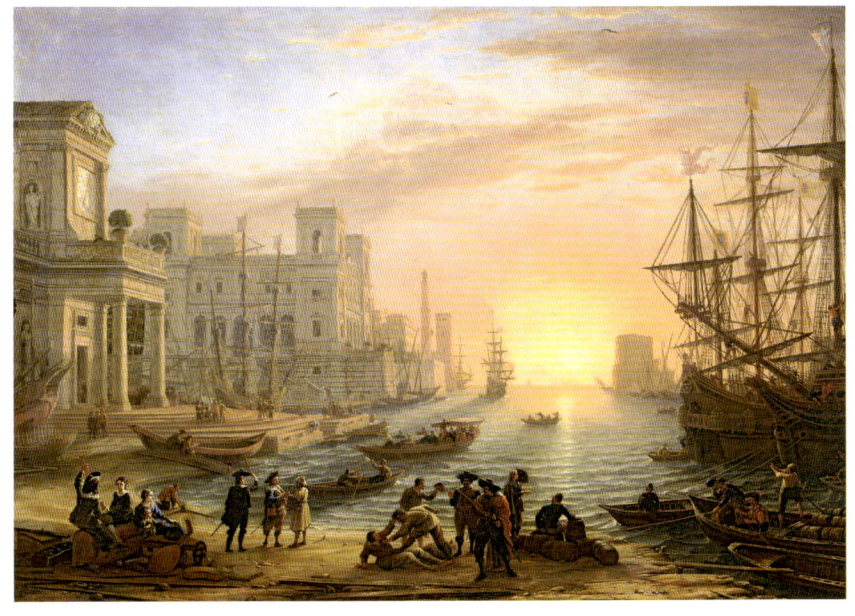

el creador de escenas mitológicas y heroicos paisajes el que volvió, decepcionado, desde París a la Academia de Francia en Roma. Claude Lorrain (1600–1682), en muchos sentidos su opuesto, vivía ya hace tiempo en Roma donde creó sus mejores paisajes mitológicos con sus ambientes románticos, dada la cantidad de melancólicos restos de la Antigüedad. Pintores con influencia flamenca como los hnos. Antoine (ca. 1600–1648), Louis (ca. 1602–1648) y Mathieu Le Nain (ca. 1610–1677) se dedicaron a "indignos" temas costumbristas, considerando la cotidianeidad de los campesinos un tema digno de ser representado. El pintor de la región de Lorena Georges de La Tour (1593–1652) adoptó los contrastes de claroscuro de Caravaggio pero no su disposición de los objetos, orientada a la realidad cotidiana. Sus escenas nocturnas están construidas de manera artificial, sustentadas por una espiritualización religiosa. El genial grabador Jacques Callot (ca. 1592/93–1635), formado en Florencia, contribuyó más a la

Claude Lorrain (1600–1682) viveva già da tempo a Roma, dove creò i suoi migliori paesaggi mitologici dall'atmosfera romantica considerando gli antichi resti con il loro carisma malinconico. Pittori influenzati dai fiamminghi come i fratelli Antoine (1600–1648 circa), Louis (1602–1648 circa) e Mathieu Le Nain (1610–1677 circa), si dedicavano al contrario a temi di genere "basso" e trovavano degna di essere dipinta anche la vita quotidiana dei contadini. Il lorenese Georges de La Tour (1593–1652) prese da Caravaggio proprio i drammatici contrasti chiaro-scuro, ma non l'interpretazione oggettiva orientata all'importanza della vita quotidiana. Le sue immagini notturne erano inscenate artisticamente, ma anche sostenute dalla spiritualizzazione religiosa. Anche l'eccellente incisore Jacques Callot (1592/1593–1635), che studiò a Firenze, contribuì alla grandezza della pittura francese del XVII secolo più di tutti i pittori accademici residenti a Parigi, senza escludere Charles Le Brun.

zelf, schepper van mythologische taferelen en heroïsche landschappen, die Parijs teleurgesteld verliet en terugkeerde naar de Franse Academie in Rome. Zijn tegenhanger Claude Lorrain (1600–1682) woonde daar al langer en schiep er zijn mooiste mythologische landschappen, waarin hij een romantische sfeer van weemoed naar het klassieke verleden opriep. Schilders die onder Vlaamse invloed stonden, onder wie de gebroeders Antoine (rond 1600–1648), Louis (rond 1602–1648) en Mathieu Le Nain (rond 1610–1677), richtten zich daarentegen op 'lagere' genres en vonden het alledaagse boerenleven waardig genoeg om uit te beelden. De Lotharinger Georges de La Tour (1593–1652) sloot aan op Caravaggio's dramatische licht-donkercontrasten, maar niet op diens aandachtige uitbeelding van alledaagse voorwerpen. De la Tours nachtelijke taferelen komen ietwat geënsceneerd over, maar worden ook door religieuze verhevenheid gedragen. De in Florence geschoolde meester-etser Jacques Callot (rond 1592/93–1635) droeg evenals de overige in

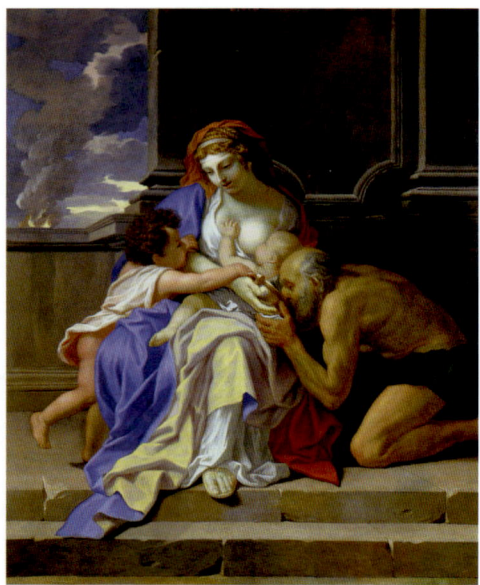

Charles le Brun (1619–1690)

An Allegory of Charity

Allégorie de la charité

Allegorie der Nächstenliebe

Alegoría de la Caridad

Allegoria della carità

Allegorie van de Naastenliefde

c. 1642–1648, Oil on canvas/Huile sur toile, 167 × 134 cm, Musée des Beaux-Arts, Caen

The anti-academic, Caravaggio-influenced stimulus of French painting found its way, for a while, into the chambers of the King's collection. Louis XIII had all of his paintings removed from his room in order to hang just one picture of La Tour. In his bedroom hung five pictures by the Flemish influenced Valentin de Boulogne (1591–1632). Moreover, the king had also bought paintings by Caravaggio.

Whilst "baroque" was no contemporary concept and asserted itself first in the 19th century, there was already the phrase "goût rococo" in the 18th century, which described overelaborate, curving furniture and stucco. Rocaille utilised shell-like forms in stucco decoration. Painting was understood to be portrayal of pleasing, contented genre subjects, as was popular with the nobility in pre-revolutionary France. This style, however, was not limited only to France, but also displaced the empty pathos of the Baroque in Austria, Germany, Spain and Italy. Even Louis XIV had, in the age of ostentatious

La tendance anti-académique de la peinture française, d'inspiration caravagesque, trouve aussi temporairement l'accès aux appartements royaux. Louis XIII avait fait ôter tous les tableaux de son cabinet pour y accrocher en leur lieu et place seulement un tableau de La Tour. Dans sa chambre à coucher figurent en revanche cinq tableaux de Valentin de Boulogne (1591–1632), d'influence flamande. Le monarque fait aussi acheter des tableaux de Caravage.

Alors que le terme « baroque » ne représente aucun concept de style contemporain, l'expression de « goût rococo » s'impose dès le XVIIIe siècle pour caractériser des meubles et des décors stuqués, délicatement travaillés – le terme « rocaille » désignant une forme de coquillage dans la décoration stuquée. En peinture, on entend par là d'agréables scènes de genre, fort appréciées des milieux nobiliaires dans la France d'avant la Révolution. Ce style n'est cependant pas limité à la France et supplante aussi en Autriche, en Allemagne, en Espagne et en Italie la rhétorique et le

bei, als alle in Paris ansässigen akademischen Maler – Charles Le Brun nicht ausgenommen.

Der anti-akademische, an Caravaggio geschulte Impuls der französichen Malerei hielt sogar zeitweise in den Gemächern des Königs Einzug. Ludwig XIII. hatte aus seinem Zimmer alle Bilder entfernen lassen und dafür nur ein Gemälde von La Tour aufgehängt. In seinem Schlafzimmer hingen fünf Bilder des flämisch beeinflussten Valentin de Boulogne (1591–1632). Überdies hatte der König auch Bilder von Caravaggio eingekauft.

Während „Barock" kein zeitgenössischer Stilbegriff war und sich erst im 19. Jahrhundert durchsetzte, gab es den Begriff „goût rococo" schon im 18. Jahrhundert und bezeichnete geschnörkelte, gedrechselte Möbel und Stuckarbeiten. Rocaille war eine Muschelform in der Stuckdekoration. In der Malerei verstand man darunter dann gefällige, heitere Genrethemen, wie sie in der Adelsschicht des vorrevolutionären Frankreichs beliebt waren. Dieser Stil war jedoch nicht auf Frankreich beschränkt, sondern verdrängte

Georges de La Tour (1593–1652)

St. Joseph, the Carpenter
Saint Joseph charpentier
Der heilige Joseph als Zimmermann
San José carpintero
San Giuseppe il falegname
De heilige Jozef als timmerman

c. 1642, Oil on canvas/Huile sur toile, 137 × 102 cm,
Musée du Louvre, Paris

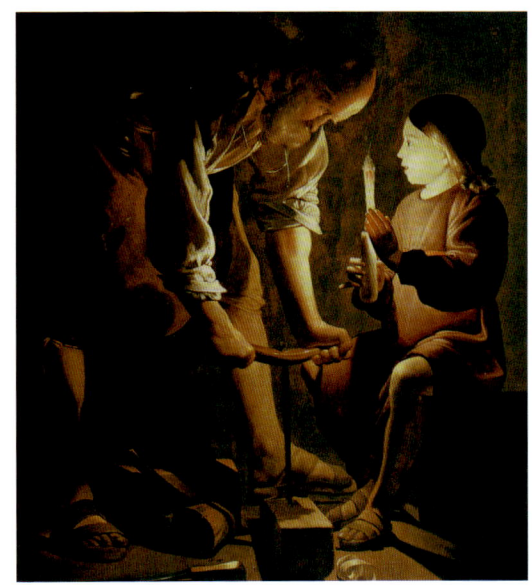

grandeza de la pintura francesa del XVII que todos los pintores académicos parisinos –sin excluir a Charles Le Brun.

El impulso anti-académico de la pintura francesa, proveniente de Caravaggio, se introdujo incluso en las estancias del Rey. Luis XIII mandó retirar todas las pinturas de su habitación, colgando en su lugar una pintura de La Tour. En su dormitorio había cinco cuadros de Valentin de Boulogne (1591–1632), de influencia flamenca. El Rey también había adquirido pinturas de Caravaggio.

Si bien el término "barroco" no se utilizaba en su tiempo, estableciéndose por primera vez en el XIX, sí existía ya en el XVIII el "gusto rococó" que describía muebles y trabajos en estuco torneados y de formas redondeadas. El rocaille era un tipo de decoración en estuco con forma de concha. En la pintura se refería a los joviales y atractivos temas costumbristas tan de moda en la clase noble en Francia antes de la Revolución. Este estilo sin embargo no se limitaba a Francia, sino que desplazó también en Austria, Alemania, España e

L'impulso anti-accademico ispirato a Caravaggio della pittura francese fece ingresso temporaneamente persino nelle stanze del re. Luigi XIII fece rimuovere tutti i quadri dalla sua stanza per appendere al loro posto un dipinto di La Tour. Nella sua camera da letto sono appesi cinque dipinti del pittore influenzato dai fiamminghi Valentin de Boulogne (1591–1632). Oltre a questi il re aveva acquistato anche quadri di Caravaggio.

Anche se "barocco" non era un concetto stilistico contemporaneo e si affermò soltanto nel XIX secolo, già nel XVIII secolo esisteva il concetto di "goût rococo" per denominare mobili e opere in stucco arabescati e torniti. Il rocaille era un forma di conchiglia nella decorazione in stucco. Nella pittura si intendono tra gli altri temi di genere piacevole e sereno, che erano amati dal ceto nobiliare della Francia pre-rivoluzionaria. Questo stile non era però limitato alla Francia, ma sostituiva anche in Austria, Germania, Spagna e Italia il pathos vacuo del barocco. Già Luigi XIV all'epoca fu disgustato dalla

Parijs werkende academische kunstenaars, met inbegrip van Le Brun, bij aan de bloei van de Franse kunst in de zeventiende eeuw.

De anti-academische, op Caravaggio geënte impuls binnen de Franse schilderkunst wist zelfs korte tijd de vertrekken van de Zonnekoning te bereiken. Lodewijk XIII liet alle doeken uit zijn salon verwijderen en in plaats daarvan maar één schilderij van La Tour ophangen. In zijn slaapkamer hingen vijf doeken van de in Vlaamse stijl schilderende Valentin de Boulogne (1591–1632). Bovendien had de koning schilderijen van Caravaggio aangekocht.

Terwijl de term 'barok' in dit tijdperk zelf niet als stijlbegrip werd gebruikt en pas in de negentiende eeuw werd ingevoerd, dook de term 'goût rococo' al in de achttiende eeuw op. Het woord stond voor weelderig versierde en gedraaide meubels en uitbundig stucwerk en was afgeleid van de rocaille, een schelpmotief dat veel in stucdecoraties werd toegepast. In de schilderkunst kenmerkte de rococo zich door lieflijke en plezierige genrestukken waaraan de adel van het prerevolutionaire Frankrijk de

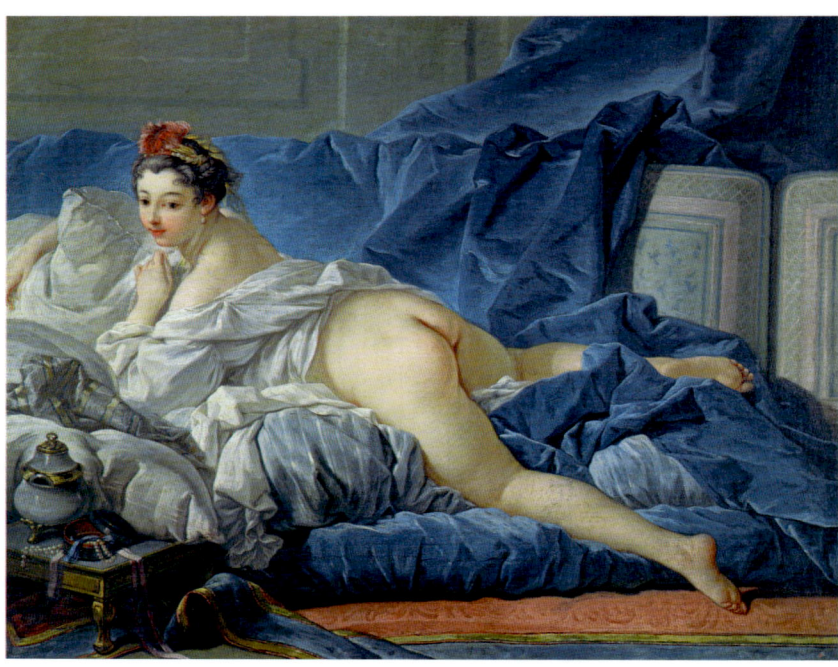

François Boucher (1703–1770)

The Odalisque
L'Odalisque
Die Odaliske
La odalisca
L'odalisca
De odalisk

1745, Oil on canvas/Huile sur toile, 53 × 64 cm, Musée du Louvre, Paris

pomposity, grown tired of the Baroque art which had been served by Colbert and Le Brun to the glorification of the authority of the royal rule. The king now favored a freer, merrier art in which the strict formal rules of the Academy were no longer valid. Classicists such as Poussin went out of fashion and had to vacate their places for artists who could create sensual and picturesque effects and whose painting would please the eye. Painters such as François Boucher (1703–1770) and Jean-Honoré Fragonard (1732–1806) delivered these works in astonishing quality and abundance. The support of Madame Pompadour, who was the official mistress of Louis XV, helped Boucher to attain a special position at the court, which he used to enable him to complete his numerous boudoir scenes with their lustfully decorated nudes, mostly featuring the king's other lovers.

The quintessence of French Rococo painting was, however, the painting of Jean-Antoine Watteau (1684–1721) with the island of Kythera,

pathos creux du baroque. Louis XIV déjà, en vieillissant, se lasse de la prétention pompeuse de l'art baroque dont Colbert et Le Brun s'étaient servis pour célébrer l'autorité de la majesté royale. Le roi préfère désormais un art plus libéré et plus sensuel, dans lequel les sévères règles formelles de l'Académie perdent de leur validité. Les artistes académiques comme Poussin sont passés de mode et doivent laisser la place à des peintres capables de créer des effets de sensualité picturale et dont les œuvres flattent avant tout le regard. Des artistes comme François Boucher (1703–1770) et Jean-Honoré Fragonard (1732–1806) fournissent ce type de tableaux en qualité et en quantité étonnantes. L'appui de Madame de Pompadour, maîtresse officielle de Louis XV, procure à Boucher une position toute particulière à la cour, qu'il utilise pour peindre d'innombrables scènes de boudoir avec des nus très sensuels – le plus souvent des maîtresses secondaires du monarque.

auch in Österreich, Deutschland, Spanien und Italien den hohlen Pathos des Barock. Bereits Ludwig XIV. wurde im Alter der prunkvollen Großspurigkeit der Barockkunst überdrüssig, derer sich Colbert und Le Brun bedient hatten, um die Autorität der königlichen Herrschaft zu preisen. Der König bevorzugte nun eine freiere, sinnesfrohe Kunst, in der die strengen formalen Regeln der Akademie ihre Gültigkeit verloren. Klassizisten wie Poussin kamen aus der Mode und mussten ihren Platz Malern räumen, die malerisch-sinnliche Effekte schaffen konnten und deren Malerei vor allem dem Augensinn schmeichelte. Maler wie François Boucher (1703–1770) und Jean-Honoré Fragonard lieferten (1732–1806) diese Werke in erstaunlicher Qualität und Fülle. Die Unterstützung der Madame Pompadour, der offiziellen Geliebten Ludwig XV. verhalf Boucher zu einer Sonderstellung am Hof, die er für seinen zahlreichen Boudoir-Szenen mit ihren lustvollen dekorierten Akten – meist andere Geliebte des Königs – nutzte.

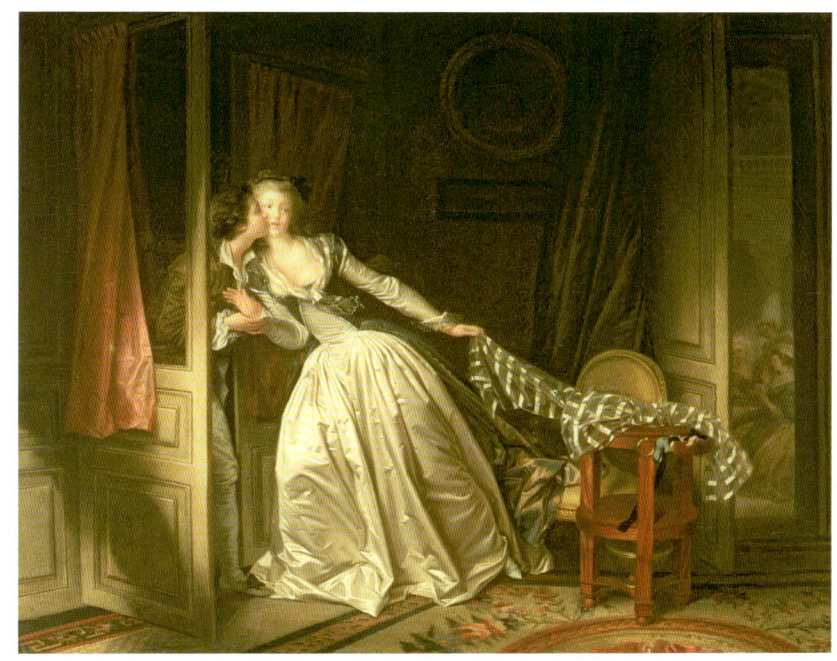

Jean-Honoré Fragonard (1732–1806)

The Stolen Kiss

Le Baiser dérobé

Der gestohlene Kuss

El beso robado

Il bacio rubato

De gestolen kus

c. 1786, Oil on canvas/Huile sur toile, 45 × 55 cm,
The State Hermitage Museum, St Petersburg

Italia el patetismo vacío del Barroco. Incluso Luis XIV en su vejez se cansó de la suntuosa pompa del arte barroco de la que se habían servido Colbert y Le Brun para glorificar el régimen real. El Rey prefería ahora un arte más libre y sensual, en el que las estrictas reglas académicas perdieron su validez. Clasicistas como Poussin dejaron de estar de moda y se vieron obligados a ceder su lugar a pintores que creaban efectos pictóricos sensuales y cuya pintura consistía principalmente en un halago a la vista. Pintores como François Boucher (1703–1770) o Jean-Honoré Fragonard (1732–1806) realizaban estas obras con maestría y profusión. El apoyo de Madame Pompadour, la amante oficial de Luis XIV, ayudó a Boucher a alcanzar una posición de excepción en la corte, que utilizó para sus muchas escenas de boudoir con sus desnudos en sensuales decorados –por lo general de amantes del rey–.

Las pinturas de Jean-Antoine Watteau (1684–1721) sin embargo también se incluyen

sfarzosa pomposità dell'arte barocca, della quale si erano serviti Colbert e Le Brun per elogiare l'autorità del potere reale. Il re preferiva infatti un'arte più libera e sensuale, in cui le severe regole formali dell'accademia perdevano la loro validità. Classicisti come Poussin passarono di moda e dovettero cedere il campo a pittori che potessero creare effetti pittorici sensuali e la cui pittura lusingava soprattutto la vista. Pittori come François Boucher (1703–1770) e Jean-Honoré Fragonard (1732–1806) realizzarono queste opere in sorprendente qualità e quantità. Madame Pompadour, l'amante ufficiale di Luigi XV, appoggiò Boucher procurandogli una posizione privilegiata a corte, che egli utilizzò dipingendo le sue numerose scene nel boudoir con voluttuosi nudi decorati, per la maggior parte altre amanti del re.

La quintessenza della pittura rococò francese è però rappresentata dai dipinti di Jean-Antoine Watteau (1684–1721) con l'isola

voorkeur gaf. Deze stijl beperkte zich echter niet tot Frankrijk maar verdrong ook in Oostenrijk, Duitsland, Spanje en Italië het holle pathos van de barok. Op latere leeftijd was Lodewijk XIV al uitgekeken op de overdreven en protserige gebaren van de barokkunst die door Colbert en Le Brun was uitgedragen om de autoriteit van de koninklijke heerschappij te verheerlijken. De Zonnekoning gaf nu de voorkeur aan een vrijere en opgewekter stijl, waarin de strenge formele regels van de Academie niet langer golden. Classicisten als Poussin raakten uit de mode en moesten plaatsmaken voor schilders die met picturaal en zinnelijk effectbejag konden werken en wier schilderijen vooral het oog streelden. Schilders als François Boucher (1703–1770) en Jean-Honoré Fragonard (1732–1806) wisten dit soort werken in buitengewone kwaliteit en ook kwantiteit te produceren. Dankzij de ondersteuning van madame de Pompadour, de officiële maîtresse van Lodewijk XV, kon Boucher een speciale tentoonstelling aan het

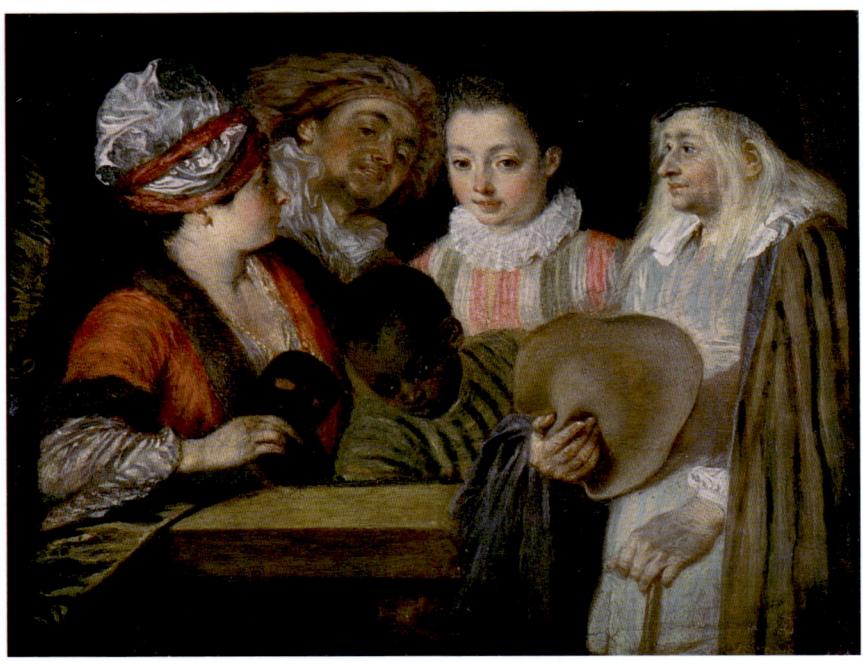

an earthly paradise, a dreamy, idyllic world in which people met for carefree flirtation and lovemaking.

The cheerful rococo style is typified by the popularity of pastel painting. The dry pens reproduce the scenes with a powdery-light coating of high color strength and great luminosity. In Paris, this technique had been popularized by the Venetian Rosalba Carriera (1675–1757). Masters of French pastels were Maurice Quentin de la Tour (1704–1788) and Jean-Étienne Liotard (1702–1789), with their portraits of the French nobility.

Jean Siméon Chardin (1699–1779) on the other hand avoided the courtly splendor and devoted himself to stillness, the unspectacular, the unheroic. Inspired by the Dutch painting of the 17th century, he painted mostly scenes of everyday life in simple interiors, or family scenes. His still lifes are among the best works of this genre and would later influence the impressionists.

La quintessence de la peinture rococo française est toutefois représentée par les tableaux de Watteau (1684–1721) sur l'île de Cythère – un « paradis terrestre », monde idyllique rêvé dans lequel les hommes se rencontrent pour des badinages et des jeux amoureux sans soucis.

Pour le style serein gai du rococo, la préférence du pastel est caractéristique. Les crayons secs rendent les scènes d'un trait léger, doté d'une haute intensité colorée et d'une grande luminosité. Cette technique est popularisée à Paris par Rosalba Carriera (1675–1757), pastelliste venue de Venise. Les maîtres français du pastel sont Maurice Quentin de la Tour (1704–1788) et Jean-Étienne Liotard (1702–1789), qui ont portraituré la société nobiliaire française.

Jean Siméon Chardin (1699–1779), au contraire, fuit le monde pour se consacrer au silencieux, au discret, au « non héroïque ». Inspiré par la peinture hollandaise du

Inbegriff der französischen Rokoko-Malerei sind aber die Gemälde von Jean-Antoine Watteau (1684–1721) mit der Insel Kythera, ein irdisches Paradies, eine verträumte, idyllische Welt, in der sich die Menschen zu sorgenfreier Tändelei und Liebesspiel treffen.

Für den heiteren Stil des Rokoko ist die Beliebtheit der Pastellmalerei bezeichnend. Die trockenen Stifte geben die Szenen mit pudrig-leichtem Strich in hoher Farbkraft und großer Leuchtkraft wieder. In Paris wurde diese Technik durch die aus Venedig stammende Rosalba Carriera (1675–1757) populär. Meister des französischen Pastells sind Maurice-Quentin de la Tour (1704–1788) und Jean-Étienne Liotard (1702–1789) mit ihren Porträts der französischen Adelsgesellschaft.

Jean Siméon Chardin (1699–1779) mied dagegen den höfischen Glanz und widmete sich dem Stillen, Unscheinbaren, Unheroischen. Angeregt durch die holländische Malerei des 17. Jahrhunderts malte er vorwiegend

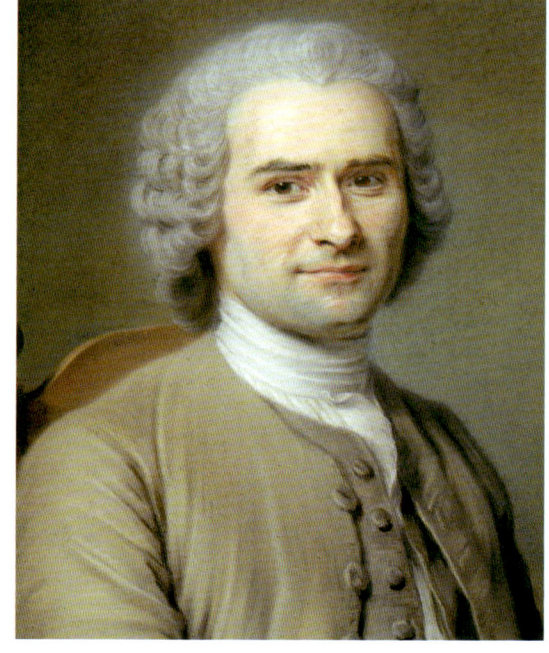

Maurice Quentin de la Tour (1704–1788)
Jean-Jacques Rousseau
c. 1764, Pastel, 43 × 34 cm, Musée Antoine Lécuyer, Saint-Quentin

en la pintura rococó, con su isla Citera, paraíso terrenal, un mundo idílico y ensoñador en el que las personas se entregan sin cuidado a flirteos y juegos amorosos.

La preferencia por la pintura al pastel es representativa del estilo jovial del Rococó. Los lápices, secos, reproducen las escenas con ligeros trazos empolvados de gran fuerza luminosa y cromática. Fue Rosalba Carriera (1675–1757), procedente de Venecia, quien popularizó esta técnica en París. Entre los maestros de la pintura al pastel francesa se cuentan Maurice-Quentin de la Tour (1704–1788) y Jean-Étienne Liotard (1702–1789) con sus retratos de la nobleza francesa.

Por otro lado Jean Siméon Chardin (1699–1779) evitó el esplendor de la corte, dedicándose a lo insignificante, lo silencioso, lo olvidado. Inspirado por la pintura holandesa del XVII pintó sobre todo escenas cotidianas en parcos interiores y escenas familiares. Sus bodegones se cuentan entre los mejores del

di Citera, un paradiso terrestre, un mondo trasognato e idilliaco in cui gli esseri umani si dedicano a flirt e giochi amorosi spensierati.

Per lo stile allegro del rococò è caratteristica la popolarità della pittura a pastello. Le matite secche restituiscono alle scene una grande forza di colore e una maggiore intensità luminosa con leggeri tratti polverosi. Questa tecnica divenne popolare a Parigi grazie a Rosalba Carriera, di origine veneziana (1675–1757). I maestri della pittura a pastello francese sono Maurice-Quentin de la Tour (1704–1788) e Jean-Étienne Liotard (1702–1789) con i loro ritratti dell'aristocrazia francese.

Al contrario Jean Siméon Chardin (1699–1779) evitò lo splendore della corte e si dedicò alla quiete, al poco appariscente, al non eroico. Stimolato dalla pittura olandese del XVII secolo, egli dipinse in prevalenza scene di vita quotidiana in modesti ambienti interni o scene familiari. Le sue nature morte

hof houden, die hij aangreep om veel van zijn boudoirstukken te tonen, oftewel taferelen met pikant geschilderde naakten, van wie de meeste eveneens geliefden van de koning waren.

Maar het hoogtepunt van de Franse rococoschilderkunst was het werk waarop Jean-Antoine Watteau (1684–1721) het eiland Kythera uitbeeldde, een aards paradijs, een geïdealiseerde wereld waarin mensen zich zorgeloos aan vertier en liefdesspel overgaven.

Binnen de opgewekte stijl van de rococo is de voorliefde voor de pastelschilderkunst veelbetekenend. Met het droge pastelkrijt konden taferelen in poederlichte streken en met een grote kleurenrijkdom en helderheid worden uitgebeeld. In Parijs werd de techniek door de uit Venetië stammende Rosalba Carriera (1675–1757) zeer populair. De meesters van de Franse pastelkunst waren Maurice-Quentin de la Tour (1704–1788) en Jean-Étienne Liotard (1702–1789), die in deze techniek de Franse adel portretteerden.

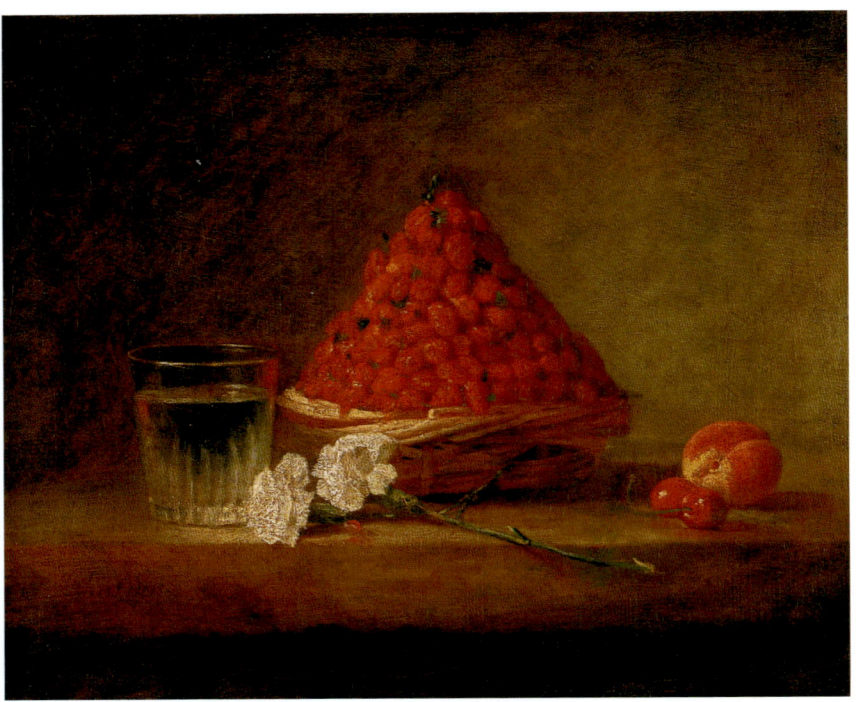

Jean-Siméon Chardin (1699–1779)

Basket with Wild Strawberries

Le Panier de fraises des bois

Korb mit wilden Erdbeeren

Cesta con fresas silvestres

Cesto di fragole di bosco

Mand met wilde aardbeien

c. 1761, Oil on canvas/Huile sur toile, 38 × 46 cm, Private collection

At the end of the 18th century there was a return to the subject of antiquity and with that a resurgence of the classical artistic stance. Following the French Revolution and the rise of Napoleon, the (neo) classical art again became the officially sanctioned art form. The most important representative of this was Jacques-Louis David (1748–1825), whose stricter, purer art was trained in the ancient style (*The Oath of Horatii*, 1784) and was elevated, especially after the seizure of power by Napoleon, to a position of being in the service of the state.

XVIIᵉ siècle, il peint de préférence des scènes de tous les jours dans des intérieurs simples, ou des scènes familiales. Ses natures mortes appartiennent aux meilleures œuvres du genre ; elles seront distinguées plus tard par les impressionnistes.

La fin du XVIIIᵉ siècle connaît un retour à l'antique – partant, au renforcement du goût classicisant. Après la Révolution française et l'ascension de Napoléon, l'art (néo) classique redevient la tendance officielle. Son représentant le plus important est Jacques-Louis David (1748–1825), dont le style sévère et pur, nourri d'Antiquité (*Le Serment des Horaces*, 1784/1785), est élevé au rang d'art officiel sous l'Empire.

Alltagsszenen in schlichten Innenräumen oder Familienszenen. Seine Stillleben gehören zu den besten Werken dieses Genres und beeindruckten später auch die Impressionisten.

Ende des 18. Jahrhunderts kam es zu einer Rückbesinnung auf die Antike und damit zur Wiedererstarkung der klassizistischen Kunstgesinnung. Nach der Französischen Revolution und dem Aufstieg Napoleons wurde die (neo) klassizistische Kunst wieder zur offiziellen Kunstrichtung. Bedeutendster Vertreter wurde Jacques-Louis David (1748–1825), dessen strenger, reiner, an der Antike geschulter Stil (*Der Schwur der Horatier*, 1784/1785) vor allem nach der Machtergreifung von Napoleon zur staatstragenden Kunst erhoben wurde.

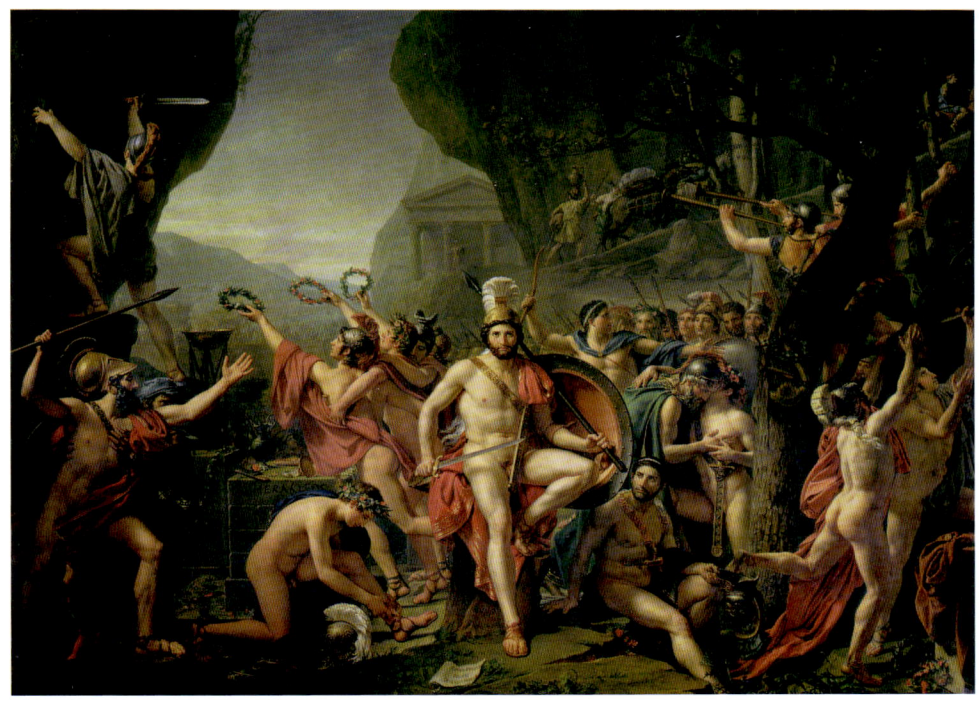

Jacques-Louis David (1748–1825)

Leonidas at Thermopylae

Léonidas aux Thermopyles

Leonidas an den Thermopylen

Leonidas y las Termopilas

Leonida alle Termopili

Leonidas bij Thermopylae

1814, Oil on canvas/Huile sur toile, 395 × 531 cm,
Musée du Louvre, Paris

género y dejaron su marca siglos después en los impresionistas.

A finales del XVIII se dio una reorientación hacia la Antigüedad clásica y con ella un refuerzo del concepto de arte clasicista. Tras la Revolución Francesa y la subida al poder de Napoleón el arte clasicista se convirtió nuevamente en la dirección oficial. Su representante más importante fue Jacques-Louis David (1748–1825), cuyo estilo puro y estricto, aprendido de los clásicos (*El juramento de los Horacios,* 1784/1785) ascendió a la categoría de arte del gobierno con la toma de poder por parte de Napoleón.

appartengono alle migliori opere di questo genere e in seguito influenzarono anche gli Impressionisti.

Alla fine del XVIII secolo si giunse al ritorno dell'antichità e quindi alla riaffermazione dei principi artistici del classicismo. Dopo la Rivoluzione francese e l'ascesa di Napoleone, l'arte (neo) classica ritornò ad essere la corrente artistica ufficiale. Il rappresentante più illustre fu Jacques-Louis David (1748–1825), il cui stile severo, puro e ispirato all'antichità (Il giuramento degli Orazi, 1784/85) fu innalzato ad arte come espressione dello Stato, soprattutto dopo la presa di potere di Napoleone.

Daarentegen meed Jean Siméon Chardin (1699–1779) de pracht van het hof en wijdde zich aan verstilde scènes van het eenvoudige en onheroïsche. Geïnspireerd door de Nederlandse meesters van de zeventiende eeuw schilderde hij overwegend alledaagse en familiaire taferelen in eenvoudige interieurs. Zijn stillevens behoren tot het beste wat ooit in dit genre is gemaakt en zouden later veel indruk op de impressionisten maken.

Aan het einde van de achttiende eeuw werd opnieuw teruggegrepen op de klassieken en trad de classicistische kunstopvatting weer op de voorgrond. Na de Franse Revolutie en de opkomst van Napoleon werd het neoclassicisme de officiële kunststroming. Belangrijke vertegenwoordigers waren Jacques-Louis David (1748–1825), wiens strenge, puristische en aan de klassieken ontleende werk (*De eed van de Horatii,* 1784/85) vooral na de machtsovername van Napoleon tot staatskunst werd verheven.

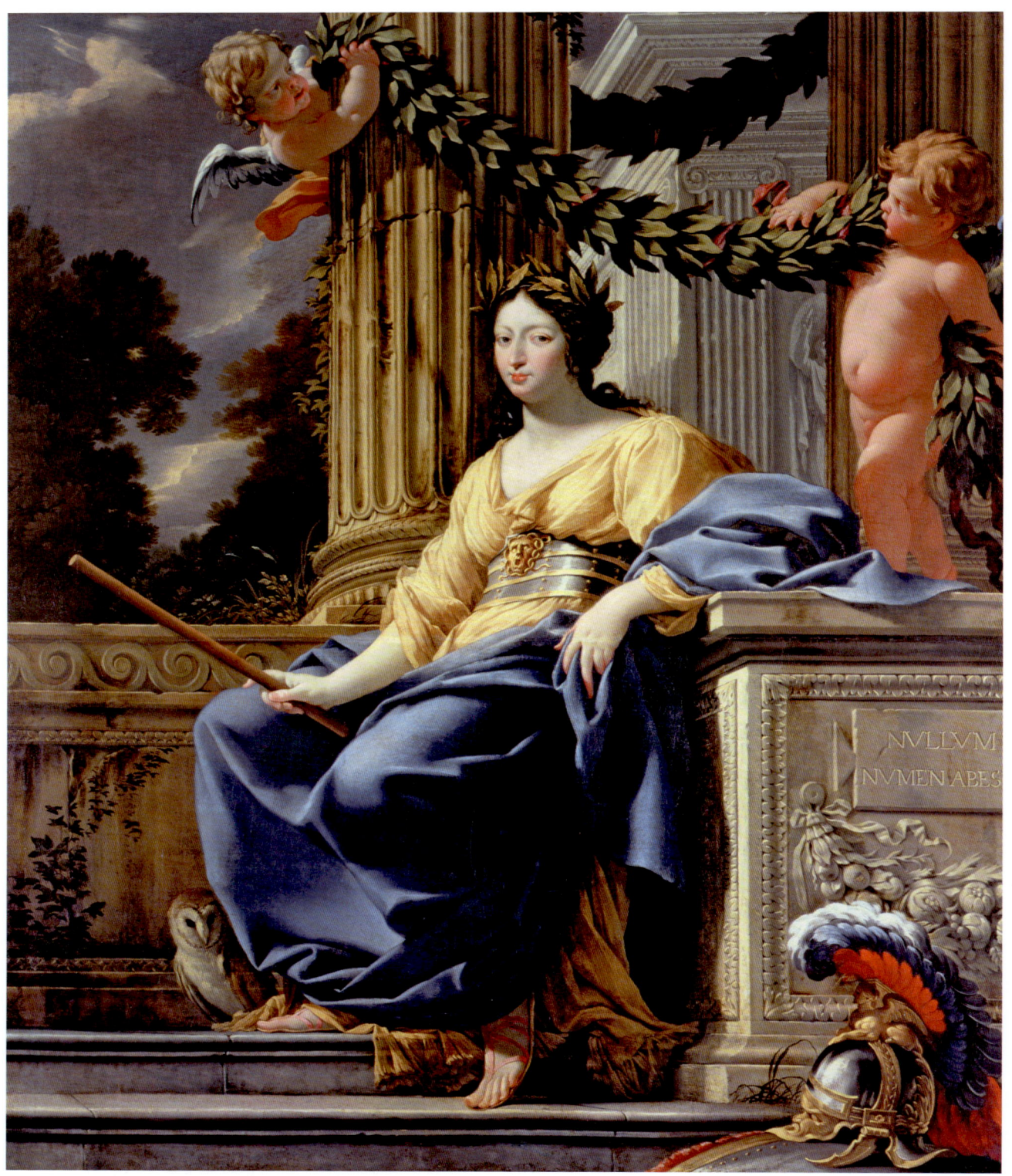

Simon Vouet (attributed to/attribué à) (1590–1649)

Allegorical Portrait of Anne of Austria

Portrait allégorique d'Anne d'Autriche

Allegorisches Porträt von Anne von Österreich

Retrato alegórico de Ana de Austria

Ritratto allegorico di Anna d'Austria

Allegorisch portret van Anna van Oostenrijk

c. 1643, Oil on canvas/Huile sur toile, 202 × 172 cm, The State Hermitage Museum, St Petersburg

Simon Vouet (1590–1649)

Prudence Leading Peace and Abundance

La Prudence amène la Paix et l'Abondance

Die Weisheit führt Frieden und Wohlstand

La Sabiduría lidera a la Paz y la Prosperidad

La prudenza porta pace e abbondanza

Wijsheid leidt Vrede en Welstand

c. 1640, Oil on canvas/Huile sur toile, 237 × 175 cm, Musée du Louvre, Paris

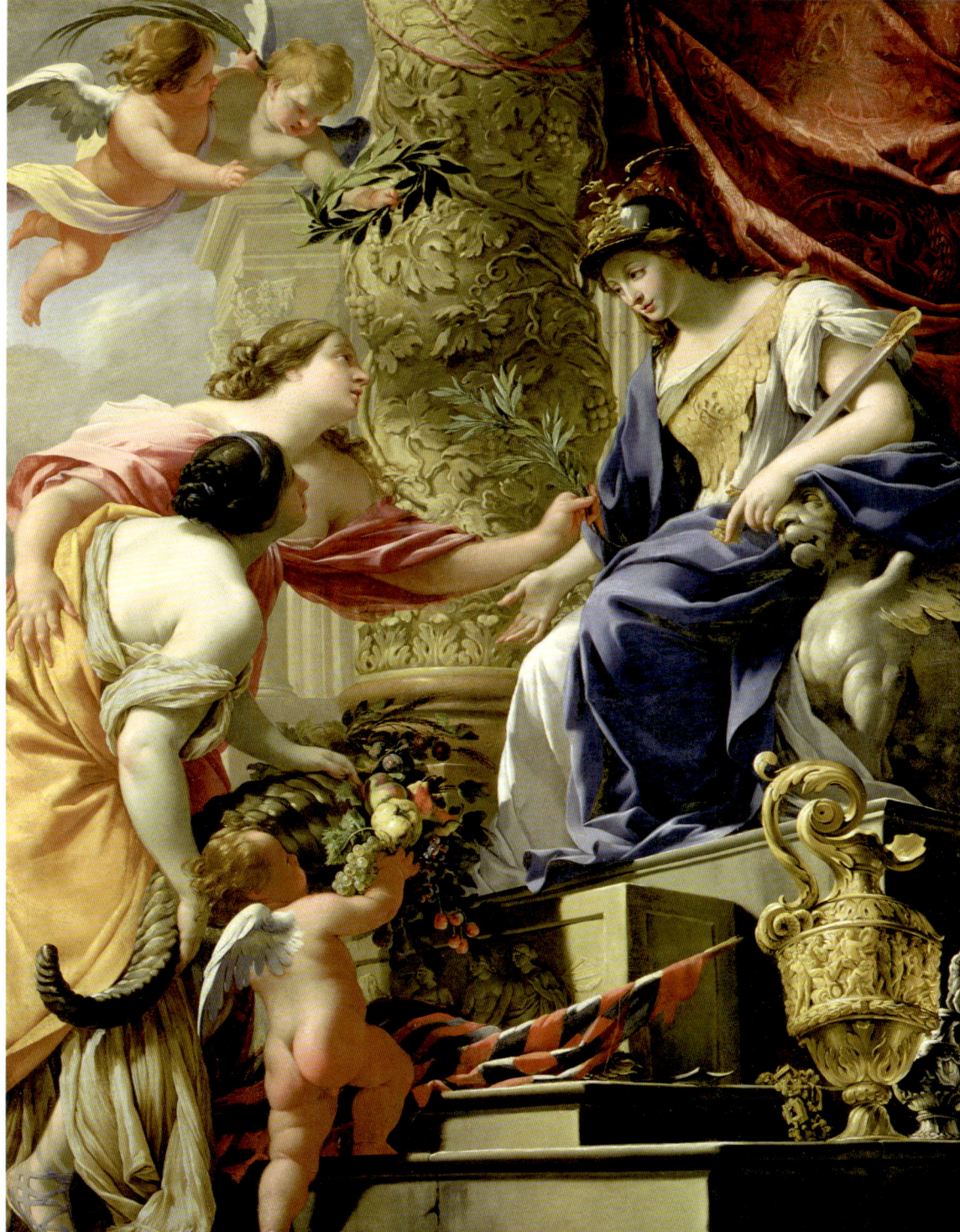

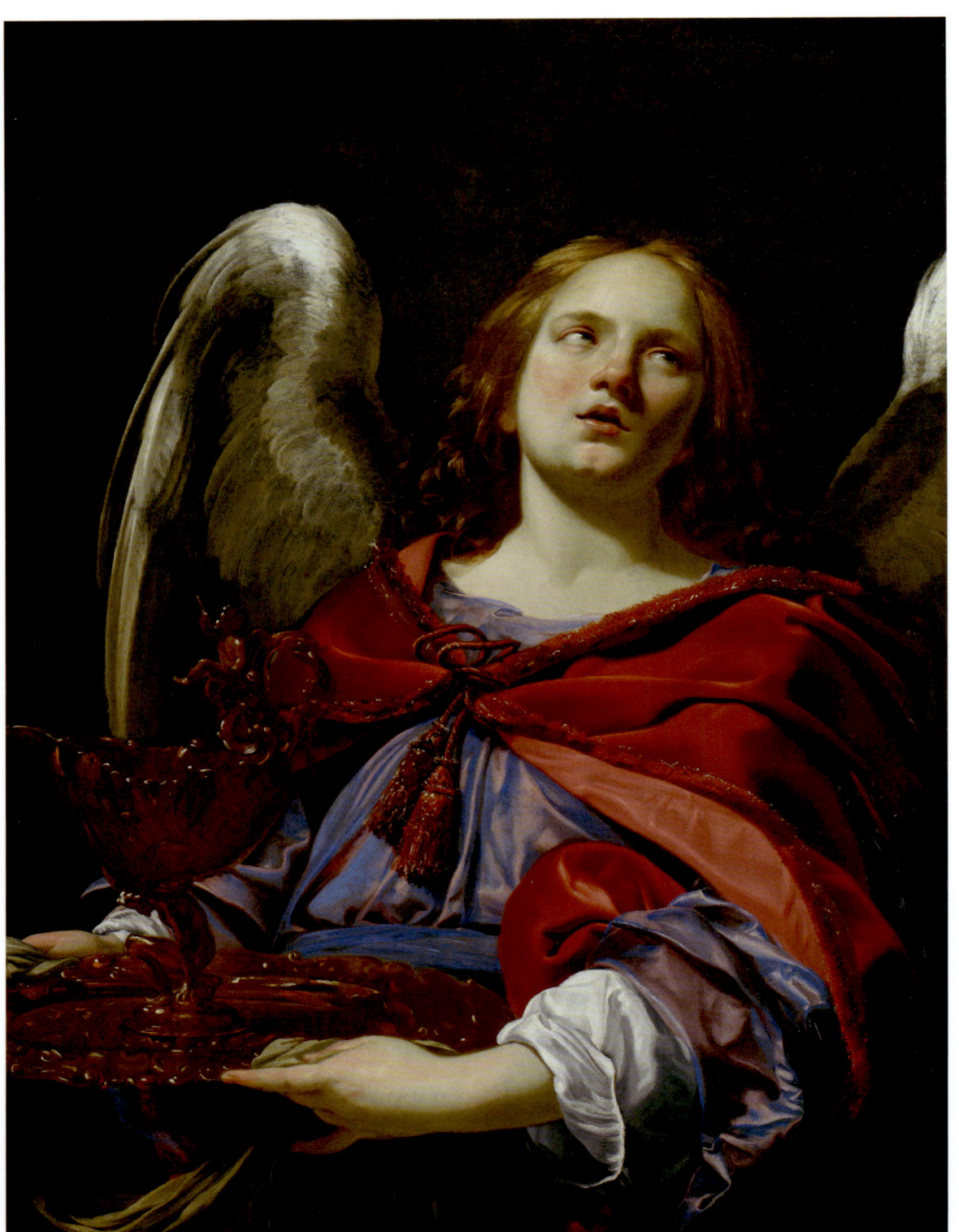

Simon Vouet (1590–1649)

Angels with Attributes of the Passion:
Angel Holding the Vessel and Towel
for washing the hands of Pontius
Pilate

Ange portant les instruments de la
Passion

Engel mit Attributen der Passion

Ángel con los atributos de la Pasión

Angelo con i simboli della passione

Engel met attributen van de Passie

1627, Oil on canvas/Huile sur toile,
104,3 × 78,42 cm, Minneapolis Institute
of Art, Minneapolis

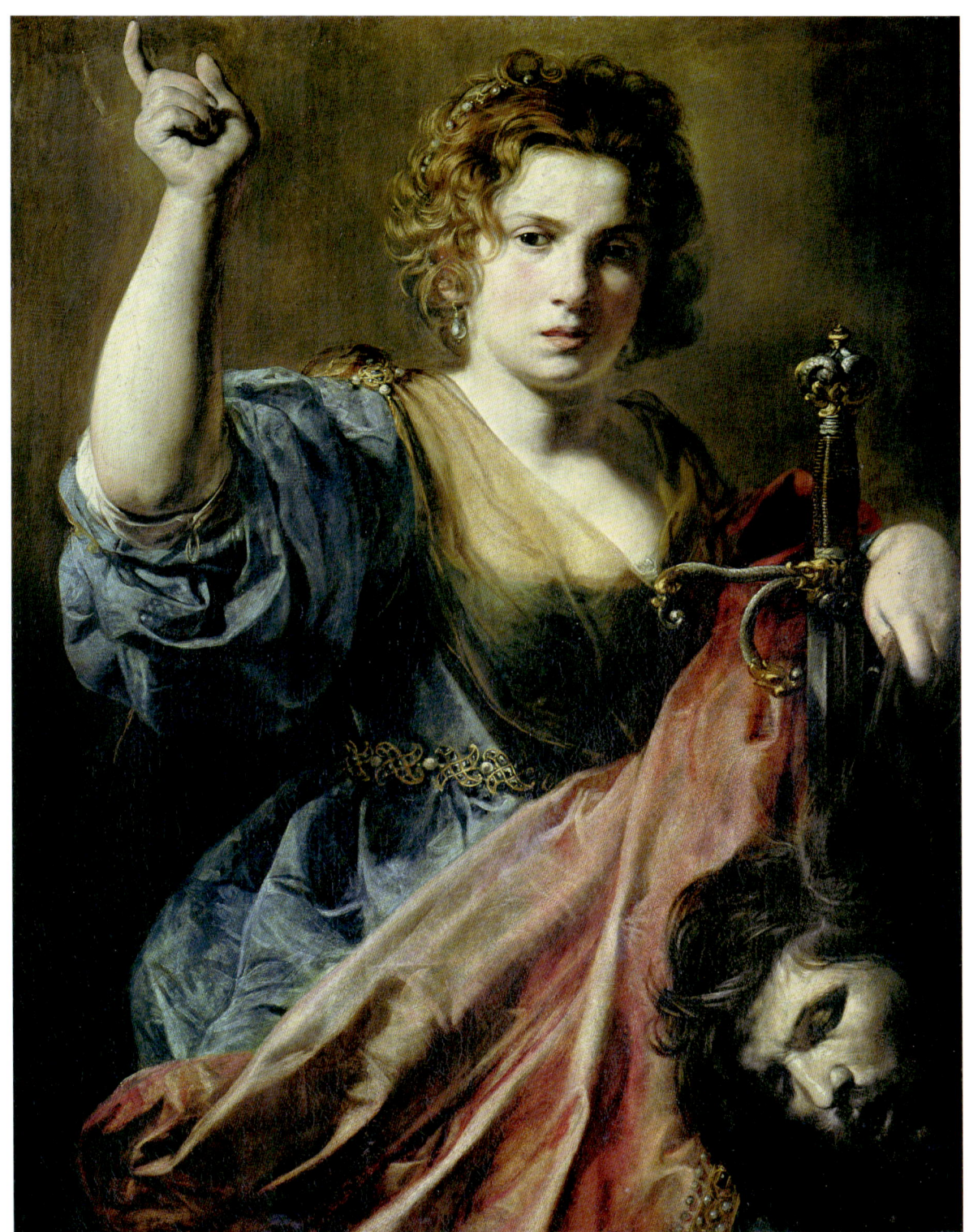

Valentin de Boulogne (1591–1632)

Judith

Judith

Judith

Judith

Giuditta

Judith

c. 1625, Oil on canvas/Huile sur toile,
97 × 74 cm, Musée des Augustins,
Toulouse

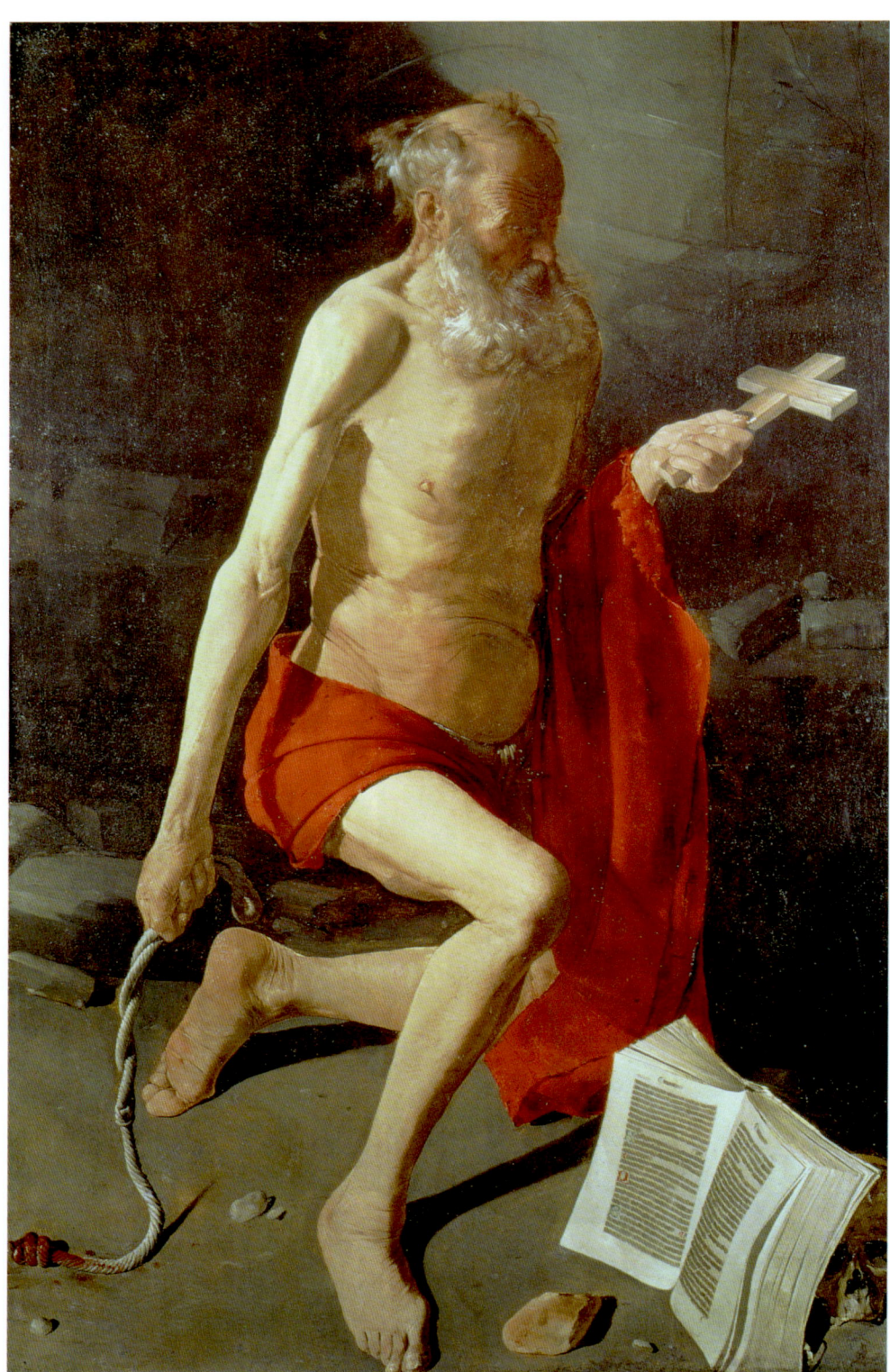

Georges de La Tour (1593–1652)

St. Jerome

Saint Jérôme

Der heilige Hieronymus

San Jerónimo

San Gerolamo

De heilige Hiëronymus

c. 1628, Oil on canvas/Huile sur toile, 157 × 100 cm,
Musée des Beaux-Arts, Grenoble

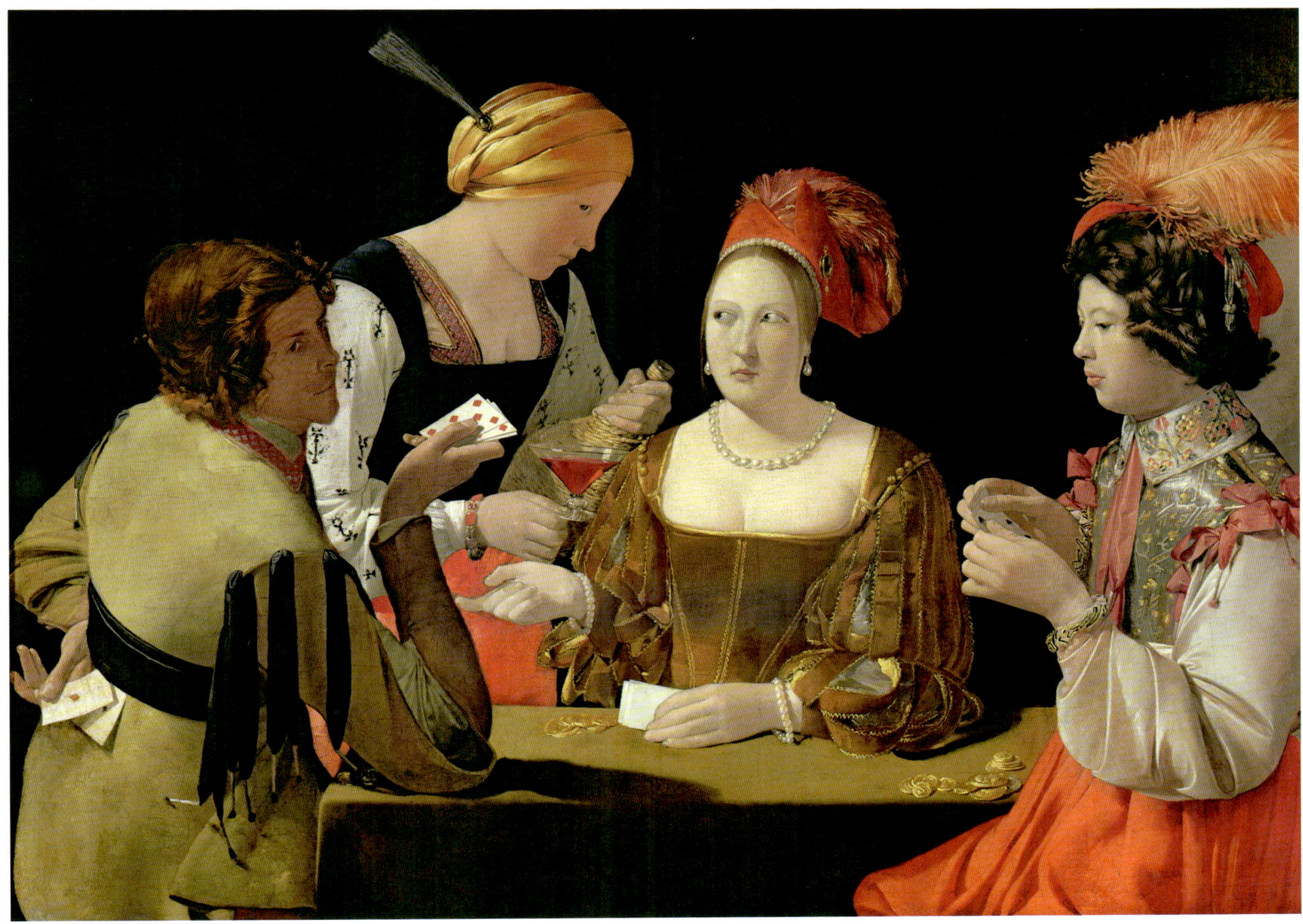

Georges de La Tour (1593–1652)

The Cheat with the Ace of Diamonds

Le Tricheur à l'as de carreau

Der Falschspieler mit dem Karo-As

El tramposo con el as de diamantes

Il baro con l'asso di quadri

De valsspeler met de ruitenaas

c. 1635, Oil on canvas/Huile sur toile, 106 × 146 cm,
Musée du Louvre, Paris

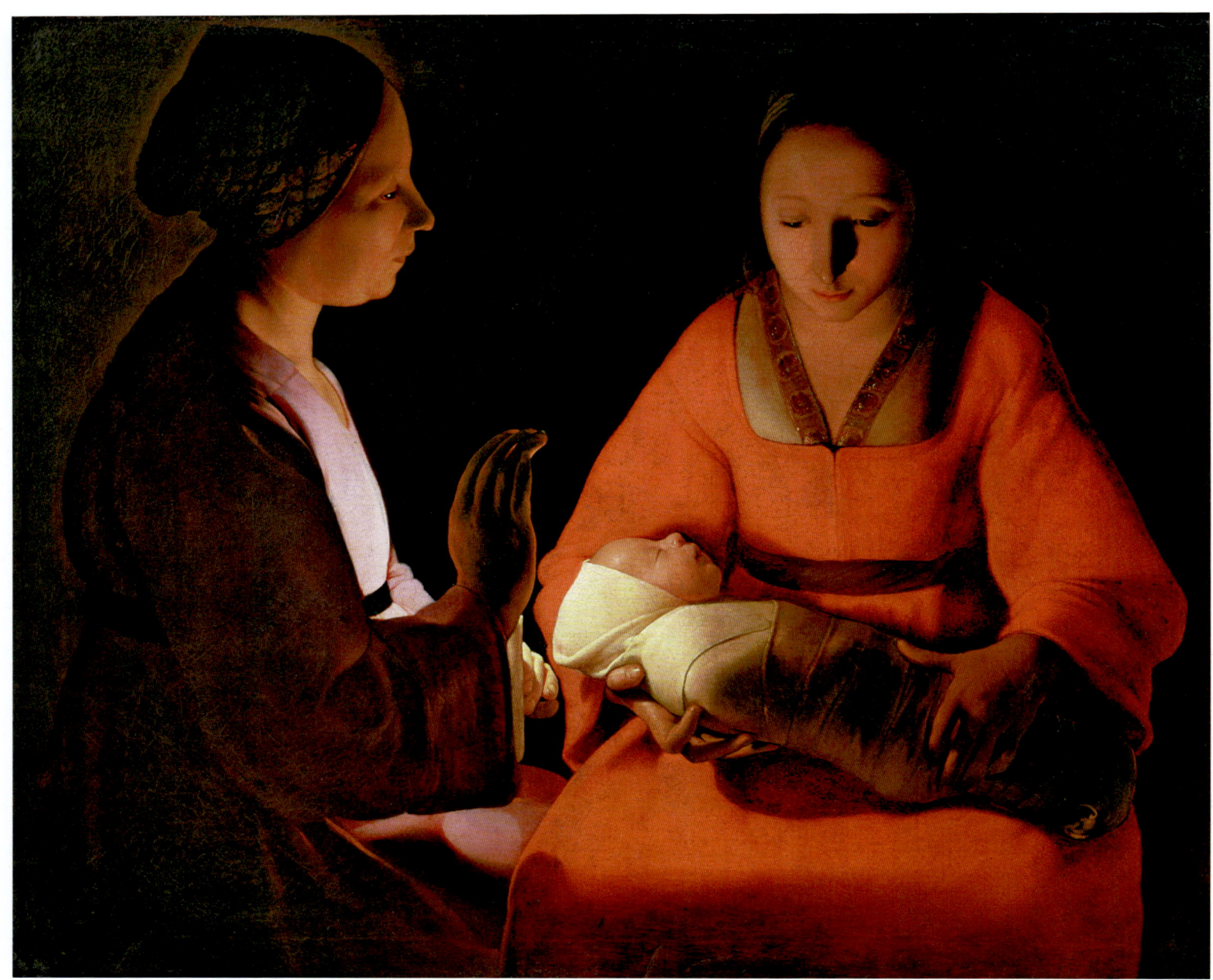

Georges de La Tour (1593–1652)

The New Born Child	Das Neugeborene	Il neonato
Le Nouveau-Né	El recién nacido	De pasgeborene

n. d., Oil on canvas/Huile sur toile, 76 × 91 cm, Musée des Beaux-Arts, Rennes

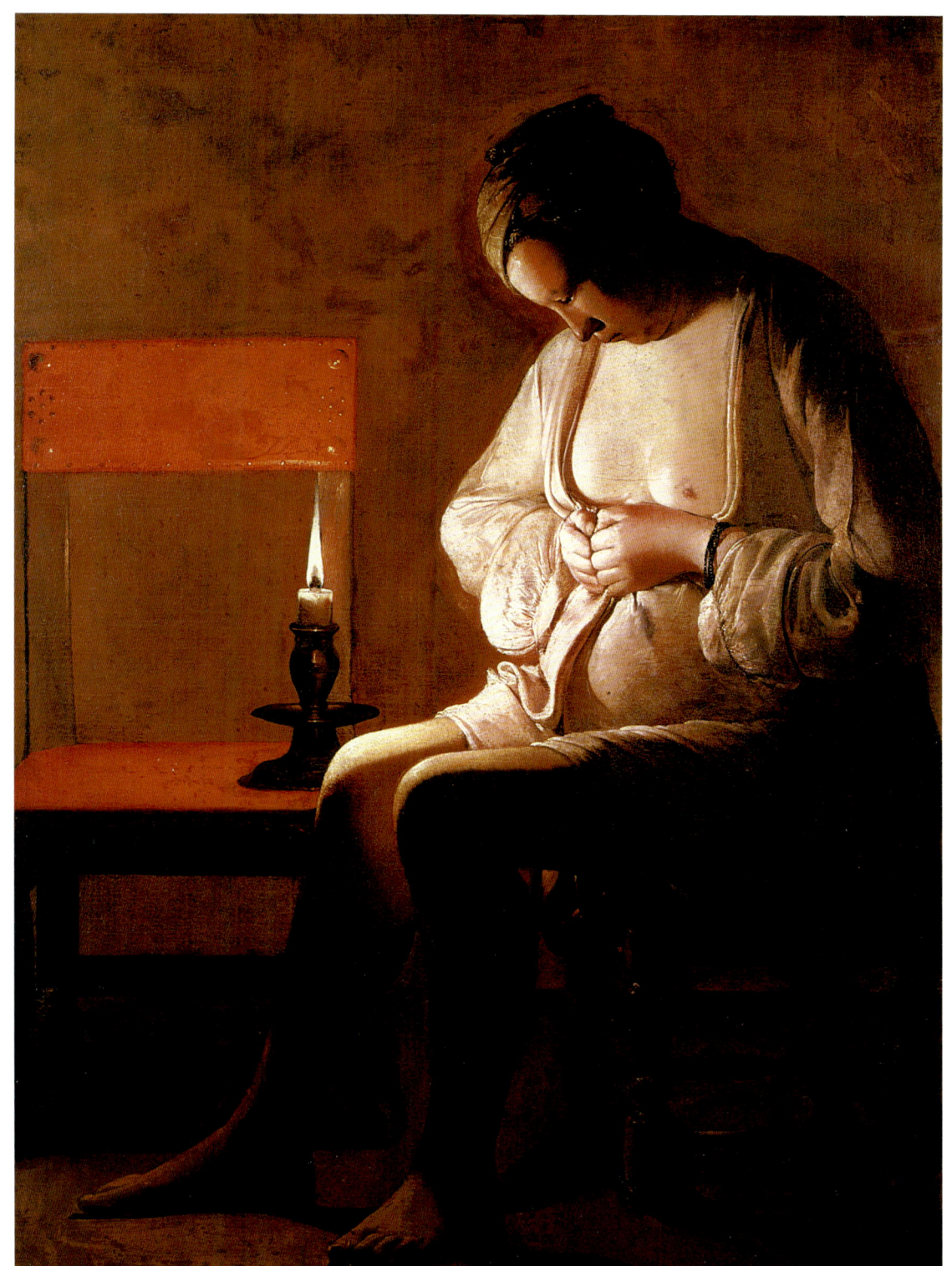

Georges de La Tour (1593–1652)

The Flea Catcher

La Femme à la puce

Die Flohfängerin

La mujer de la pulga

La donna con le pulci

De vlooienvangster

c. 1638, Oil on canvas/Huile sur toile,
121 × 89 cm, Palais des ducs de Lorraine –
Musée lorrain, Nancy

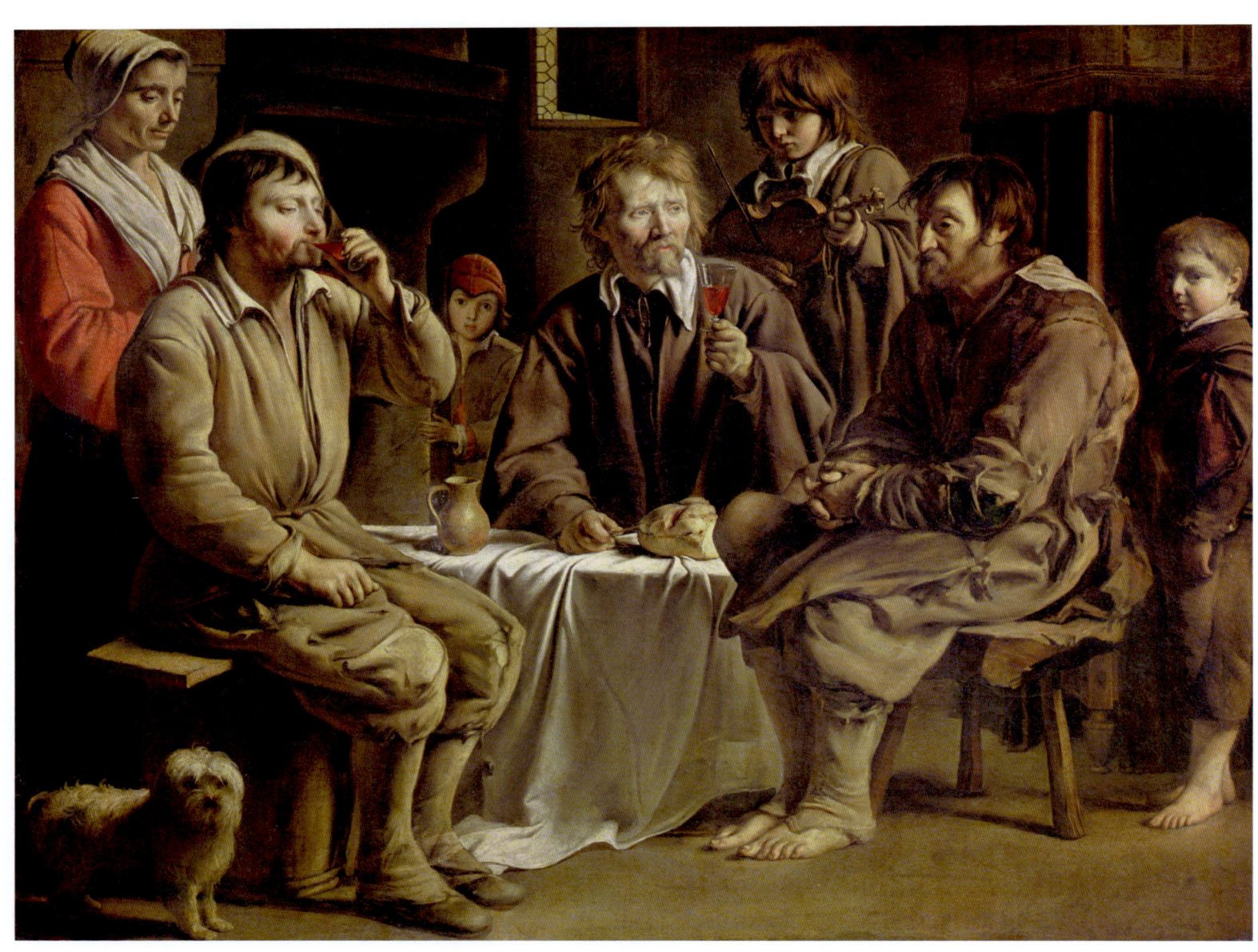

Louis Le Nain (c. 1597–1648) or/ou Antoine Le Nain (c. 1600–1648)

The Peasants' Meal   Das Mahl der Bauern   Il pasto dei contadini

Repas de paysans   La comida de los campesinos De boerenmaaltijd

1642, Oil on canvas/Huile sur toile, 97 × 122 cm, Musée du Louvre, Paris

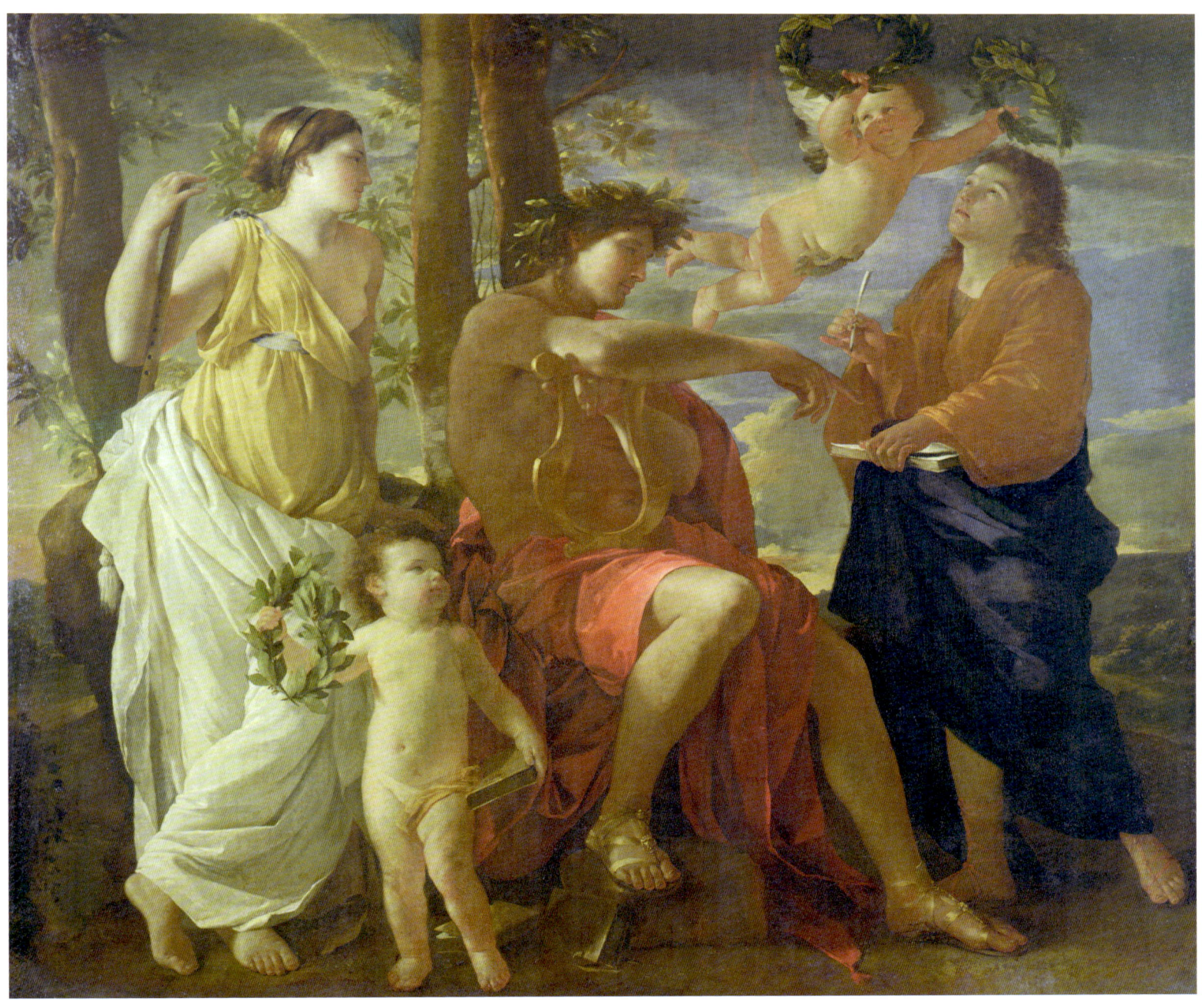

Nicolas Poussin (1594–1665)

The Inspiration of the Poet   Die Inspiration des Dichters   L'ispirazione del poeta

L'Inspiration du poète   La inspiración del poeta   De inspiratie van de dichter

c. 1629–1630, Oil on canvas/Huile sur toile, 183 × 213 cm, Musée du Louvre, Paris

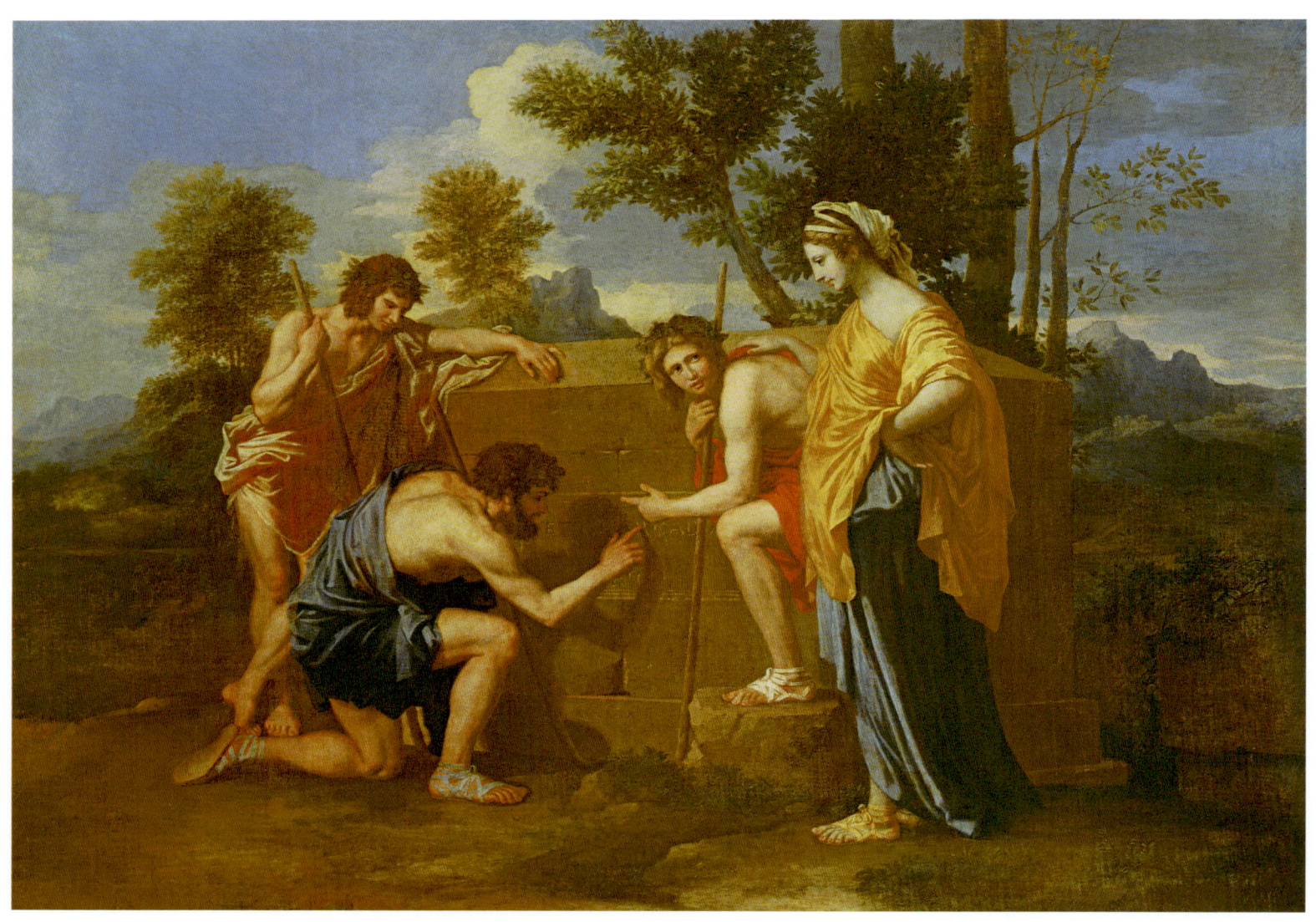

Nicolas Poussin (1594–1665)

The Shepherds of Arcadia

Les Bergers d'Arcadie, *dit aussi* Et in Arcadia ego

Die Hirten von Arkadien

Los pastores de Arcadia

I pastori d'Arcadia

De Arcadische herders

c. 1637–1638, Oil on canvas/Huile sur toile, 85 × 121 cm

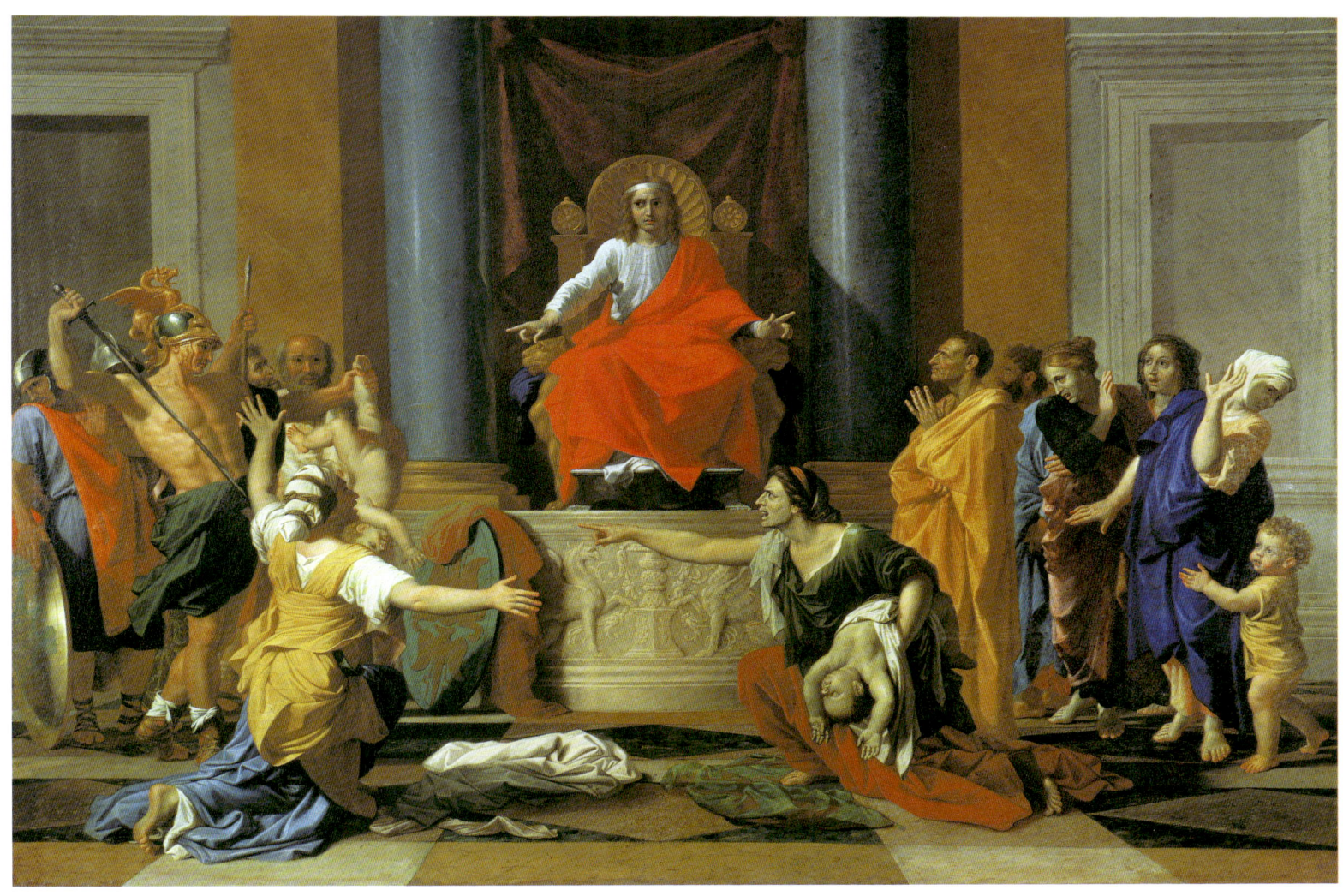

Nicolas Poussin (1594–1665)

The Judgment of Solomon

Le Jugement de Salomon

Das Urteil des Salomon

El juicio de Salomón

Il giudizio di Salomone

Salomonsoordeel

1649, Oil on canvas/Huile sur toile, 101 × 150 cm, Musée du Louvre, Paris

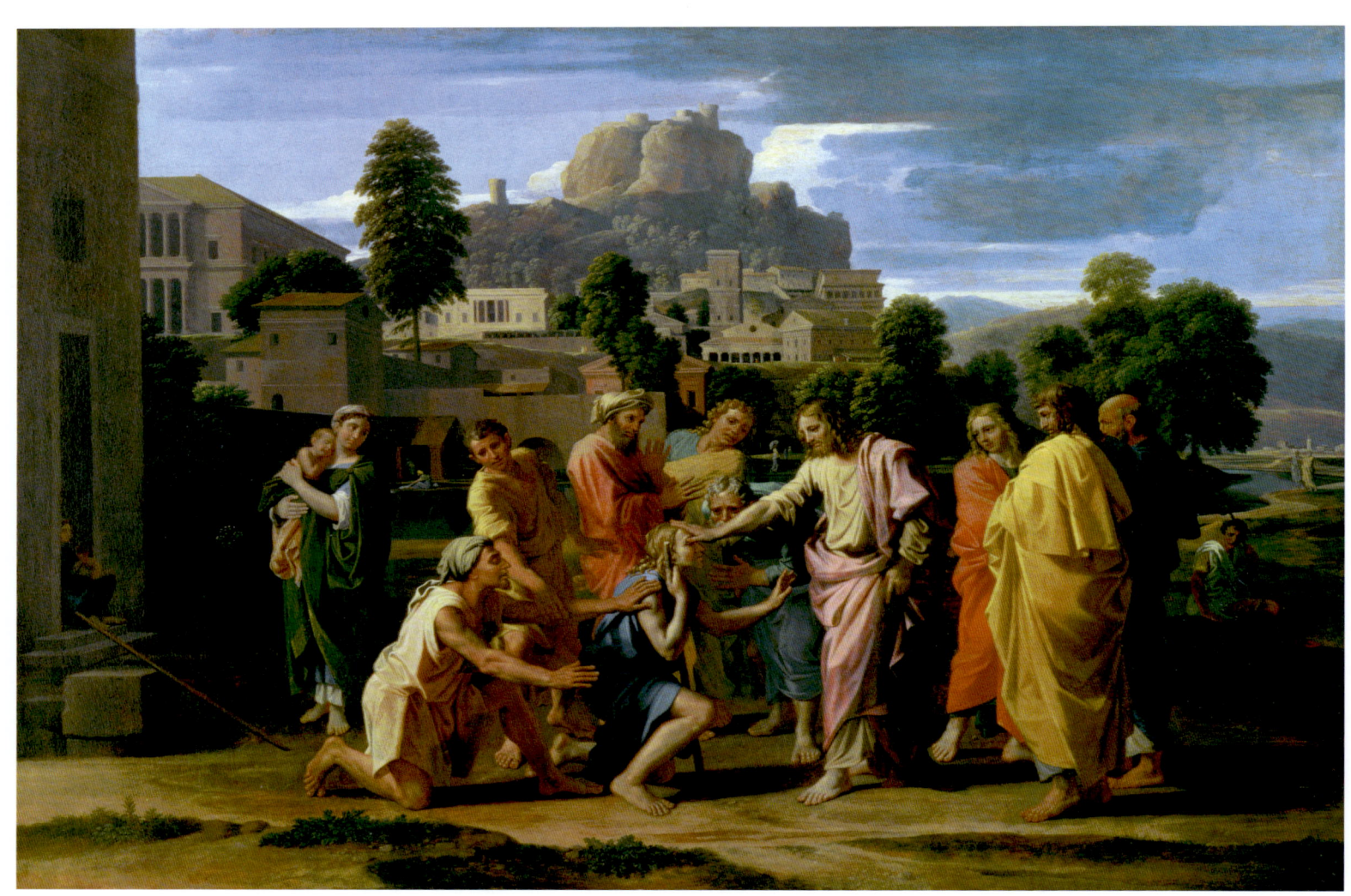

Nicolas Poussin (1594–1665)

The Blind of Jericho, *or* Christ Healing the Blind

Les Aveugles de Jéricho, *dit aussi* Le Christ guérissant les aveugles

Der Blinde von Jericho *oder* Christus heilt die Blinden

El ciego de Jericó *o* Cristo cura a los ciegos

Il cieco di Gerico *o* Gesù Cristo guarisce il cieco

De blinden te Jericho, *of:* Christus geneest de blinden

1650, Oil on canvas/Huile sur toile, 119 × 176 cm, Musée du Louvre, Paris

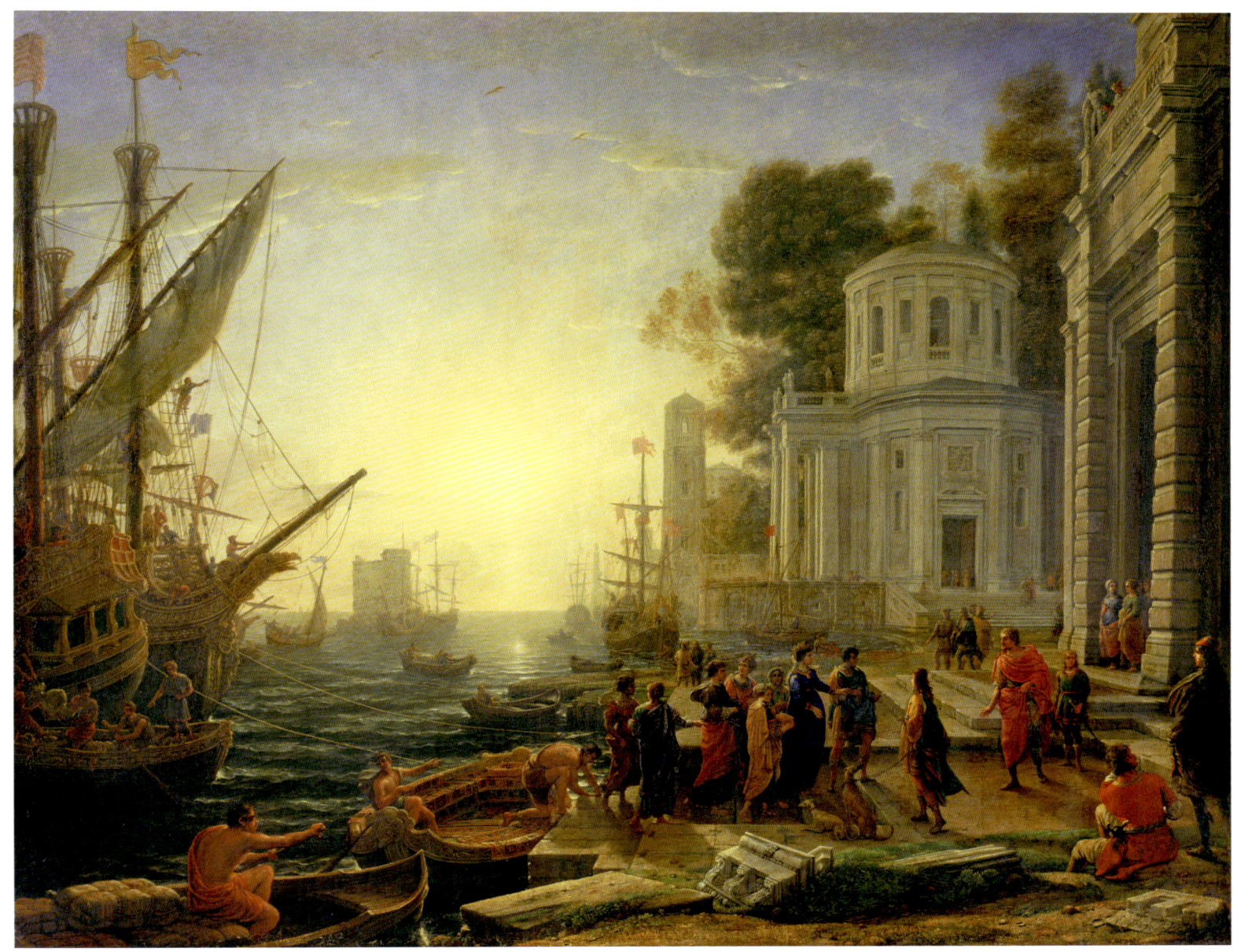

Claude Lorrain (1600–1682)

Cleopatra Disembarking at Tarsus

Le Débarquement de Cléopâtre à Tarse

Die Landung der Kleopatra in Tarsos

El desembarco de Cleopatra en Tarso

Lo sbarco di Cleopatra a Tarso

Cleopatra gaat aan land bij Tarsos

1642–1643, Oil on canvas/Huile sur toile, 119 × 168 cm, Musée du Louvre, Paris

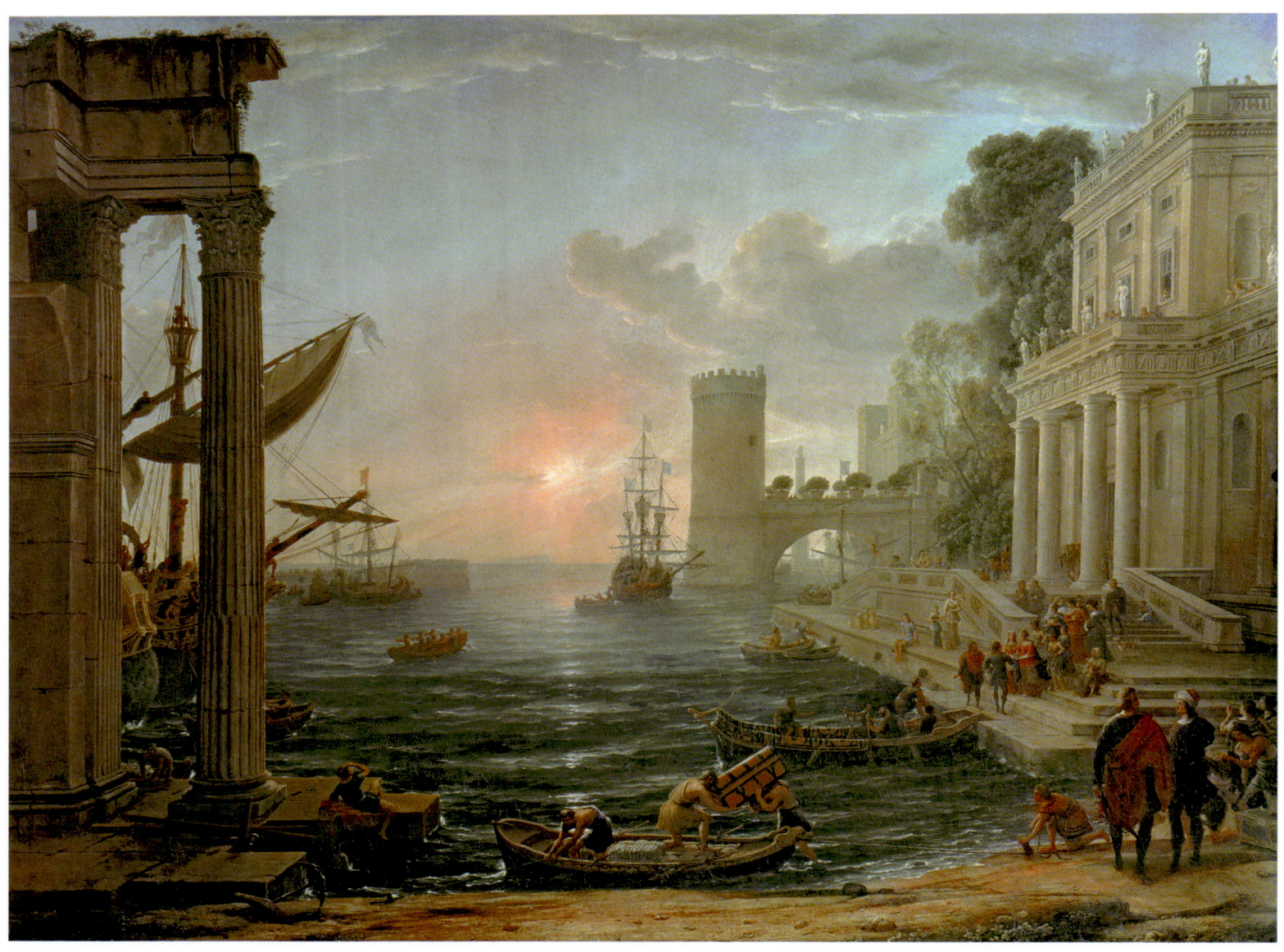

Claude Lorrain (1600–1682)

Seaport with the Embarkation of the Queen of Sheba

L'Embarquement de la reine de Saba

Seehafen mit der Einschiffung der Königin von Saba

Puerto marítimo con el embarco de la reina de Saba

Porto con l'imbarco della regina di Saba

Zeehaven met de inscheping van de koningin van Seba

1648, Oil on canvas/Huile sur toile, 149,1 × 196,7 cm, National Gallery, London

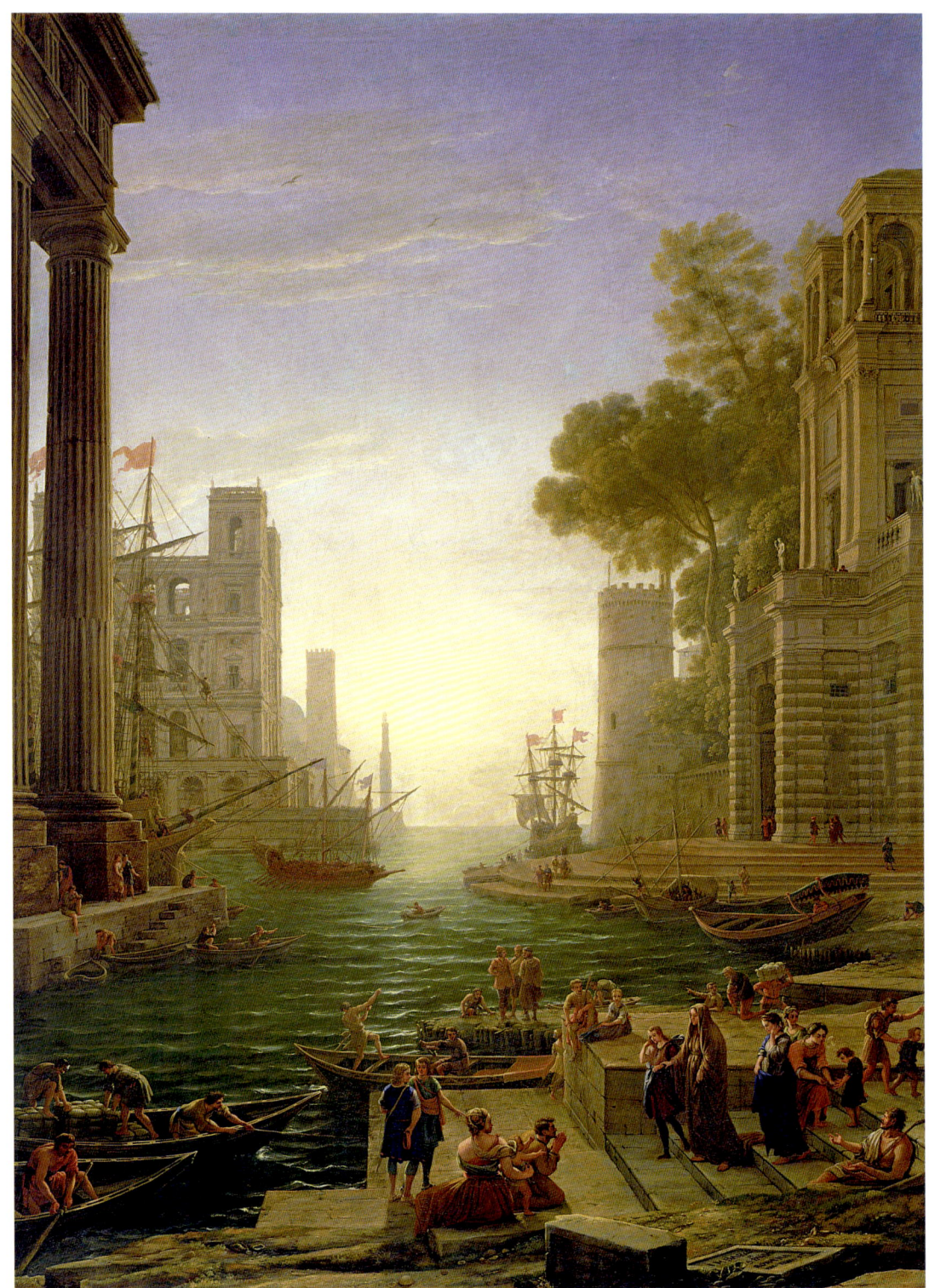

Claude Lorrain (1600–1682)

Embarkation of St. Paula Romana at Ostia

L'Embarquement de sainte Paule à Ostie

Einschiffung der Hl. Paula Romana in Ostia

Embarco de la Santa Paula Romana en Ostia

L'imbarco di Santa Paola Romana a Ostia

Inscheping van de Hl. Paula Romana in Ostia

c. 1639, Oil on canvas/Huile sur toile, 211 × 145 cm,
Museo del Prado, Madrid

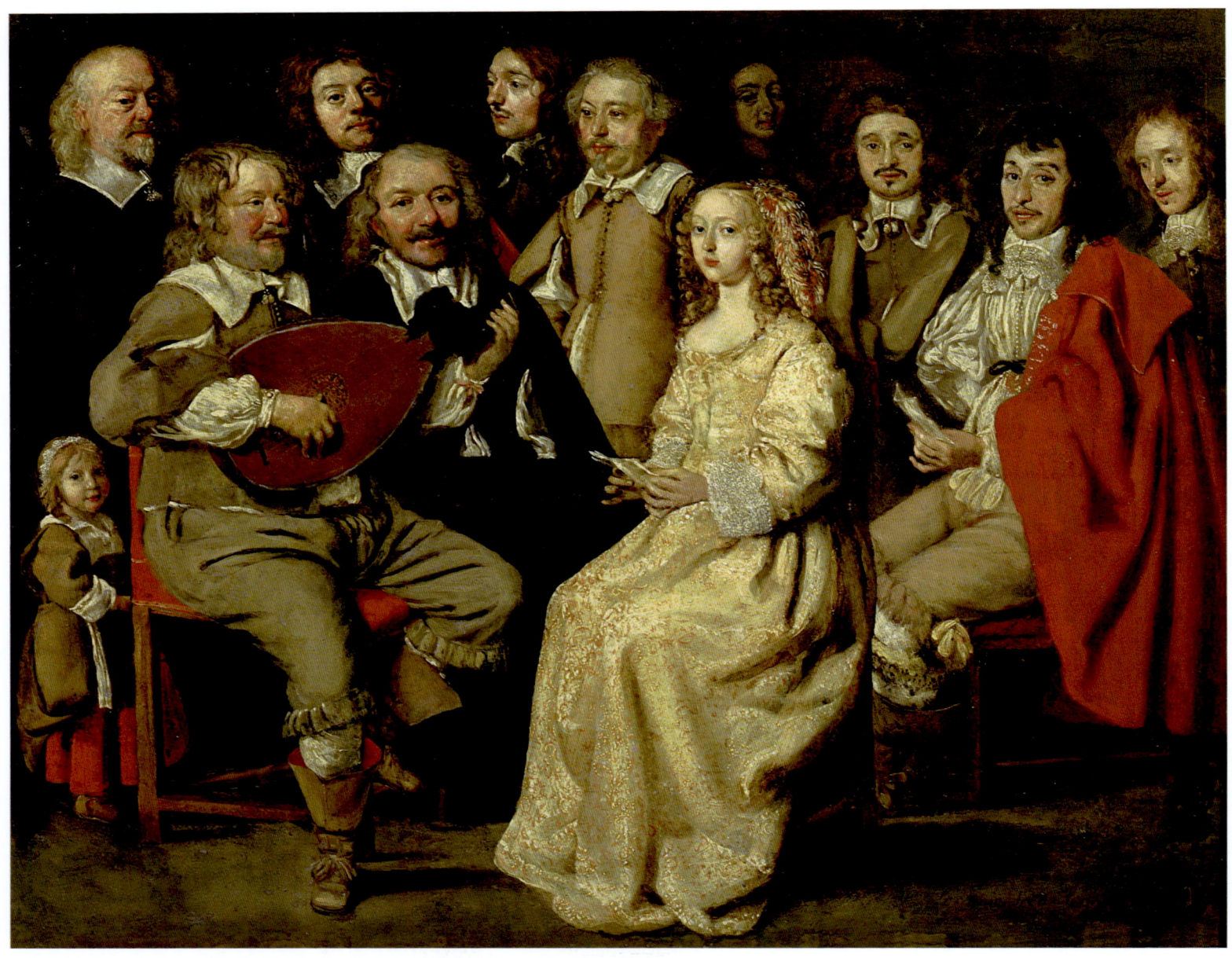

Antoine Le Nain (c. 1600–1648) or/ou Louis Le Nain (c. 1597–1648)

The Musical Reunion

Réunion Musicale

Die Musikgesellschaft

La compañía de músicos

L'intrattenimento musicale

Het muziekgezelschap

1642, Oil on copper/Huile sur cuivre, 32 × 40 cm, Musée du Louvre, Paris

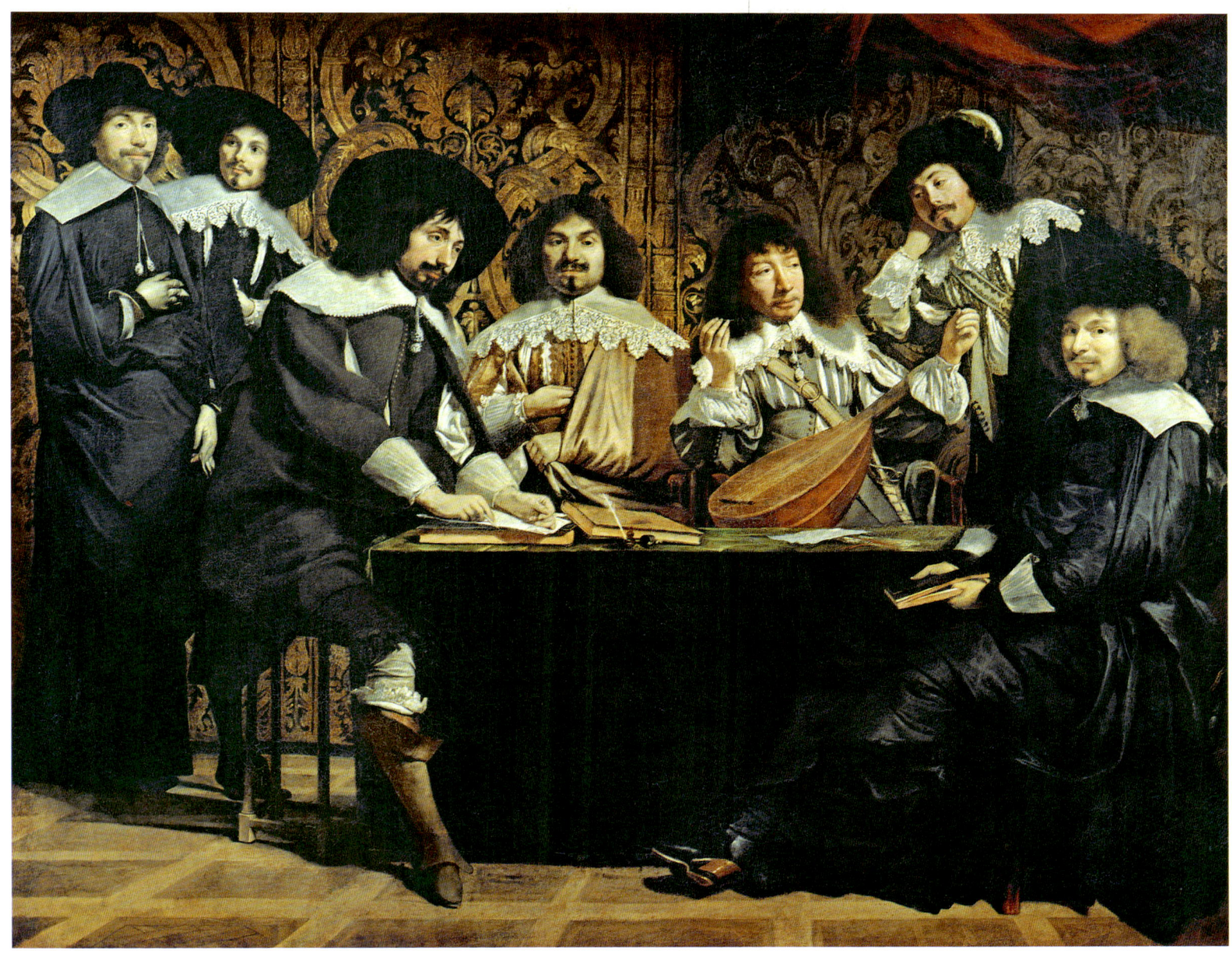

Louis Le Nain (c. 1597–1648) or/ou Antoine Le Nain (c. 1600–1648)

The Academy, *or* The Amateurs' Meeting

L'Académie, *dit aussi* Réunion d'amateurs

Die Akademie *oder* Das Treffen der Amateure

La Academia *o* El encuentro de los amateurs

L'Accademia *o* L'incontro dei dilettanti

De Academie, *of*: Bijeenkomst van de Amateurs

1640, Oil on canvas/Huile sur toile, 116 × 146 cm, Musée du Louvre, Paris

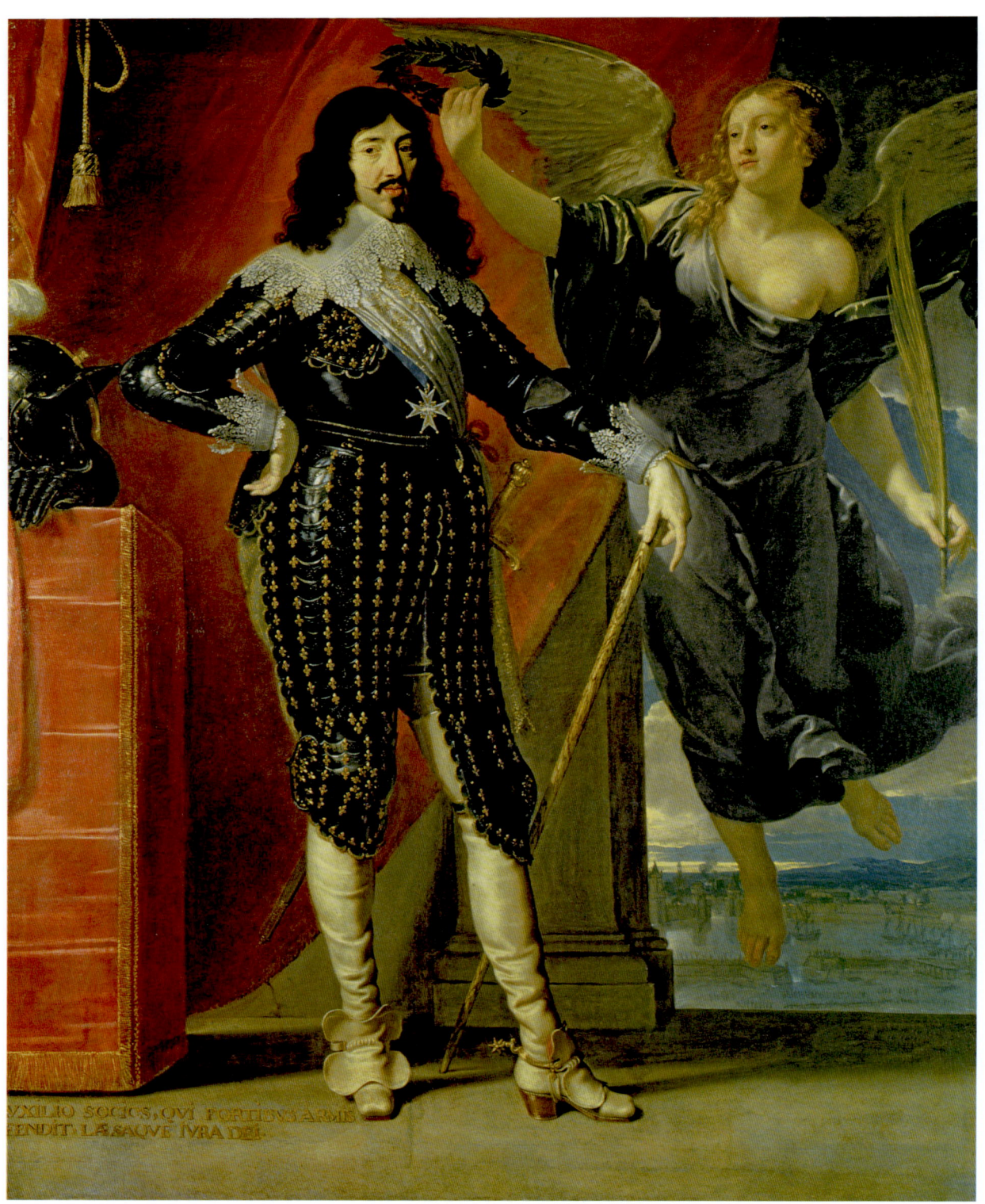

Philippe de Champaigne (1602–1674)

Louis XIII Crowned by Victory

Louis XIII couronné par la Victoire (siège de La Rochelle, 1628)

Ludwig XIII. wird vom Sieg gekrönt

Luis XIII coronado antes de la victoria

Luigi XIII incoronato dalla Vittoria

Lodewijk XIII wordt door de Overwinning gekroond

1635, Oil on canvas/Huile sur toile, 228,5 × 175 cm, Musée du Louvre, Paris

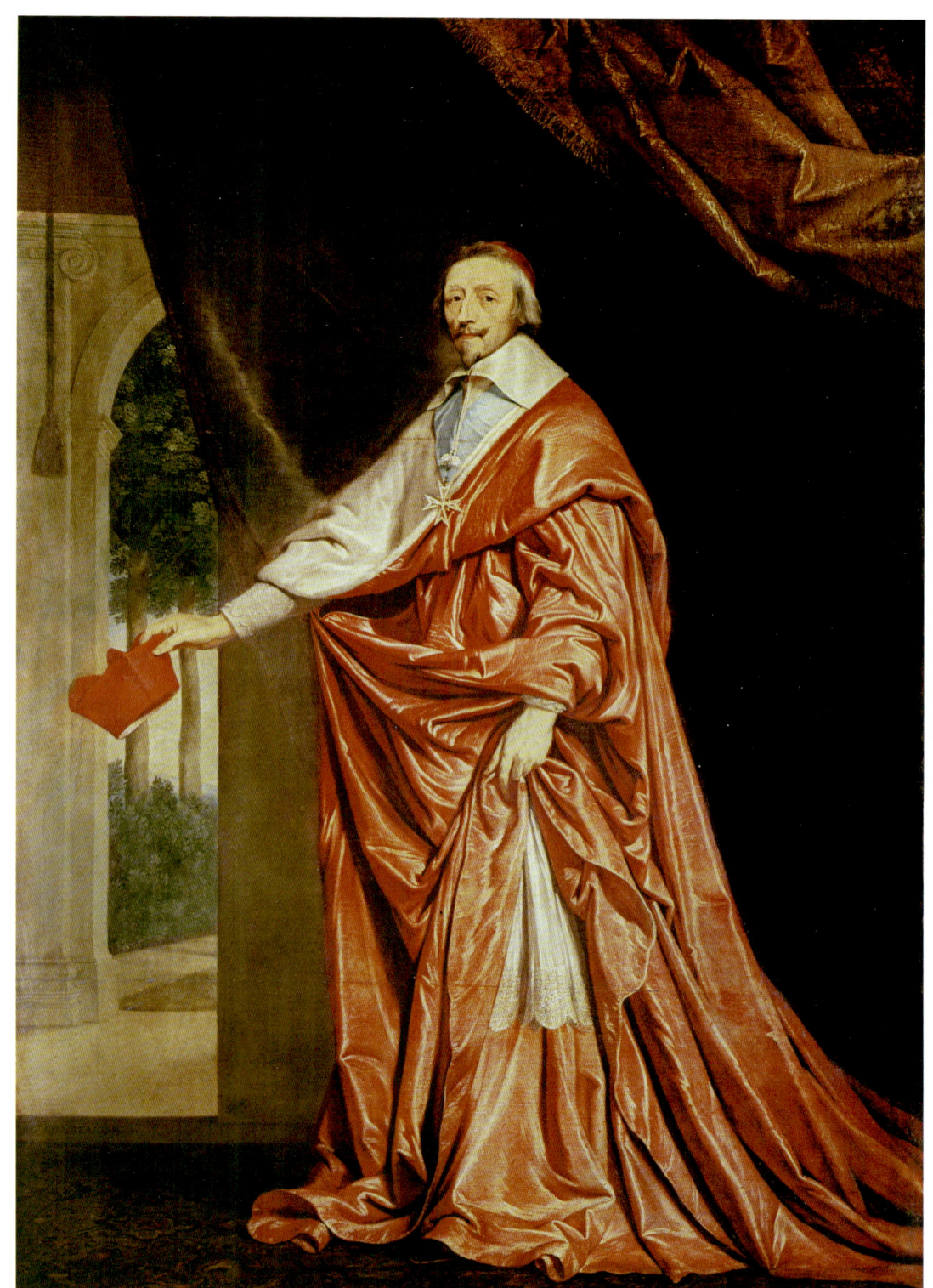

Philippe de Champaigne (1602–1674)

Portrait of Cardinal de Richelieu

Portrait du cardinal de Richelieu

Porträt des Kardinals Richelieu

Retrato del cardenal Richelieu

Ritratto del Cardinale Richelieu

Portret van kardinaal Richelieu

c. 1633–1640, Oil on canvas/Huile sur toile,
259,5 × 178,5 cm, National Gallery, London

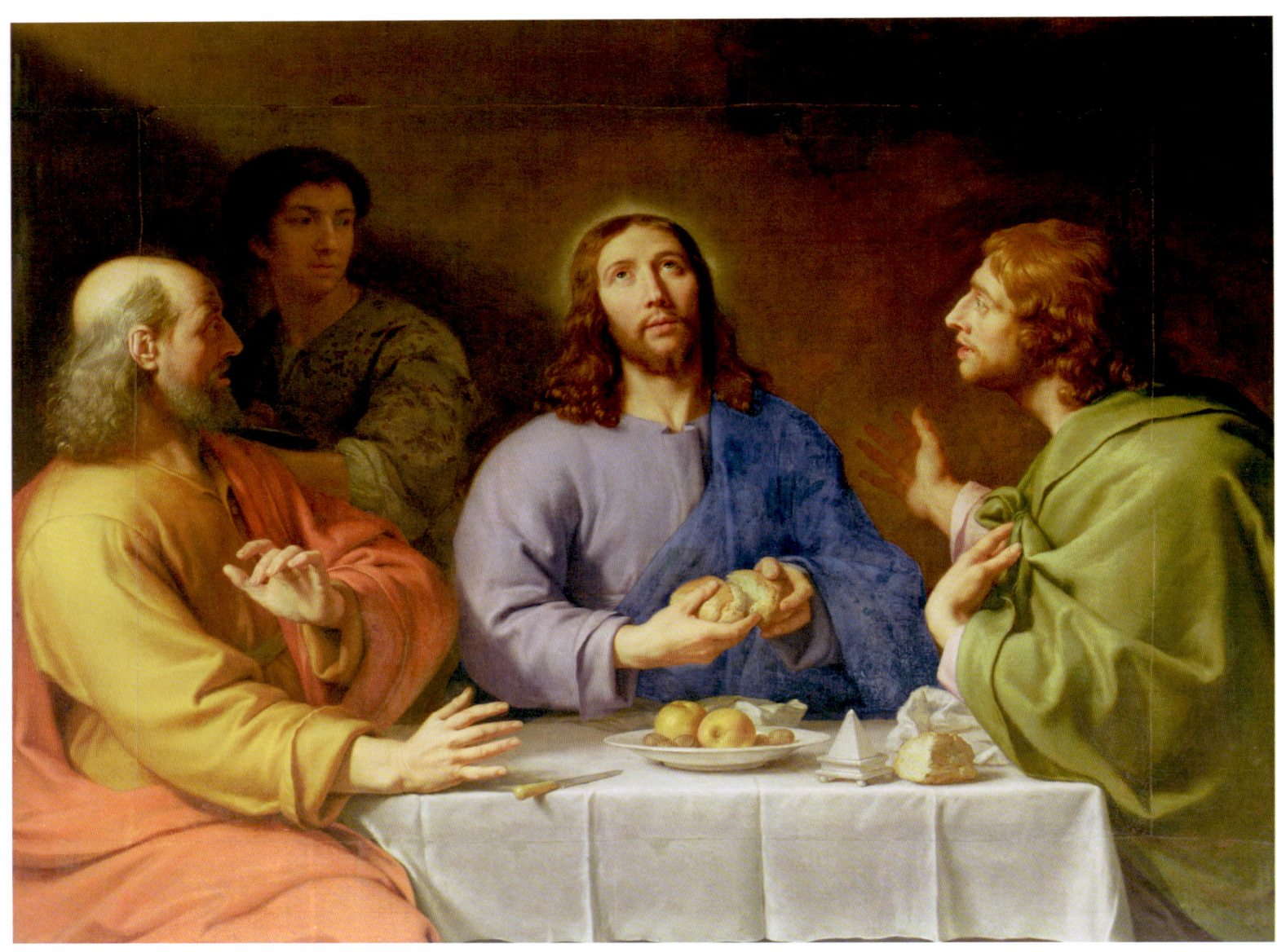

Philippe de Champaigne (1602–1674)

The Supper at Emmaus

Les Disciples d'Emmaüs

Das Abendmahl in Emmaus

La cena en Emaús

La cena di Emmaus

Het avondmaal te Emmaüs

1656, Oil on canvas/Huile sur toile, 123 × 169 cm, Musée des Beaux-Arts, Angers

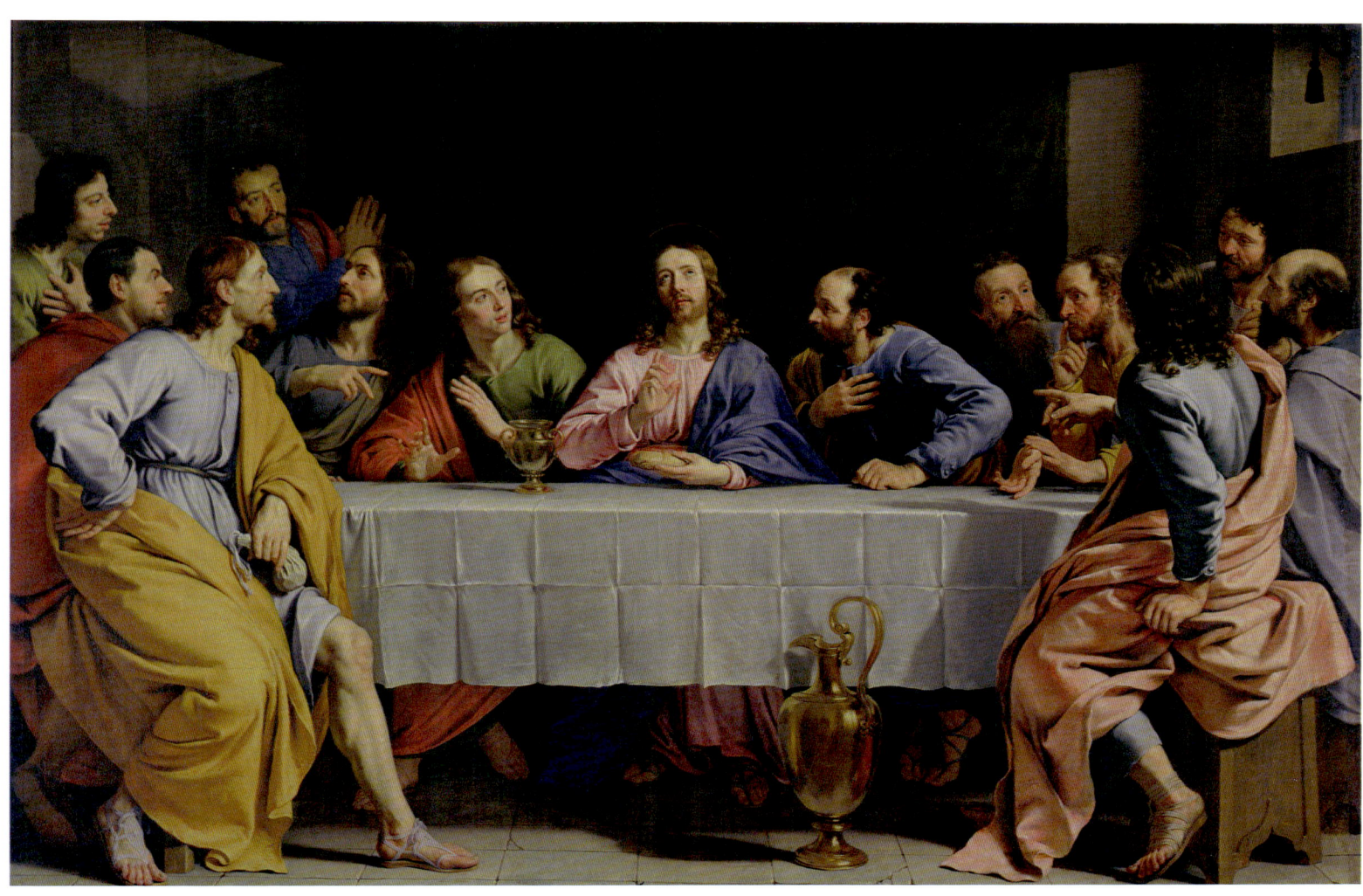

Philippe de Champaigne (1602–1674)

The Last Supper

La Cène

Das letzte Abendmahl

La última cena

L'ultima cena

Het Laatste Avondmaal

c. 1652, Oil on canvas/Huile sur toile, 158 × 233 cm, Musée du Louvre, Paris

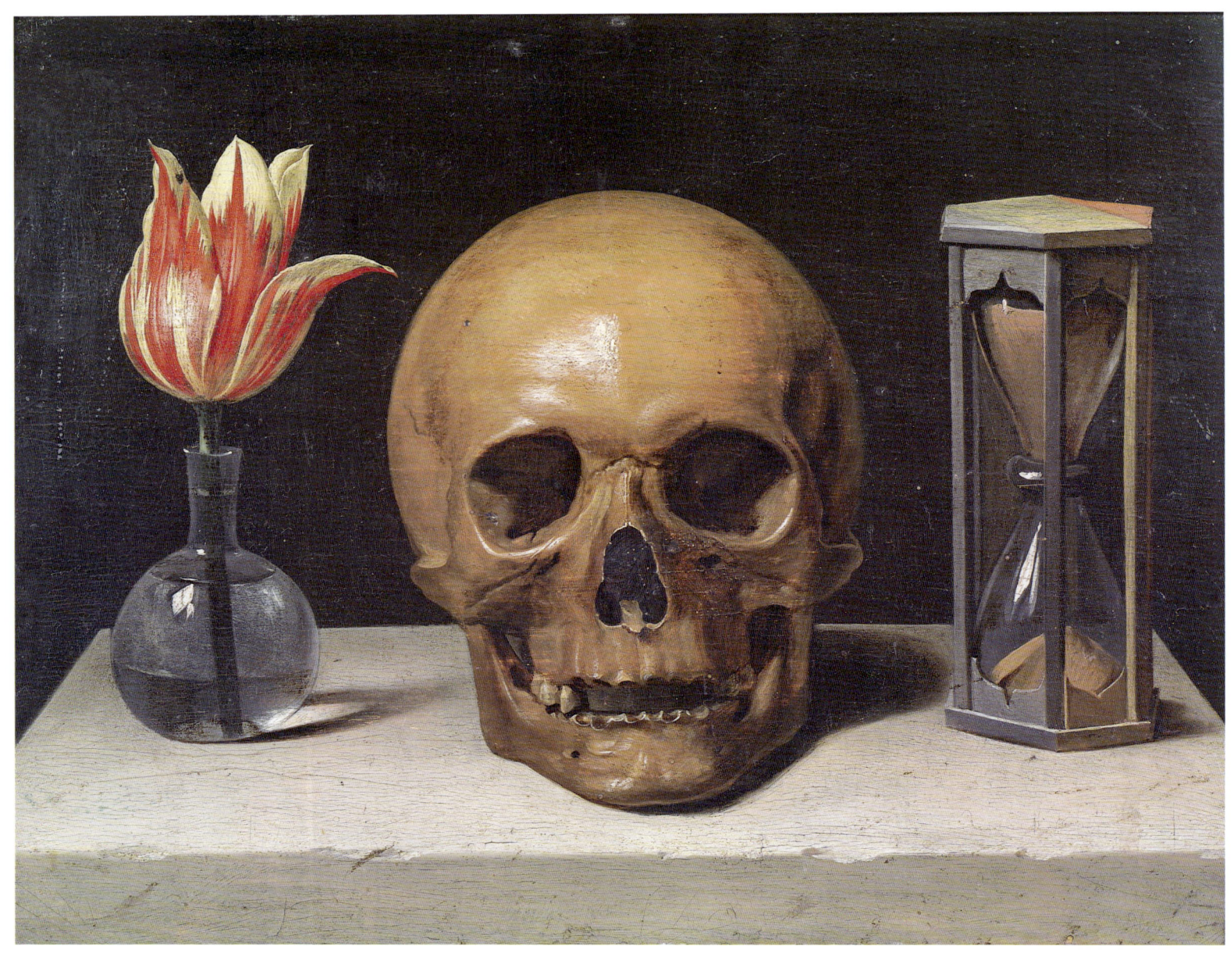

Philippe de Champaigne (1602–1674)

Vanitas Still Life with a Tulip, Skull and Hour-Glass

Vanité, *ou* Allégorie de la vie humaine

Vanitas Stillleben mit Tulpe, Totenschädel und Stundenglas

Bodegón de Vanitas con tulipán, calavera y reloj de arena

Vanitas natura morta con tulipano, teschio e clessidra

Vanitas-stilleven met tulp, schedel en zandloper

c. 1644, Oil on wood/Huile sur bois, 28 × 37 cm, Musée de Tessé, Le Mans

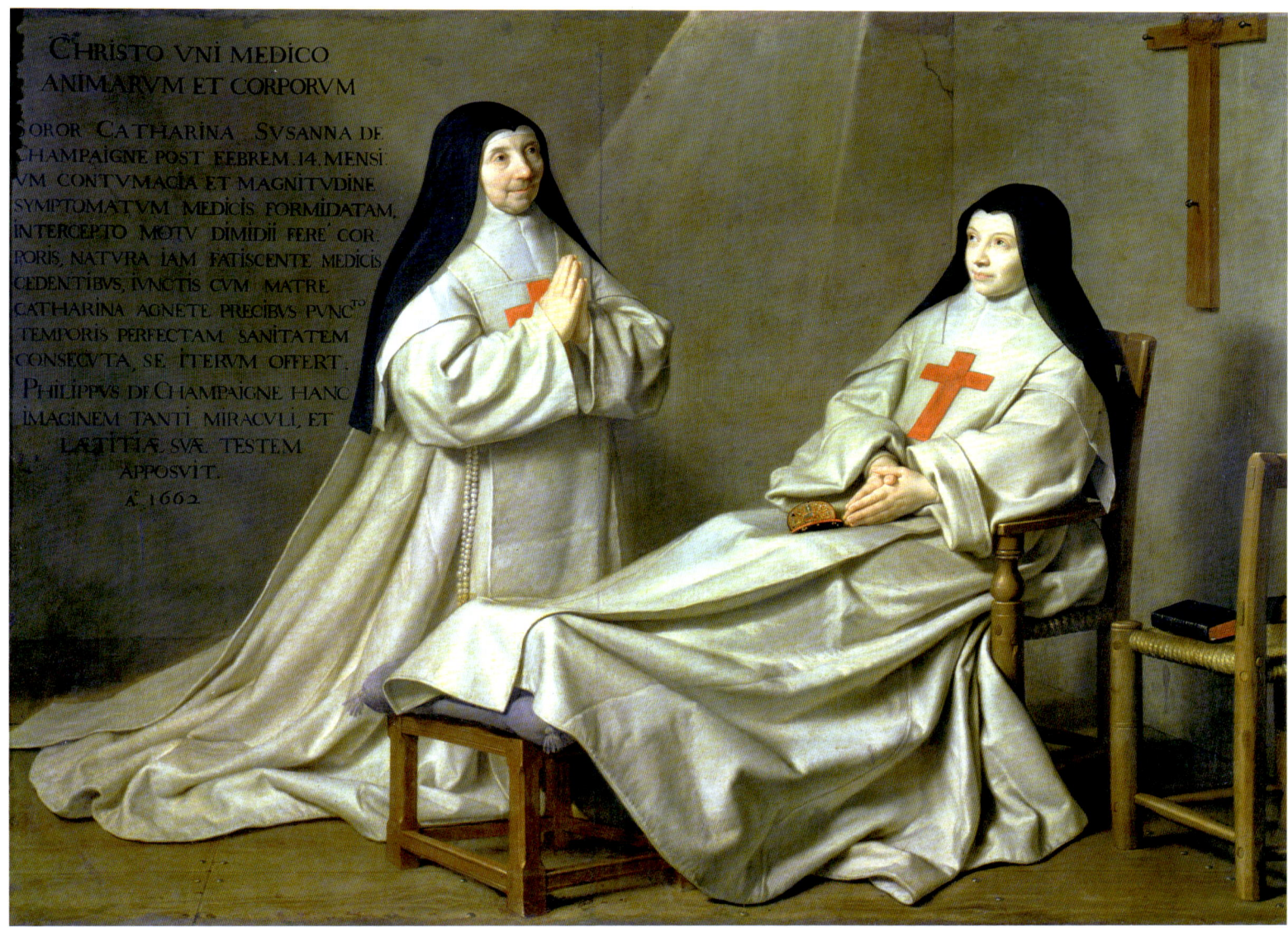

Philippe de Champaigne (1602–1674)

Ex-voto (Votive offering)

Ex-voto

Ex-Voto

Exvoto

Ex-voto

Ex voto

1662, Oil on canvas/Huile sur toile, 165 × 229 cm, Musée du Louvre, Paris

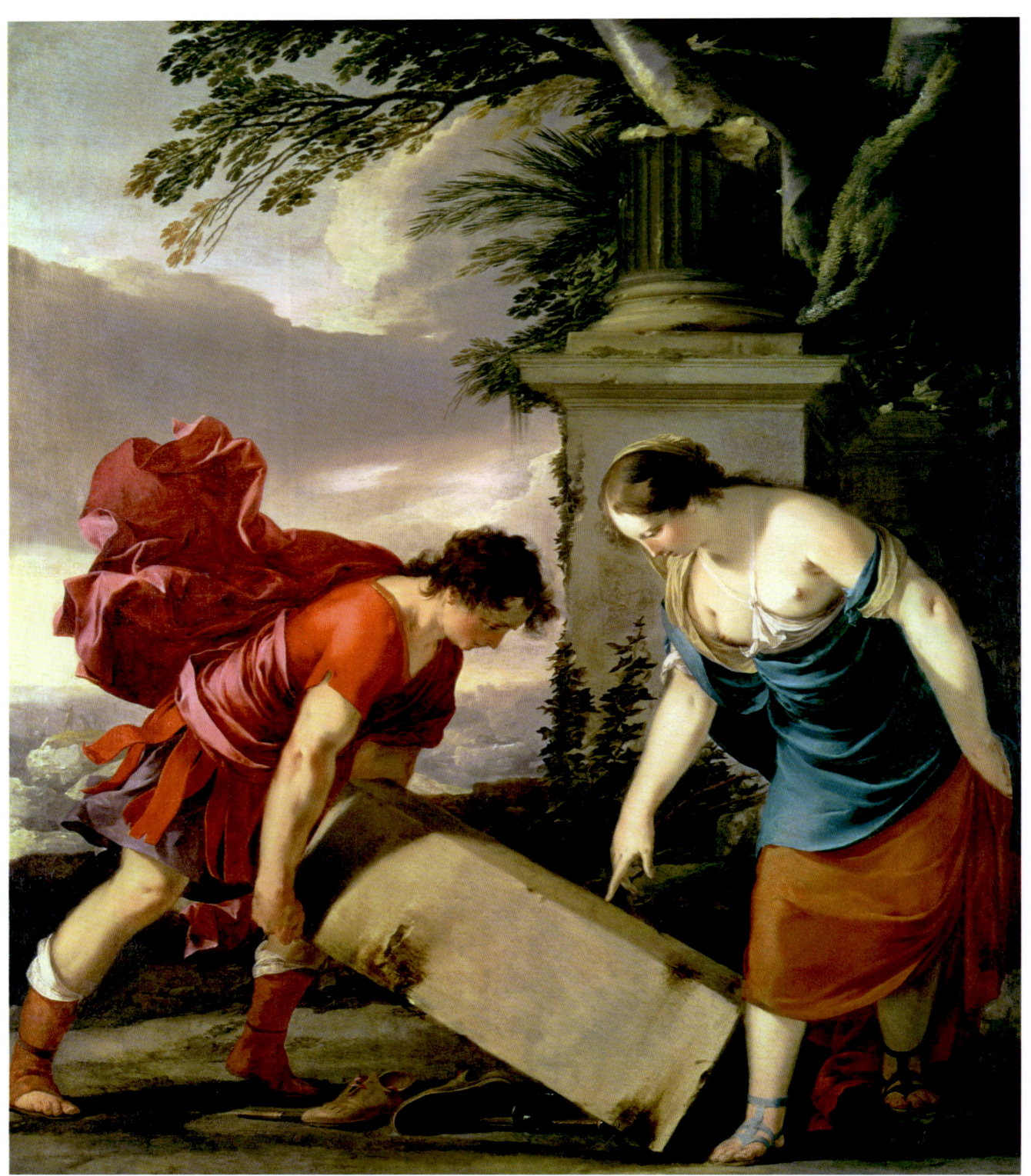

**Laurent de La Hyre
(1606–1656)**

Theseus and his
Mother Aethra

Thésée et Éthra

Theseus und seine
Mutter Aethra

Teseo y su madre
Etra

Teseo e sua madre
Etra

Theseus en zijn
moeder Aethra

c. 1635–1636, Oil on
canvas/Huile sur
toile, 141 × 118,5 cm,
Szépművészeti
Múzeum, Budapest

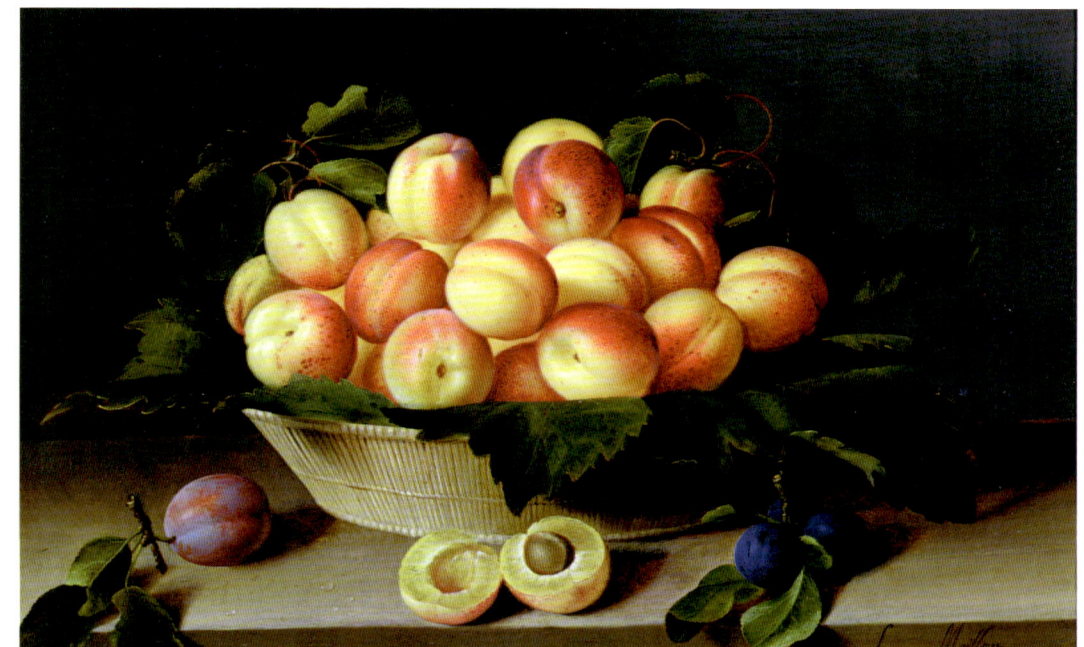

Louise Moillon (1610–1696)

Basket of Apricots

Panier d'abricots

Korb mit Aprikosen

Cesta con albaricoques

Cesto di albicocche

Mand met abrikozen

1634, Oil on canvas/Huile sur toile, 34,5 × 52,5 cm,
Musée des Augustins, Toulouse

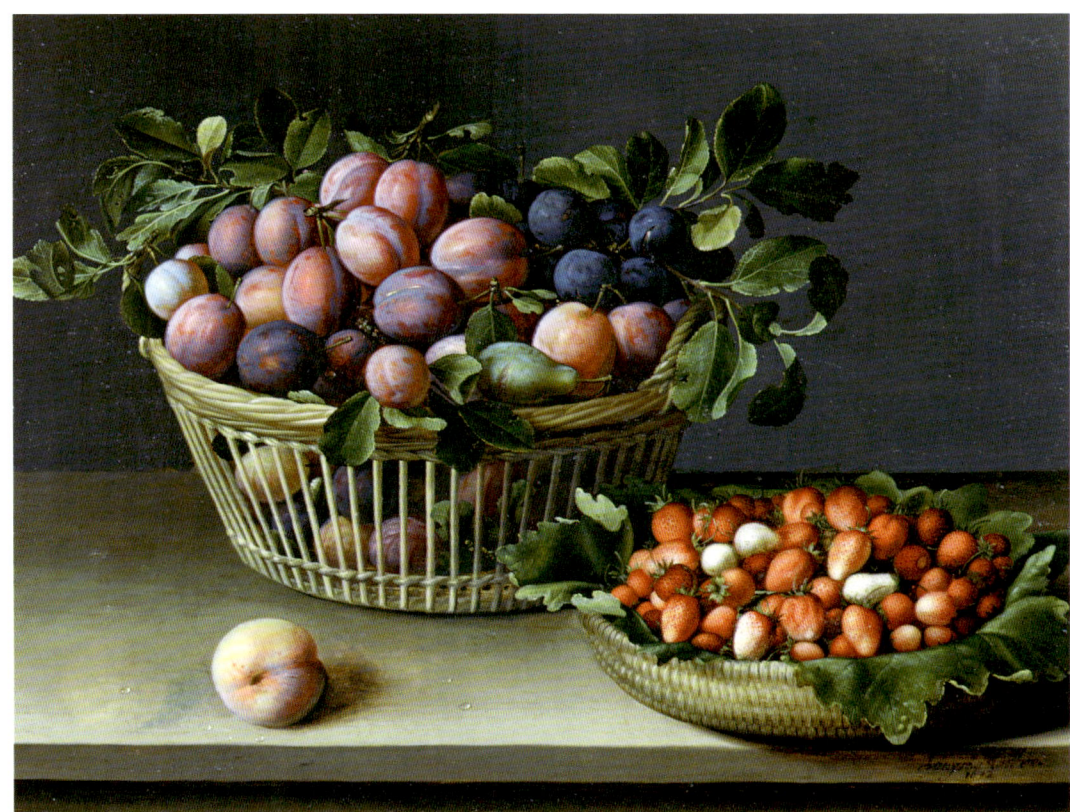

Louise Moillon (1610–1696)

Basket of Plums and Basket of Strawberries

Corbeille de prunes et panier de fraises

Korb mit Pflaumen und Korb mit Erdbeeren

Cesta de ciruelas y cesta de fresas

Cesto di prugne e cesto di fragole

Mand met pruimen en mand met aardbeien

1632, Oil on canvas/Huile sur toile, 44 × 58 cm,
Musée des Augustins, Toulouse

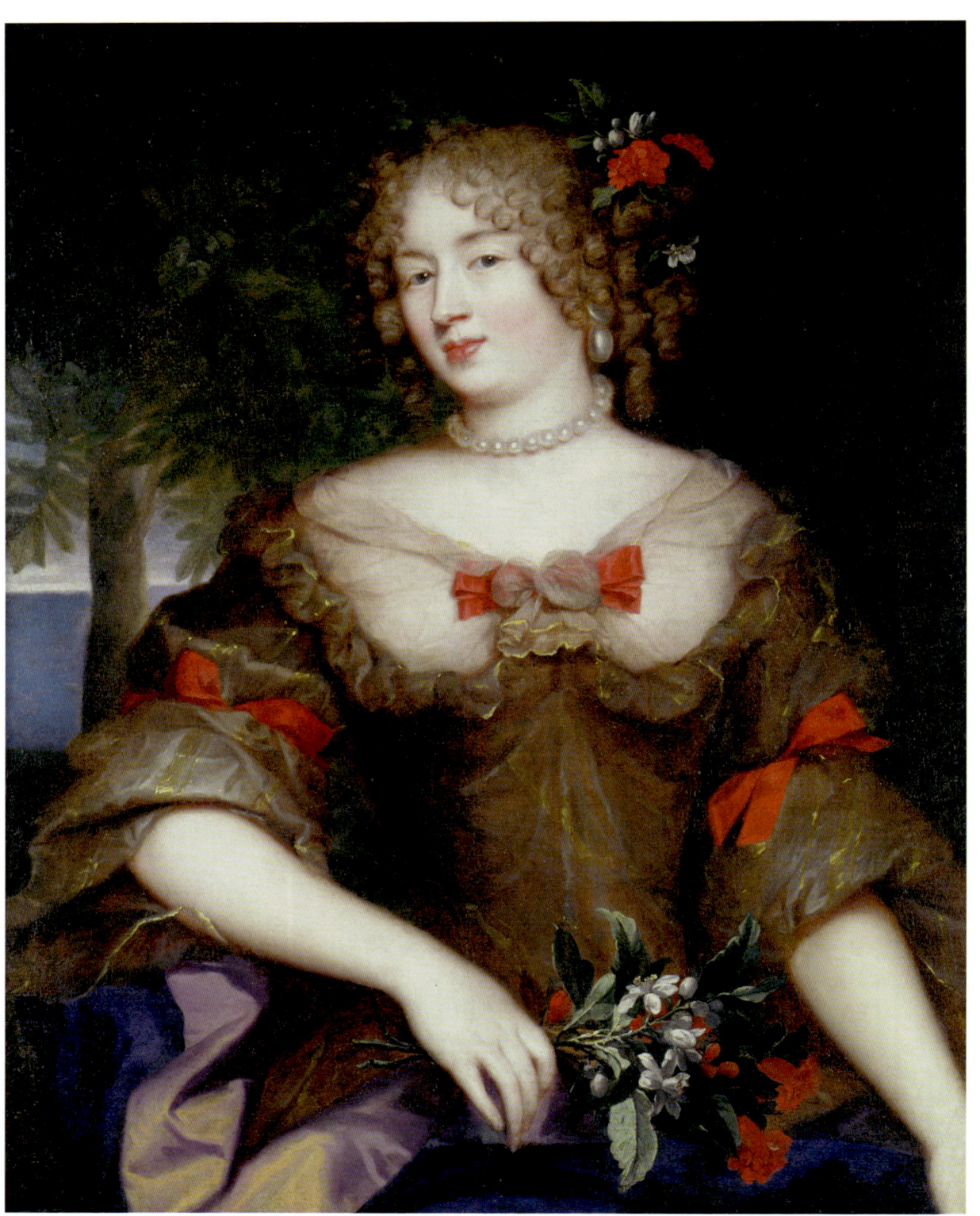

Pierre Mignard (1612–1695)

Françoise de Sevigne Countess of Grignan

Françoise de Sévigné, comtesse de Grignan

Françoise de Sevigne, Herzogin von Grignan

Françoise de Sevigne, Duquesa de Grignan

Françoise de Sevigne, duchessa di Grignan

Françoise de Sévigné, hertogin van Grignan

c. 1669, Oil on canvas/Huile sur toile, 90 × 73 cm, Musée Carnavalet, Paris

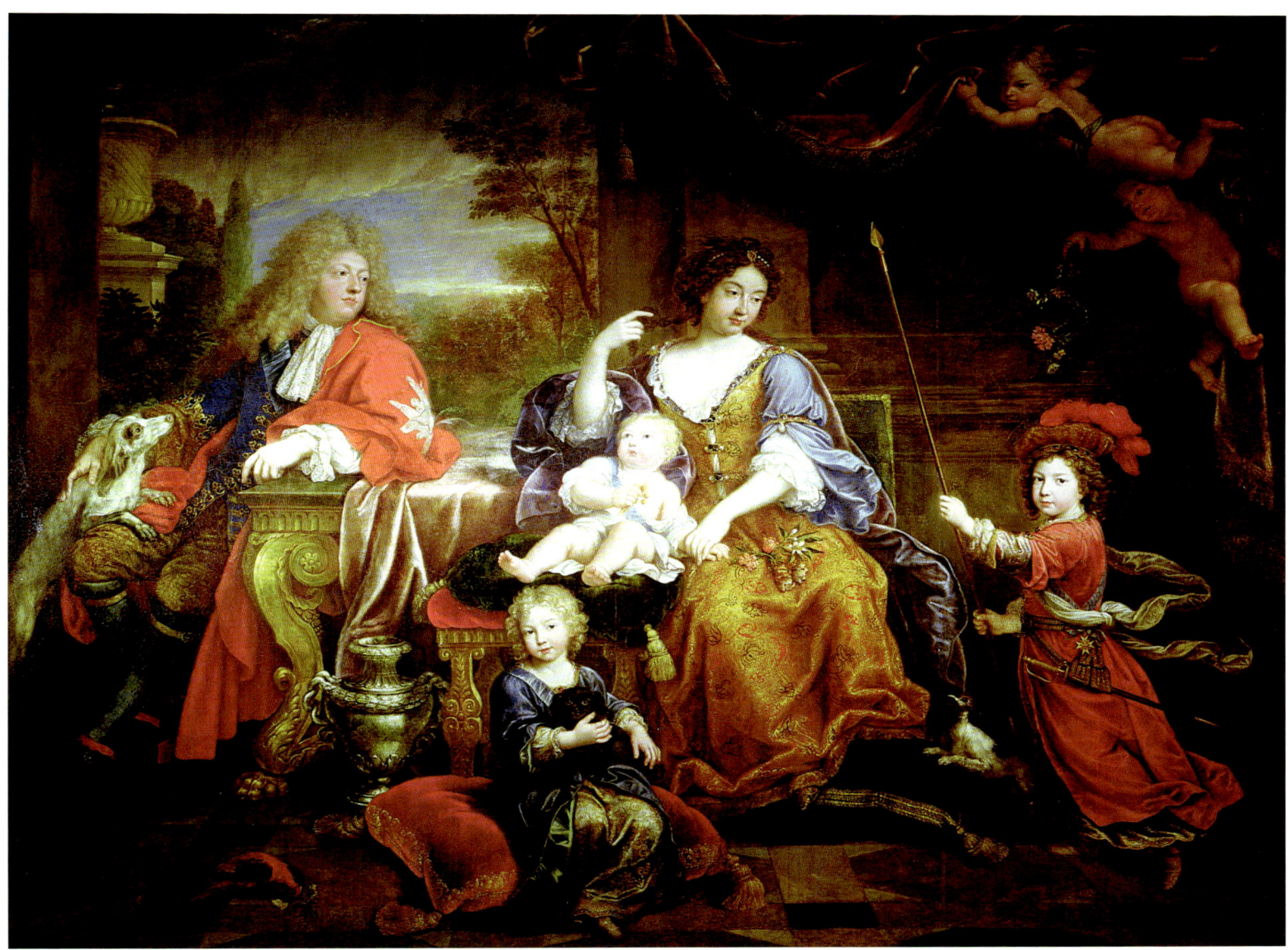

Pierre Mignard (1612–1695)

The Grand Dauphin with his Wife and Children

Le Grand Dauphin et sa famille

Der Große Dauphin mit Frau und Kindern

El Gran Delfín con mujer e hijos

Il Gran Delfino con moglie e figli

Le Grand Dauphin met vrouw en kinderen

1692, Oil on canvas/Huile sur toile, 211,5 × 201,8 cm, Château de Versailles, Versailles

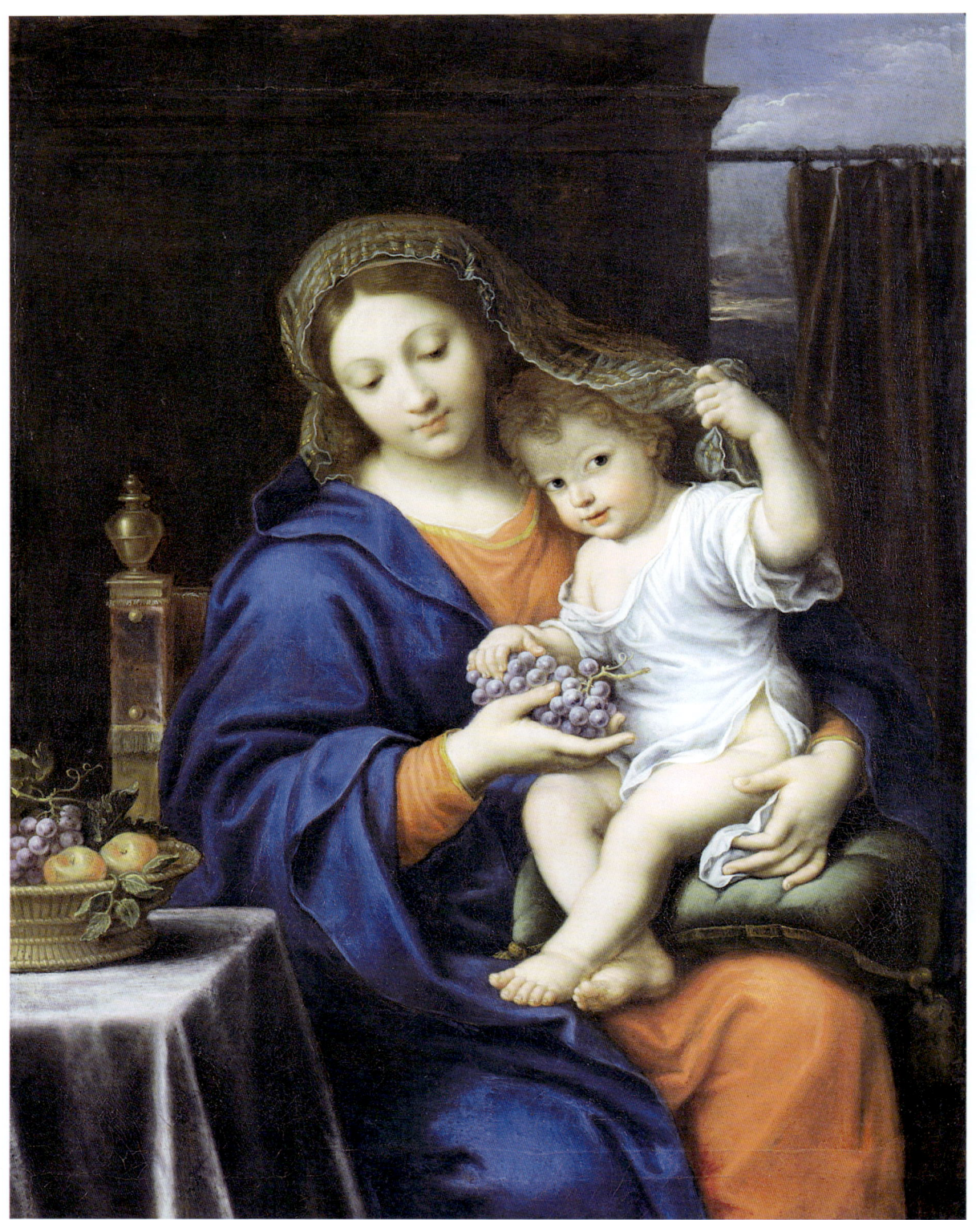

Pierre Mignard (1612–1695)

The Virgin of the Grapes

La Vierge à la grappe

Madonna mit den Trauben

Madonna con uvas

La Madonna dell'uva

De Madonna met de druiven

1640–1650, Oil on canvas/Huile sur toile, 121 × 94 cm, Musée du Louvre, Paris

Eustache Le Sueur (1616–1655)

The Muses, Clio, Euterpe and Thalia

Clio, Euterpe et Thalie

Die Musen Clio, Euterpe und Thalia

Las Musas Clío, Euterpe y Talía

Le muse Clio, Euterpe e Talia

De muzen Clio, Euterpe en Thaleia

c. 1652–1655, Oil on canvas/Huile sur toile, 130 × 130 cm, Musée du Louvre, Paris

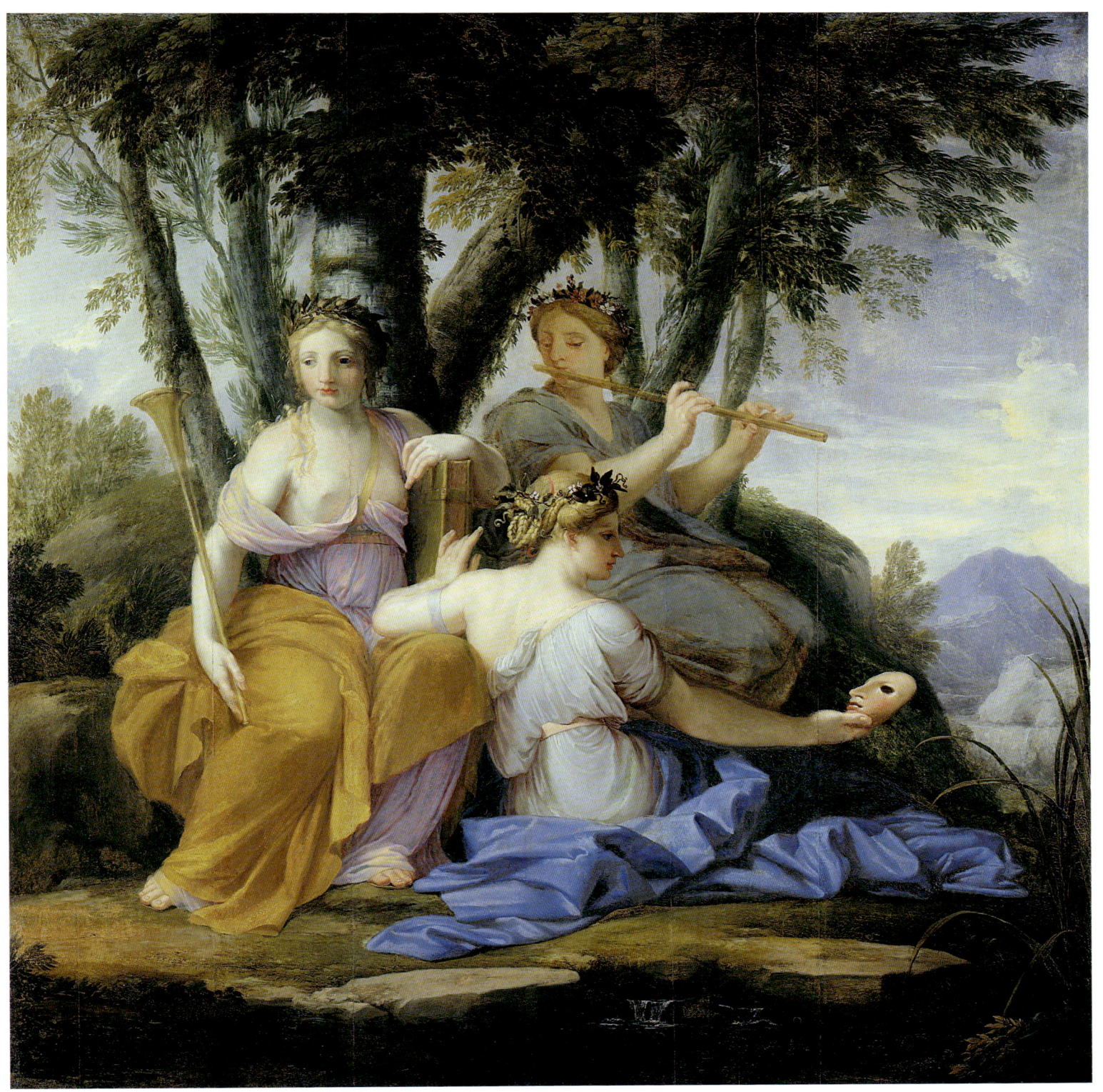

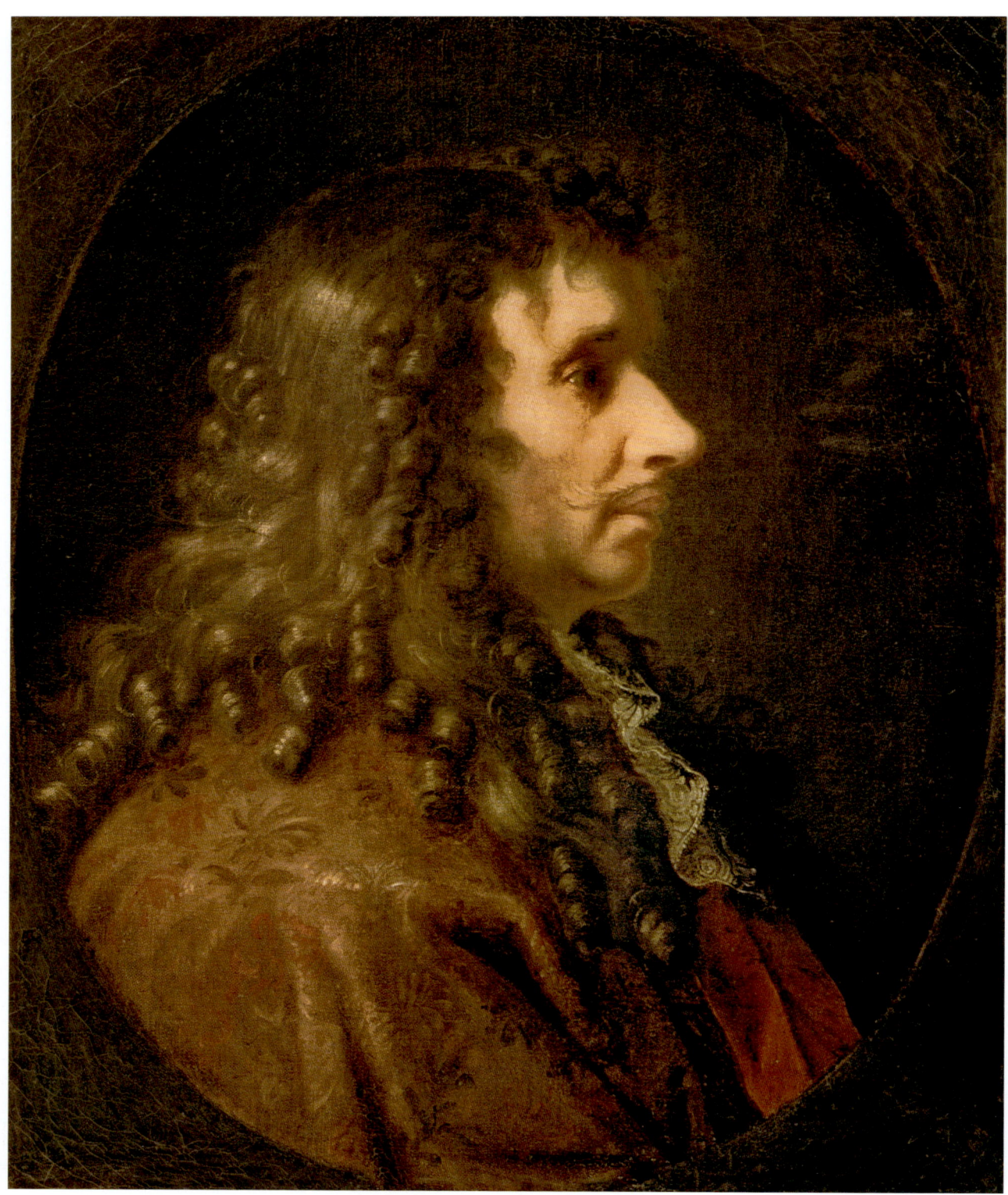

**Charles Le Brun
(1619–1690)**

Portrait of Molière

Portrait de Molière

Porträt von Molière

Retrato de Molière

Ritratto di Molière

Portret van Molière

1660, Oil on canvas/
Huile sur toile, 67 × 54 cm,
Pushkin State Museum of
Fine Arts, Moscow

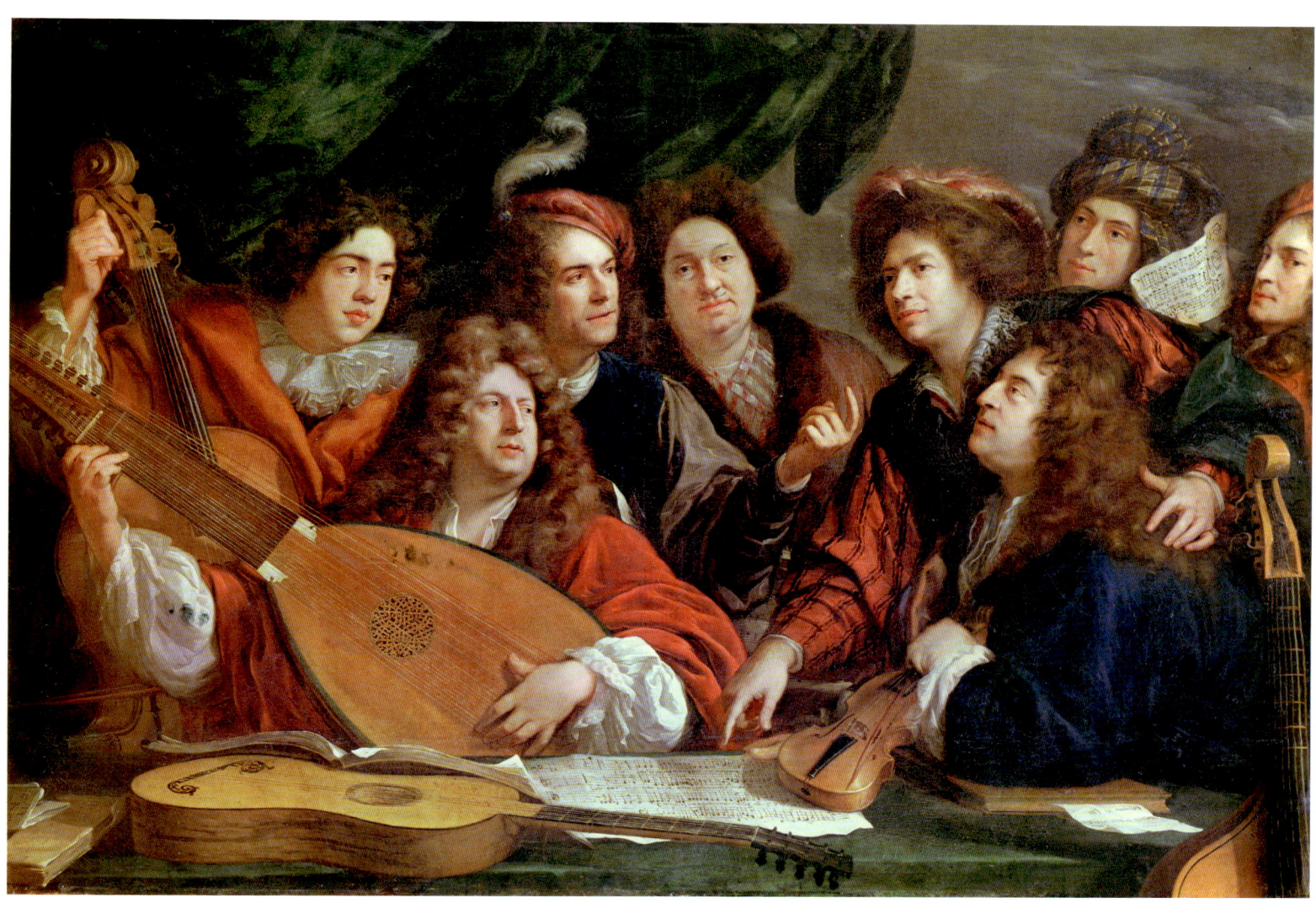

François Puget (1651–1707)

The Musical Society

Réunion de musiciens

Die Musikgesellschaft

La compañía de músicos

Riunione di musicisti

Het muziekgezelschap

1688, Oil on canvas/Huile sur toile, 147 × 212 cm, Musée du Louvre, Paris

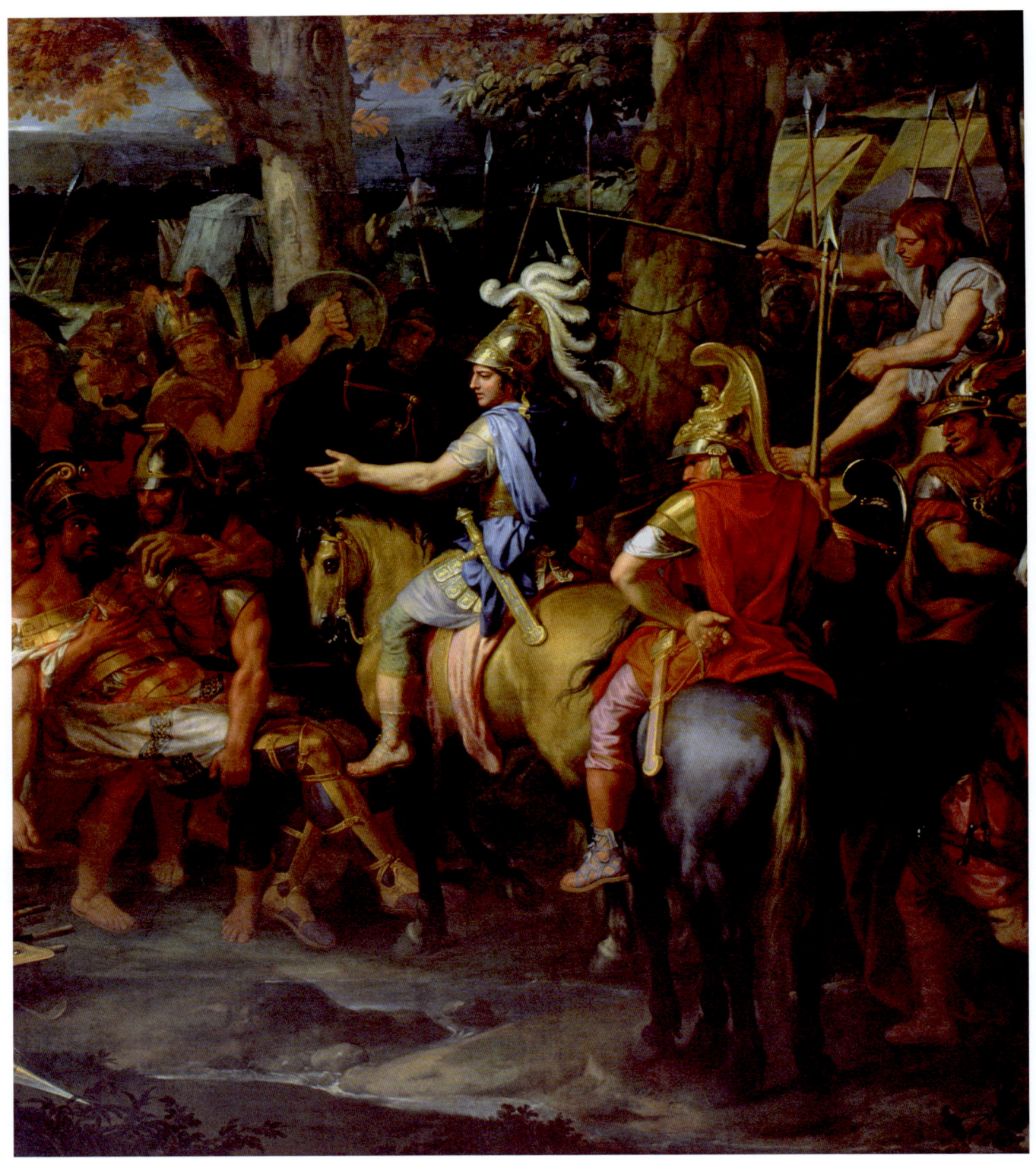

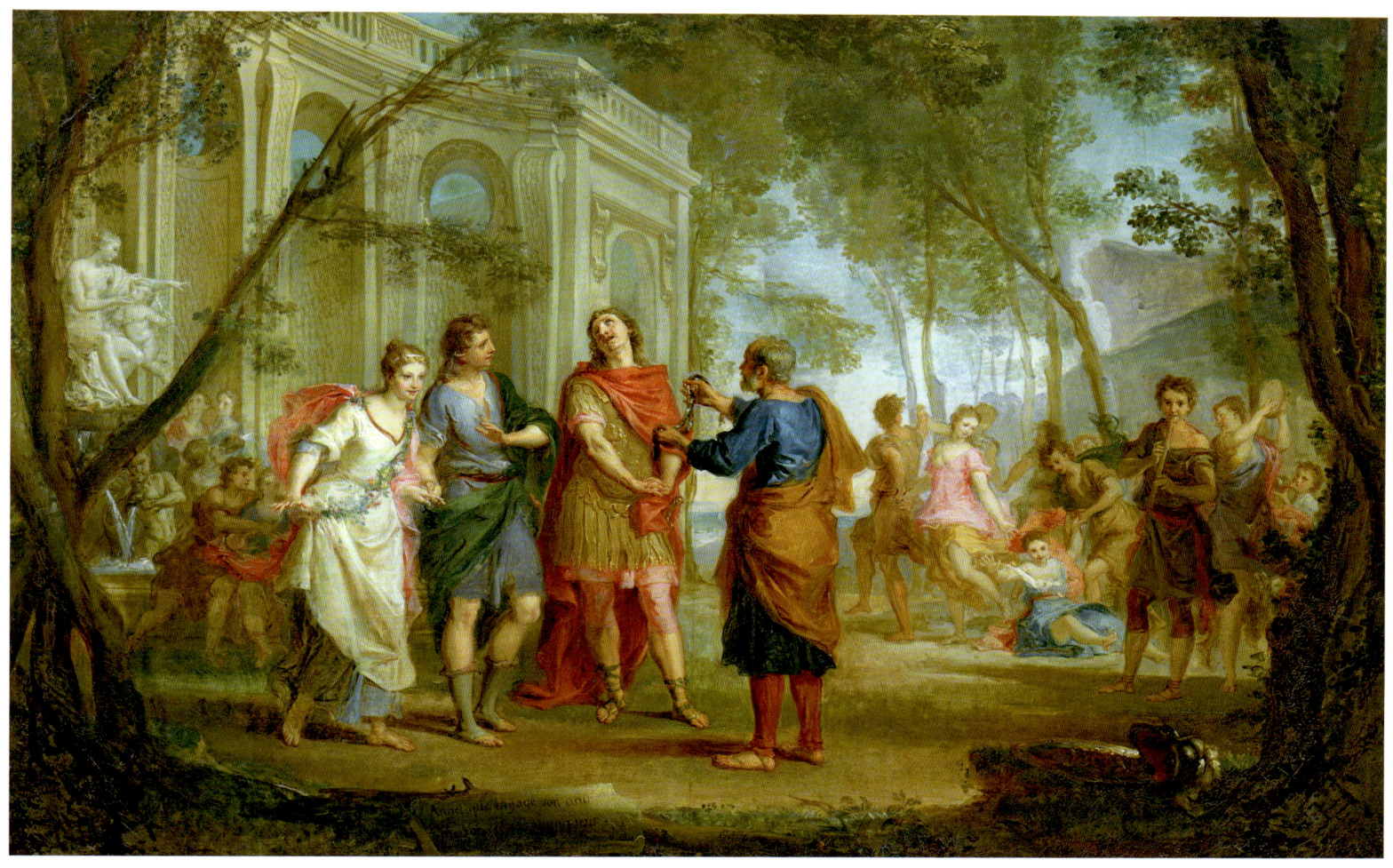

Charles Le Brun (1619–1690)

Alexander and Porus at the Battle of Hydaspes *(detail)*

Alexandre et Porus *(détail)*

Alexander und Porus in der Schlacht von Hydaspes *(Detail)*

Alejandro y Poros en la batalla de Hidaspes *(detalle)*

Alessandro e Poro nella battaglia dell'Idaspe *(dettaglio)*

Alexander en Poros in de Slag bij de Hydaspes *(detail)*

c. 1673, Oil on canvas/Huile sur toile, 470 × 126,4 cm, Musée du Louvre, Paris

Louis Galloche (1670–1761)

Roland Learns of the Love of Angelica and Medoro

Roland apprenant les amours d'Angélique et de Médor

Roland lernt aus der Liebe von Angelika und Medor

Roland aprende del amor de Angélica y Medoro

Orlando scopre l'amore di Angelica e Medoro

Roland verneemt van de liefde tussen Angelica en Medoro

c. 1733, Oil on canvas/Huile sur toile, 80 × 110 cm, Musée des Beaux-Arts, Caen

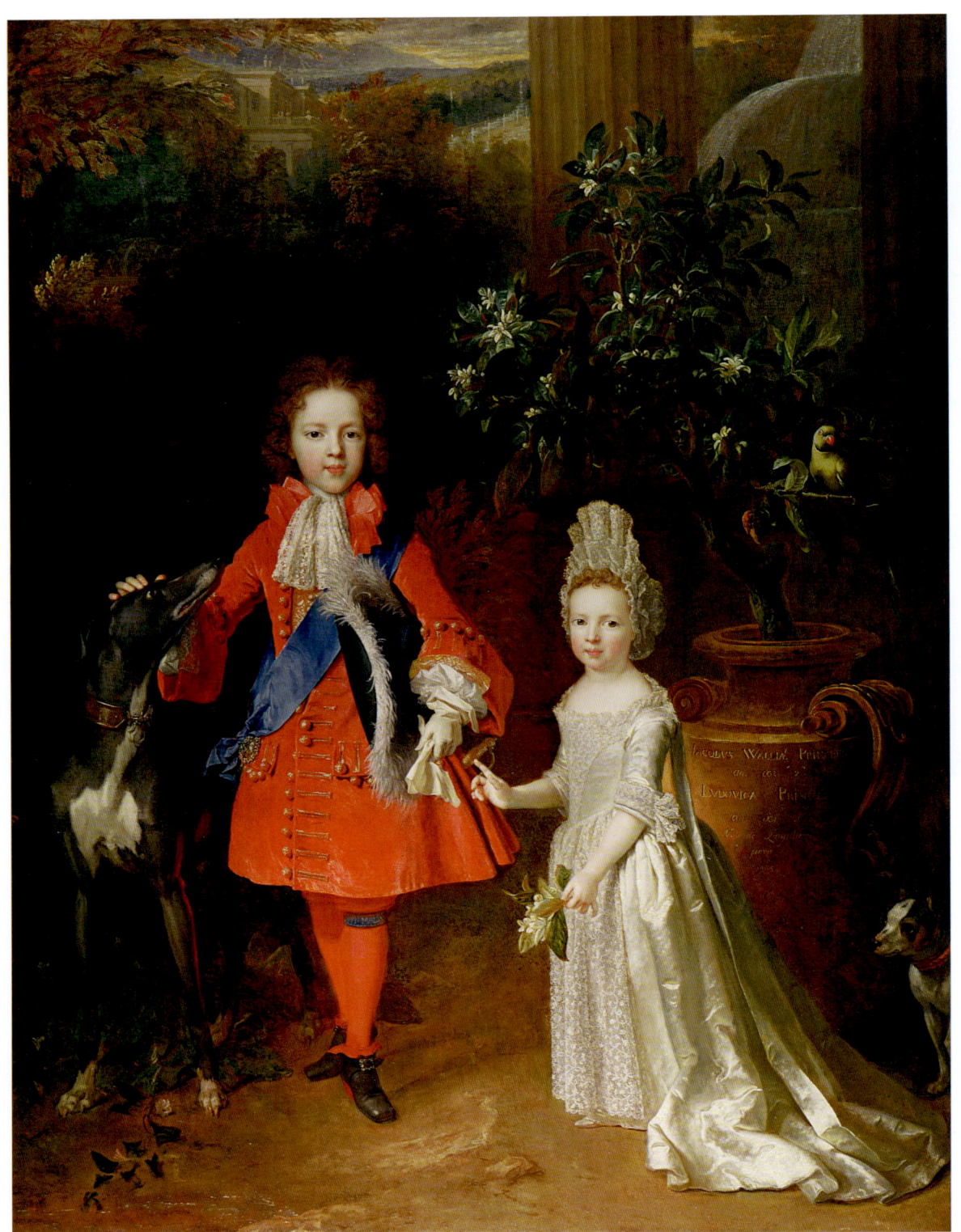

Nicolas de Largillière (1656–1746)

Prince James Francis Edward Stuart and Princess Maria Theresa Stuart

Le Prince de Galles et la Princesse sa sœur

Prinz Edward Stuart und Prinzessin Maria Stuart

Príncipe Edward Stuart y princesa Maria Stuart

Il principe Edoardo Stuart e la principessa Maria Stuart

Prins James Francis Stuart en prinses Maria Louisa Stuart

1695, Oil on canvas/Huile sur toile, 192,8 × 145,7 cm, National Portrait Gallery, London

Pierre-Denis Martin (1663–1742)

General view of the Chateau and the Pavilions at Marly

Le Château de Marly

Ansicht des Schlosses und der Pavillons von Marly

Vista del castillo y de los pabellones de Marly

Vista del castello e del padiglione di Marly

Gezicht op het slot en de paviljoens van Marly

1723, Oil on canvas/Huile sur toile, 137 × 155 cm, Château de Versailles, Versailles

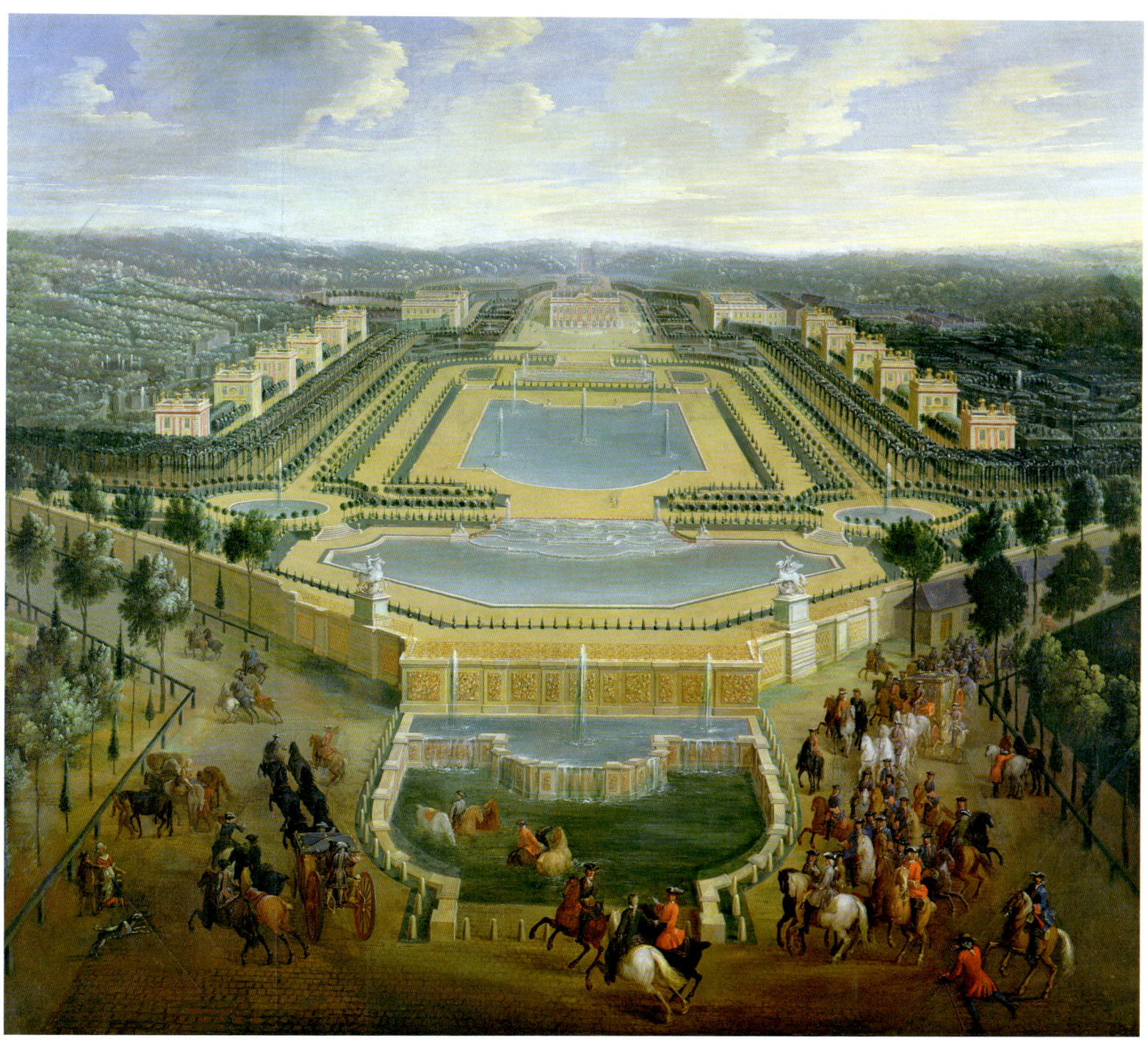

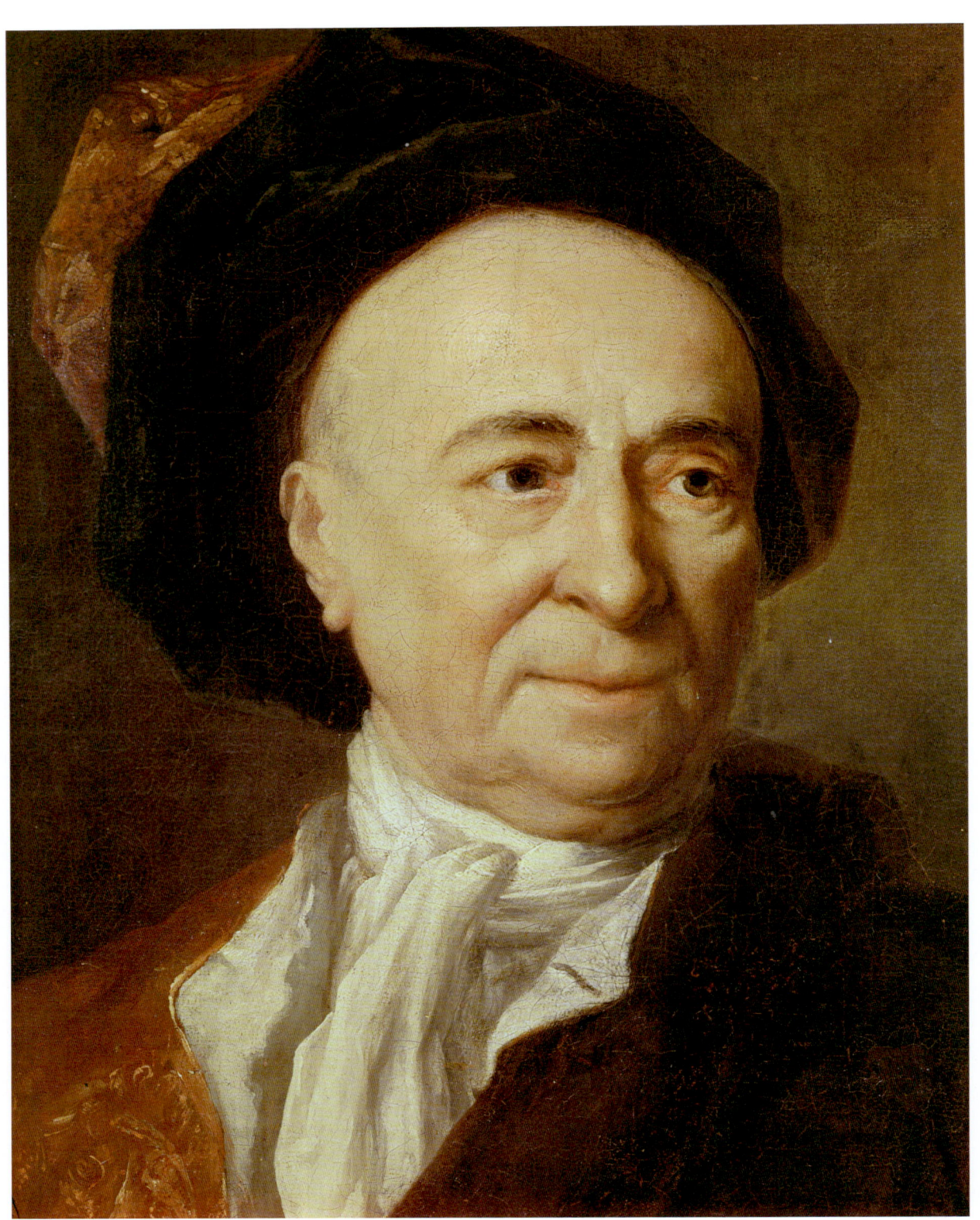

**Nicolas de Largillière
(1656–1746)**

Bernard le Bovier de Fontenelle

Portrait de Bernard le Bovier de
Fontenelle

Bildnis Bernard le Bovier de
Fontenelle

Retrato de Bernard le Bovier de
Fontenelle

Ritratto di Bernard le Bovier de
Fontenelle

Portret van Bernard Le Bovier
de Fontenelle

n. d., Oil on canvas/Huile sur toile,
Musée des Beaux-Arts, Chartres

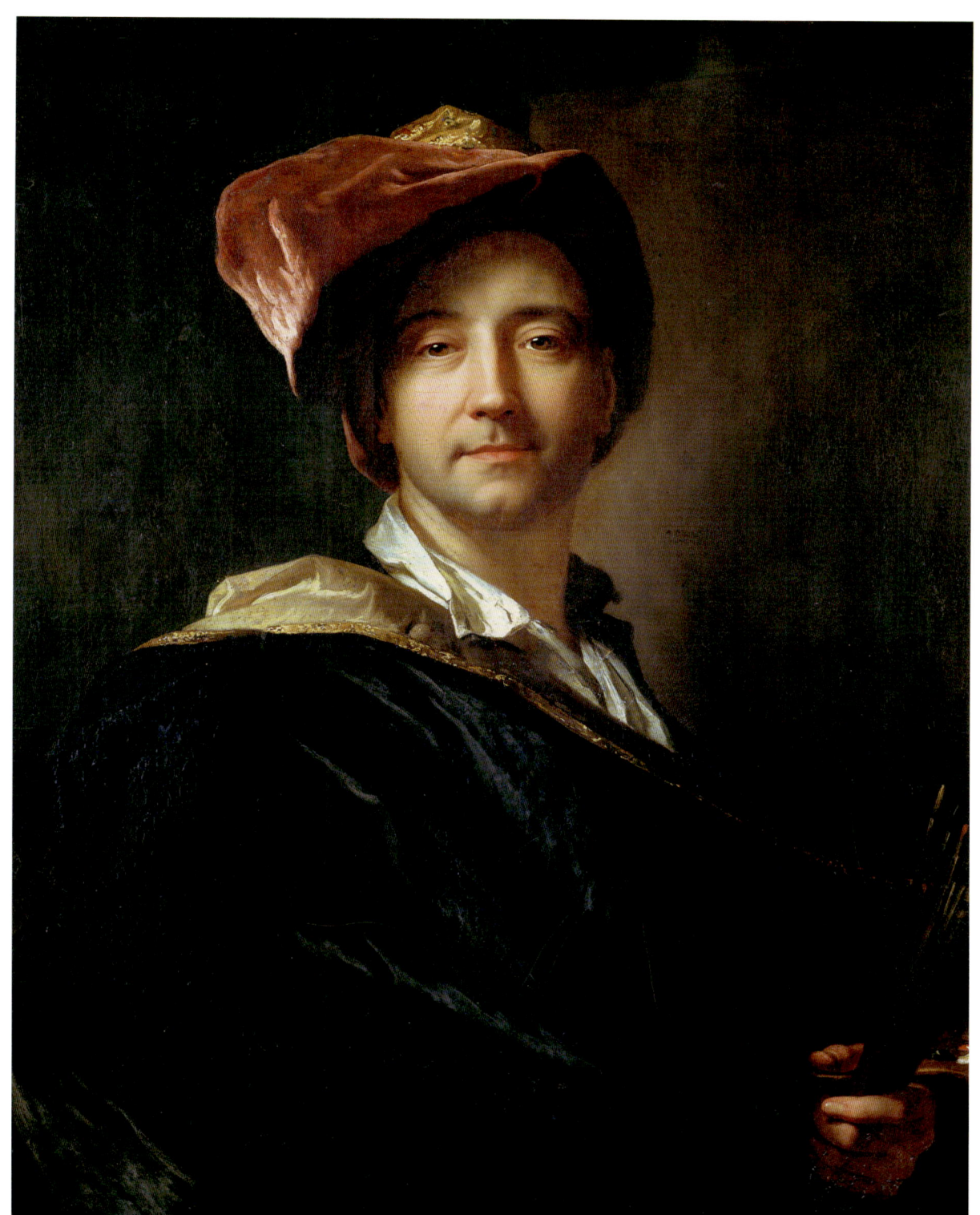

Hyacinthe Rigaud (1659–1743)

Self Portrait in a Turban

Autoportrait au turban

Selbstbildnis mit Turban

Autorretrato con turbante

Autoritratto con turbante

Zelfportret met tulband

1698, Oil on canvas / Huile sur toile,
84 × 67 cm, Musée Hyacinthe
Rigaud, Perpignan

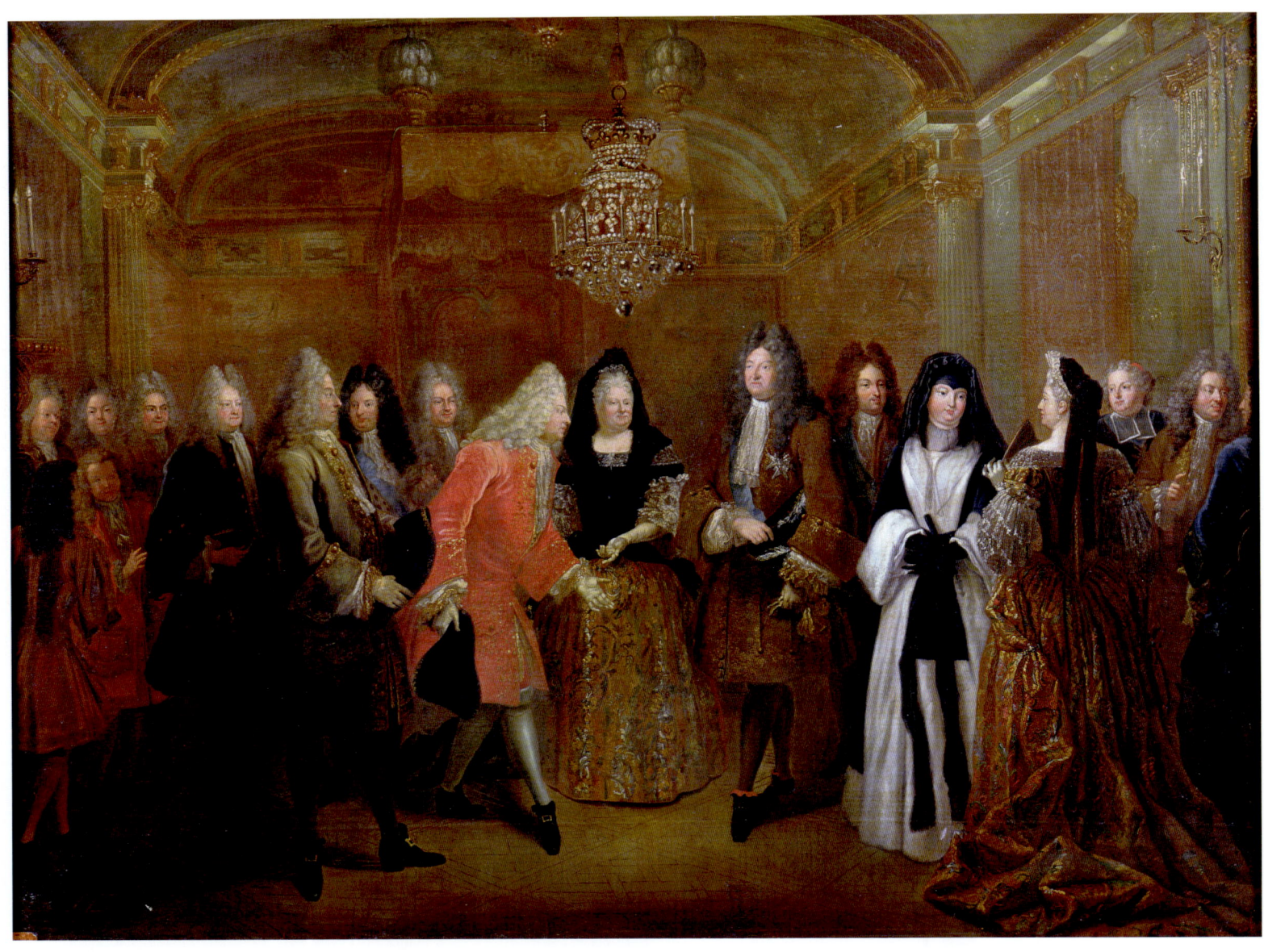

Louis de Silvestre (1675–1760)

Louis XIV Welcomes the Elector of Saxony, Frederick Augustus II to Fontainebleau, 27th September 1714

Louis XIV reçoit à Fontainebleau le prince-électeur de Saxe, 27 septembre 1714

Ludwig XIV. begrüßt den Abgesandten von Sachsen, Friedrich August II. in Fontainebleau

Luis XIV saluda al enviado de Sajonia, Federico Augusto II en Fontainebleau

Luigi XIV accoglie l'elettore di Sassonia, Federico Augusto II a Fontainebleau

Lodewijk XIV begroet de afgezant van Saksen, Frederik Augustus II, in Fontainebleau

1715, Oil on canvas/Huile sur toile, 120 × 155 cm, Château de Versailles, Versailles

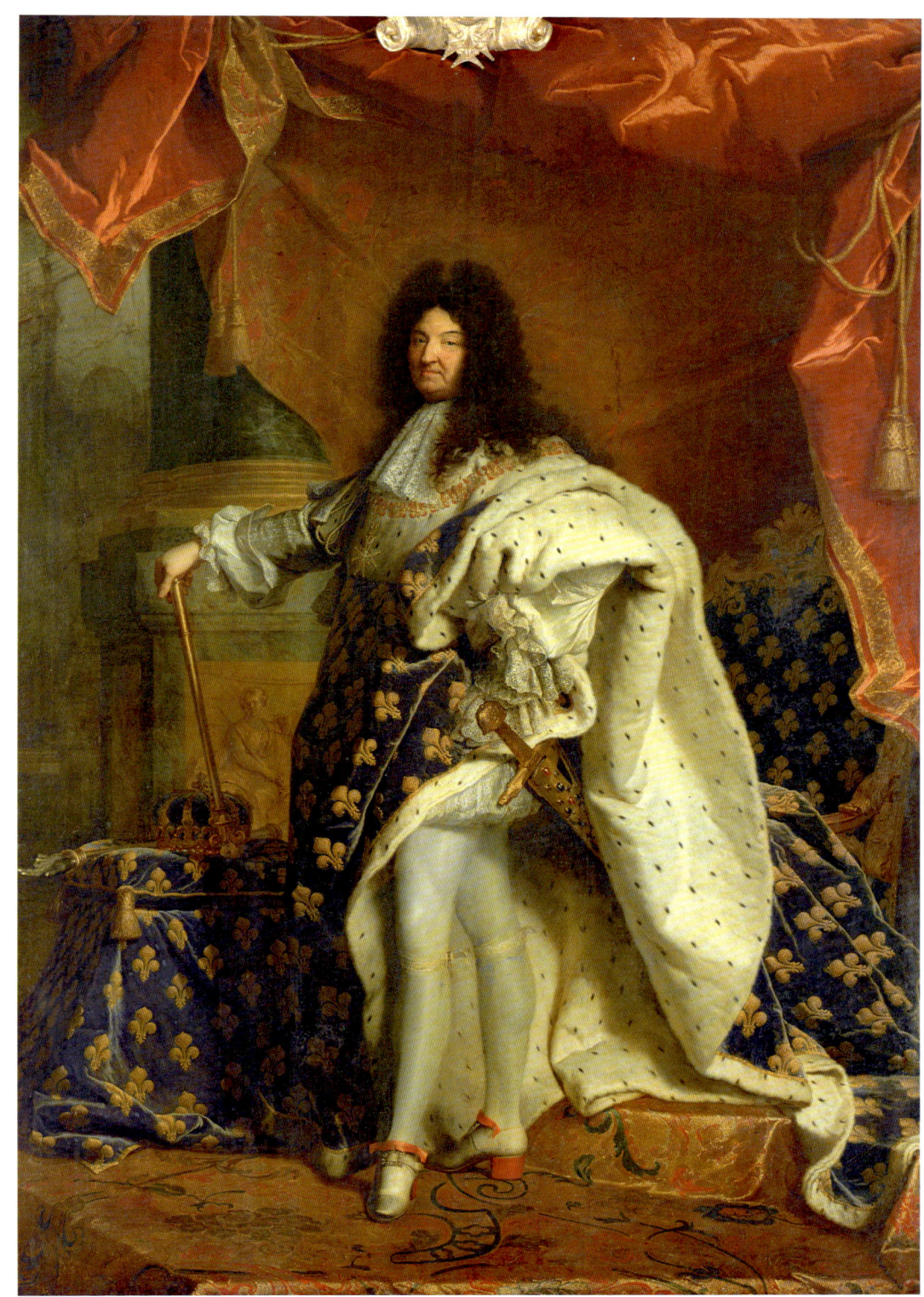

Hyacinthe Rigaud (1659–1743)
Louis XIV, King of France
Louis XIV (1638–1715)
Ludwig XIV., König von Frankreich
Luis XIV, Rey de Francia
Luigi XIV Re di Francia e di Navarra
Lodewijk XIV, koning van Frankrijk
1701, Oil on canvas/Huile sur toile, 277 × 194 cm

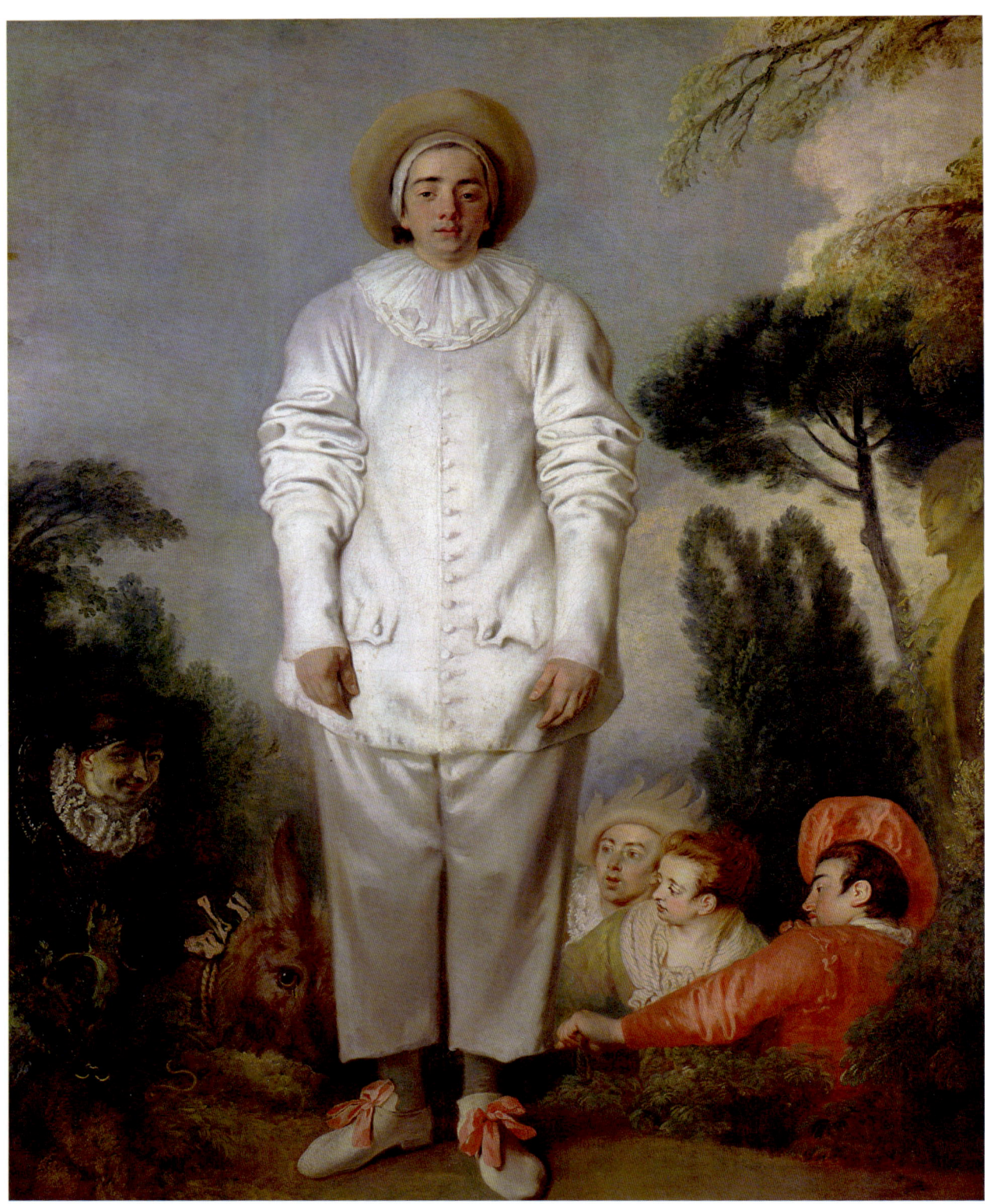

Jean-Antoine Watteau
(1684–1721)

Gilles

Pierrot, *dit autrefois* Gilles

Gilles

Gilles

Gilles

Gilles

c. 1718–1719, Oil on canvas/
Huile sur toile, 185 × 150 cm,
Musée du Louvre, Paris

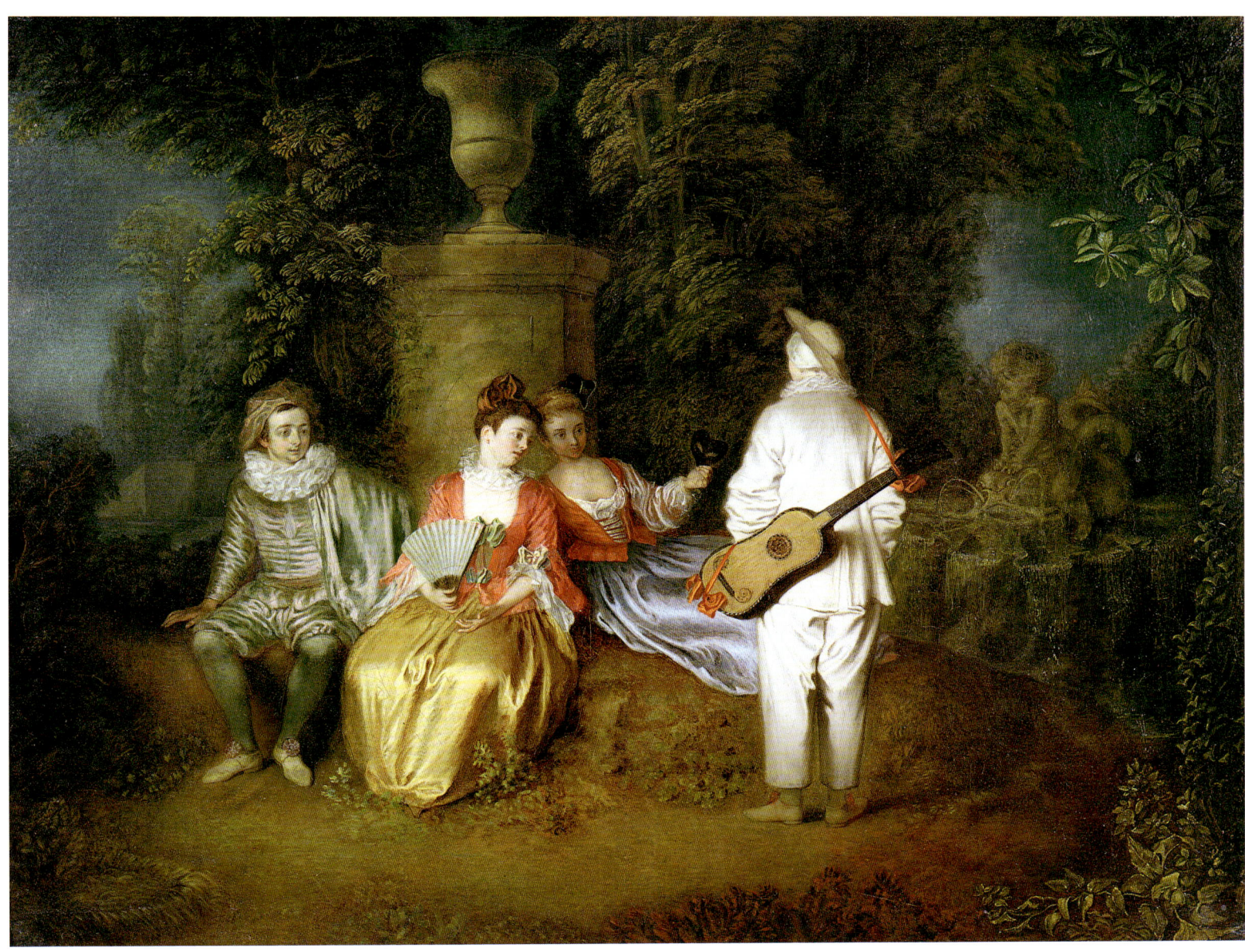

Jean-Antoine Watteau (1684–1721)

The Foursome

Les Quatre Amis

Die vier Freunde

Los cuatro amigos

I quattro amici

De vier vrienden

c. 1713, Oil on canvas/Huile sur toile, 49,5 × 62,9 cm, Legion of Honor, San Francisco

Jean-Antoine Watteau (1684–1721)

Embarkation for Cythera

Pélerinage à l'île de Cythère

Die Einschiffung nach Kythera

Embarcando hacia Citera

L'imbarco per Citera

De inscheping voor Kythera

1717, Oil on canvas/Huile sur toile, 129 × 194 cm, Musée du Louvre, Paris

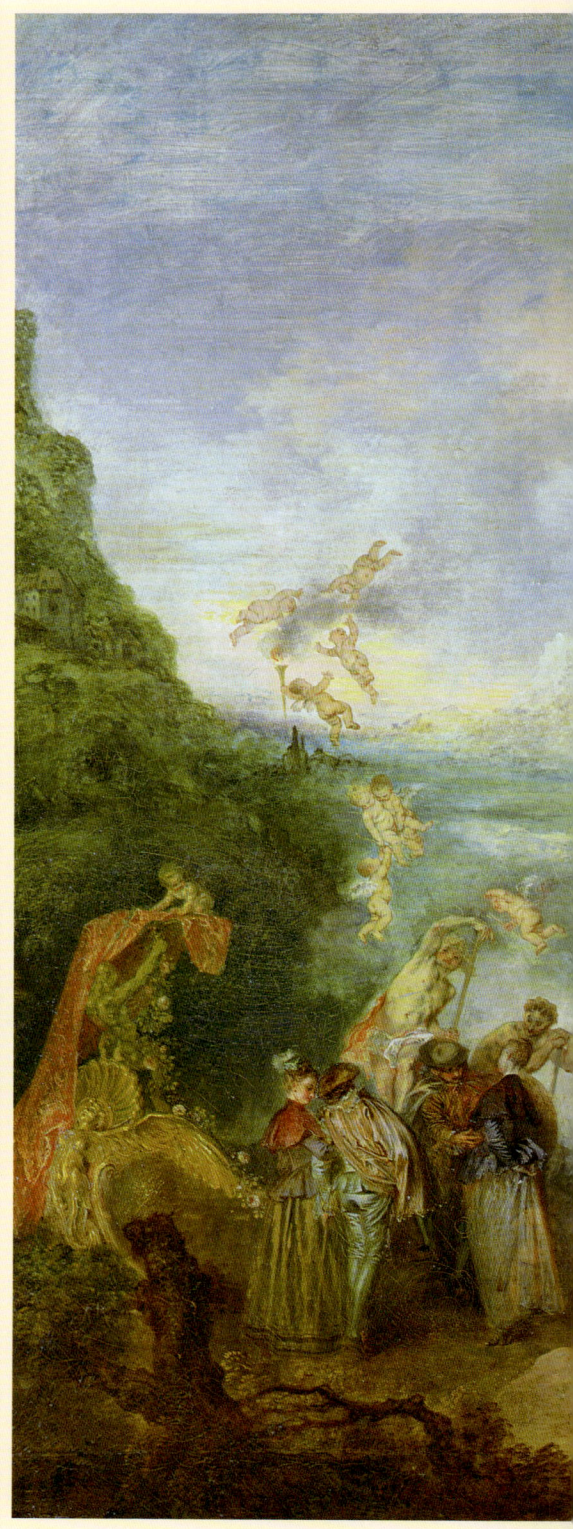

The painting shows leaving for (or, probably, the departure from) the island of Kythera, a legendary Greek island (now Kythira), upon which the goddess of love, Aphrodite, was worshiped. In Watteau's picture the stone love goddess watches benevolently the departing loving couples, who are depicted in various stages of being in love. Here Watteau avoids intrusive gestures, but lets the characters speak in delicate hints. The colors are from the school of Rubens and Titian and depict the landscape in subtle tones.

On assiste ici à l'arrivée sur – ou bien au départ de – l'île de Cythère, île grecque légendaire et près de laquelle serait née Aphrodite, déesse de l'Amour, qui y était vénérée (aujourd'hui « Kythira »). La déesse de pierre regarde avec bienveillance les couples d'amoureux, représentés à divers stades de leur liaison. Watteau évite donc les gestes dérangeants et laisse les personnages s'exprimer par tendres allusions. La palette est dans la veine de Rubens et de Titien, et fixe le paysage en tons subtils.

Das Gemälde zeigt den Aufbruch zu (oder auch die Abreise von) der Insel Kythera, einer sagenumwobenen griechischen Insel (heute: Kythira), auf der man die Göttin der Liebe Aphrodite verehrte. Auf Watteaus Bild beobachtet die steinerne Liebesgöttin wohlwollend die aufbrechenden Liebespaare, die in verschiedenen Stadien der Verliebtheit gezeigt werden. Dabei vermeidet Watteau aufdringliche Gesten, sondern lässt die Figuren in zarten Andeutungen sprechen. Die Farbigkeit ist an Rubens und Tizian geschult und hält die Landschaft in subtilen Tönen fest.

La pintura muestra el desembarco en (o partida desde) la isla de Citera, una mítica isla griega en la que se veneraba a la diosa del amor Afrodita. En el cuadro de Watteau la diosa del amor, estatua, observa con bondad a las diversas parejas de enamorados, que aparecen representados en diversos estadios del cortejo. Watteau evita aquí gestos comprometidos, haciendo hablar a sus figuras de forma más bien insinuada. El uso del color está en deuda con Tiziano y Rubens, y captura el paisaje en tonos sutiles.

Il dipinto mostra la partenza o il ritorno dall'isola di Citera, una leggendaria isola greca (oggi: Cerigo), sulla quale si venera la dea dell'amore, Afrodite. Nel quadro di Watteau la dea dell'amore sotto forma di busto di pietra osserva benevolmente le coppie di innamorati in partenza, che vengono ritratti in diverse fasi della storia d'amore. Watteau evita gesti importuni, lasciando invece parlare le figure con tenere allusioni. La cromaticità è ispirata a Rubens e Tiziano e fissa il paesaggio in sfumature sottili.

Het schilderij toont het vertrek naar (of misschien wel het vertrek van) het eiland Kythera, een met mythen omgeven Grieks eiland (nu Kythira) waar men de godin van de liefde Aphrodite vereerde. Op het doek van Watteau ziet de in steen uitgehouwen liefdesgodin welwillend toe op de vertrekkende paartjes, die in verschillende stadia van verliefdheid worden getoond. Daarbij vermijdt Watteau al te brede gebaren en laat de figuren in tedere zinspelingen spreken. Het kleurgebruik is ontleend aan het voorbeeld van Rubens en Titiaan, waarbij Watteau het landschap in subtiele tonen heeft vastgelegd.

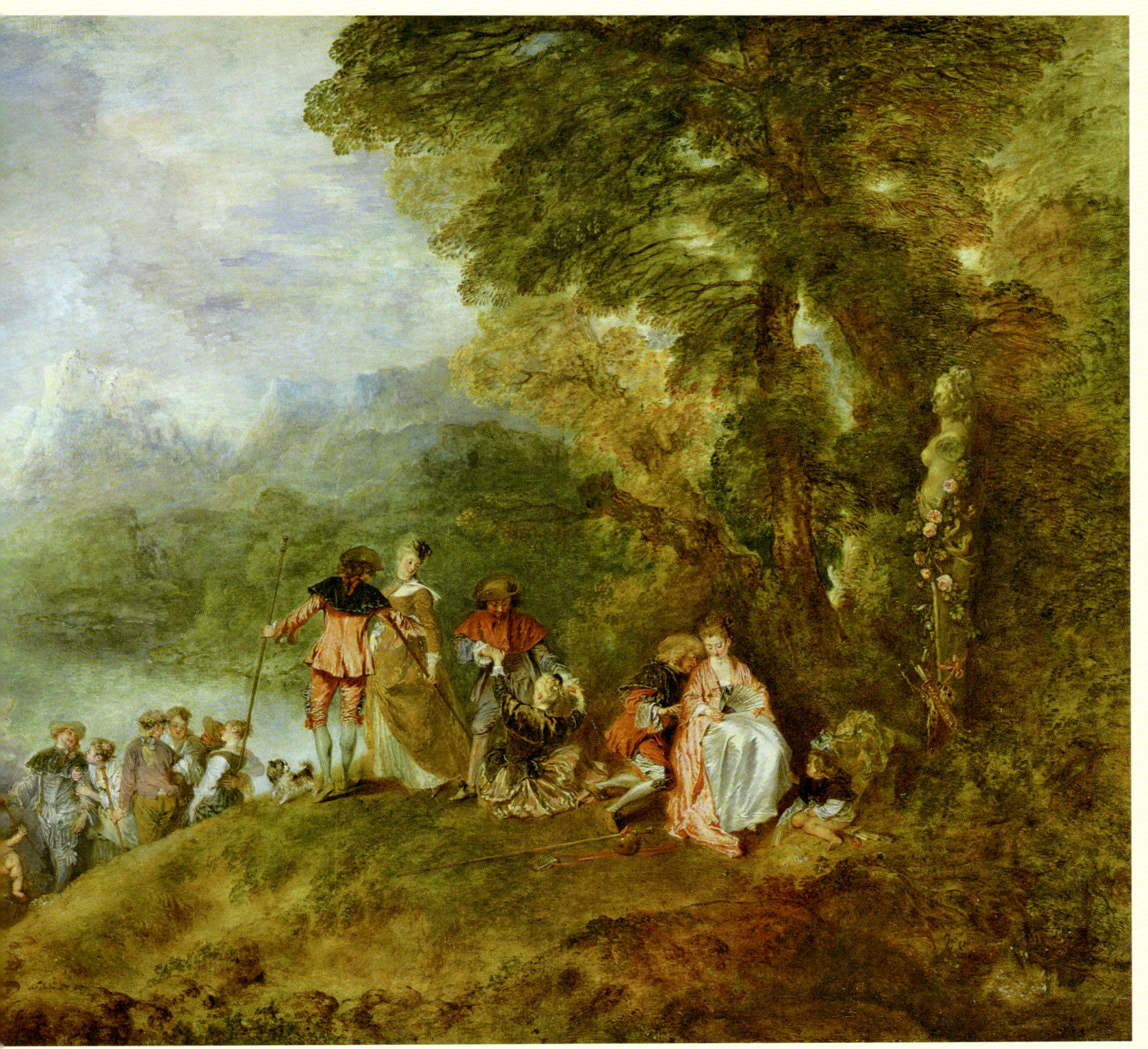

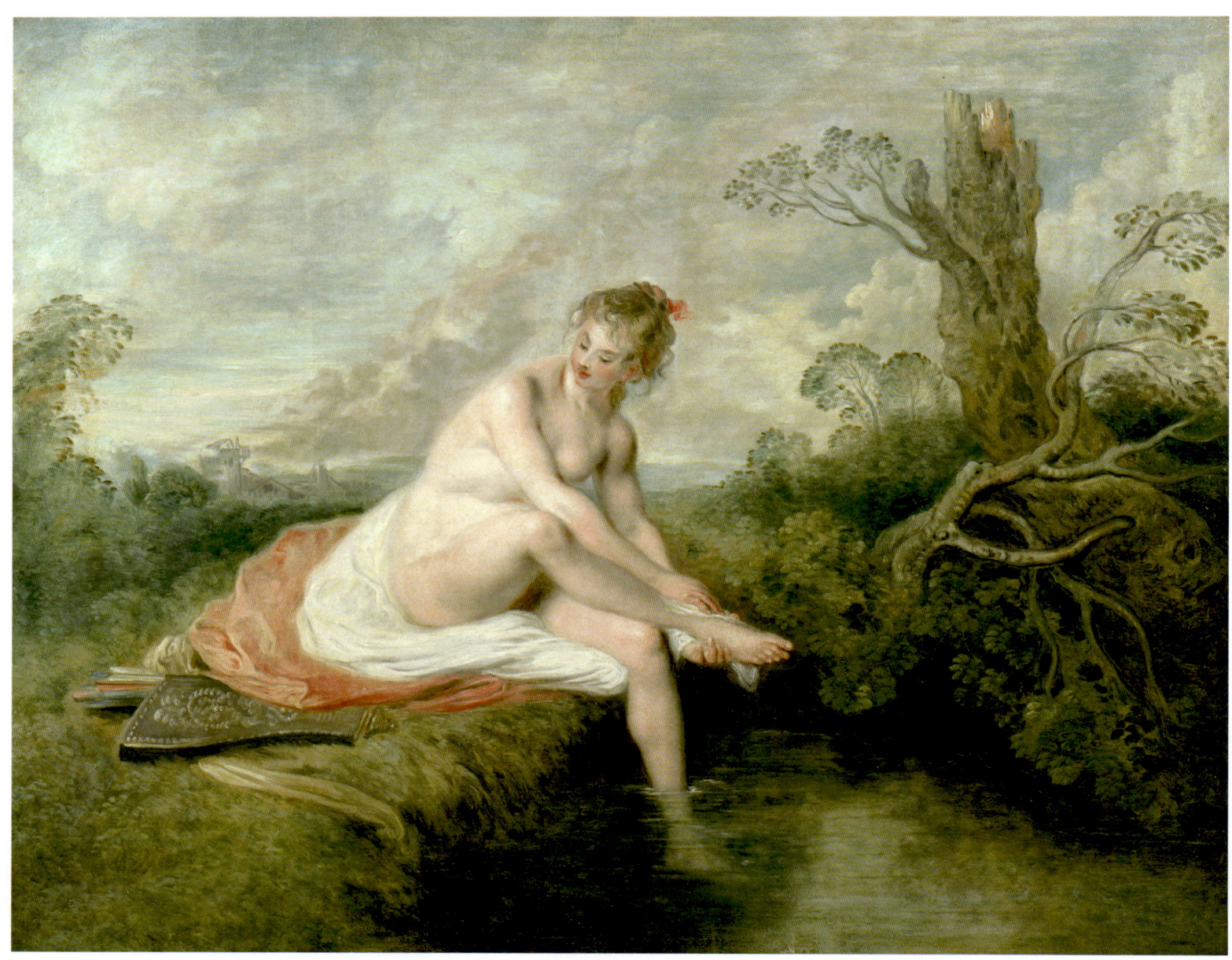

Jean-Antoine Watteau (1684–1721)

The Bath of Diana	Das Bad der Diana	Il bagno di Diana
Diane au bain	El baño de Diana	Het bad van Diana

c. 1715–1716, Oil on canvas/Huile sur toile, 80 × 101 cm, Musée du Louvre, Paris

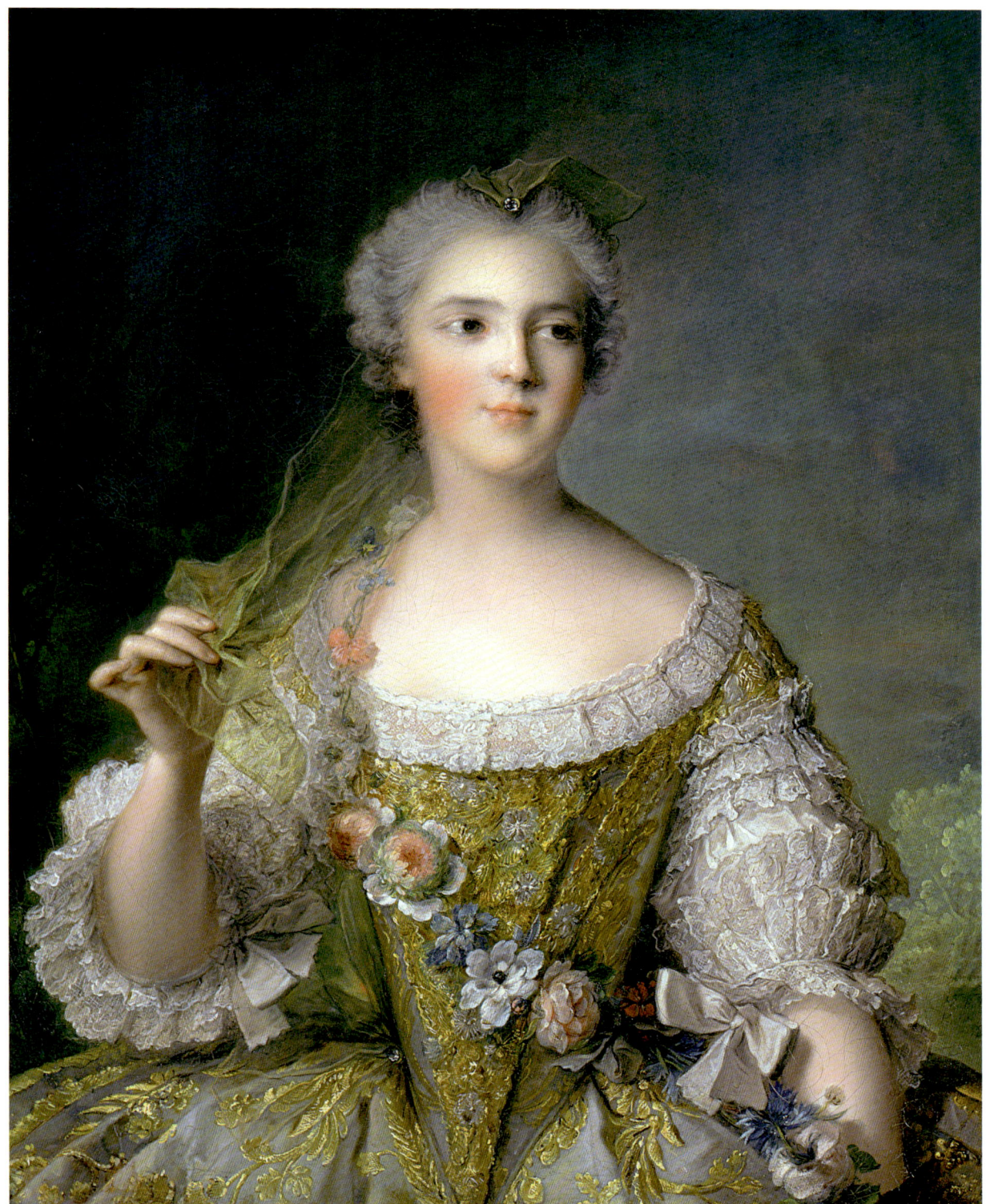

**Jean-Marc Nattier
(1685–1766)**

Portrait of Madame Sophie,
daughter of Louis XV, at
Fontevrault,

Madame Sophie, fille de
Louis XV, à Fontevrault

Porträt Madame Sophie,
Tochter von Luwig XV. in
Fontevrault

Retrato de Madame Sophie,
hija de Luis XV en Fontevrault

Ritratto di Madame Sophie,
figlia di Luigi XV, a Fontevrault

Portret van madame Sophie,
dochter van Lodewijk XV, in
Fontevrault

1748, Oil on canvas/Huile sur toile,
81 × 65 cm, Château de Versailles,
Versailles

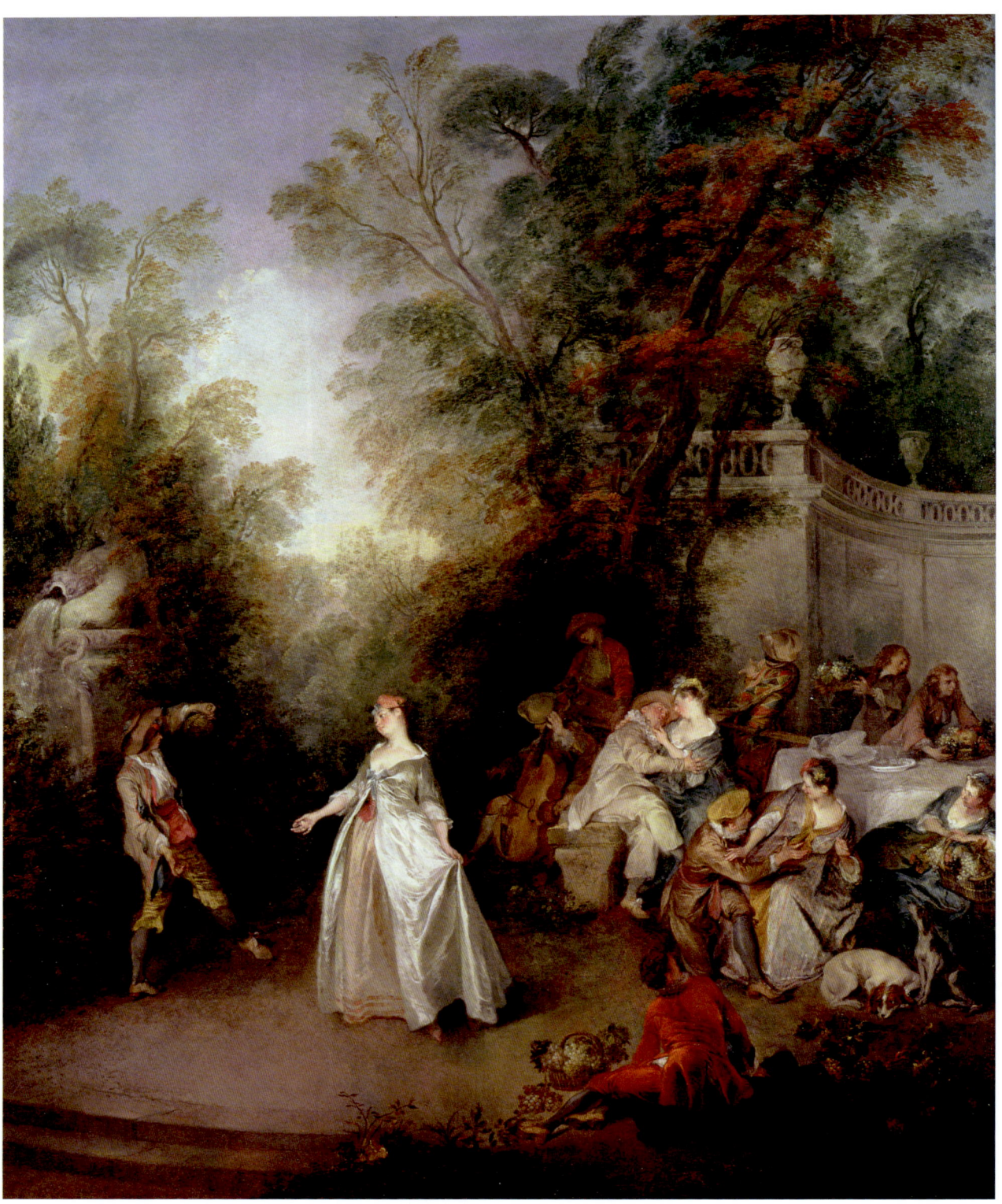

Nicolas Lancret
(1690–1743)

A Feast

Une Fête galante

Ein Fest

Fiesta

Una festa

Een feest

n. d., Oil on canvas/Huile sur
toile, Private collection

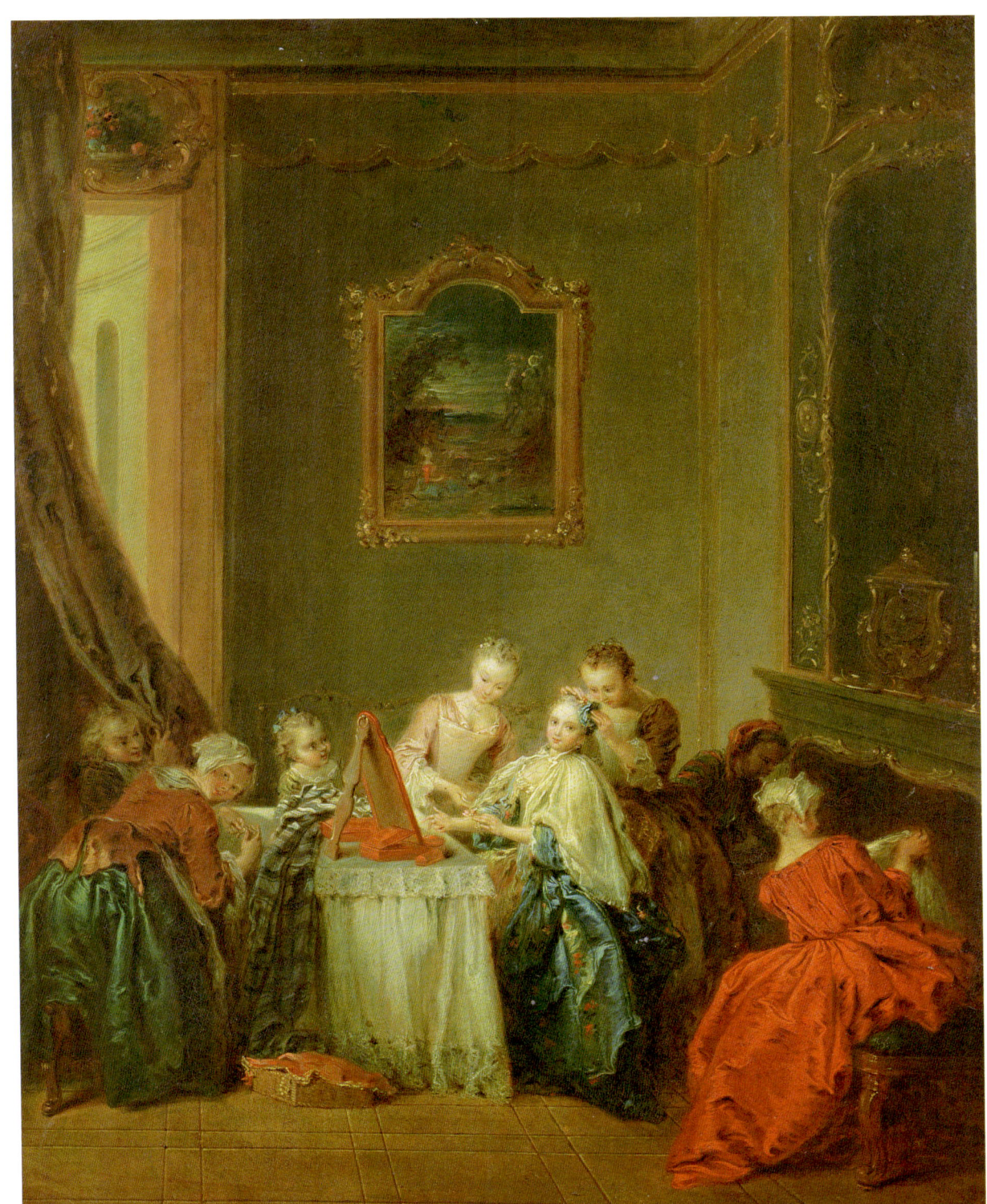

**Jean-Baptiste Joseph Pater
(1695–1736)**

The Toilet: Young woman at her
Dressing Table

La Toilette, jeune femme à sa
coiffeuse

Die Toilette: Junge Frau am
Ankleidetisch

El baño: Mujer joven en el
tocador

Giovane donna alla toeletta

Het toilet: jonge vrouw aan de
kaptafel

n. d., Oil on canvas/Huile sur toile,
47 × 37,5 cm, Musée du Louvre,
Paris

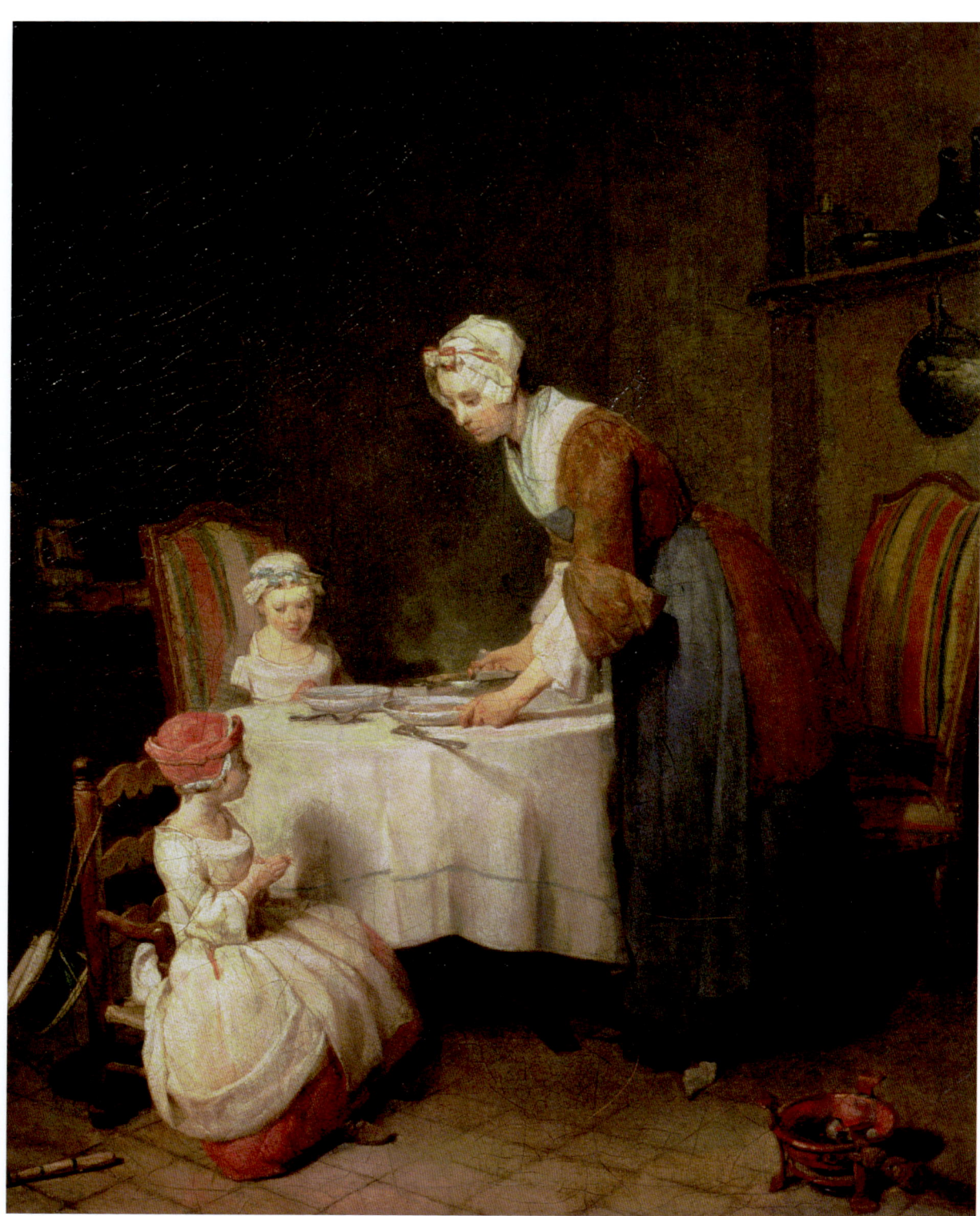

**Jean-Siméon Chardin
(1699–1779)**

The Grace

Le Bénédicité

Die Anmut

La Gracia

La grazia

De bevalligheid

1740, Oil on canvas/Huile sur toile,
49 × 38 cm, Musée du Louvre,
Paris

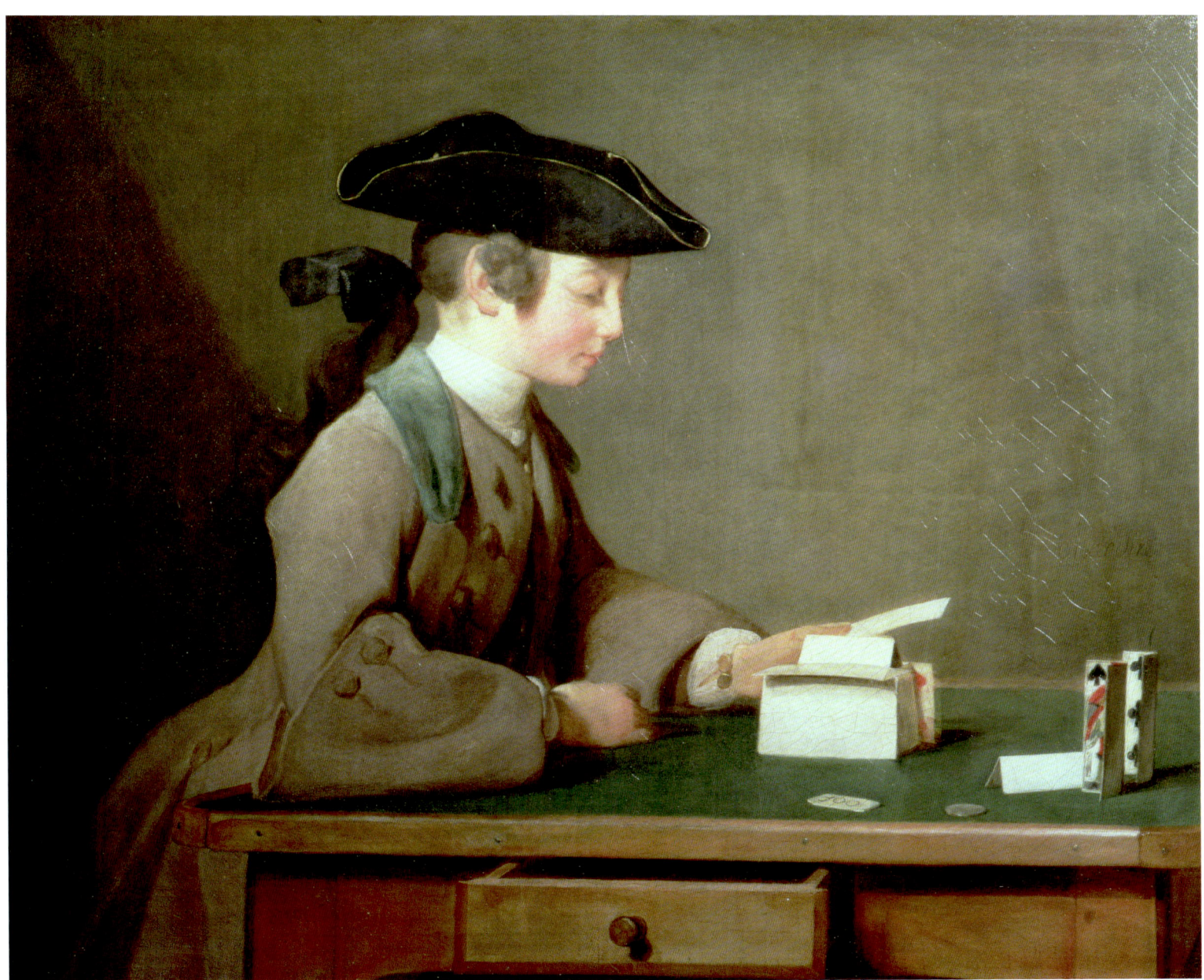

Jean-Siméon Chardin (1699–1779)

The House of Cards	Das Kartenspiel	Il castello di carte
Le Château de cartes	El juego de cartas	Het kaartspel

c. 1736–1737, Oil on canvas/Huile sur toile, 60,3 × 71,8 cm, National Gallery, London

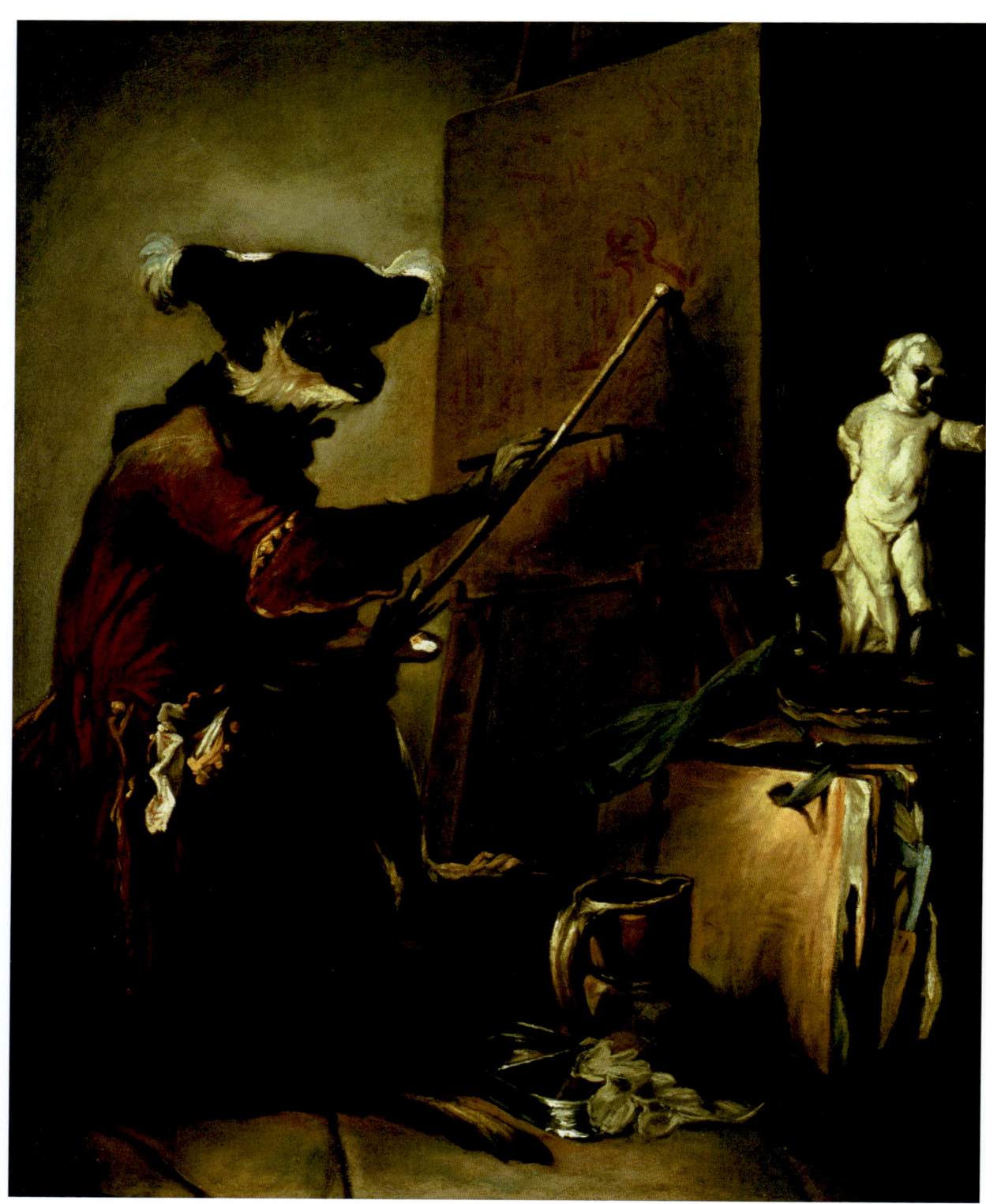

Jean-Siméon Chardin (1699–1779)

The Monkey Painter

Le Singe peintre

Der Maleraffe

El mono pintor

La scimmia pittrice

De schilderende aap

c. 1740, Oil on canvas/Huile sur toile, 73 × 59 cm, Musée du Louvre, Paris

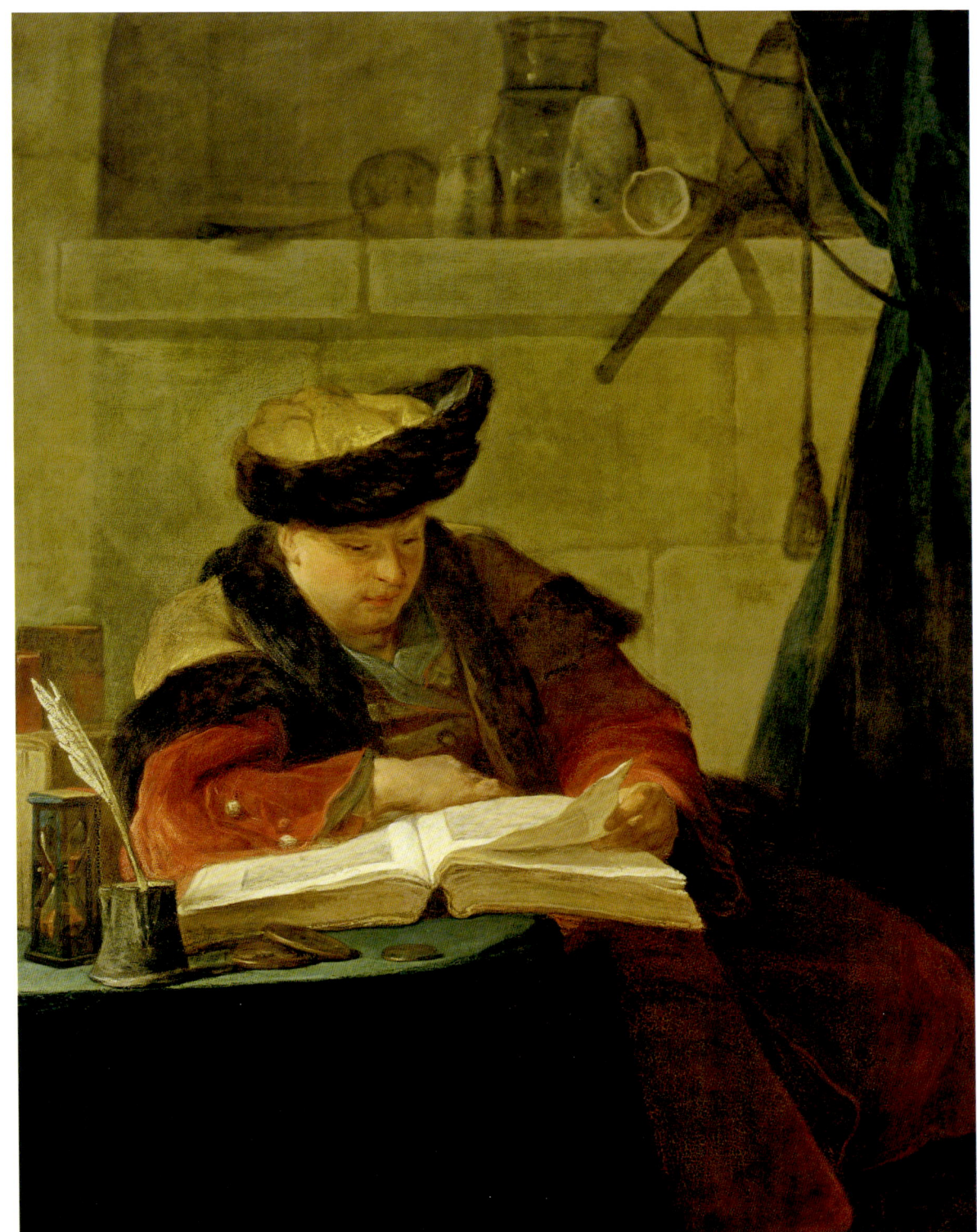

Jean-Siméon Chardin (1699–1779)

A Chemist in his Laboratory, *or* The Prompter, *or* A Philosopher giving a Lecture (Portrait of the painter Joseph Aved

Chimiste dans son laboratoire (Portrait du peintre Joseph Aved, *dit* Le Souffleur)

Der Alchemist *oder* Der Souffleur (Porträt des Malers Joseph Aved)

El alquimista *o* El filósofo leyendo (Retrato del pintor Joseph Avedo

L'alchimista *o* Il suggeritore (ritratto del pittore Joseph Aved)

De alchemist, *of:* De souffleur (Portret van de schilder Joseph Aved)

1734, Oil on canvas/Huile sur toile, 138 × 105 cm, Musée du Louvre, Paris

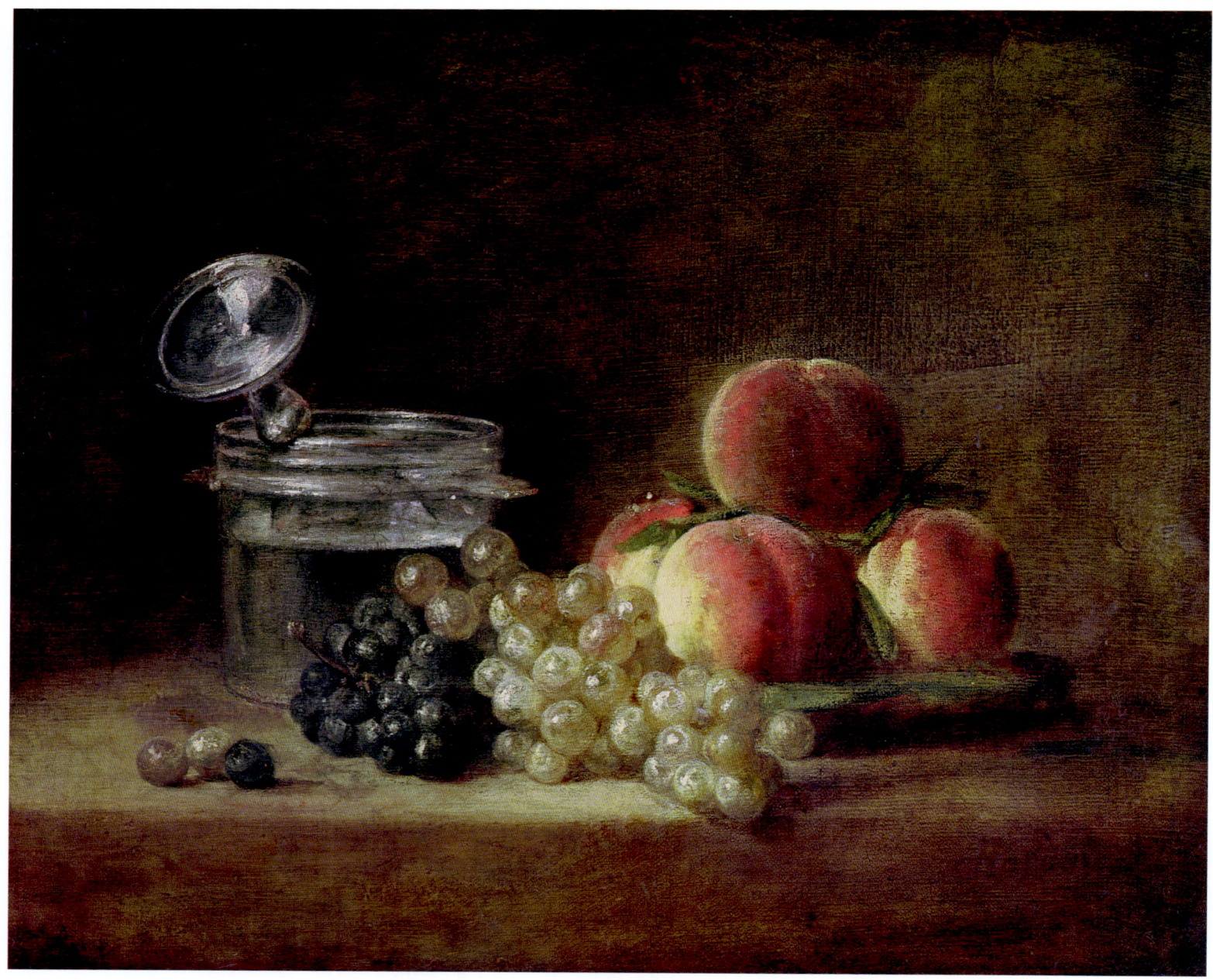

Jean-Siméon Chardin (1699–1779)

Still Life with a Basket of Peaches, White and Black Grapes with Cooler and Wineglass

Pêches et raisins avec un rafraîchissoir

Stillleben mit einem Korb Pfirsiche, weißen und roten Trauben, Kühler und Weinglas

Bodegón con una cesta de melocotones, uvas rojas y blancas y vaso

Natura morta con cesto di pesche, uva bianca e rossa, caraffa e bicchiere

Stilleven met een mand met perziken en witte en rode druiven, wijnkoeler en wijnglas

c. 1759, Oil on canvas/Huile sur toile, 38 × 46 cm, Musée des Beaux-Arts de Rennes, Rennes

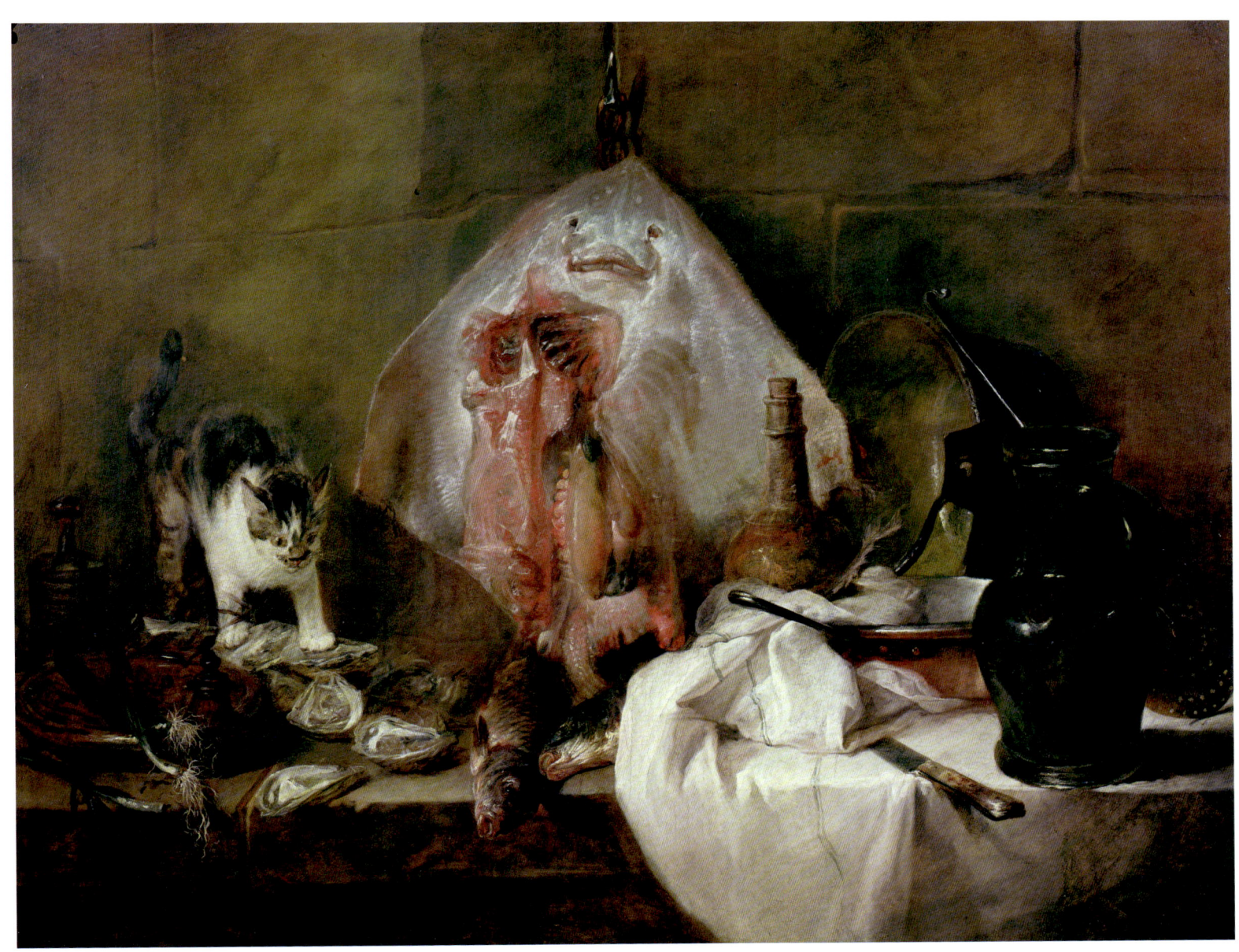

Jean-Siméon Chardin (1699–1779)

The Skate, *or* Kitchen Interior	Der Rochen, *oder* Kücheninterieur	La razza
La Raie	La raya, *o* interior de una cocina	De rog, *of* Het keukeninterieur

c. 1725–1726, Oil on canvas/Huile sur toile, 114 × 146 cm, Musée du Louvre, Paris

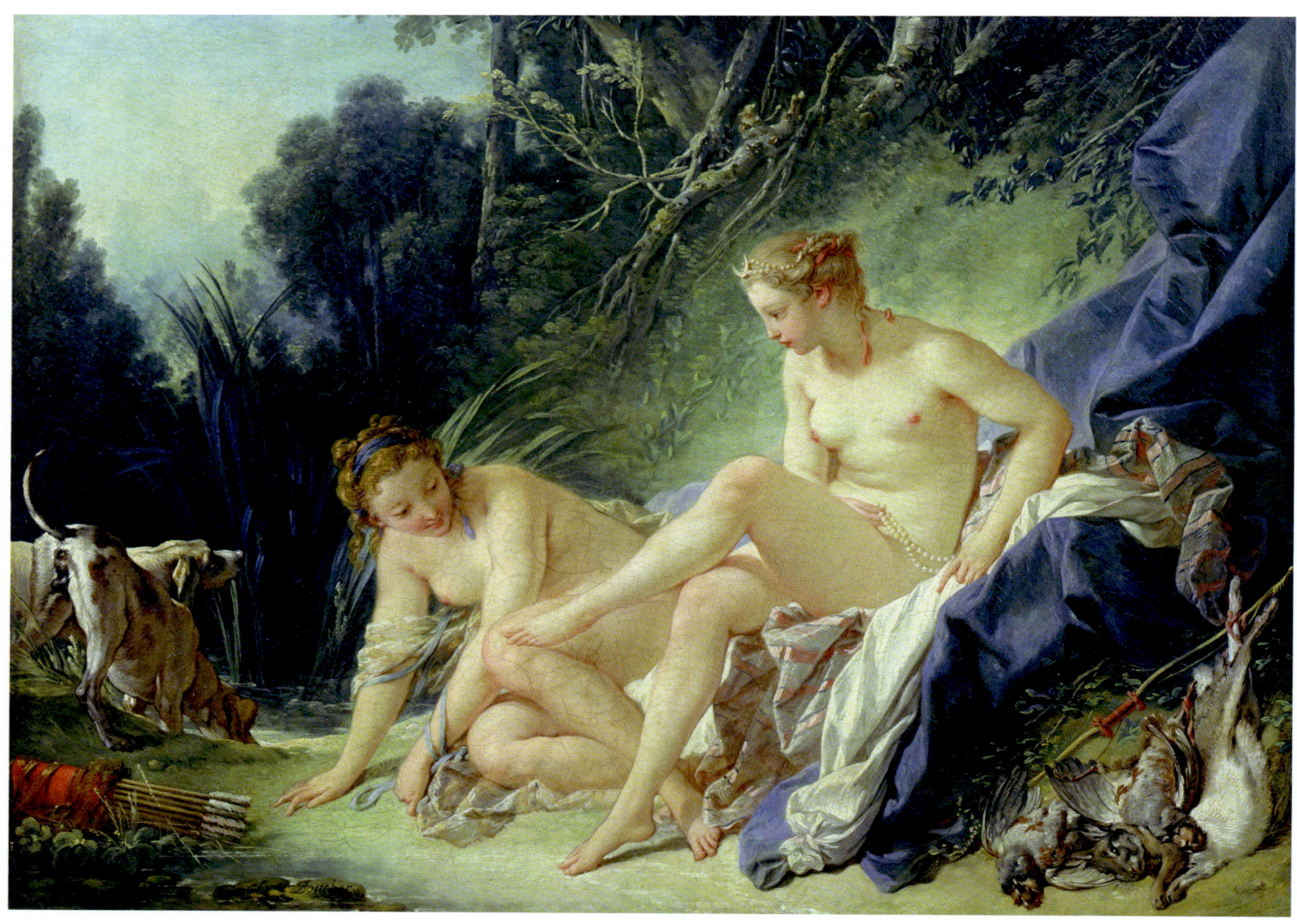

François Boucher (1703–1770)

Diana Getting out of her Bath

Diane sortant du bain

Diana steigt aus dem Bad

Diana saliendo del baño

Diana esce dal bagno

Diana na het baden

1742, Oil on canvas/Huile sur toile, 57 × 73 cm, Musée du Louvre, Paris

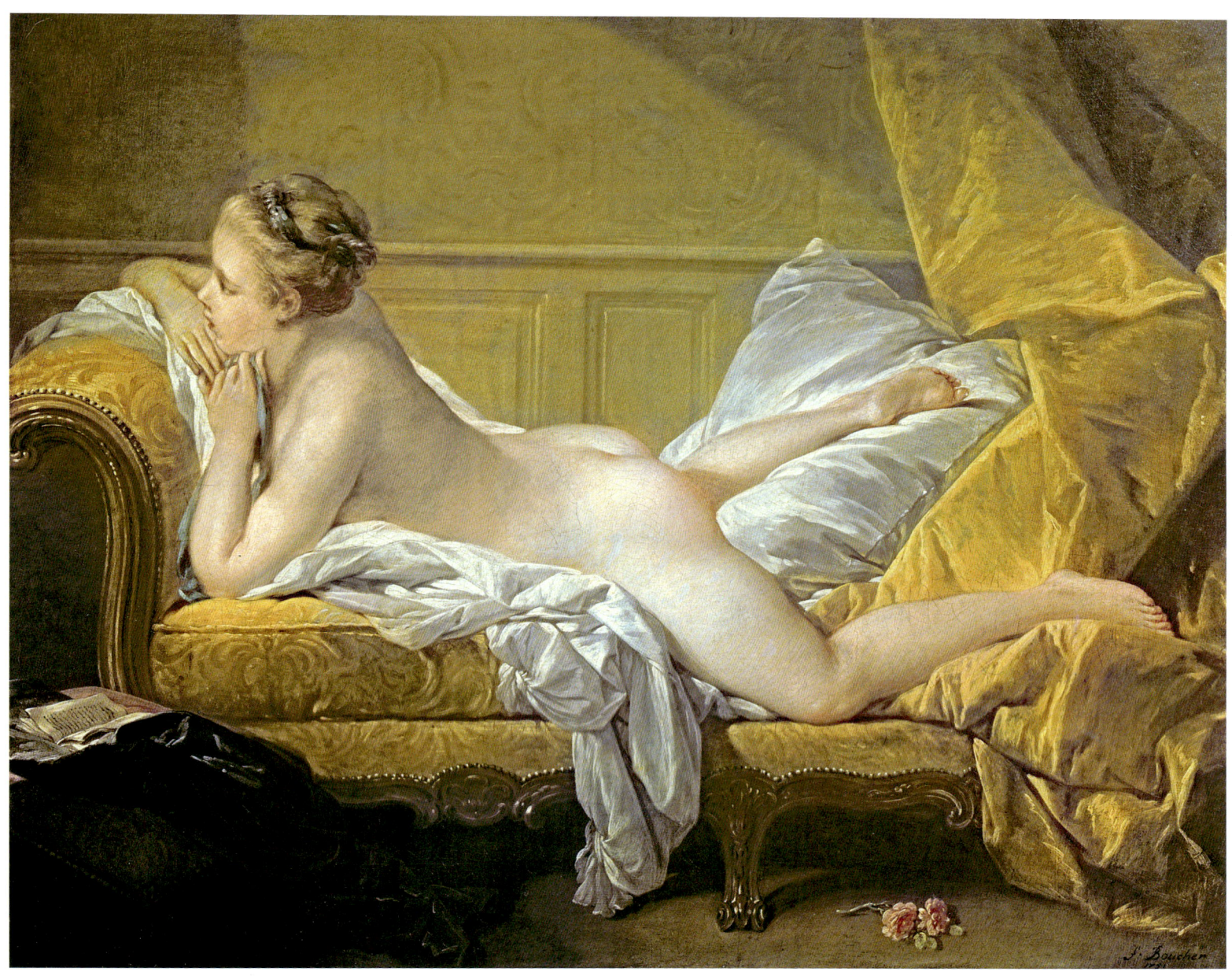

François Boucher (1703–1770)

Reclining Nude (Miss O'Murphy)   Ruhendes Mädchen (Miss O'Murphy)   Ragazza distesa (Miss O'Murphy)

L'Odalisque blonde (Miss O'Murphy)   Joven descansando (Miss O'Murphy)   Liggend meisje (miss O'Murphy)

1751, Oil on canvas/Huile sur toile, 59,5 × 73,5 cm, Wallraf-Richartz-Museum & Fondation Corboud, Köln

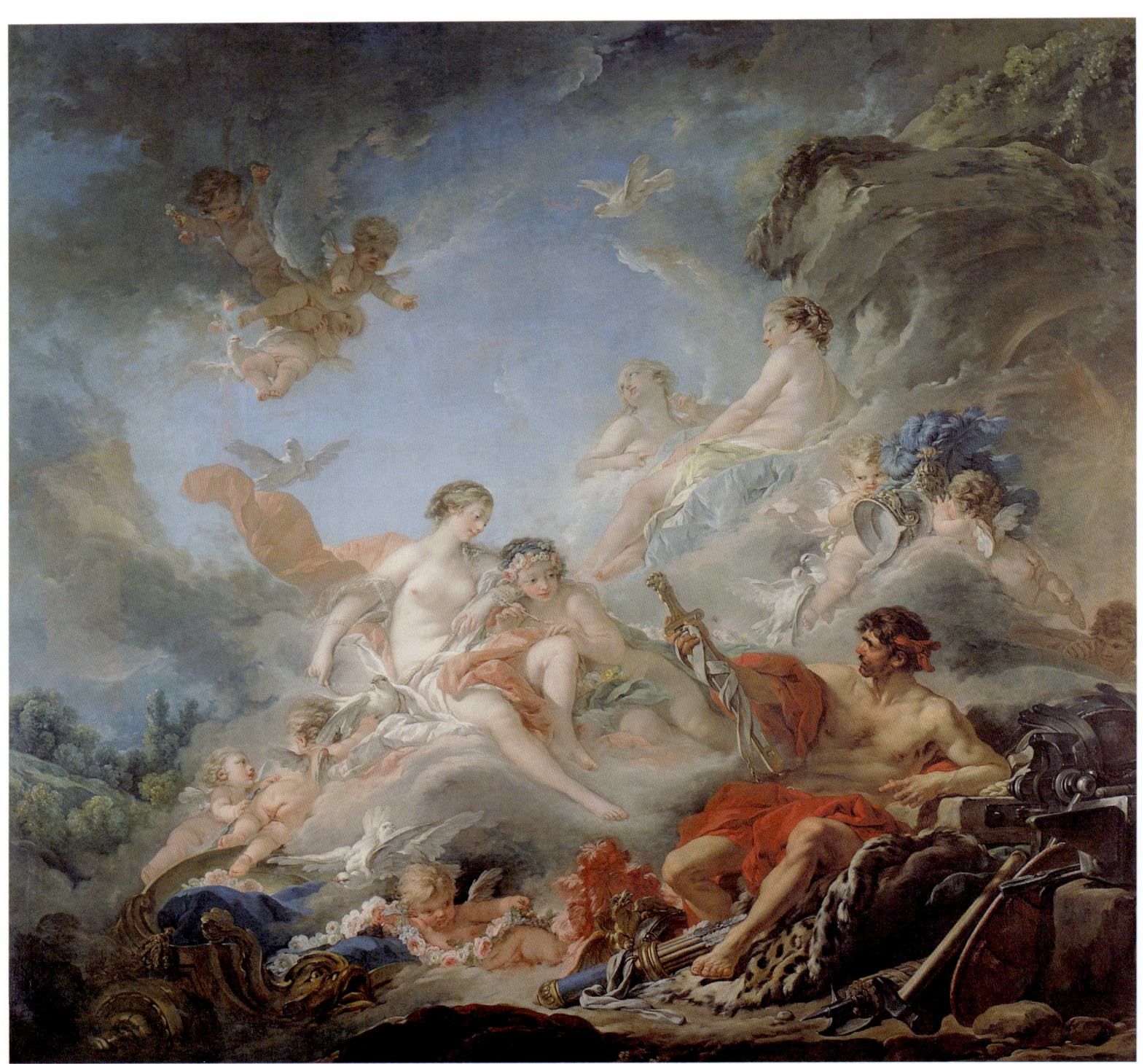

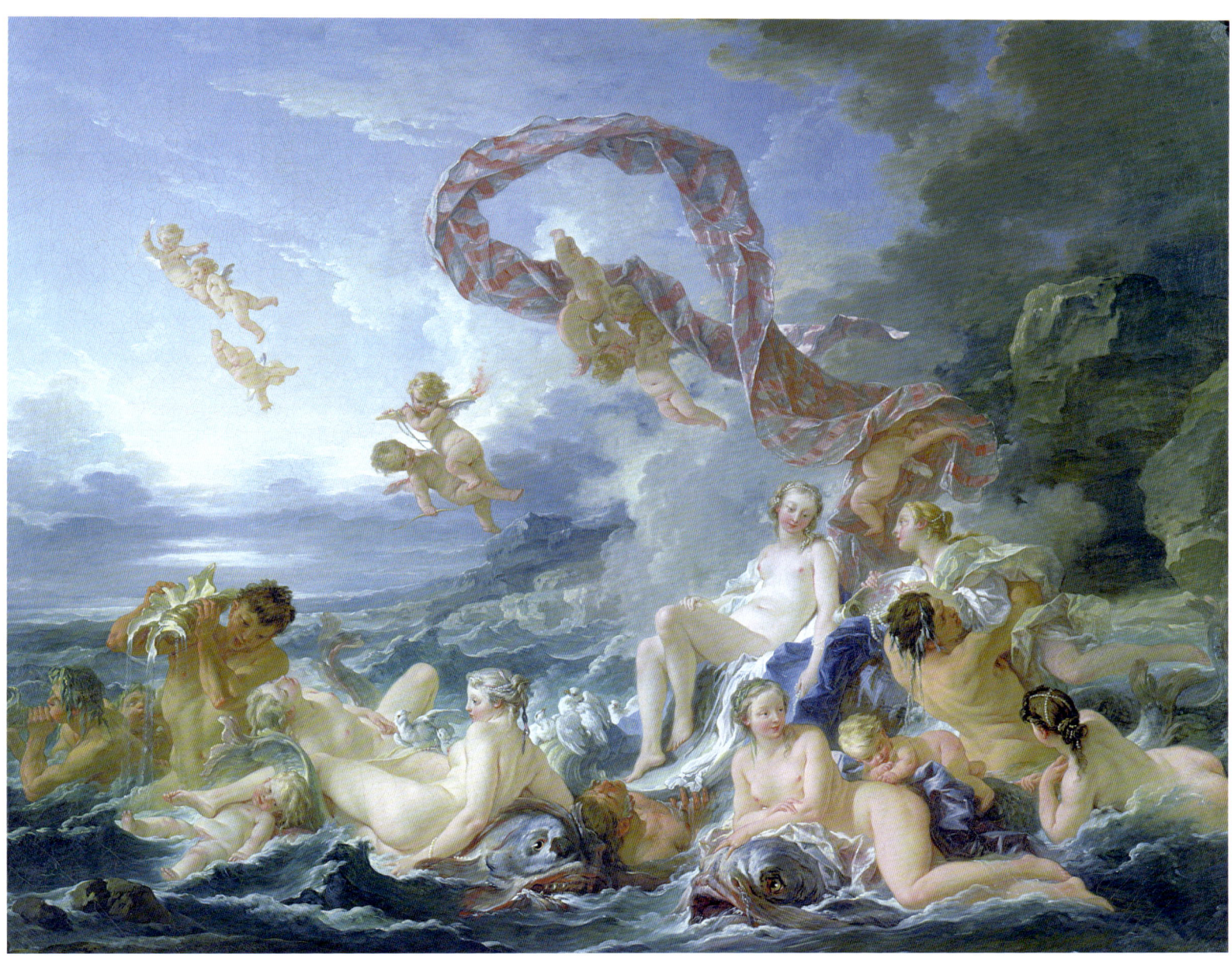

François Boucher (1703–1770)

The Forge of Vulcan, *or* Vulcan Presenting Arms for Aeneas to Venus

Les Forges de Vulcain

Die Schmiede des Vulkan

La fragua de Vulcano

La fucina di Vulcano

De smidse van Vulcanus

1757, Oil on canvas/Huile sur toile, 320 × 320 cm, Musée du Louvre, Paris

François Boucher (1703–1770)

The Triumph of Venus

Le Triomphe de Vénus

Triumph der Venus

Triunfo de Venus

Il trionfo di Venere

De Triomf van Venus

1740, Oil on canvas/Huile sur toile, 130 × 162 cm, Nationalmuseum, Stockholm

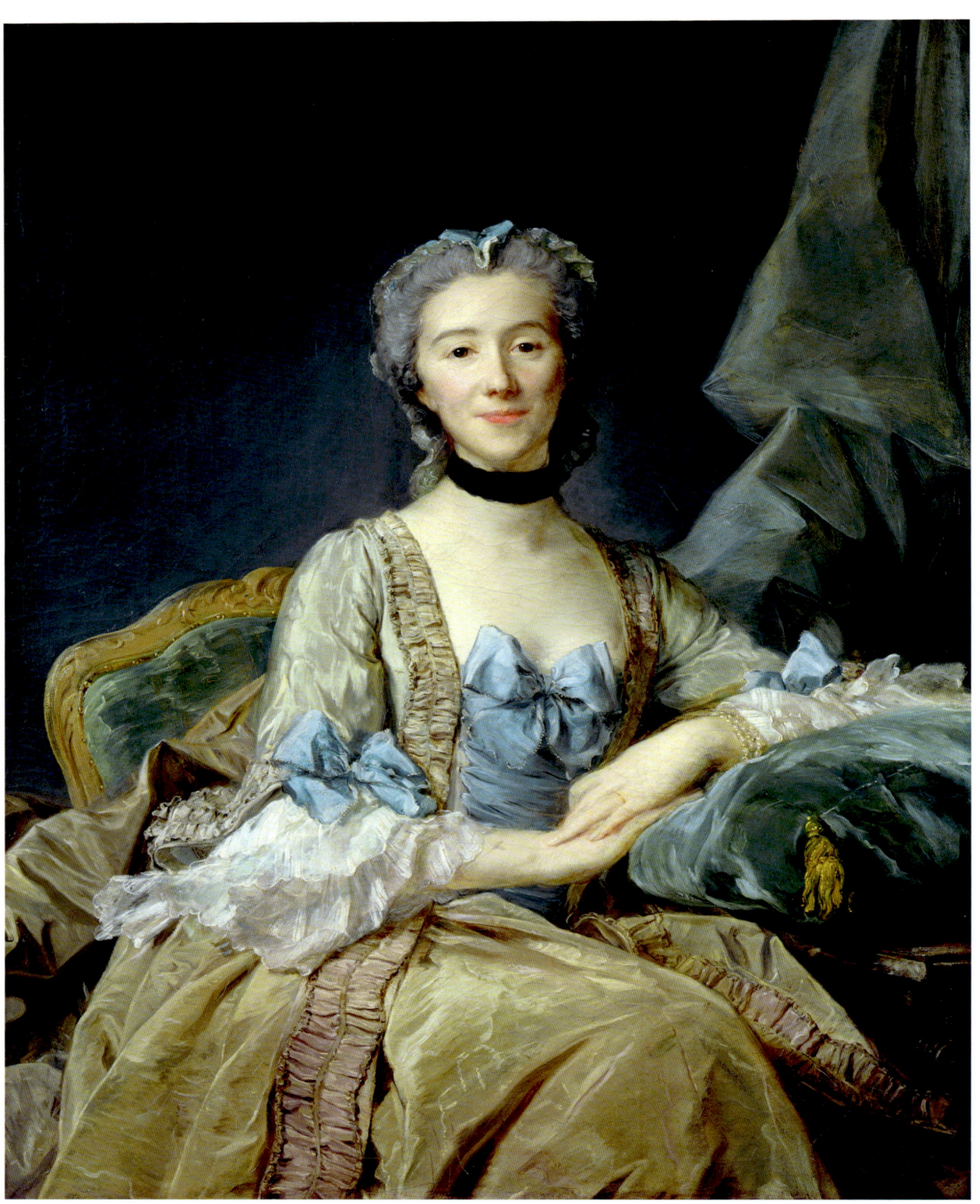

**Jean-Baptiste Perronneau
(1715–1783)**

Madame de Sorquainville

1749, Oil on canvas/Huile sur
toile, 101 × 81 cm, Musée du
Louvre, Paris

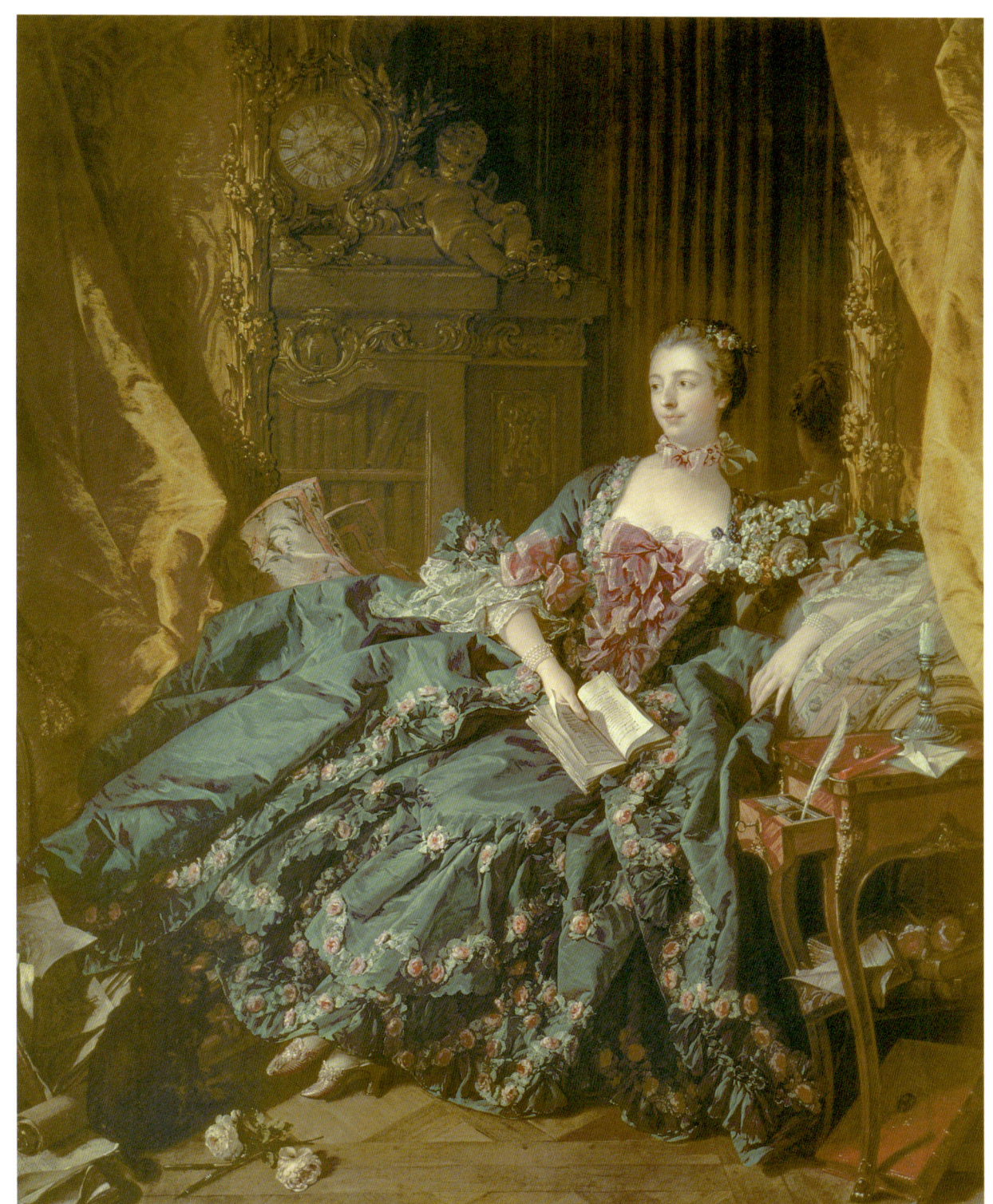

François Boucher (1703–1770)

Madame de Pompadour

Portrait de
madame de Pompadour

Bildnis der
Madame de Pompadour

Retrato de
Madame de Pompadour

Ritratto di
Madame de Pompadour

Portret van
madame de Pompadour

1756, Oil on canvas/Huile sur toile,
201 × 157 cm, Alte Pinakothek,
München

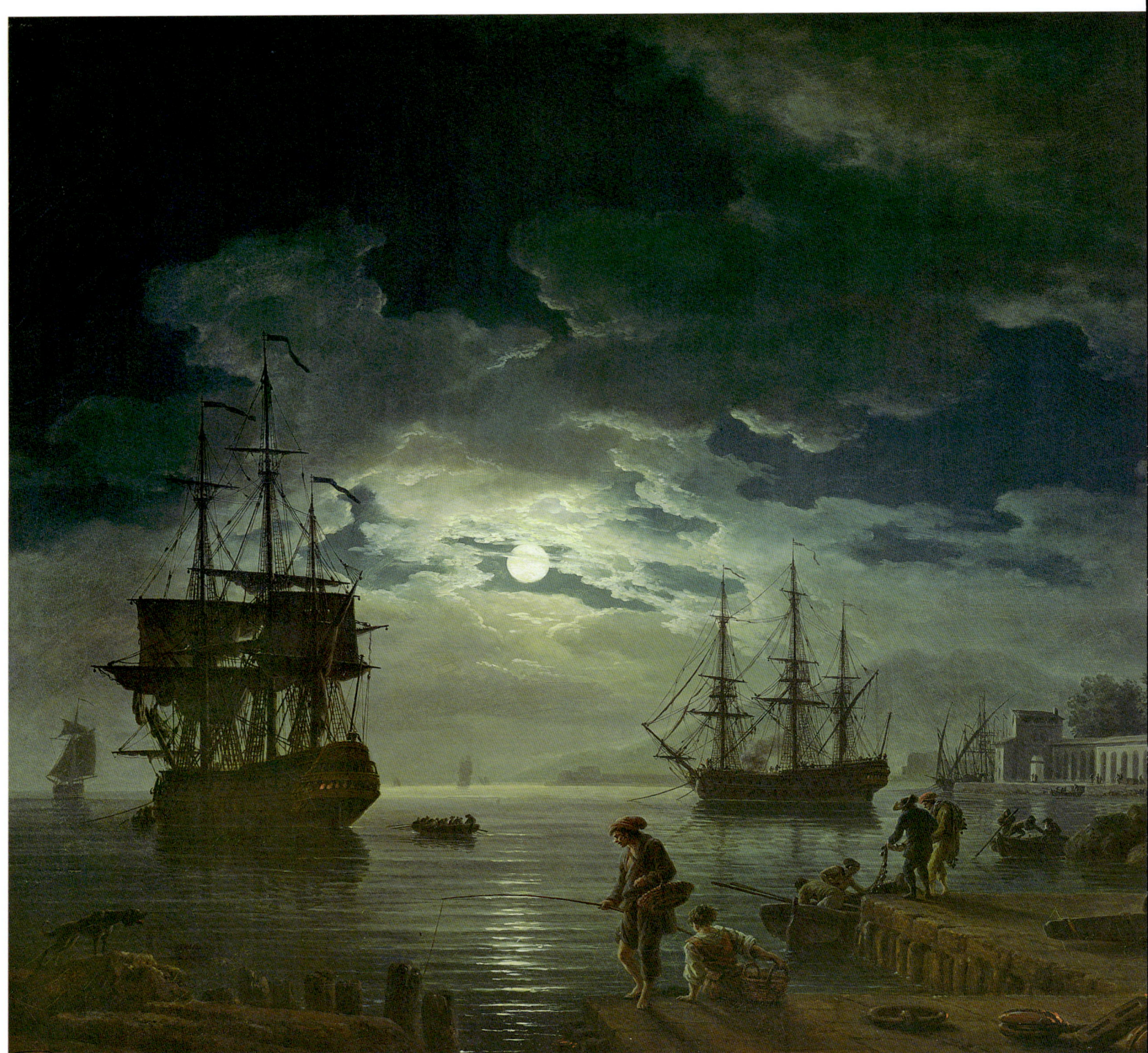

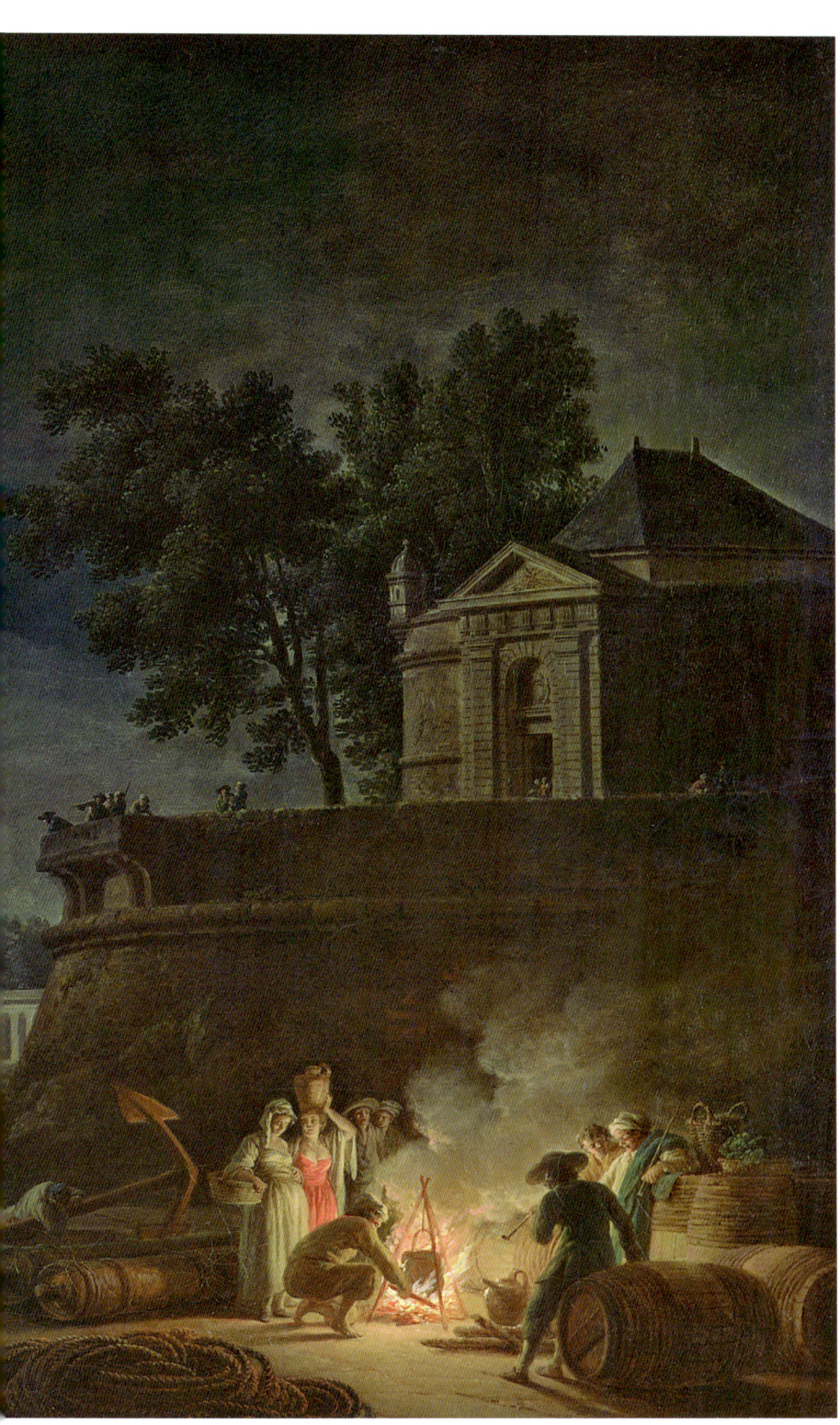

Joseph Vernet (1714–1789)

Night: A Port in the Moonlight

La Nuit : un port de mer au clair de lune

Nacht: ein Hafen im Mondlicht

Noche: un puerto a la luz de la luna

Notte: un porto al chiaro di luna

Haven in het maanlicht

1771, Oil on canvas/Huile sur toile, 98 × 164 cm, Musée du Louvre, Paris

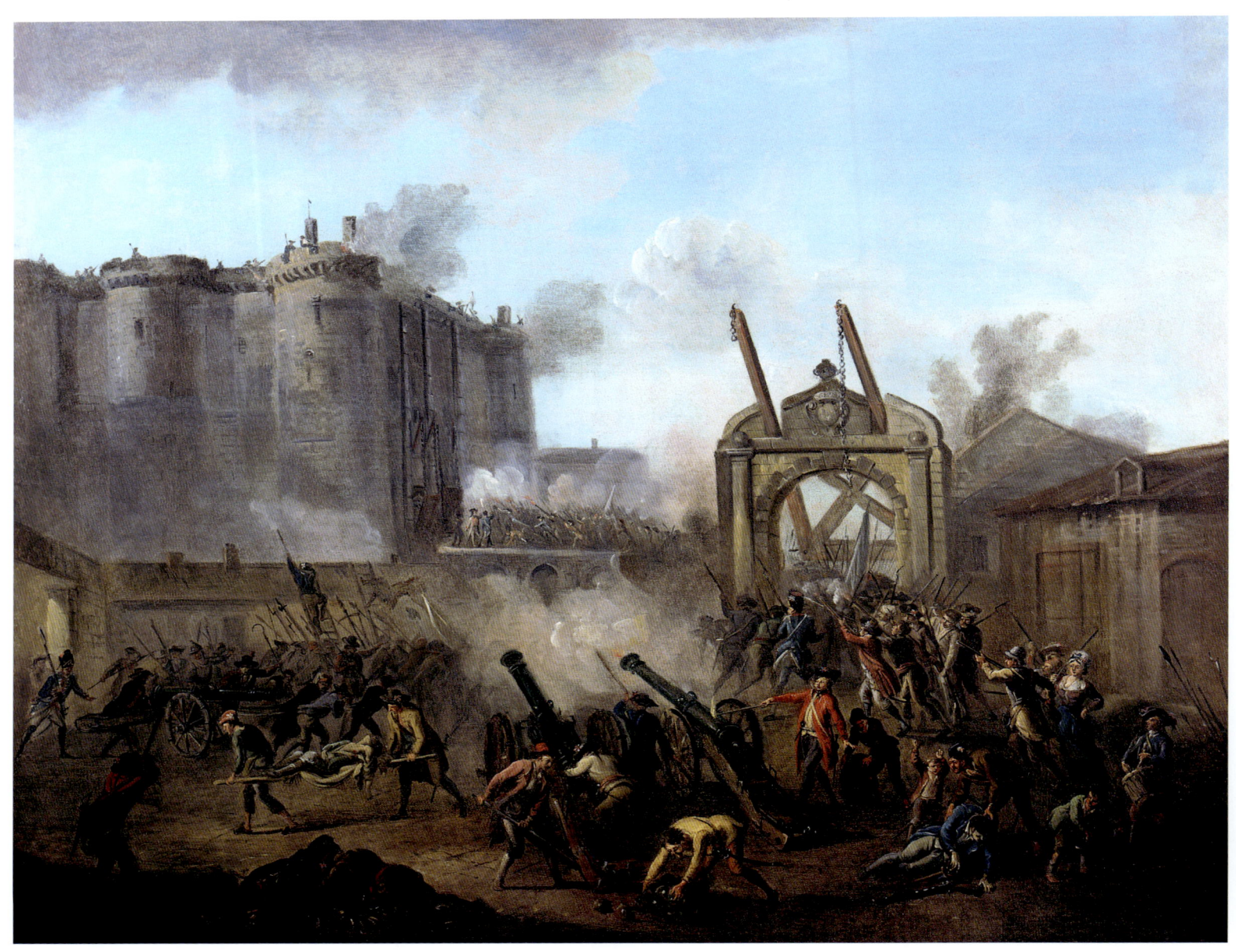

Jean-Baptiste Lallemand (1716–1803)

The Taking of the Bastille, 14th July 1789

La Prise de la Bastille, le 14 juillet 1789

Der Fall der Bastille 14. Juli 1789

La toma de la Bastilla 14 de julio 1789

La presa della Bastiglia, 14 luglio 1789

De val van de Bastille op 14 juli 1789

c. 1789, Oil on canvas/Huile sur toile, 80 × 104 cm, Musée Carnavalet, Paris

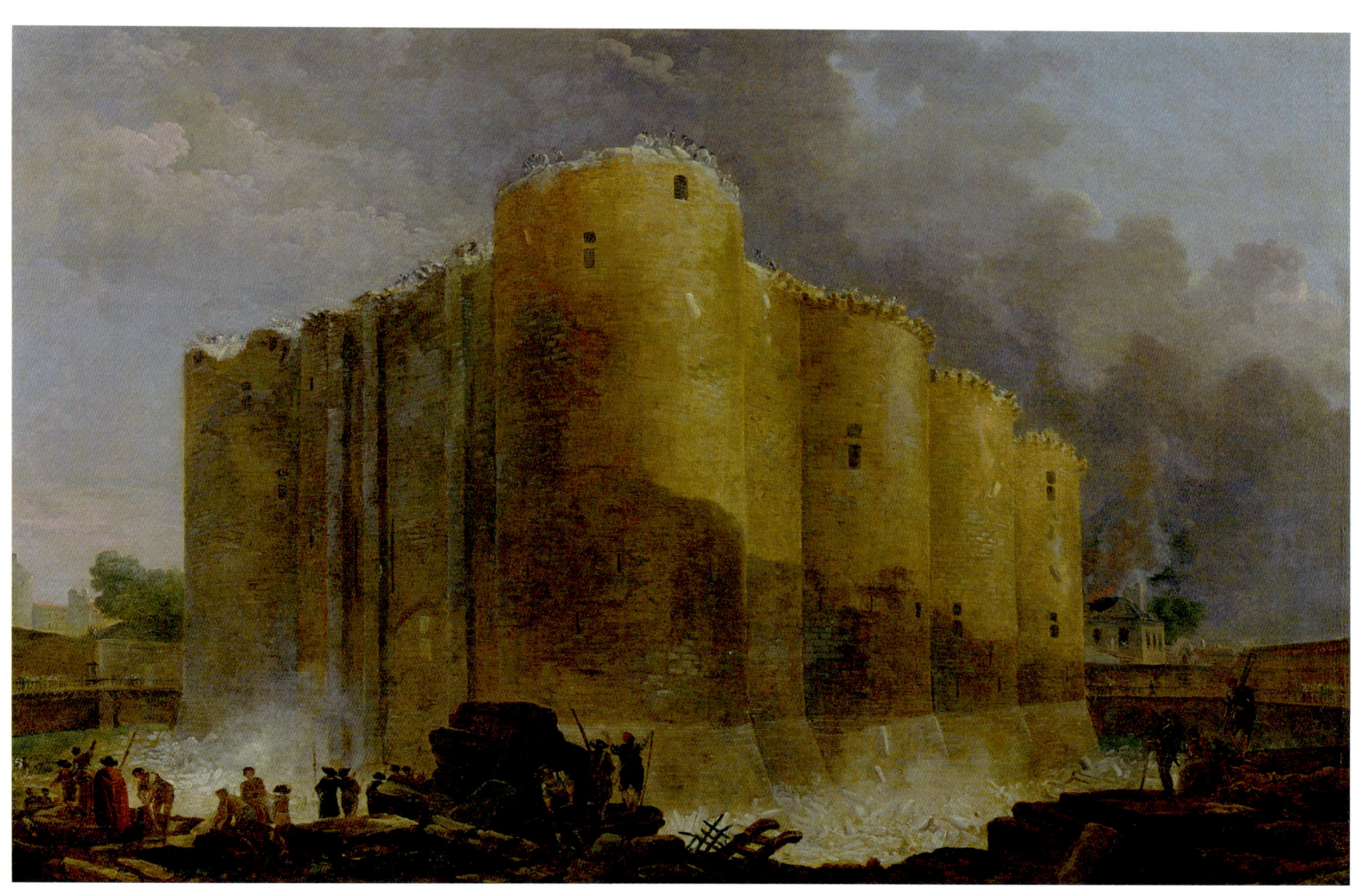

Hubert Robert (1733–1808)

Demolition of the Bastille

La Bastille dans les premiers jours de sa démolition

Der Abriss der Bastille

Demolición de la Bastilla

La demolizione della Bastiglia

De sloop van de Bastille

1789, Oil on canvas/Huile sur toile, 77 × 114 cm, Musée Carnavalet, Paris

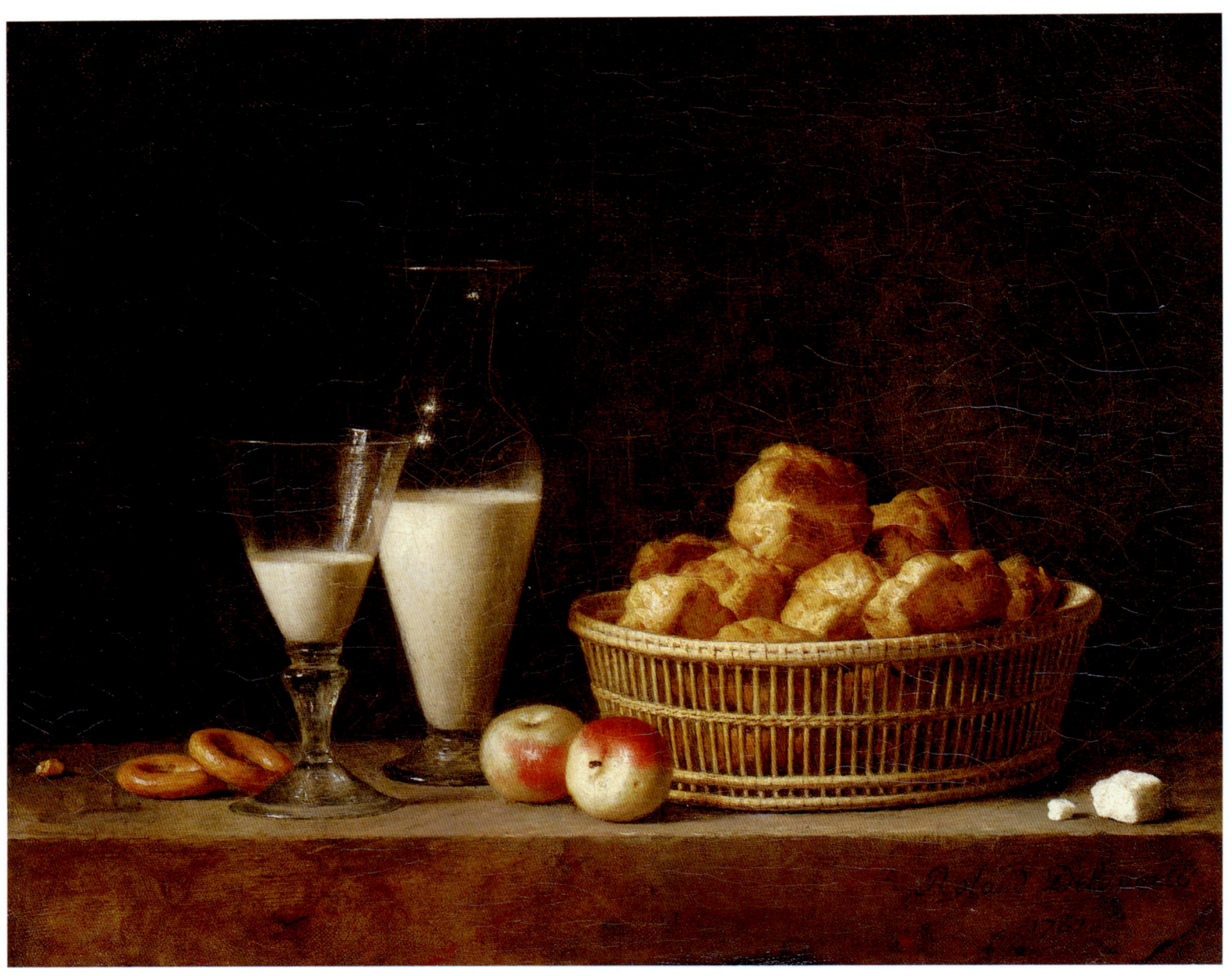

Henri-Horace Roland de la Porte (1724–1793)

The Small Collation, *or* The Carafe of Orgeat

La Petite Collation, *dit aussi* La Carafe d'orgeat

Das kleine Frühstück

El pequeño desayuno

La piccola colazione

Le petit déjeuner

1787, Oil on canvas/Huile sur toile, 37 × 46 cm, Musée du Louvre, Paris

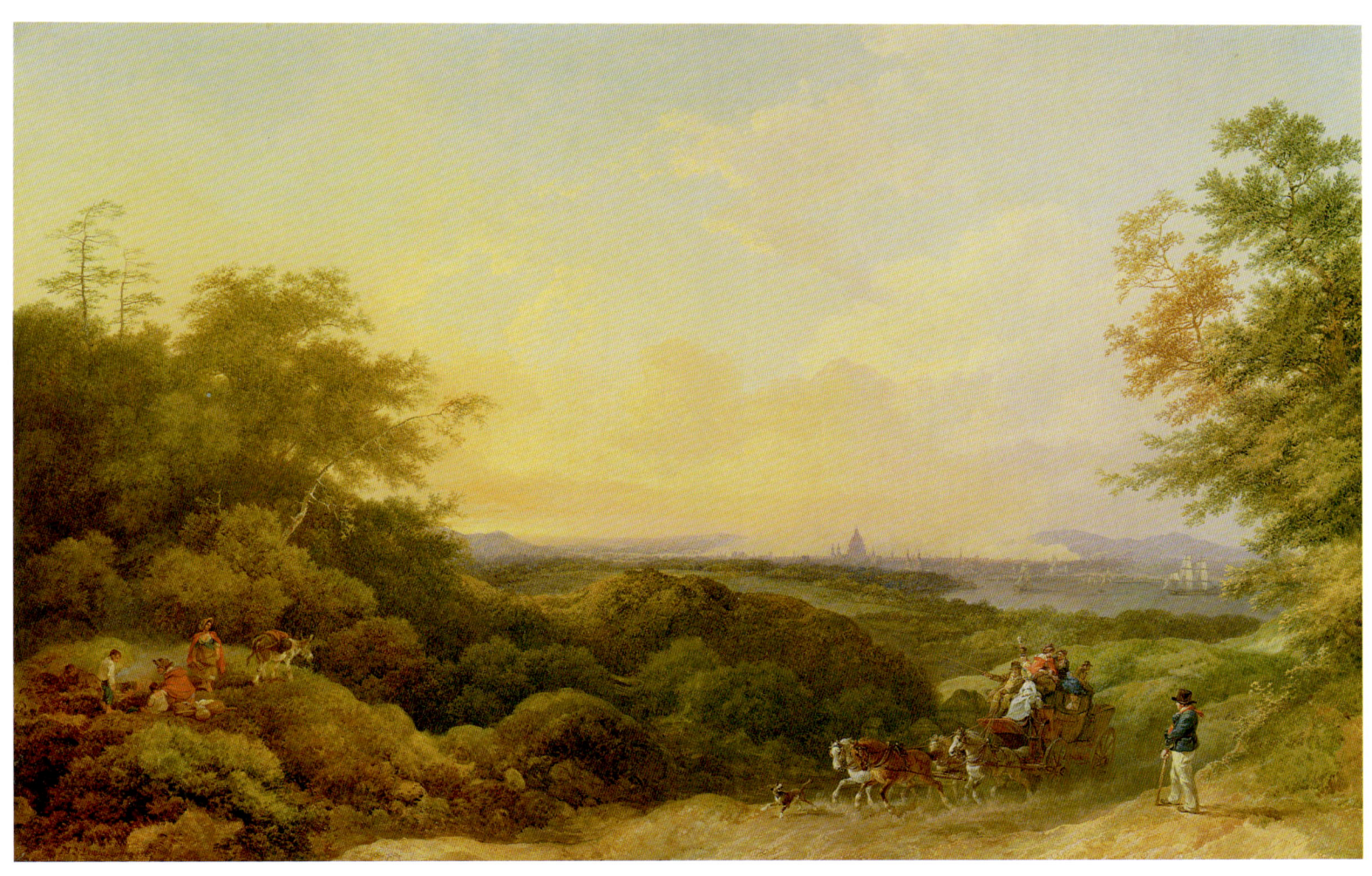

Philippe Jacques de Loutherbourg (1740–1812)

The Evening Coach, London from Greenwich

La Calèche du soir, de Londres à Greenwich

Die Abendkutsche, von London nach Greenwich

La carroza de la tarde, de Londres a Greenwich

La carrozza notturna da Londra a Greenwich

De avondkoets van Greenwich naar Londen

1805, Oil on canvas/Huile sur toile, 75 × 117 cm, Yale Center for British Art, New Haven

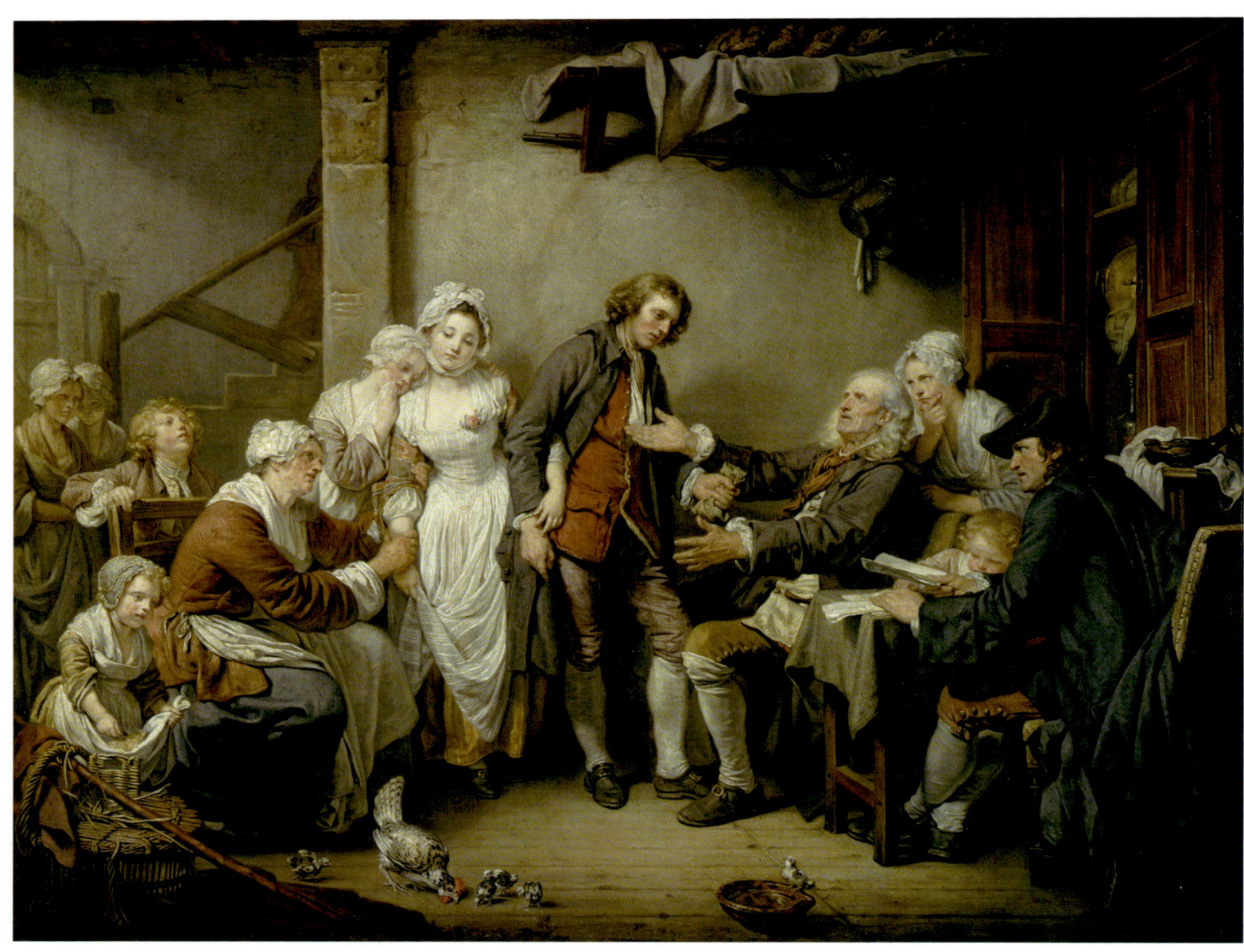

Jean-Baptiste Greuze (1725–1805)

The Village Agreement

L'Accordée de village

Die Dorfhochzeit

La boda del pueblo

Accordo di matrimonio al villaggio

De dorpsbruiloft

1761, Oil on canvas/Huile sur toile, 92 × 117 cm, Musée du Louvre, Paris

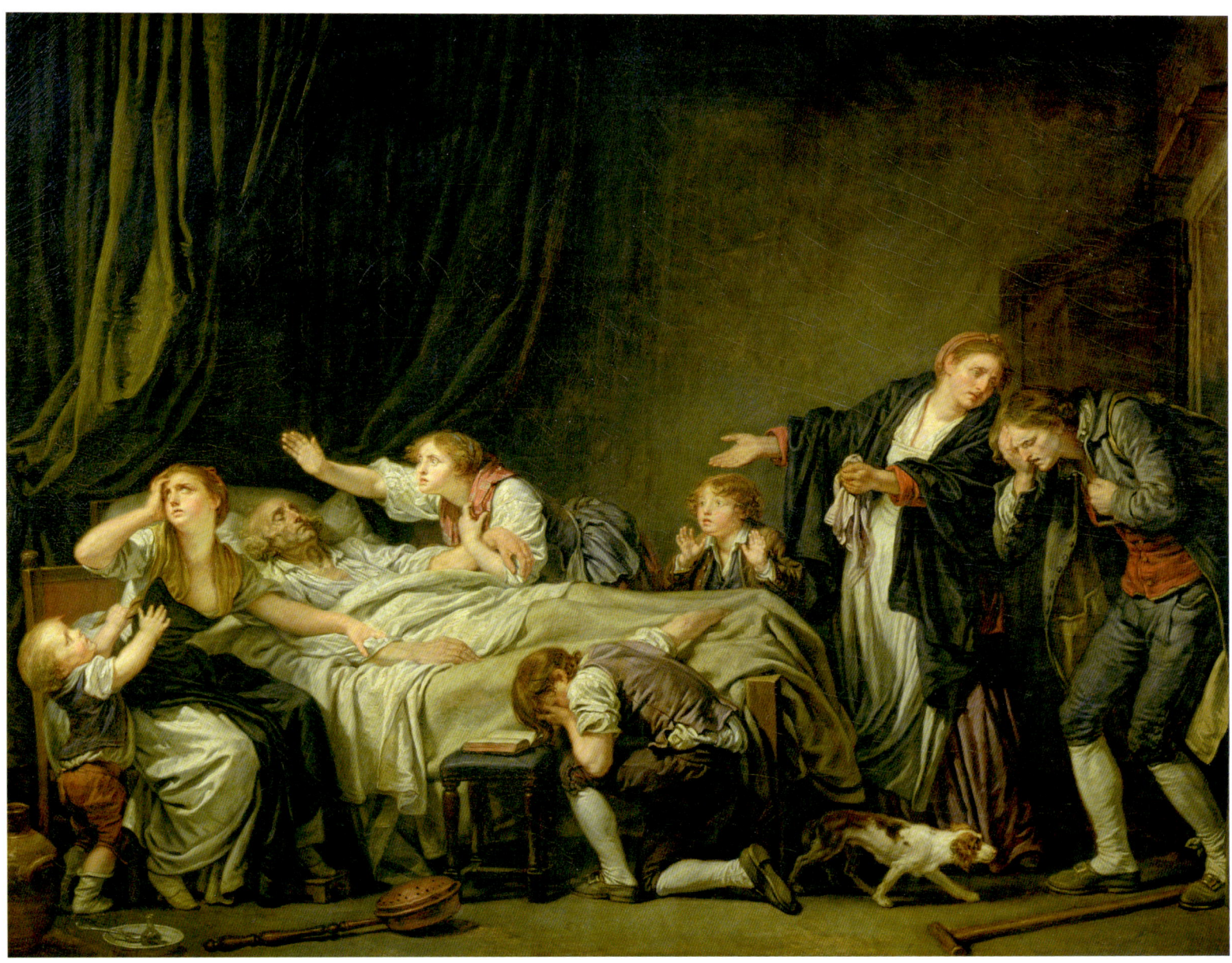

Jean Baptiste Greuze (1725–1805)

The Punished Son

Le Fils puni

Der bestrafte Sohn

El hijo castigado

Il figlio punito

De bestrafte zoon

1778, Oil on canvas/Huile sur toile, 130 × 163 cm, Musée du Louvre, Paris

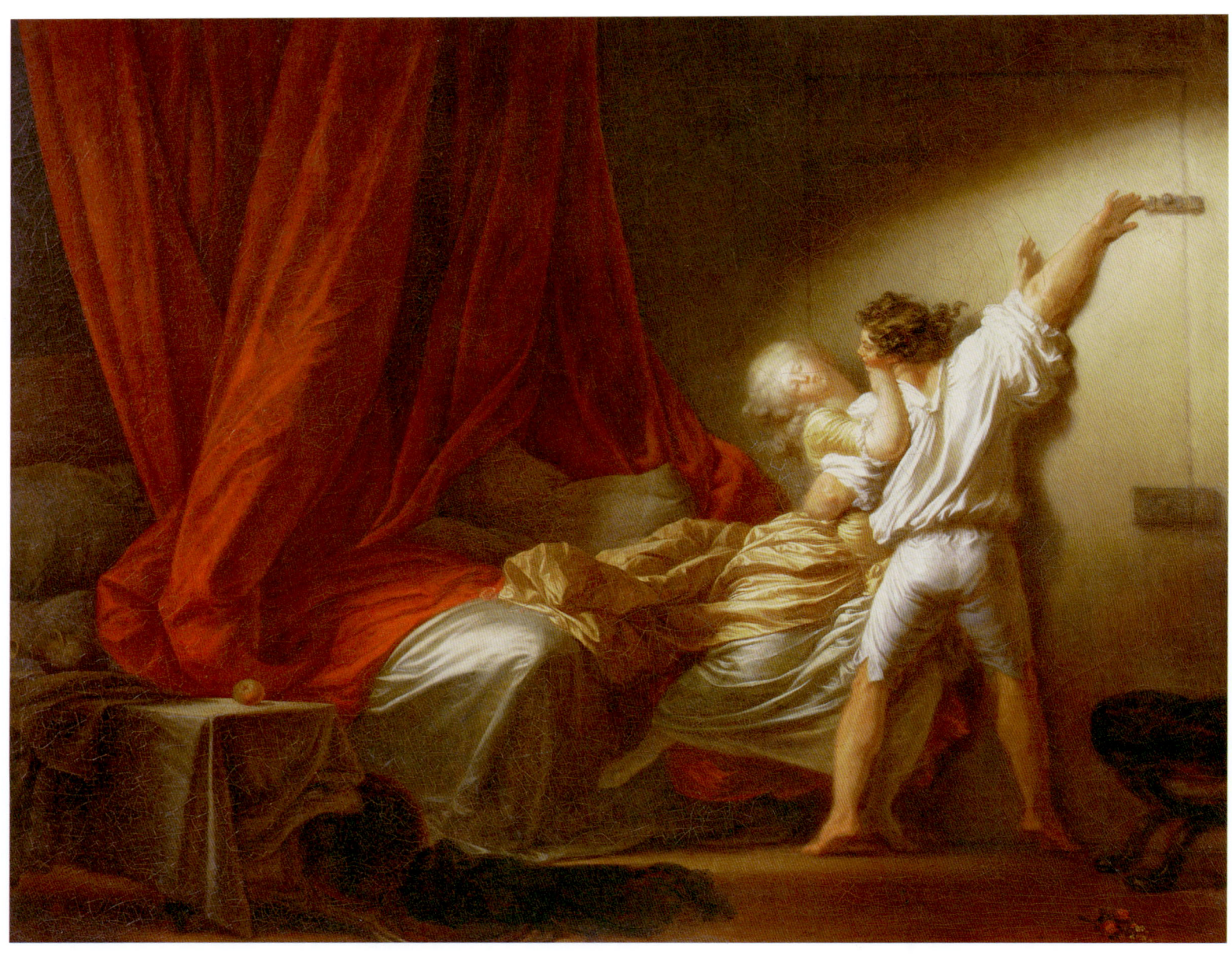

Jean-Honoré Fragonard (1732–1806)

The Bolt

Le Verrou

Der Riegel

El cerrojo

Il chiavistello

De klink

c. 1777, Oil on canvas/Huile sur toile, 74 × 94 cm, Musée du Louvre, Paris

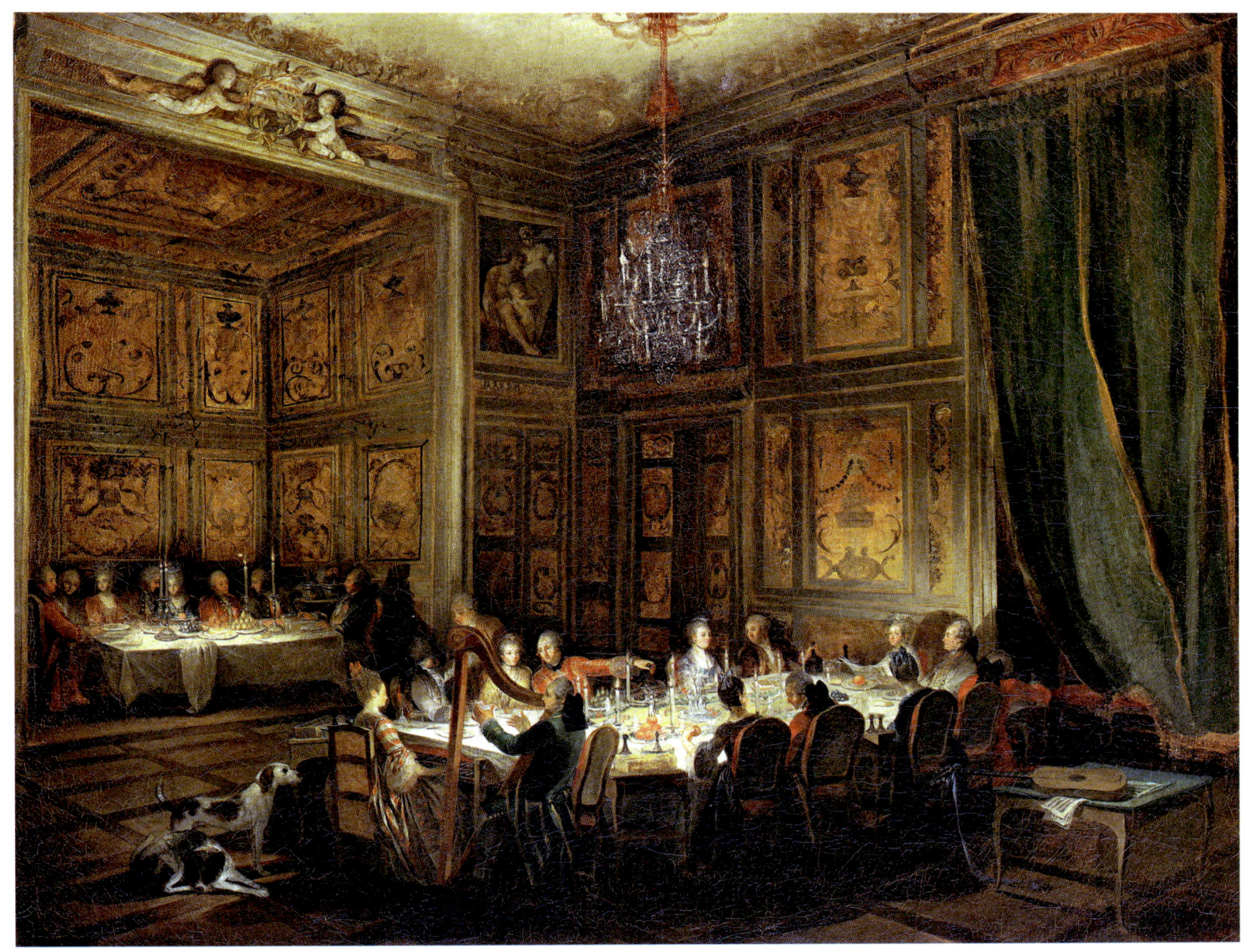

Michel Barthélemy Olivier (1712–1784)

Dinner of the Prince of Conti in the Temple

Le Souper du prince de Conti au Temple

Abendessen des Prinzen Conti im Tempel

Cena del príncipe Conti en el templo

Cena del principe di Conti nel tempio

Avondmaal van de prins van Conti in de tempel

1766, Oil on canvas/Huile sur toile, 56 × 71 cm, Château de Versailles, Versailles

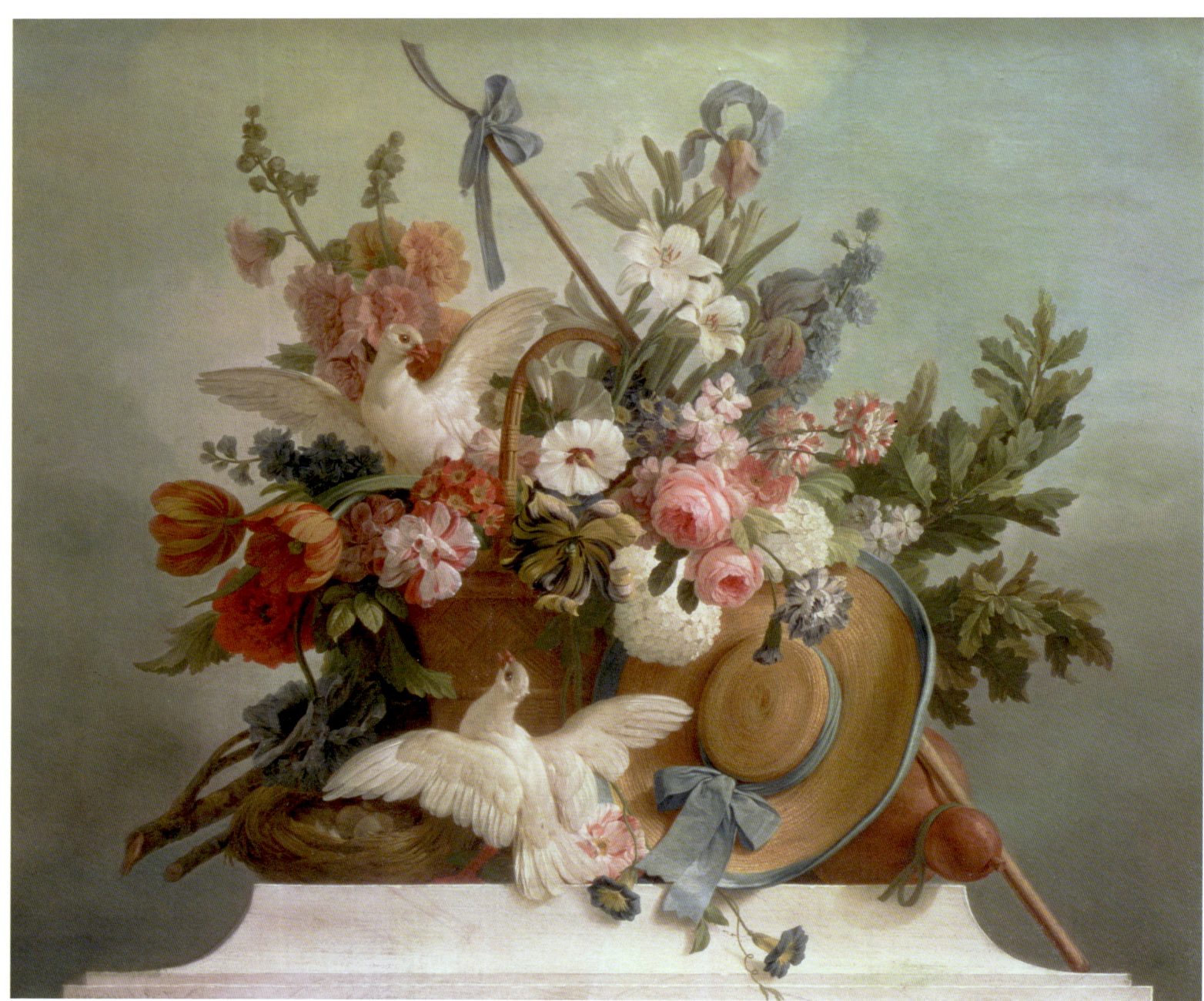

Jean-Baptiste Huet (1745–1811)

Peace	Frieden	Pace
La Paix	Paz	Vrede

1790, Oil on canvas/Huile sur toile, 112 × 131 cm, Private collection

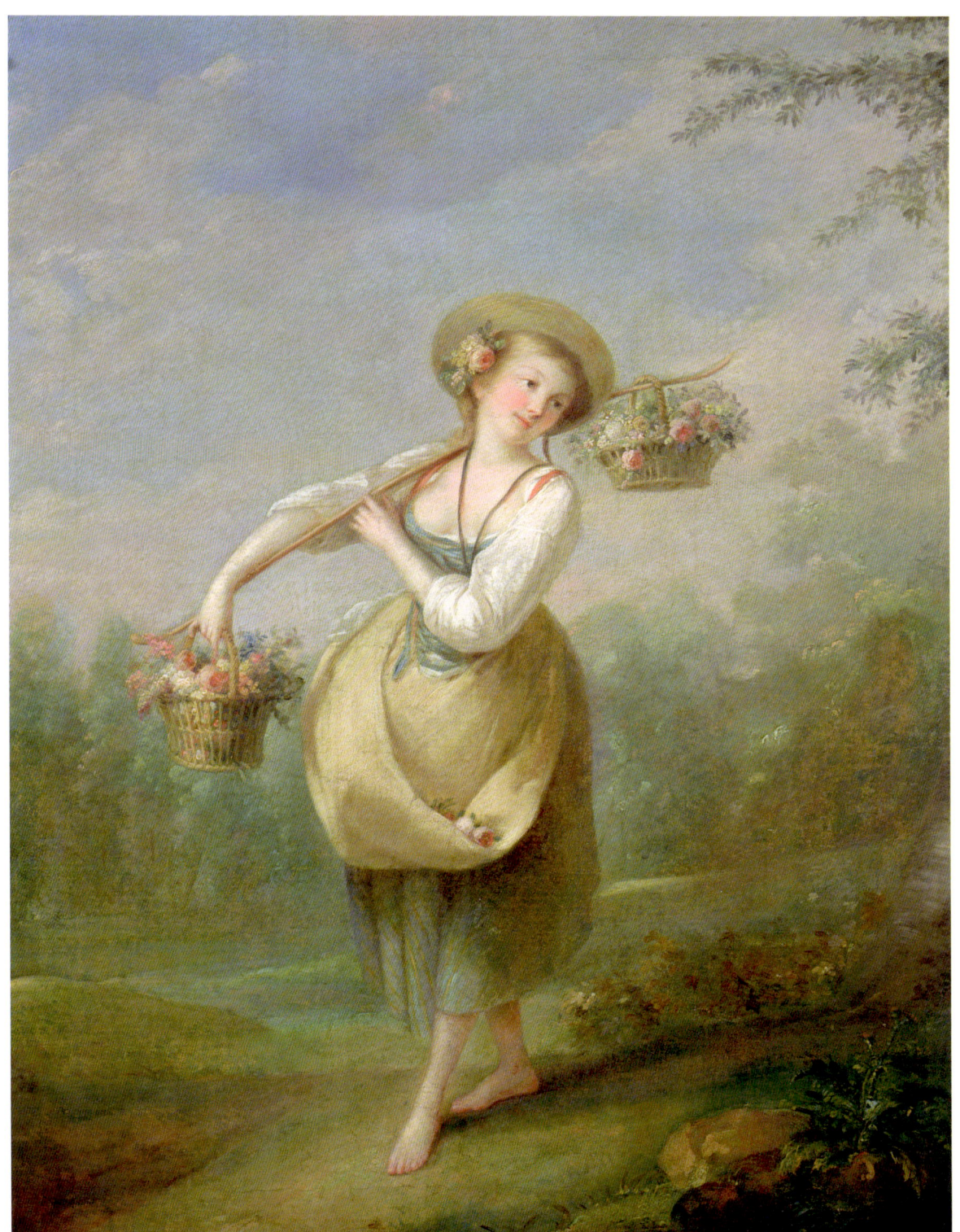

Jean-Baptiste Huet (1745–1811)

The Flower Girl

La Bouquetière

Das Blumenmädchen

La joven de las flores

La ragazza con i fiori

Het bloemenmeisje

n. d., Oil on canvas/Huile sur toile, 67,5 × 50,5 cm, Musée Cognacq-Jay, Paris

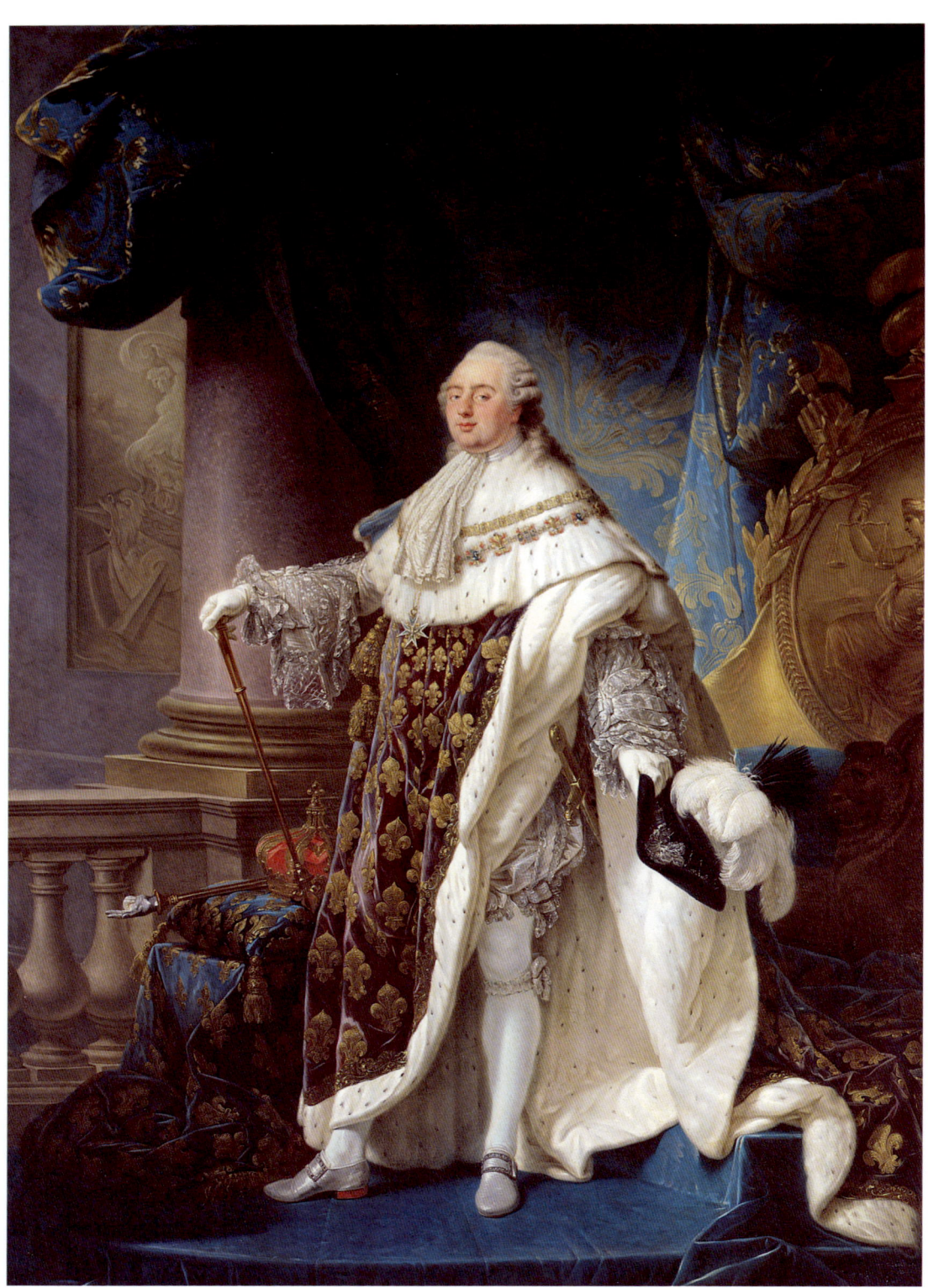

Antoine François Callet (1741–1823)

Louis XVI

Louis XVI, roi de France et de Navarre

Ludwig XVI.

Luis XVI

Luigi XVI

Lodewijk XVI

1789, Oil on canvas/Huile sur toile, 278 × 196 cm,
Château de Versailles, Versailles

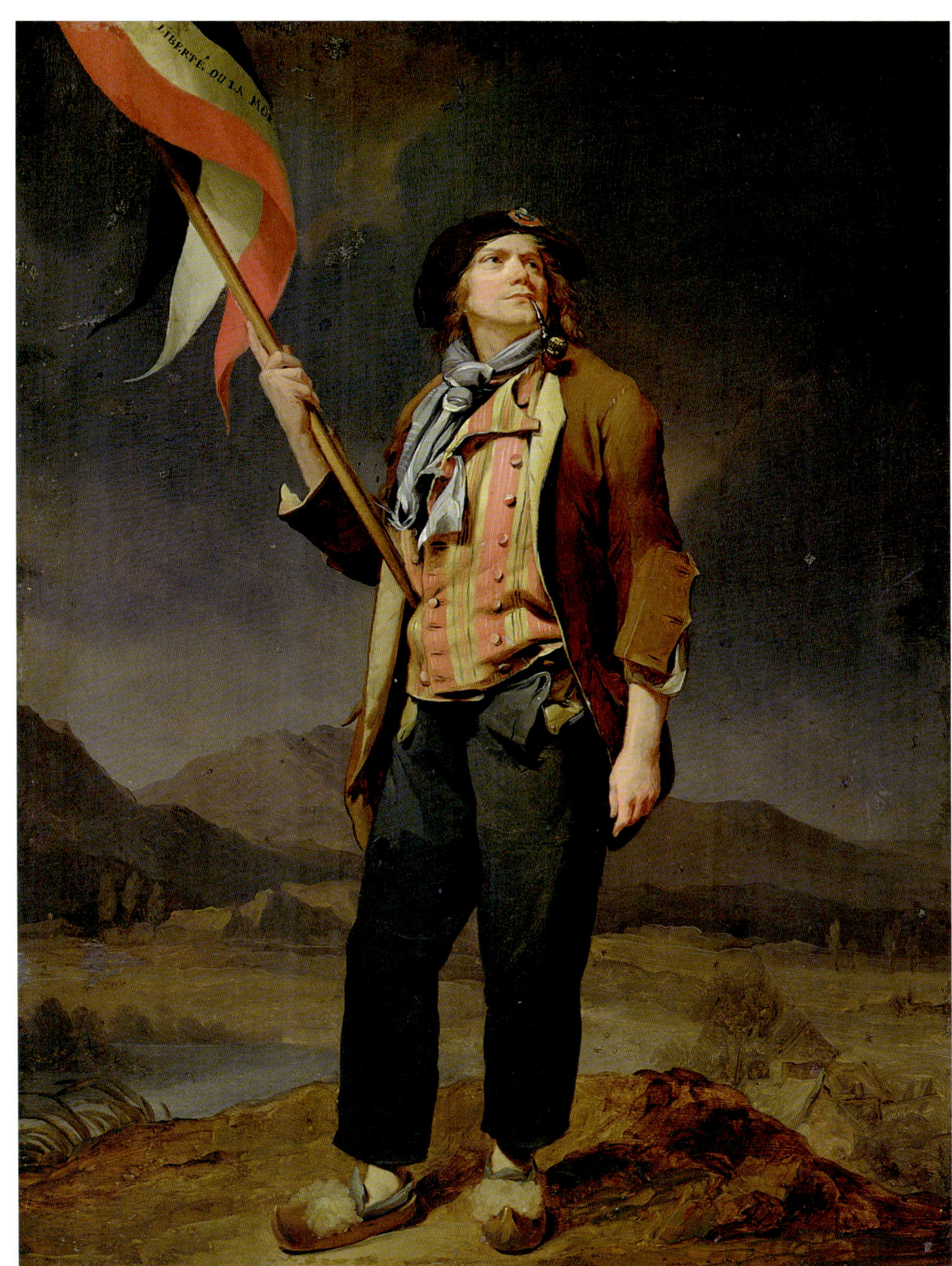

Louis Léopold Boilly (1761–1845)

The Singer Chenard, as a Sans-Culotte

Le Chanteur Simon Chenard, en costume de sans-culotte

Der Sänger Chenard als Sans-Culotte

El cantante Chenard como Sans-Culotte

Il cantante Chenard in veste di sanculotto

De zanger Chenard als sansculotte

1792, Oil on wood/Huile sur bois, 33,5 × 22,5 cm, Musée Carnavalet, Paris

FROM NEOCLASSICISM TO POST IMPRESSIONISM

DU NÉOCLASSICISME AU POSTIMPRESSIONNISME

VOM NEOKLASSIZISMUS ZUM POST-IMPRESSIONISMUS

DEL NEOCLASICISMO AL POSTIMPRESIONISMO

DAL NEOCLASSICISMO AL POST-IMPRESSIONISMO

VAN NEOCLASSICISME TOT POSTIMPRESSIONISME

Eugène Delacroix (1798–1863)

Liberty Leading the People (28 July 1830)

La Liberté guidant le peuple (28 juillet 1830)

Die Freiheit führt das Volk an (28. Juli 1830)

La Libertad guiando al pueblo (28 de julio de 1830)

La libertà che guida il popolo (28 luglio 1830)

De vrijheid voor het volk (28 juli 1830)

1830–1831, Oil on canvas/Huile sur toile, 260 × 325 cm, Musée du Louvre, Paris

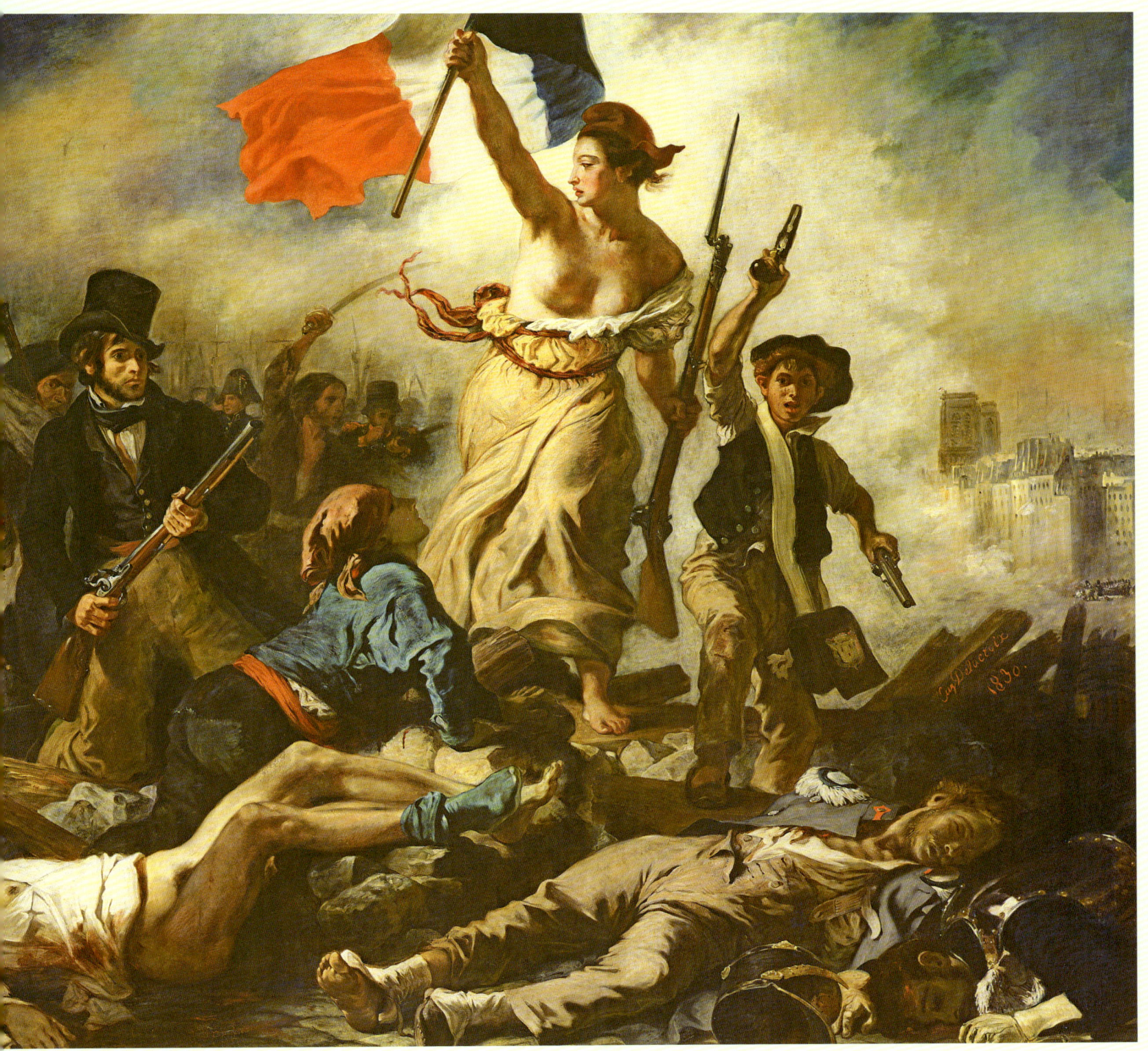

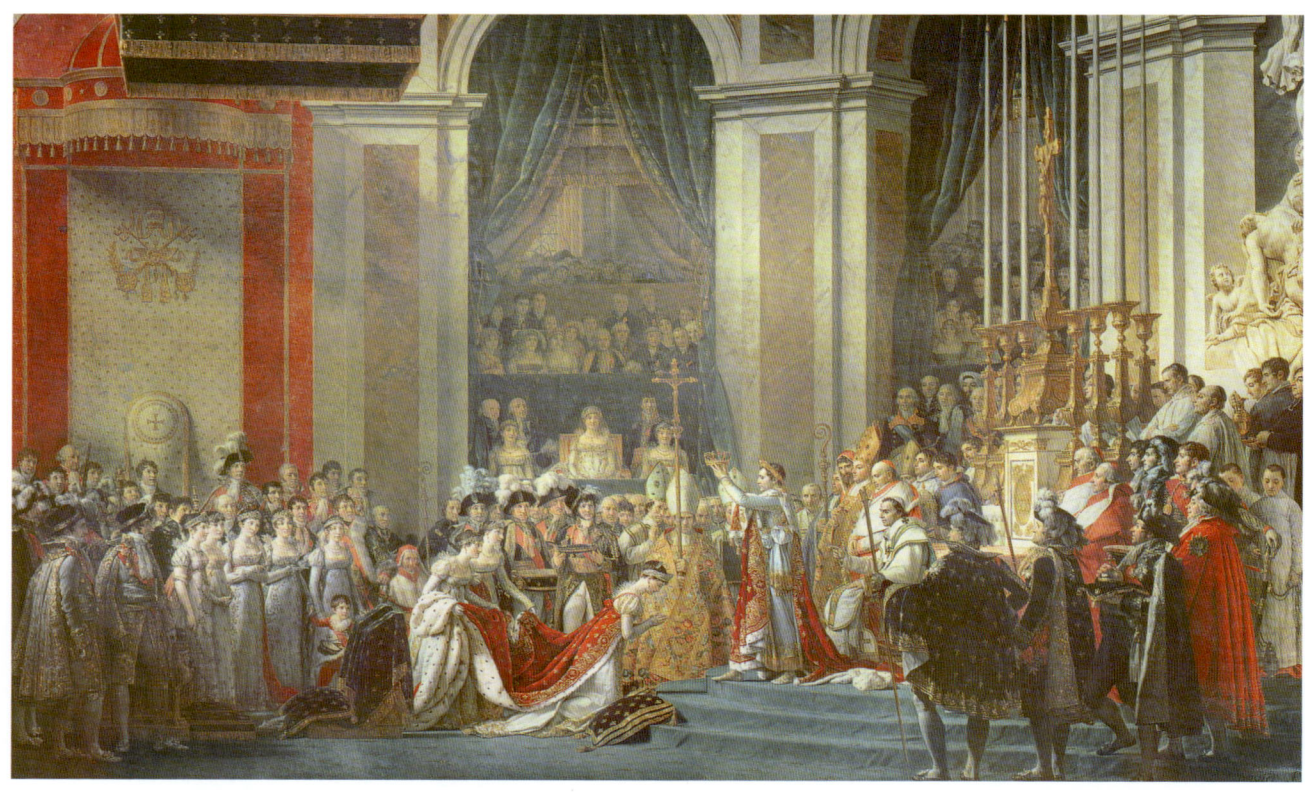

Revolt and renewal

The French Revolution and the subsequent reign of Napoleon I had far-reaching effects across the whole of Europe.

Napoleon I (Emperor from 1804) had, through the conquest of large parts of Europe, created a supremacy reminiscent of the Roman Empire. Accordingly, Roman antiquity became the model for the French arts, be it in architecture (the triumphal arches, the Victory Column at Place Vendôme, the columns of La Madeleine), in sculpture (Antonio Canova) or in painting (David). The emperor was glorified in many portraits and busts of him were exhibited. After the fall of Napoleon (1815) and the subsequent Congress of Vienna, this rearrangement was again shattered. However, the gulf between the old rulers and the new revolutionary aspirations of Europe were no

Révolte et renouveau

La Révolution française et le règne consécutif de Napoléon ont eu des effets considérables dans toute l'Europe.

Avec ses conquêtes de grandes parties de celle-ci, Napoléon Ier (empereur à partir de 1804) a constitué un empire dont l'extension évoque celle de l'*imperium romanum*. L'Antiquité romaine devient donc le modèle des arts français, qu'il s'agisse d'architecture (arcs de triomphe, colonne Vendôme, église-temple de La Madeleine), la sculpture (Antonio Canova) ou de peinture (David). La personne de l'Empereur est exaltée par des bustes et des portraits multipliés en grand nombre. Après la chute de l'Empire (1815) et le congrès de Vienne, cet ordre nouveau est jeté à bas. Mais le fossé creusé entre les anciens maîtres revenus au pouvoir et les aspirations

Revolte und Erneuerung

Die Französische Revolution und die folgende Herrschaft von Napoleon I. hatten weitreichende Nachwirkungen auf ganz Europa.

Napoleon I. (ab 1804 Kaiser) hatte durch die Eroberung weiter Teile Europas ein Reich geschaffen, das in seiner Ausdehnung an das römische Imperium erinnerte. Dementsprechend wurde die römische Antike zum Vorbild der französischen Künste, sei es in der Architektur (Triumphbögen, Siegessäule Place Vendôme, Säulenordnung La Madeleine), in der Plastik (Antonio Canova) oder in der Malerei (David). Der Kaiser wurde in vielen Porträts verherrlicht und in Büsten zur Schau gestellt. Nach dem Sturz Napoleons (1815) und dem nachfolgenden Wiener Kongress wurde diese Neuordnung wieder zerschlagen. Aber

Revuelta y renovación

La Revolución Francesa y posterior gobierno de Napoleón I tuvieron consecuencias de gran calado para toda Europa.

Napoleón I (Emperador a partir de 1804) había creado con la conquista de diversas partes de Europa un imperio que recordaba por su extensión al Imperio romano. Consecuentemente la antigua Roma se erigió en ejemplo para el arte francés, ya fuera en la arquitectura (arcos de triunfo, columna Vendôme, la columnata de la Madeleine), artes plásticas (Antonio Canova) o en la pintura (David). El Emperador fue glorificado en multitud de retratos y bustos. Tras la caída de Napoleón (1815) y el posterior Congreso de Viena este nuevo ordenamiento desapareció, pero las diferencias entre los antiguos gobernantes y el nuevo ansia revolucionaria

Rivolta e rinnovamento

La rivoluzione francese e il conseguente dominio di Napoleone I ebbero ampie ripercussioni in tutta Europa.

Napoleone I (imperatore dal 1804) grazie alla conquista di varie parti d'Europa aveva creato un impero che per la sua estensione ricordava l'Impero romano. Conformemente l'antichità romana divenne il modello delle arti francesi, che si trattasse di architettura (archi di trionfo, Colonna della Vittoria di Place Vendôme, colonnato de La Madeleine), scultura (Antonio Canova) o pittura (David). L'imperatore fu glorificato in molti ritratti e dipinto con il busto in vista. Dopo la caduta di Napoleone (1815) e il conseguente Congresso di Vienna questo nuovo ordine fu di nuovo distrutto. Ma non era più possibile superare i fossati tra gli antichi detentori del potere

Revolutie en vernieuwing

De Franse Revolutie en de daaropvolgende heerschappij van Napoleon I hadden ingrijpende gevolgen voor heel Europa.

Napoleon I (vanaf 1804 keizer) creëerde door zijn verovering van grote delen van Europa een imperium dat in zijn omvang herinnerde aan het Romeinse Rijk. De Romeinse oudheid werd dan ook een voorbeeld voor de Franse kunsten, in de architectuur (triomfbogen, de overwinningszuil op de Place Vendôme, de zuilenorde van La Madeleine), in de beeldhouwkunst (Antonio Canova) en in de schilderkunst (David). De keizer werd in talloze portretten vereeuwigd en in bustes verheerlijkt. Na de val van Napoleon in 1815 en het daaropvolgende Congres van Wenen werd Napoleons nieuwe orde ongedaan gemaakt. Maar de kloof tussen de oude machthebbers en

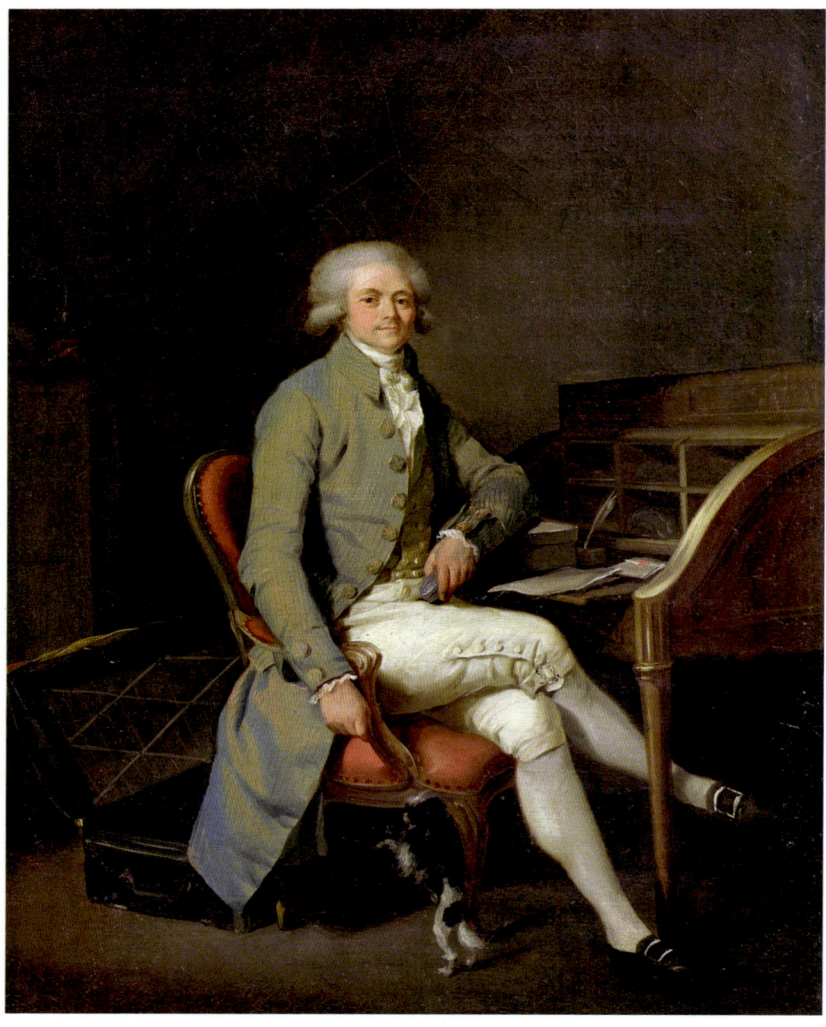

Louis Léopold Boilly (1761–1845)

Maximilien de Robespierre

c. 1791, Oil on canvas/Huile sur toile, 41 × 32 cm, Palais des Beaux-Arts, Lille

longer to be bridged, leading to deep social upheavals. Freed from the constraints of academies and without royal and ecclesiastical patronage, the artists had to turn to the public with their paintings and sculptures and trust the free market. There began a contest within the arts to win the public's favor, as well as an expansion of the old themes and motifs: art became the personal creed of the artist, whose subjects were able to explain all aspects of society. The community had, however, changed greatly under the pressure of industrialization.

progressistes nouvelles en Europe est devenu infranchissable et cette situation provoque de profondes fractures sociales. Libérés des carcans académiques, mais désormais privés des commandes ecclésiastiques et princières, les artistes se tournent vers le public pour vendre leurs tableaux et leurs sculptures sur le marché libre. Les arts commencent à se disputer les faveurs de la clientèle et de nouveaux sujets et motifs apparaissent : l'art devient proclamation de foi personnelle, dont les sujets peuvent aborder tous les domaines de la société. Or

die Gräben zwischen den alten Machthabern und den neuen revolutionären Bestrebungen in Europa waren nicht mehr zu überbrücken und führten zu tiefen gesellschaftlichen Verwerfungen. Frei von den Zwängen der Akademien und ohne die königlichen und kirchlichen Auftraggeber mussten sich die Künstler an die Öffentlichkeit wenden und ihre Bilder und Plastiken dem freien Markt anvertrauen. Es begann ein Wettstreit der Künste um die Gunst des Publikums, wie auch eine Ausweitung der alten Themen

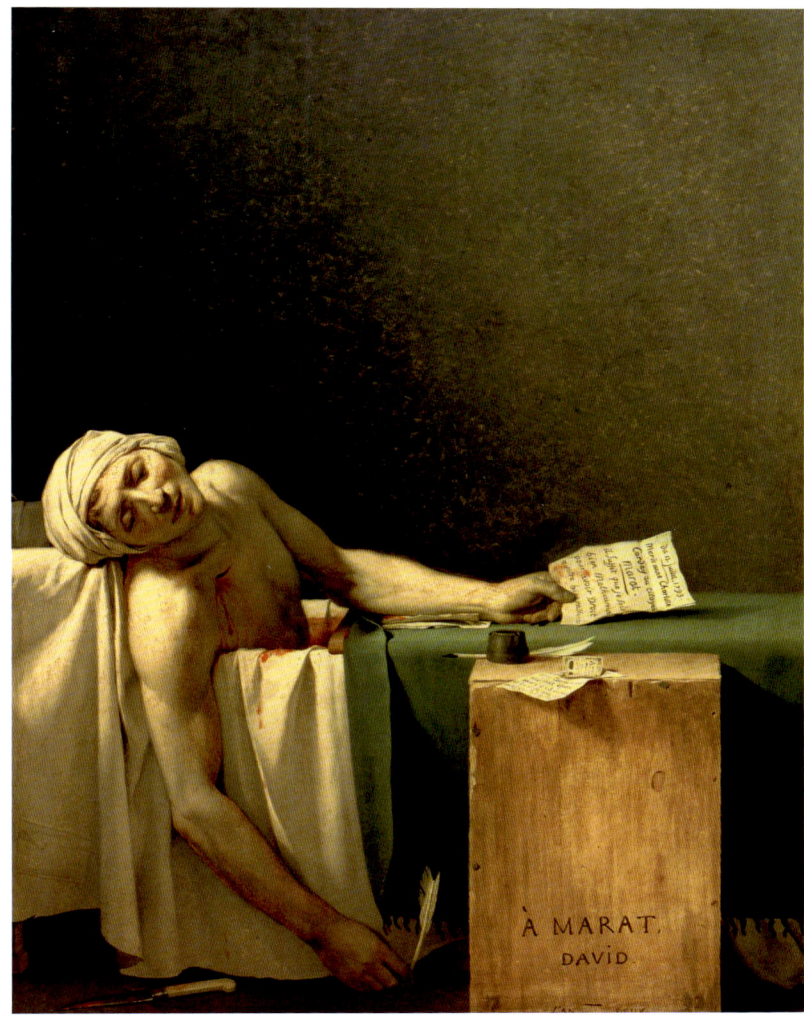

Jacques-Louis David (1748–1825)

The Death of Marat

La Mort de Marat

Der Tod des Marat

La muerte de Marat

La morte di Marat

De dood van Marat

1793, Oil on canvas/Huile sur toile, 165 × 128 cm, Musées royaux des Beaux-Arts de Belgique, Brussels

en Europa eran irreconciliables y llevaron a un importante rechazo por parte de la sociedad. Liberados del corsé académico y sin sus mecenas reales y religiosos, los artistas se dirigieron a la sociedad, confiando sus imágenes y obras al libre mercado. Comenzó entonces una competición por ganar el favor del público junto con una expansión de antiguos temas y motivos: el arte se convirtió en el particular credo del artista, y sus temas podían encontrarse en cualquier área de la vida social. La sociedad sin embargo había

e i nuovi tentativi rivoluzionari in Europa e questo portò a profonde opposizioni sociali. Liberi dalle pressioni delle accademie e senza i committenti reali ed ecclesiastici, gli artisti dovettero rivolgersi al pubblico e affidare i loro quadri e sculture al libero mercato. Cominciò una competizione delle arti per conquistare il favore del pubblico, come anche un ampliamento di vecchi temi e motivi: l'arte divenne una professione di fede personale dell'artista, i suoi temi potevano occuparsi di tutti i settori della società. La società era però

een nieuw revolutionair streven in Europa was niet meer te overbruggen en leidde tot diepe sociale schisma's. Los van de voorschriften van de academies en zonder vorstelijke en kerkelijke opdrachtgevers moesten kunstenaars zich nu tot het grote publiek wenden en hun schilderijen en beeldhouwwerken op de vrije markt brengen. Er begon een wedloop om de gunst van het publiek en ook het aantal artistieke thema's en motieven begon zich uit te breiden: kunst werd steeds meer een uiting van de persoonlijke zienswijze van de kunstenaar,

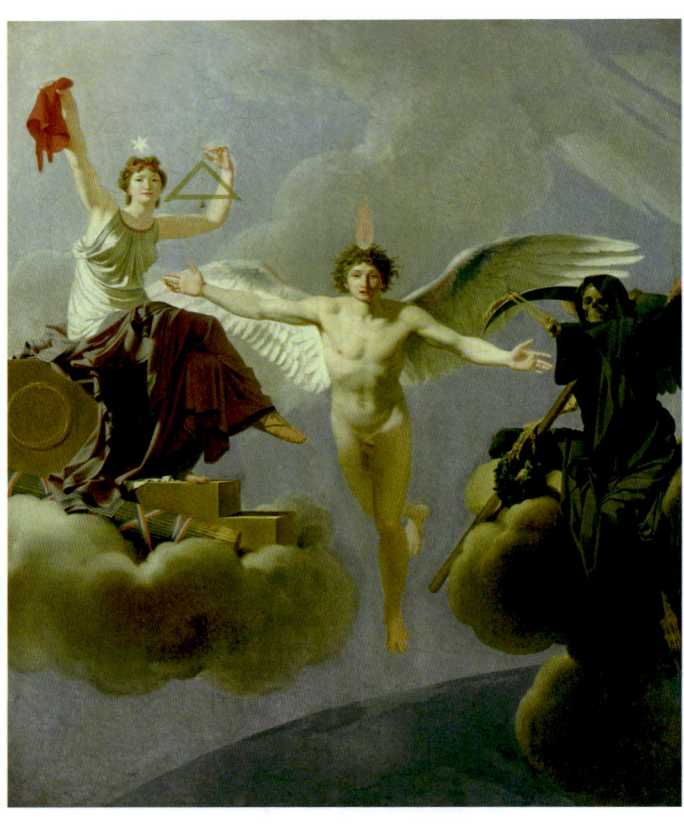

Jean-Baptiste Regnault (1754–1829)

Freedom or Death

La Liberté ou la mort

Freiheit oder Tod

La Libertad o la Muerte

Libertà o morte

Vrijheid of dood

1795, Oil on canvas/Huile sur toile, 60 × 49,3 cm, Kunsthalle, Hamburg

This was associated with the dramatic increase of urban populations and a correspondingly sharp deterioration in the living conditions of the new urban underclass of workers. Increasingly to be seen was the desire for social and political reform. Nevertheless, the established layers of society refused to abandon their traditional privileges and set against this development with considerable resistance.

This unresolved political tension inevitably led to outbreaks of violence and riots throughout Europe, which were usually bloodily suppressed. In France, following the Revolution of 1848, Louis Bonaparte came to power, ruling from 1852 onwards as Emperor Napoleon III. He introduced a strictly authoritarian regime and had all of Paris

celle-ci s'était profondément modifiée, sous la pression de l'industrialisation.

À cela s'ajoute un accroissement dramatique des populations citadines, accompagné d'une dégradation drastique des conditions de vie d'une nouvelle classe urbaine inférieure, celle des ouvriers. La demande de réformes sociales et politiques se fait ainsi de plus en plus forte. Les classes supérieures de la société, bien établies, refusent évidemment de remettre en cause leurs privilèges et opposent à cette évolution une résistance opiniâtre.

Ces tensions politiques et sociales non résolues conduisent inévitablement à des explosions de violences et des révoltes dans toute l'Europe. En France, après l'échec de la révolution républicaine de 1848, Louis Napoléon Bonaparte s'empare du pouvoir

und Motive: Kunst wurde zum persönlichen Glaubensbekenntnis des Künstlers, seine Themen konnten sich mit sämtlichen Bereiche der Gesellschaft auseinandersetzen. Die Gesellschaft hatte sich aber unter dem Druck der Industrialisierung stark verändert. Damit verbunden war ein dramatischer Anstieg der Stadtbevölkerung mit einer drastischen Verschlechterung der Lebensbedingungen der neuen städtischen Unterschicht, der Arbeiter. Immer stärker wurde das Verlangen nach sozialen und politischen Reformen. Die etablierten Schichten der Gesellschaft weigerten sich jedoch, ihre traditionellen Privilegien aufzugeben und setzen dieser Entwicklung erheblichen Widerstand entgegen. Diese politisch nicht umgesetzte Spannung führte unweigerlich zu Gewaltausbrüchen

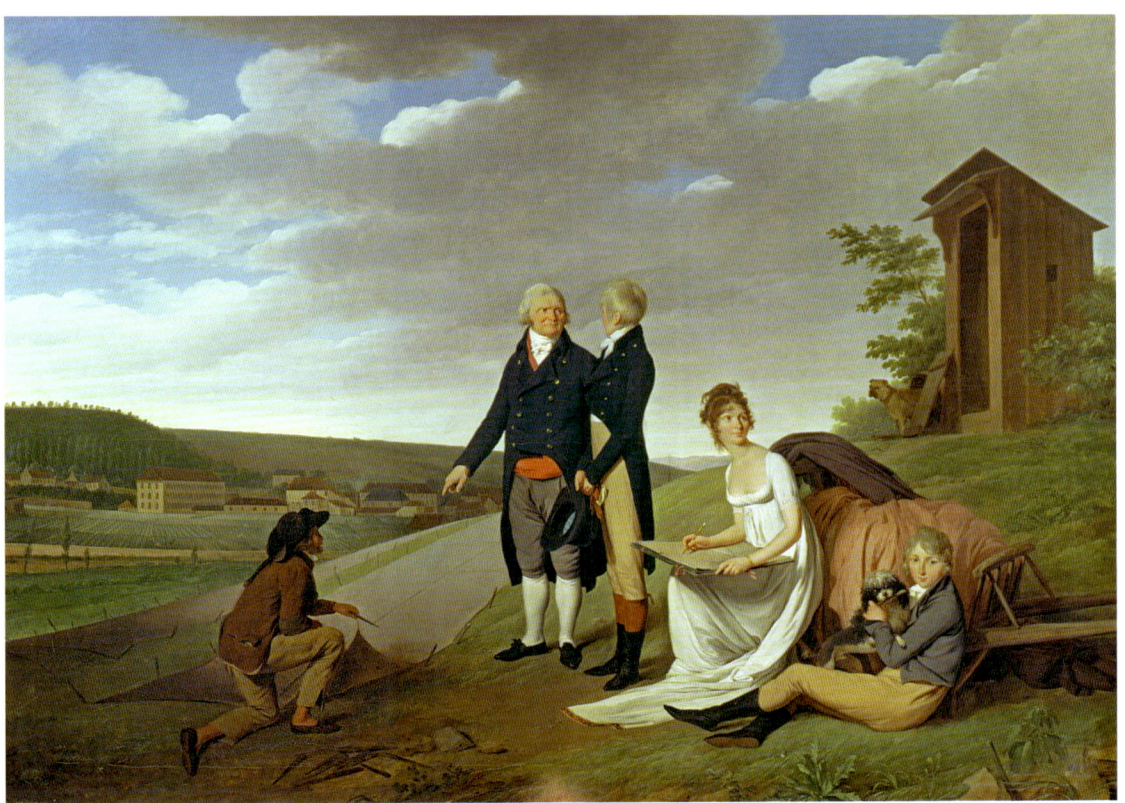

cambiado de manera acusada bajo las presiones de la industrialización.

Con esta había llegado un dramático aumento de la población en las ciudades, con el consiguiente empeoramiento de la calidad de vida de la nueva clase baja de las ciudades, los trabajadores. El deseo de reformas políticas y sociales fue cada vez mayor. Las clases más establecidas de la sociedad sin embargo se negaron a renunciar a sus tradicionales privilegios y presentaron una dura oposición a esta evolución.

Esta tensión, que no encontraba resolución política, llevó irremediablemente a episodios de violencia y revueltas en toda Europa, que fueron a su vez sangrientamente reprimidas. En Francia Louis Bonaparte asumió el poder tras la Revolución de 1848, como emperador

profondamente cambiata sotto la pressione dell'industrializzazione.

Perciò l'aumento drammatico della popolazione urbana era legato ad un drastico peggioramento delle condizioni di vita del nuovo ceto inferiore delle città, i lavoratori. Vi era una richiesta sempre più forte di riforme sociali e politiche. I ceti affermati della società si rifiutarono però di rinunciare ai loro privilegi tradizionali e opposero una notevole resistenza a questo sviluppo.

Questa tensione non trovò sbocco in politica e causò immancabilmente scoppi di violenza e rivolte in tutta Europa, che furono però repressi nel sangue. In Francia dopo la Rivoluzione del 1848 prese il potere Luigi Bonaparte, che dal 1852 introdusse un regime fortemente autoritario come Imperatore

die zich in zijn of haar motieven met een breed scala van maatschappelijke onderwerpen kon bezighouden. Maar die maatschappij was onder druk van de industriële revolutie ingrijpend veranderd.

Er deed zich een dramatische toename van de stedelijke bevolking voor, en daarmee een drastische verslechtering van de leefomstandigheden van de nieuwe stedelijke onderlaag, de arbeider. Steeds sterker klonk de roep om sociale en politieke hervormingen. Maar de gevestigde machten weigerden om hun bevoorrechte positie op te geven en verzetten zich verbeten tegen deze ontwikkelingen.

Spanningen die nog geen politieke uitlaatklep hadden gevonden, leidden onontkoombaar tot uitbarstingen van geweld en revoltes in heel Europa, die echter bloedig

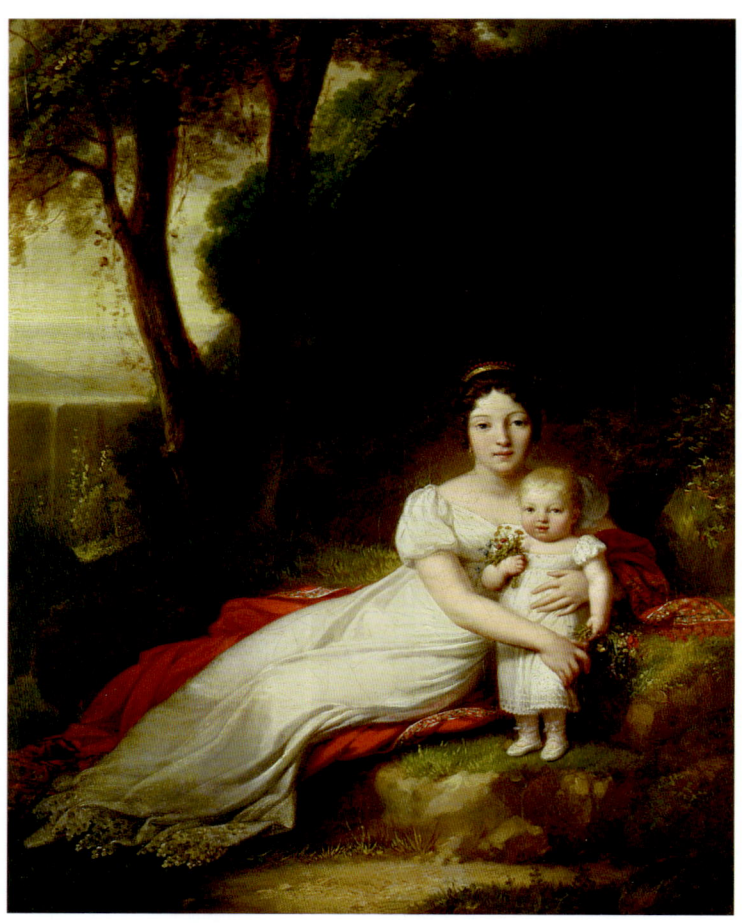

rebuilt under Baron Haussmann, in order to better control any rioting. The revolutions in the German Confederation failed, whilst in Italy there were calls for democratic reforms, with the goal of national unification.

The dissatisfaction with the political and social conditions allowed criticism in many areas to grow loud, as an increased awareness developed of the social problems brought by the unequal distribution of wealth, which was illustrated by the deep gulf existing between the splendor of the bourgeoisie and the miserable lives of the working class. Charles Baudelaire challenged the artists to represent the "heroism of modern

et devient empereur en 1852 sous le nom de Napoléon III, à la tête d'un régime autoritaire et répressif. Une grande partie de Paris est reconstruite afin de mieux pouvoir contrôler les soulèvements dans la capitale. Les révolutions échouent en Allemagne et en Italie, où elles associent les demandes de réformes démocratiques à des exigences de création d'États nationaux.

L'insatisfaction relative aux conditions politiques et sociales provoque de violentes critiques dans de nombreux domaines, avec la conscience de plus en plus vive des problèmes sociaux : répartition injuste des richesses, gouffre choquant entre le prestige

und Revolten in ganz Europa, die allerdings blutig niedergeschlagen wurden. In Frankreich kam nach der Revolution von 1848 Louis Bonaparte an die Macht, der ab 1852 als Kaiser Napoleon III. ein streng autoritäres Regime einführte und ganz Paris von Baron Haussmann umbauen ließ, um Aufstände besser kontrollieren zu können. Ebenso scheiterten die Revolutionen im Deutschen Bund und in Italien, die Forderungen nach demokratischen Reformen mit den Zielen nationalstaatlicher Einigung verbanden. Die Unzufriedenheit mit den politischen und gesellschaftlichen Zuständen ließ in vielen Bereichen Kritik laut werden, und es

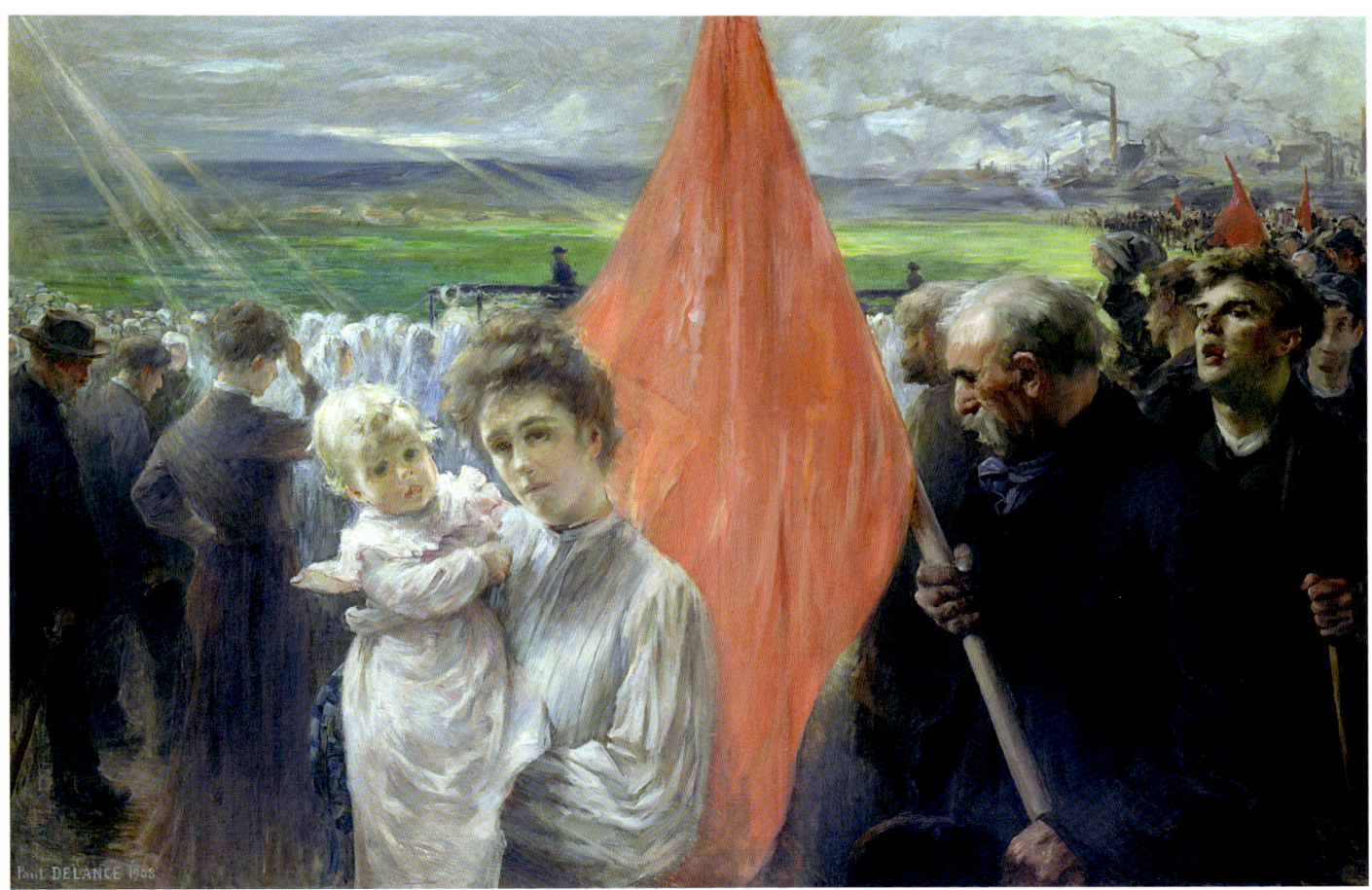

Napoleón III a partir de 1852, e introdujo
un estricto régimen autoritario a la vez que
encargó al Barón Haussmann la renovación de
París para poder controlar mejor las revueltas.
También fracasaron las revueltas en Italia y la
Confederación Germánica, que tenían como
meta además de las reformas democráticas la
unificación nacional.

El descontento con la situación política y
social hizo que las críticas en muchas áreas
fueran evidentes; se desarrolló una consciencia
creciente de los problemas sociales, la desigual
distribución de los bienes, la enorme brecha
entre la suntuosidad de la burguesía y el horror
de la clase trabajadora. Charles Baudelaire

Napoleone III e fece restaurare l'intera Parigi
dal Barone Haussmann, per poter meglio
controllare le sommosse. Allo stesso modo le
rivoluzioni nella Confederazione germanica
e in Italia fallirono nel collegare le richieste
di riforme democratiche con gli obiettivi di
unificazione nazionalistica.L'insoddisfazione
per le condizioni politiche e sociali causò forti
critiche in molti ambiti, e si sviluppò in una
crescente consapevolezza per i problemi sociali,
l'ingiusta distribuzione dei beni, la profonda
spaccatura tra lo splendore della borghesia
e la miseria della classe lavoratrice. Charles
Baudelaire sfidò gli artisti a rappresentare

werden neergeslagen. Na de revolutie van 1848
kwam in Frankrijk Lodewijk Napoleon aan
de macht, die vanaf 1852 als keizer Napoleon
III een autoritair regime leidde en heel Parijs
liet herinrichten door baron Haussmann,
om eventuele oproeren beter te kunnen
controleren. Ook in de Duitse Bond en Italië
mislukten deze revoluties, waarin de roep om
democratische hervormingen samenviel met
het nationalistische streven naar eenwording.

De onvrede met de politieke en sociale
situatie leidde op talloze gebieden tot kritiek,
waarbij zich een steeds scherper bewustzijn
voor maatschappelijke problemen ontwikkelde,
voor de onrechtvaardige verdeling van de

life", instead of continuing to follow in the traditions of art.

In literature, philosophy and art, Romanticism brought about a radical upheaval. Instead of looking towards the worlds of antiquity for cultural inspiration, they turned to the present and developed an individual and intense feeling for nature, which was expressed by an emphasis on color. The revolutionary changes in the industrial, social and economic fields led to an extensive artistic freedom, which allowed passionate experiments with color and form to arise, eventually leading to an artistic movement with far-reaching international importance, namely impressionism.

The impressionists were interested not only in the appearance of objects in the changing light, but also in the discovery and perception of new metropolitan themes, such as the discovery of the concept of leisure time in the picturesque suburbs of Paris

The idea of a comprehensive renewal of not only artistic, but also social structures inspired the art nouveau of around 1900, with the goal of unifying all design areas. From here onwards, the path of art led to the radical '-isms' of the of the 20th century, which would break with all previous styles to rely only on the autonomy of the art and the creativity of the individual.

de la bourgeoisie aisée et la misère des classes laborieuses. Charles Baudelaire exhorte les artistes à représenter l'« héroïsme de la vie moderne », au lieu de continuer à perpétuer les traditions routinières de l'art.

En littérature, en art et en philosophie, le romantisme marque une rupture : au lieu de chercher dans le monde éteint de l'Antiquité des modèles pour rendre compte des réalités culturelles du moment, on se tourne vers le présent et on développe un sentiment de la Nature puissant et individuel, qui s'exprime dans l'accentuation du coloris. Les bouleversements révolutionnaires dans les domaines de la société, de l'industrie et du commerce conduisent ainsi à une plus grande liberté artistique et font naître des expérimentations passionnées sur les formes et les couleurs – qui finissent par déboucher sur un mouvement artistique de vaste portée internationale : l'impressionnisme.

Les impressionnistes ne s'intéressent pas seulement à l'apparence des choses en fonction de lumières changeantes, mais aussi à la découverte et à la perception de nouveaux sujets dans la grande ville et – en complément – à la représentation du temps libre dans les faubourgs et les banlieues pittoresques de Paris.

La conception d'un renouveau global, non seulement artistique mais aussi social, conduit vers 1900 l'Art nouveau à une unité souhaitée de tous les domaines de création. De là, la suite du parcours de l'art mène à la radicalité des nombreux « -ismes » du xxᵉ siècle, lesquels rompent résolument avec tous les styles antérieurs et ne se fondent plus que sur l'autonomie revendiquée de l'art et de l'individu créatif.

entwickelte sich ein wachsendes Bewusstsein für die gesellschaftlichen Probleme, die ungerechte Verteilung der Güter, die tiefe Kluft zwischen dem Glanz der Bürgertums und dem Elend der Arbeiterklasse. Charles Baudelaire forderte die Künstler heraus, den „Heroismus des modernen Lebens" darzustellen anstatt den Traditionen der Kunst weiterhin zu folgen. In der Literatur, Philosophie und Kunst bewirkte die Romantik einen Umbruch. Anstatt in der vergangenen Welt der Antike Vorbilder für die kulturelle Gestaltung zu suchen, wandte man sich der Gegenwart zu und entwickelte ein individuelles und intensives Naturgefühl, das sich auch in der Betonung der Farbe ausdrückte. Die revolutionären Veränderungen auf industriellem, sozialem und wirtschaftlichem Gebiet führten zu einer weitgehenden künstlerischen Freiheit und ließen leidenschaftliche Experimente mit Farbe und Form aufkommen, die schließlich zu einer künstlerischen Bewegung mit weitreichender internationaler Bedeutung führten: dem Impressionismus.

Das Interesse der Impressionisten galt aber nicht allein der Erscheinung der Gegenstände im wechselnden Licht, sondern auch der Entdeckung und Wahrnehmung neuer großstädtischer Motive, wie auch als Ergänzung dazu der Entdeckung der Freizeit in den malerischen Vororten von Paris. Der Gedanke einer umfassenden, nicht nur künstlerischen, sondern gesellschaftlichen Erneuerung bewegte den Jugendstil um 1900 mit dem Ziel einer Einheit aller Gestaltungsbereiche. Von hier aus führt der weitere Weg der Kunst in die Radikalität der Ismen des 20. Jahrhunderts, die mit allen vorhergegangenen Stilen brechen und sich nur noch auf die Autonomie der Kunst und des schöpferischen Individuums stützen.

retó a los artistas a captar "el heroísmo de la vida moderna" en vez de perpetuar tradiciones artísticas.

En la literatura, la filosofía y el arte el Romanticismo supuso una ruptura. En vez de buscar ejemplos para la concepción artística en el mundo pasado de la Antigüedad se volvió al presente y se desarrolló un sentido del naturalismo individual e intenso, que se expresó por medio de acentos cromáticos. Los cambios revolucionarios en lo social, industrial y económico llevaron a una gran libertad artística y permitieron la creación de apasionados experimentos de color y forma, que llevarían en última instancia a un movimiento de importancia y significación internacionales: el impresionismo.

El interés de los impresionistas no solo se centraba en la apariencia de los objetos bajo la luz cambiante, sino también en el descubrimiento y percepción de nuevos motivos en la gran ciudad, así como la pintura al aire libre en los alrededores de París.

El concepto de una renovación profunda, no solo artística sino social, impulsó al *Art Noveau* alrededor del cambio de siglo, con su objetivo de una unificación de todas las disciplinas. A partir de aquí el camino del arte llevó a la radicalidad de los -ismos en el XX que rompieron con todos los estilos previos, apoyándose tan solo en la autonomía del arte y del sujeto creador.

"l'eroismo della vita moderna", invece di seguire ancora le tradizioni dell'arte.

In letteratura, filosofia e arte il romanticismo causò un cambiamento radicale. Invece di cercare modelli per la forma culturale nel mondo passato dell'antichità, ci si rivolse al presente sviluppando un senso della natura individuale e intenso, che si esprimeva anche nell'accentuazione del colore. I cambiamenti rivoluzionari in campo industriale, sociale ed economico favorirono un'ampia libertà artistica e causarono esperimenti appassionati con il colore e la forma, che alla fine diedero origine ad un movimento artistico di grande portata internazionale: l'Impressionismo.

L'interesse degli impressionisti non era soltanto la visione degli oggetti nella luce mutevole, ma anche la scoperta e percezione di nuovi motivi metropolitani, come anche il completamento della scoperta della libertà nei pittoreschi sobborghi di Parigi.

Il pensiero di un rinnovamento completo, non solo artistico ma anche sociale, diede origine allo *Jugendstil* intorno al 1900 con lo scopo di una unificazione in tutti i campi creativi. Da questo momento in poi il percorso artistico condusse alla radicalizzazione degli "ismi" del XX secolo, che rompe con tutti gli stili precedenti e si basa soltanto sull'autonomia dell'arte e dell'individuo creativo.

welvaart, voor de kloof die gaapte tussen de welvaart van de gegoede burgerij en de armoede van de arbeiders. Charles Baudelaire daagde kunstenaars uit om het "heroïsme van het dagelijks leven" uit te beelden en de tradities van de kunst niet langer klakkeloos te volgen.

In de literatuur, de filosofie en de kunsten zorgde de Romantiek voor een omwenteling. In plaats van op de klassieke oudheid terug te grijpen en te zoeken naar classicistische thema's, richtte men zich nu op het heden en ontwikkelde een individueel en intensief gevoel voor de natuur, die zich in een nadruk op kleurgebruik uitdrukte. De revolutionaire veranderingen op industrieel, sociaal en economisch gebied leidden tot een grote artistieke vrijheid en inspireerden tot gepassioneerde experimenten in kleur en vorm. Uiteindelijk leidde dit alles tot een stroming die internationaal haar stempel op de kunst zou drukken: het impressionisme.

De impressionisten richtten zich niet alleen op de verschijningsvorm van de wereld zoals deze zich in het veranderende licht toont, maar ook op het ontdekken en weergeven van het leven in de grote stad, zij het als aanvulling op de ontdekking van de vrijetijdsbesteding in de schilderachtige voorstadjes van Parijs.

Het idee van een alomvattende, niet alleen schilderkunstige maar algemeen maatschappelijke vernieuwing was wat de Jugendstil rond 1900 met het streven naar een versmelting van alle kunstvormen wilde bereiken. Vanaf de Jugendstil is de ontwikkeling naar het radicalisme van de moderne kunststromingen van de twintigste eeuw duidelijk door te trekken. In deze stromingen werd tenslotte gebroken met voorgaande stijlen en richtte men zich louter nog op de autonomie van de kunst en het scheppende individualisme van de kunstenaar.

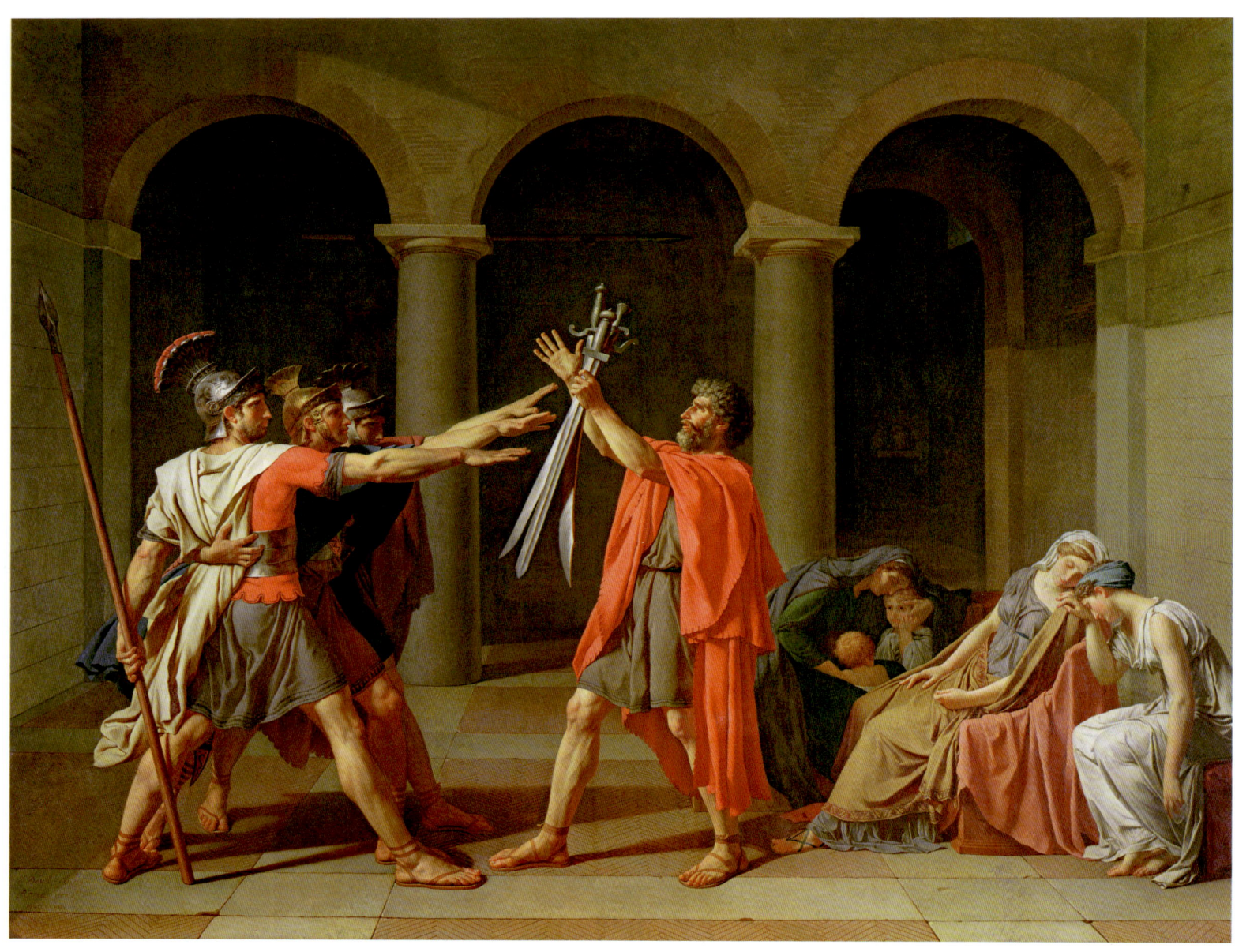

Jacques-Louis David (1748–1825)

The Oath of Horatii

Le Serment des Horaces

Der Schwur der Horatier

El juramento de los Horacios

Il giuramento degli Orazi

De eed van de Horatii

1784, Oil on canvas/Huile sur toile, 330 × 425 cm, Musée du Louvre, Paris

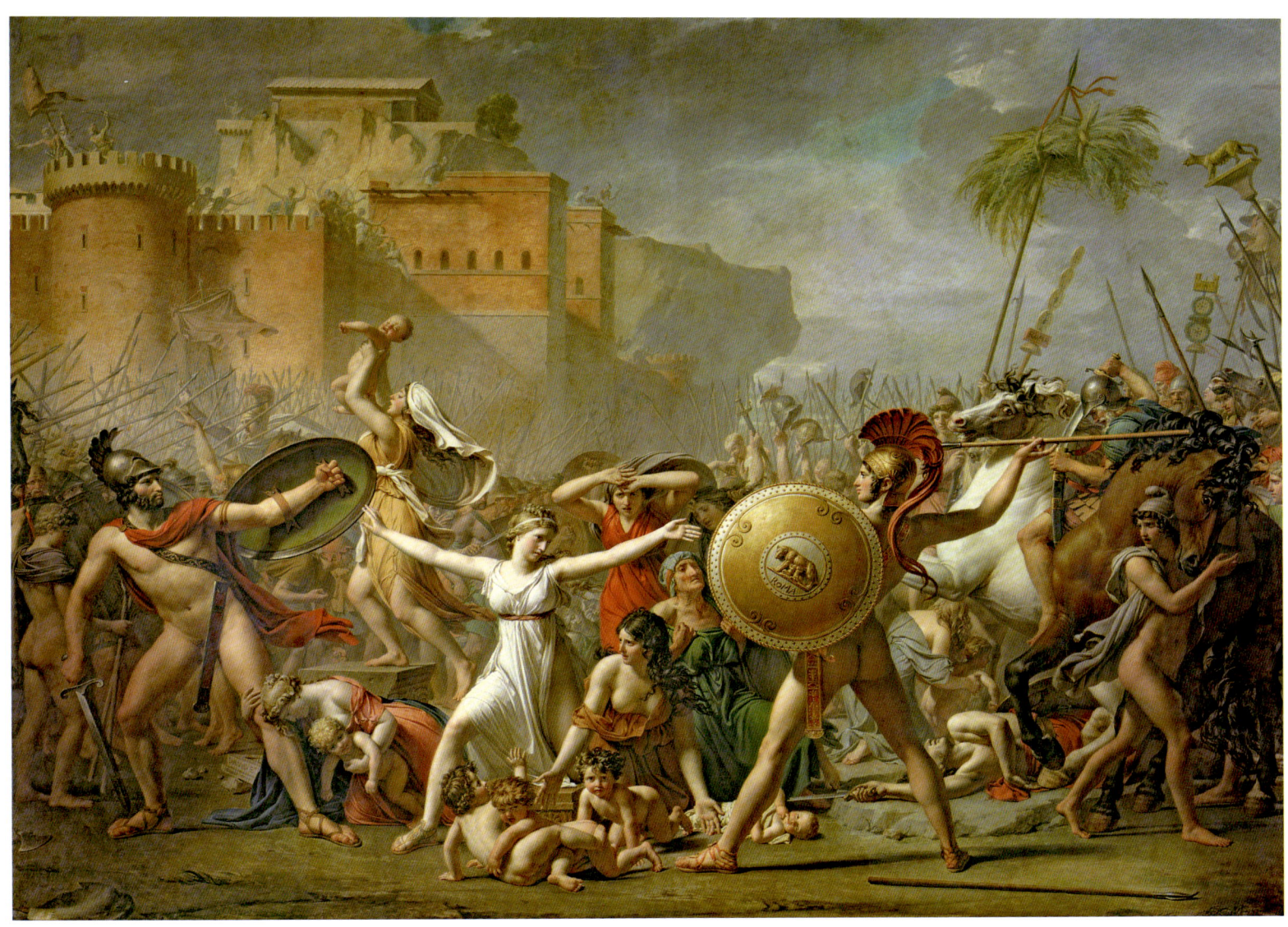

Jacques-Louis David (1748–1825)

The Sabine Women

Les Sabines

Die Sabinerinnen

Las Sabinas

Le donne sabine

De Sabijnse maagden

1799, Oil on canvas/Huile sur toile, 385 × 522 cm, Musée du Louvre, Paris

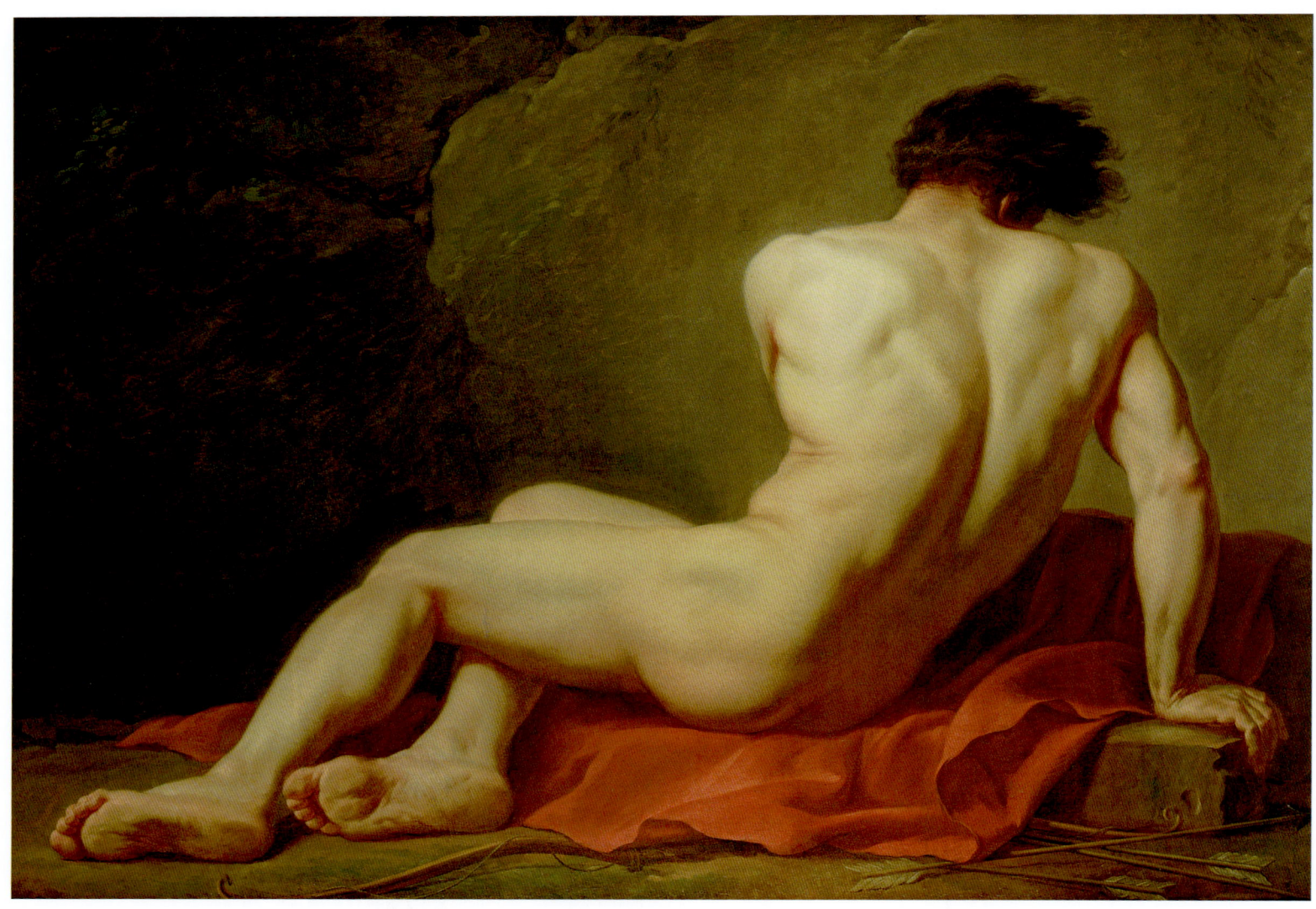

Jacques-Louis David (1748–1825)

Patrocles

Patrocle

Patrokles

Patrocles

Patroclo

Patroklos

1778, Oil on canvas/Huile sur toile, 122,5 × 170 cm, Musée Thomas Henry, Cherbourg

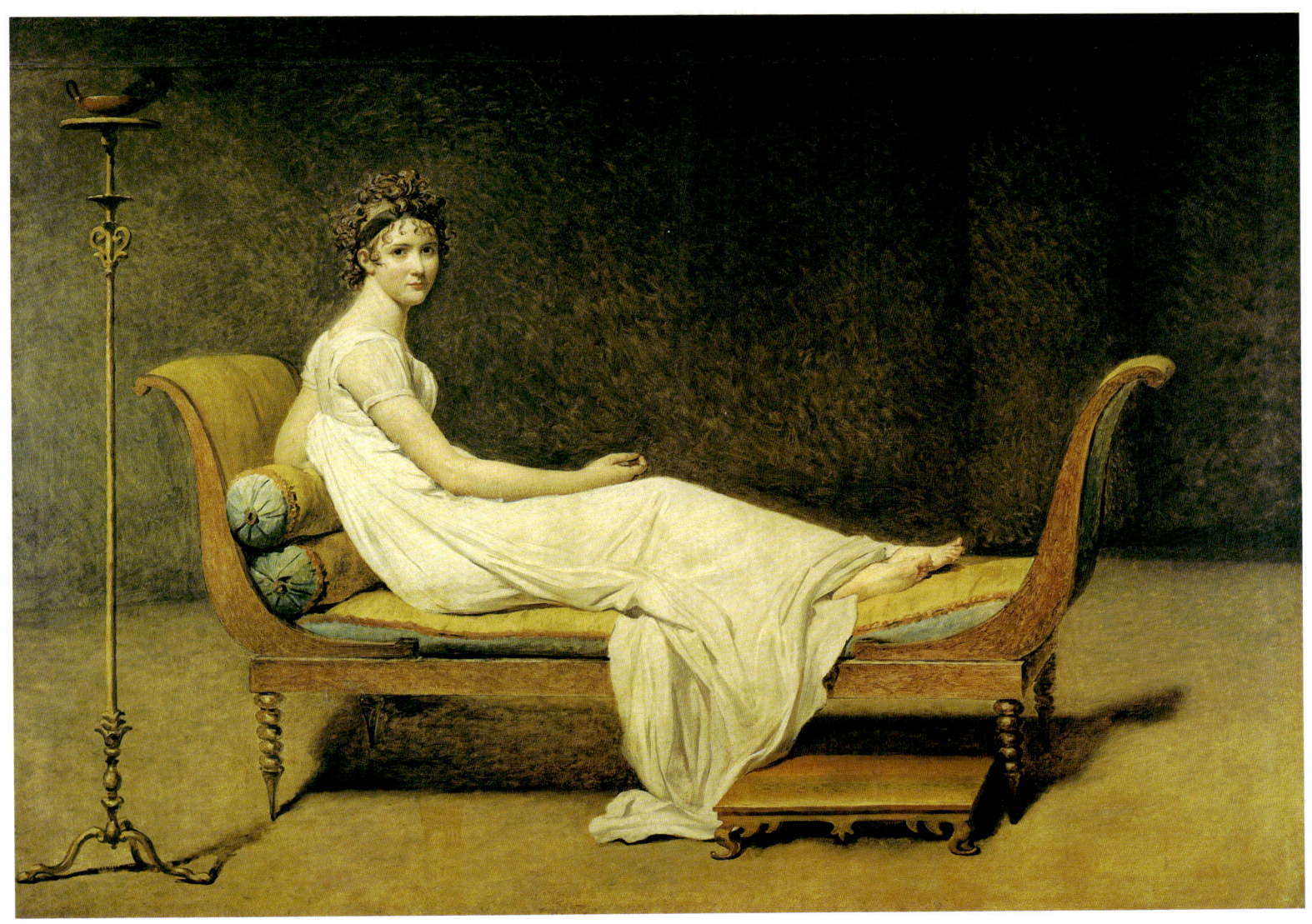

Jacques-Louis David (1748–1825)

Madame Récamier

1800, Oil on canvas/Huile sur toile, 174 × 244 cm, Musée du Louvre, Paris

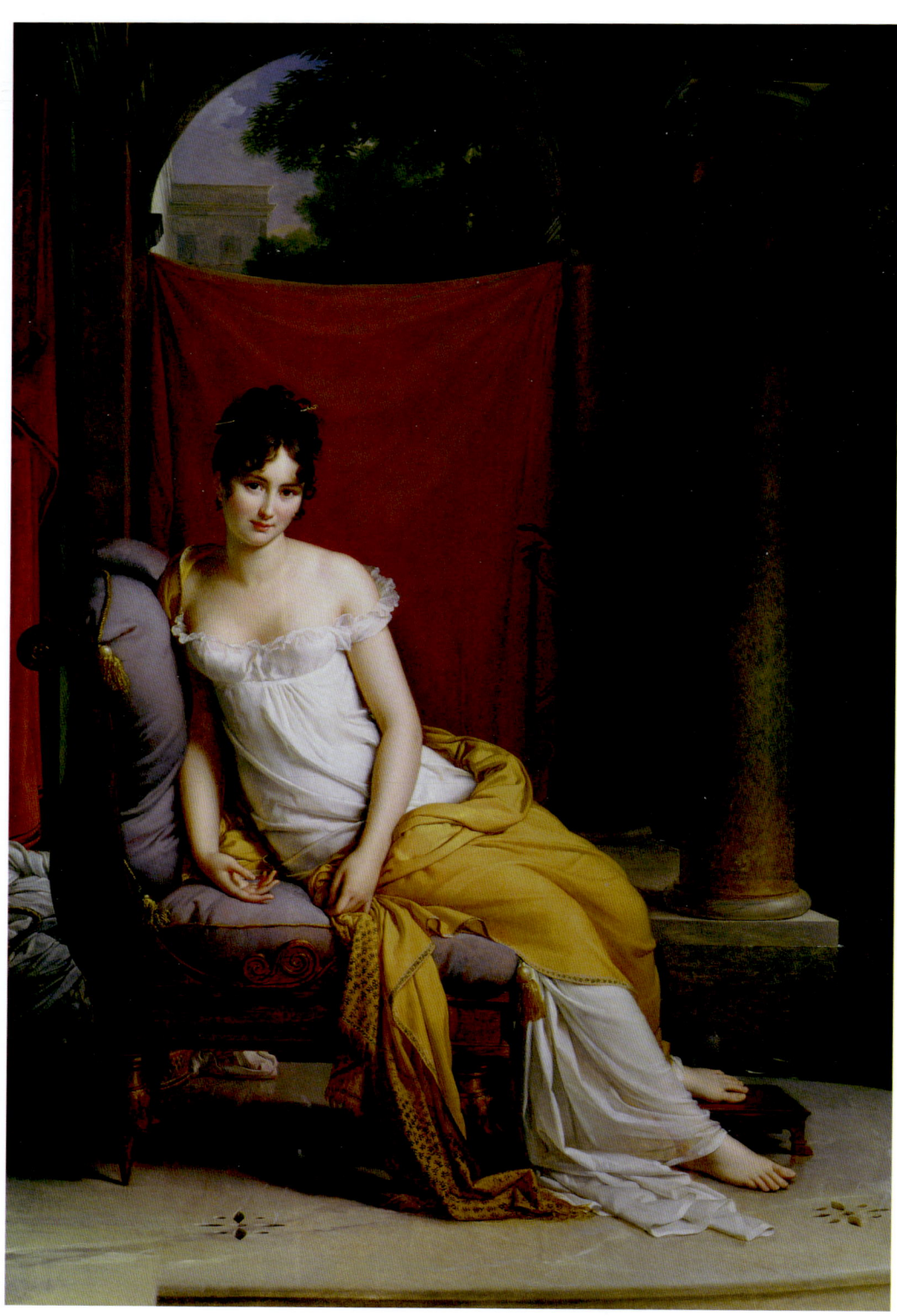

François Gérard (1770–1837)

Portrait of Madame Recamier

Portrait de madame Récamier

Bildnis der Madame Recamier

Retrato de Madame Recamier

Ritratto di Madame Recamier

Portret van madame Recamier

c. 1805, Oil on canvas/Huile sur toile, 225 × 148 cm,
Musée Carnavalet, Paris

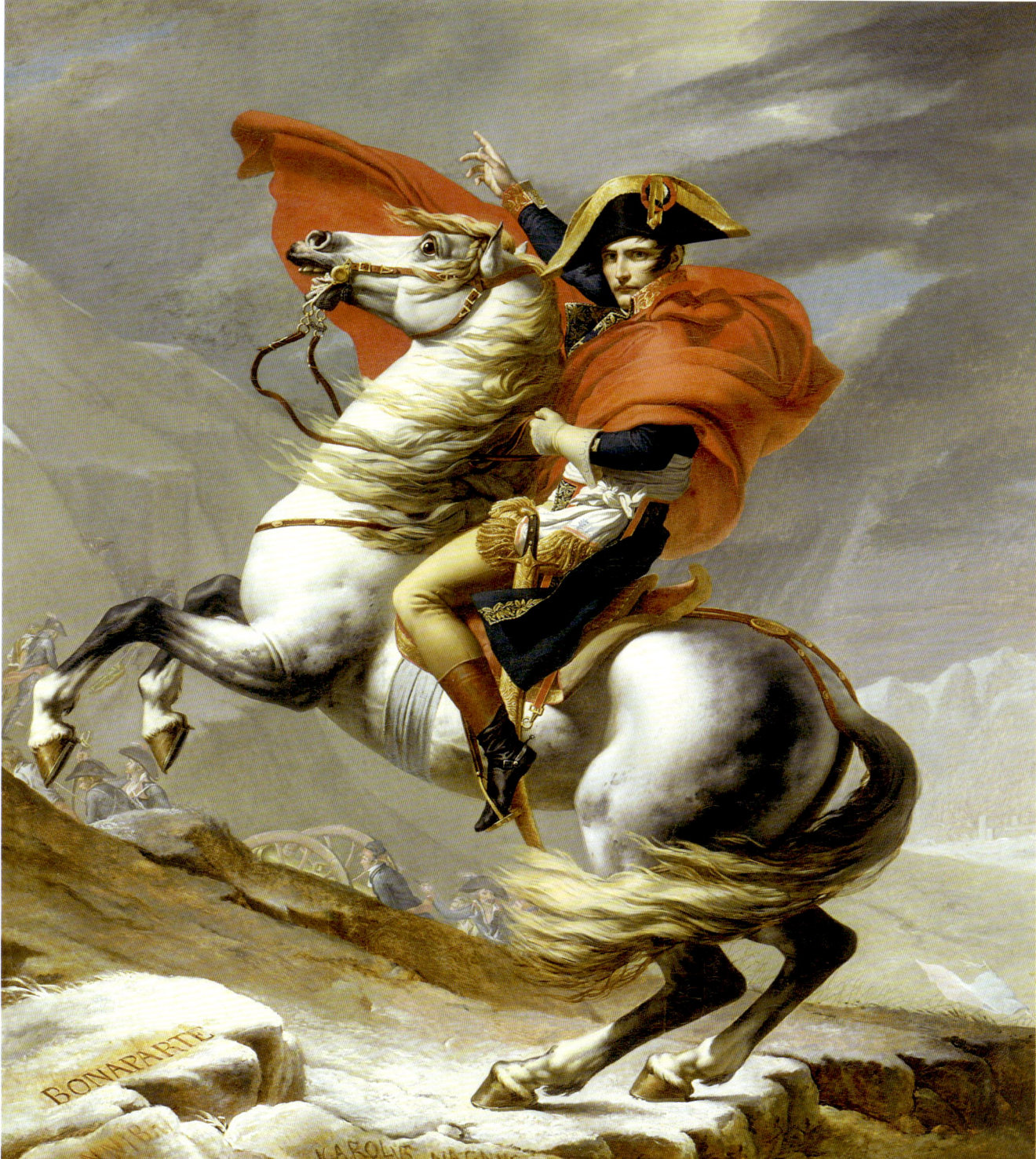

Jacques-Louis David (1748–1825)

Napoleon Crossing the Grand Saint-Bernard Pass, 20th May 1800

Bonaparte, premier consul, franchissant le Grand Saint-Bernard, 20 mai 1800

Napoleon bei der Überquerung des Großen St.-Bernhard-Passes, 20. Mai 1800

Napoleón cruzando el paso de San Bernardo, 20 de≈mayo 1800

Napoleone attraversa il Passo del Gran San Bernardo, 20 maggio 1800

Napoleon tijdens het oversteken van de Grote Sint-Bernhardpas, 20 mei 1800

1802, Oil on canvas/ Huile sur toile, 268 × 224,2 cm, Château de Versailles, Versailles

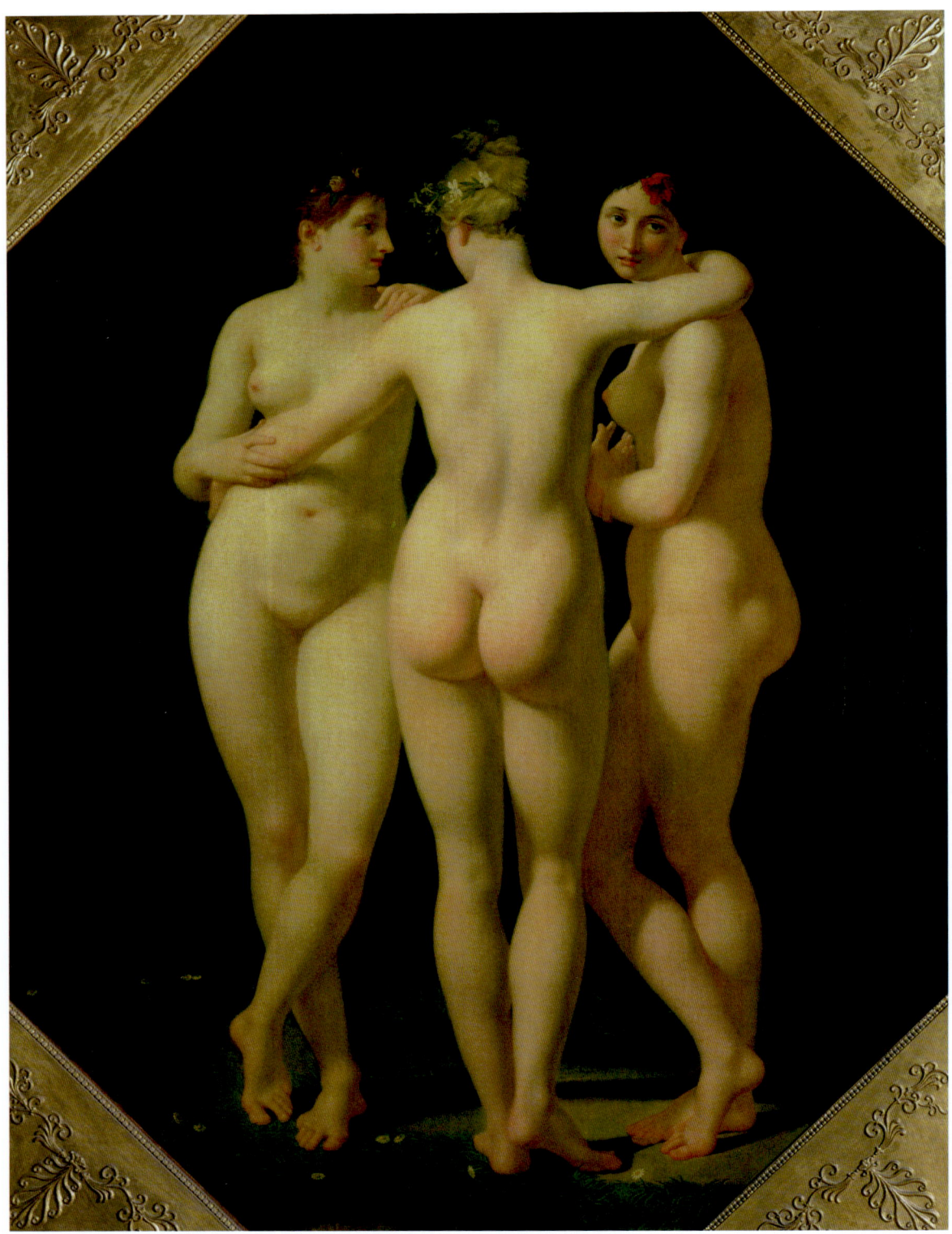

Jean-Baptiste Regnault (1754–1829)

The Three Graces

Les Trois Grâces

Die drei Grazien

Las tres Gracias

Le tre Grazie

De Drie Gratiën

1794, Oil on canvas/Huile sur toile,
204 × 153 cm, Musée du Louvre, Paris

Louis Hersent (1777–1860)

The Bathers

Les Baigneuses

Die Badenden

Las bañistas

I bagnanti

De baadsters

1830, Oil on canvas/Huile sur toile,
130,8 × 138,4 cm, Private collection

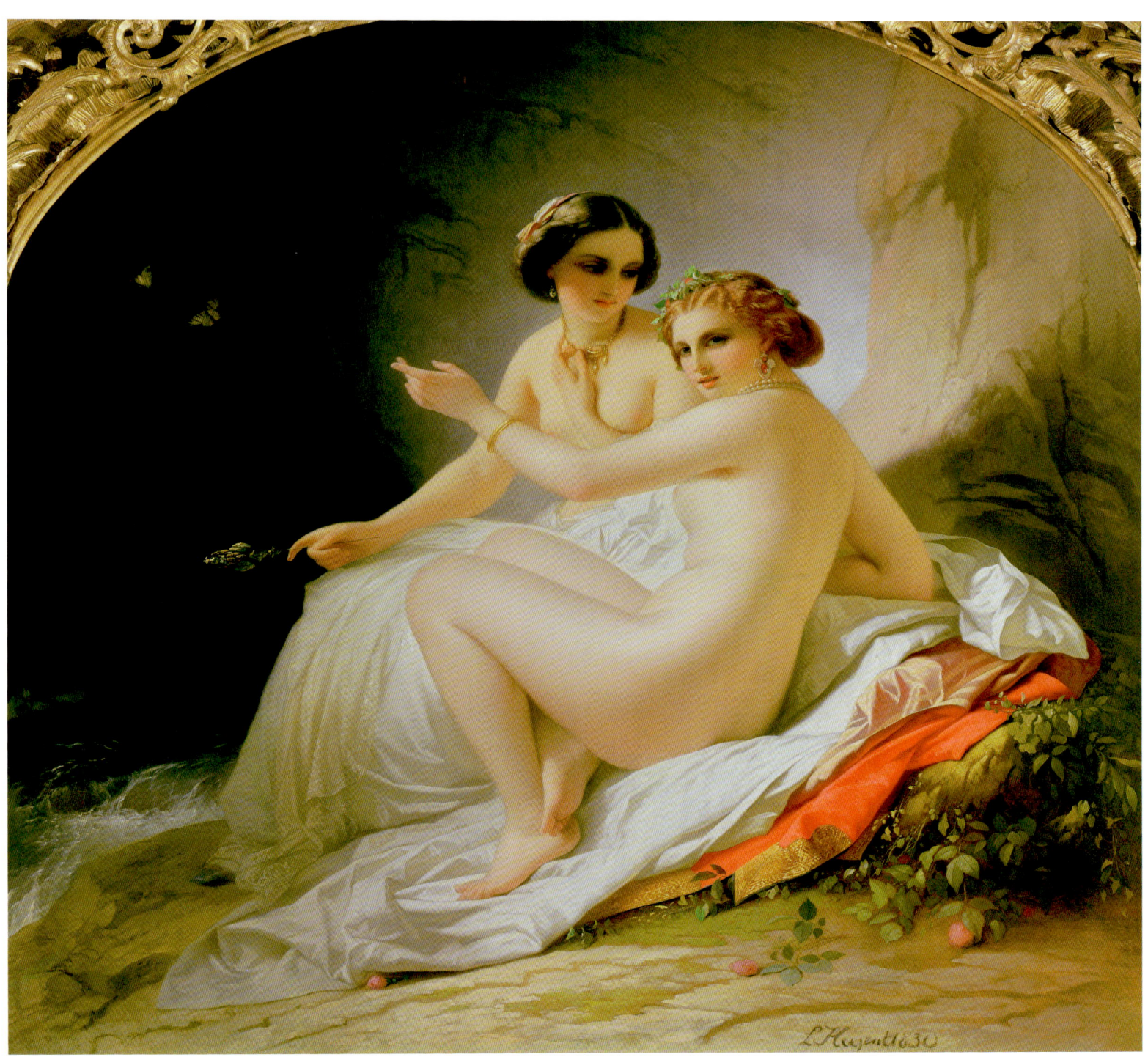

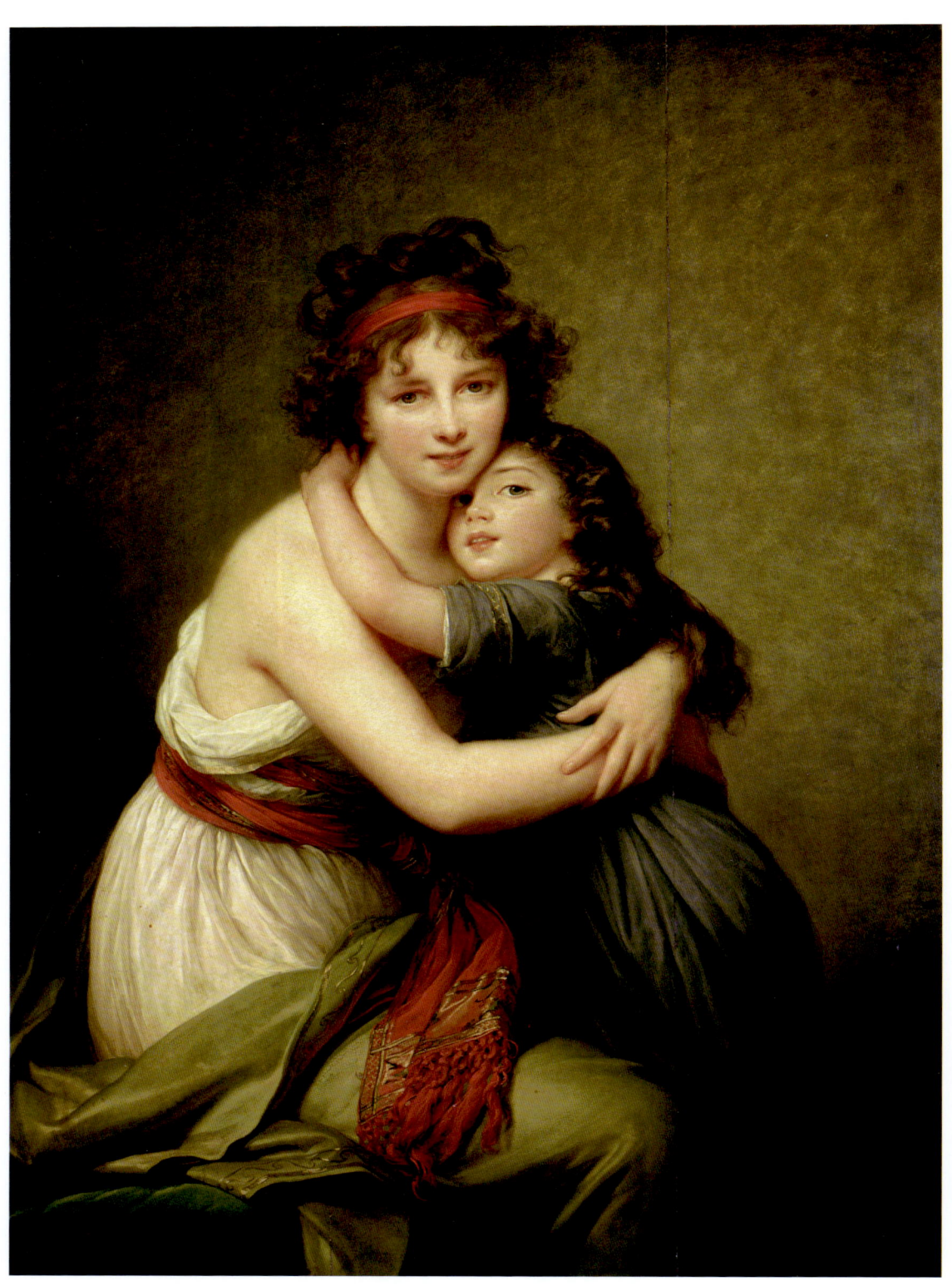

**Élisabeth-Louise Vigée-Lebrun
(1755–1842)**

Madame Vigée-Lebrun and her Daughter,
Jeanne-Lucie-Louise

Madame Vigée-Le Brun et sa fille,
Jeanne-Lucie-Louise, dite Julie

Madame Vigée-Lebrun und ihre Tochter
Jeanne-Lucie-Louise

Madame Vigée-Lebrun y su hija Jeanne-
Lucie-Louise

Madame Vigée-Lebrun e sua figlia
Jeanne-Lucie-Louise

Madame Vigée-Lebrun en haar dochter
Jeanne-Lucie-Louise

1789, Oil on canvas/Huile sur toile,
130 × 94 cm, Musée du Louvre, Paris

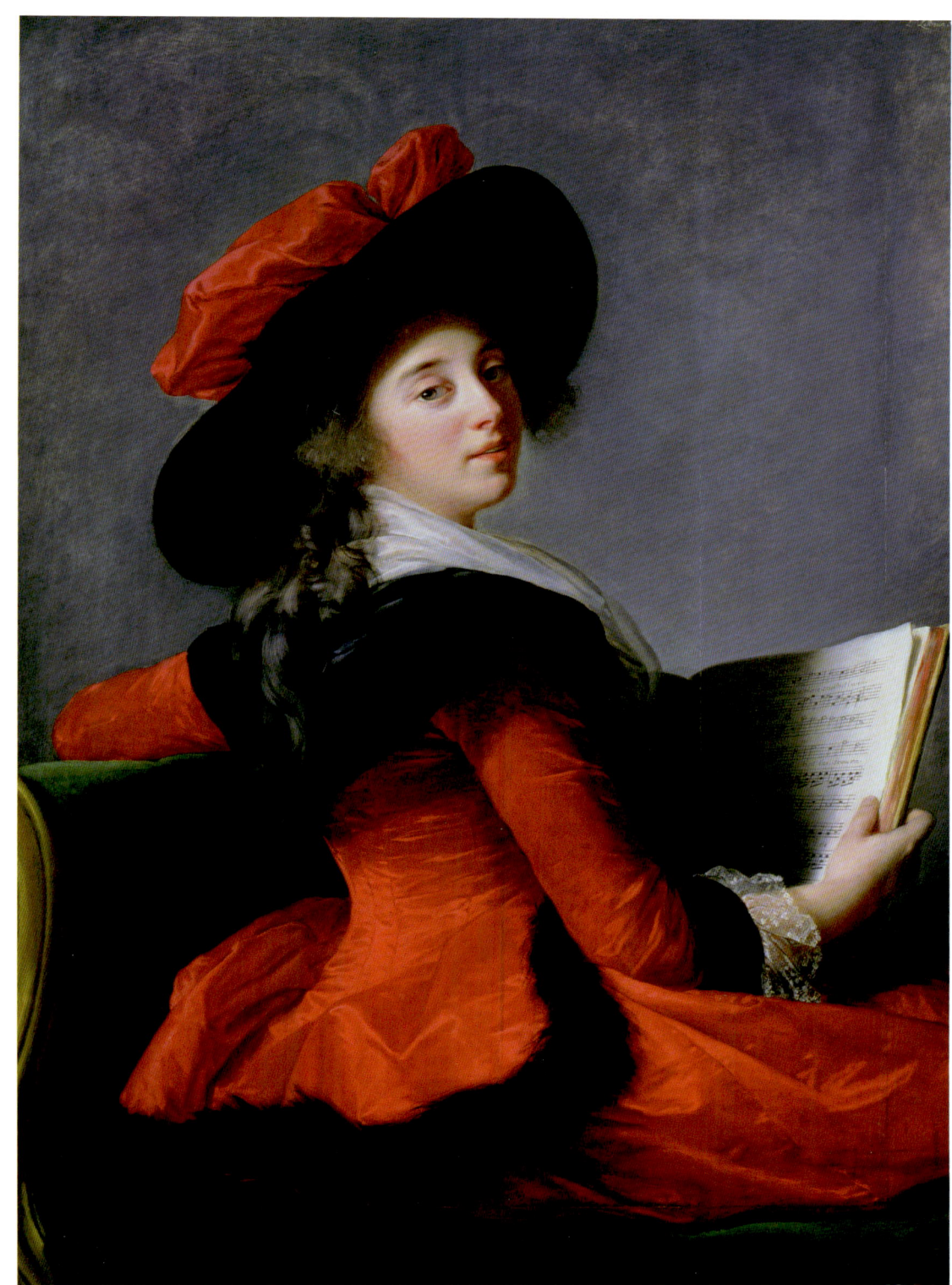

Élisabeth-Louise Vigée-Lebrun
(1755–1842)

La Baronne de Crussol

La Baronne de Crussol

Die Baronin de Crussol

La baronesa de Crussol

La baronessa de Crussol

De barones van Crussol

1785, Oil on wood/Huile sur bois, 114 × 84 cm,
Musée des Augustins, Toulouse

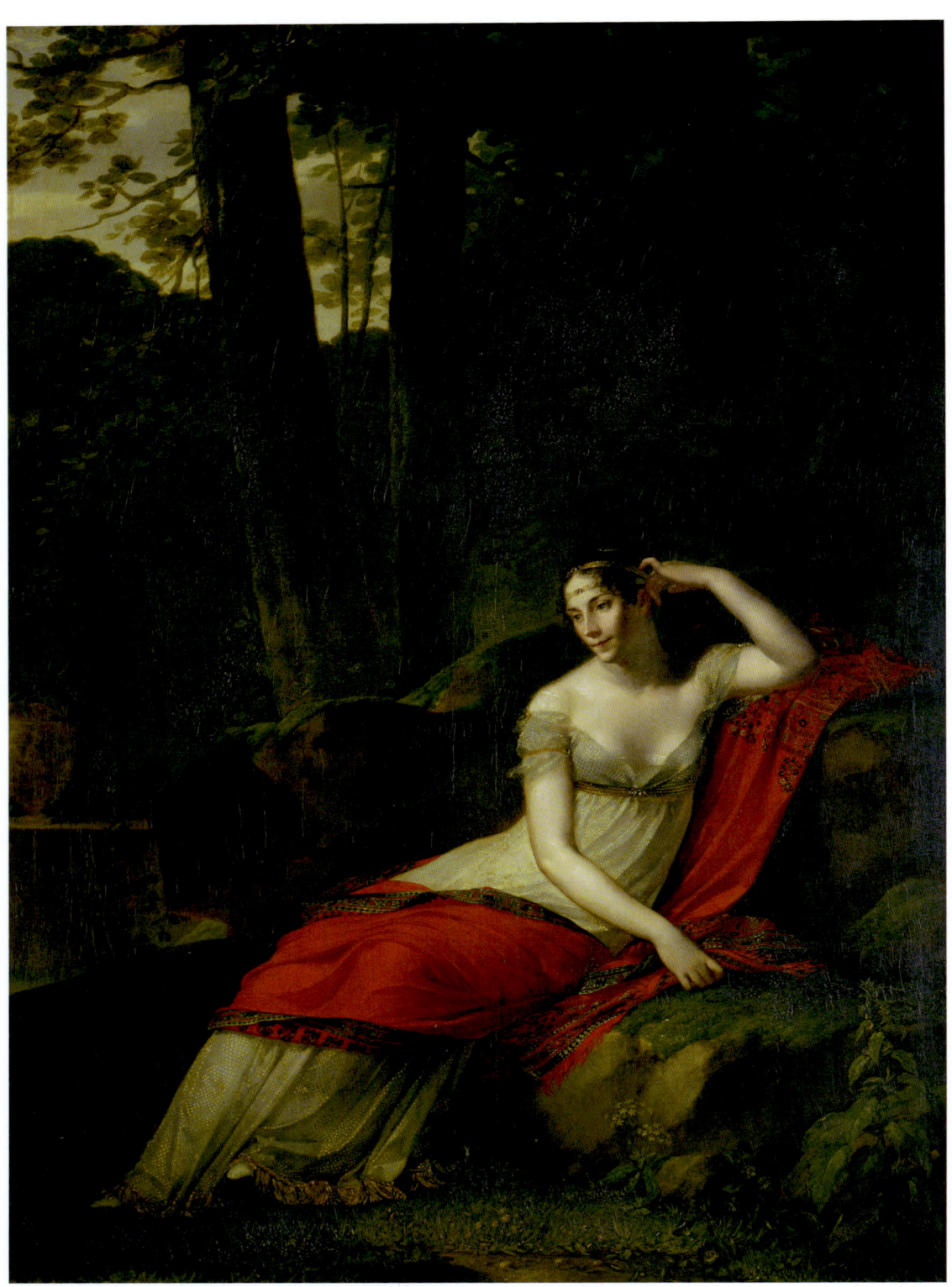

Pierre-Paul Prud'hon (1758–1823)

Portrait of the Empress Josephine

L'Impératrice Joséphine

Bildnis der Kaiserin Josephine

Retrato de la emperatriz Josefina

Ritratto dell'imperatrice Josephine

Portret van keizerin Josephine

1805, Oil on canvas/Huile sur toile,
244 × 179 cm, Musée du Louvre, Paris

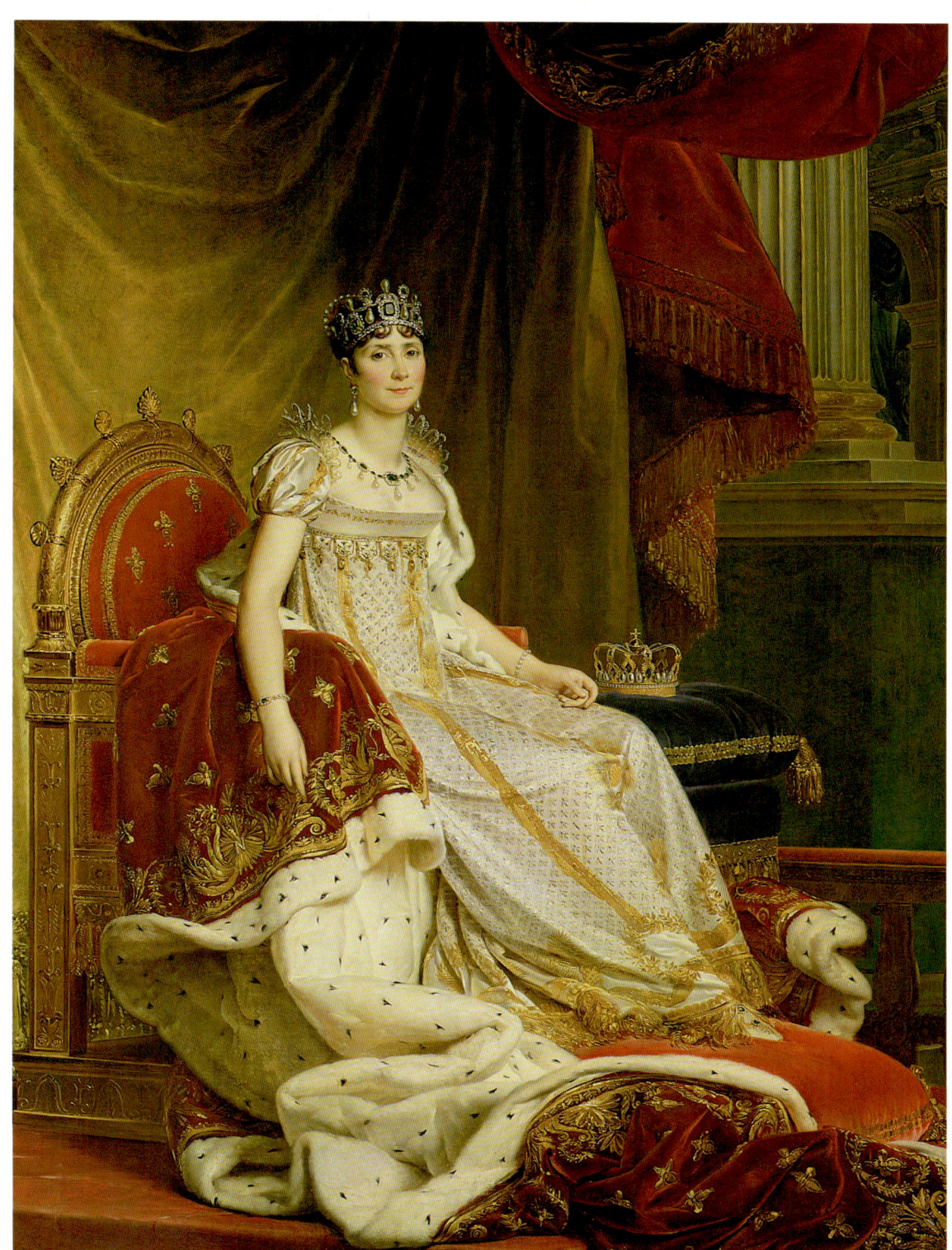

François Gérard (1770–1837)

Empress Josephine

Joséphine en costume de sacre

Kaiserin Josephine

La emperatriz Josefina

L'imperatrice Josephine

Keizerin Josephine

1808, Oil on canvas/Huile sur toile,
215 × 160 cm, Château de Fontainebleau,
Fontainebleau

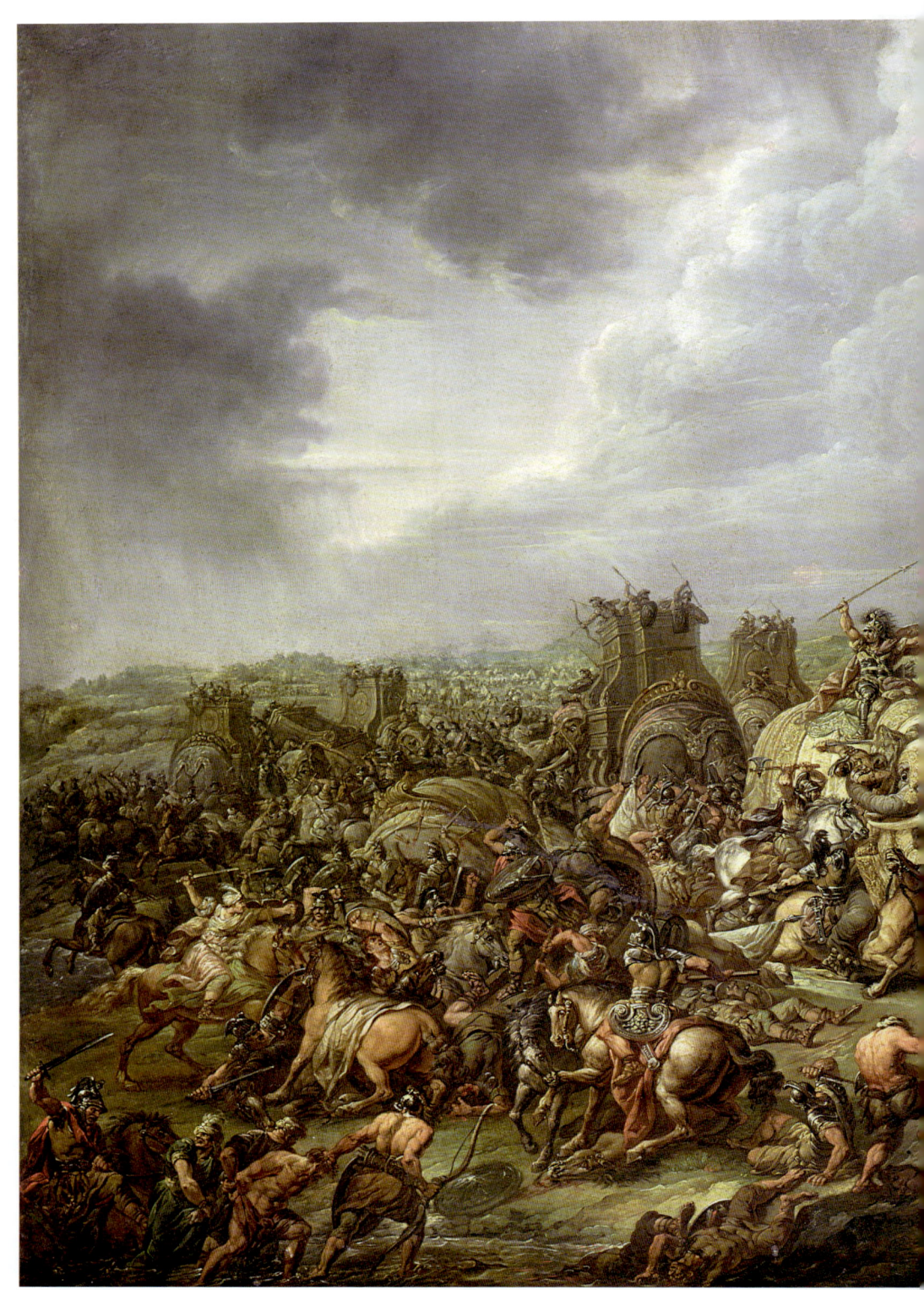

François Watteau (1758–1823)

The Defeat of Porus by Alexander the Great

La Défaite de Porus par Alexandre

Der Sieg des Alexander des Großen über Porus

La victoria de Alejandro Magno sobre Poros

La vittoria di Alessandro Magno su Poro

De zege van Alexander de Grote op Poros

1802., Oil on canvas/Huile sur toile, 86 × 140 cm,
Palais des Beaux-Arts, Lille

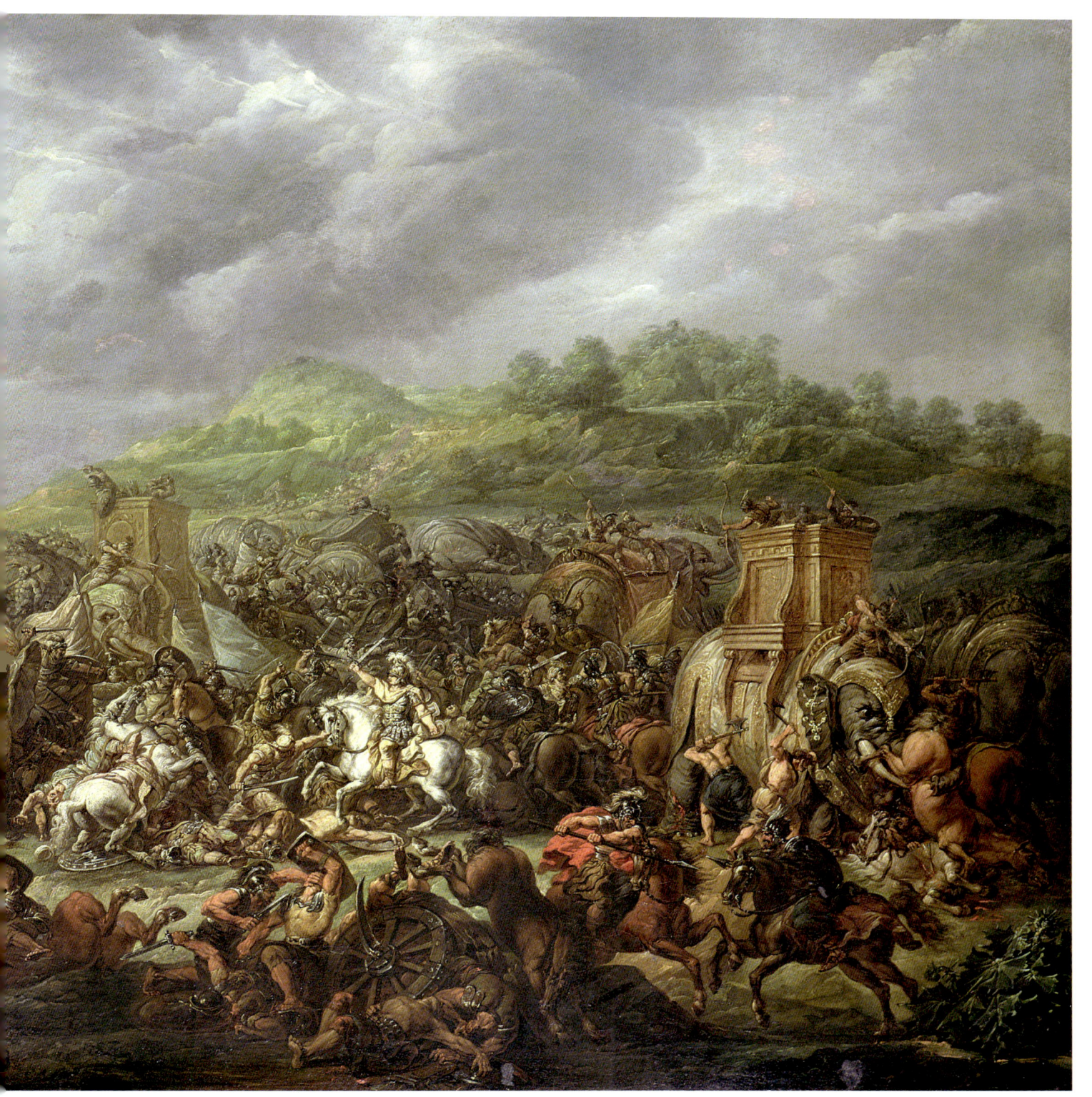

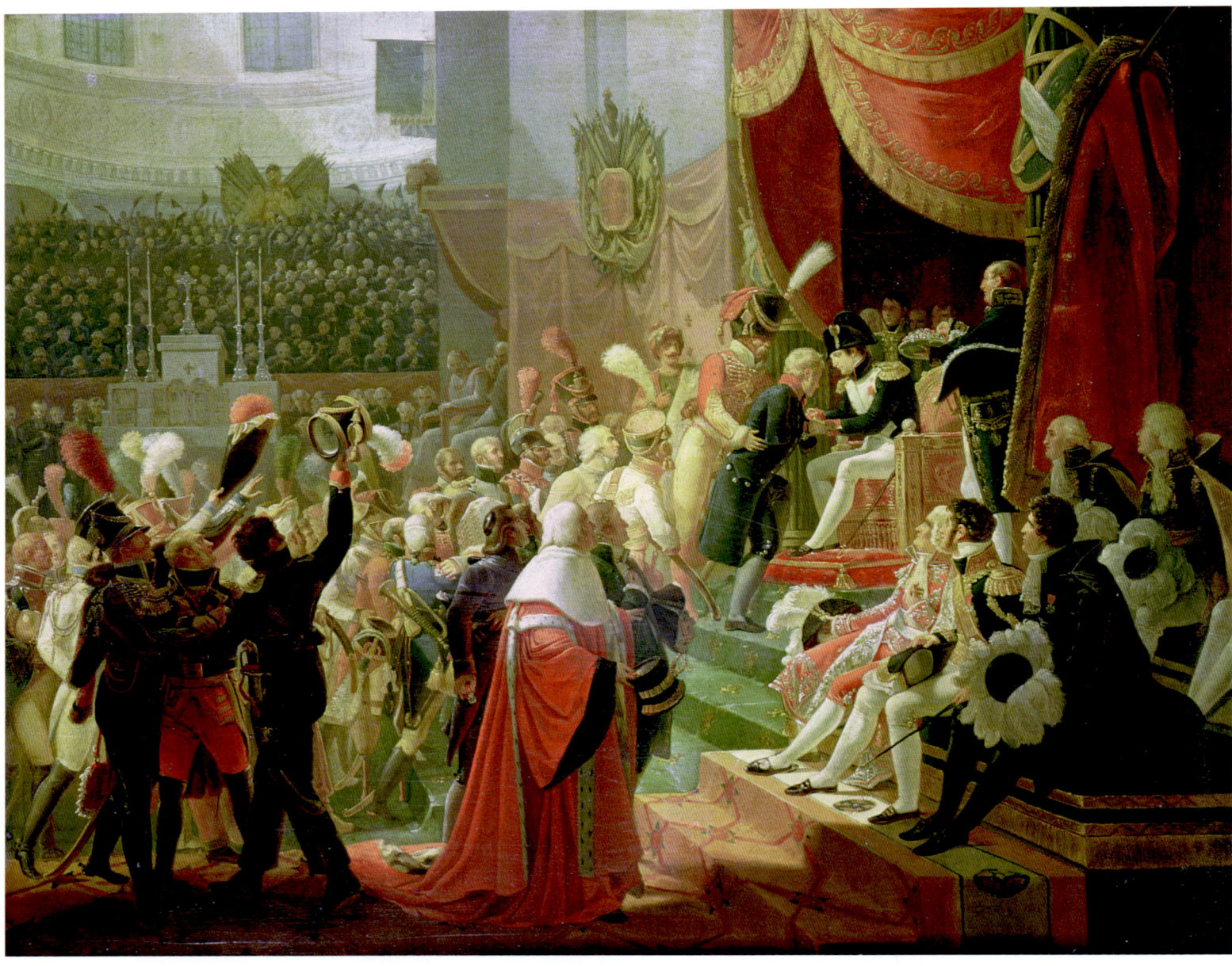

Jean-Baptiste Debret (1768–1848)

The First Distribution of Crosses of the Legion of
Honour in the Church of the Invalides, 14th July 1804

La Première Distribution de la Légion d'honneur à
l'église des Invalides

Die erste Verleihung der Kreuze der Ehrenlegion
in der Kirche der Invaliden, 14. Juli 1804

La primera concesión de la Cruz de la Legión de
Honor en la Iglesia de los inválidos, 14 de julio 1804

La prima distribuzione delle croci della Legion d'Onore
nella Chiesa degli Invalidi, 14 luglio 1804

De eerste onderscheiding met het Kruis van het Legioen
van Eer in de Cathédrale des Invalides, 14 juli 1804

1812, Oil on canvas/Huile sur toile, 403 × 531 cm, Château de Versailles, Versailles

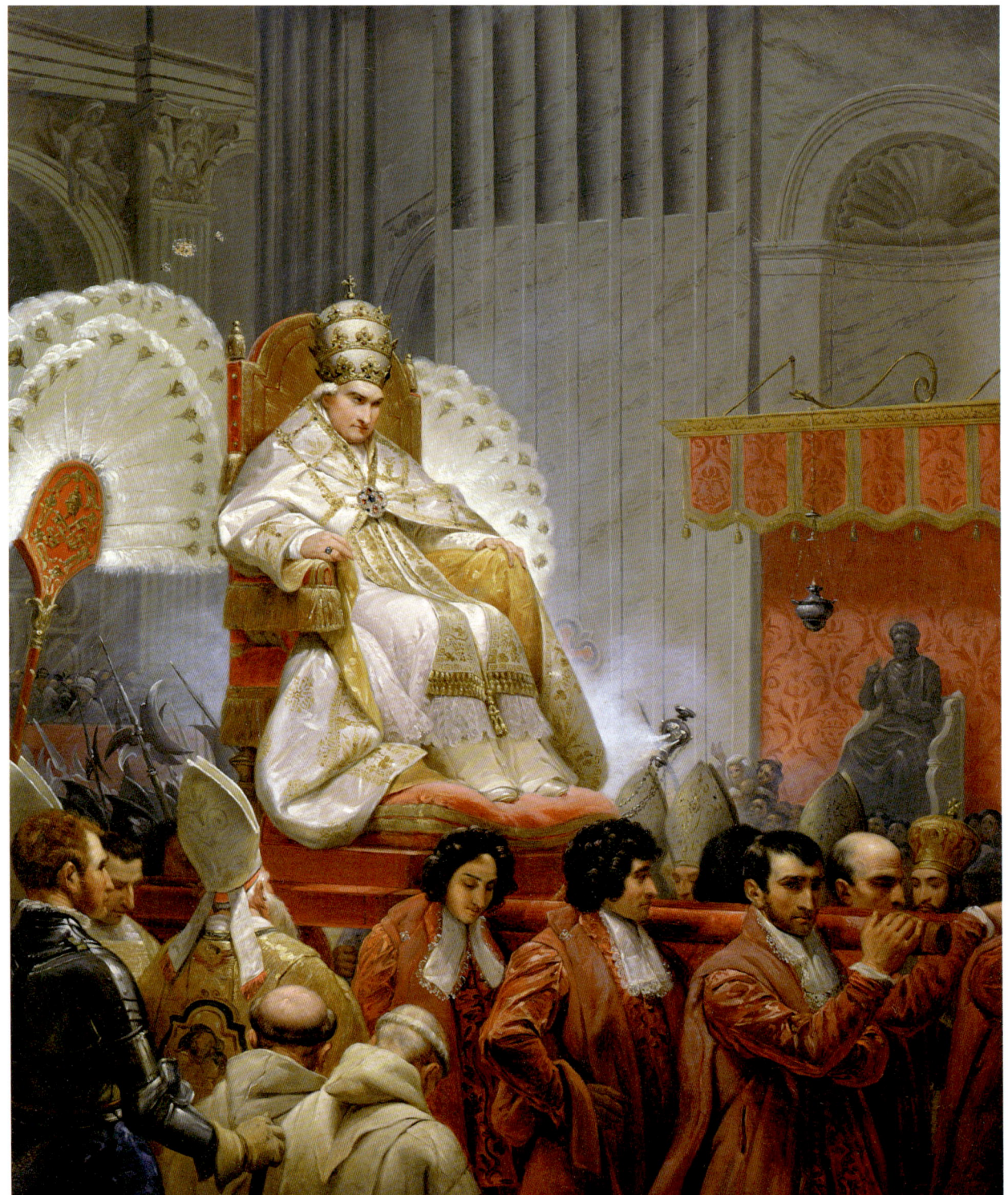

Horace Vernet (1789–1863)

Pope Pius VIII in St. Peter's on the Sedia Gestatoria

Pie VIII à Saint-Pierre de Rome sur la Sedia Gestatoria

Papst Pius VIII. im Dom von St. Peter anläßlich der Sedia Gestatoria

El Papa Pío VIII en la Basílica de San Pedro con la Sedia Gestatoria

Papa Pio VIII nella basilica di San Pietro sulla Sedia Gestatoria

Paus Pius VIII in de Sint-Pieter ter gelegenheid van de Sedia Gestatoria

1829, Oil on canvas/Huile sur toile, 385 × 329 cm, Château de Versailles, Versailles

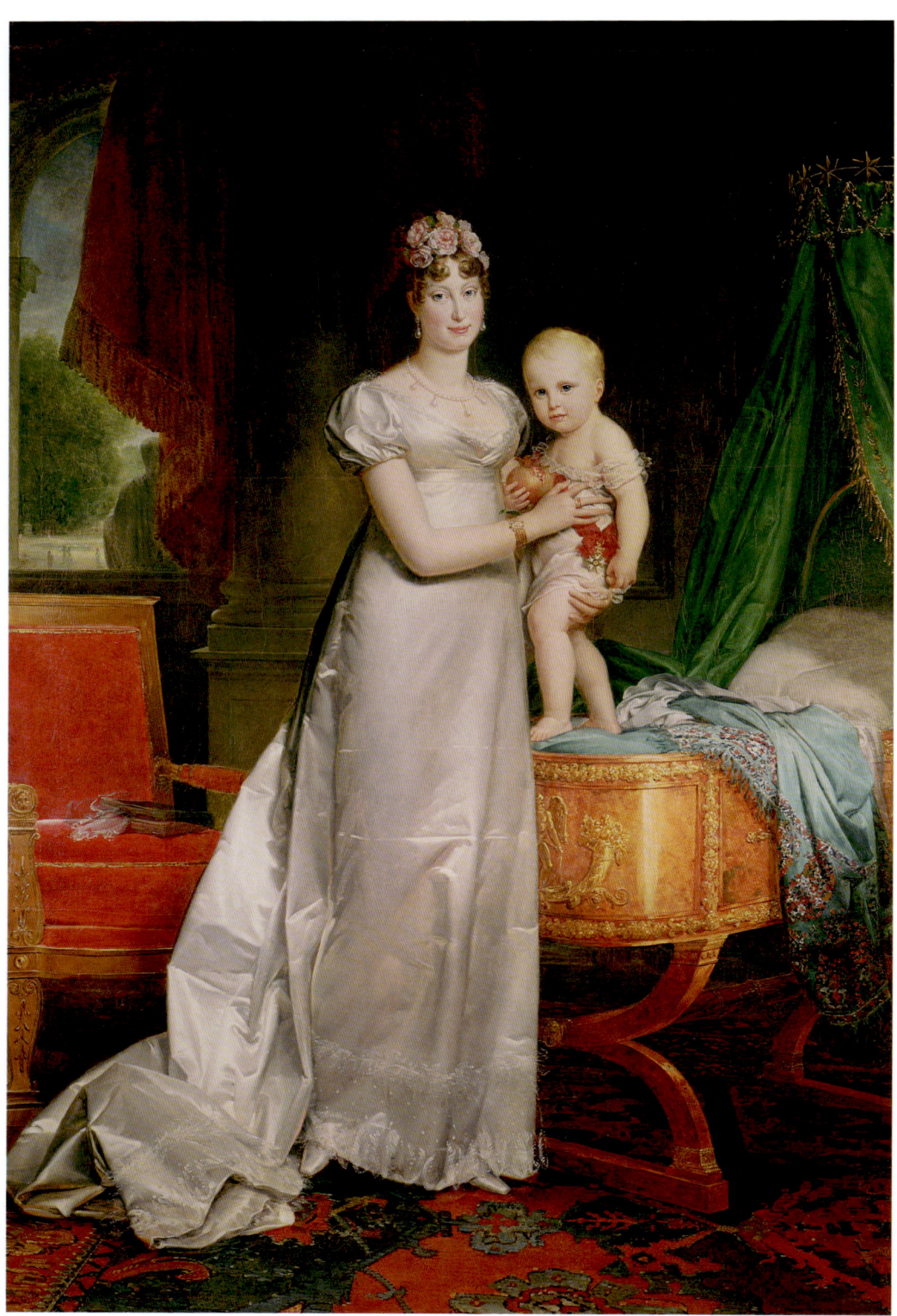

François Gérard (1770–1837)

Marie Louise and the King of Rome

L'Impératrice Marie-Louise et le roi de Rome

Marie Louise und der König von Rom

Maria Luisa y el rey de Roma

Maria Luisa e il re di Roma

Marie Louise en de koning van Rome

1812, Oil on canvas/Huile sur toile, 32,5 × 22,9 cm, Château de Versailles, Versailles

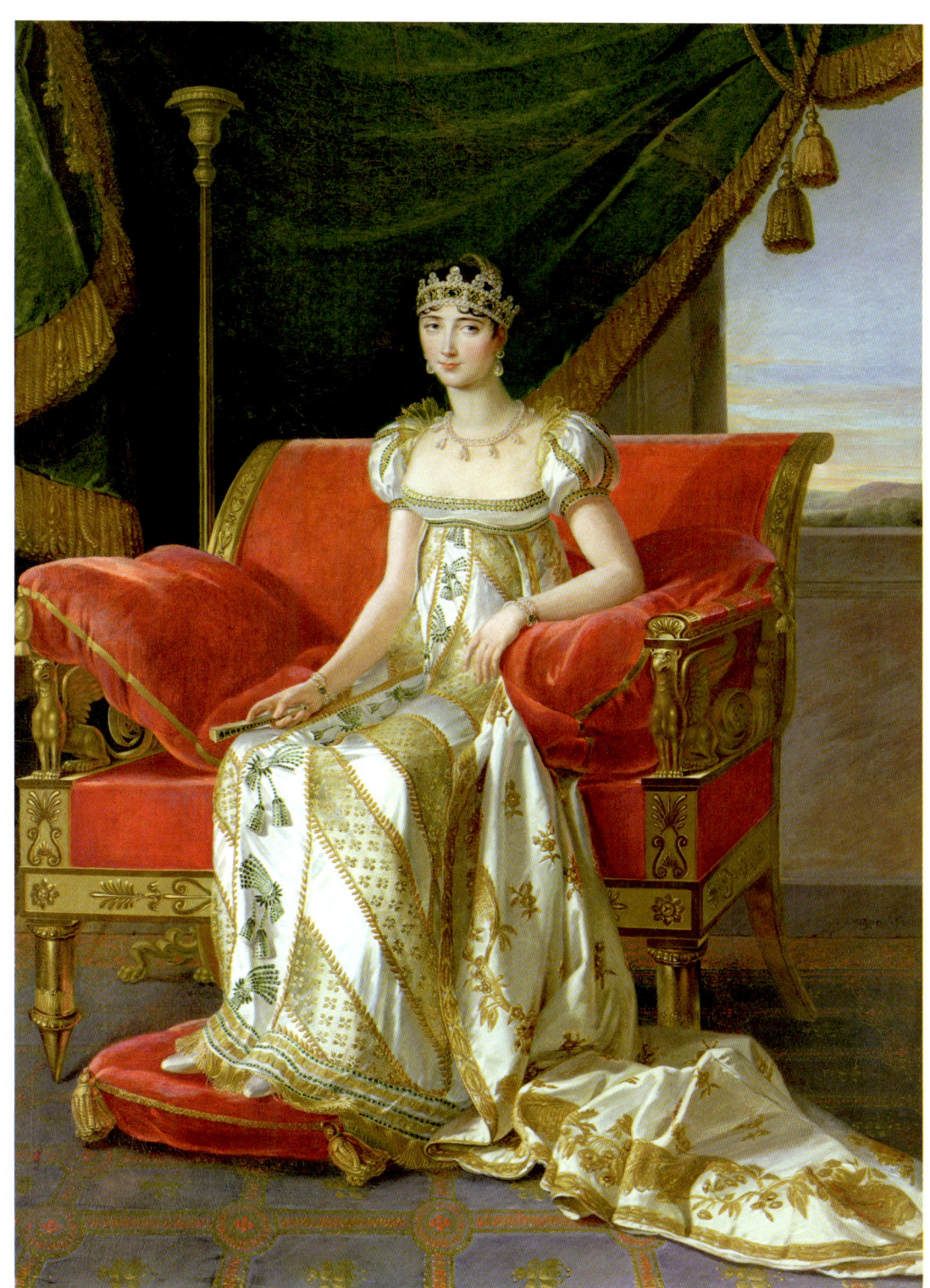

Marie-Guillemine Benoist (1768−1826)

Marie Pauline Bonaparte

Portrait de Pauline Bonaparte

Marie Pauline Bonaparte

Marie Pauline Bonaparte

Marie Pauline Bonaparte

Pauline Bonaparte

1808, Oil on canvas/Huile sur toile, 200 × 142 cm,
Château de Fontainebleau, Fontainebleau

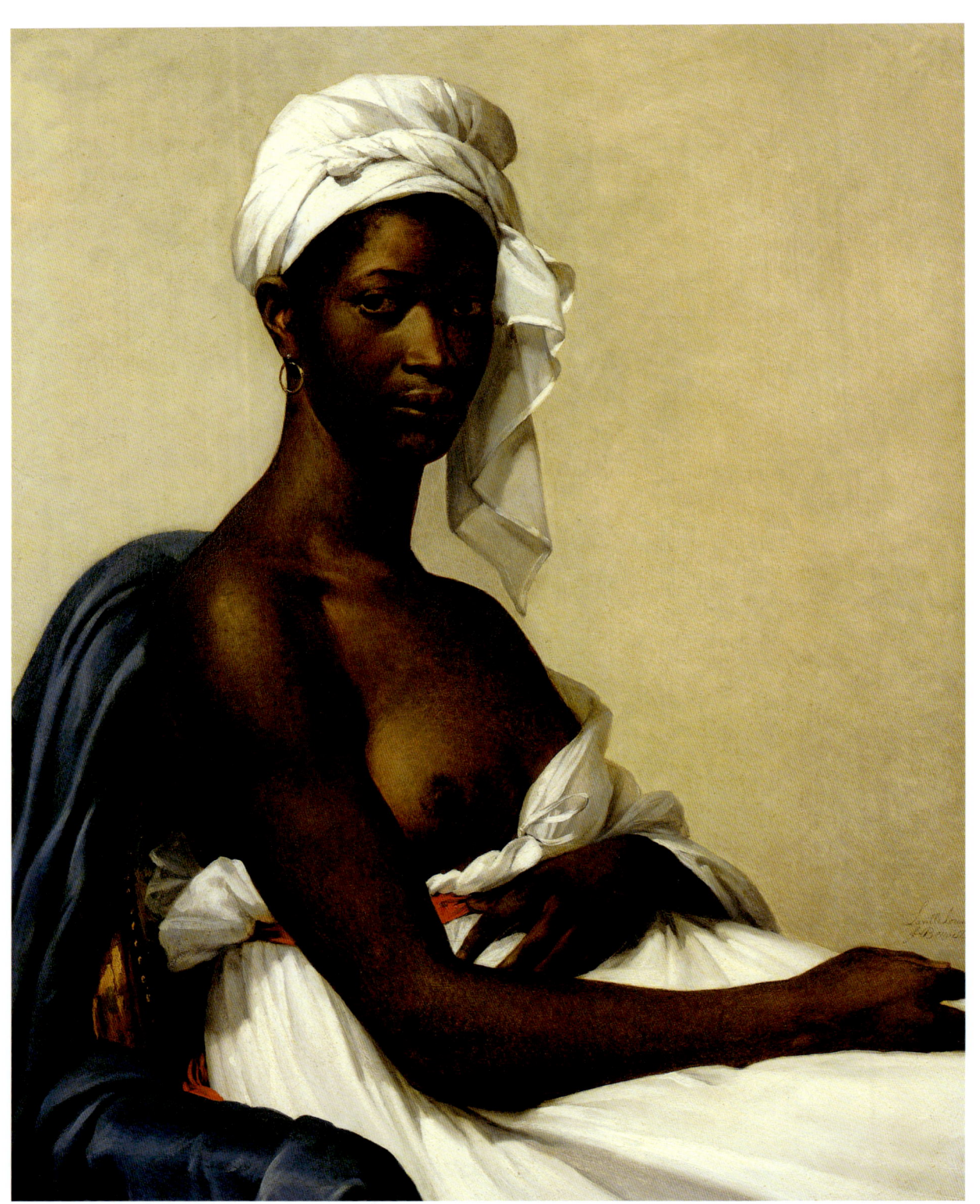

**Marie-Guillemine Benoist
(1768–1826)**

Portrait of a Negress

Portrait d'une femme noire

Bildnis einer Negerin

Retrato de una negra

Ritratto di una negra

Portret van een negerin

c. 1800, Oil on canvas/Huile
sur toile, 81 × 65 cm, Musée du
Louvre, Paris

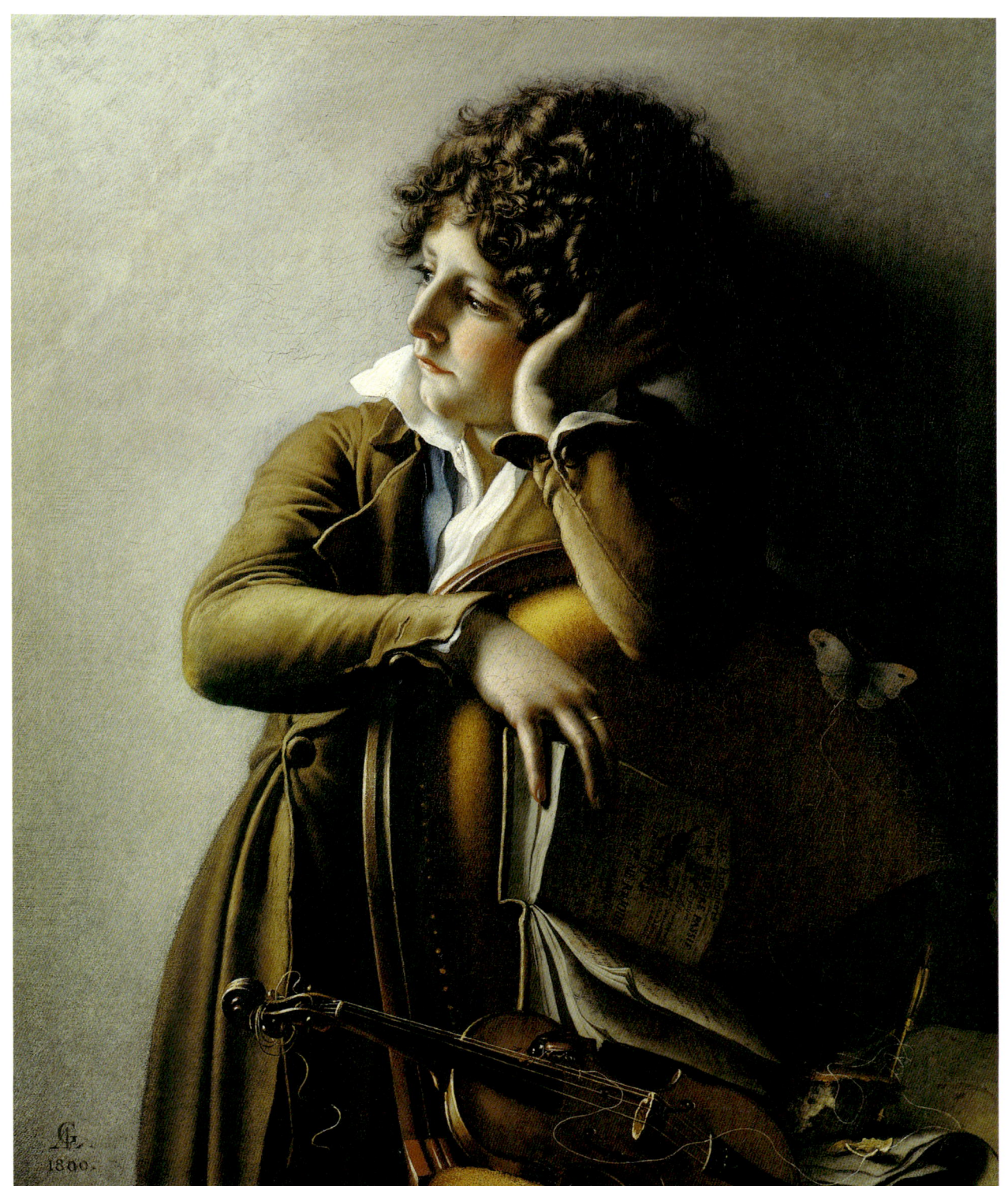

**Anne-Louis Girodet
de Roussy-Trioson
(1767–1824)**

Portrait of
Benoît Agnès Trioson

Benoît-Agnès Trioson,
dit Ruehaus *ou* Ruoz

Porträt von
Benoît Agnès Trioson

Retrato de
Benoît Agnès Trioson

Ritratto di
Benoît Agnès Trioson

Portret van
Benoît Agnès Trioson

c. 1800, Oil on canvas/Huile
sur toile, 73 × 59 cm, Musée
du Louvre, Paris

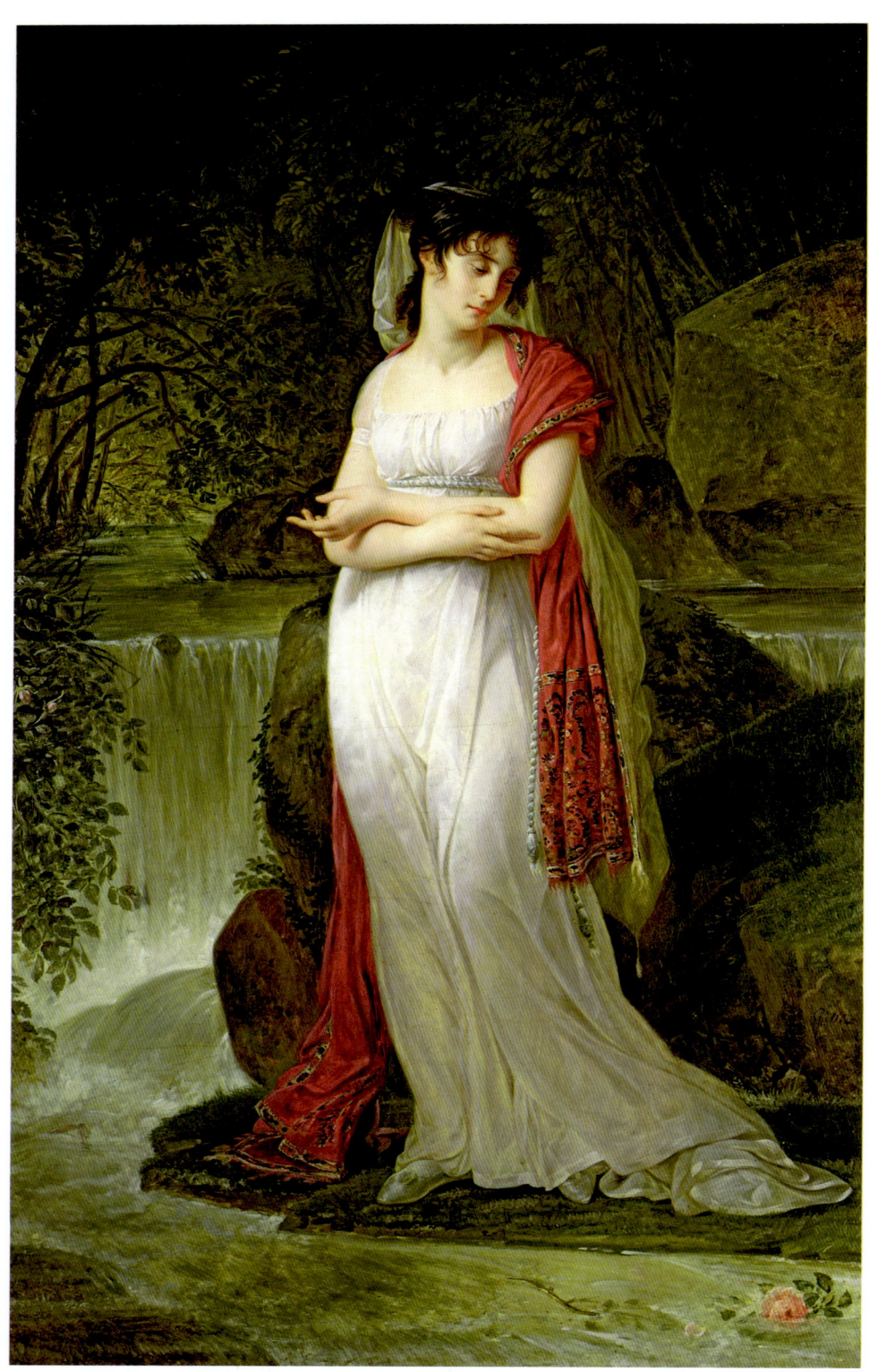

Antoine-Jean Gros (1771–1835)

Christine Boyer

n. d., Oil on canvas/Huile sur toile, 214 × 134 cm,
Musée du Louvre, Paris

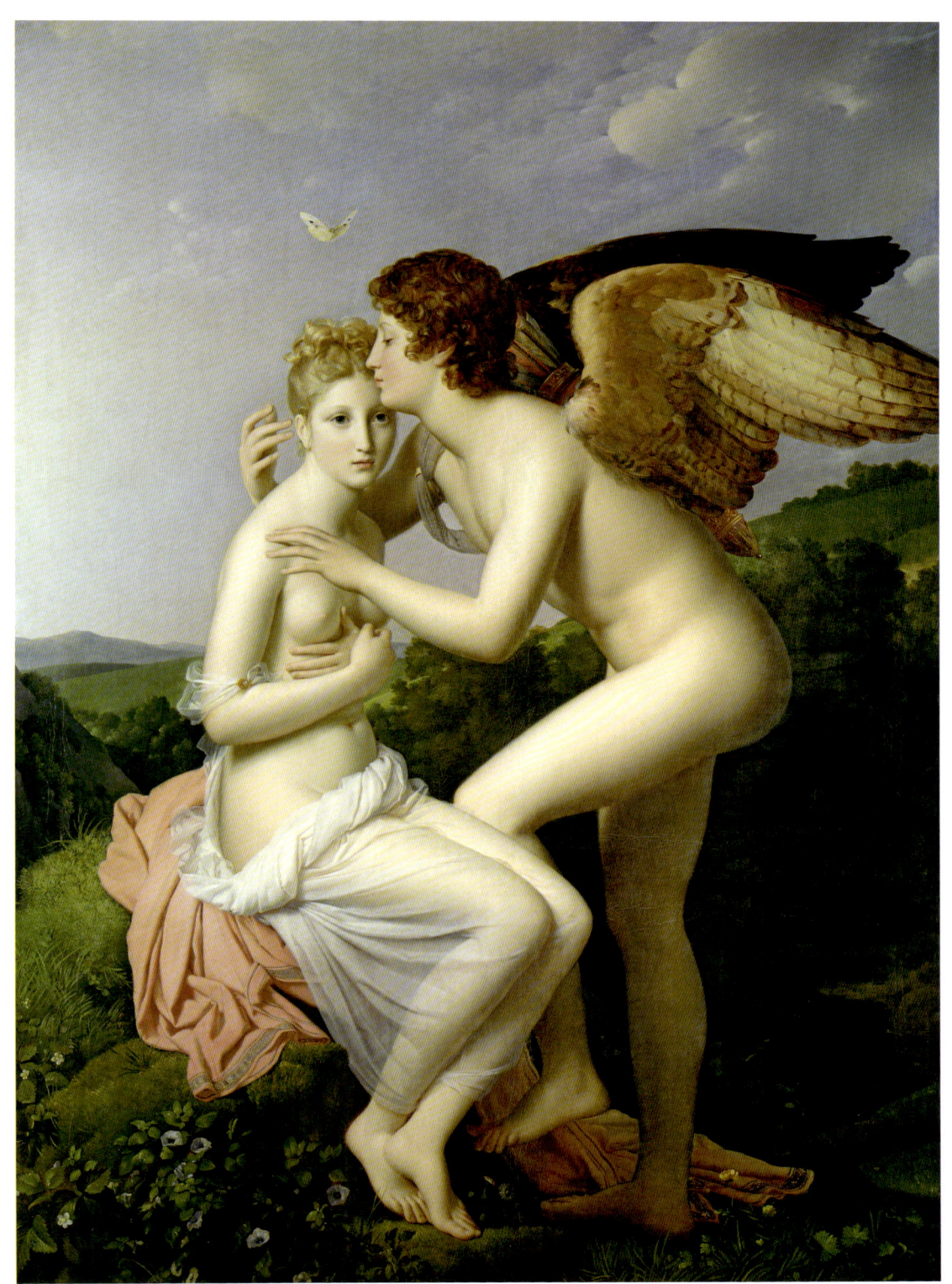

François Gérard (1770–1837)

Psyche Receiving the First Kiss of Cupid

Psyché et l'Amour

Psyche erhält ihren ersten Kuss von Cupido

Psique recibiendo el primer beso de Cupido

Psiche riceve il suo primo bacio da Cupido

Psyche ontvangt de eerste kus van Cupido

1798, Oil on canvas/Huile sur toile,
186 × 132 cm, Musée du Louvre, Paris

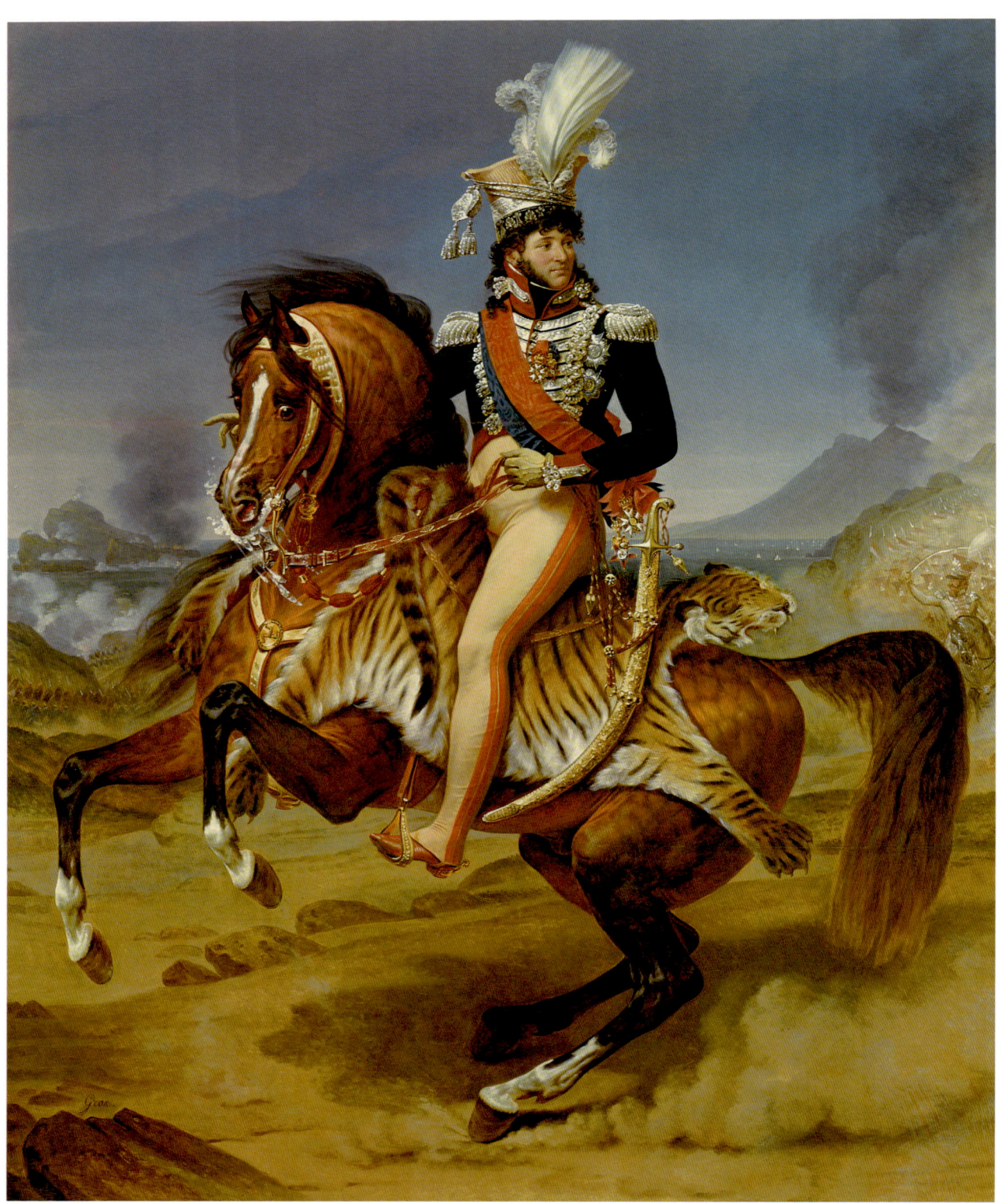

**Antoine-Jean Gros
(1771–1835)**

Equestrian Portrait of
Joachim Murat

Portrait équestre de
Joachim Murat

Reiterbildnis von Joachim
Murat

Retrato ecuestre de
Joachim Murat

Ritratto equestre di
Gioacchino Murat

Ruiterportret van Joachim
Murat

1812, Oil on canvas/Huile sur
toile, 343 × 280 cm, Musée
du Louvre, Paris

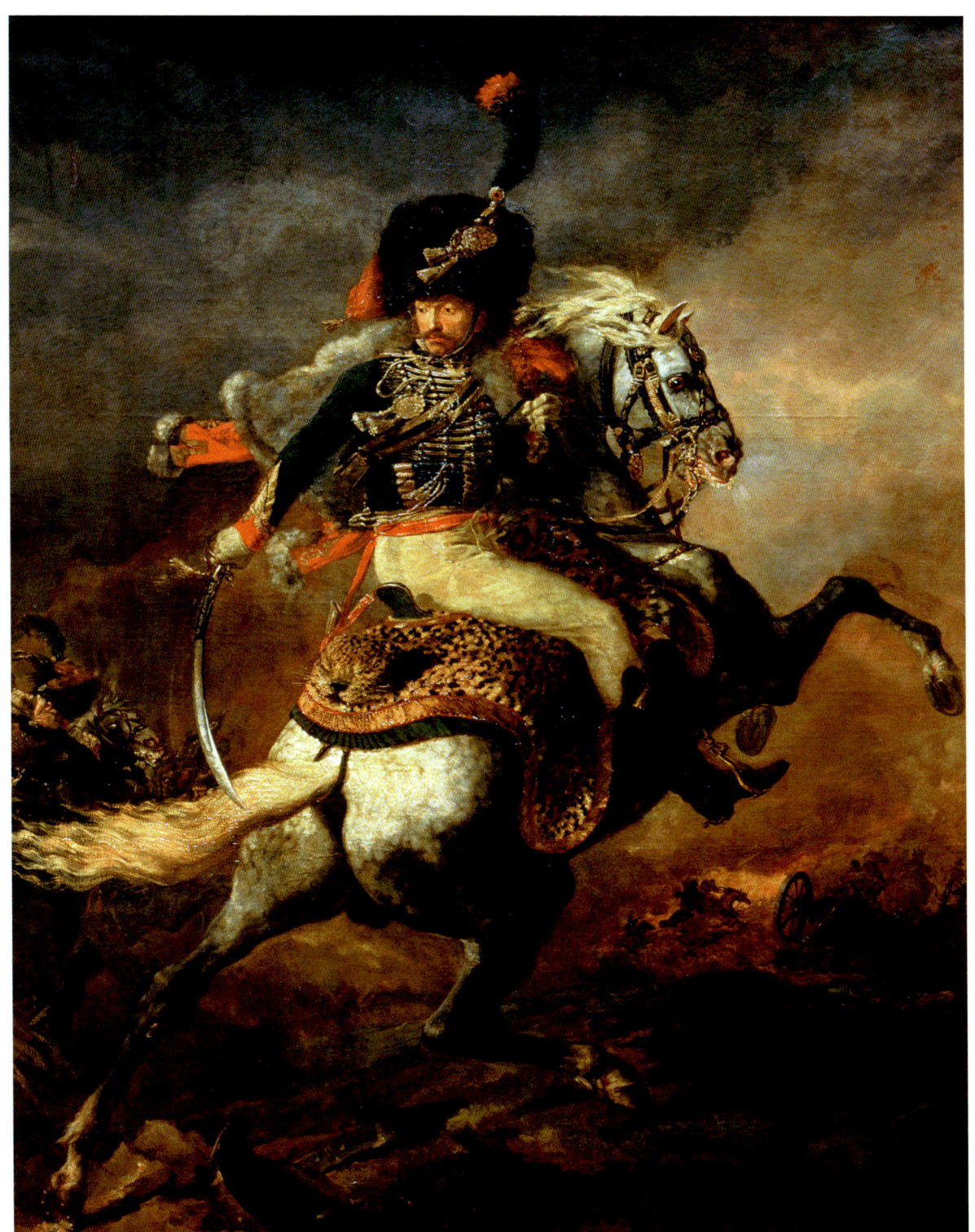

Théodore Géricault (1791–1824)

Officer of the Hussars

Officier de chasseurs à cheval de la
garde impériale chargeant

Offizier der kaiserlichen Gardejäger
beim Angriff

Oficial de cazadores a caballo de la
guardia imperial, a la carga

Ufficiale della fanteria imperiale
all'attacco

Officier van de Keizerlijke Garde in
de aanval

1812, Oil on canvas/Huile sur toile,
349 × 266 cm, Musée du Louvre, Paris

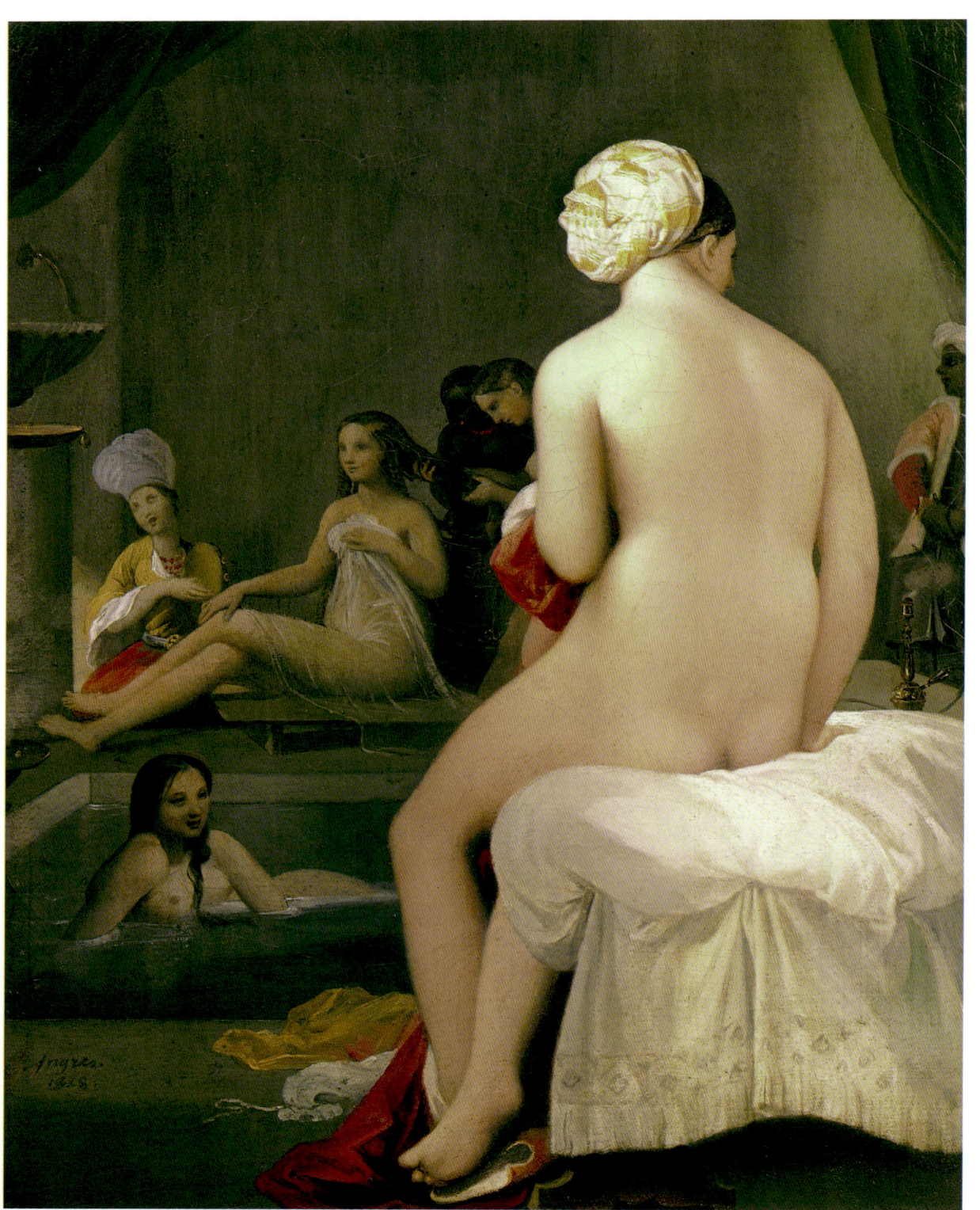

Jean-Auguste-Dominique Ingres (1780–1867)

The Little Bather in the Harem

La Petite Baigneuse. Intérieur de harem

Die kleine Badende im Harem

Las pequeñas bañistas en el harén

La piccola bagnante nell'arem

De kleine baadster in de harem

1828, Oil on canvas/Huile sur toile, 35 × 27 cm, Musée du Louvre, Paris

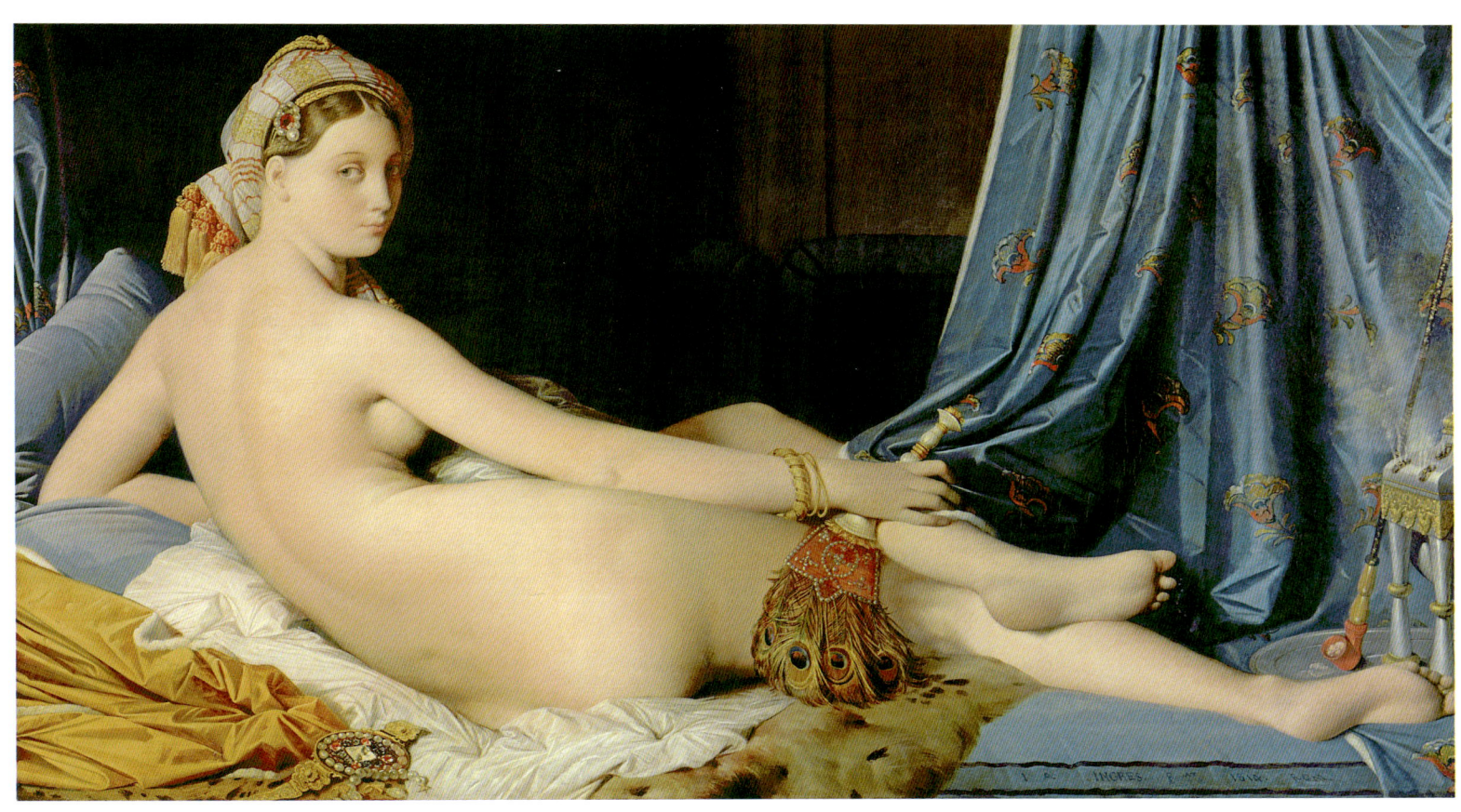

Jean-Auguste-Dominique Ingres (1780–1867)

The Grande Odalisque

Une Odalisque, *dite* La Grande Odalisque

Die Große Odaliske

La gran odalisca

La grande odalisca

La Grande odalisque

1814, Oil on canvas/Huile sur toile, 91 × 162 cm, Musée du Louvre, Paris

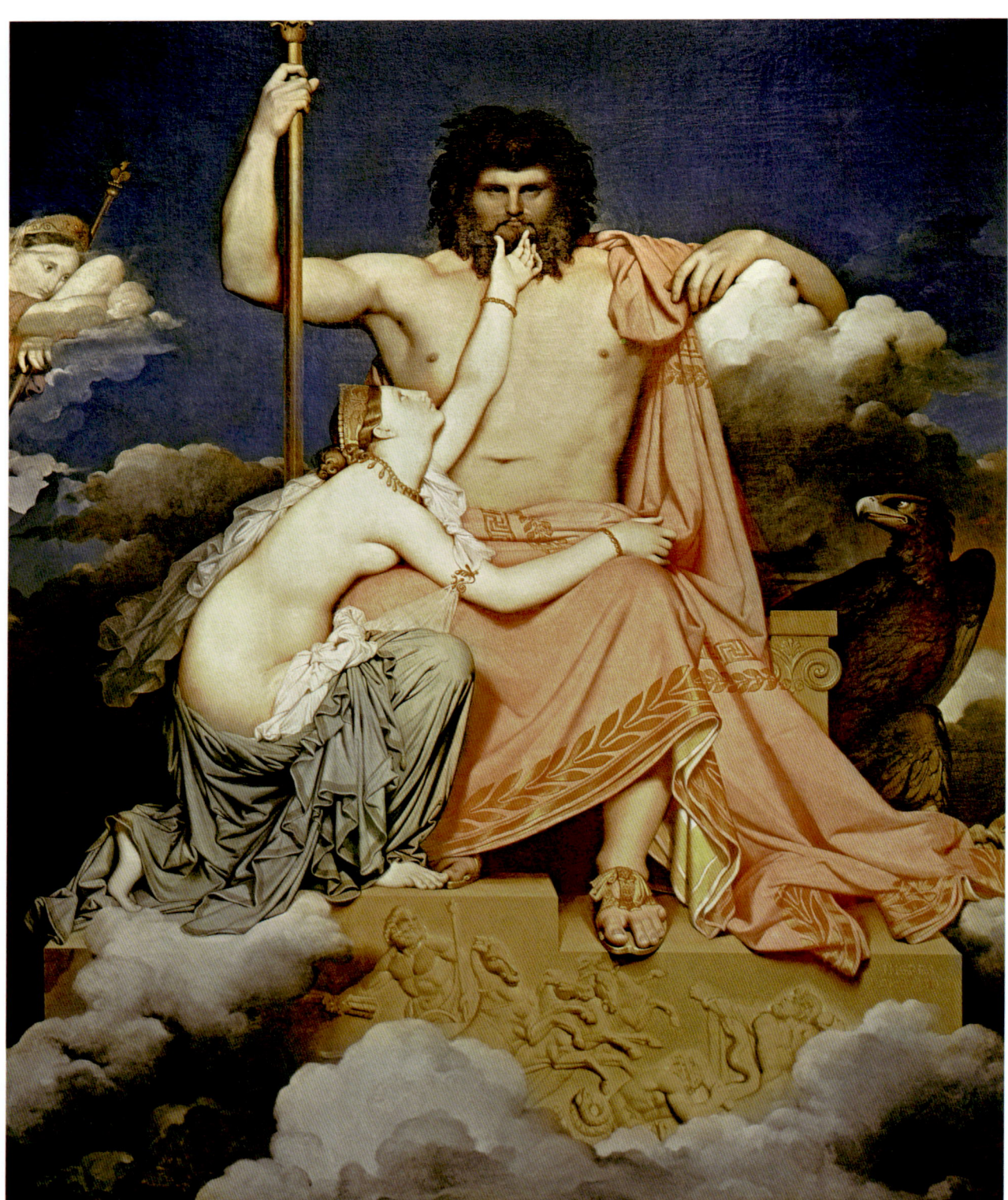

Jean-Auguste-Dominique Ingres (1780–1867)

Jupiter and Thetis

Jupiter et Thétis

Jupiter und Thetis

Júpiter y Tetis

Giove e Teti

Jupiter en Thetis

1811, Oil on canvas/Huile sur toile, 324 × 260 cm, Musée Granet, Aix-en-Provence

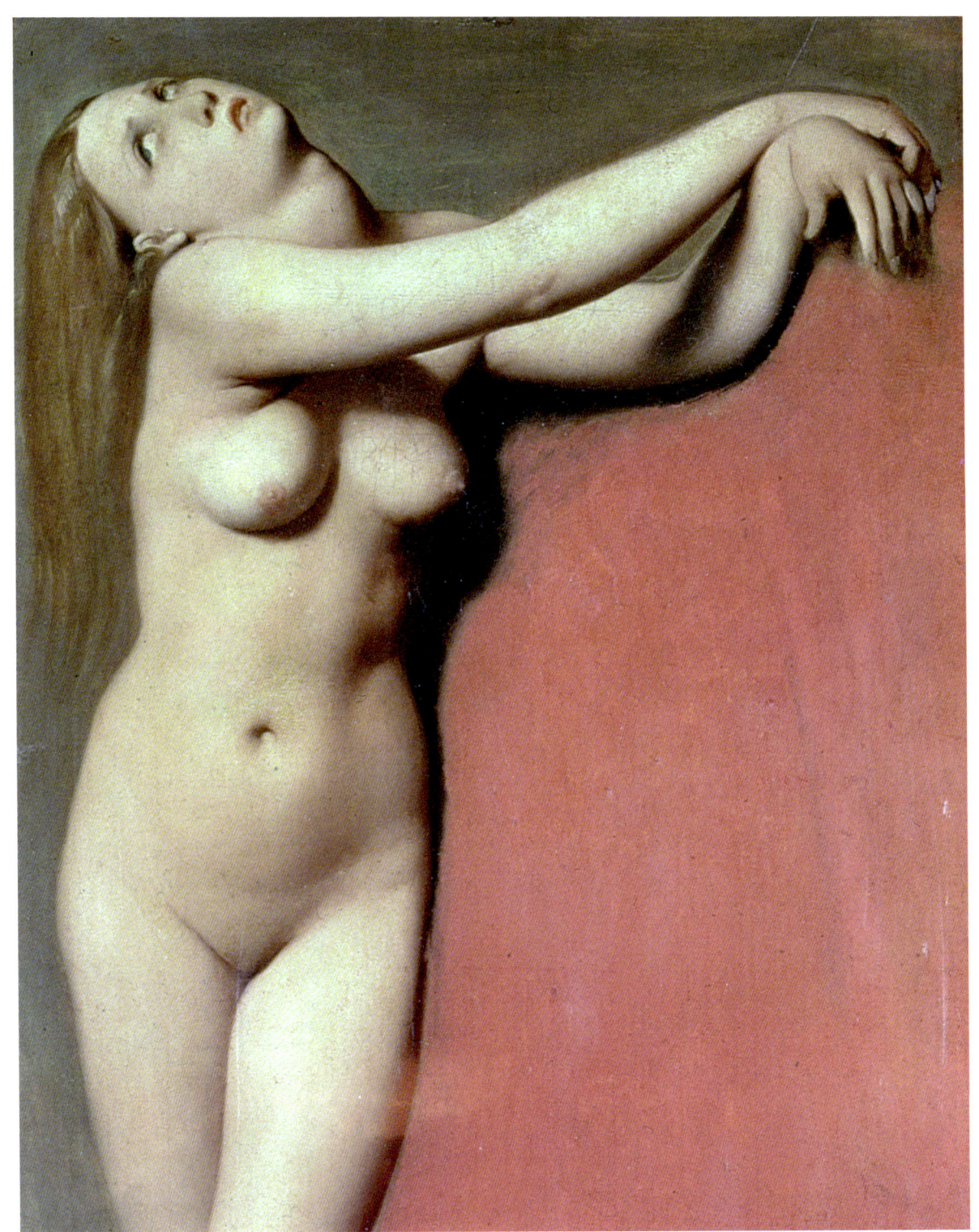

**Jean-Auguste-Dominique Ingres
(1780–1867)**

Angelique *(detail)*

Angélique *(détail)*

Angelika *(Detail)*

Angélica *(detalle)*

Angelica *(dettaglio)*

Angelica *(detail)*

c. 1819, Oil on canvas/Huile sur toile,
85,4 × 42,5 cm, Musée du Louvre, Paris

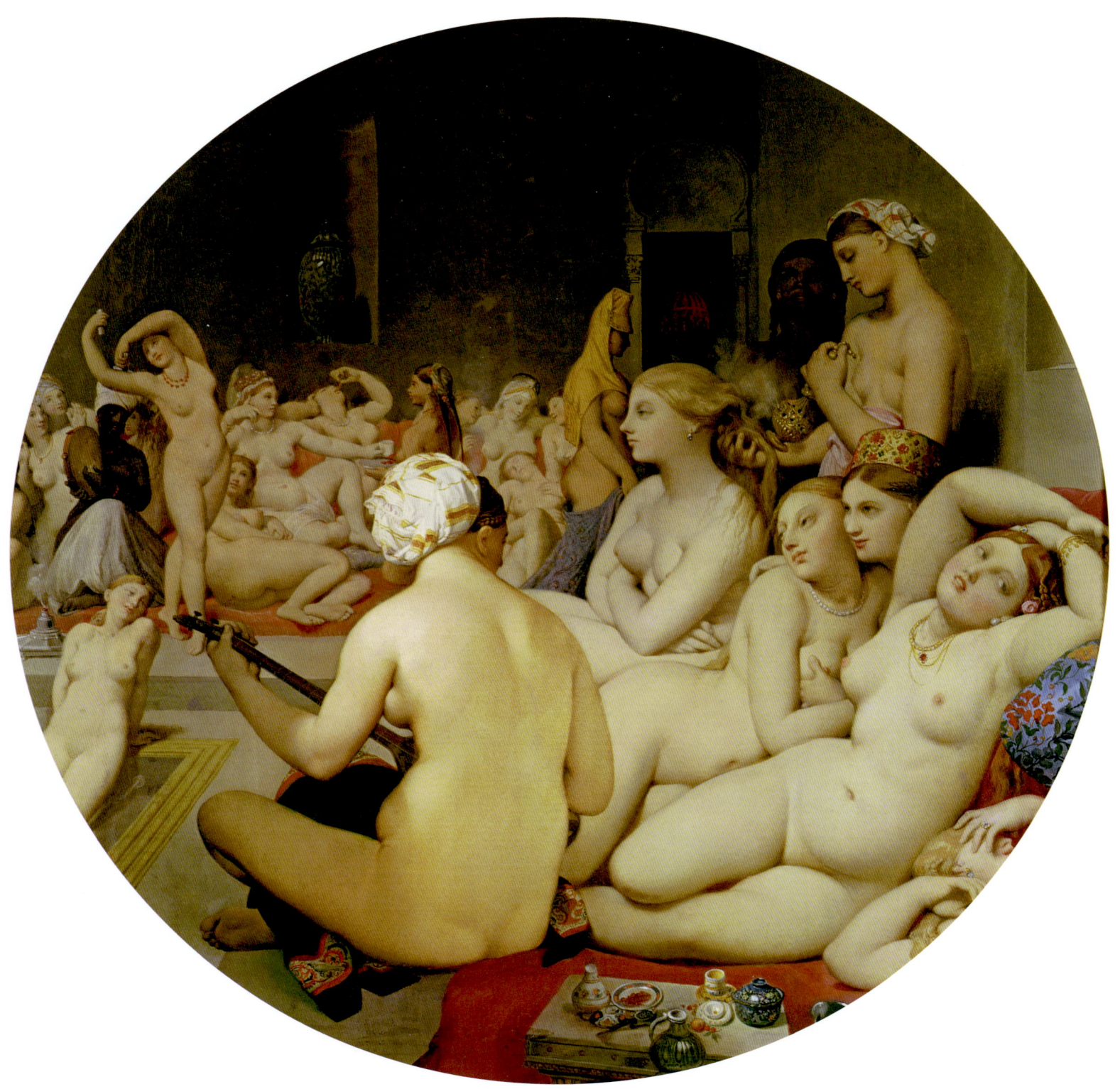

**Jean-Auguste-Dominique Ingres
(1780–1867)**

The Turkish Bath

Le Bain turc

Das türkische Bad

El baño turco

Il bagno turco

Het Turkse bad

1862, Oil on panel/Huile sur bois, 108 cm,
Musée du Louvre, Paris

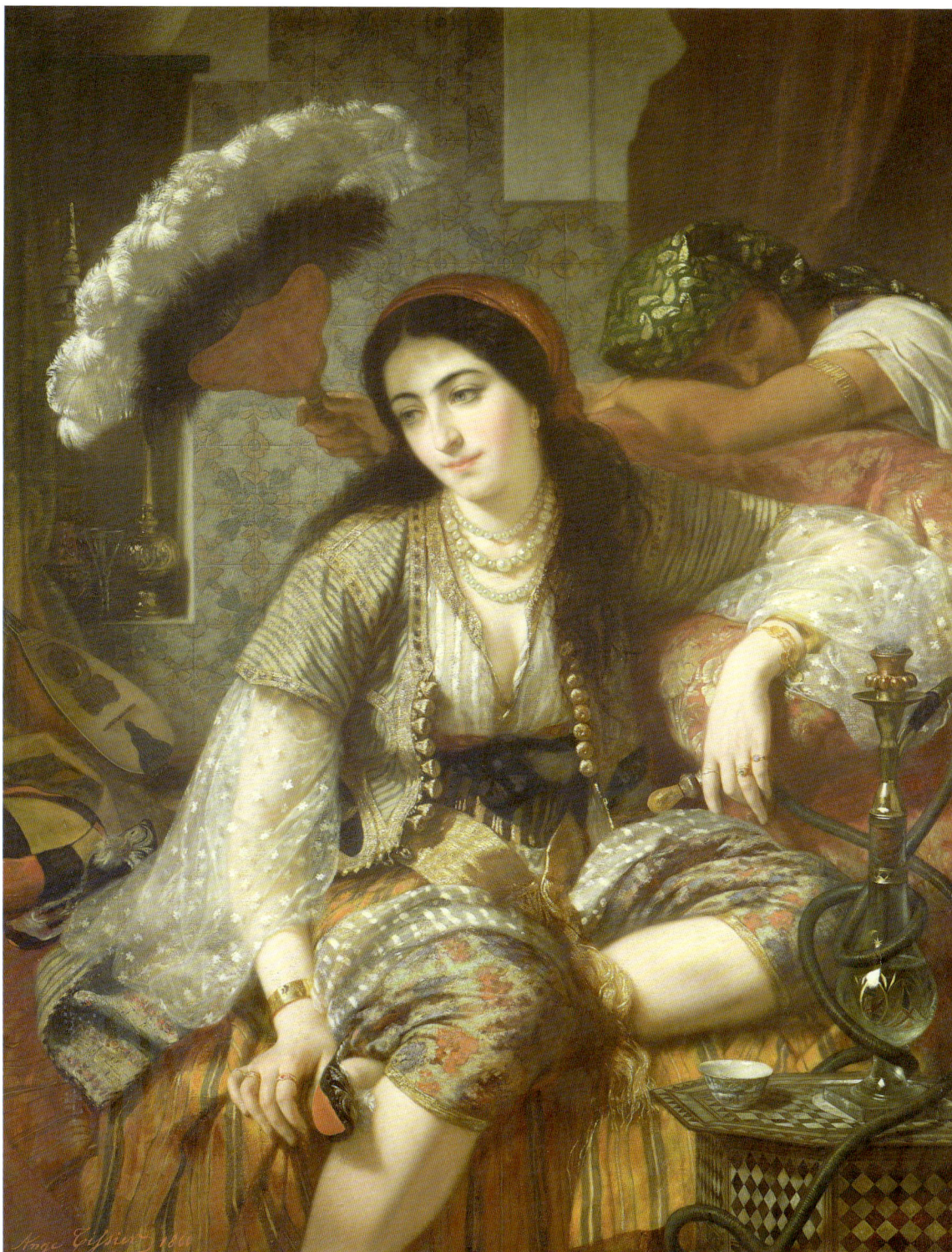

**Jean Baptiste Ange Tissier
(1814–1876)**

Odalisque

Une Algérienne et son esclave

Odaliske

Odalisca

Odalisca

Odalisk

1860, Oil on canvas/Huile sur toile,
130 × 97,5 cm, Musée du quai Branly-
Jacques Chirac, Paris

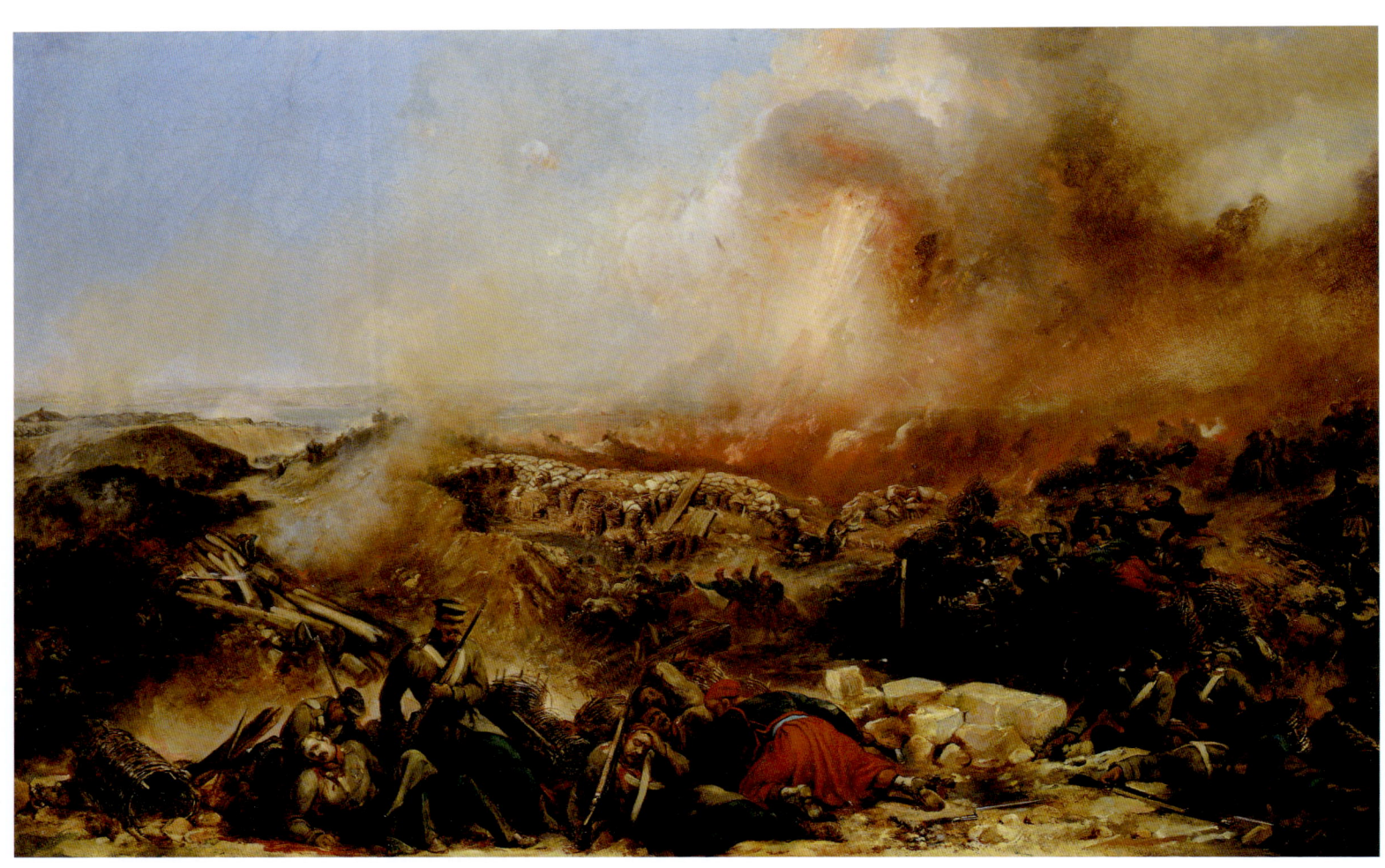

Jean-Charles Langlois (1789–1870)

The Battle of Sebastopol *(left section of triptych)*

La Bataille de Sébastopol *(volet gauche du triptyque)*

Die Schlacht von Sewastopol *(linker Teil des Triptychon)*

La batalla de Sebastopol *(panel izquierdo de un tríptico)*

La battaglia di Sebastopoli *(parte sinistra del trittico)*

De Slag bij Sebastopol *(linkerdeel van het triptiek)*

1855, Oil on canvas/Huile sur toile, 46 × 61 cm, Musée des Beaux-Arts, Caen

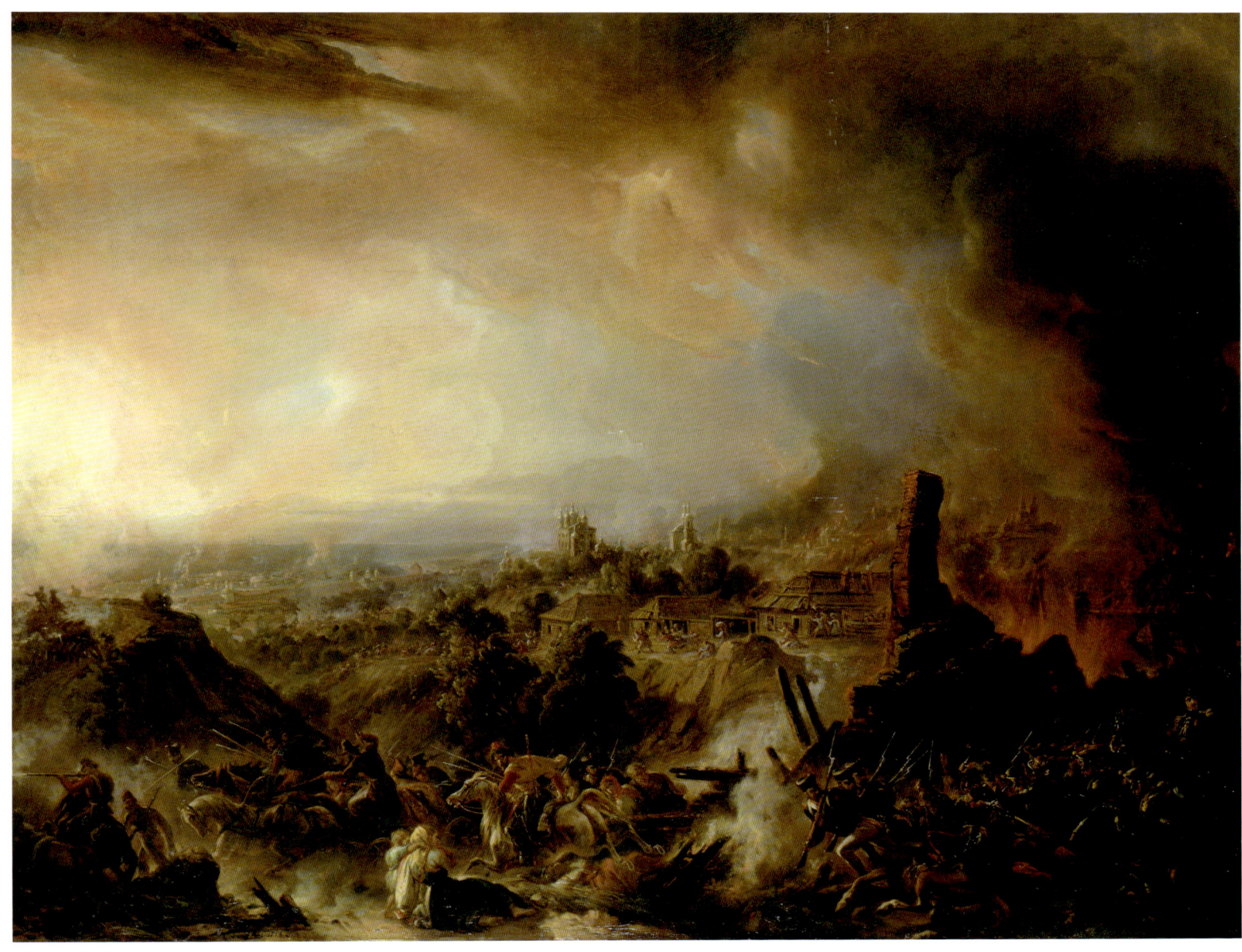

Jean-Charles Langlois (1789–1870)

The Burning of Moscow in 1812

L'Incendie de Moscou, en 1812

Der Brand von Moskau 1812

El incendio de Moscú 1812

L'incendio di Mosca nel 1812

De brand van Moskou, 1812

1854, Oil on canvas/Huile sur toile, 112,5 × 145 cm, Musée des Beaux-Arts, Caen

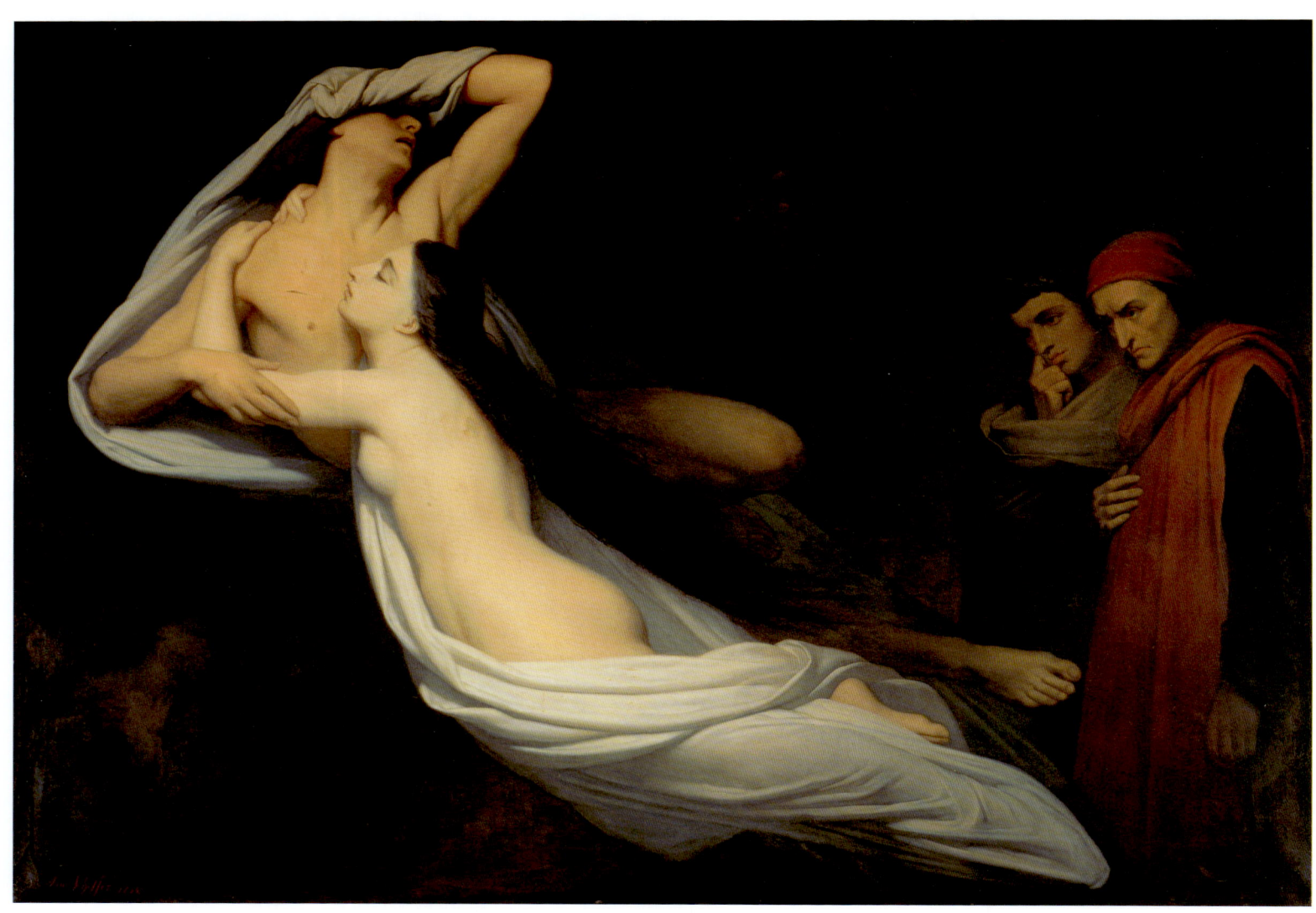

Ary Scheffer (1795–1858)

The Figures of Francesca da Rimini and Paolo da Verrucchio Appear to Dante and Virgil

Les ombres de Francesca da Rimini et de Paolo Malatesta apparaissent à Dante et à Virgile

Die Schatten der Francesca da Rimini und des Paolo Malatesta erscheinen Dante und Vergil

Las sombras de Francesca da Rimini y de Paolo Malatesta se aparecen a Dante y Virgilio

Gli spettri di Francesca da Rimini e Paolo Malatesta appaiono a Dante e Virgilio

De schimmen van Francesca da Rimini en Paolo Malatesta verschijnen aan Dante en Vergilius

1855, Oil on canvas/Huile sur toile, 171 × 239 cm, Musée du Louvre, Paris

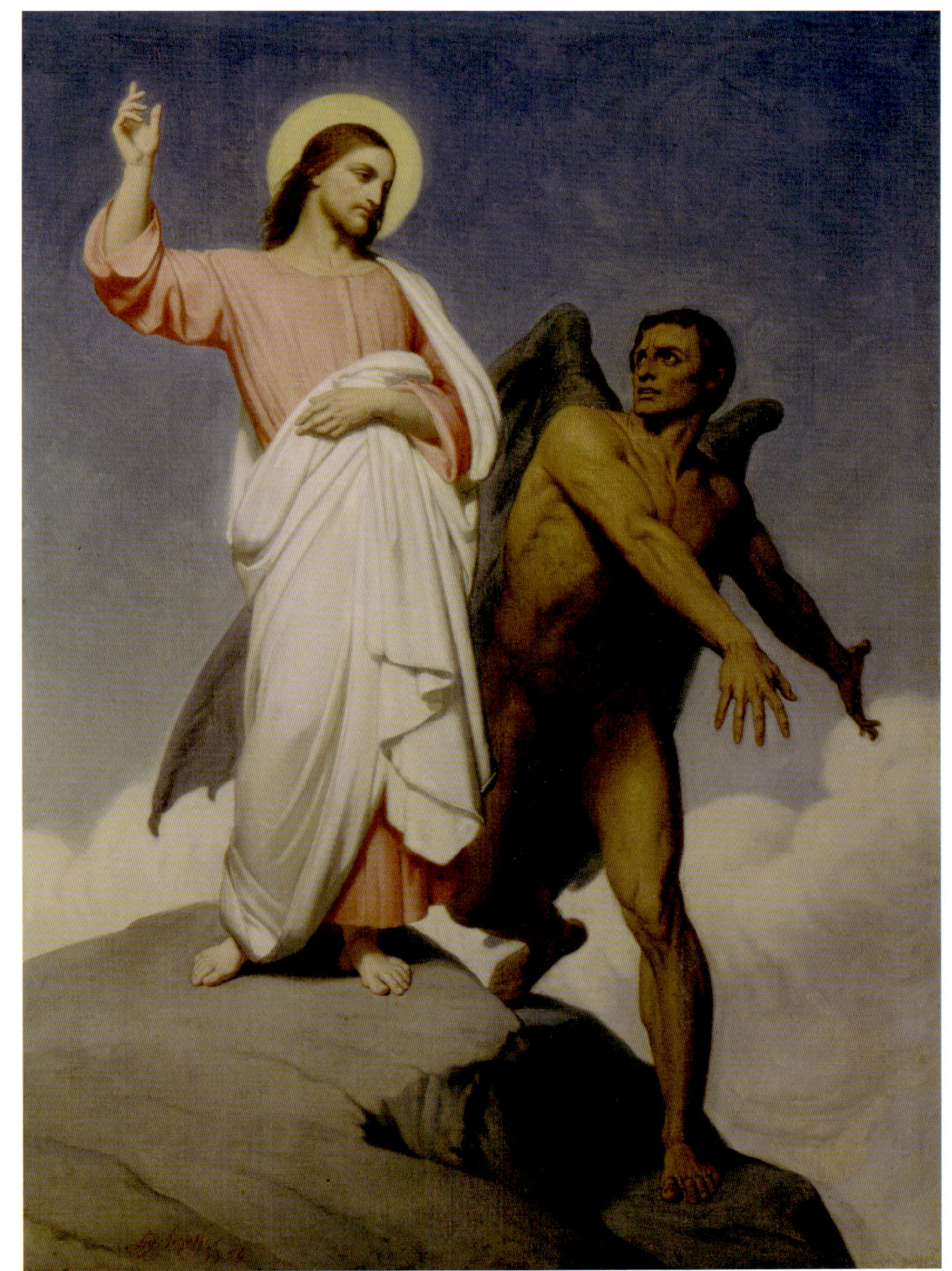

Ary Scheffer (1795–1858)

The Temptation of Christ

La Tentation du Christ

Die Versuchung Christi

La tentación de Cristo

La tentazione di Gesù Cristo

De verzoeking van Christus

1854, Oil on canvas/Huile sur toile, 75,5 × 55 cm,
National Gallery of Victoria, Melbourne

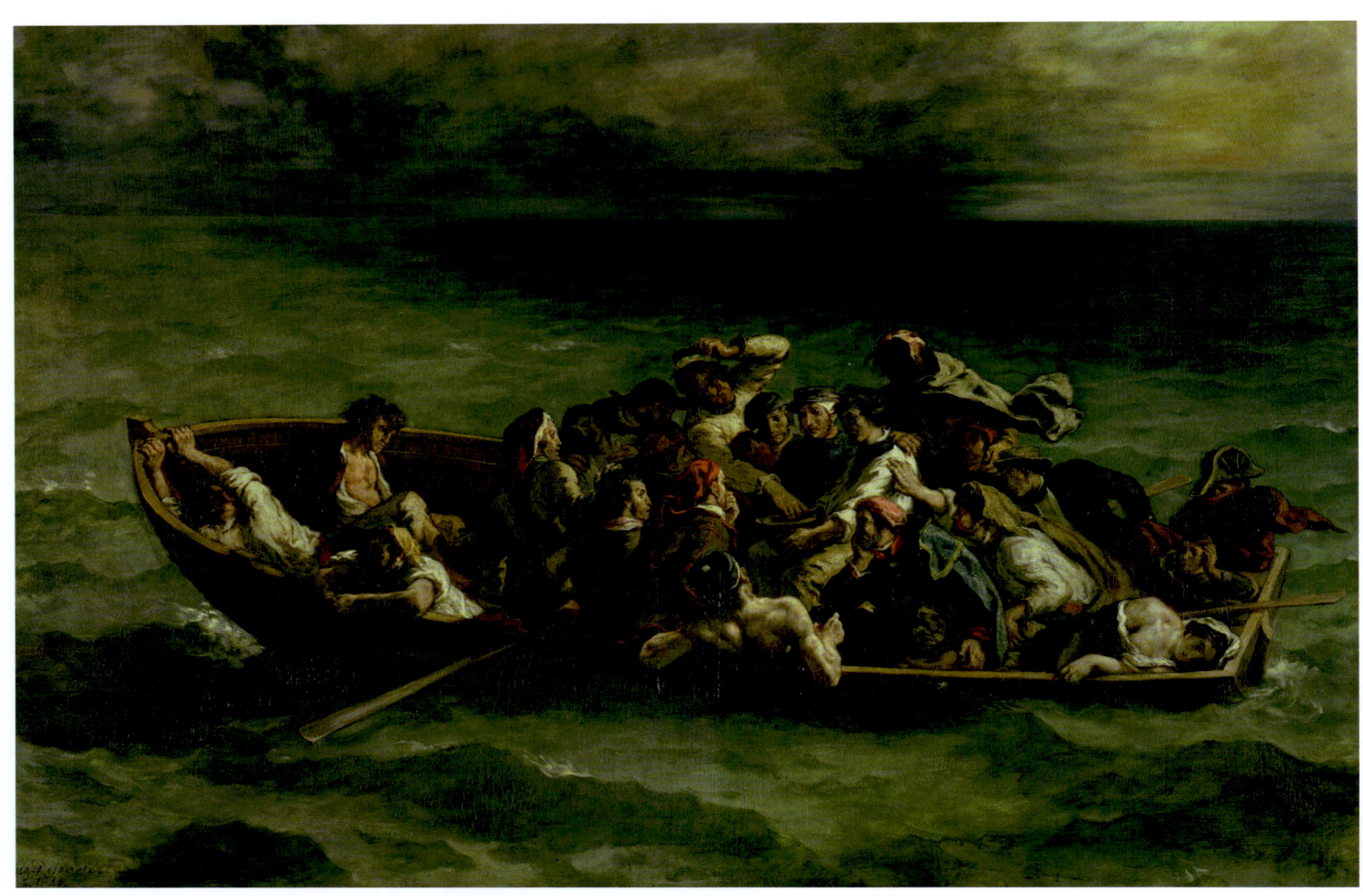

Eugène Delacroix (1798–1863)

The Shipwreck of Don Juan

Le Naufrage de Don Juan

Der Schiffsbruch von Don Juan

El naufragio del Don Juan

Il naufragio di Don Giovanni

De schipbreuk van Don Juan

1840, Oil on canvas/Huile sur toile, 135 × 196 cm, Musée du Louvre, Paris

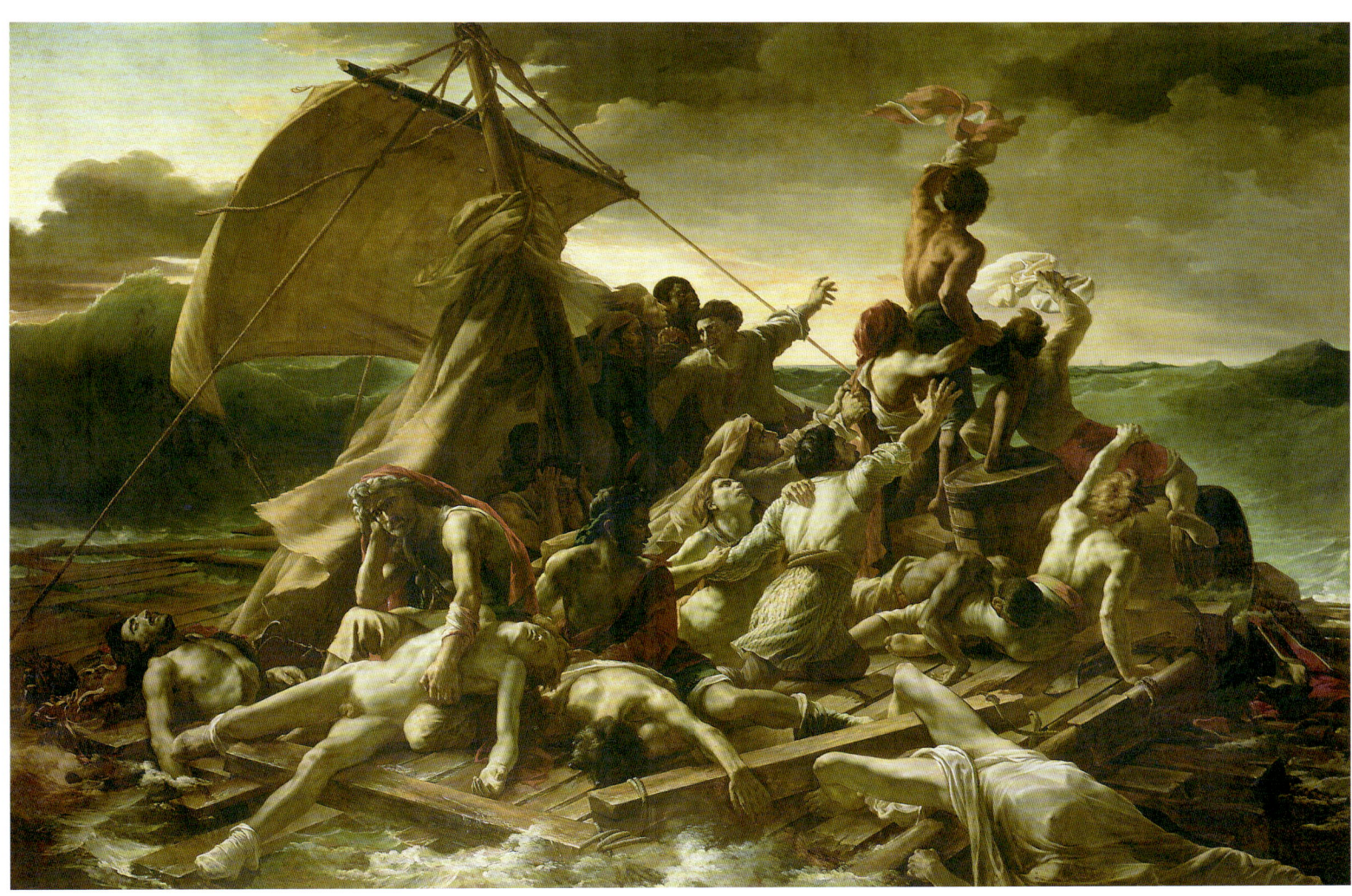

Théodore Géricault (1791–1824)

The Raft of the Medusa

Le Radeau de la Méduse

Das Floß der Medusa

La balsa de la Medusa

La zattera della Medusa

Het vlot van de Medusa

1819, Oil on canvas/Huile sur toile, 491 × 716 cm, Musée du Louvre, Paris

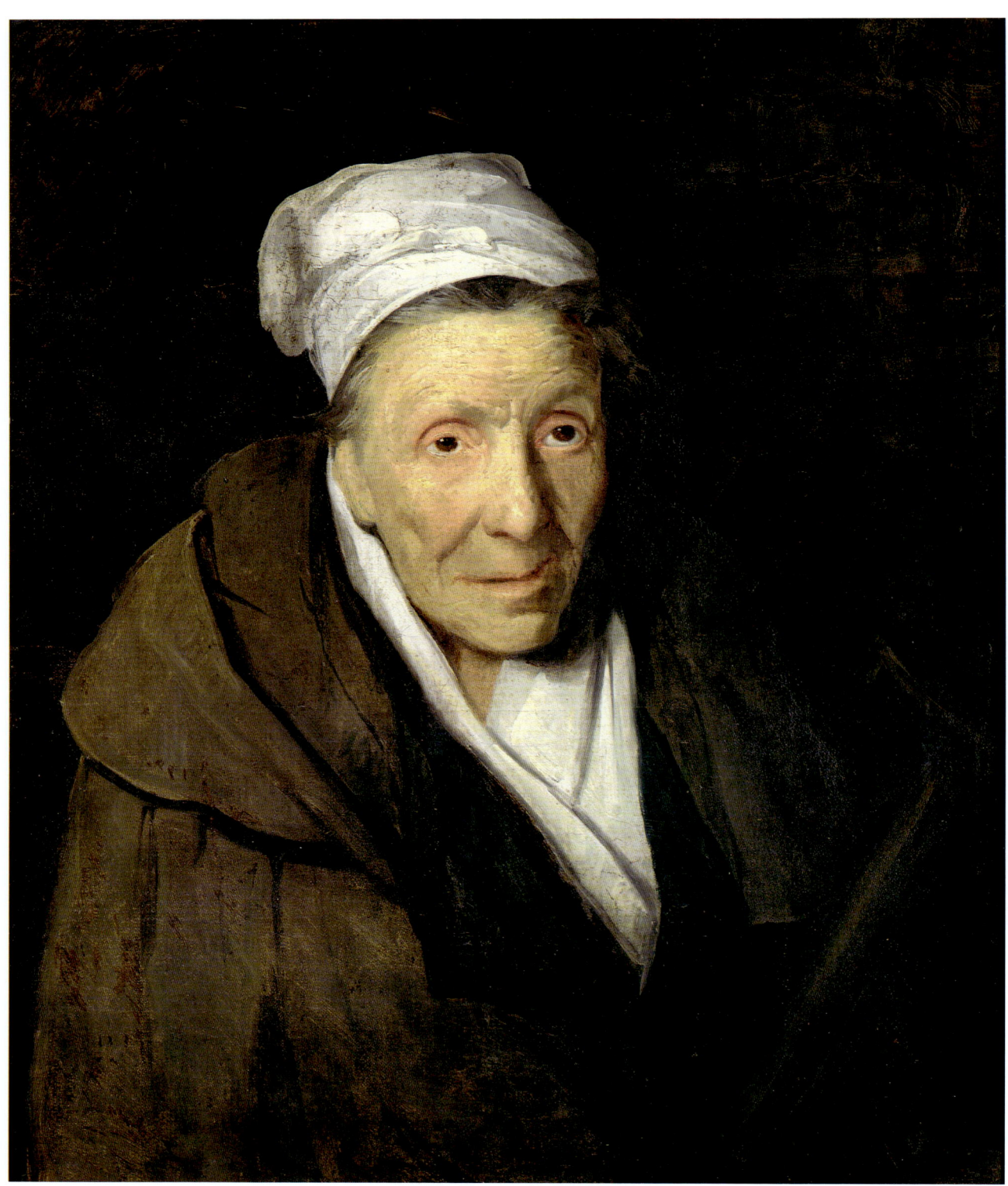

**Théodore Géricault
(1791–1824)**

The Woman with
Gambling Mania

La Folle monomane
du jeu

Die irrsinnige Spielerin

La ludópata

Alienata con la
monomania del gioco

De krankzinnige
speelster

c. 1820, Oil on canvas/
Huile sur toile, 77 × 65 cm,
Musée du Louvre, Paris

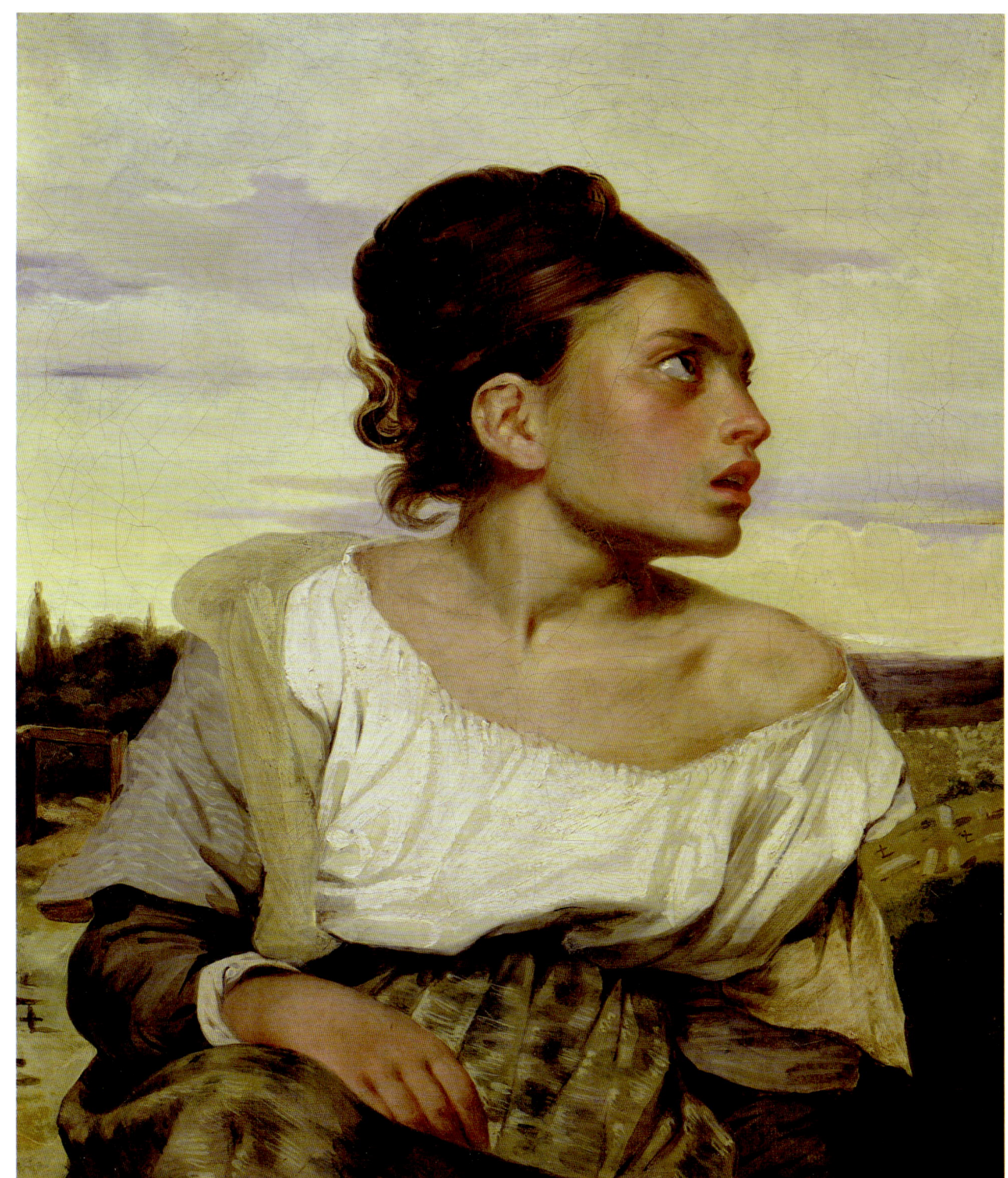

**Eugène Delacroix
(1789–1863)**

Young Orphan in the
Cemetery

Jeune Orpheline au
cimetière

Junge Waise auf dem
Friedhof

Joven huérfana en el
cementerio

Orfanella al cimitero

Weesje op het kerkhof

c. 1824, Oil on canvas/Huile
sur toile, 66,5 × 54,5 cm,
Musée du Louvre, Paris

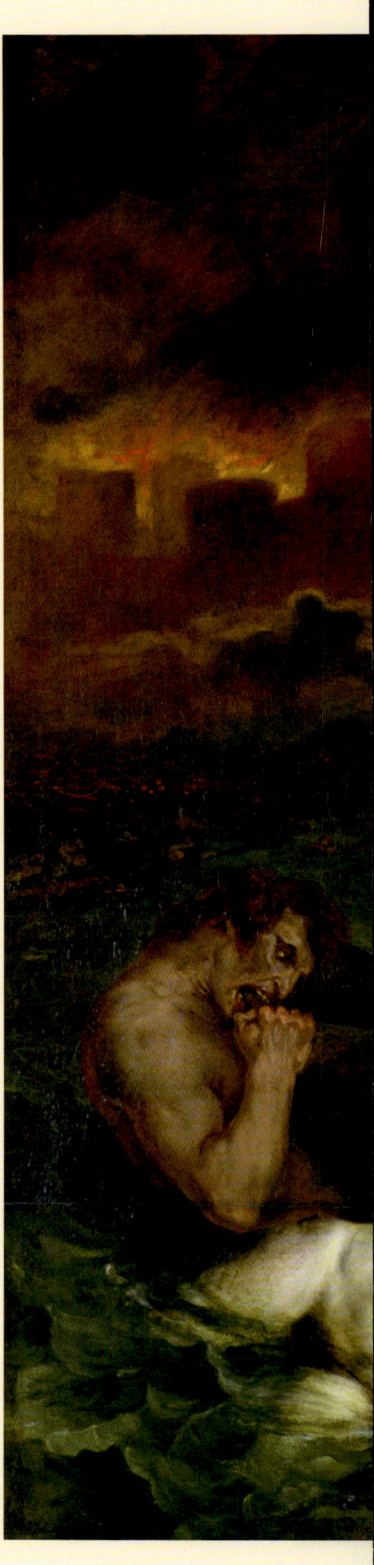

Eugène Delacroix (1798–1863)

Dante and Virgil in the Underworld

Dante et Virgile aux enfers, *dit aussi* La Barque de Dante

Dante und Vergil in der Unterwelt

Dante y Virgilio en el ultramundo

Dante e Virgilio negli Inferi

Dante en Vergilius in de onderwereld

1822, Oil on canvas/Huile sur toile, 189 × 241 cm, Musée du Louvre, Paris

Delacroix here represents the crossing, by Dante and his guide Virgil, of the mythological river Styx. Shocked, Dante recoils from the dead who are floating in the water and clinging to the boat, whilst Virgil looks on unflinchingly. Against the background of burning houses, the main figure Dante stands out in strong complementary colors red and green.

Delacroix représente ici la traversée du Styx – le fleuve des Enfers – par Dante et son guide Virgile. Effrayé, Dante défaille devant les morts qui essaient de s'accrocher à la barque, cependant que Virgile, impavide, guide l'embarcation droit devant. Sur le fond des maisons en flammes, Dante se détache en puissantes couleurs complémentaires, rouge et vert.

Delcroix stellt hier die Überfahrt von Dante und seinem Führer Vergil über den Todesfluss Styx dar. Erschrocken weicht Dante vor den sich an den Nachen klammernden, im Wasser treibenden Toten zurück, während Vergil unbeirrt hinschaut. Vor dem Hintergrund der brennenden Häuser hebt sich die Hauptfigur Dante in kräftigen Komplementärfarben Rot und Grün ab.

Delacroix presenta aquí a Dante y su guía Virgilio atravesando el río Estigia. Dante, sorprendido, se aparta de los muertos que, desde el agua, se apilan contra la barca, mientras que Virgilio mira inmutable hacia adelante. Sobre el fondo de casas en llamas se resalta la figura principal de Dante en sus intensos colores complementarios (rojo y verde).

Delacroix qui raffigura la traversata di Dante e della sua guida Virgilio sullo Stige, il fiume infernale. Dante indietreggia spaventato aggrappandosi alla barchetta, ricacciando i morti nell'acqua, mentre Virgilio osserva impassibile. Davanti allo sfondo delle case in fiamme la figura principale di Dante si distingue nei potenti colori complementari del rosso e il verde.

Delacroix beeldt hier Dante en zijn gids Vergilius uit bij het oversteken van de Styx, de rivier die naar de onderwereld leidt. Verschrikt deinst Dante terug voor de in het water drijvende doden, die zich vastklampen aan de boorden van het bootje, terwijl Vergilius toekijkt. Tegen een achtergrond van brandende huizen verheft de hoofdpersoon Dante zich in de krachtige complementaire kleuren rood en groen.

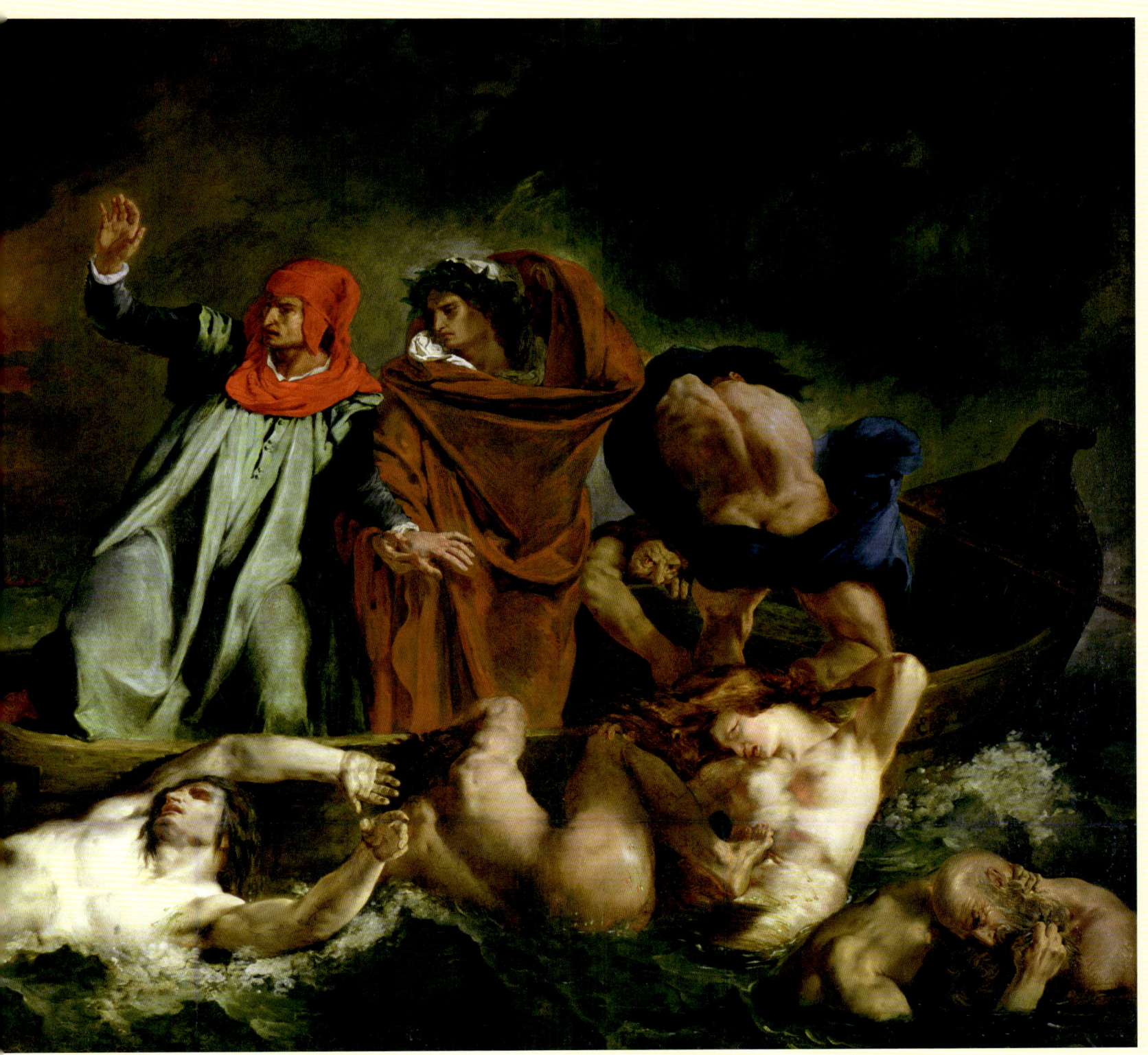

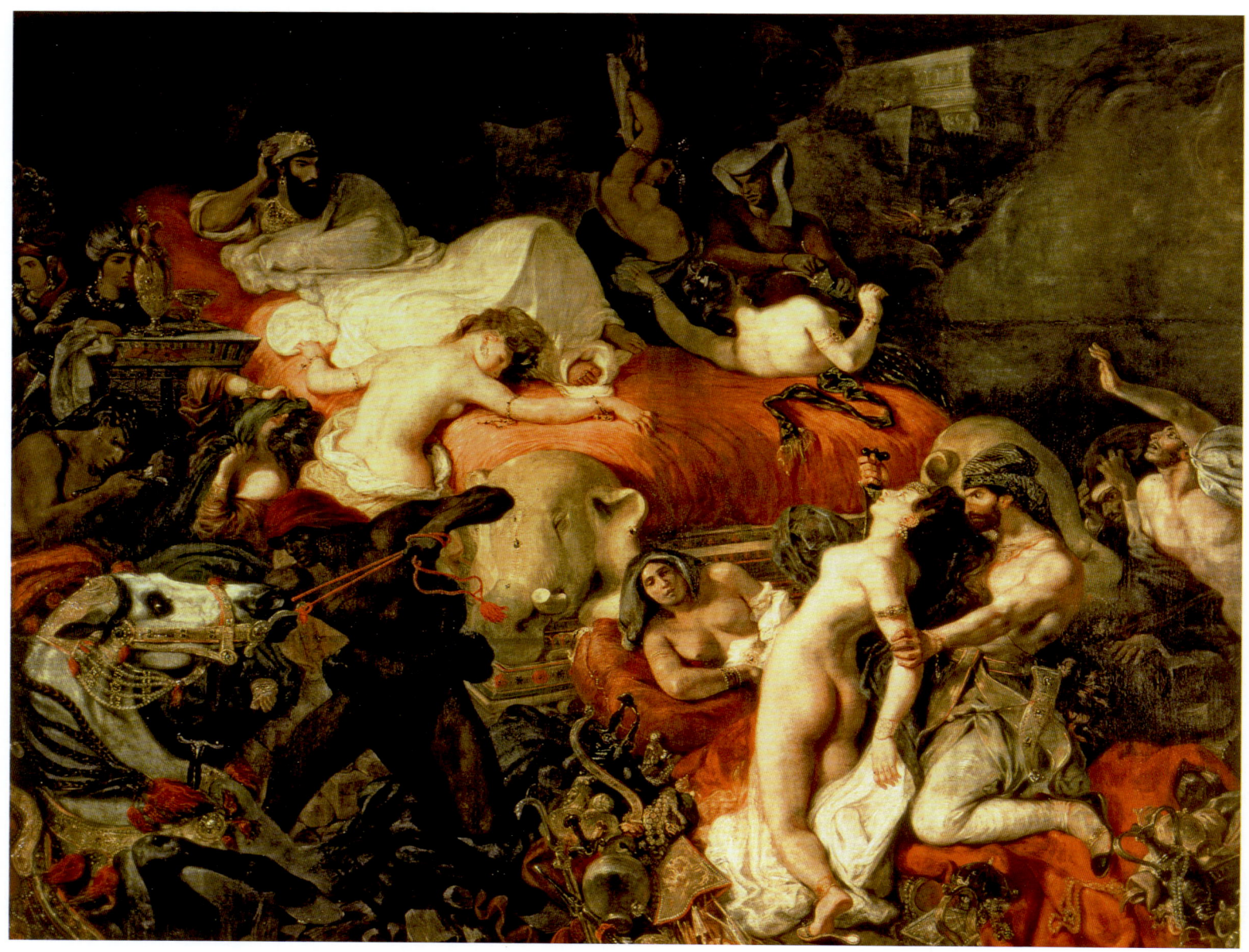

Eugène Delacroix (1798–1863)

The Death of Sardanapalus

Mort de Sardanapale

Der Tod des Sardanapalus

La muerte de Sardanápalo

La morte di Sardanapalo

De dood van Sardanapalus

1827, Oil on canvas/Huile sur toile, 392 × 496 cm, Musée du Louvre, Paris

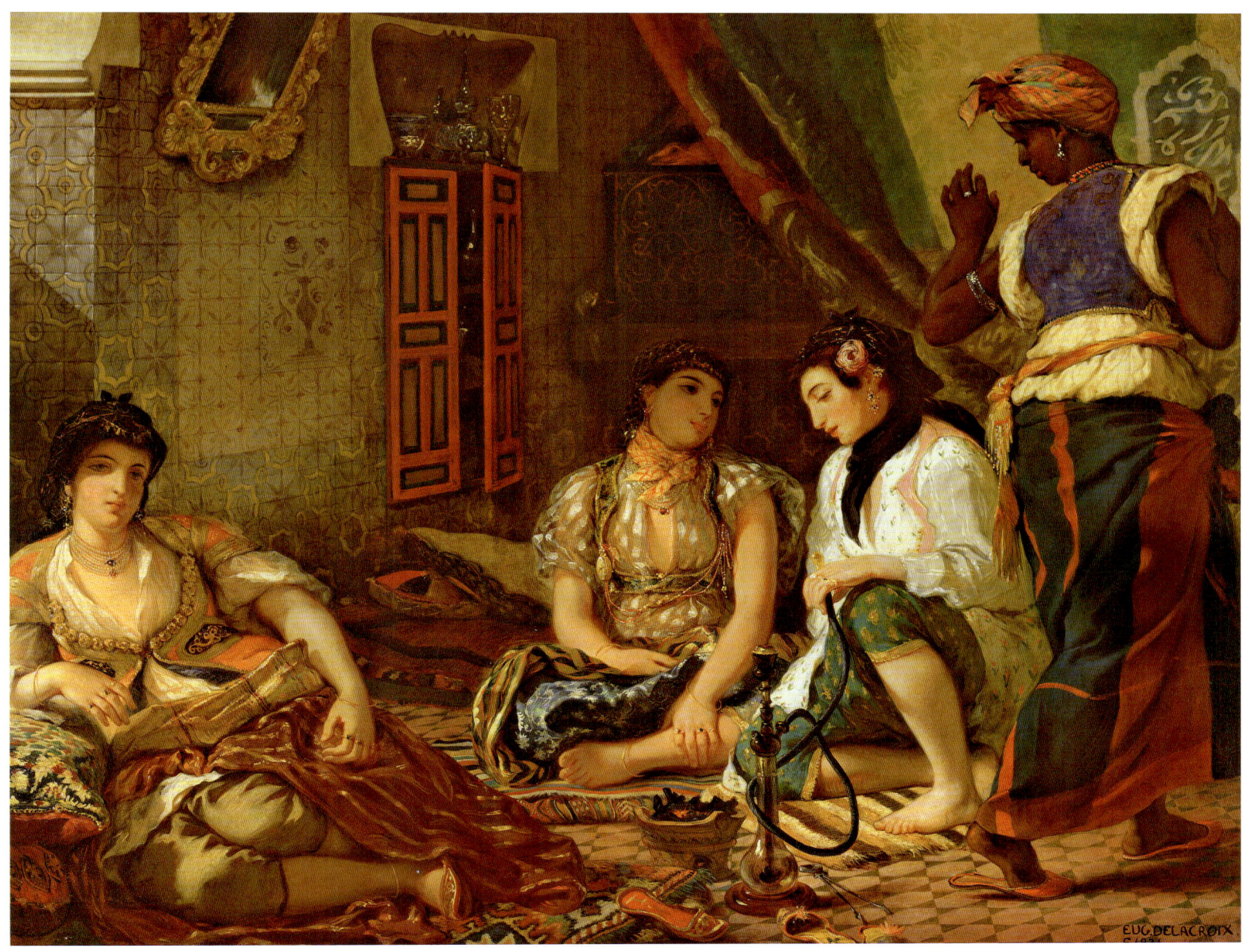

Eugène Delacroix (1798–1863)

Women of Algiers in their Quarters

Femmes d'Alger dans leur appartement

Frauen von Algier in ihrem Gemach

Mujeres de Argel

Donne di Algeri nei loro appartamenti

Vrouwen van Algiers in hun vertrek

1834, Oil on canvas/Huile sur toile, 180 × 229 cm, Musée du Louvre, Paris

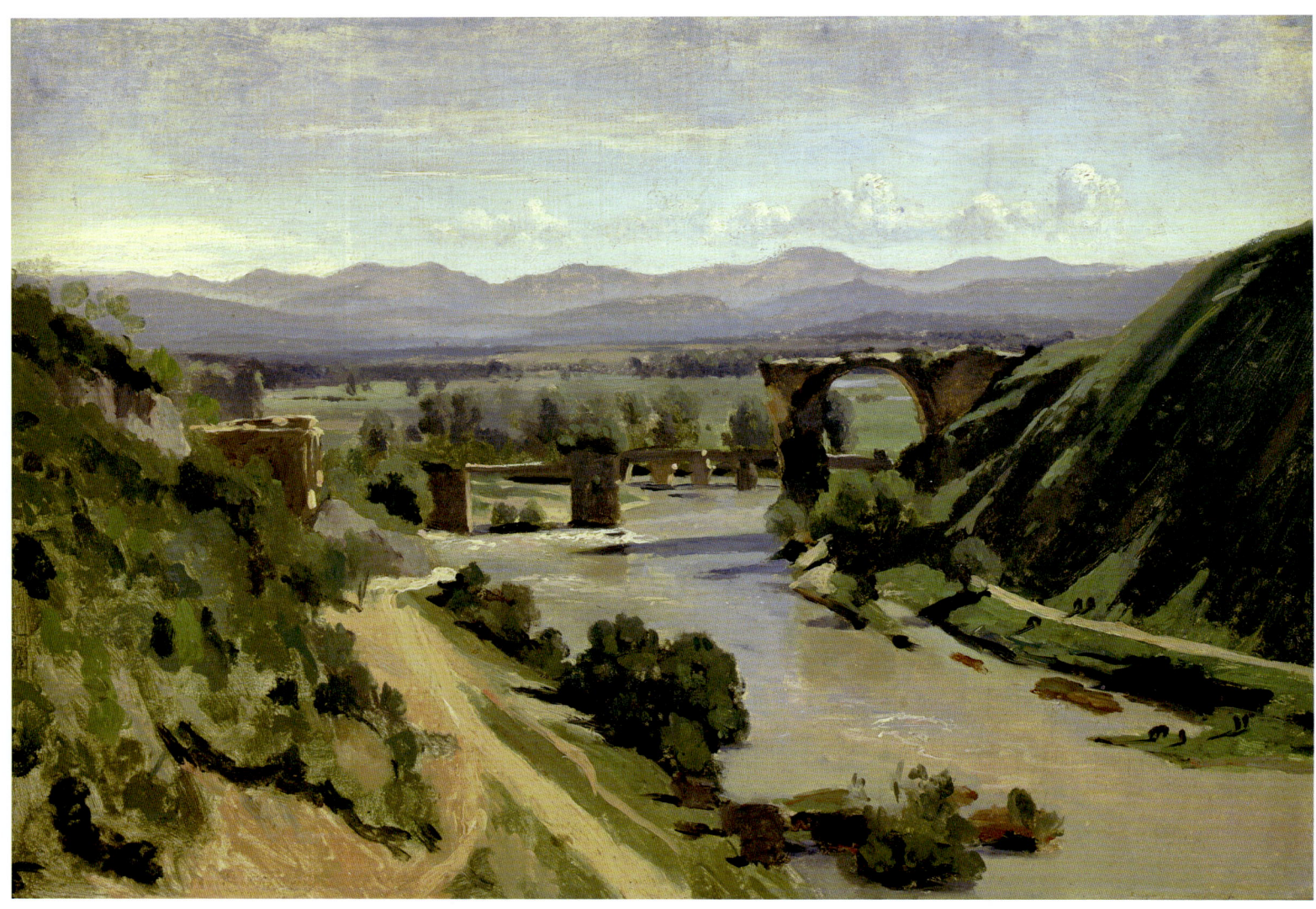

Jean-Baptiste Camille Corot (1796–1875)

Narni, The Bridge of Augustus over the Nera

Le Pont de Narni

Die Brücke von Narni

El puente de Narni

Il ponte di Narni

De brug van Narni

1826, Oil on paper mounted on canvas/ Huile sur papier marouflé sur toile, 34 × 48 cm, Musée du Louvre, Paris

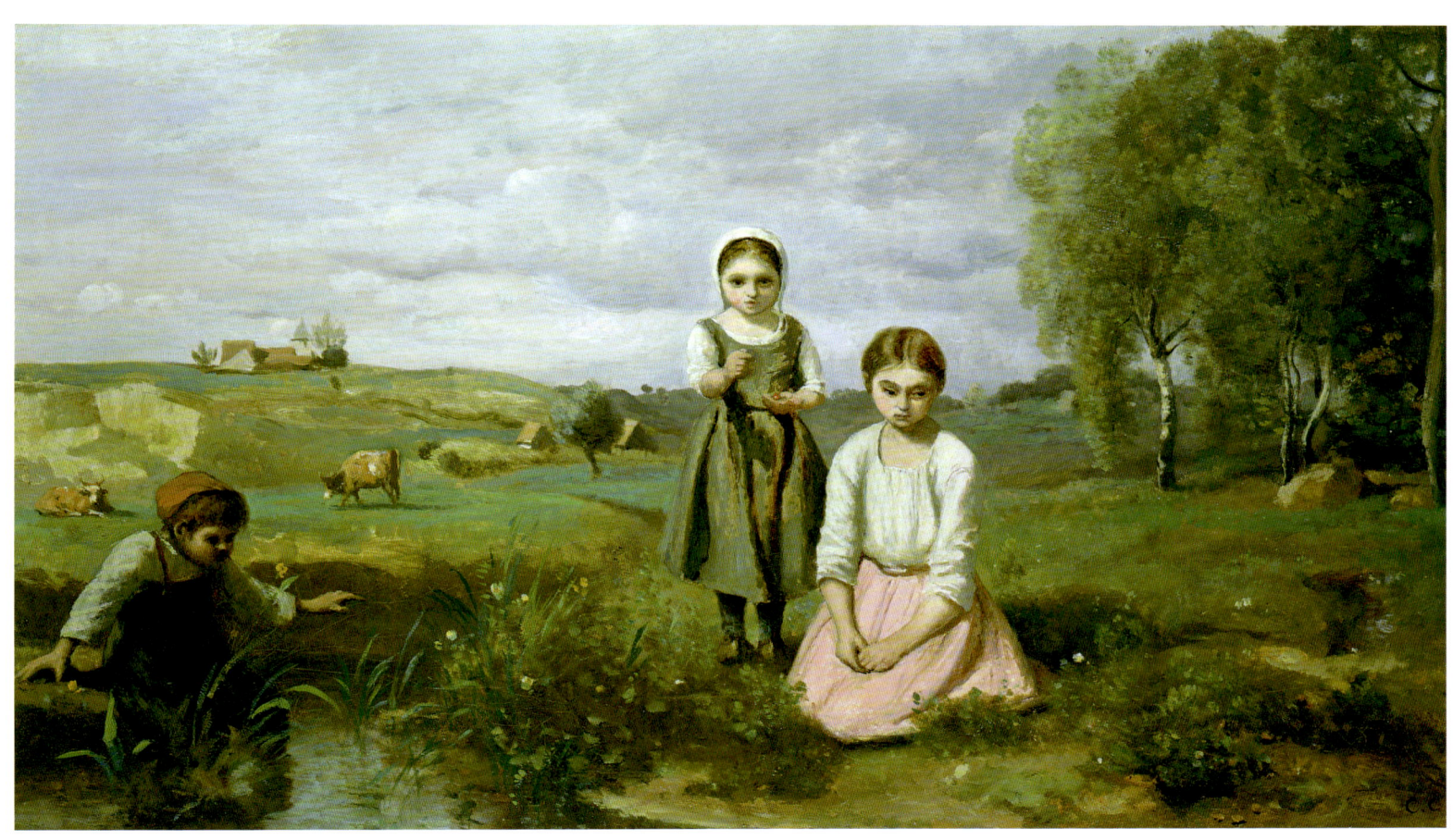

Jean-Baptiste Camille Corot (1796–1875)

Children beside a brook in the countryside, Lormes

Enfants au bord d'un ruisseau dans la campagne à Lormes

Kinder neben einem Bach auf dem Land

Niños junto a un arroyo en el capo

Bambini vicino a un ruscello in campagna

Kinderen bij een beek op het platteland

c. 1840, Oil on canvas/Huile sur toile, 43 × 74 cm, Private collection

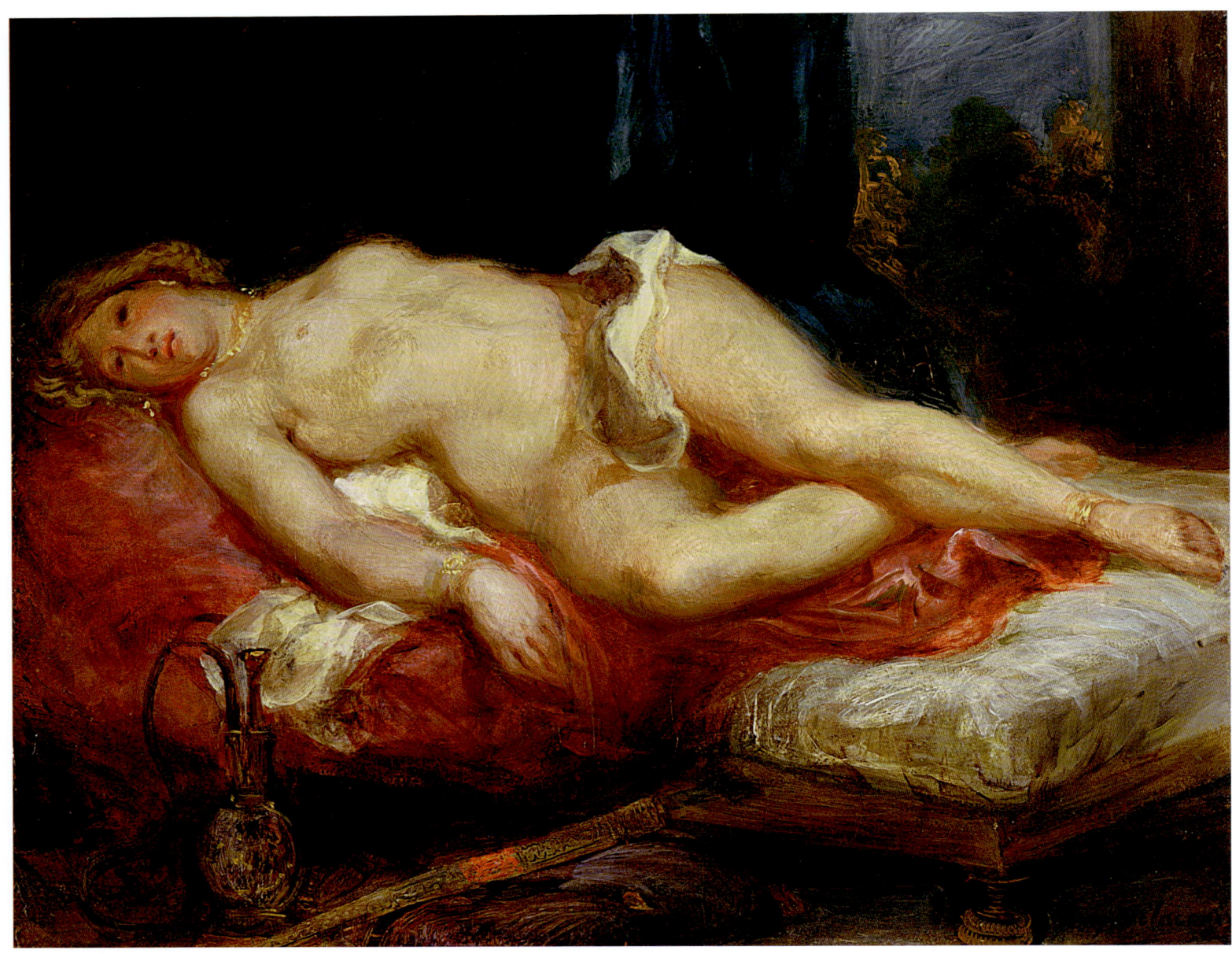

Eugène Delacroix (1798–1863)

Odalisque

Odalisque

Odaliske

Odalisca

Odalisca

Odalisk

c. 1825, Oil on canvas/Huile sur toile, 37,8 × 46,4 cm, Fitzwilliam Museum, Cambridge

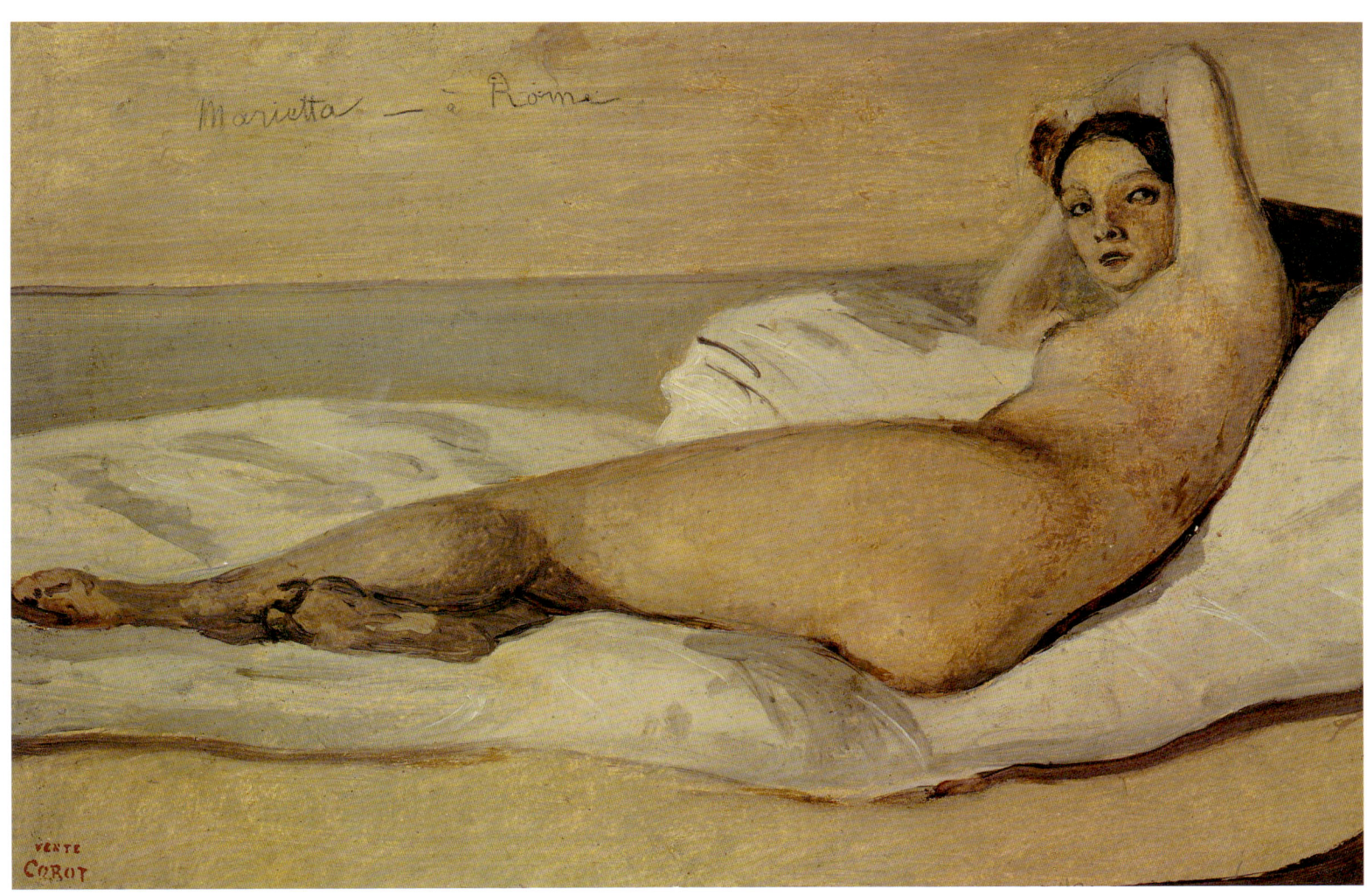

Jean-Baptiste Camille Corot (1796–1875)

The Roman Odalisque (Marietta)

L'Odalisque romaine (Marietta)

Die römische Odaliske (Marietta)

La odalisca romana (Marietta)

L'odalisca romana (Marietta)

De Romeinse odalisk (Marietta)

1843, Oil on canvas/Huile sur toile, 29,3 × 44,2 cm, Musée du Petit Palais, Paris

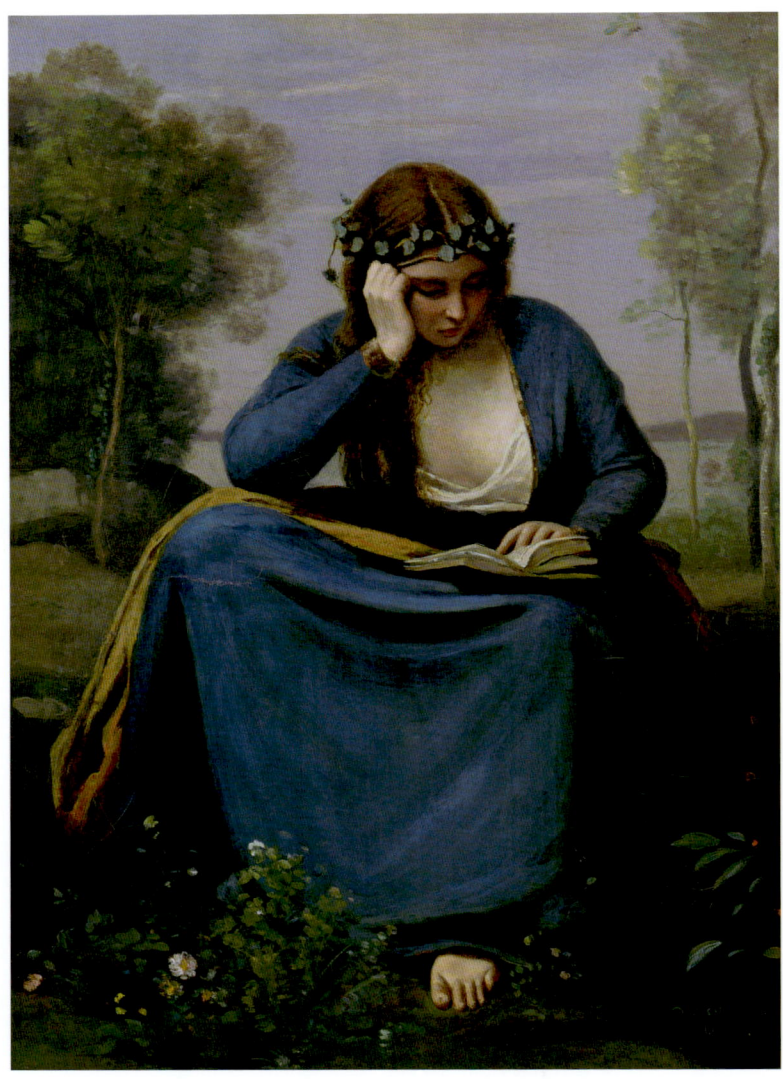

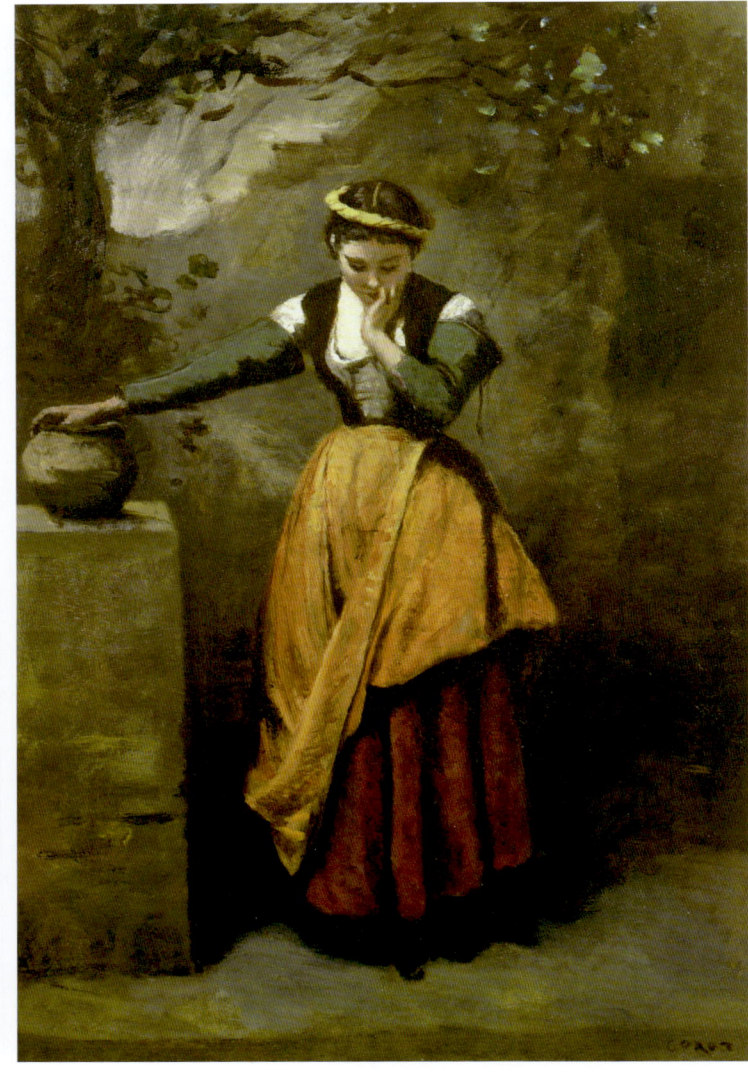

Jean-Baptiste Camille Corot (1796–1875)

The Reader Crowned with Flowers, *or* Virgil's Muse

Liseuse couronnée de fleurs *ou* La Muse de Virgile

Die Lesende mit Blumen gekrönt *oder* Vergils Muse

Lectora con corona de flores *o* La musa de Virgilio

La lettrice con corona di fiori *o* la musa di Virgilio

Leesster met bloemenkrans, *of:* De muze van Vergilius

1845, Oil on canvas/Huile sur toile, 47 × 34 cm, Musée du Louvre, Paris

Jean-Baptiste Camille Corot (1796–1875)

Dreamer at the Fountain

La Rêveuse à la fontaine

Träumerin am Brunnen

Soñadora en la fuenta

Sognatrice alla fontana

Droomster bij de fontein

c. 1860, Oil on canvas/Huile sur toile, 64 × 43 cm, Private collection

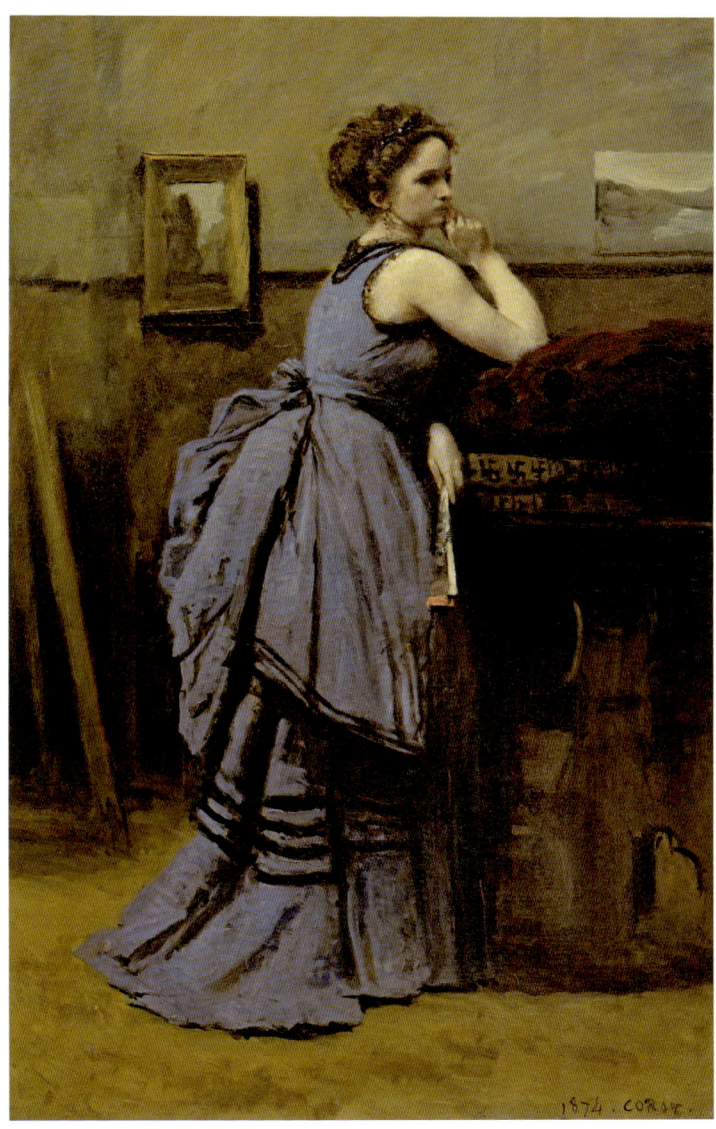

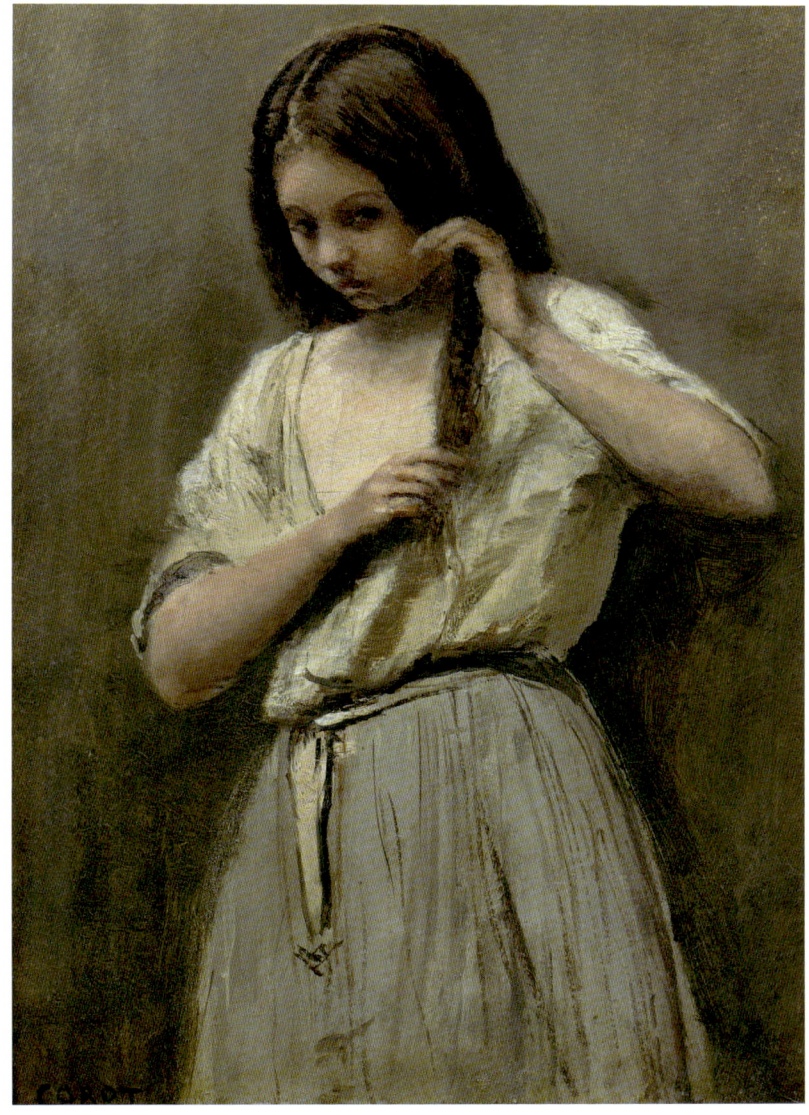

Jean-Baptiste Camille Corot (1796–1875)

The Woman in Blue

La Dame en bleu

Die Frau in Blau

La dama de azul

La donna in blu

De vrouw in het blauw

1874, Oil on canvas/Huile sur toile, 80 × 50,5 cm, Musée du Louvre, Paris

Jean-Baptiste Camille Corot (1796–1875)

Young Girl at her Toilet

Fillette à sa toilette

Junges Mädchen bei der Toilette

Mujer joven en el aseo

Giovane ragazza alla toeletta

Jong meisje bij het toilet

c. 1860–1865, Oil on canvas/Huile sur toile, 34 × 24 cm, Musée du Louvre, Paris

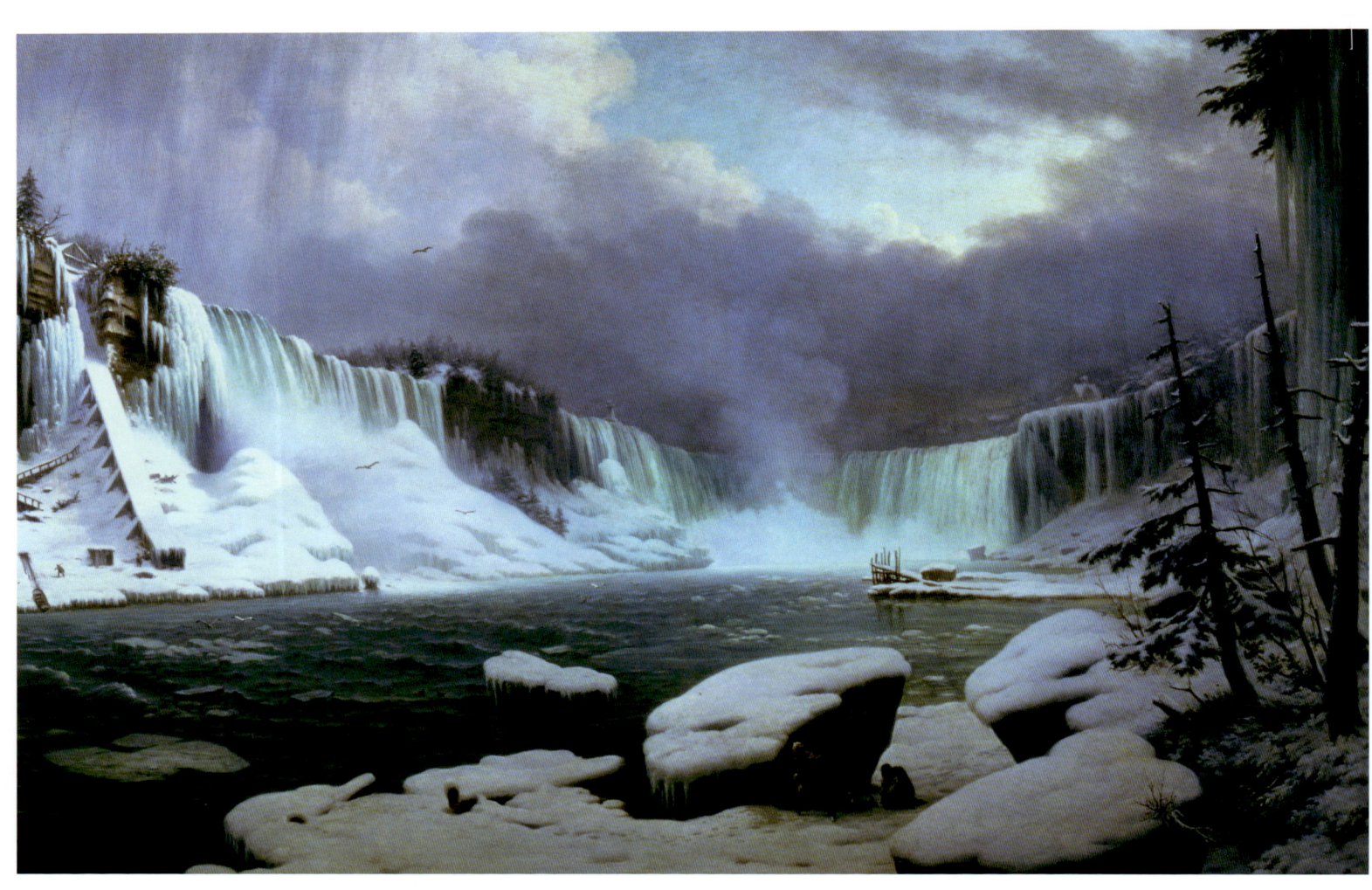

Hippolyte-Victor-Valentin Sebron (1801–1879)

Niagara Falls

Chutes du Niagara enhiver

Die Niagarafälle im Winter

Las cataratas del Niágara en invierno

Le cascate del Niagara in inverno

De Niagarawatervallen in de winter

1857, Oil on canvas/Huile sur toile, 137 × 212 cm, Musée des Beaux-Arts, Rouen

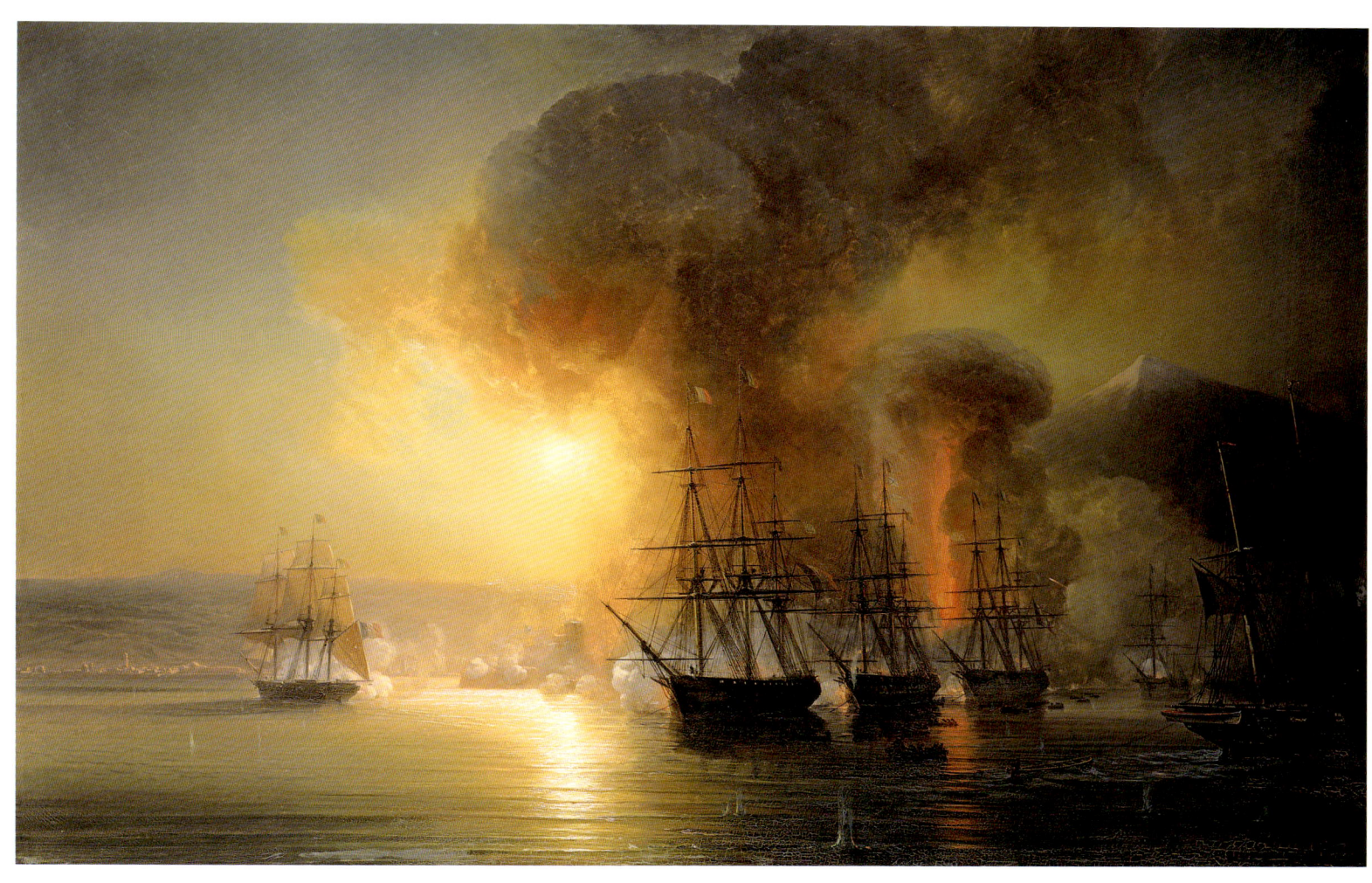

Jean Antoine Théodore Gudin (1802–1880)

Capture of the Fort of Saint-Jean-d'Ulloa on 23rd November 1838

Prise du fort de Saint-Jean-d'Ulloa le 23 novembre 1838

Einnahme des Fort von Saint-Jean-d'Ulloa am 23. November 1838

La toma del fuerte de Saint-Jean-d'Ulloa el 23 de noviembre de 1838

Cattura del Forte di Saint Jean d'Ulloa, 23 novembre 1838

Inname van het Fort Saint-Jean-d'Ulloa op 23 november 1838

1839, Oil on canvas/Huile sur toile, 153,2 × 228 cm, Château de Versailles, Versailles

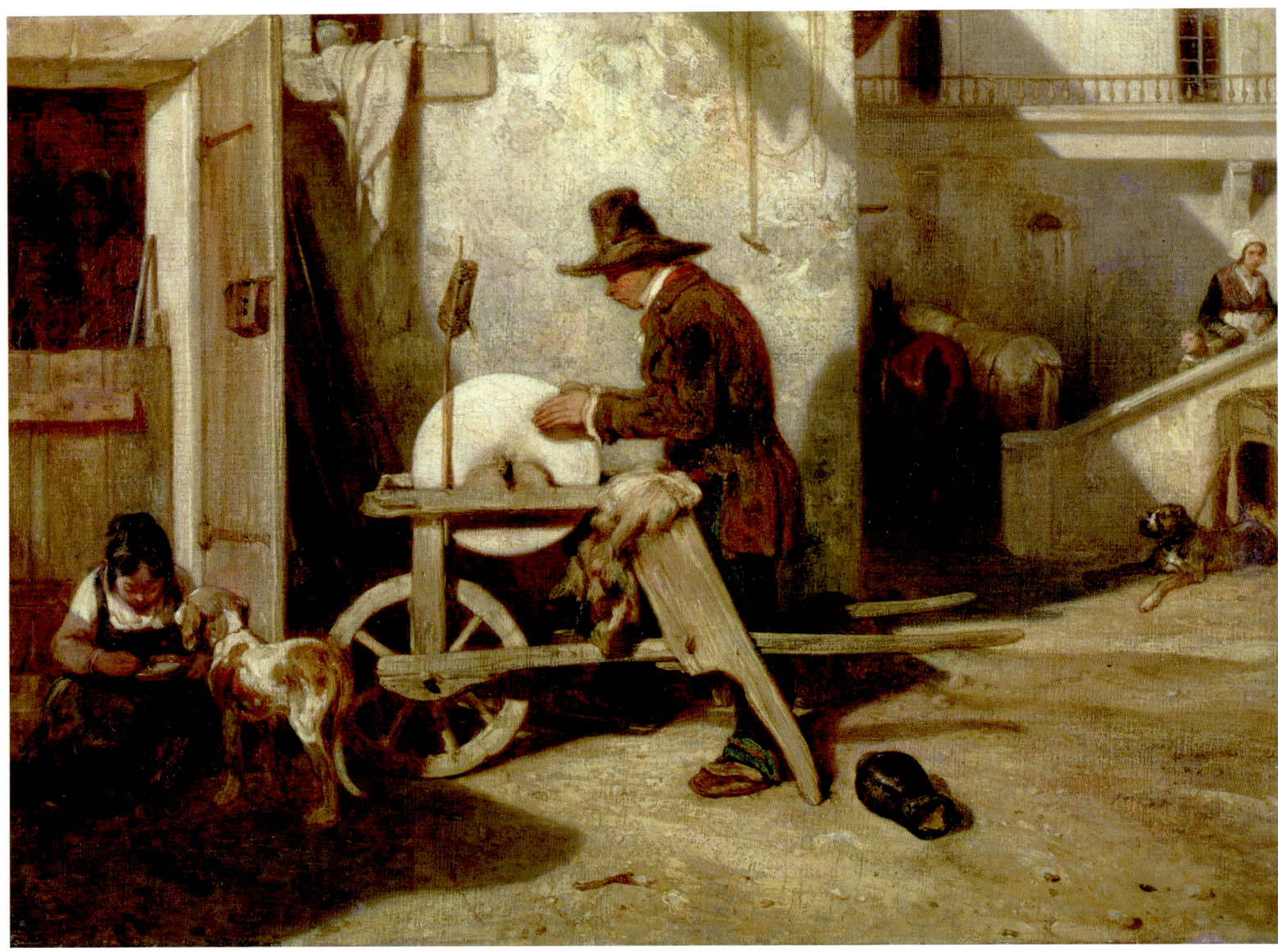

Alexandre-Gabriel Decamps (1803–1860)

The Knife-grinder

Le Rémouleur

Der Scherenschleifer

El afilador

L'arrotino

De scharensliep

n. d., Oil on canvas/Huile sur toile, 38 × 51 cm, Musée du Louvre, Paris

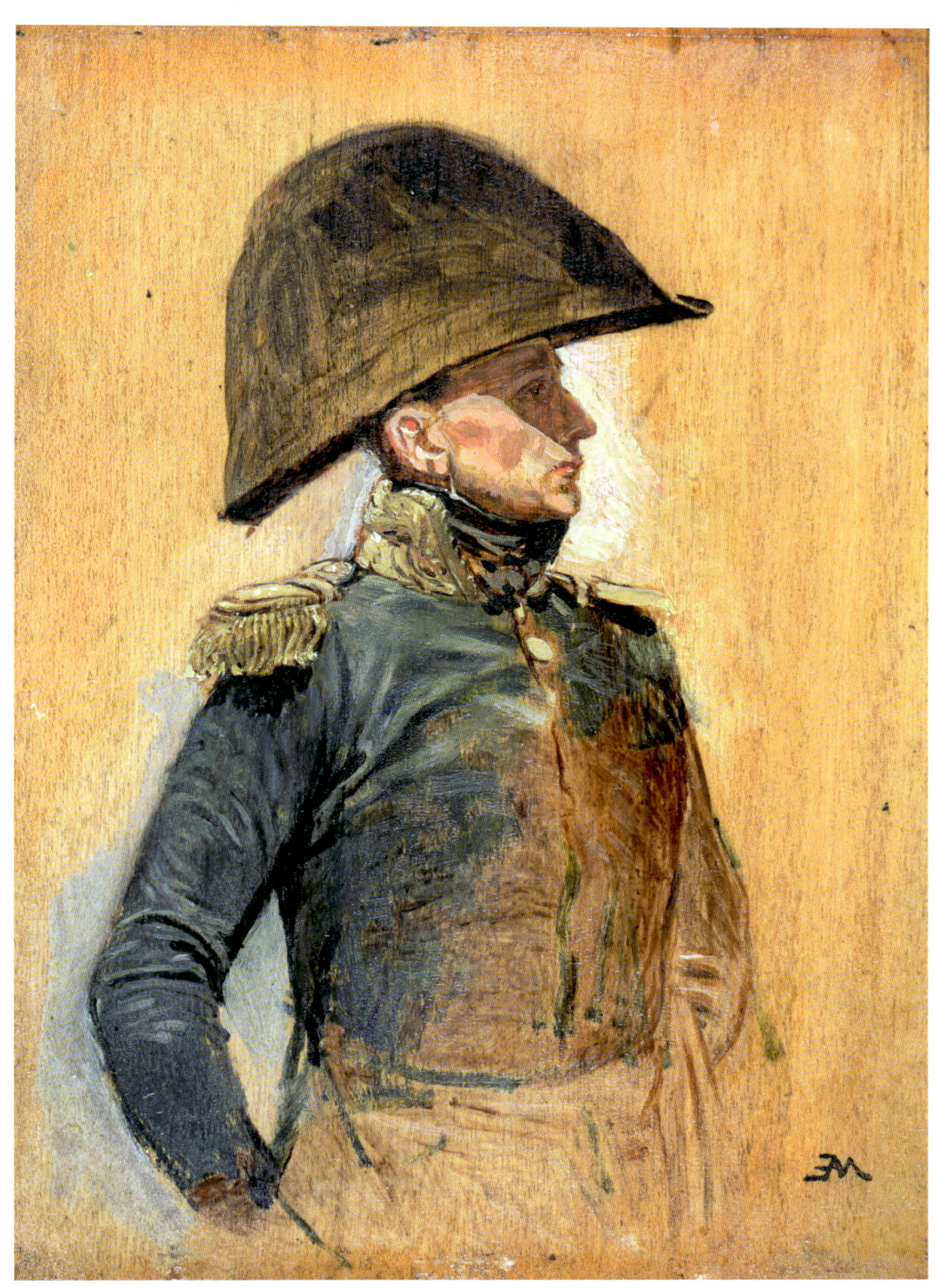

Jean-Louis-Ernest Meissonier (1815–1891)

A General Officer

Un Général

Ein General

Un General

Un generale

Een generaal

1835–1891, Oil on wood/Huile sur bois,
12,9 × 9,4 cm, Manchester Art Gallery,
Manchester

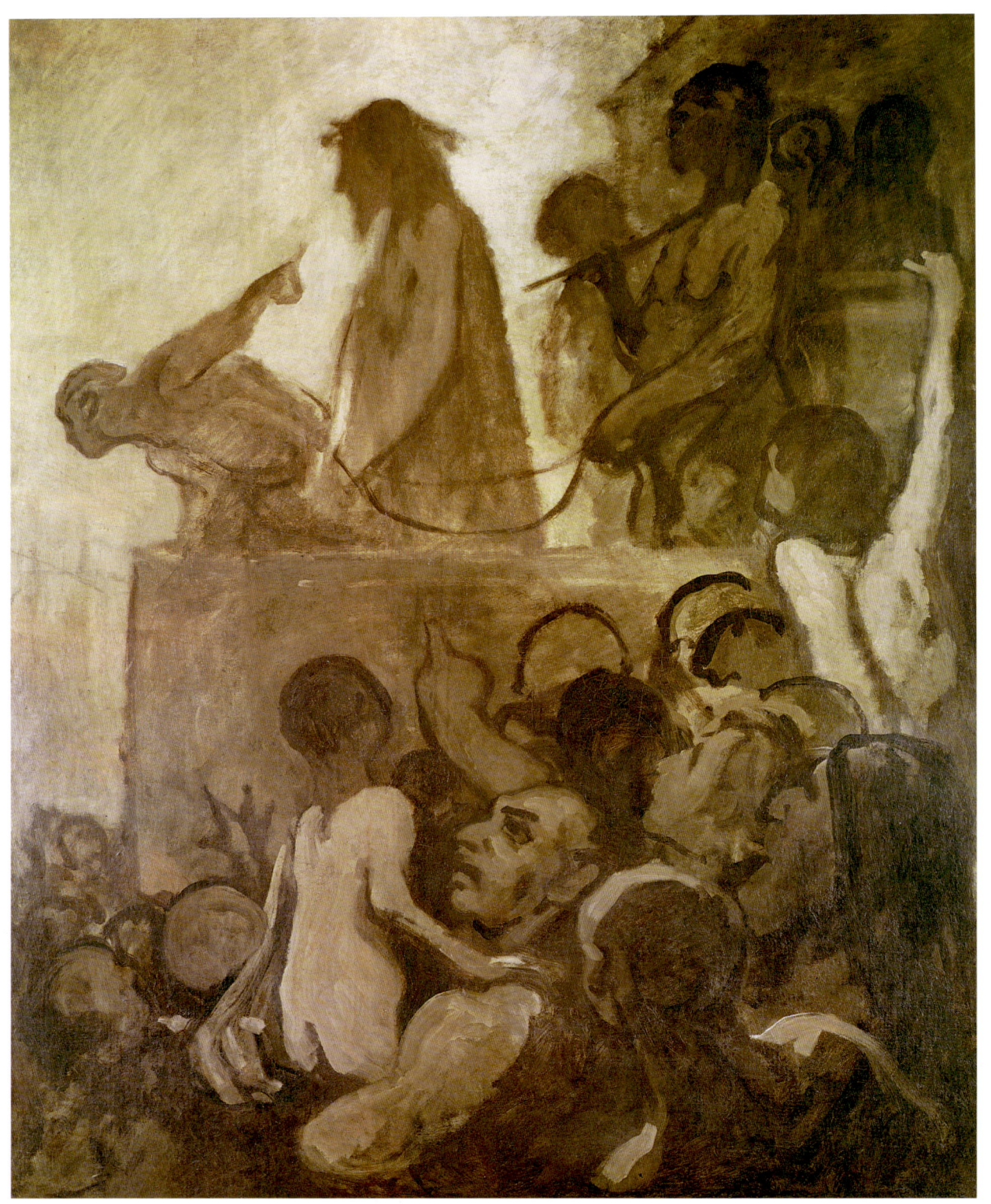

Honoré Daumier (1808–1879)

Ecce Homo

c. 1851, Oil on canvas/Huile sur
toile, 162,5 × 130 cm, Museum
Folkwang, Essen

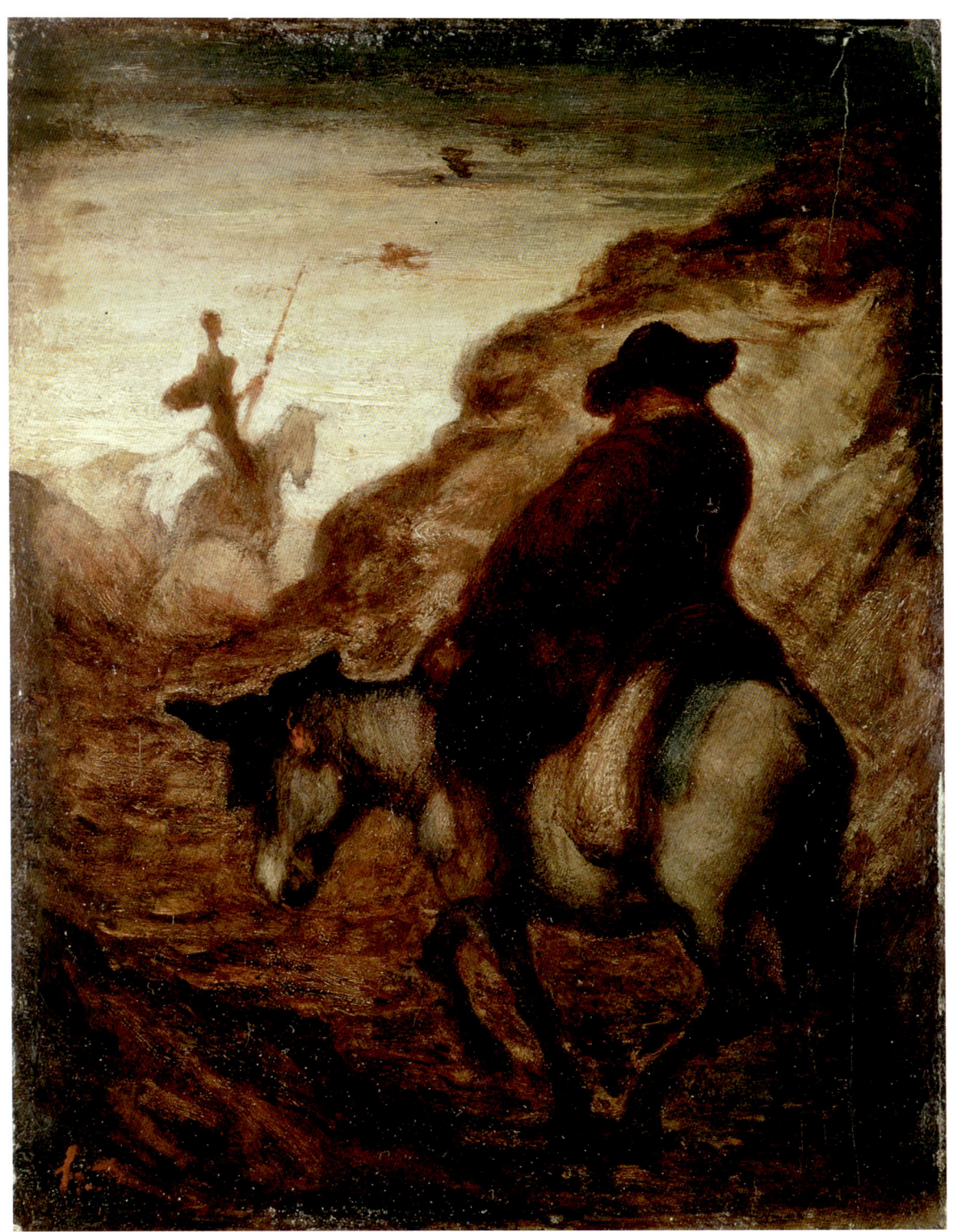

Honoré Daumier (1808–1879)

Sancho and Don Quixote

Don Quichotte et Sancho Pança

Sancho und Don Quichote

Sancho y Don Quijote

Sancho Panza e Don Chisciotte

Sancho Panza en Don Quichot

n. d., Oil on canvas/Huile sur toile,
32,4 × 24,1 cm, Burrell Collection,
Glasgow

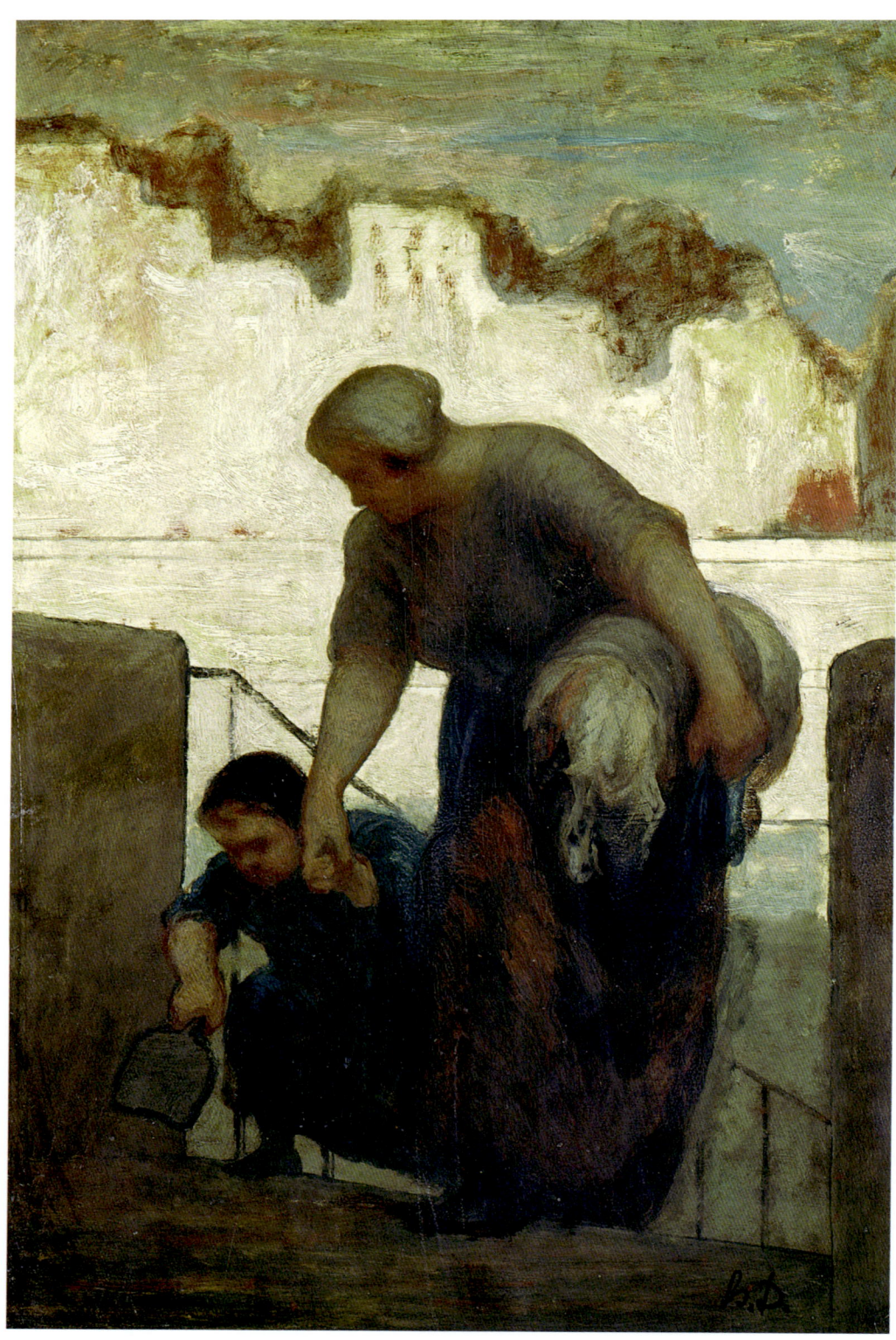

Honoré Daumier (1808–1879)

The Washerwoman

La Laveuse ou La Blanchisseuse

Die Wäscherin

La lavandera

La lavandaia

De wasvrouw

c. 1863, Oil on wood/Huile sur bois, 49 × 33,4 cm,
Musée d'Orsay, Paris

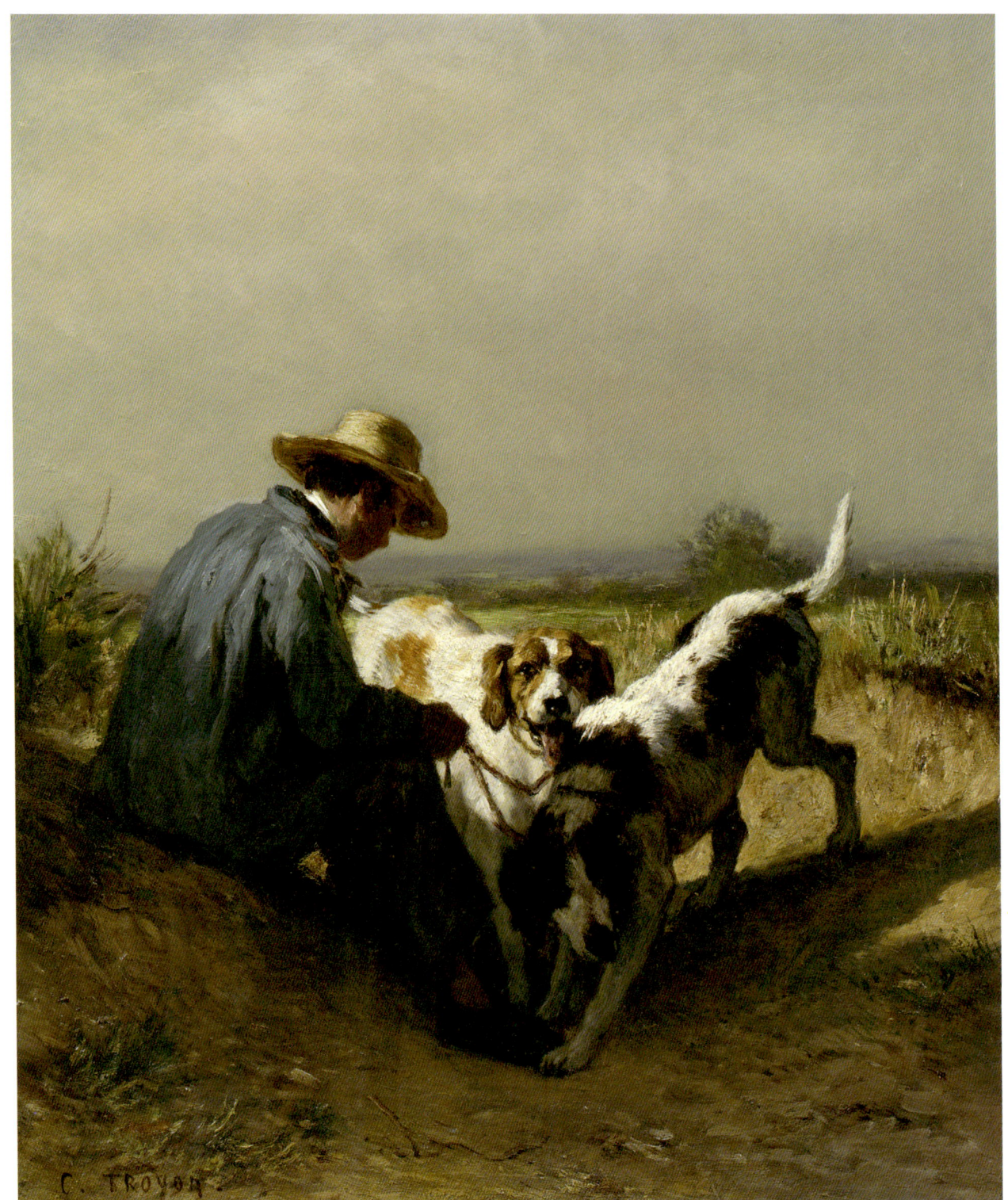

**Constant Troyon
(1810–1865)**

The Gamekeeper

Le Garde-chasses

Der Hundehalter

El dueño de los perros

Il guardiacaccia

De wildopzichter

c. 1850, Oil on wood/Huile sur
bois, 46 × 37,4 cm, Clark Art
Institute, Williamstown

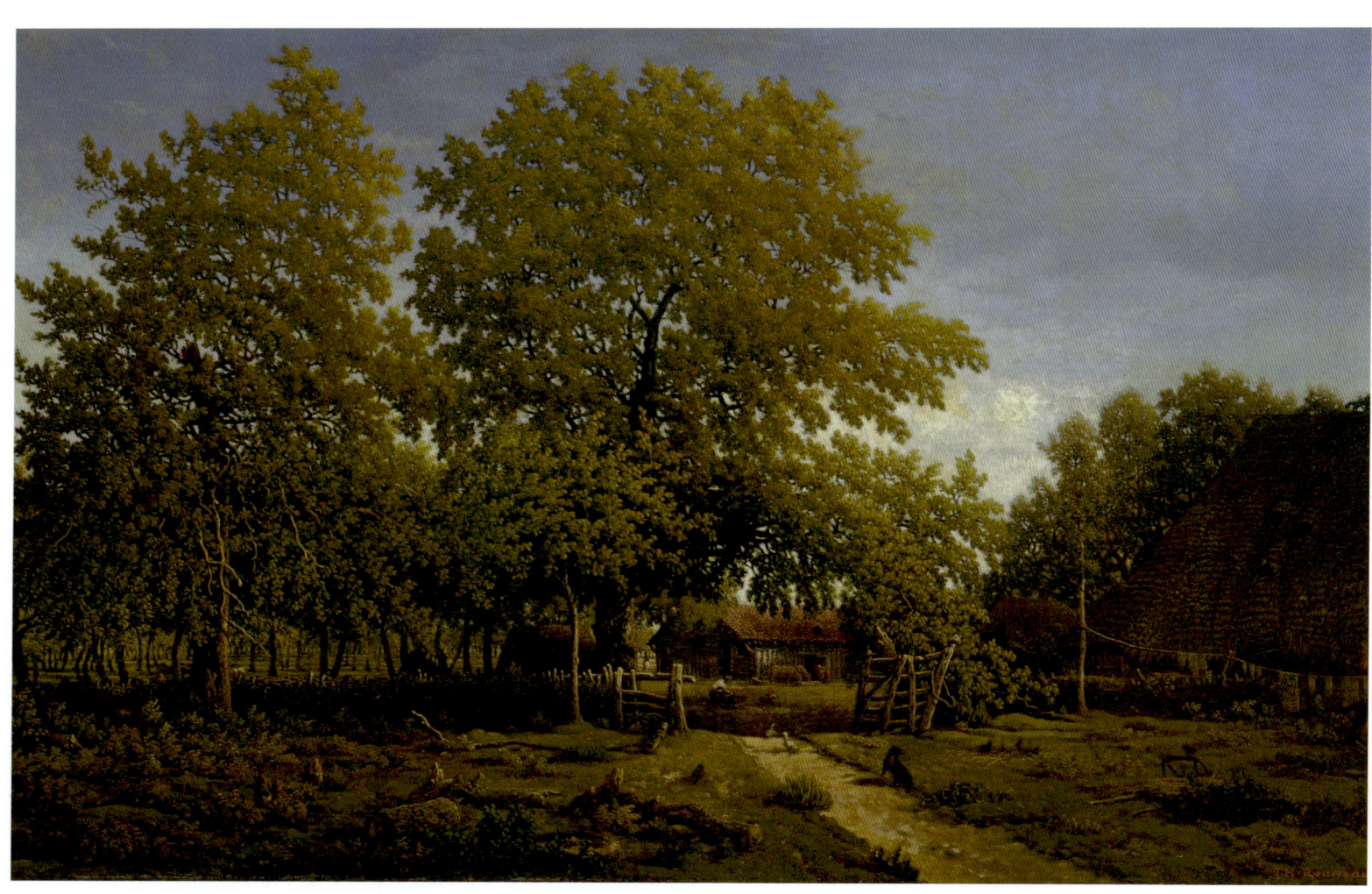

Théodore Rousseau (1812–1867)

Farm in the Landes

Une Ferme dans les Landes

Bauernhof in den Landes

Granja en el campo

Fattoria nelle Landes

Boerenhoeve in Les Landes

1844–1867, Oil on canvas/Huile sur toile, 64,8 × 99,1 cm, Clark Art Institute, Williamstown

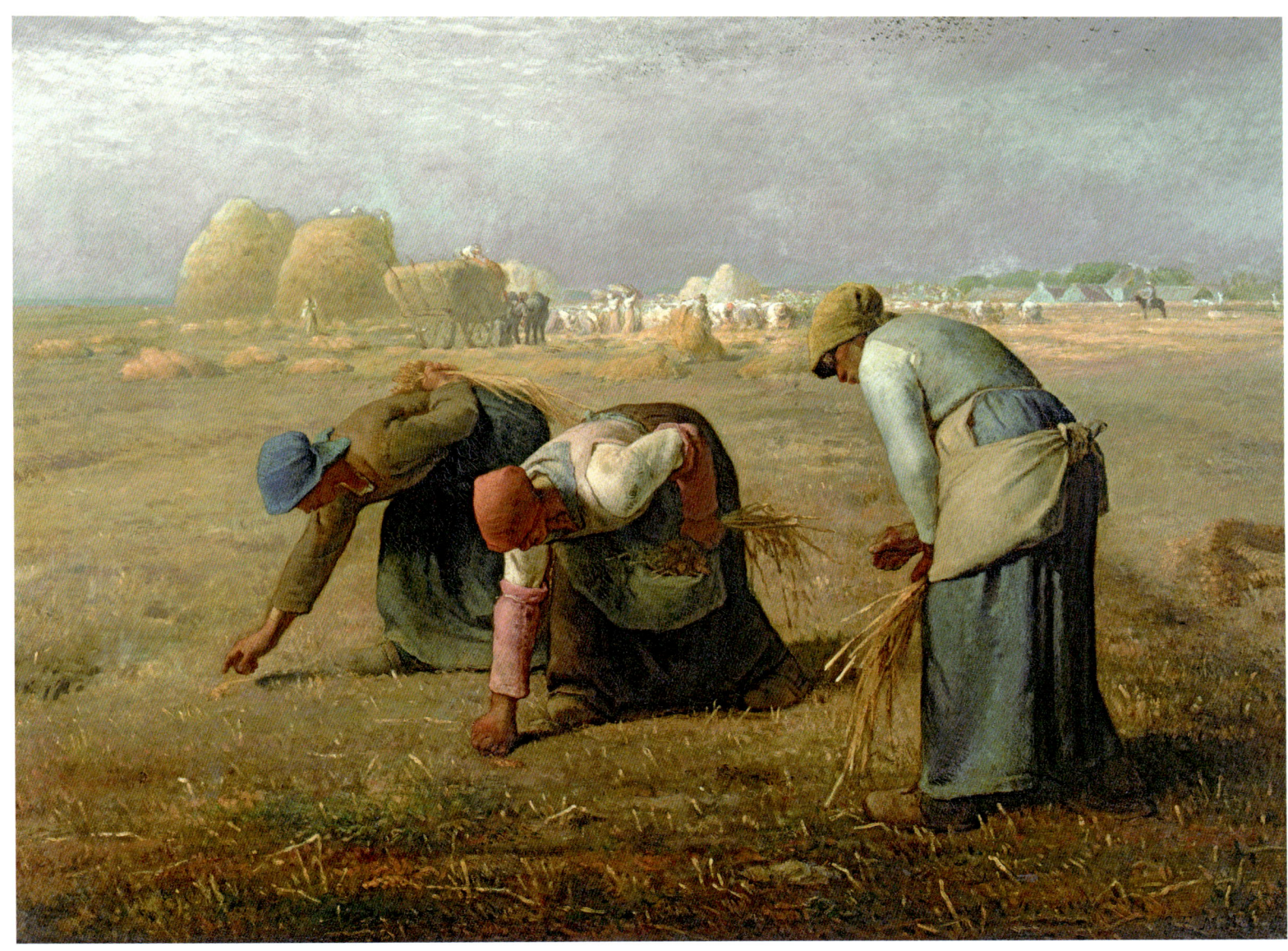

Jean-François Millet (1814–1875)

The Gleaners

Des glaneuses

Die Ährenleserinnen

Las portadoras de espigas

Le spigolatrici

De arenleessters

1857, Oil on canvas/Huile sur toile, 83,5 × 110 cm, Musée d'Orsay, Paris

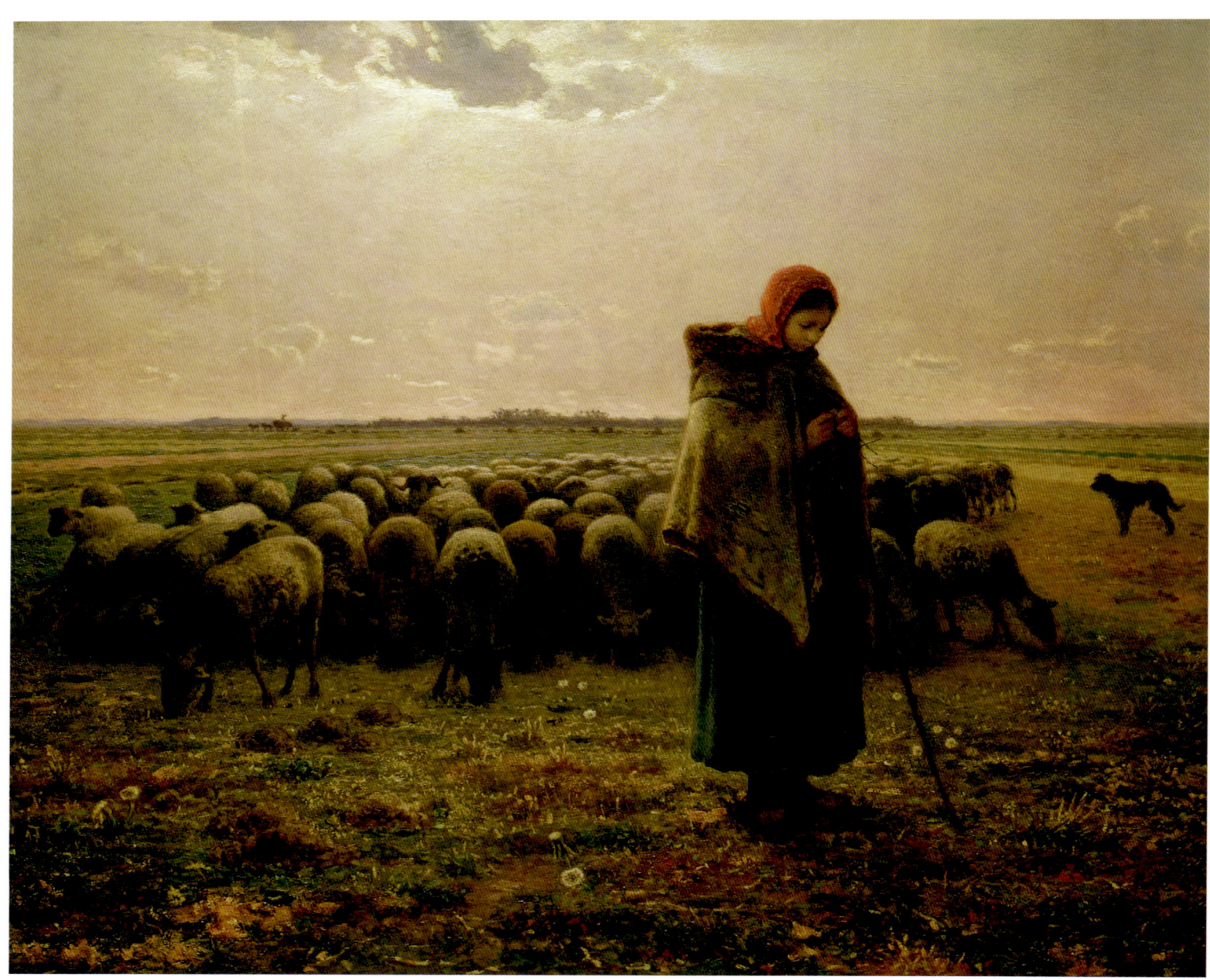

Jean-François Millet (1814–1875)

Shepherdess with her Flock   Schafhirtin mit ihrer Herde   Pastorella con il suo gregge

Bergère avec son troupeau   Pastora con su rebaño   Schapenhoedster met haar kudde

c. 1863, Oil on canvas/Huile sur toile, 81 × 101 cm, Musée d'Orsay, Paris

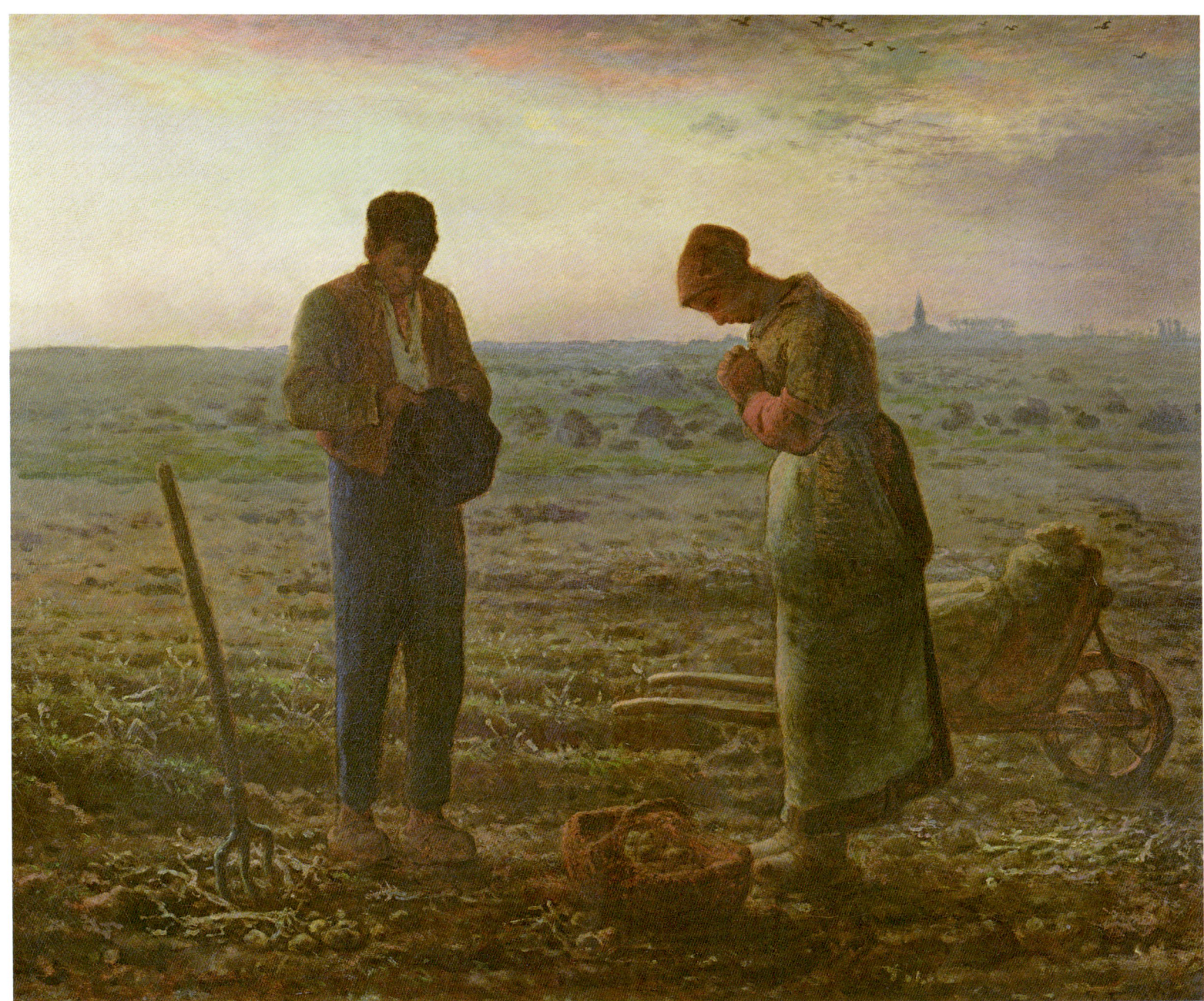

Jean-François Millet (1814–1875)

| The Angelus | Das Angelusläuten | L'Angelus |
| L'Angélus | El Ángelus | Het luiden voor het angelus |

1857–1859, Oil on canvas/Huile sur toile, 55,5 × 66 cm, Musée d'Orsay, Paris

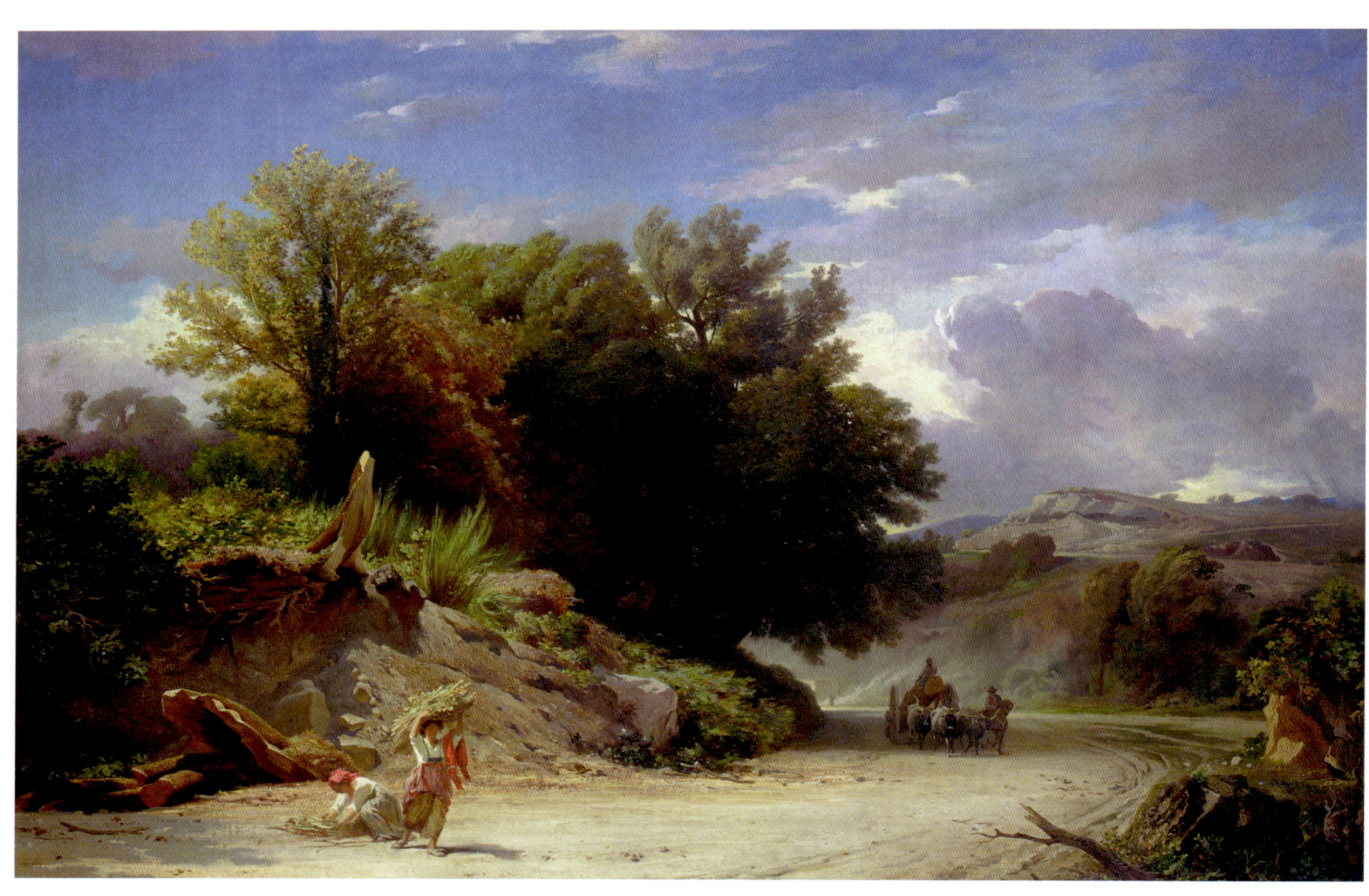

Jean-Achille Benouville (1815–1891)

Landscape on the Outskirts of Rome

Paysage des environs de Rome

Landschaft am Rande von Rom

Paisaje en los exteriores de Roma

Paesaggio alla periferia di Roma

Landschap aan de rand van Rome

1853, Oil on canvas/Huile sur toile, 117 × 175 cm, Musée des Beaux-Arts, Rouen

Charles-François Daubigny
(1817–1878)

The Harvest

La Moisson

Die Ernte

La cosecha

Il raccolto

De oogst

1851, Oil on canvas/Huile sur toile,
135 × 196 cm, Musée d'Orsay, Paris

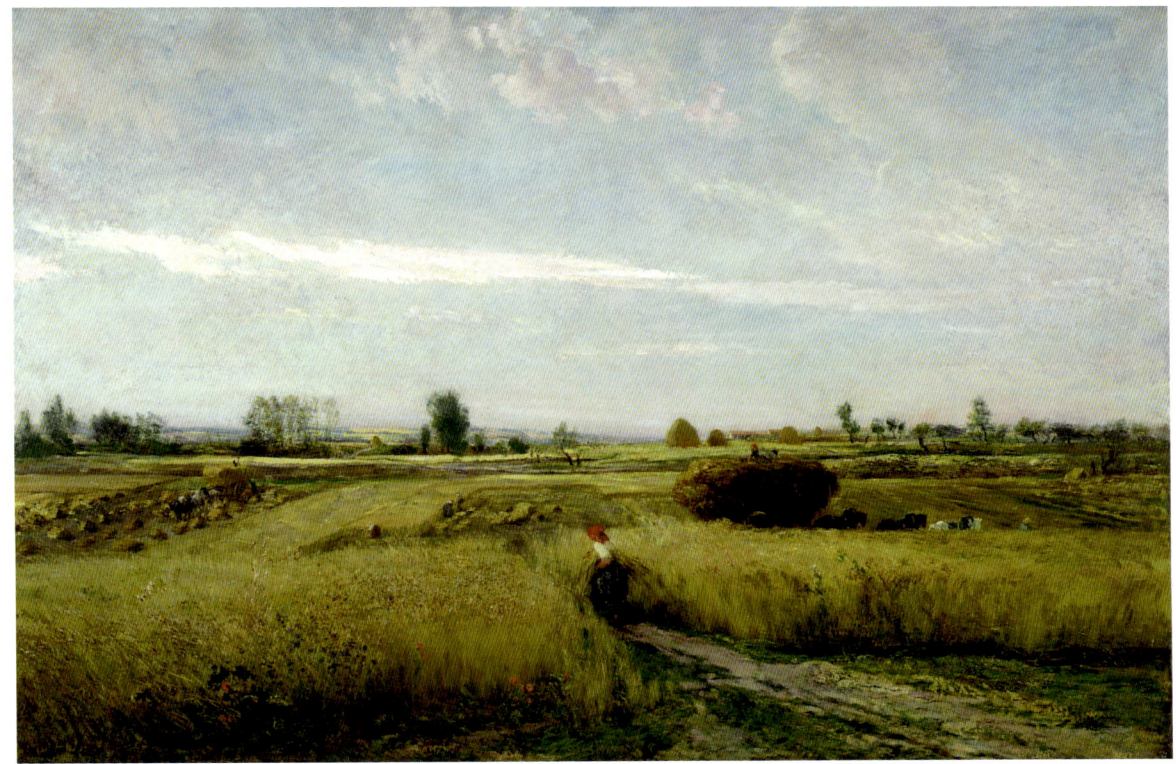

Charles-François Daubigny
(1817–1878)

The pond at Gylieu

L'Etang de Gylieu

Der Teich von Gylieu

El estanque de Gylieu

Lo stagno di Gylieu

De vijver van Gylieu

1853, Oil on canvas/Huile sur toile,
62 × 99,7 cm, Cincinnati Art Museum,
Cincinnati

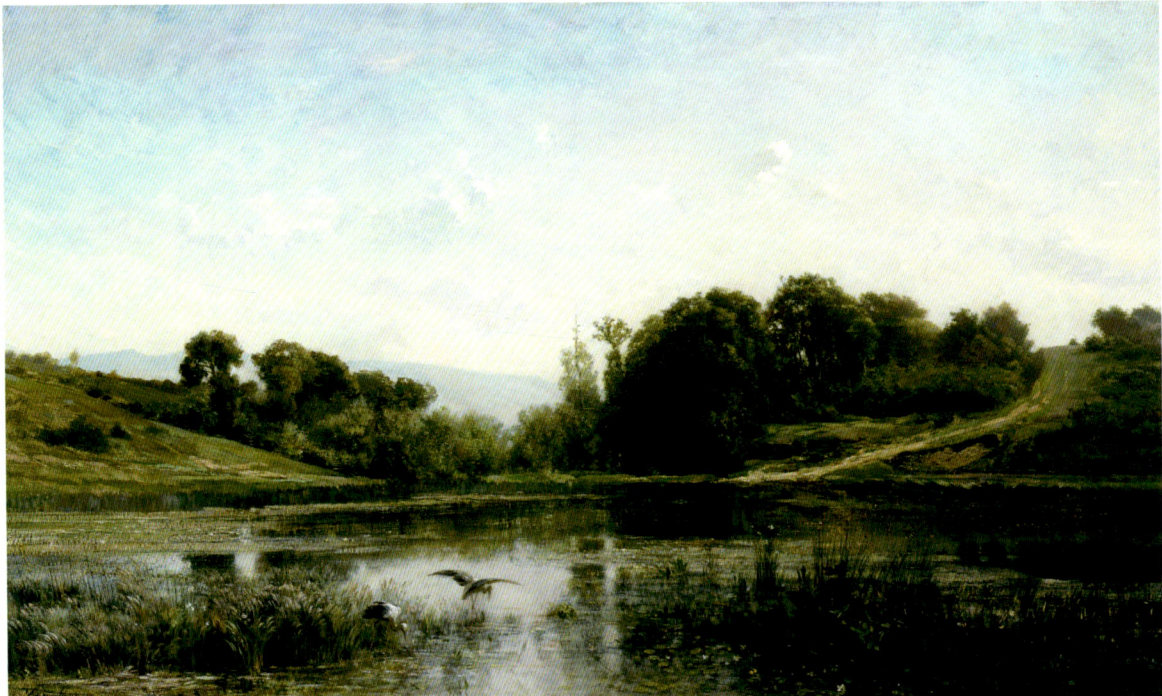

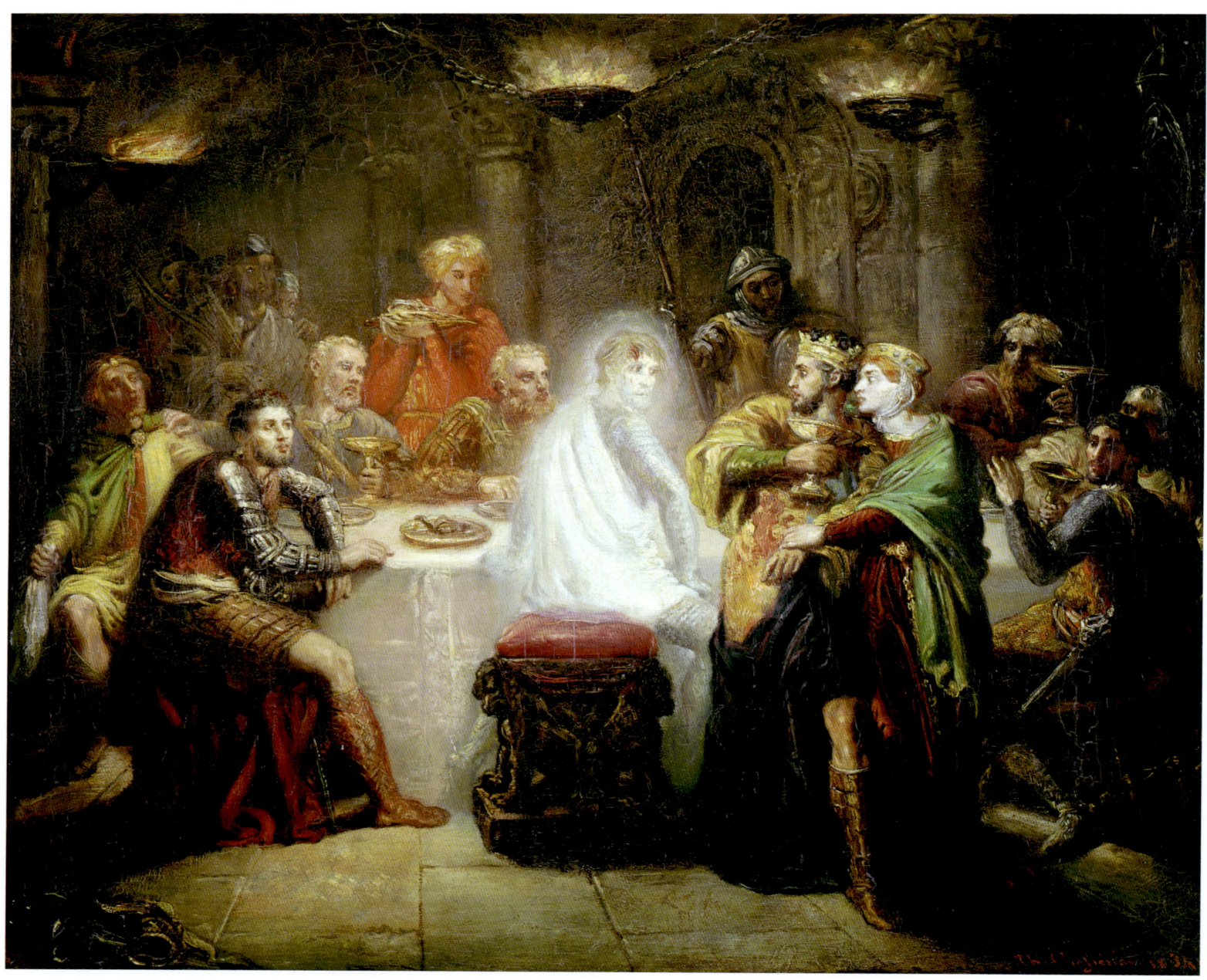

Théodore Chassériau (1819–1856)

The Ghost of Banquo   Der Geist von Banquo   Lo spirito di Banquo

Le Spectre de Banquo   El fantasma de Banquo   De geest van Banquo

1854–1855, Oil on canvas/Huile sur toile, 53,8 × 65,3 cm, Musée des Beaux-Arts, Reims

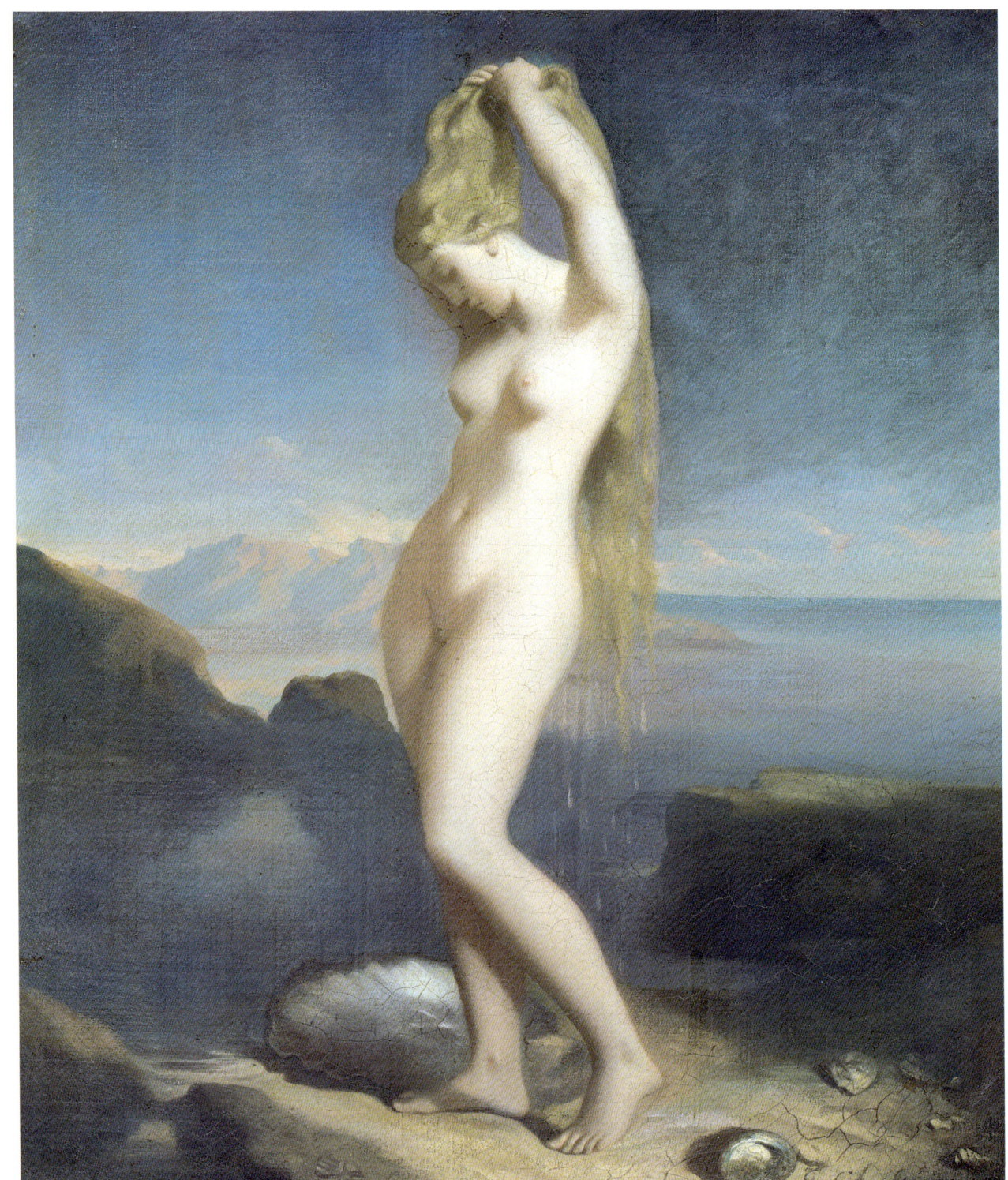

**Théodore Chassériau
(1819–1856)**

Venus Anadyomene, *or*
Venus of the Sea

Vénus anadyomène, *dite
aussi* Vénus marine

Venus Anadyomene *oder*
Venus des Meeres

Venus Anadiomena *o*
La Venus del mar

Venere Anadiomene *o la*
Venere dei mari

Venus Anadyomene *of*
de Venus uit de Zee

1838, Oil on canvas/Huile sur
toile, 65 × 55 cm, Musée du
Louvre, Paris

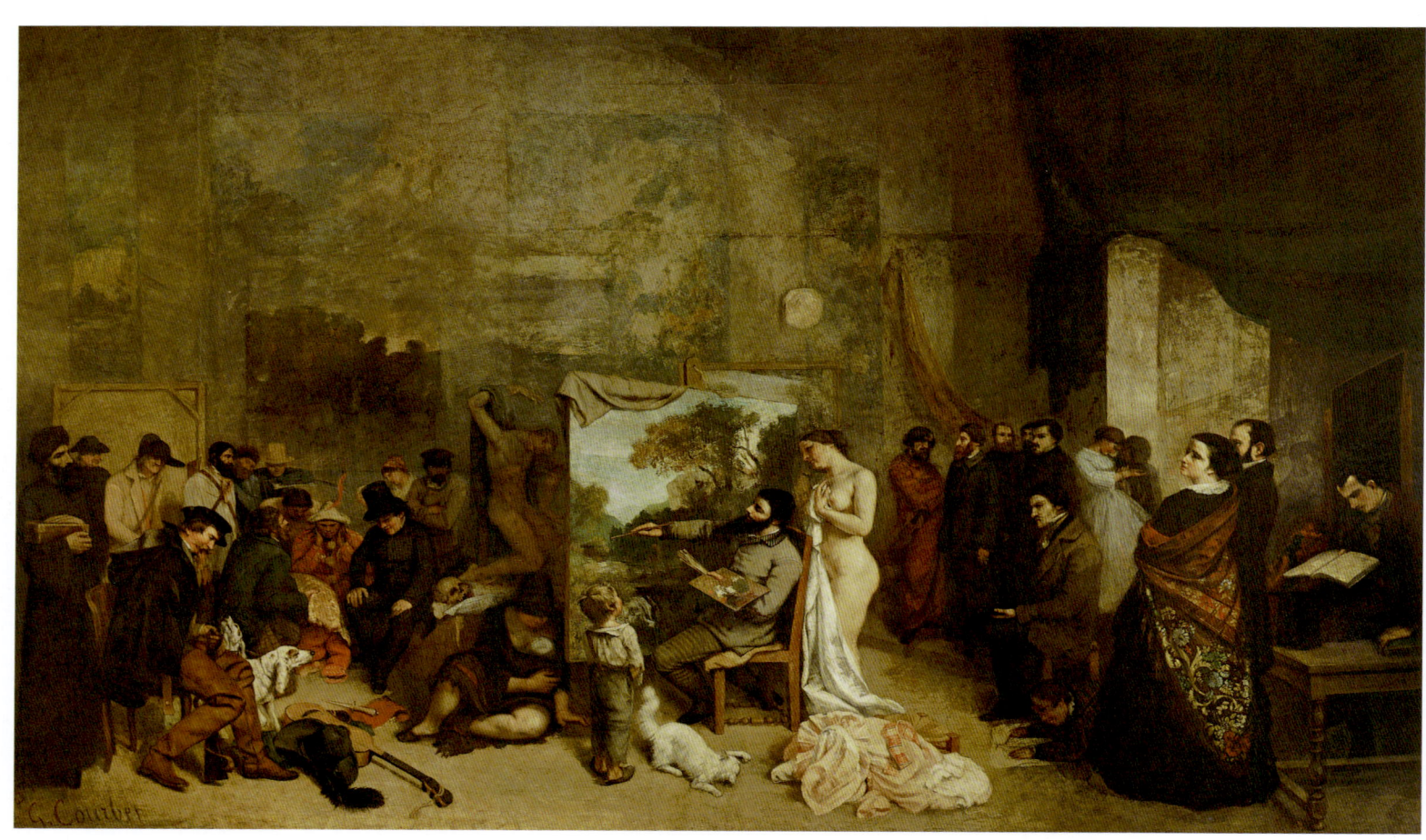

Gustave Courbet (1819–1877)

The Painter's Studio

L'Atelier du peintre

Das Atelier des Künstlers

El taller del pintor

L'atelier dell'artista

Het atelier van de kunstenaar

1865, Oil on canvas/Huile sur toile, 361 × 598 cm, Musée d'Orsay, Paris

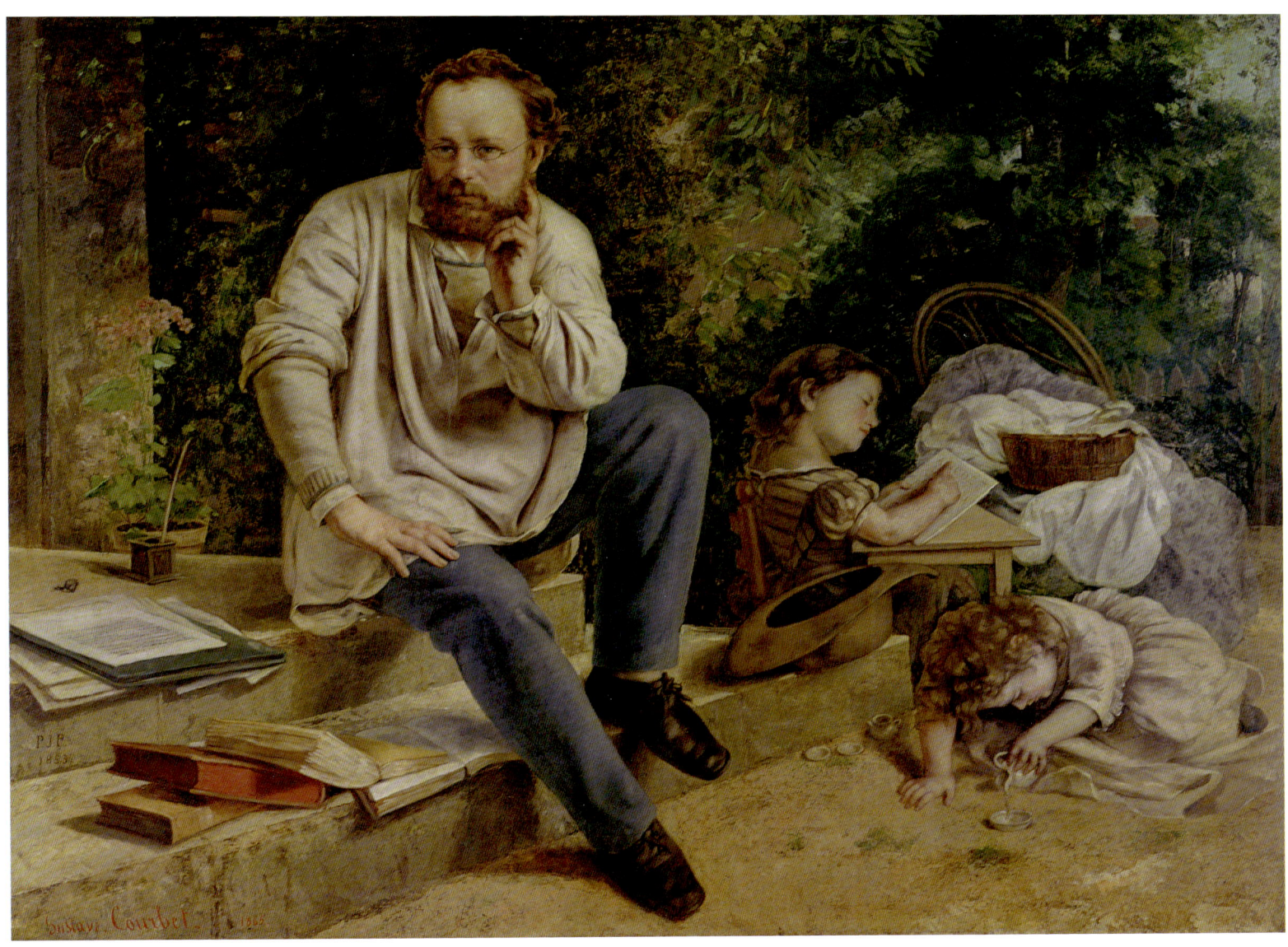

Gustave Courbet (1819–1877)

Pierre Joseph Proudhon and his Children in 1853

Pierre Joseph Proudhon et ses enfants en 1853

Pierre Joseph Proudhon und seine Kinder im Jahr 1853

Pierre Joseph Proudhon y sus hijos en 1853

Pierre Joseph Proudhon e i suoi bambini nel 1853

Pierre Joseph Proudhon en zijn kinderen in het jaar 1853

1865, Oil on canvas/Huile sur toile, 147 × 198 cm, Musée du Petit Palais, Paris

pp. 218–219

Gustave Courbet (1819–1877)

A Burial at Ornans

Un enterrement à Ornans

Ein Begräbnis in Ornans

Entierro en Ornans

Funerale a Ornans

Een begrafenis in Ornans

1849–1850, Oil on canvas/Huile sur toile, 315 × 668 cm, Musée d'Orsay, Paris

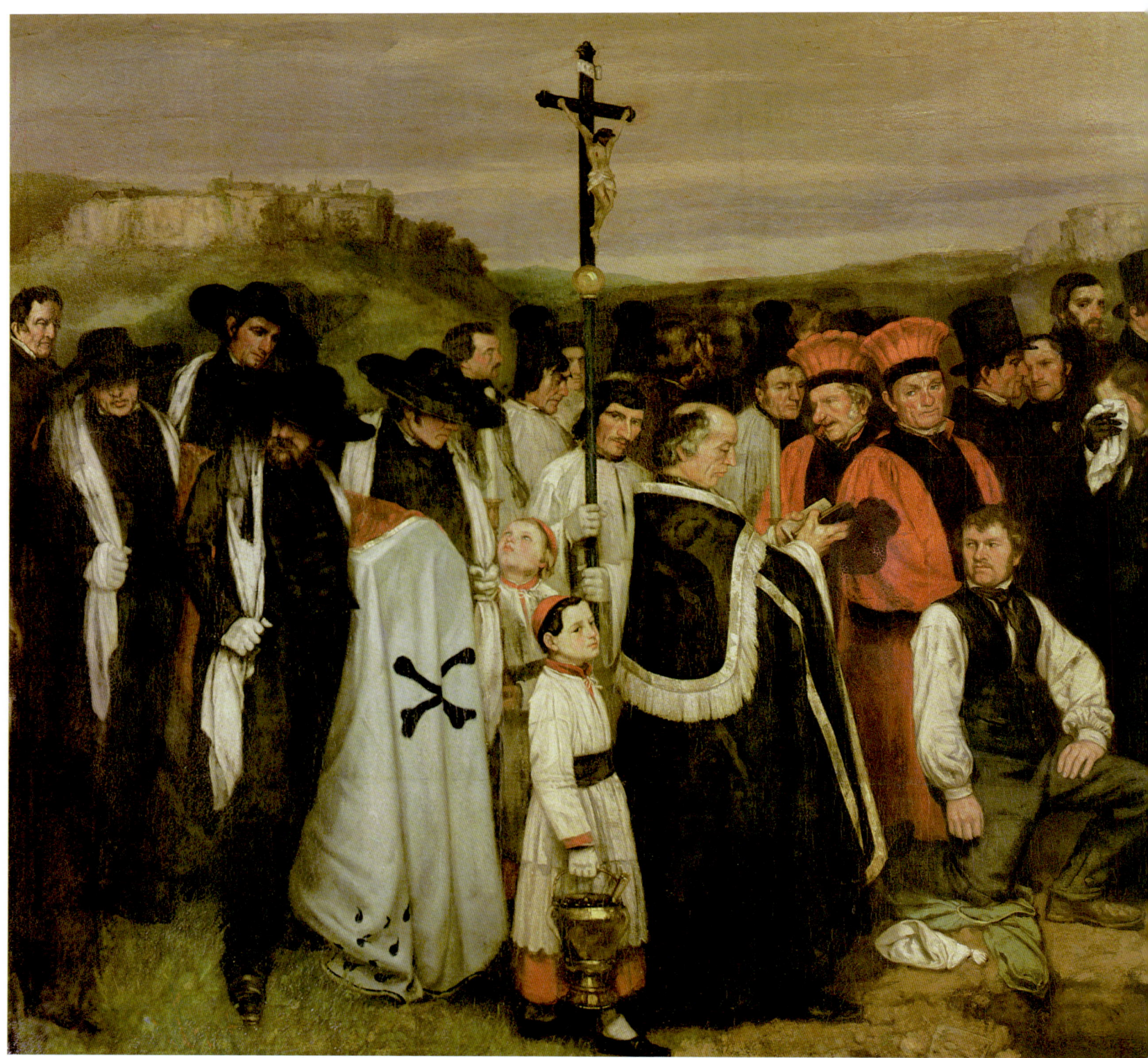

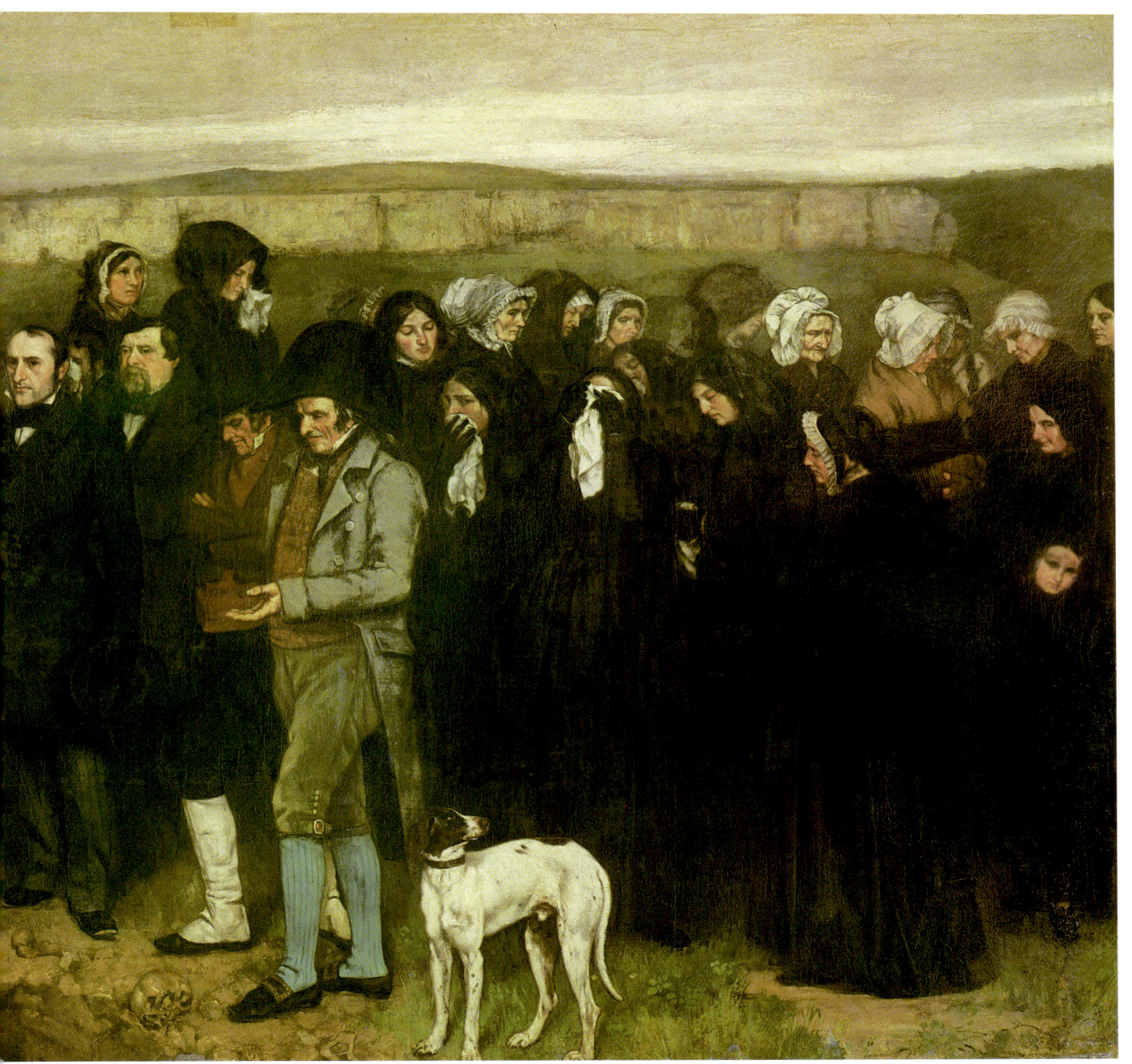

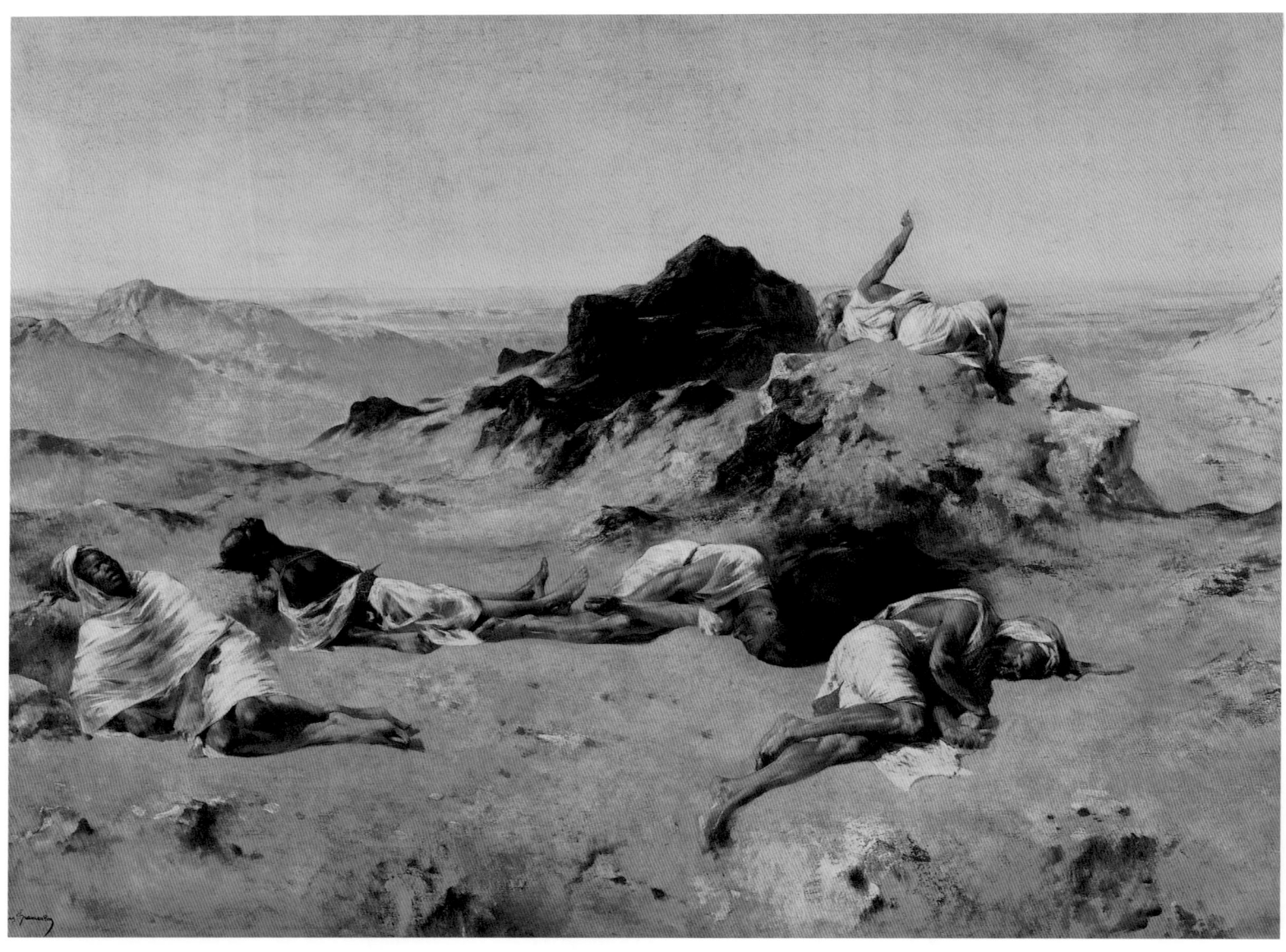

Eugène Fromentin (1820–1876)

The Land of Thirst

Le Pays de la soif

Das Land des Durstes

El país de la sed

La terra di sete

Het land van de dorst

c. 1869, Oil on canvas/Huile sur toile, 103 × 143,2 cm, Musée d'Orsay, Paris

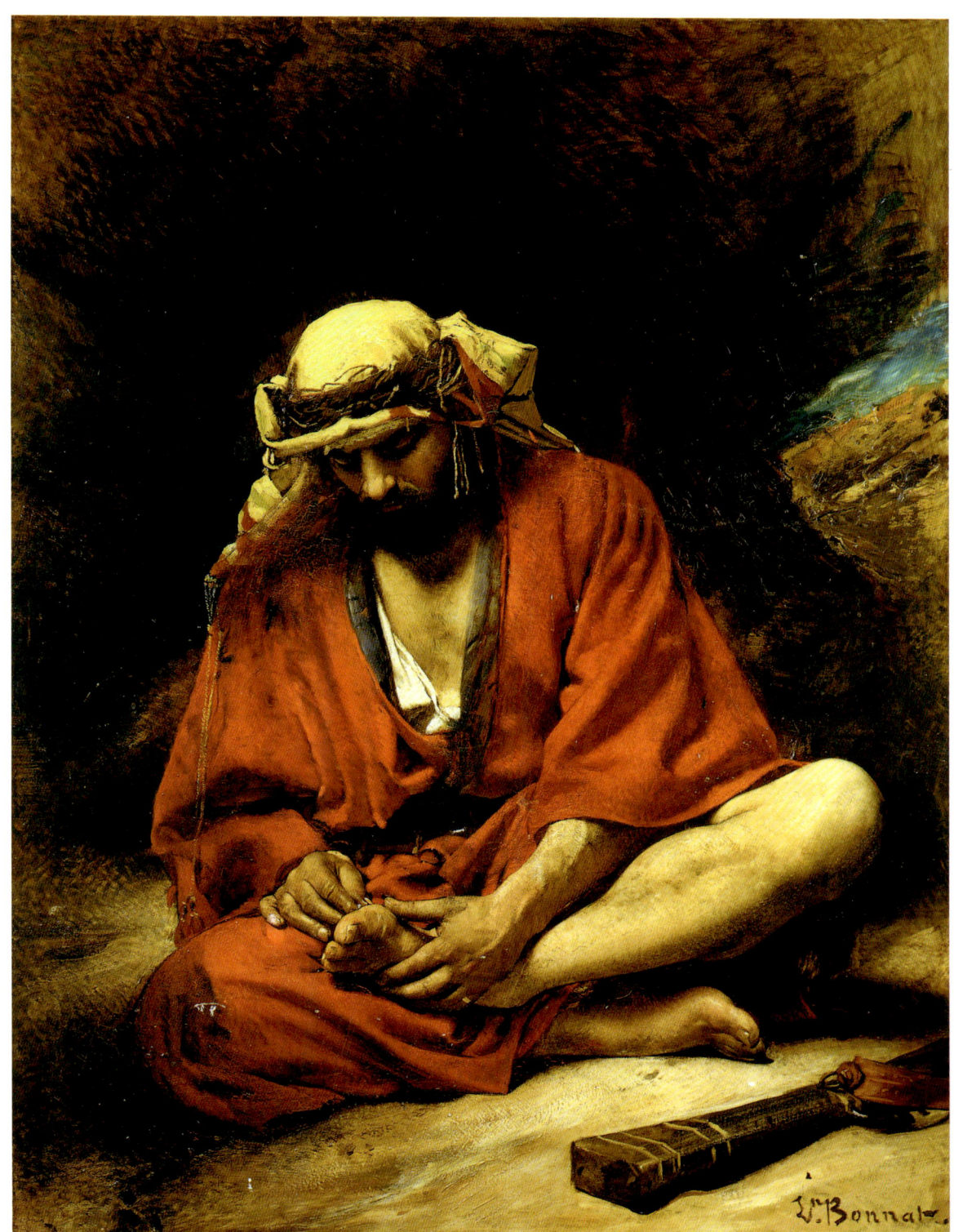

Léon Bonnat (1833–1922)

An Arab Plucking a Thorn
from his Foot

Le Tireur d'épine arabe

Ein Araber zieht sich einen Dorn
aus dem Fuß

Un árabe se saca una espina del pie

Un arabo si toglie una spina dal piede

Een Arabier trekt zich een doorn
uit de voet

n. d., Oil on canvas/Huile sur toile,
140 × 105 cm, Private collection

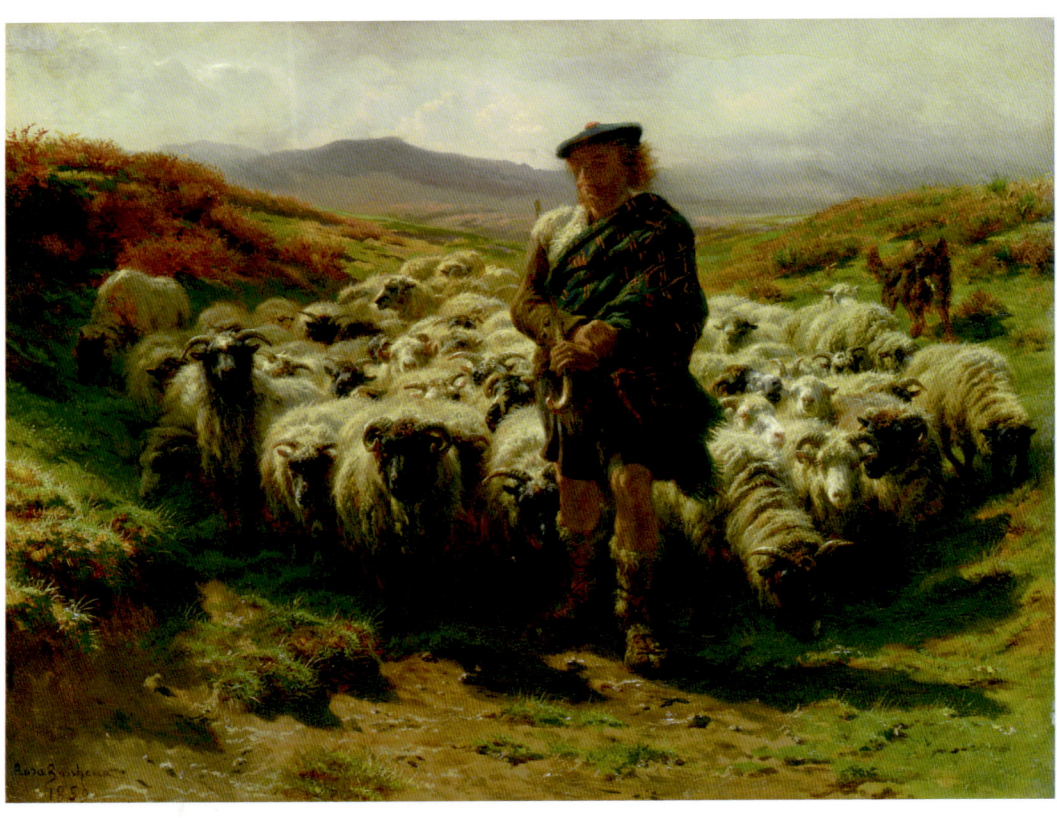

Rosa Bonheur (1822–1899)

The Highland Shepherd

Berger des Highlands

Hochlandschäfer

Pastor de tierras altas

Il pastore delle Highland

Schaapherder in de Highlands

1859, Oil on canvas/Huile sur toile, 49 × 63 cm,
Kunsthalle, Hamburg

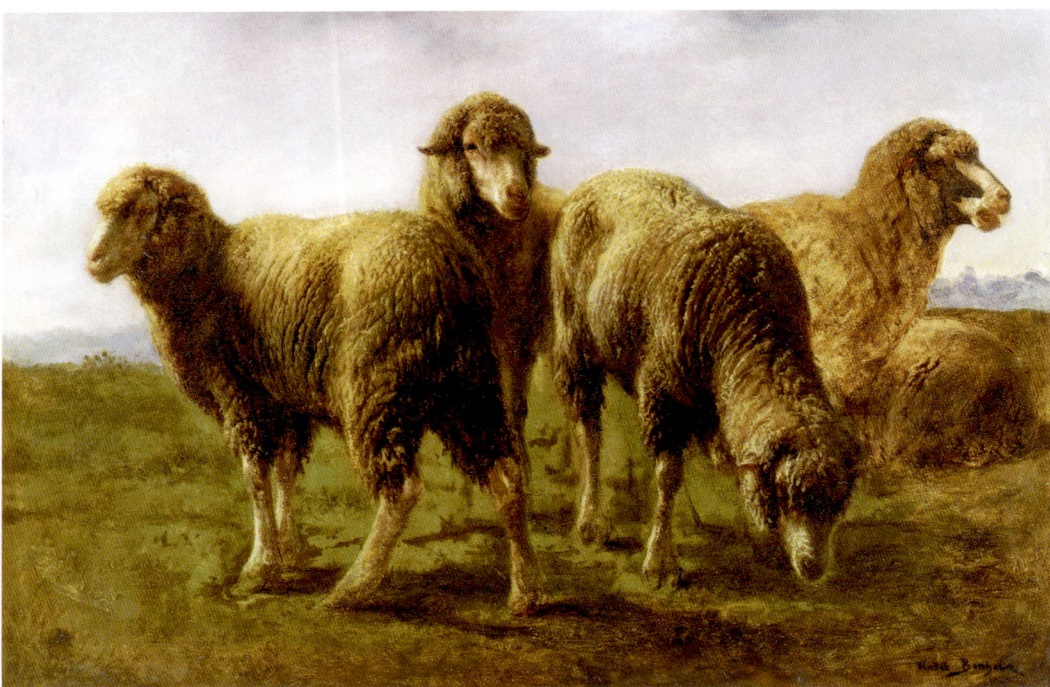

Rosa Bonheur (1822–1899)

Sheep Grazing in a Meadow

Moutons dans un pré

Grasende Schafe auf einer Wiese

Ovejas pastando en una pradera

Pecora che pascola su un prato

Grazende schapen op een weide

n. d., Oil on canvas/Huile sur toile, 36,8 × 53,4 cm,
Private collection

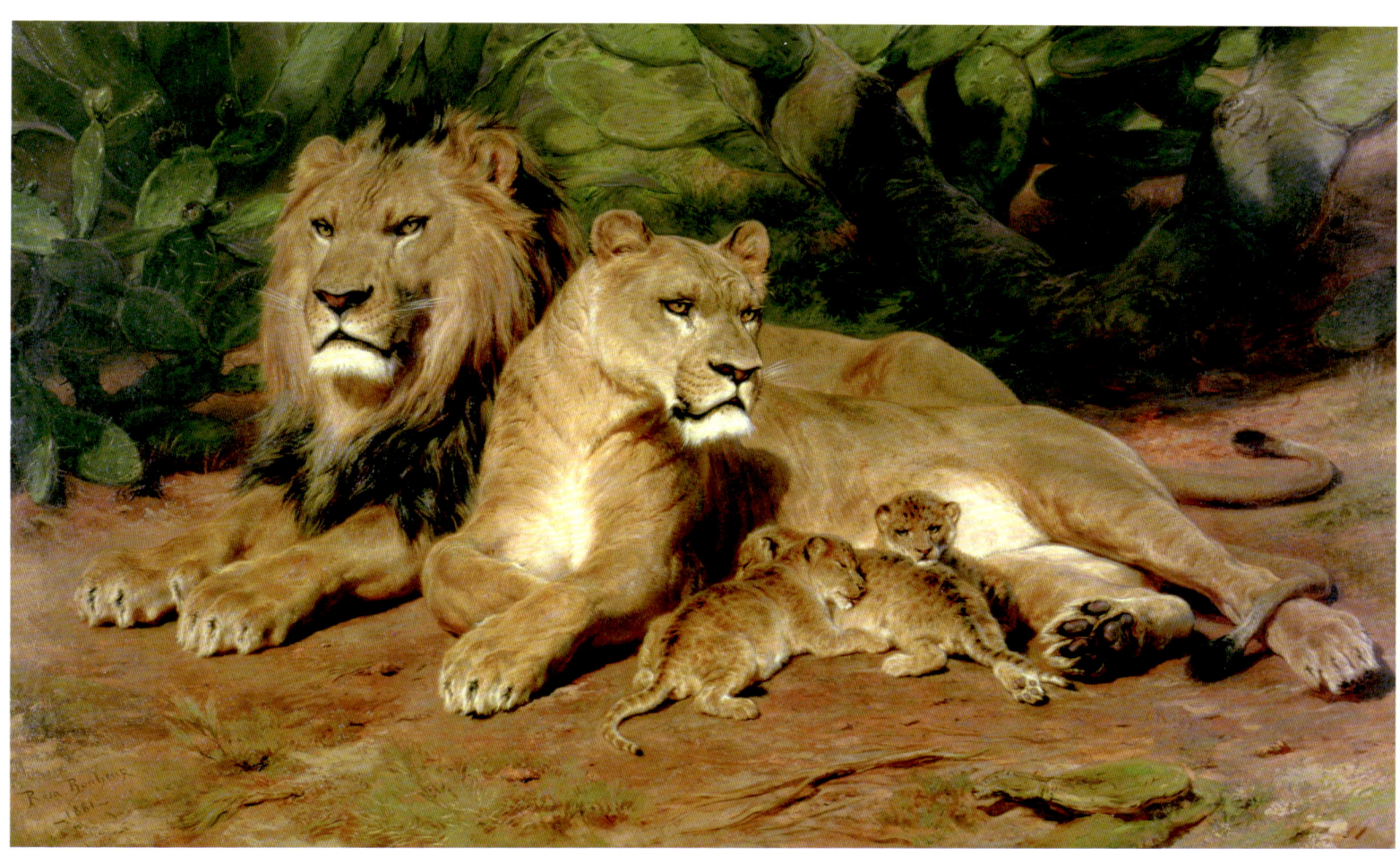

Rosa Bonheur (1822–1899)

The Lions at Home

Les Lions

Löwen in ihrer Heimat

Leones en su patria

Leoni nel loro habitat

Leeuwen in hun vaderland

1881, Oil on canvas/Huile sur toile, 162,3 × 262,3 cm, Ferens Art Gallery, Hull

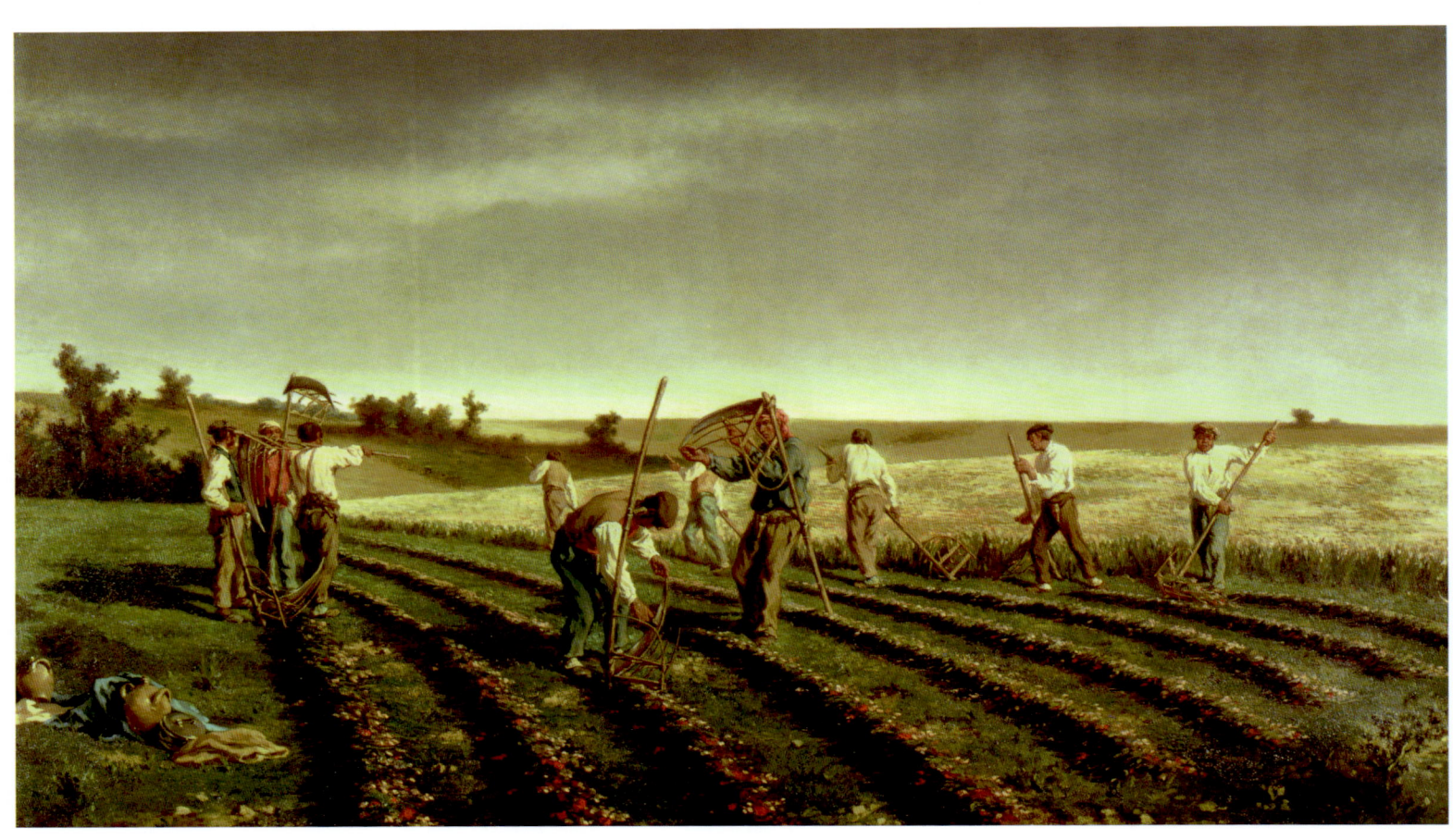

Pierre Edmond Alexandre Hédouin (1820–1889)

Reaping Sainfoin in Chambaudouin

Les Faucheurs de sainfoin à Chambaudoin

Ernte in Chambaudoin

Cosecha en Chambaudoin

Raccolto a Chambaudoin

Oogst in Chambaudoin

1852, Oil on canvas/Huile sur toile, 110 × 190 cm, Palais des Beaux-Arts, Lille

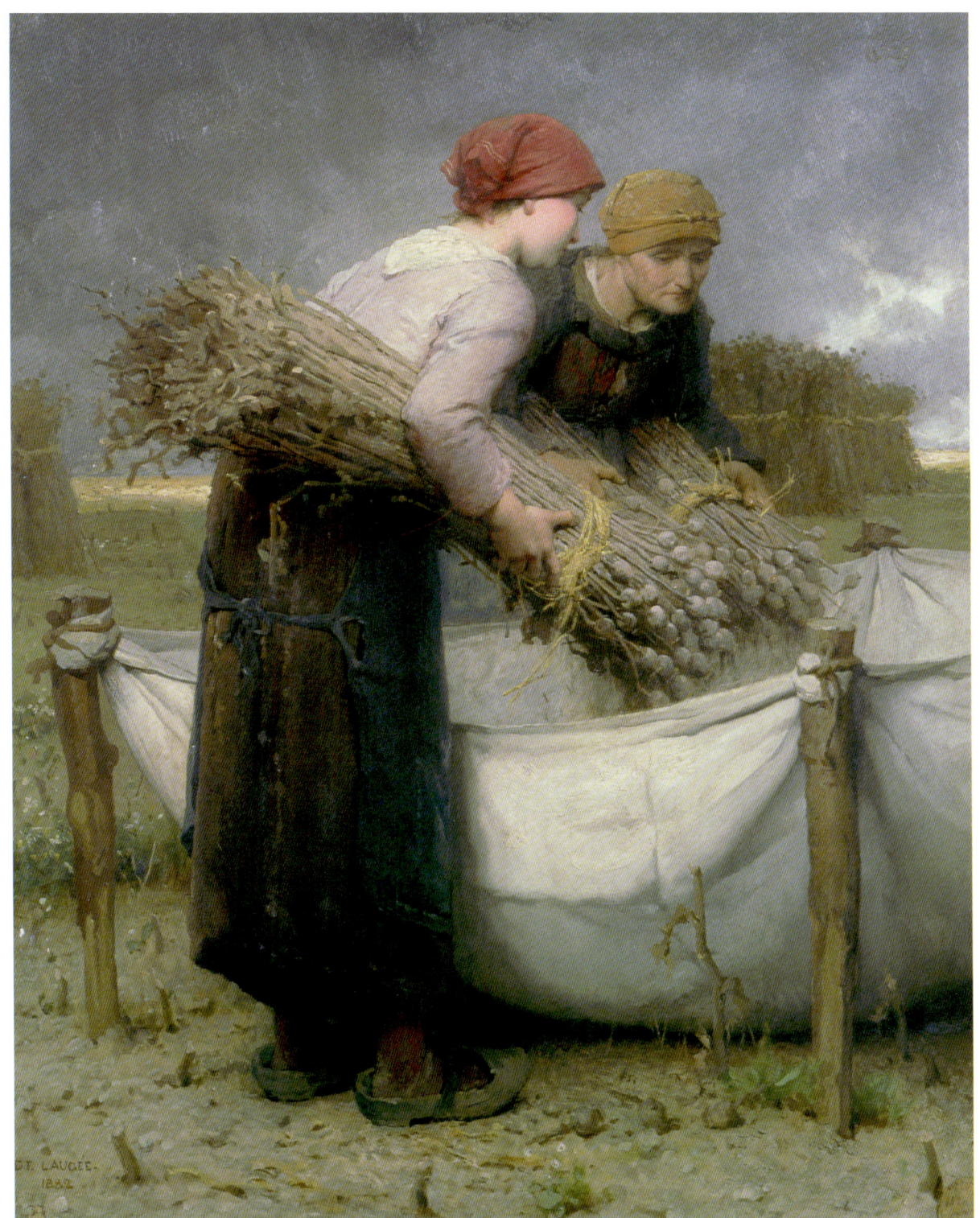

Desiré François Laugée
(1823–1896)

Women in the Field

Femmes aux champs

Frauen auf dem Feld

Mujeres en el campo

Donne nel campo

Vrouwen op het veld

1882, Oil on canvas/Huile sur toile,
93,5 × 73 cm, Musée des Beaux-Arts,
Rouen

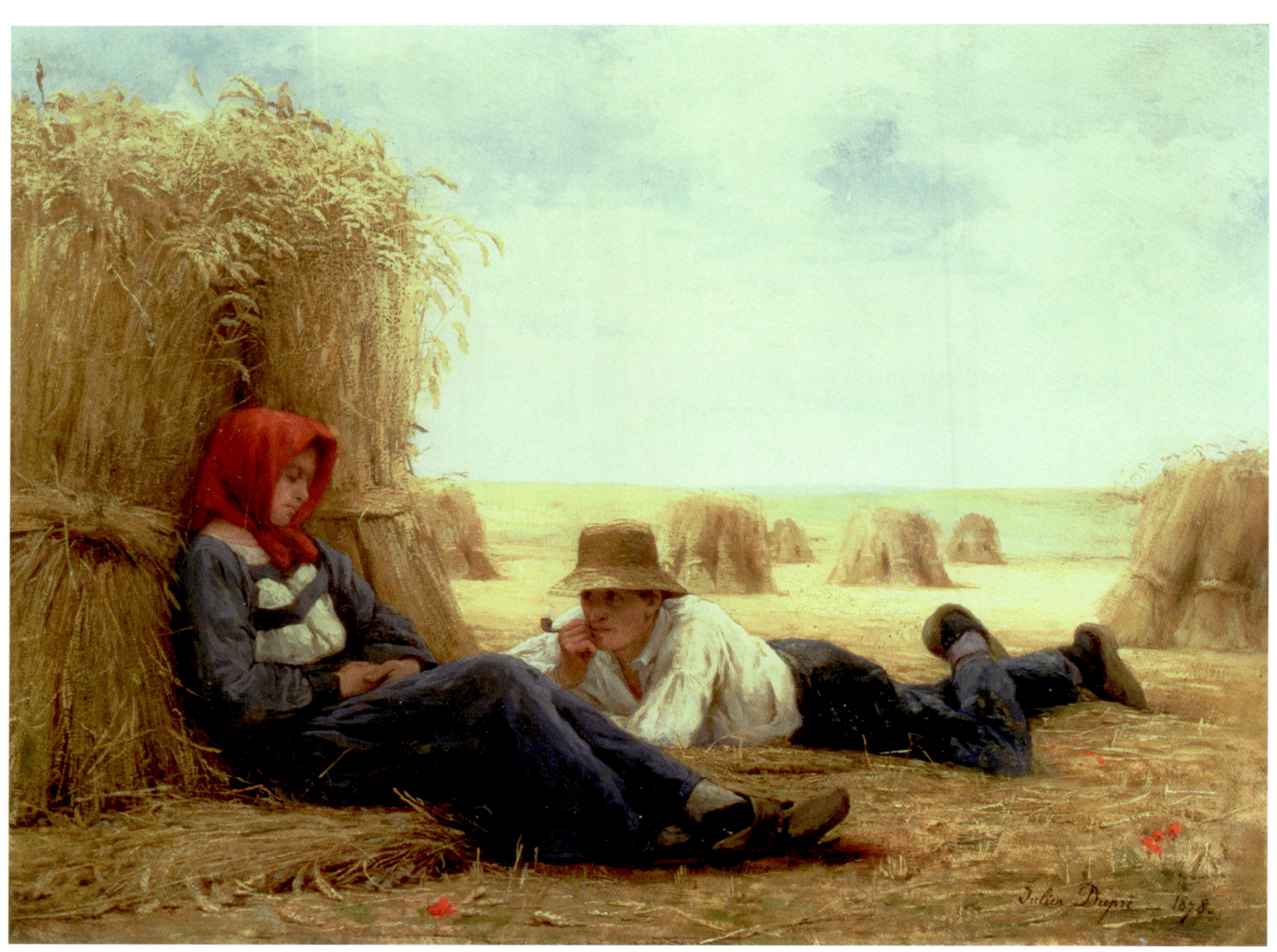

Julien Dupré (1851–1910)

Harvest Time	Erntezeit	Tempo di raccolto
La Moisson	Tiempo de cosecha	Oogsttijd

1880, Oil on canvas/Huile sur toile, 64,8 × 81,3 cm, Private collection

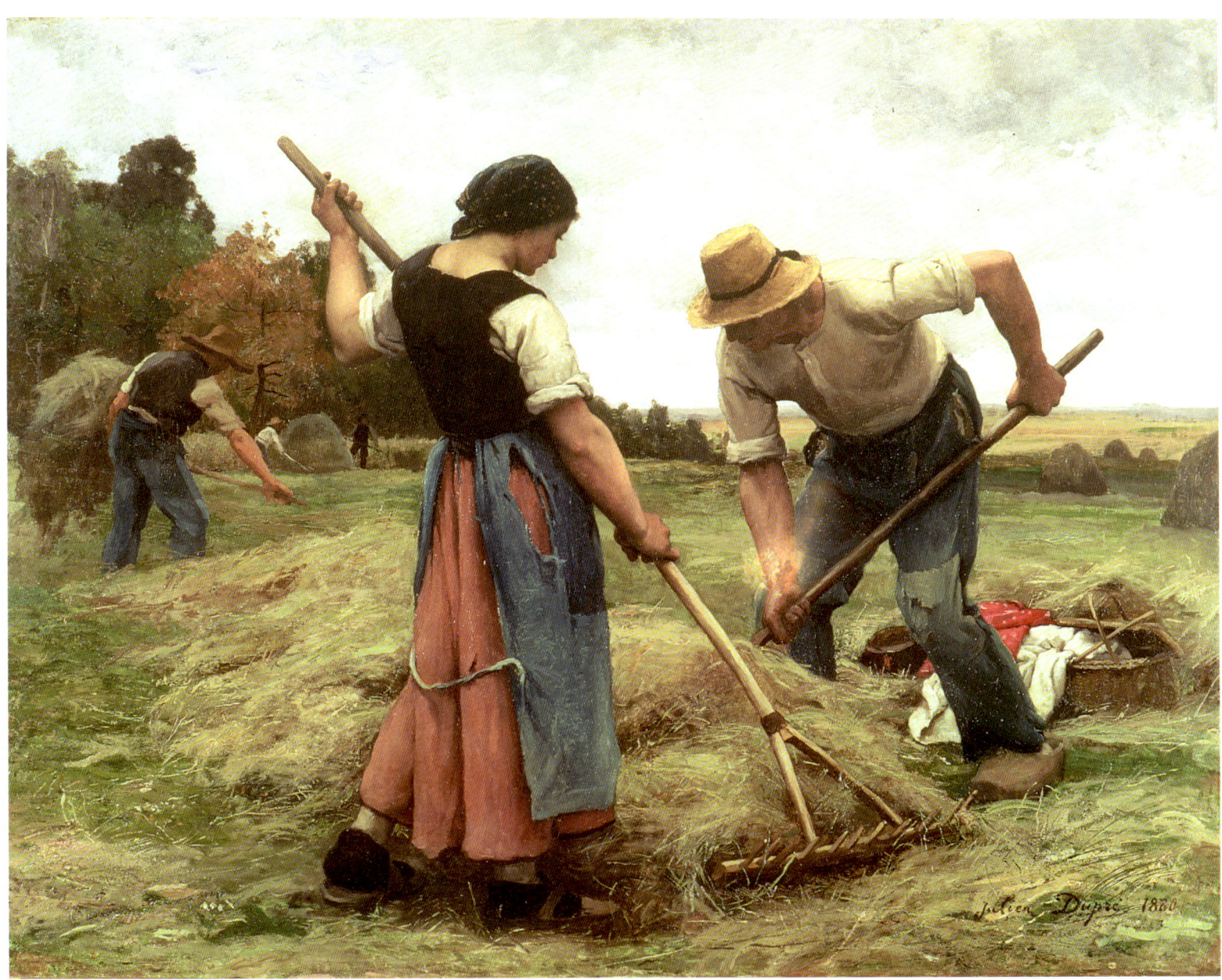

Julien Dupré (1841–1919)

Haymaking	Heuernte	Raccoglitrici di fieno
La Fenaison	La cosecha del heno	Hooioogst

1880, Oil on canvas/Huile sur toile, 64,8 × 81,3 cm, Private collection

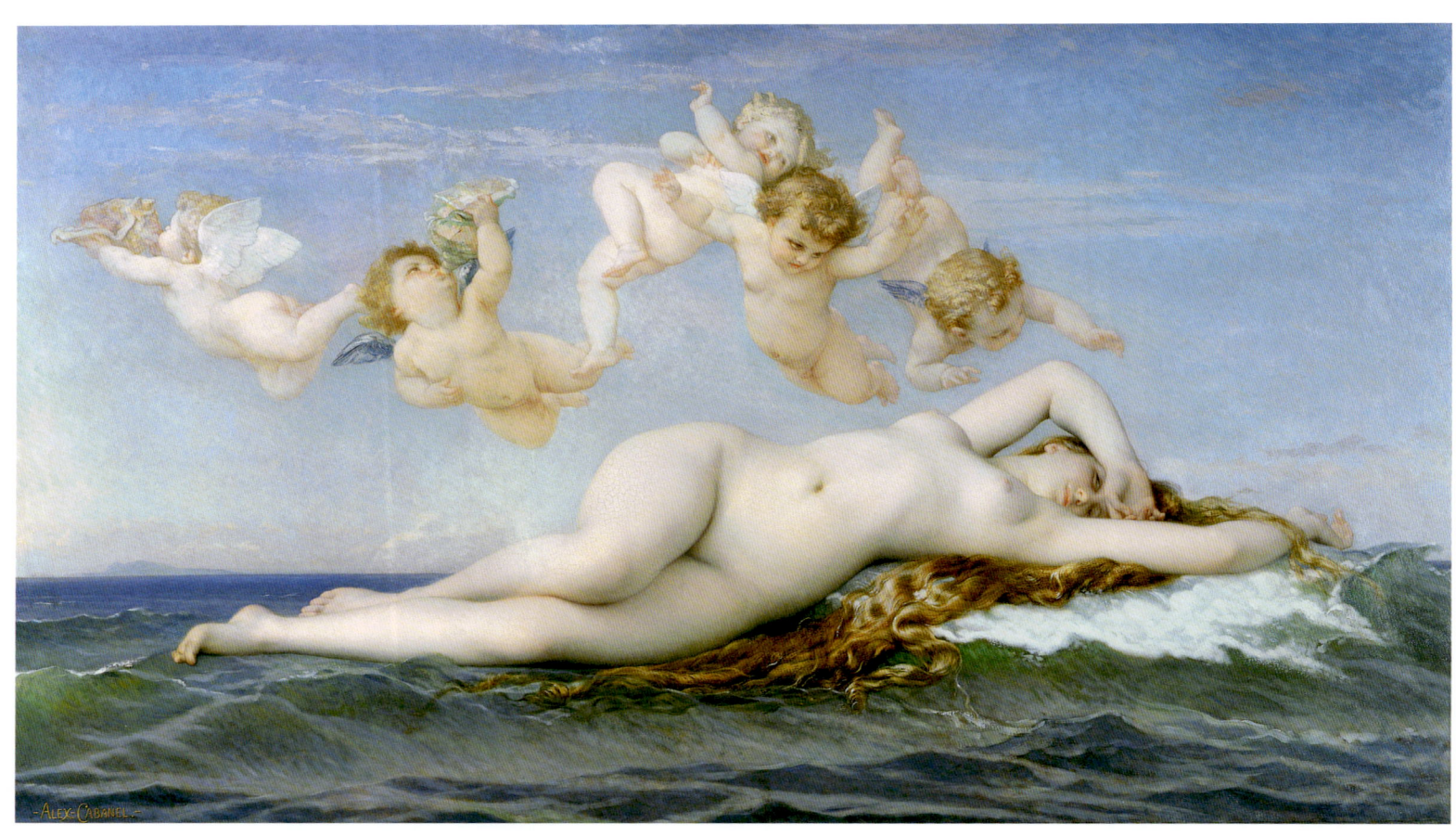

Alexandre Cabanel (1823–1889)

Birth of Venus

La Naissance de Vénus

Die Geburt der Venus

El nacimiento de Venus

La nascita di Venere

De geboorte van Venus

1863, Oil on canvas/Huile sur toile, 130 × 225 cm, Musée d'Orsay, Paris

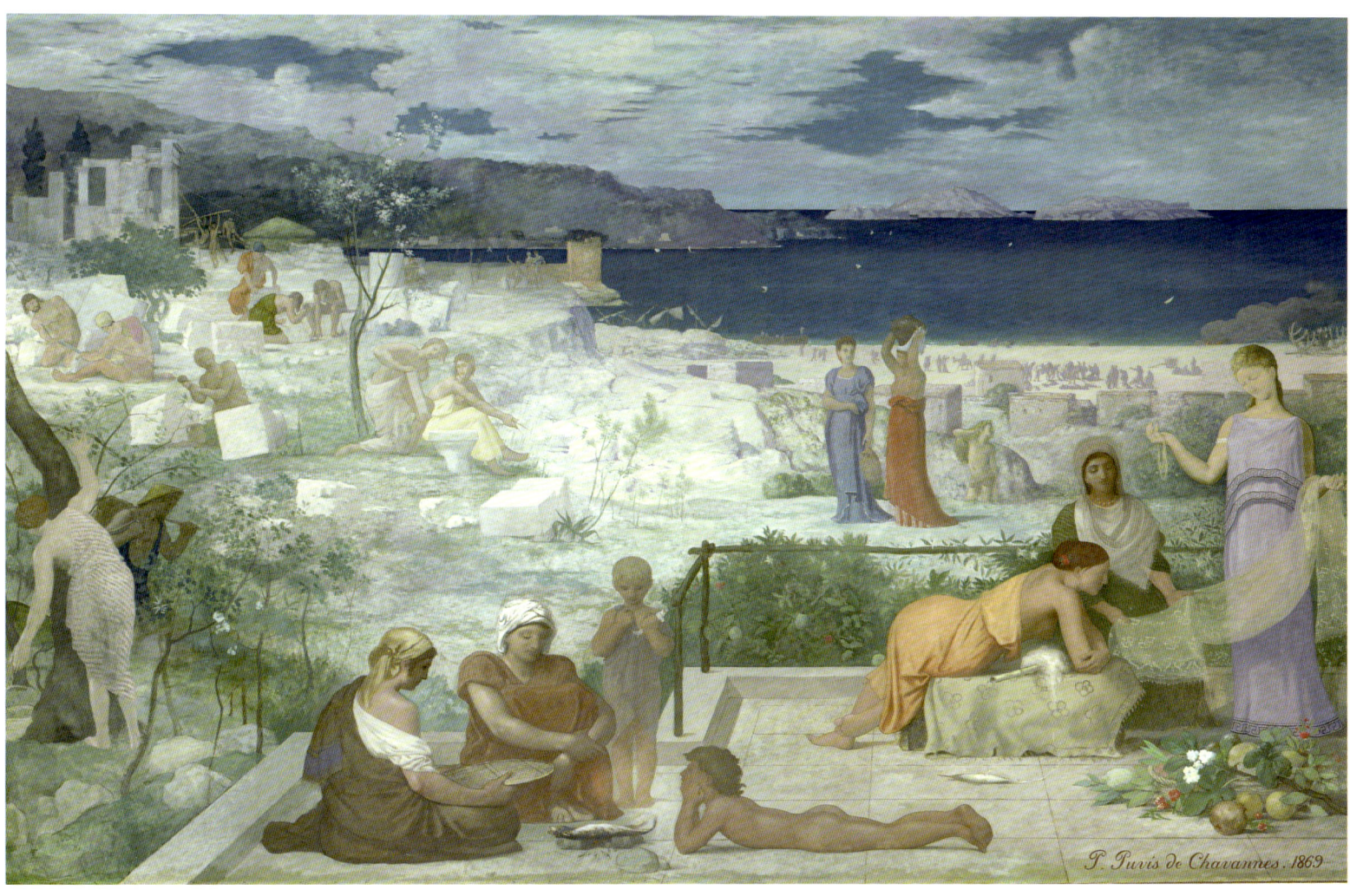

Pierre Puvis de Chavannes (1824–1898)

The Greek Colony, Marseille

Marseille, colonie grecque

Die griechische Kolonie in Marseille

La colona griega en Marsella

La colonia greca a Marsiglia

De Griekse kolonie Massalia (Marseille)

1869, Oil on canvas/Huile sur toile, 423 × 565 cm, Musée des Beaux-Arts, Marseille

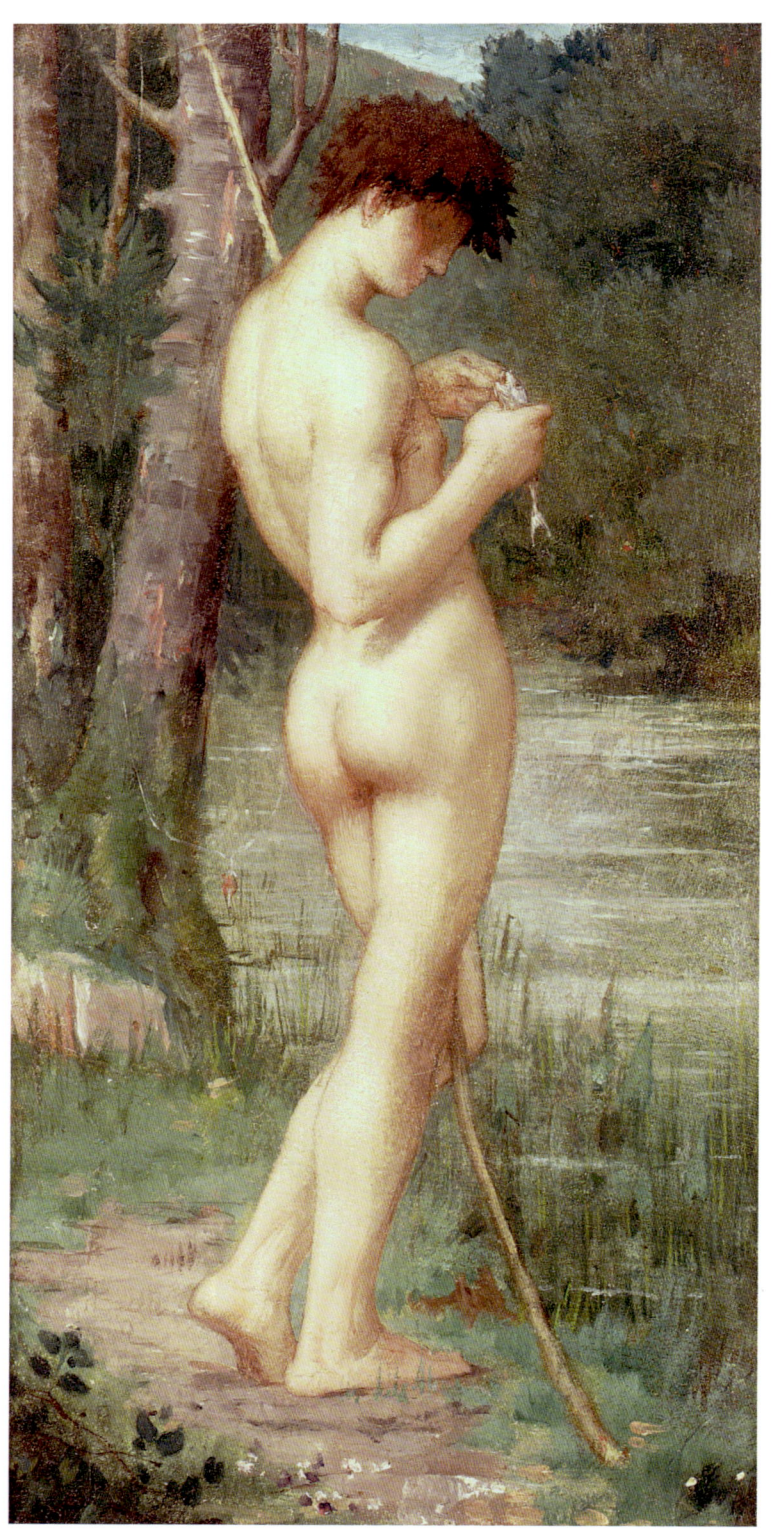

Pierre Puvis de Chavannes (1824–1898)

The Little Fisherman

Le Petit pêcheur

Der Fischerjunge

El pescador

Il giovane pescatore

De vissersjongen

n. d., Oil on canvas/Huile sur toile, 28,1 × 14,5 cm, Private collection

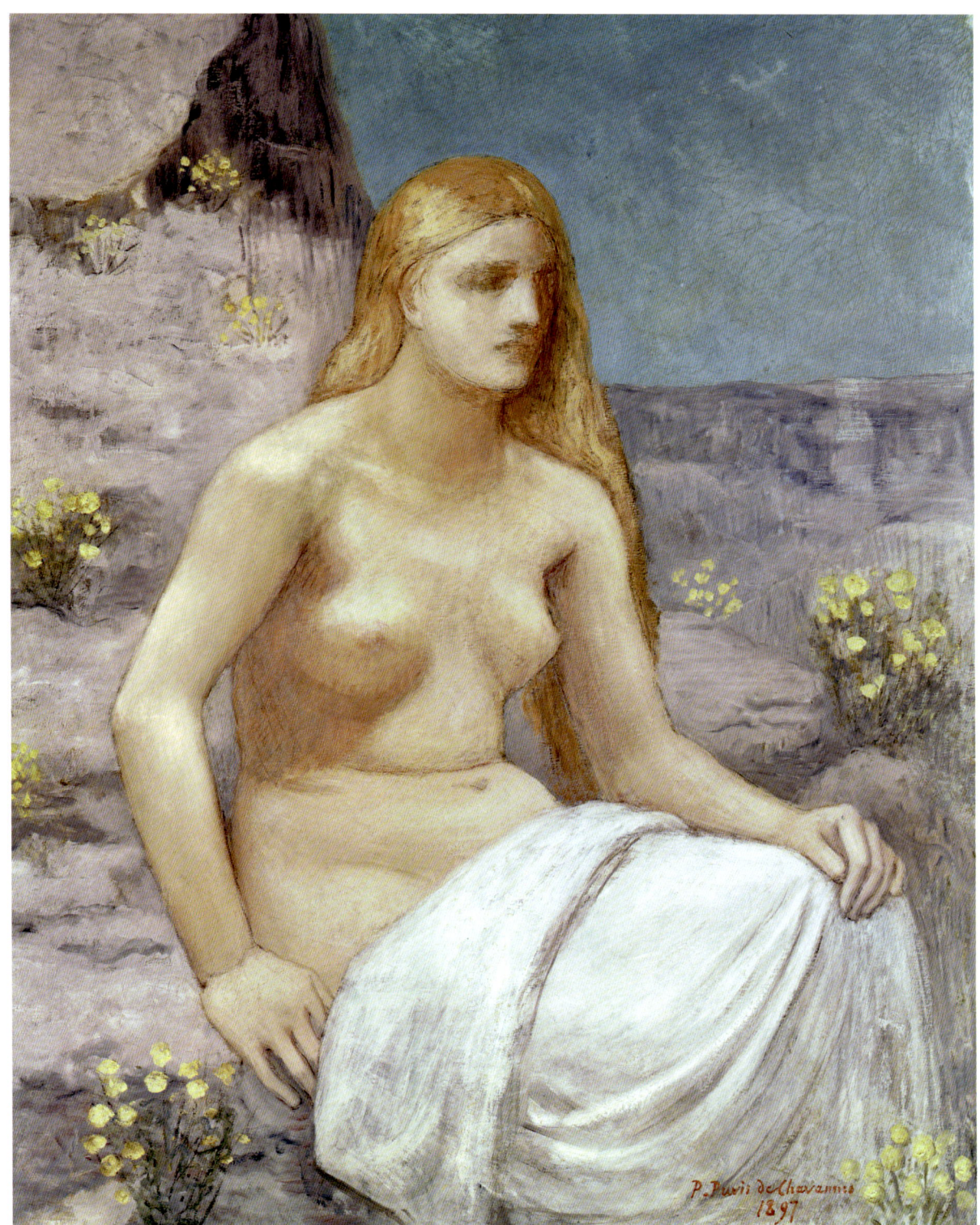

**Pierre Puvis de Chavannes
(1824–1898)**

St. Mary Magdalene

Marie Madeleine

Die Hl. Maria Magdalena

Santa María Magdalena

Santa Maria Maddalena

De heilige Maria Magdalena

1897, Oil on canvas/Huile sur toile,
116,5 × 89,5 cm, Szépművészeti
Múzeum, Budapest

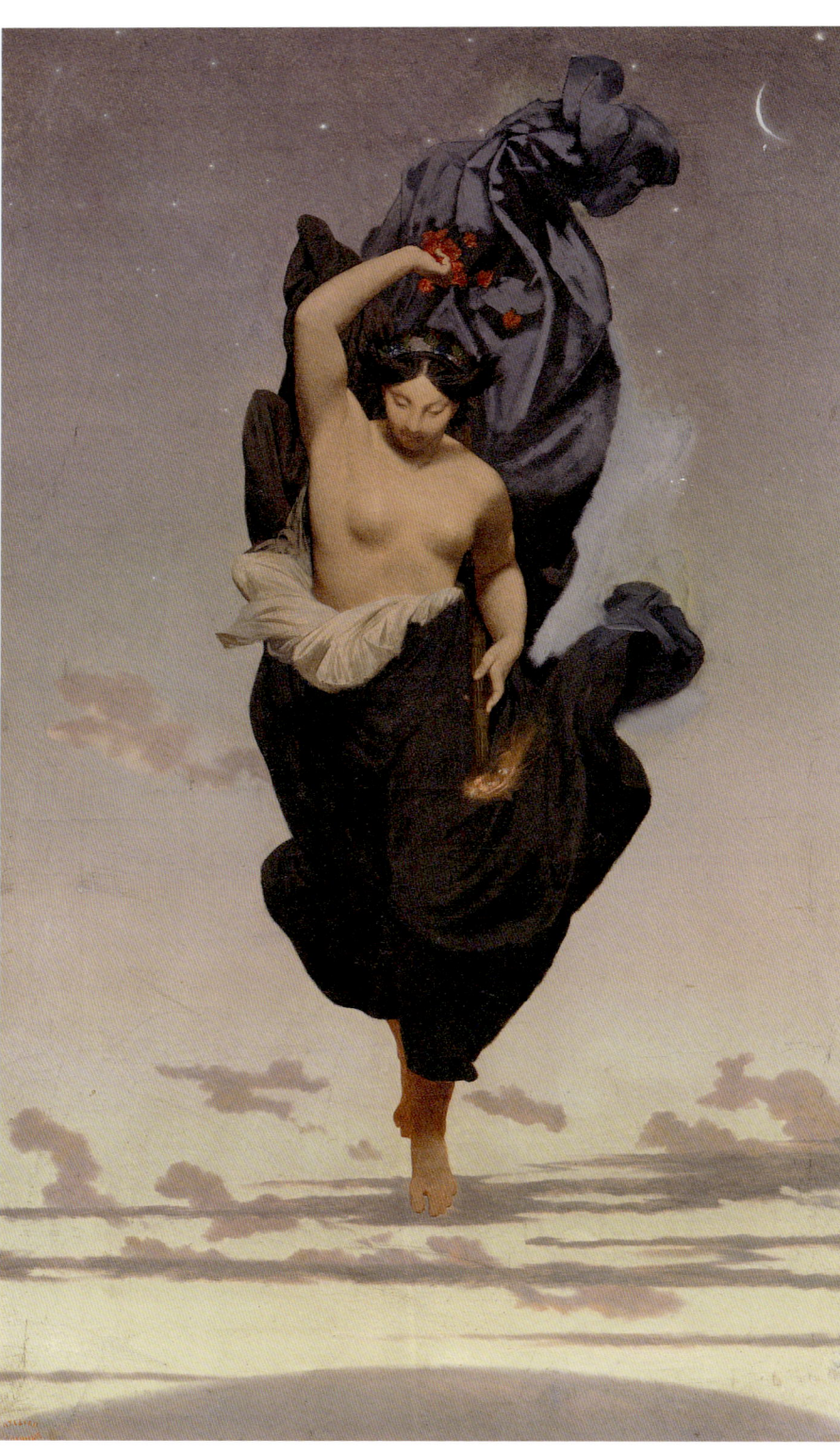

Jean-Léon Gérôme (1824–1904)

Night

La Nuit

Die Nacht

La noche

La notte

De nacht

1850–1855, Oil on canvas/Huile sur toile,
76,5 × 46 cm, Musée d'Orsay, Paris

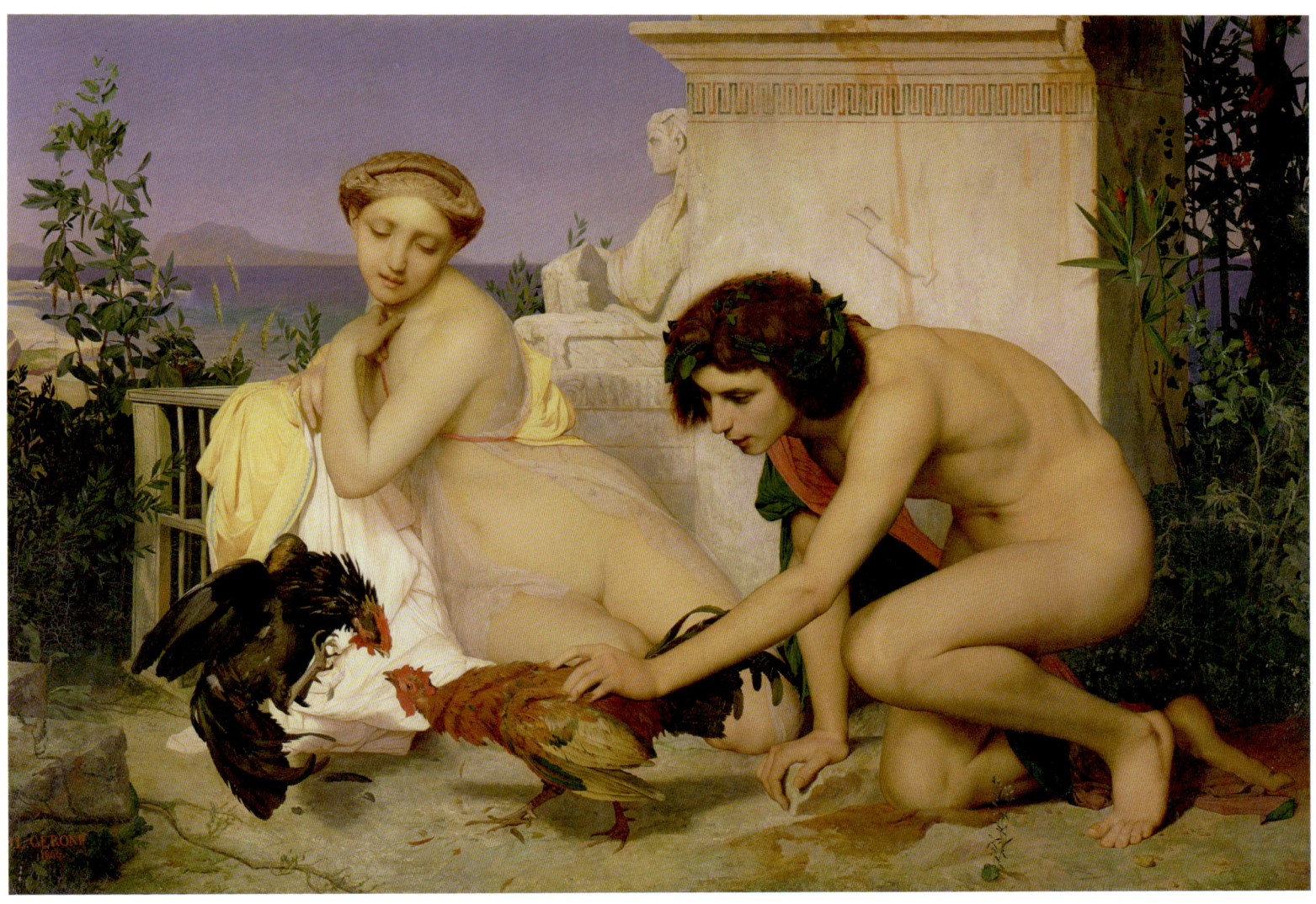

Jean-Léon Gérôme (1824–1904)

Young Greeks Encouraging Cocks to Fight

Jeunes grecs faisant battre des coqs *ou* Un combat de coqs

Junge Griechen beim Hahnenkampf

Jóvenes griegos poniendo dos gallos a pelear *o* Pelea de gallos

Giovani greci che fanno combattere dei galli *o* Un combattimenti di galli

Jonge Grieken bij het hanengevecht *of:* Een hanengevecht

1846, Oil on canvas/Huile sur toile, 143 × 204 cm, Musée d'Orsay, Paris

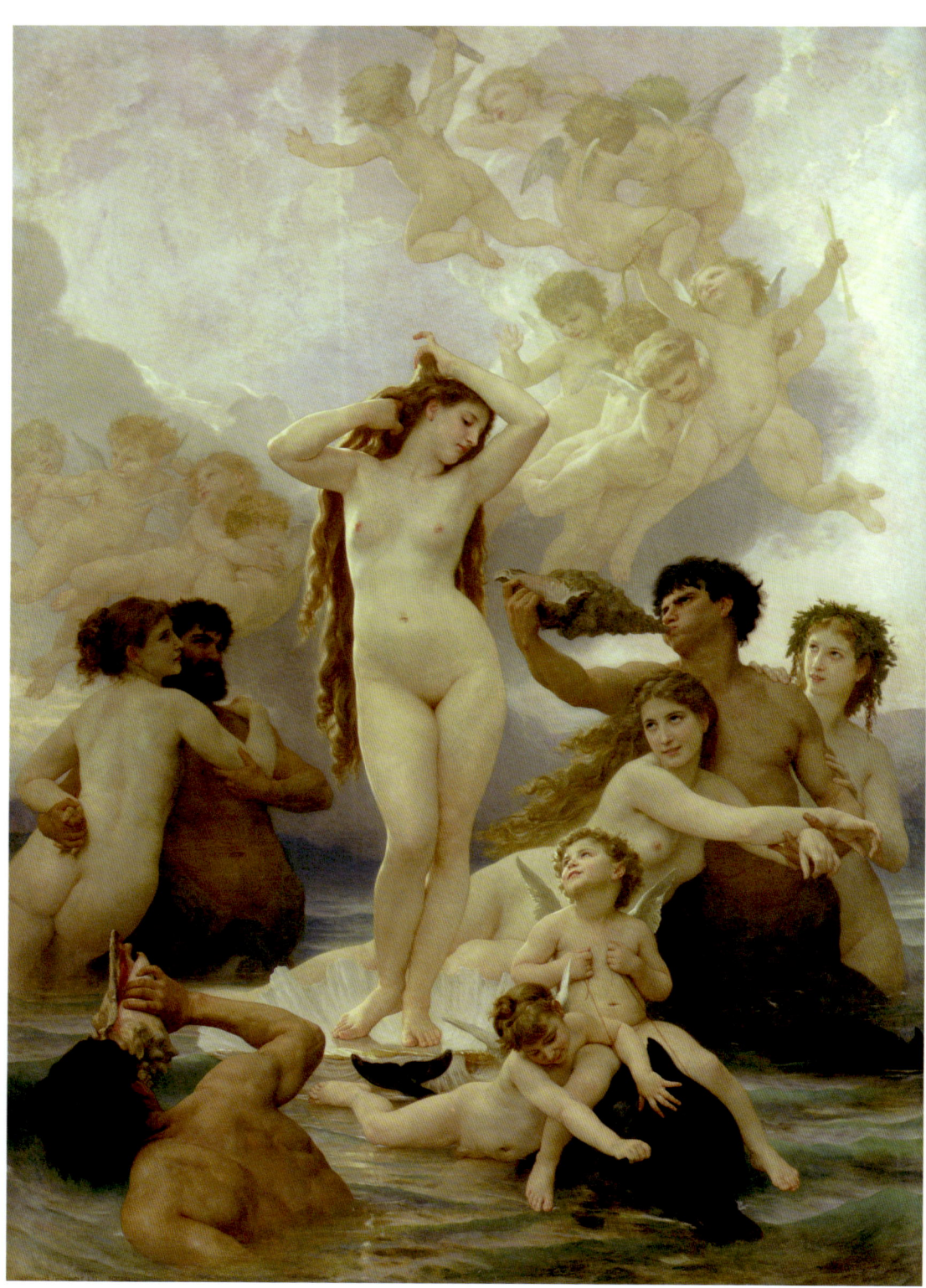

William Bouguereau (1825–1905)

The Birth of Venus

La Naissance de Vénus

Die Geburt der Venus

El nacimiento de Venus

La nascita di Venere

De geboorte van Venus

1879, Oil on canvas/Huile sur toile,
300 × 215 cm, Musée d'Orsay, Paris

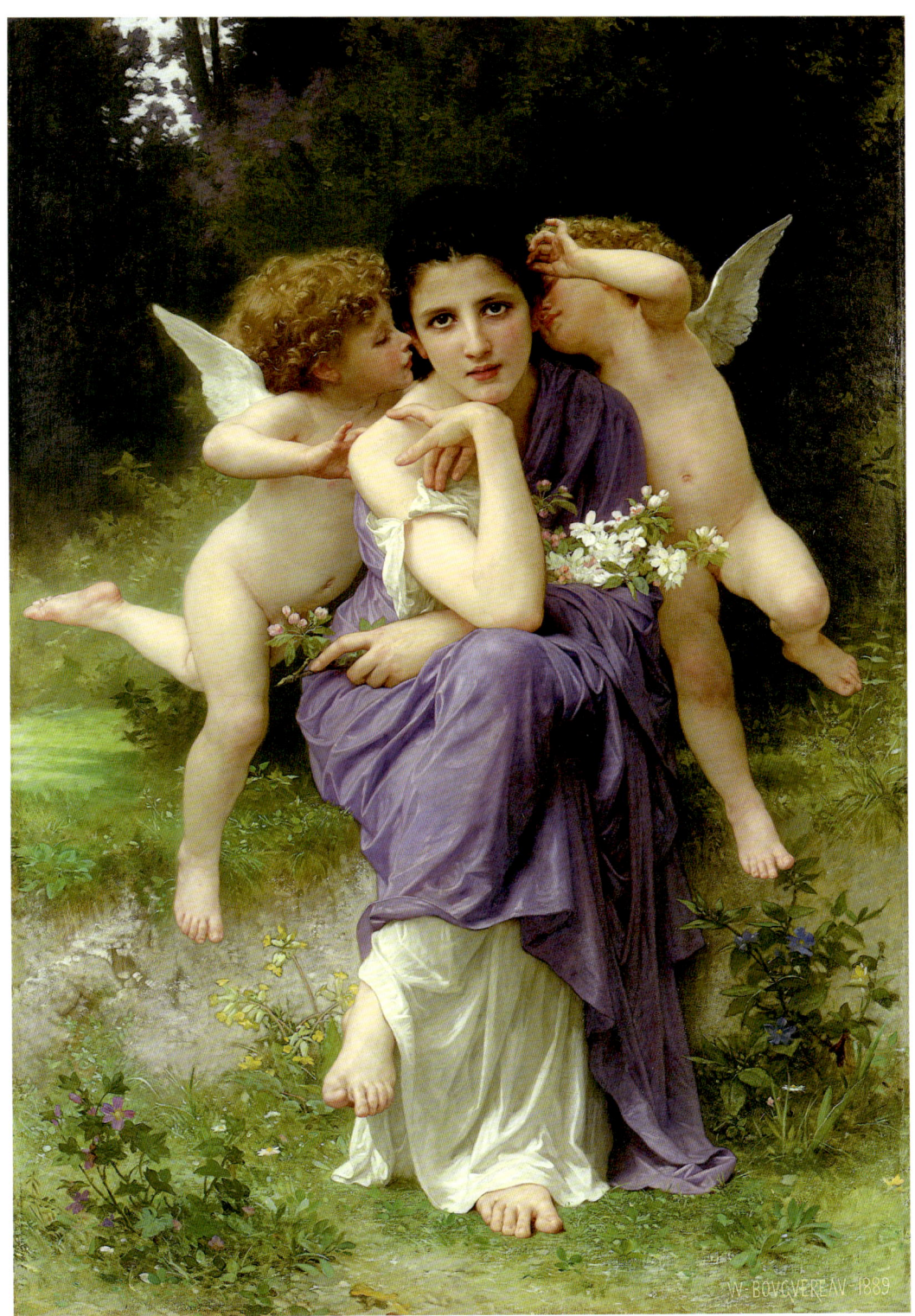

William Bouguereau (1825–1905)

Chansons de Printemps

Chansons de Printemps

Lieder des Frühlings

Canciones de primavera

Canzoni della primavera

Chansons de printemps

1889, Oil on canvas/Huile sur toile, 148,6 × 99,7 cm,
Private collection

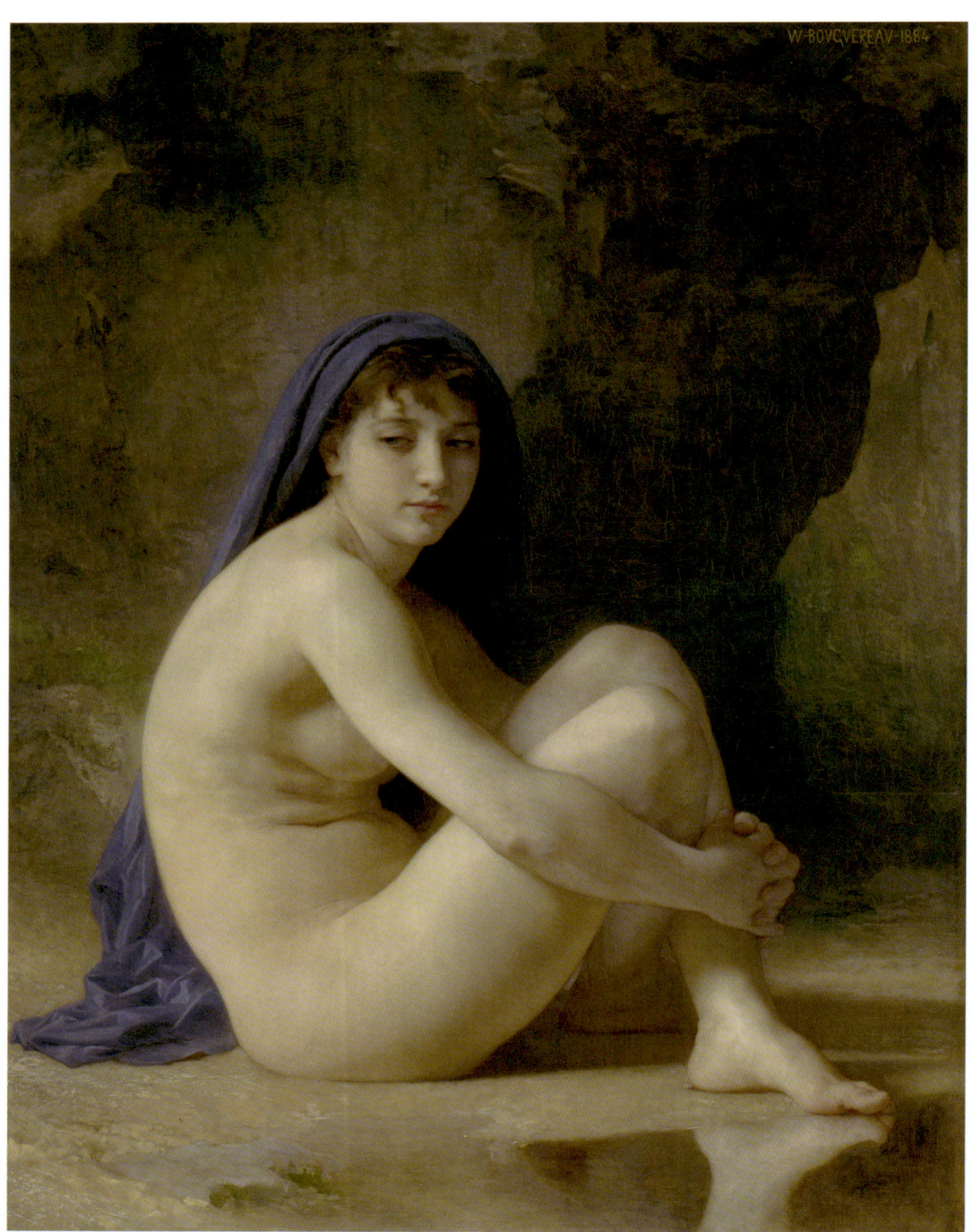

William Bouguereau (1825–1905)

Seated Nude

Nu assis

Sitzender Akt

Desnudo sentado

Nudo seduto

Zittend naakt

1884, Oil on canvas/Huile sur toile, 116,5 × 89,8 cm, Clark Art Institute, Williamstown

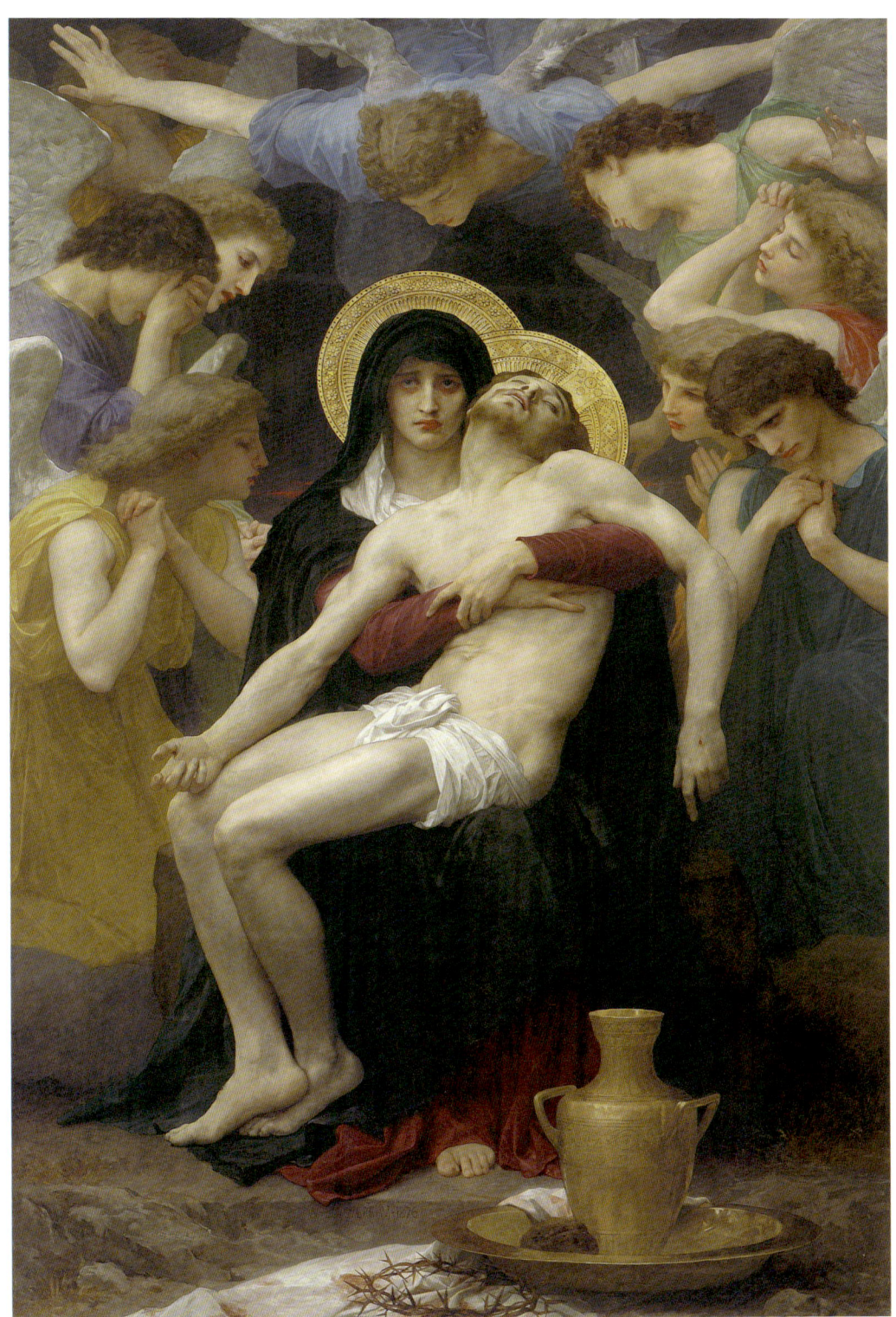

William Bouguereau (1825–1905)

Pieta
Pietà
Pieta
Pietá
Pietà
Pietà

1876, Oil on canvas/Huile sur toile, 222,9 × 149,2 cm,
Private collection

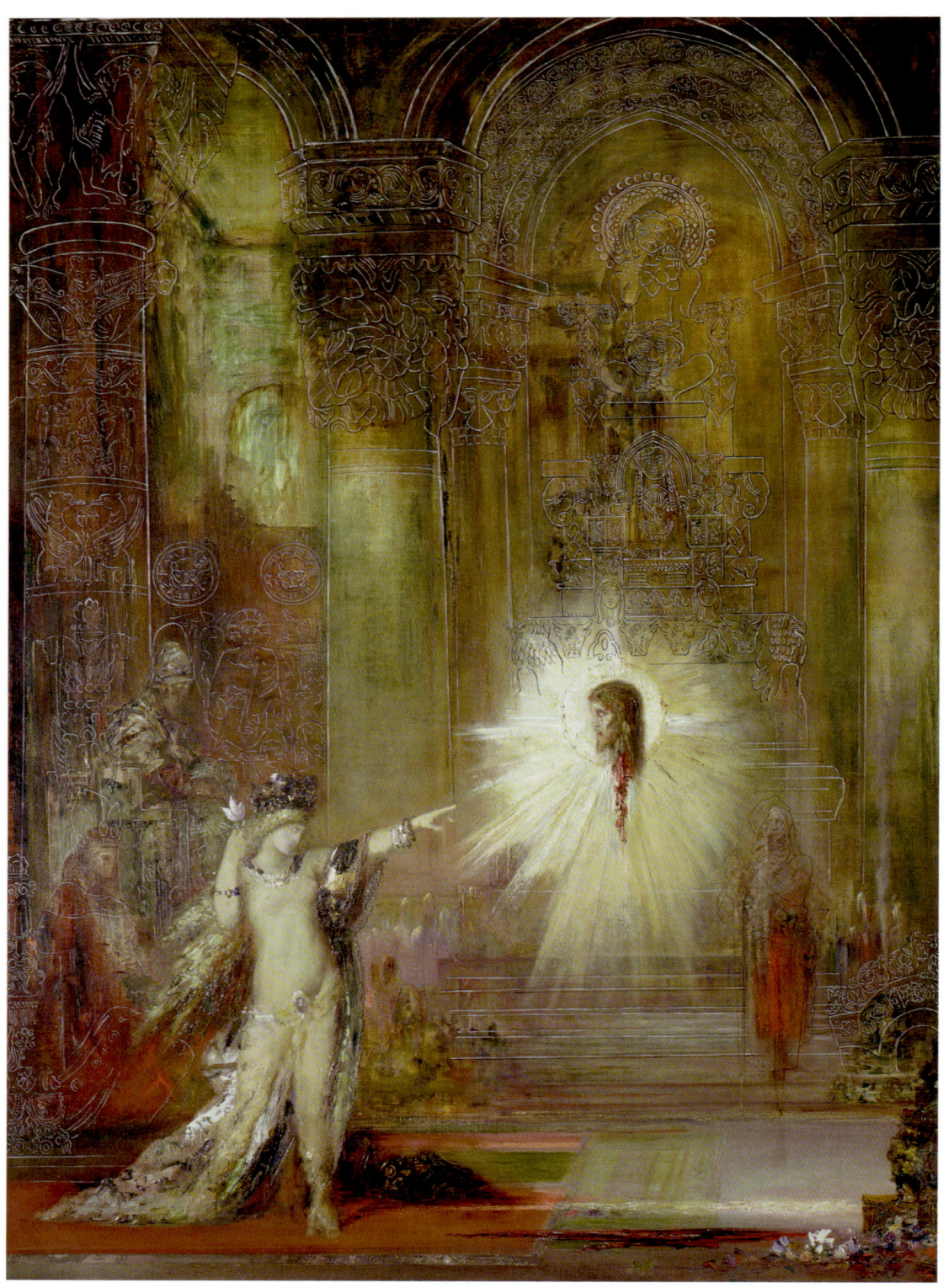

Gustave Moreau (1826–1898)

The Apparition

L'Apparition

Die Erscheinung

La aparición

L'apparizione

De verschijning

1876–1898, Oil on canvas/Huile sur toile,
142 × 103 cm, Musée national Gustave
Moreau, Paris

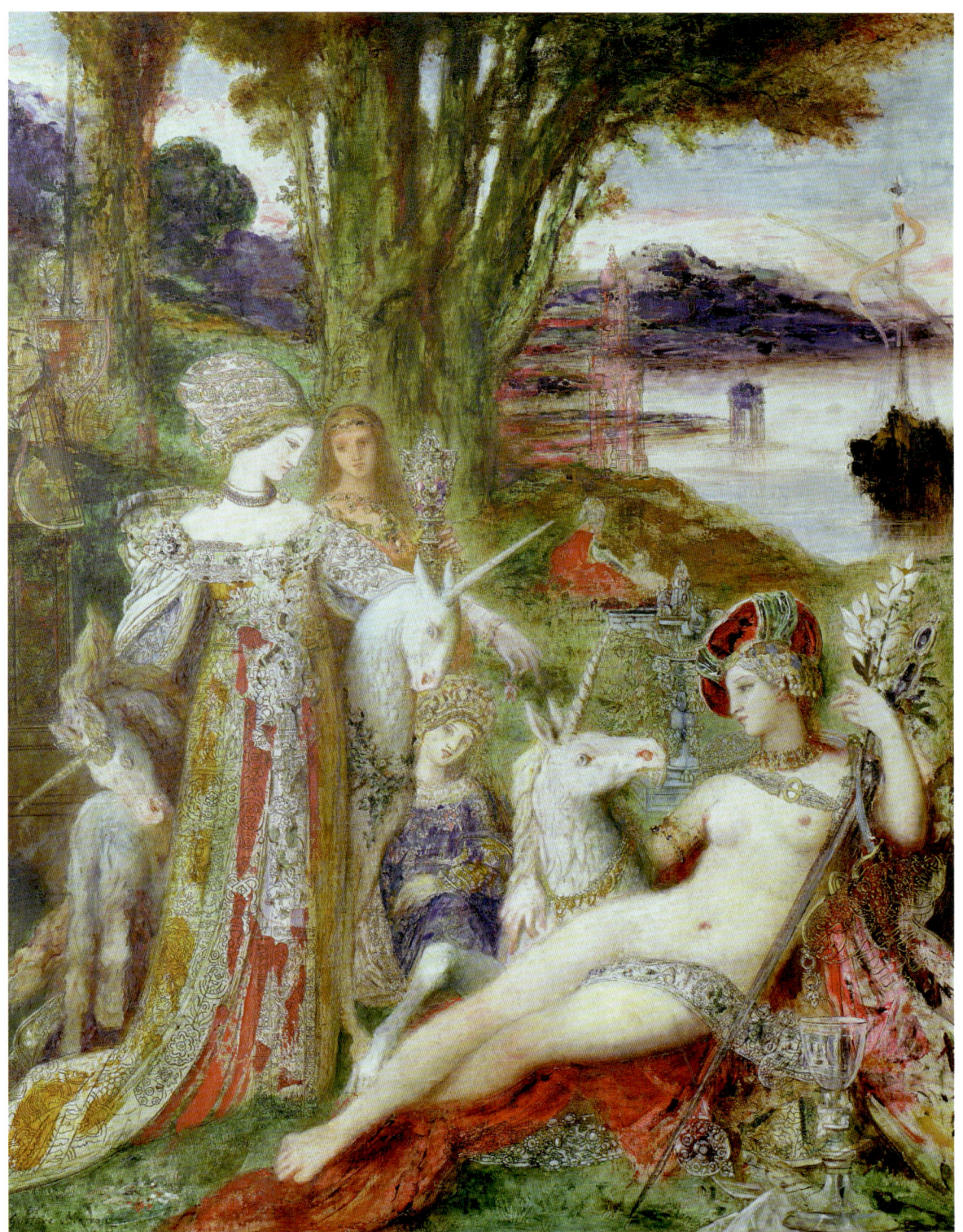

Gustave Moreau (1826–1898)

The Unicorns

Les Licornes

Die Einhörner

Los unicornios

Gli unicorni

De eenhoorns

n. d., Oil on canvas/Huile sur toile,
115 × 90 cm, Musée national Gustave
Moreau, Paris

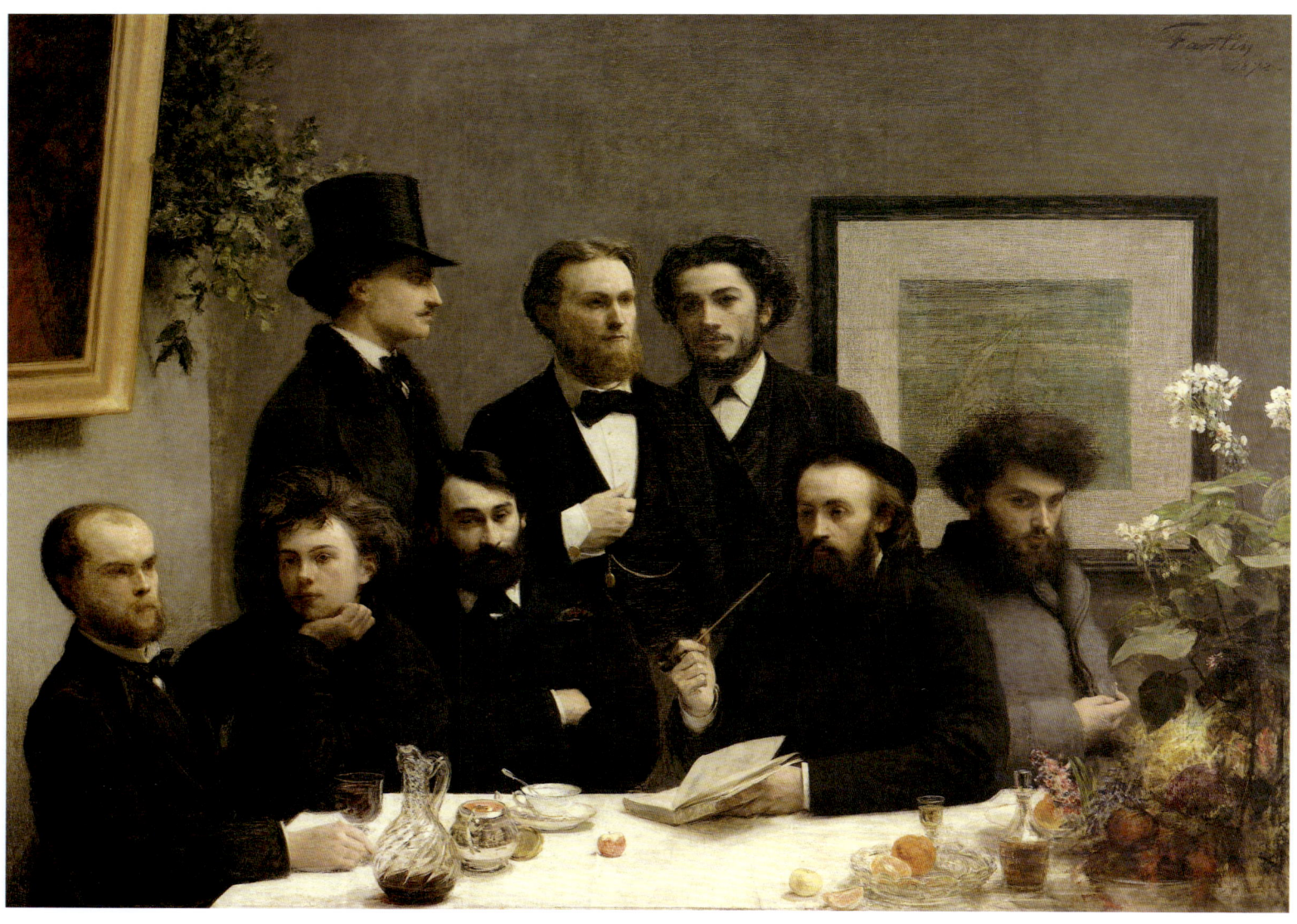

Henri Fantin-Latour (1836–1904)

A Corner of the Table

Un Coin de table

Eine Seite des Tisches

Un lado de la mesa

Un angolo del tavolo

Een tafelkant

1872, Oil on canvas/Huile sur toile, 161 × 223,5 cm, Musée d'Orsay, Paris

Henri Fantin-Latour (1836–1904)

Flowers and Fruit

Fleurs et fruits

Blumen und Früchte

Flores y frutos

Fiori e frutta

Bloemen en fruit

1865, Oil on canvas/Huile sur toile, 64 × 57 cm, Musée d'Orsay, Paris

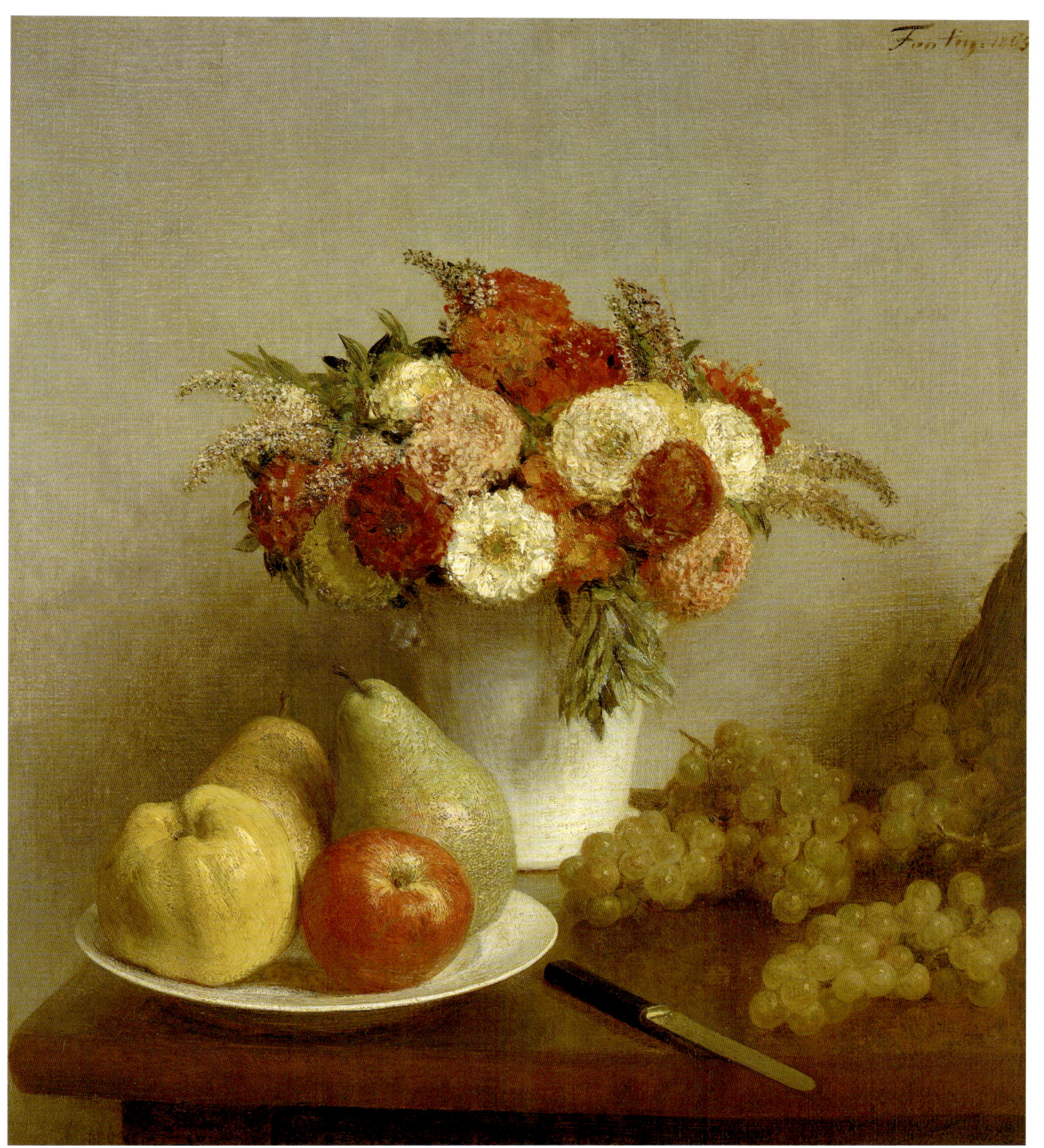

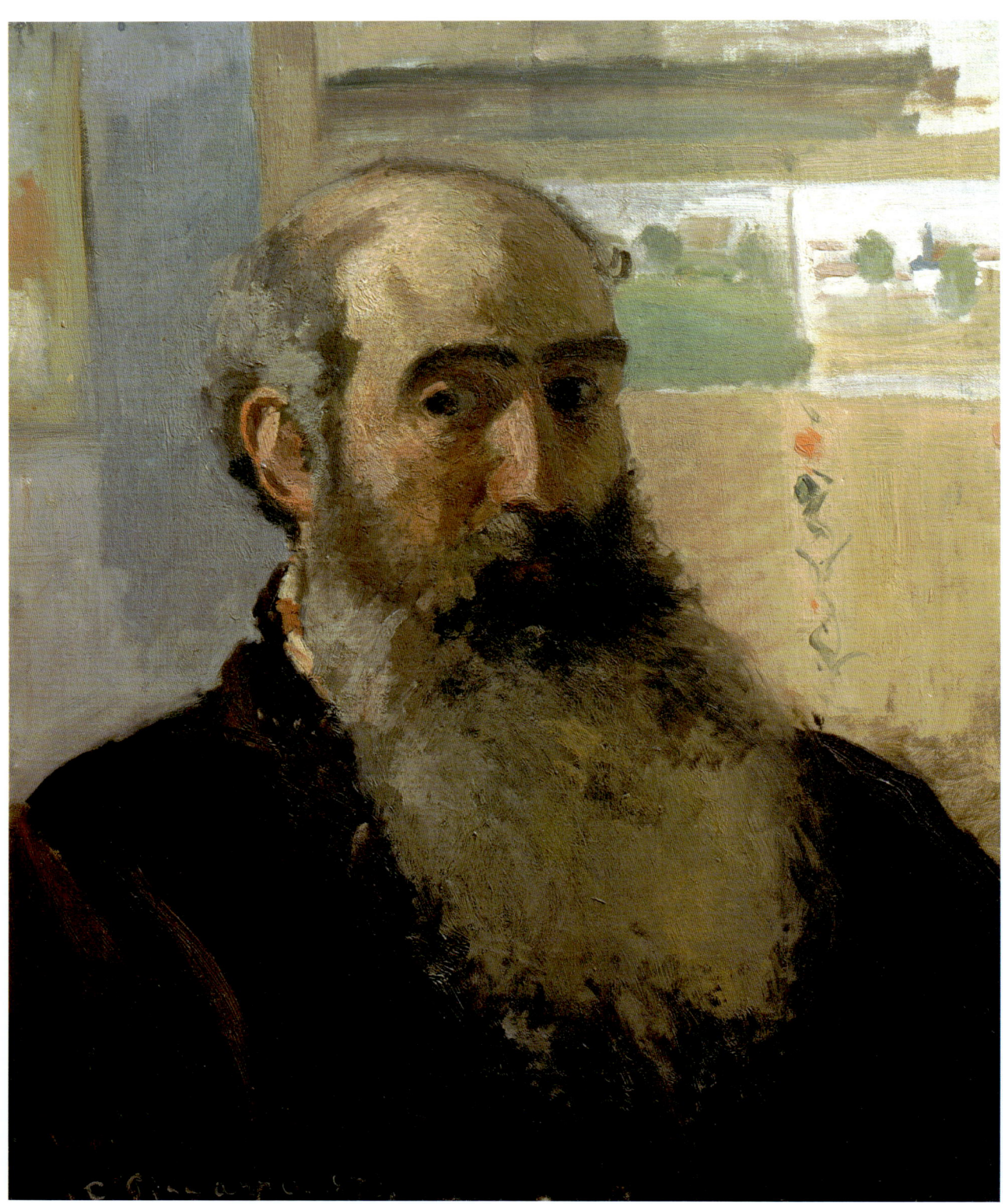

**Camille Pissarro
(1830–1903)**

Self Portrait

Portrait de l'artiste

Selbstporträt

Autorretrato

Autoritratto

Zelfportret

1873, Oil on canvas/Huile sur toile, 55,5 × 46 cm, Musée d'Orsay, Paris

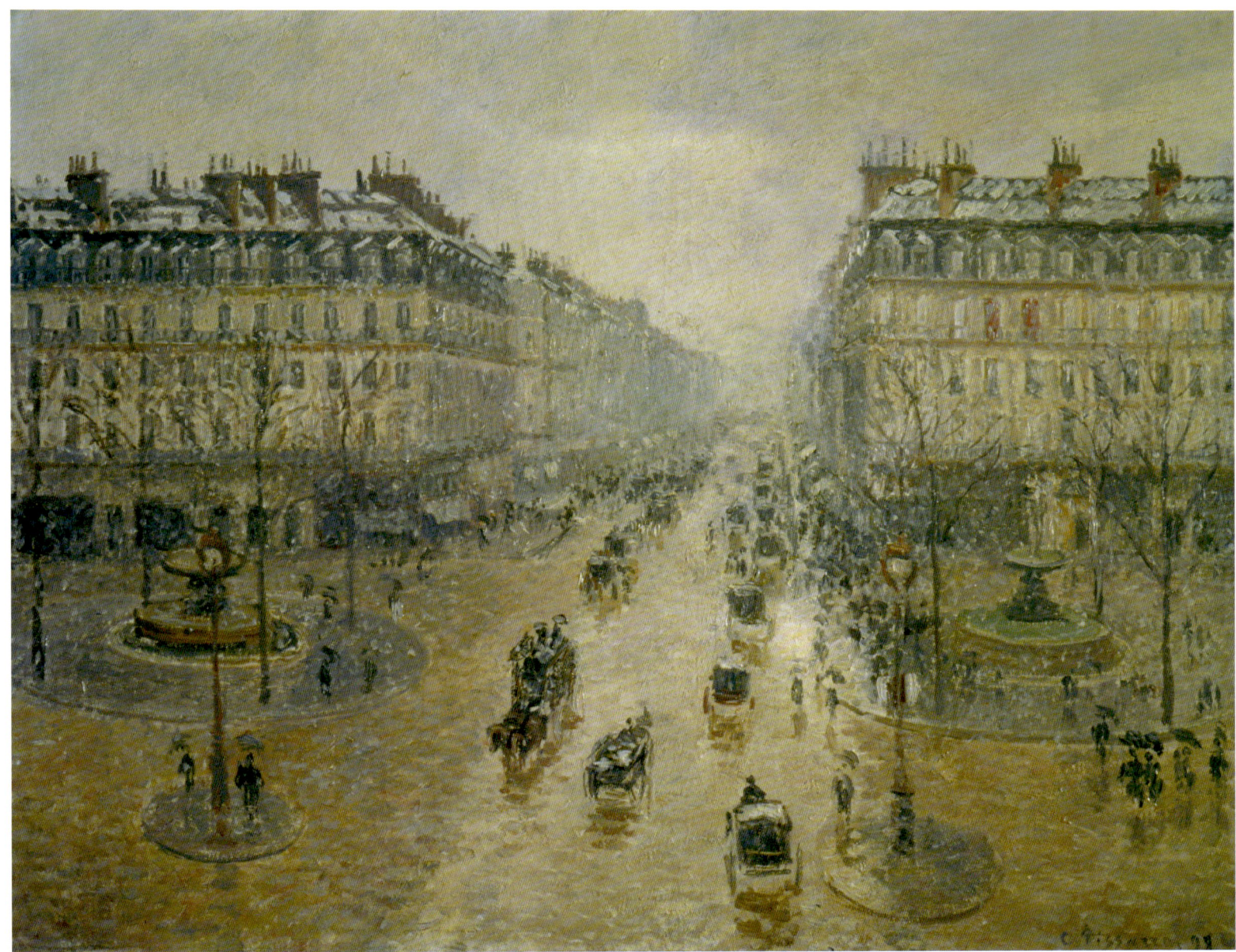

Camille Pissarro (1830–1903)

Avenue de L'Opera, Paris

Avenue de l'Opéra, Paris

Avenue de l'Opera, Paris

Avenue de l'Opera, París

Avenue de l'Opéra, Parigi

Avenue de l'Opéra, Parijs

1898, Oil on canvas/Huile sur toile, 65 × 82 cm, Pushkin State Museum of Fine Arts, Moscow

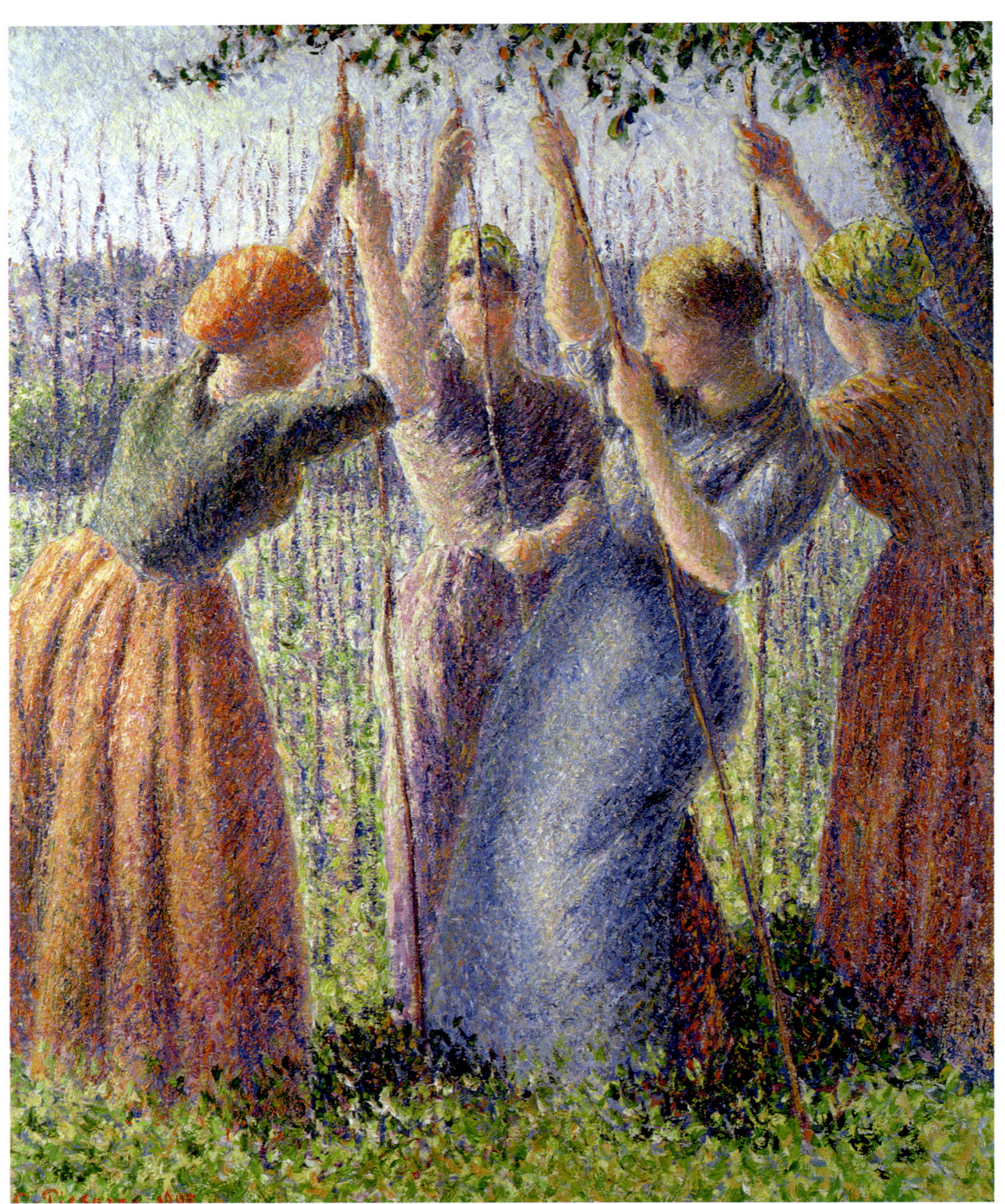

**Camille Pissarro
(1830–1903)**

Women Planting Peasticks

Paysannes plantant des rames

Frauen pflanzen Erbsenstöcke

Campesinas plantando estacas

Donne che piantano paletti per i piselli

Vrouwen bij het planten van erwtenstaken

1891, Oil on canvas/Huile sur toile, 55 × 46 cm, Private collection

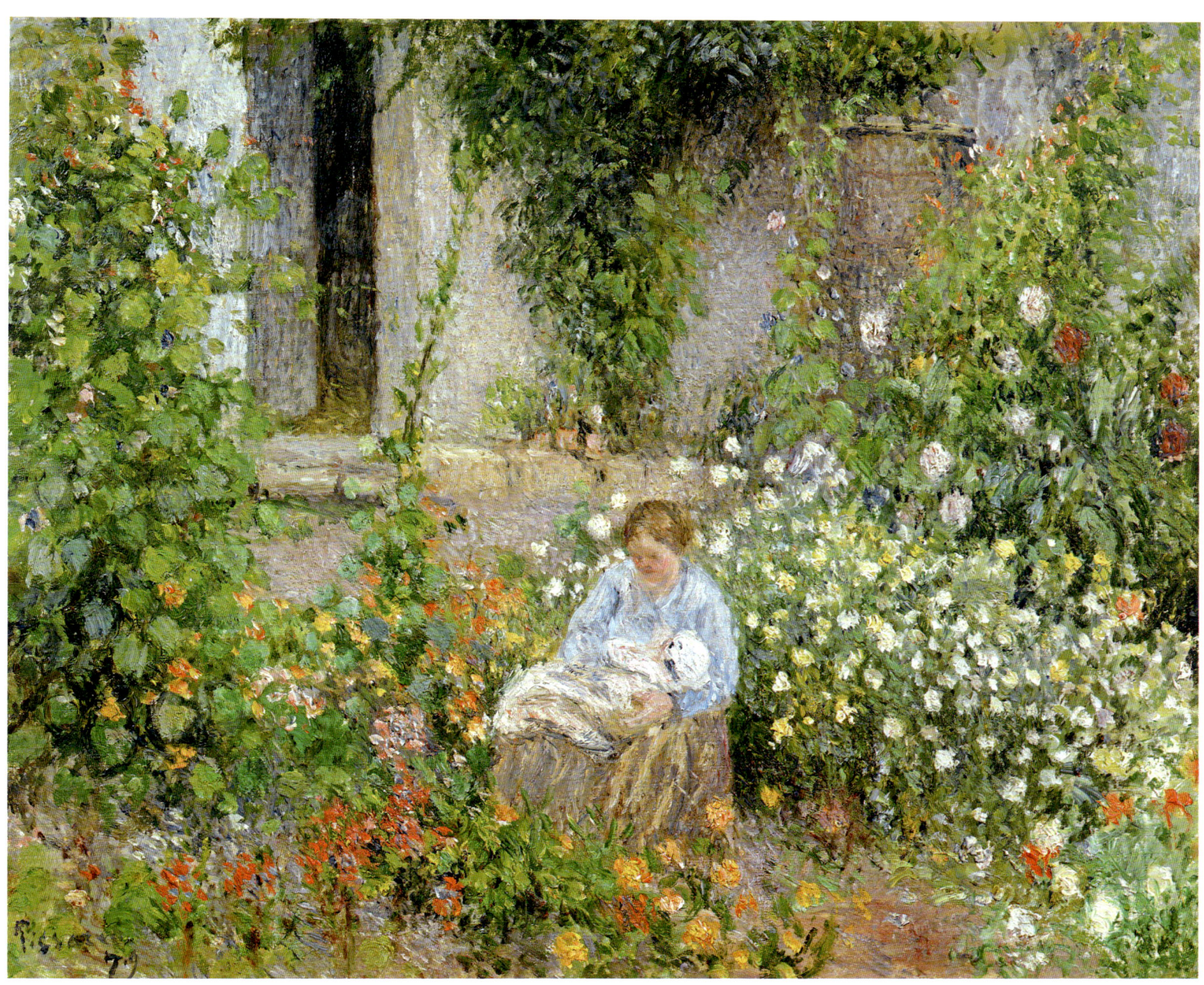

Camille Pissarro (1830–1903)

Mother and Child in the Flowers	Mutter und Kind zwischen den Blumen	Madre e figlio tra i fiori
Femme et enfant dans les fleurs	Madre e hijo en las flores	Moeder en kind tussen de bloemen

1879, Oil on canvas/Huile sur toile, 38 × 46 cm, Private collection

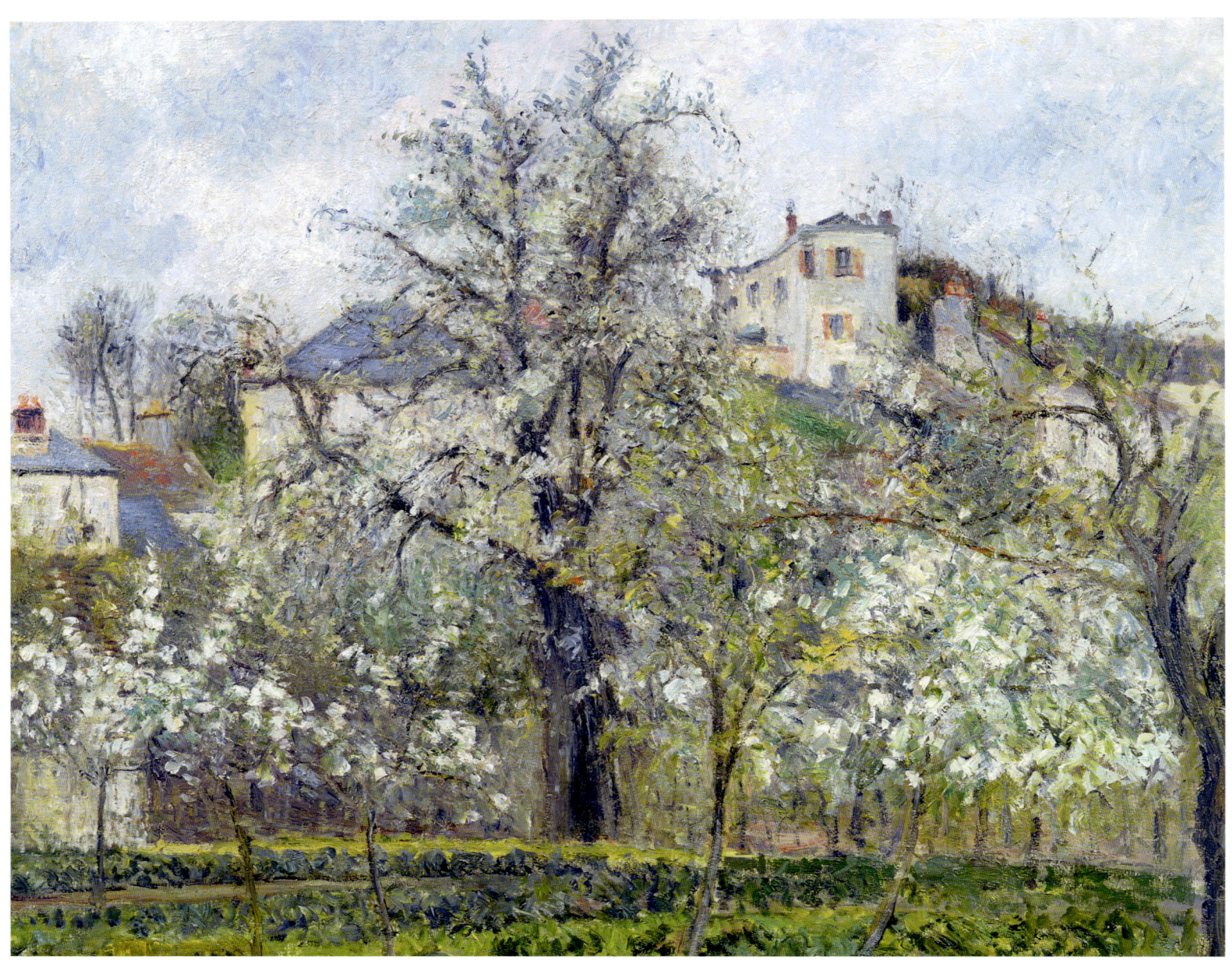

Camille Pissarro (1830–1903)

The Vegetable Garden with Trees in Blossom, Spring, Pontoise

Printemps. Pruniers en fleurs

Der Gemüsegarten in Pontoise im Frühling

El huerto de Pontoise en primavera

L'orto a Pontoise in primavera

De moestuin in Pontoise in het voorjaar

1877, Oil on canvas/Huile sur toile, 65,5 × 81 cm, Musée d'Orsay, Paris

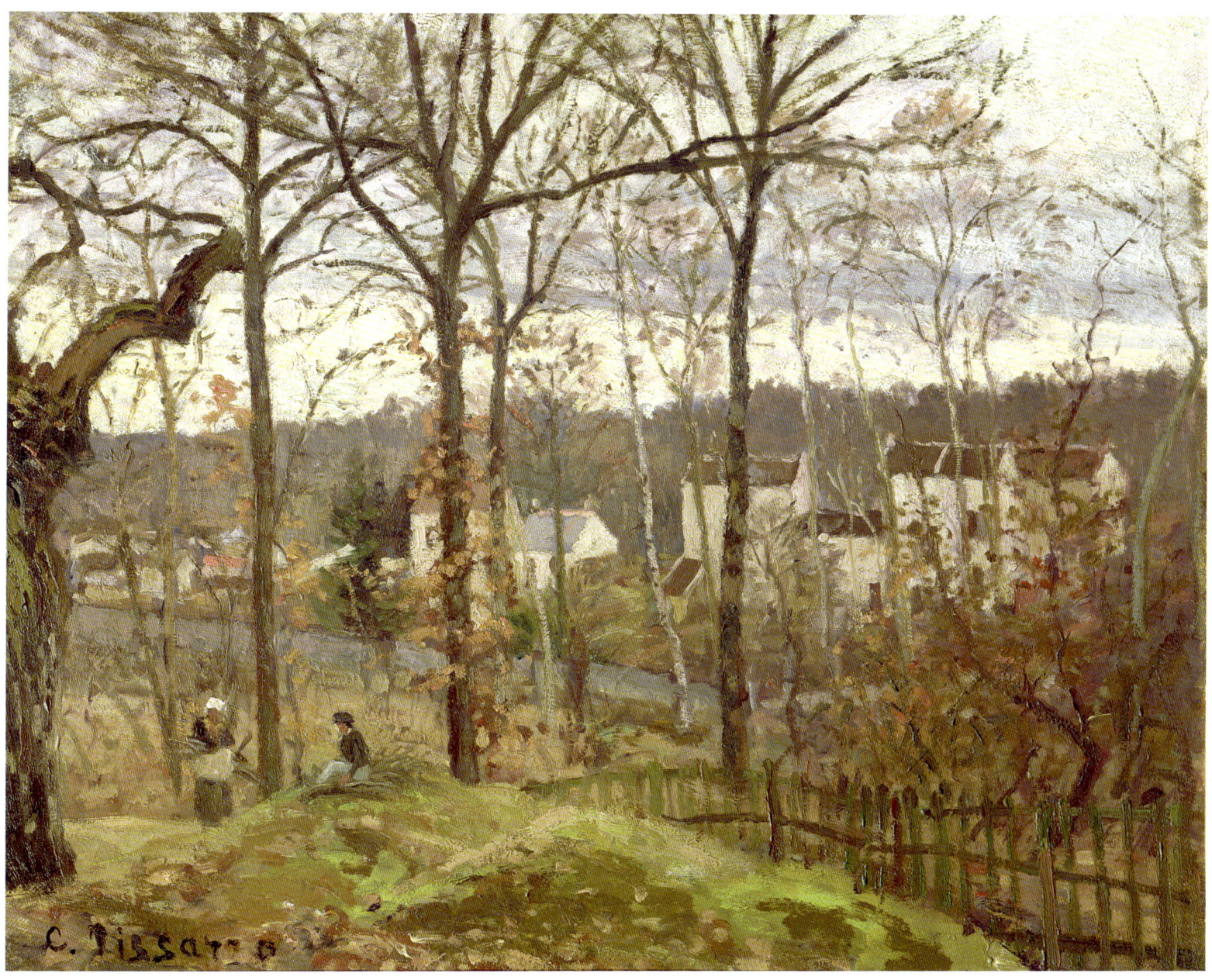

Camille Pissarro (1830–1903)

Winter Landscape at Louveciennes   Winterlandschaft in Louveciennes   Paesaggio invernale a Louveciennes

Paysage d'hiver à Louveciennes   Paisaje invernal en Louveciennes   Winterlandschap bij Louveciennes

c. 1870, Oil on canvas/Huile sur toile, 37 × 46 cm, Musée d'Orsay, Paris

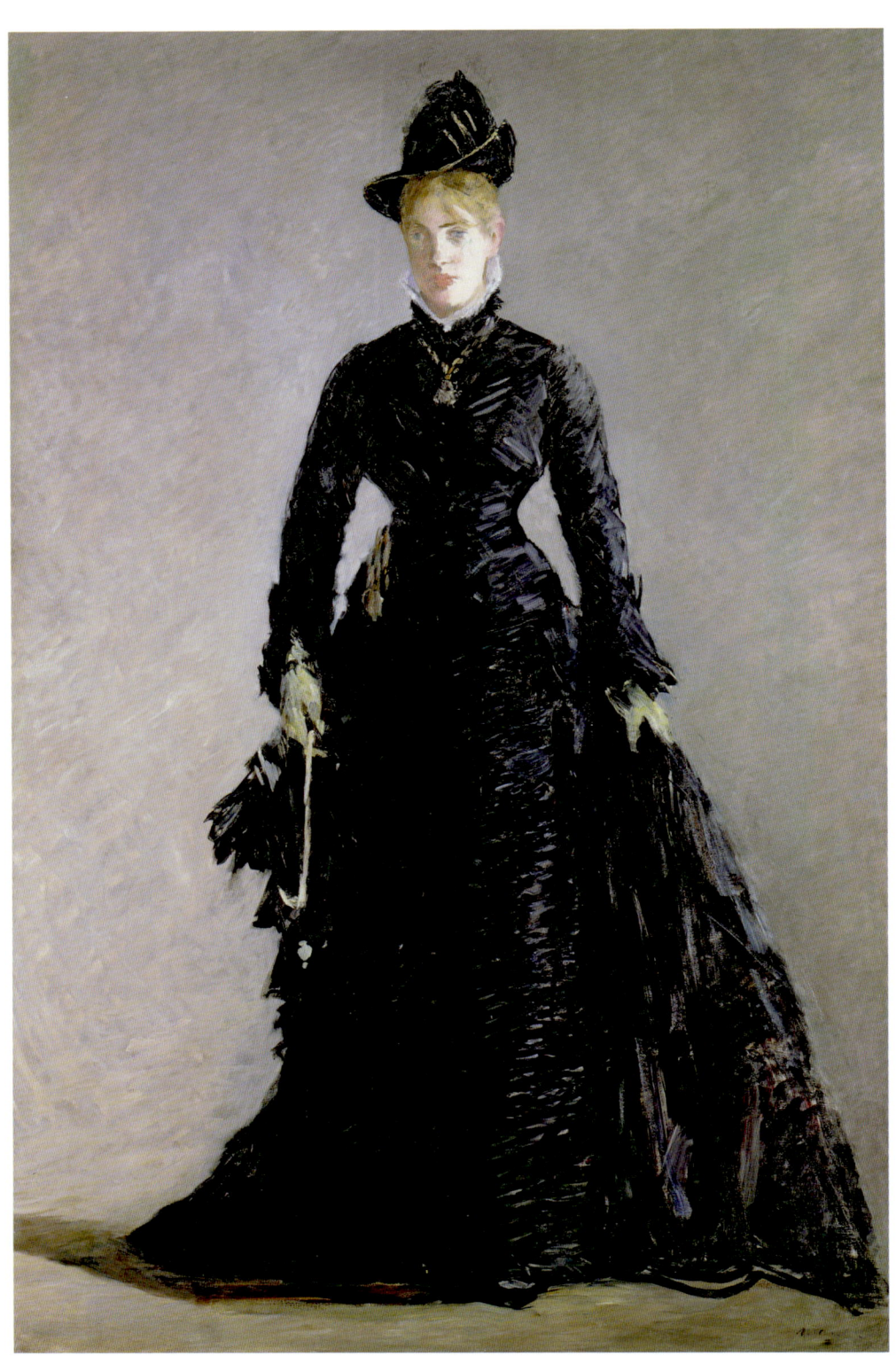

Édouard Manet (1832–1883)

A Parisian Lady

La Parisienne

Eine Pariser Dame

Una dama parisina

Una dama parigina

Een Parijse dame

n. d., Oil on canvas/Huile sur toile, 192 × 125 cm,
Nationalmuseum, Stockholm

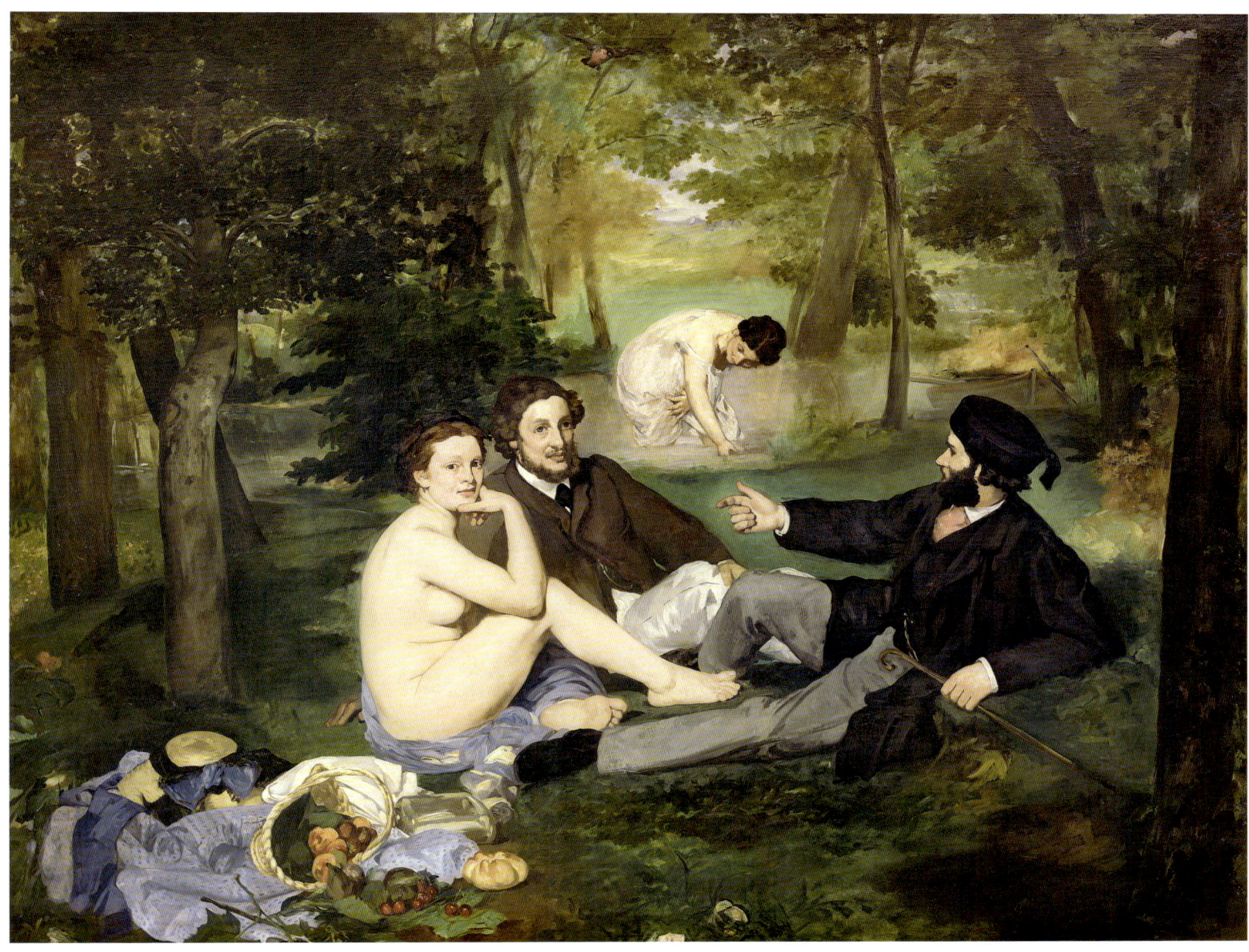

Édouard Manet (1832–1883)

The Luncheon on the Grass

Le Déjeuner sur l'herbe

Das Frühstück im Grünen

El almuerzo sobre la hierba

Colazione sull'erba

Lunch op het gras

1863, Oil on canvas/Huile sur toile, 207 × 265 cm, Musée d'Orsay, Paris

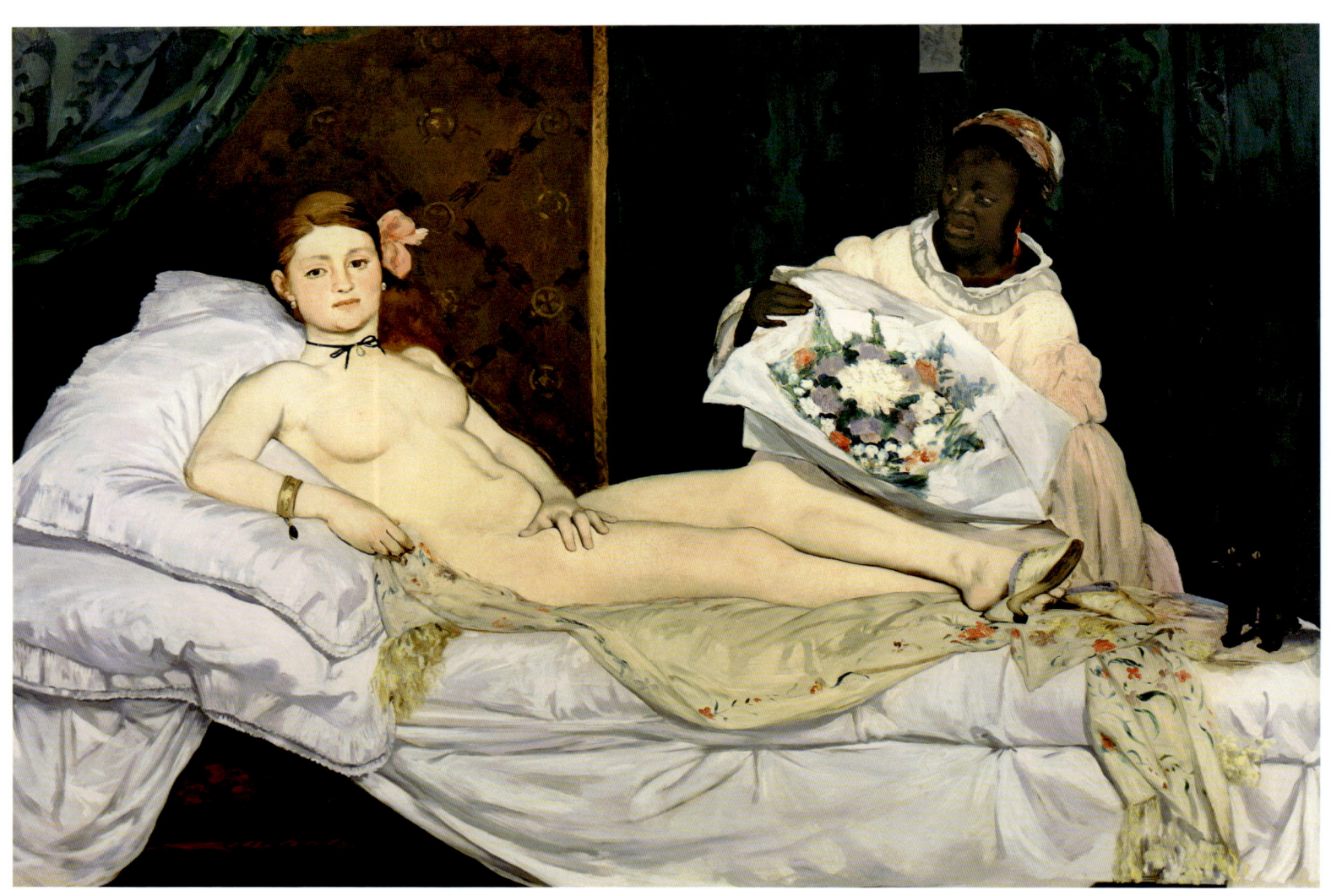

Édouard Manet (1832–1883)

Olympia

1863, Oil on canvas/Huile sur toile, 130,5 × 191 cm, Musée d'Orsay, Paris

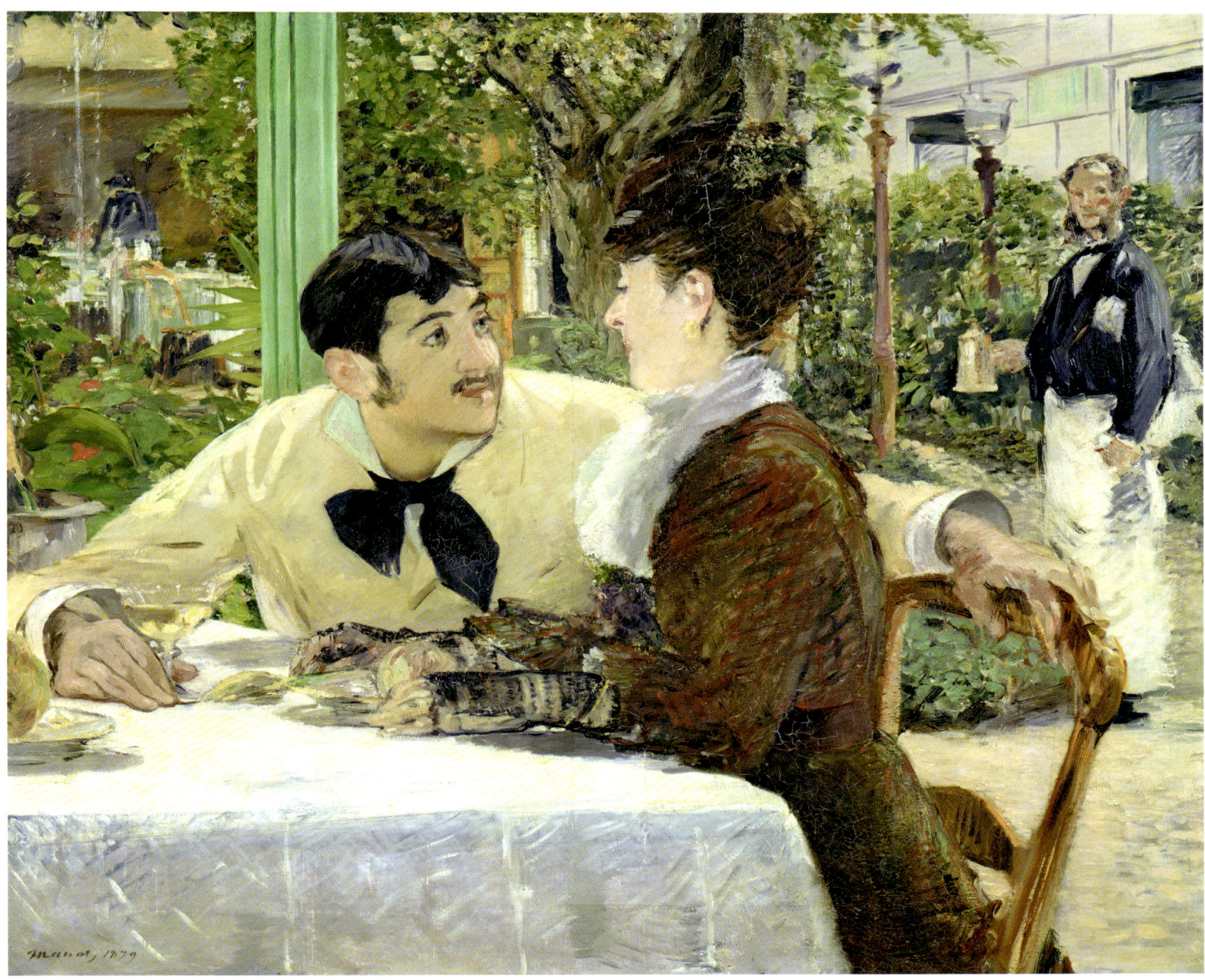

Édouard Manet (1832–1883)

| The Garden of Père Lathuille | Bei Père Lathuille | Chez Père Lathuille |
| Chez le Père Lathuille | Con Père Lathuille | Bij Père Lathuille |

1879, Oil on canvas/Huile sur toile, 93,5 × 112,5 cm, Musée des Beaux-Arts, Tournai

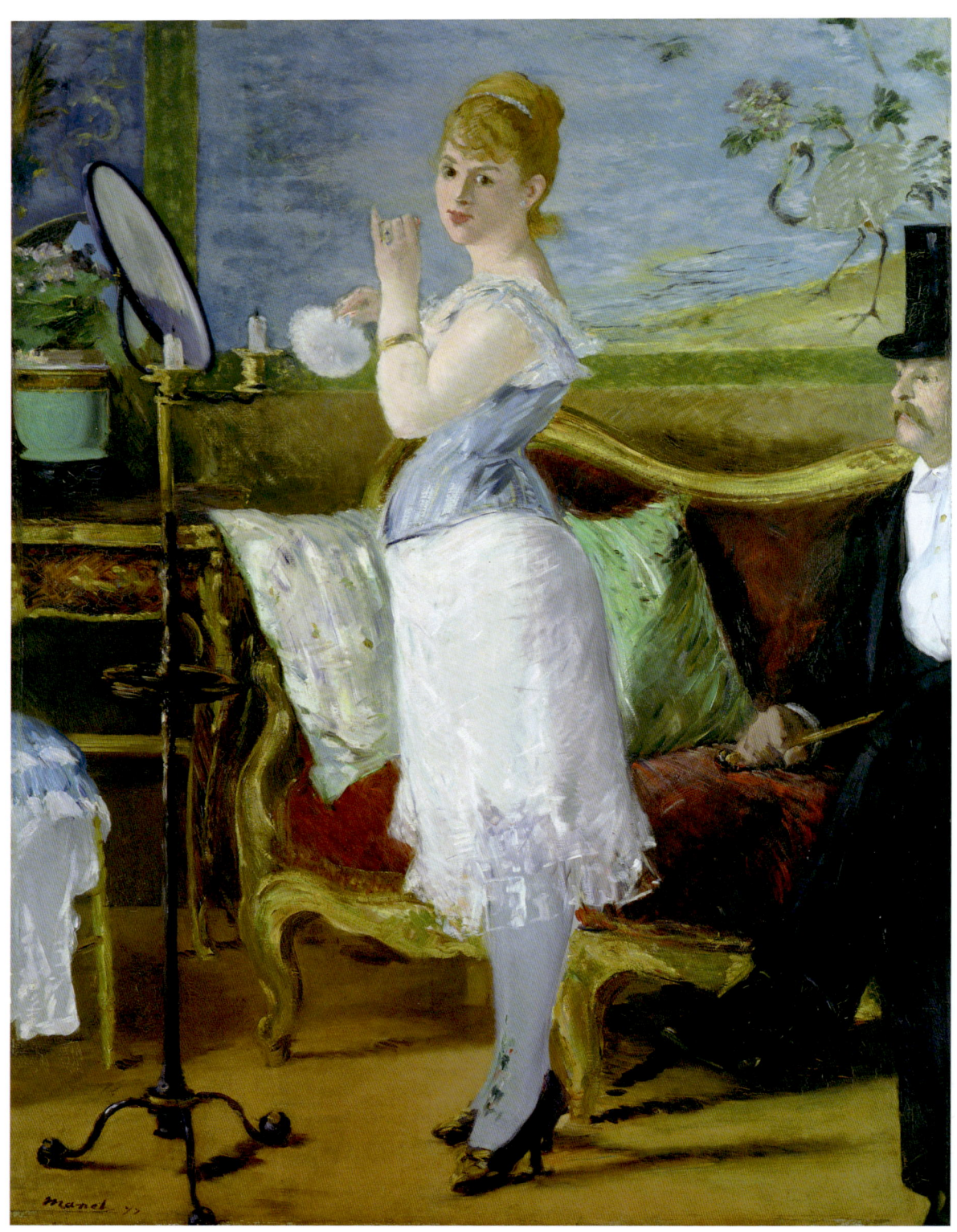

Édouard Manet (1832–1883)

Nana

1877, Oil on canvas/Huile sur toile,
154 × 115 cm, Kunsthalle, Hamburg

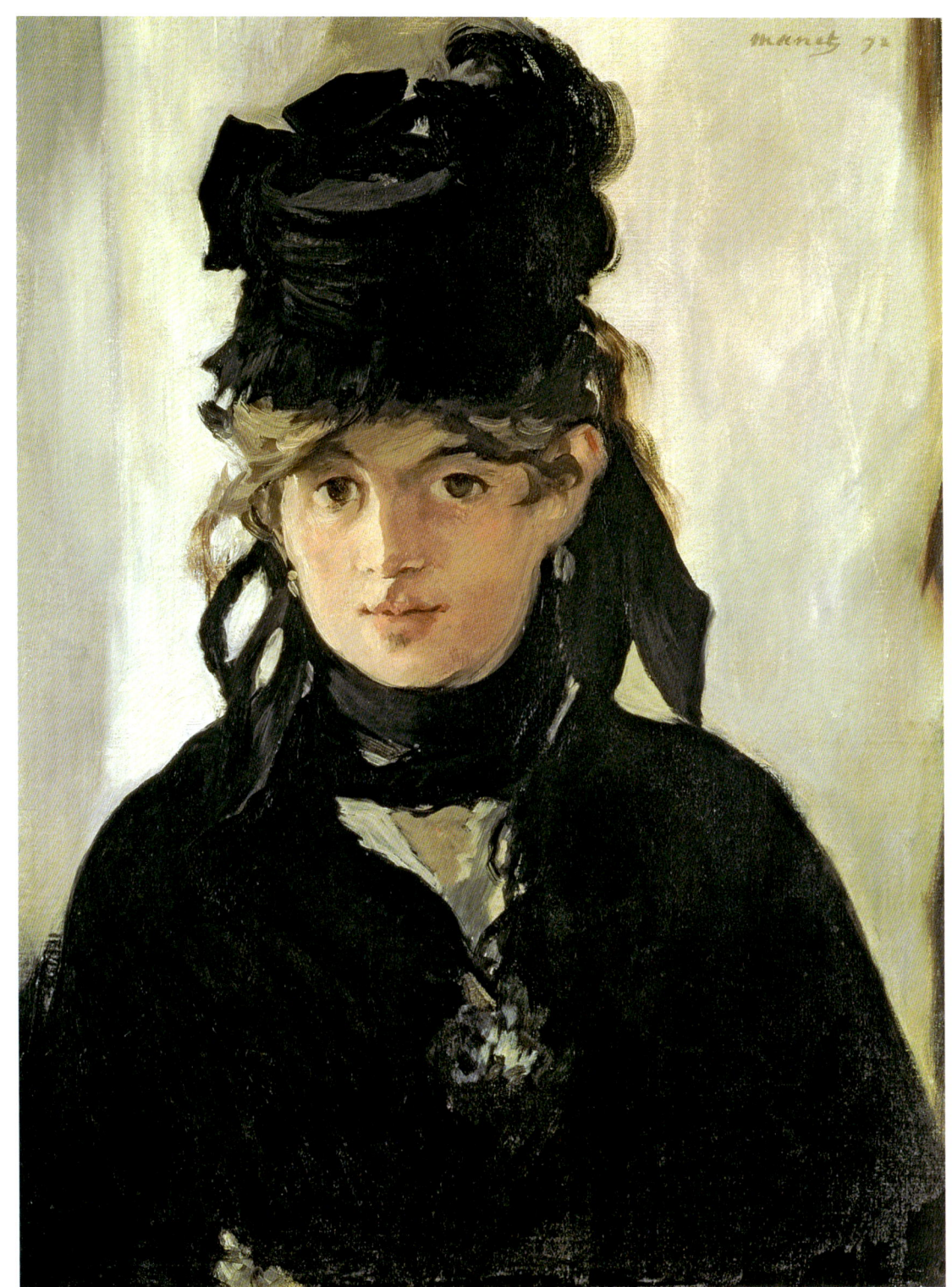

Édouard Manet (1832–1883)

Berthe Morisot with a Bouquet of Violets

Berthe Morisot au bouquet de violettes

Berthe Morisot mit einem Veilchen-
Sträußchen

Berthe Morisot con un ramito de violetas

Berthe Morisot con un mazzo di violette

Berthe Morisot met een boeket viooltjes

1872, Oil on canvas/Huile sur toile,
55,5 × 40,5 cm, Musée d'Orsay, Paris

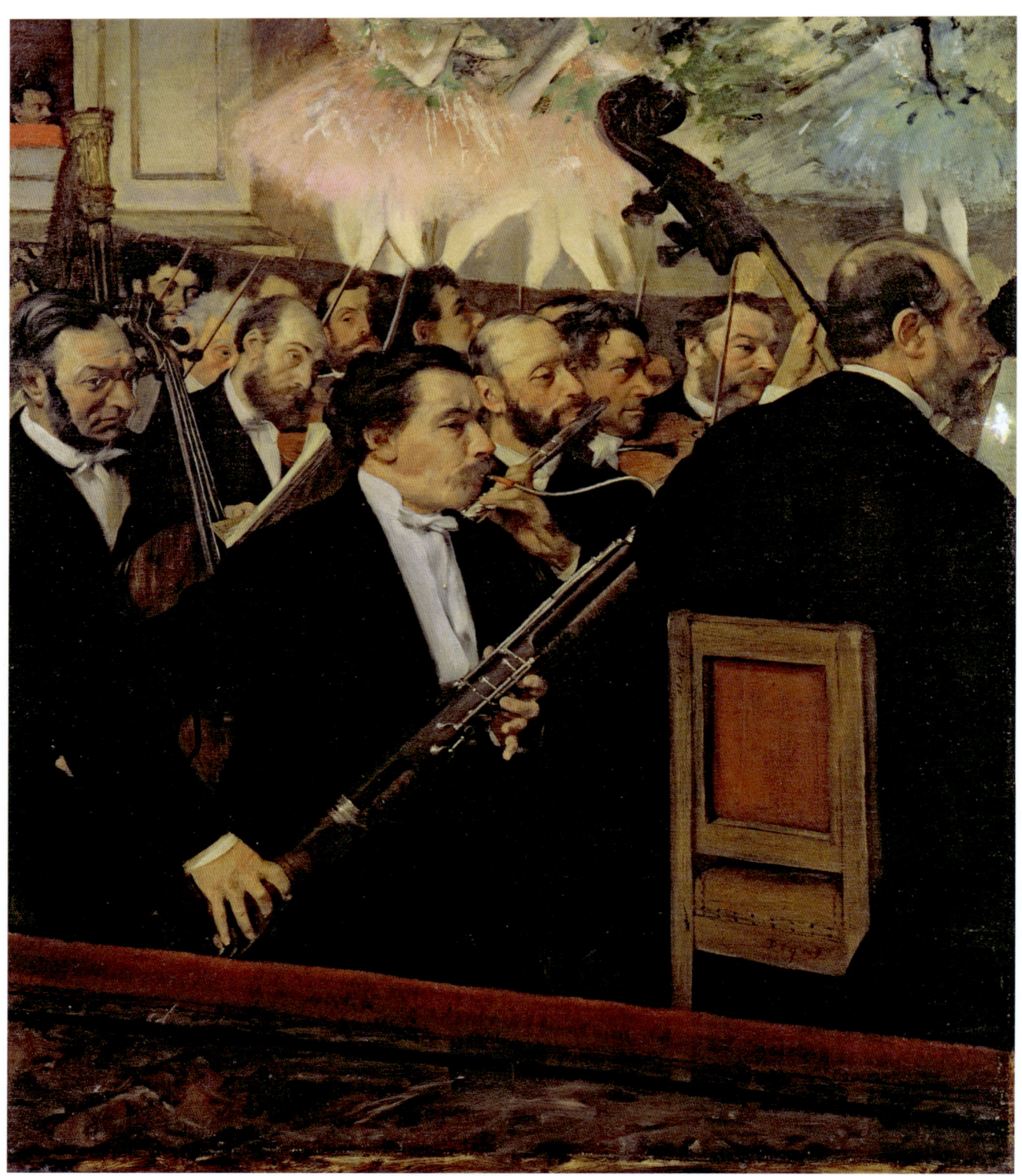

Edgar Degas (1834–1917)

The Opera Orchestra

L'Orchestre de l'Opéra

Das Orchester der Oper

La orquesta de la Ópera

L'orchesta dell'opera

Het Orchestre de l'Opéra

c. 1870, Oil on canvas/ Huile sur toile, 56,6 × 46 cm, Musée d'Orsay, Paris

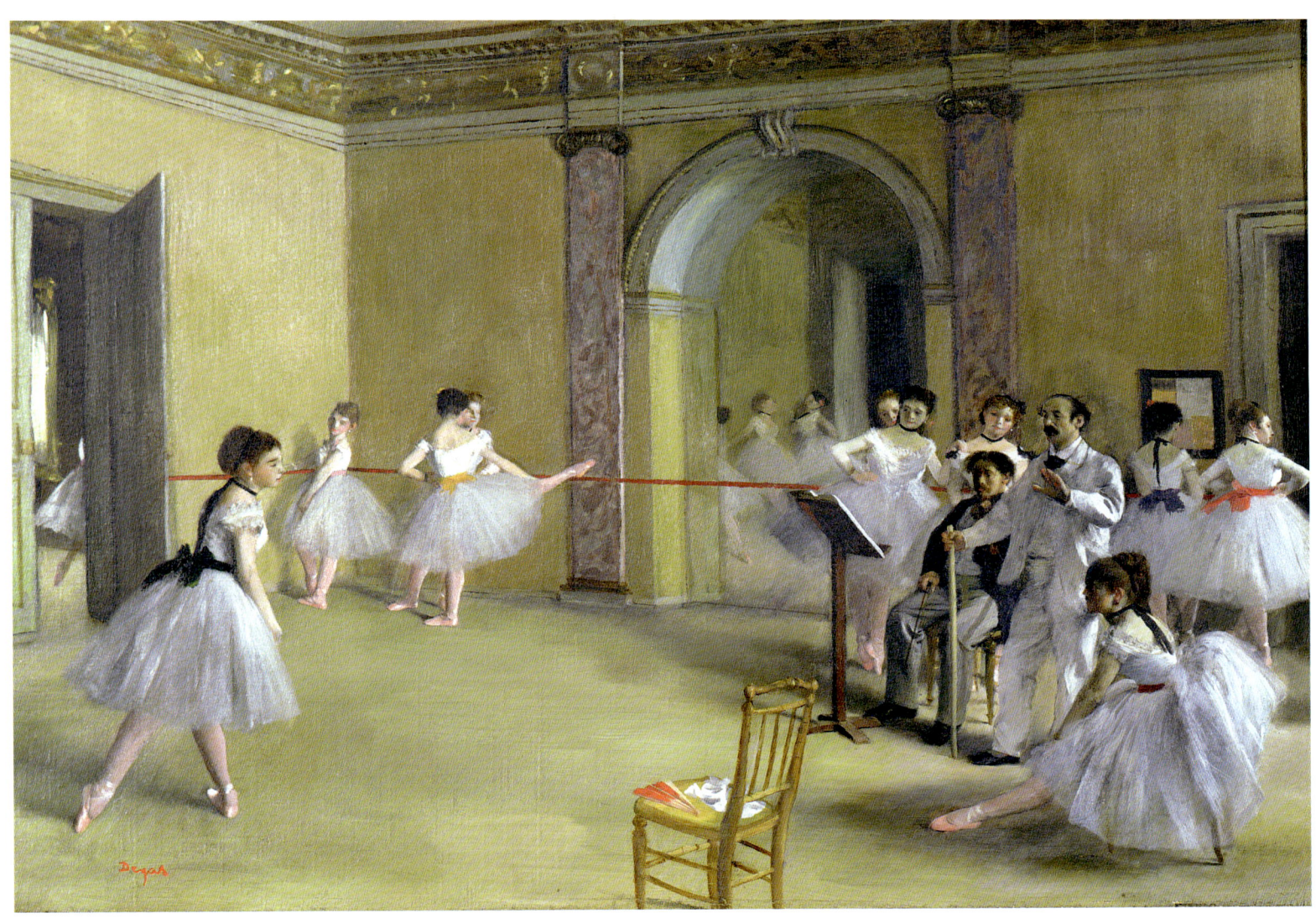

Edgar Degas (1834–1917)

The Dance Foyer at the Opera on the rue Le Peletier

Le Foyer de la danse à l'Opéra de la rue Le Peletier

Der Proberaum in der Oper an der Rue Le Peletier

El local de ensayos en la Ópera de la calle Le Peletier

Il foyer della danza al teatro dell'Opera in Rue Le Peletier

Repetitiezaal in de Opéra aan de Rue Le Peletier

1872, Oil on canvas/Huile sur toile, 32,7 × 46 cm, Musée d'Orsay, Paris

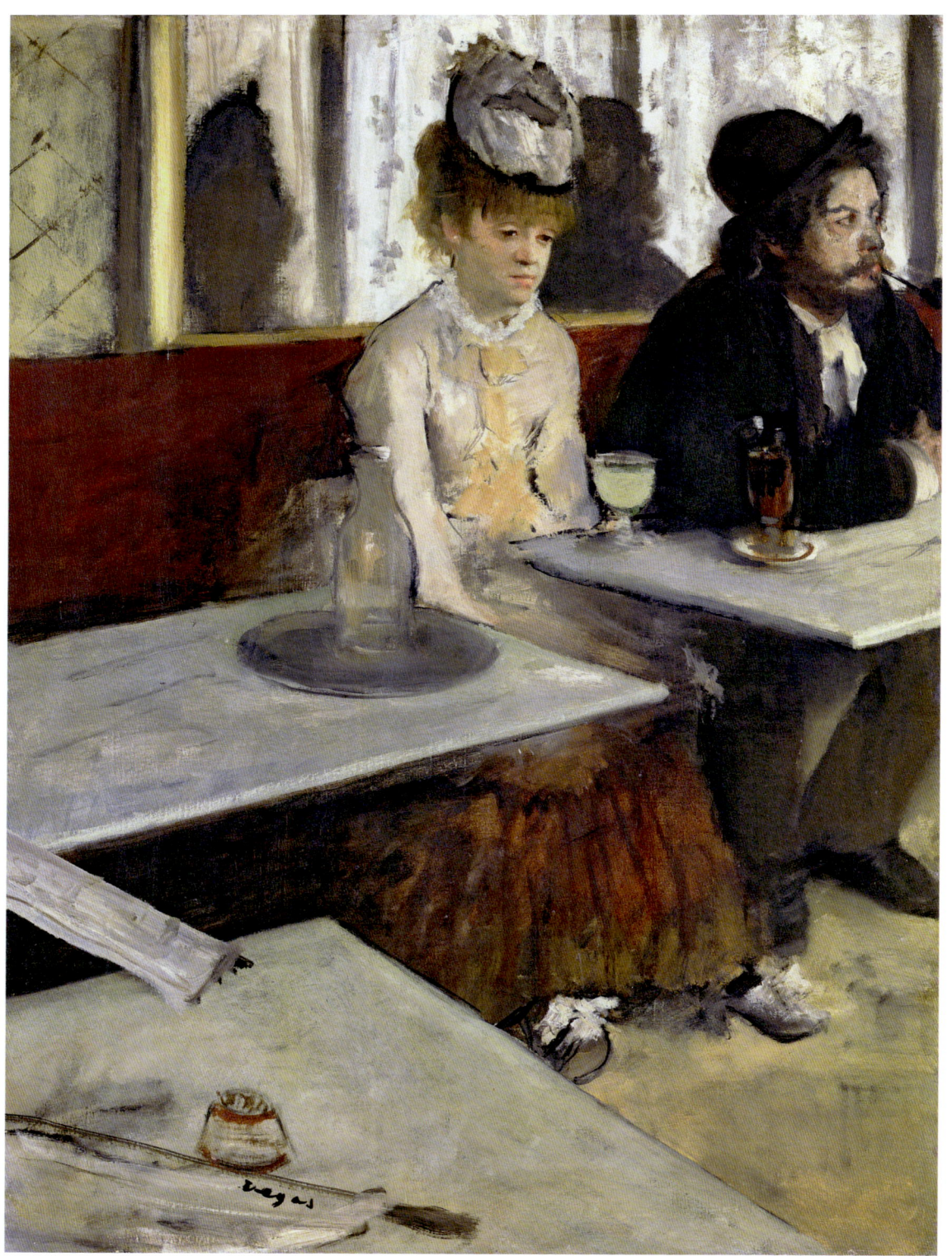

Edgar Degas (1834–1917)

In a Cafe, *or* The Absinthe

Dans un café, *dit aussi* L'Absinthe

Der Absinth

Absenta

L'assenzio

De absint

c. 1875–1876, Oil on canvas/Huile sur toile,
92 × 68,5 cm, Musée d'Orsay, Paris

Edgar Degas (1834–1917)

Dancers in blue

Danseuses en bleues

Tänzerinnen in Blau

Bailarinas de azul

Ballerine in blu

Danseressen in het blauw

c. 1890, Oil on canvas/Huile sur toile,
85,3 × 75,3 cm, Musée d'Orsay, Paris

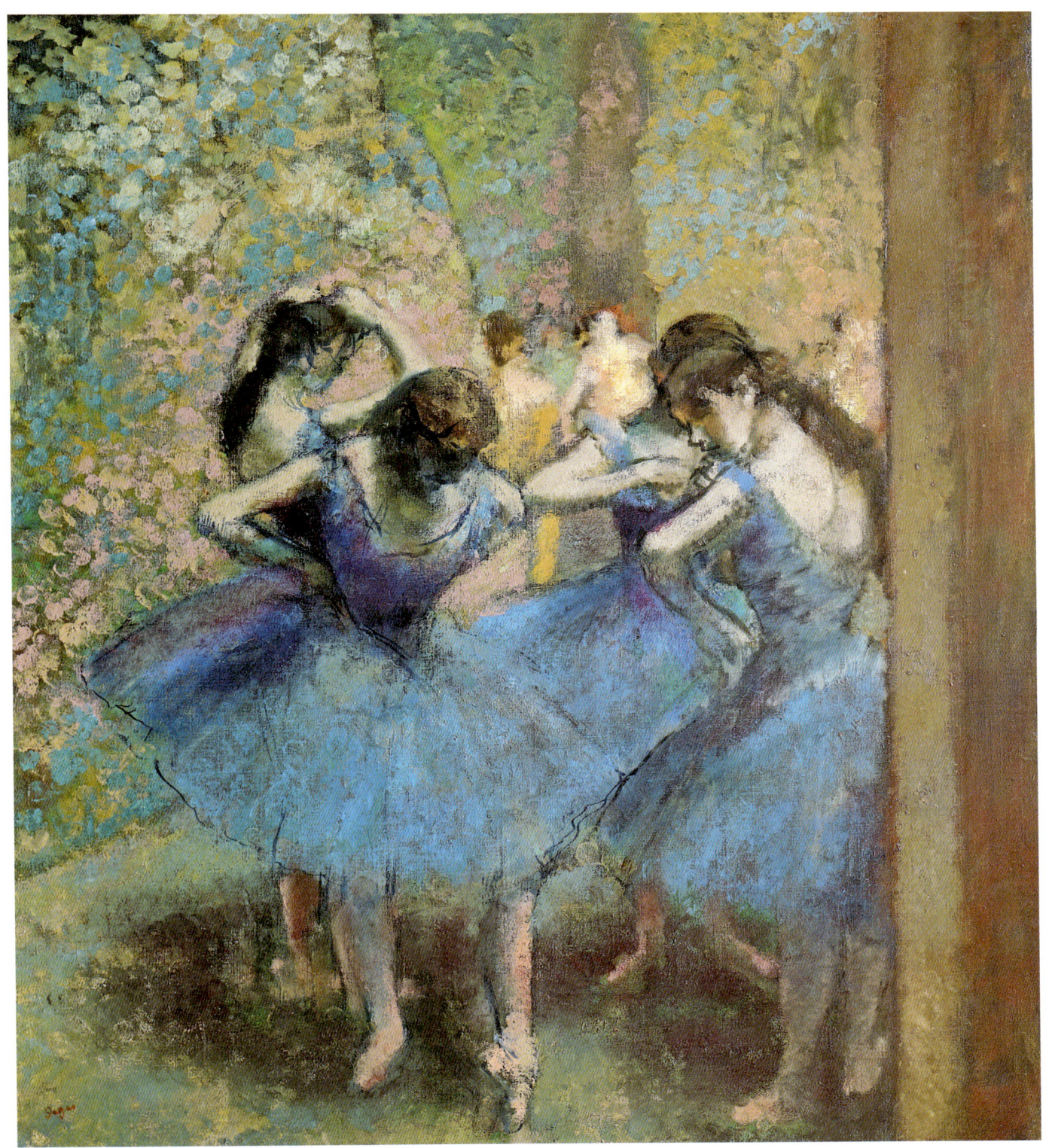

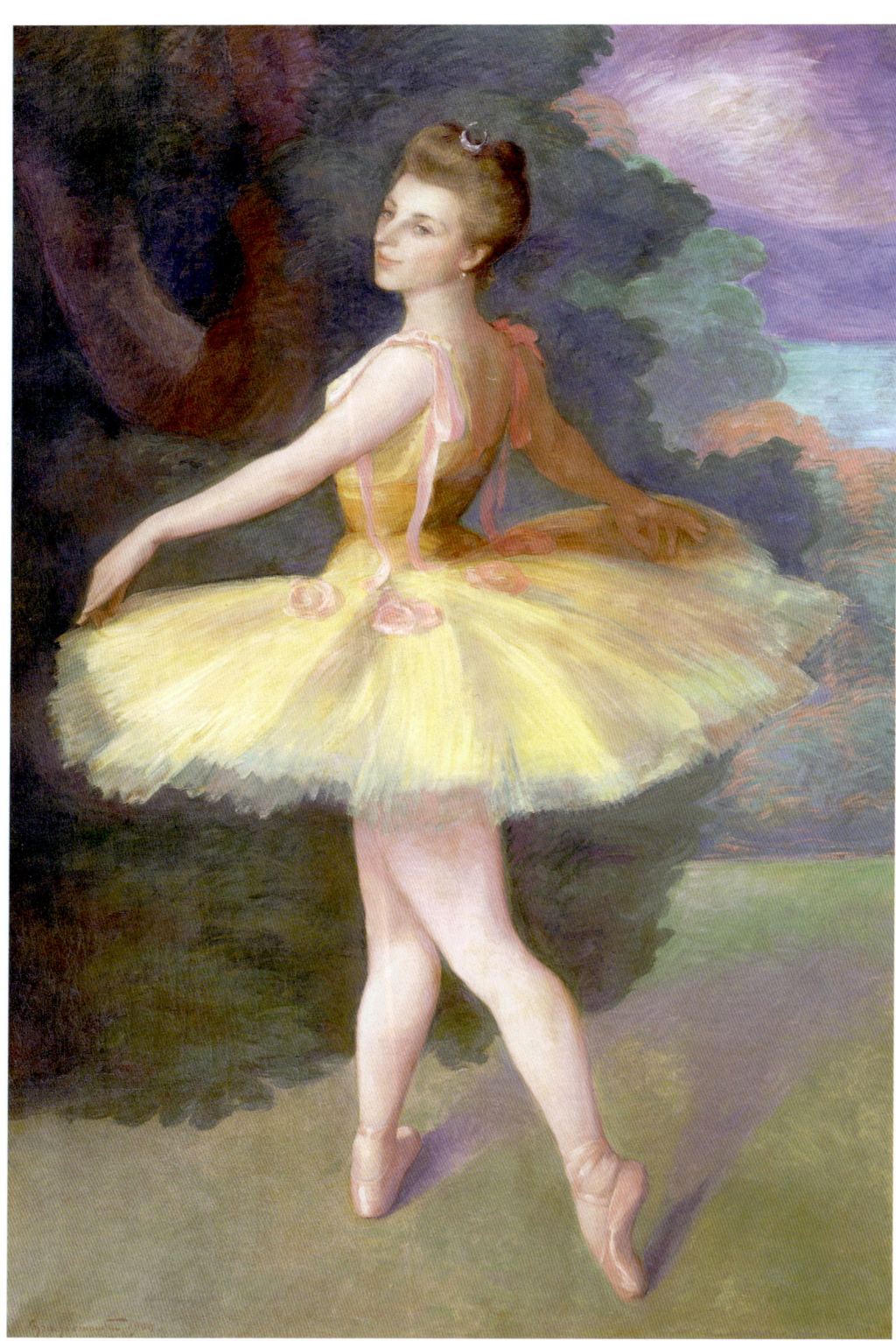

Félix Bracquemond (1833–1914)

The Song of Spring

Chanson de printemps

Das Lied vom Frühling

La canción de primavera

La canzone della primavera

Het lied van het voorjaar

1900, Oil on canvas/Huile sur toile, 195,6 × 141 cm,
Private collection

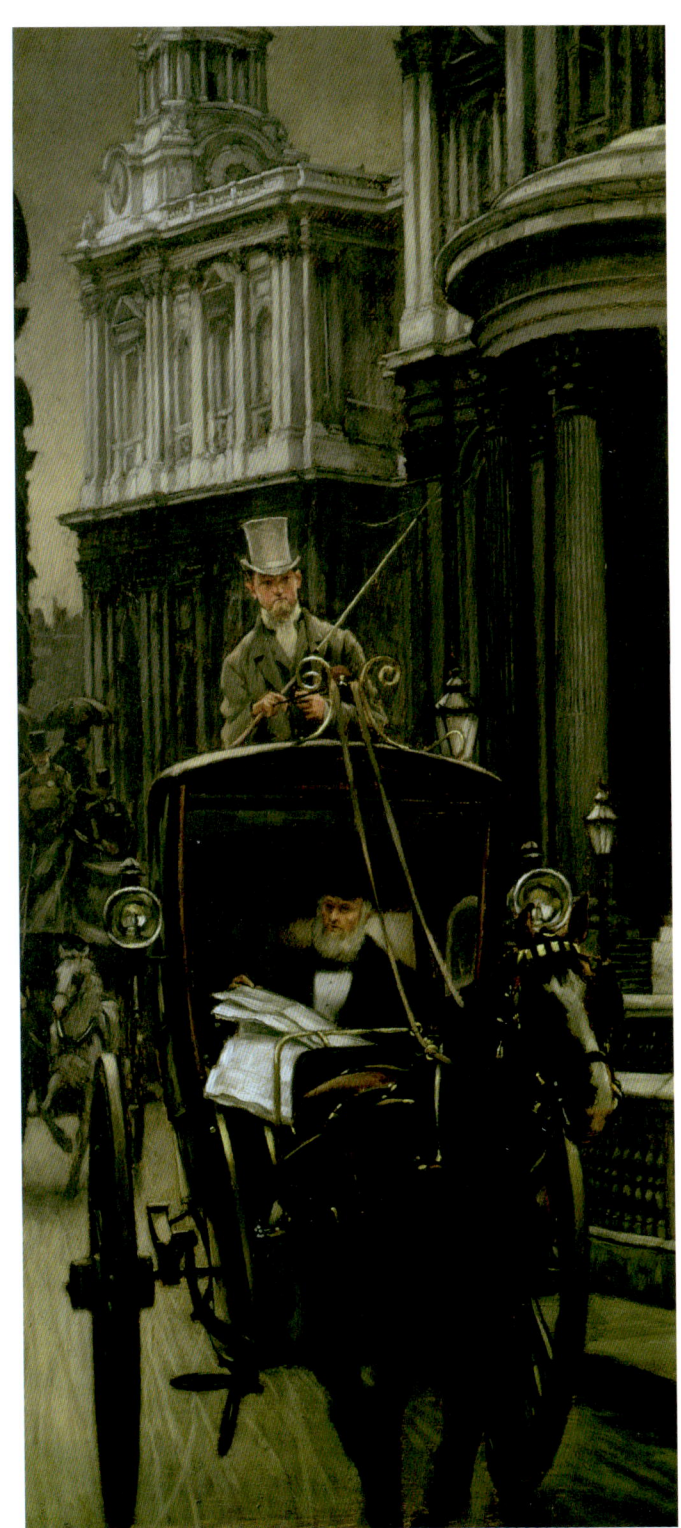

James Tissot (1836–1902)

Going to Business (Going to the City)

Départ pour le travail

Zur Arbeit fahren

Camino del trabajo

Andando al lavoro

Op weg naar het werk

c. 1879, Oil on wood/Huile sur bois, 43,8 × 25,4 cm,
Private collection

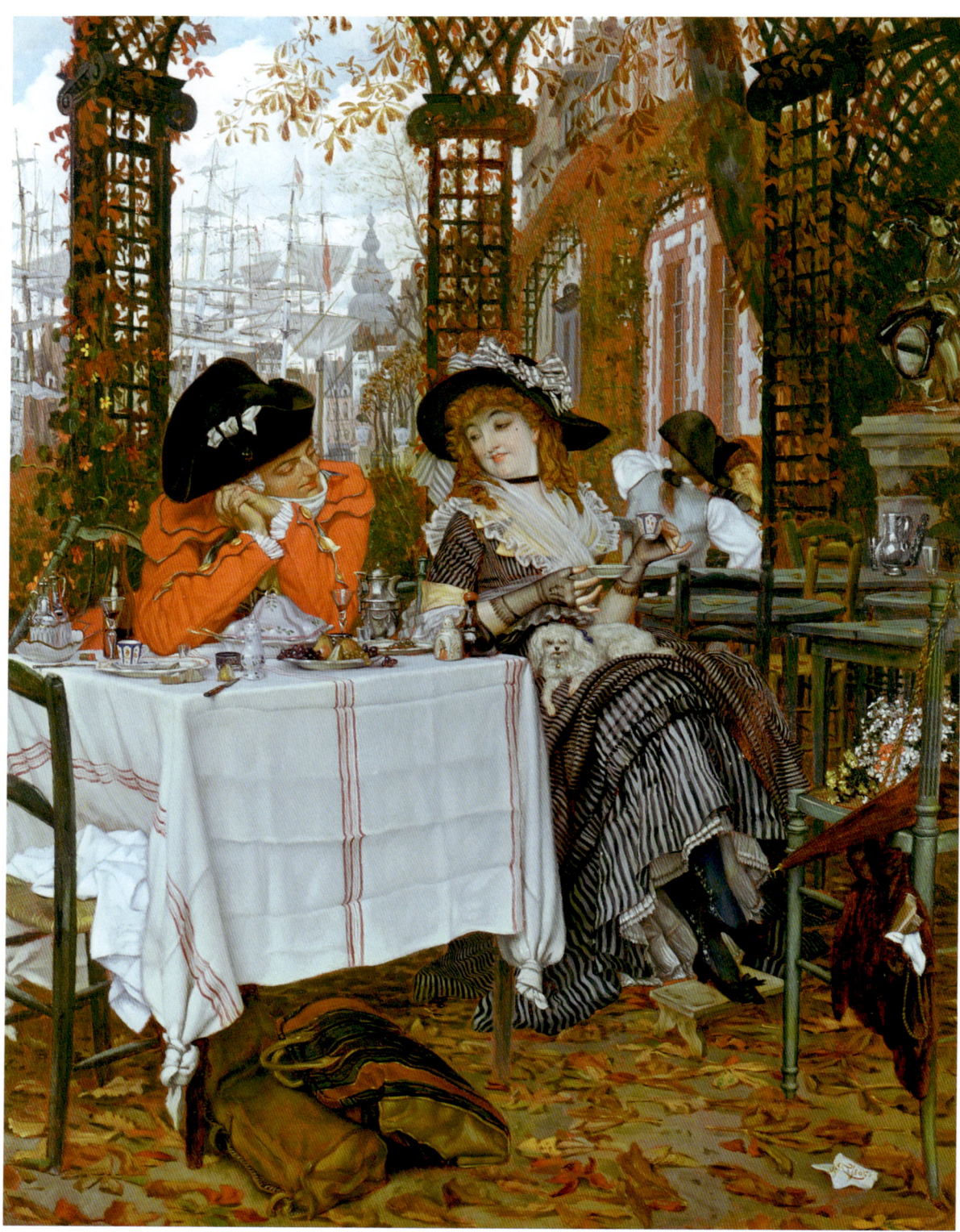

**James Jacques Joseph Tissot
(1836–1902)**

A Luncheon

Un Déjeuner

Ein Frühstück

Un desayuno

Una colazione

Een ontbijt

c. 1868, Oil on canvas/Huile sur toile,
78,7 × 58,4 cm, Private collection

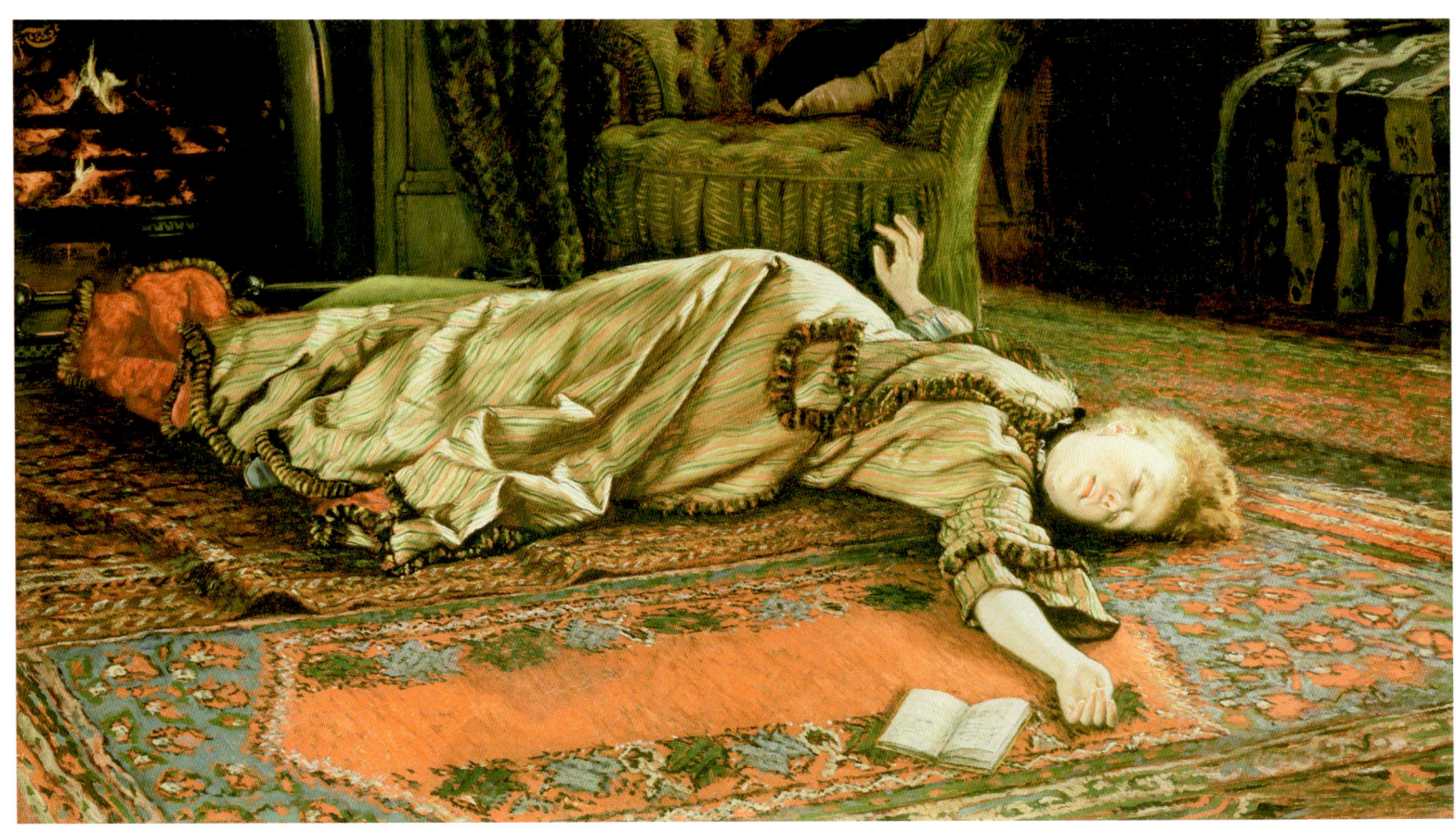

James Jacques Joseph Tissot (1836–1902)

Abandoned

Abandonnée

Verlassen

Abandonado

Abbandonato

Verlaten

c. 1881–1882, Oil on wood/Huile sur bois, 31,7 × 52,1 cm, Private collection

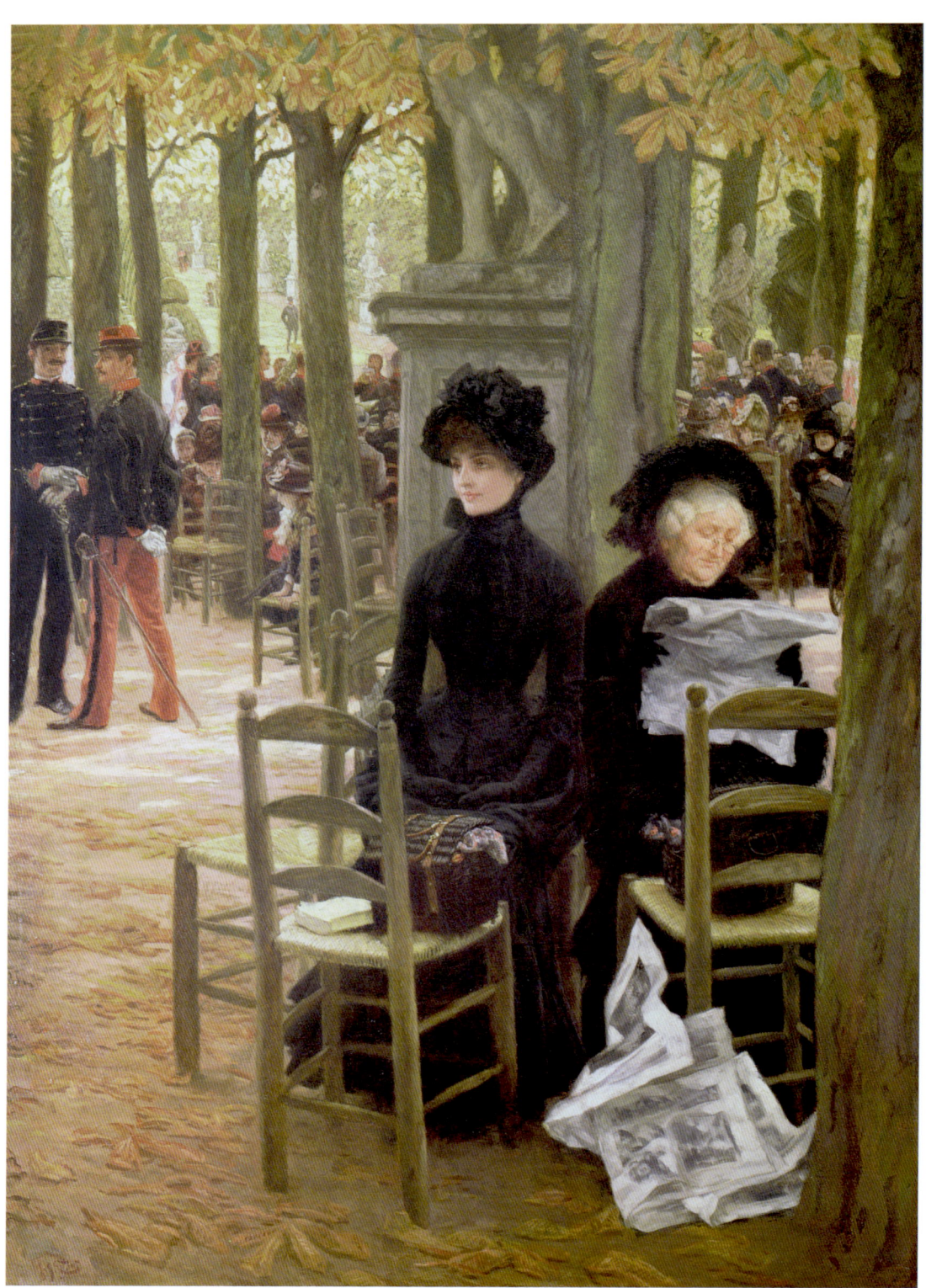

James Jacques Joseph Tissot (1836–1902)

Without a Dowry

Sans dot

Ohne Mitgift

Sin dote

Senza dote

Zonder bruidsschat

1883–1885, Oil on canvas/Huile sur toile,
147,1 × 105 cm, Private collection

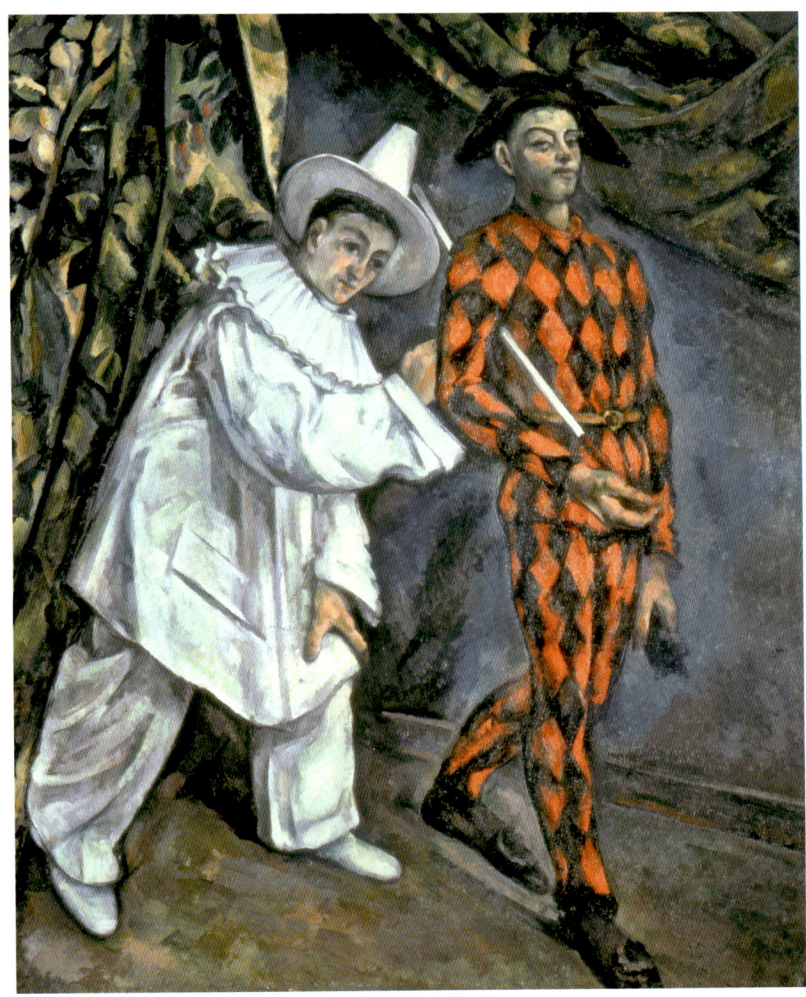

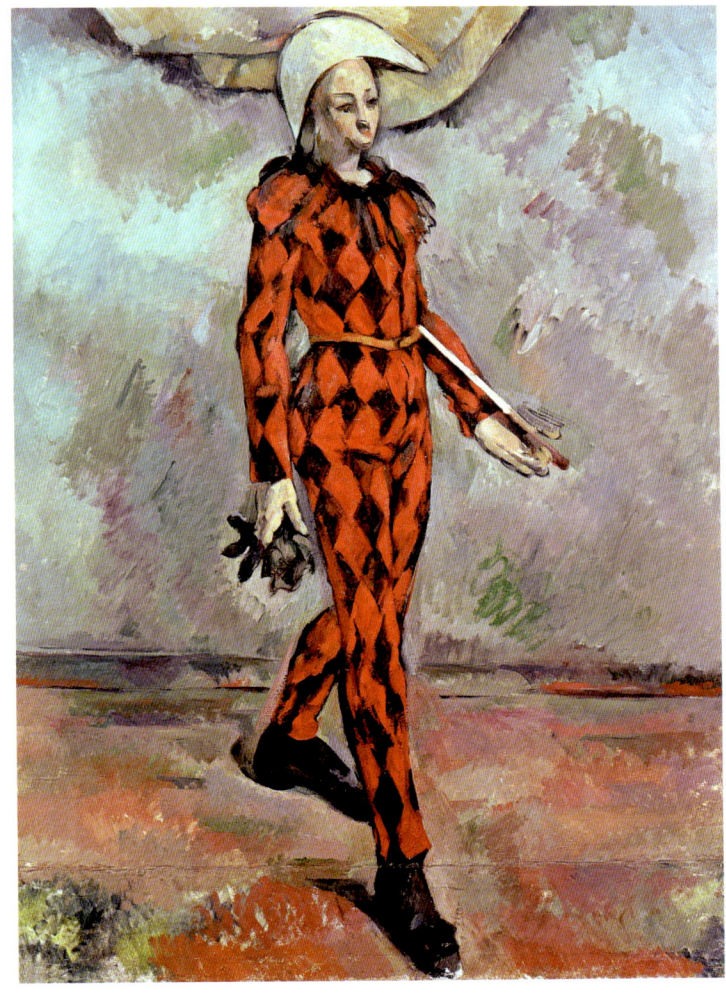

Paul Cézanne (1839–1906)

Pierrot and Harlequin

Pierrot et Arlequin (Mardi gras)

Pierrot und Harlekin

Pierrot y Arlequín

Pierrot e Arlecchino

Pierrot en Harlekijn

1888, Oil on canvas/Huile sur toile, 102 × 81 cm,
Pushkin State Museum of Fine Arts, Moscow

Paul Cézanne (1839–1906)

Harlequin

Arlequin

Harlekin

Arlequín

Arlecchino

Harlekijn

1890, Oil on canvas/Huile sur toile, 92 × 65 cm, Private collection

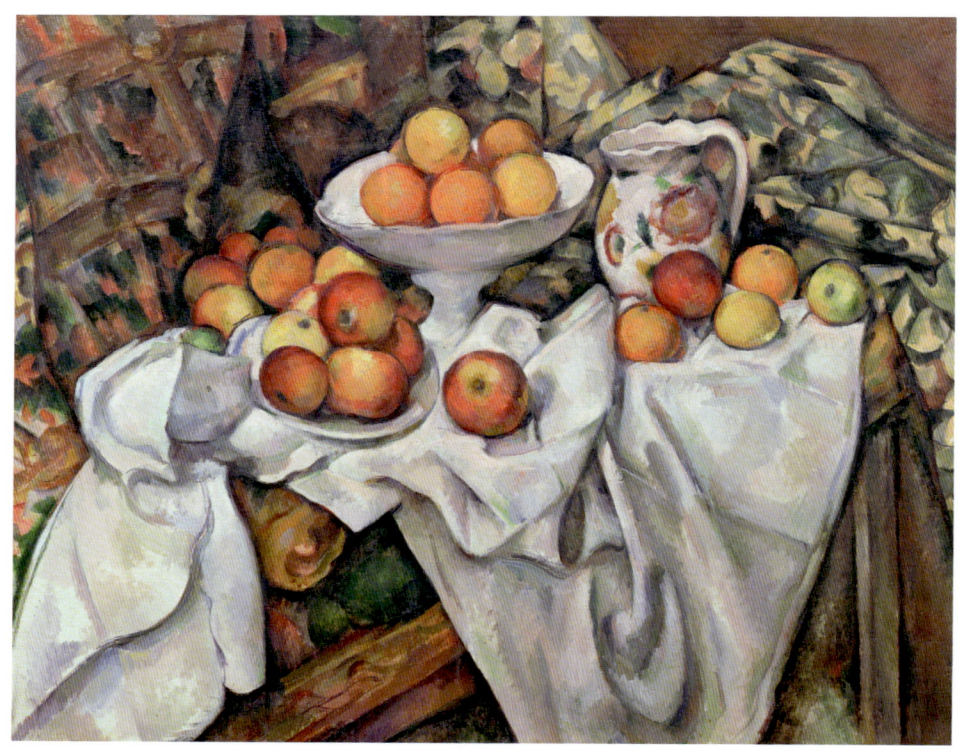

Paul Cézanne (1839–1906)

Apples and Oranges

Pommes et oranges

Stillleben mit Äpfeln und Orangen

Bodegón con manzanas y naranjas

Natura morta con mele e arance

Stilleven met appels en sinaasappels

c. 1899, Oil on canvas/Huile sur toile, 74 × 93 cm,
Musée d'Orsay, Paris

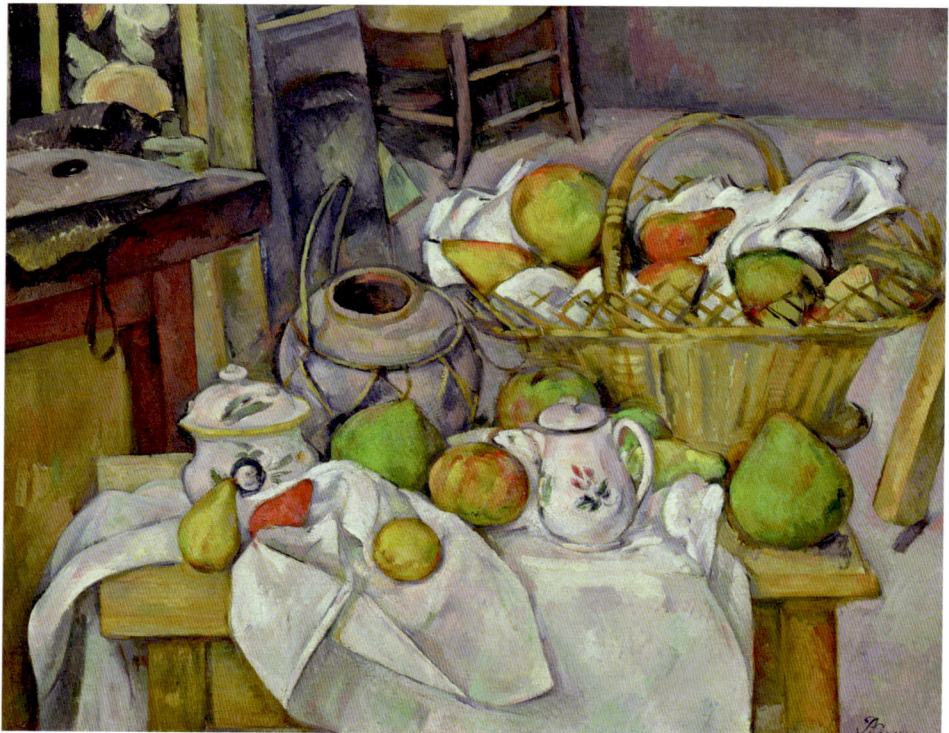

Paul Cézanne (1839–1906)

Still Life with Basket

La Table de cuisine

Stillleben mit Früchtekorb

Bodegón con cesta de fruta

Natura morta con cesto di frutta

Stilleven met fruitmand

1888–1890, Oil on canvas/Huile sur toile, 65 × 81,5 cm,
Musée d'Orsay, Paris

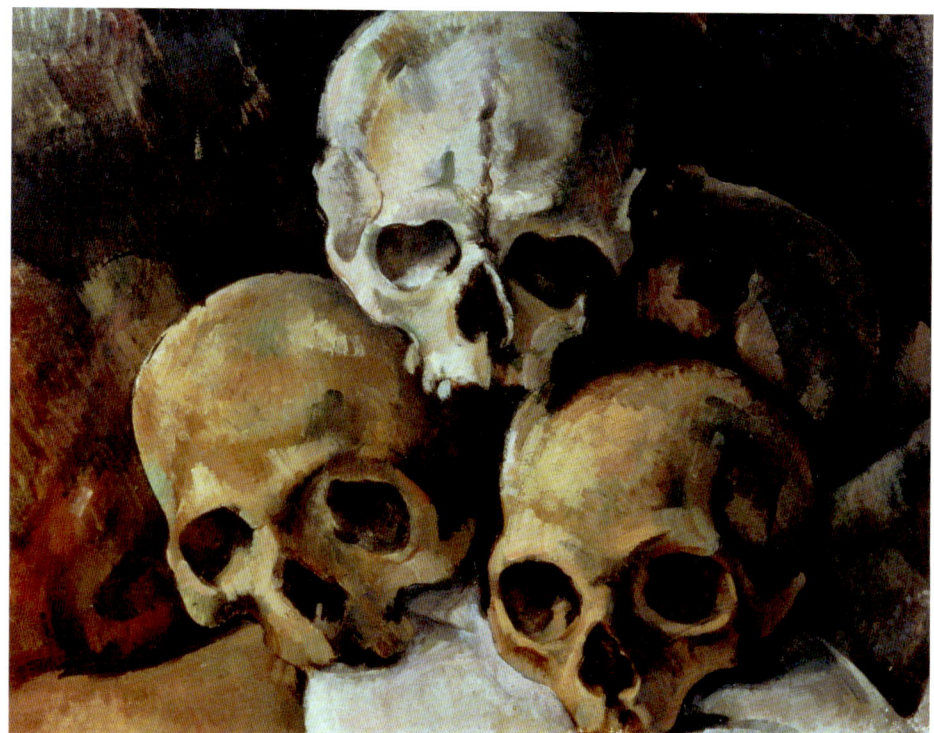

Paul Cézanne (1839–1906)

Pyramid of skulls

Pyramide de crânes

Stillleben mit Totenköpfen

Bodegón con calaveras

Natura morta con teschi

Schedelpiramide

1898–1900, Oil on canvas/Huile sur toile, 39 × 46,5 cm,
Private collection

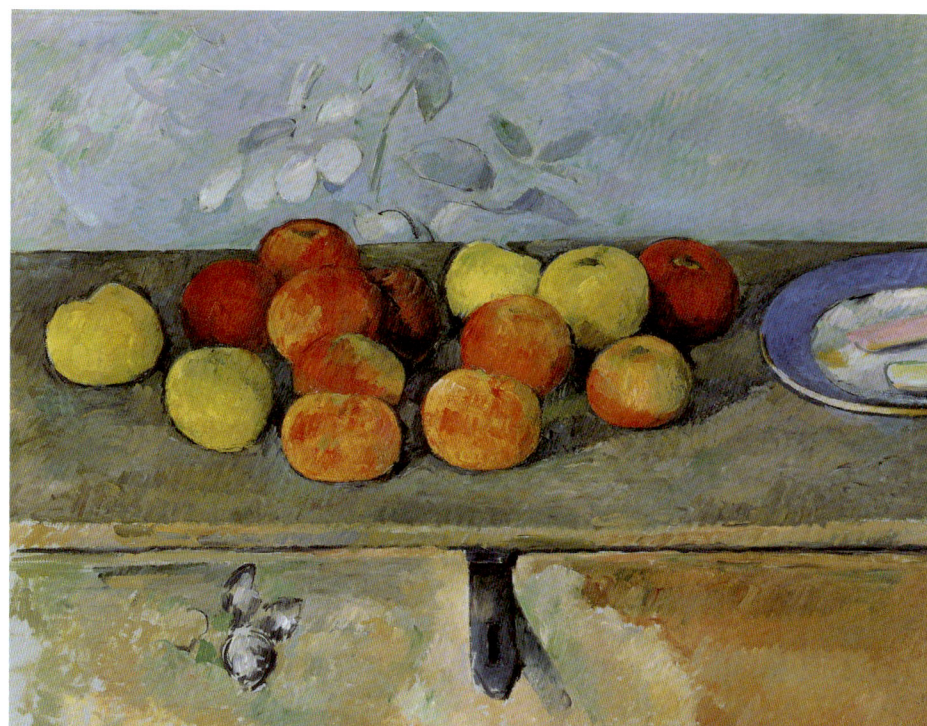

Paul Cézanne (1839–1906)

Still Life of Apples and Biscuits

Pommes et biscuits

Stillleben mit Äpfeln und Biscuits

Bodegón con manzanas y galletas

Natura morta con mele e biscotti

Stilleven met appels en koekjes

c. 1879–1880, Oil on canvas/Huile sur toile, 45 × 55 cm,
Musée de l'Orangerie, Paris

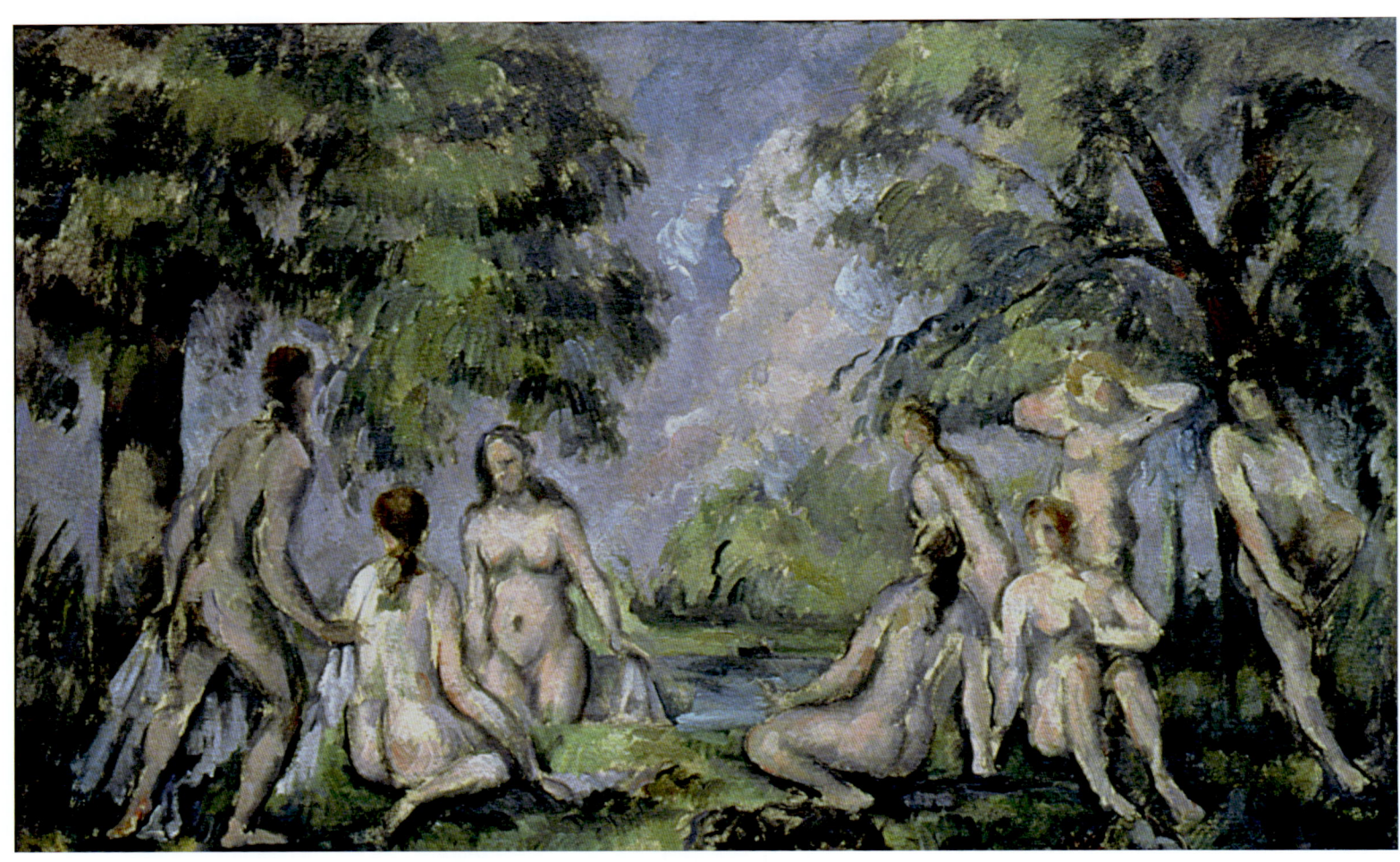

Paul Cézanne (1839–1906)

The Bathers

Baigneuses

Die Badenden

Las bañistas

I bagnanti

De baadsters

c. 1890, Oil on canvas/Huile sur toile, 29 × 45 cm, Musée d'Orsay, Paris

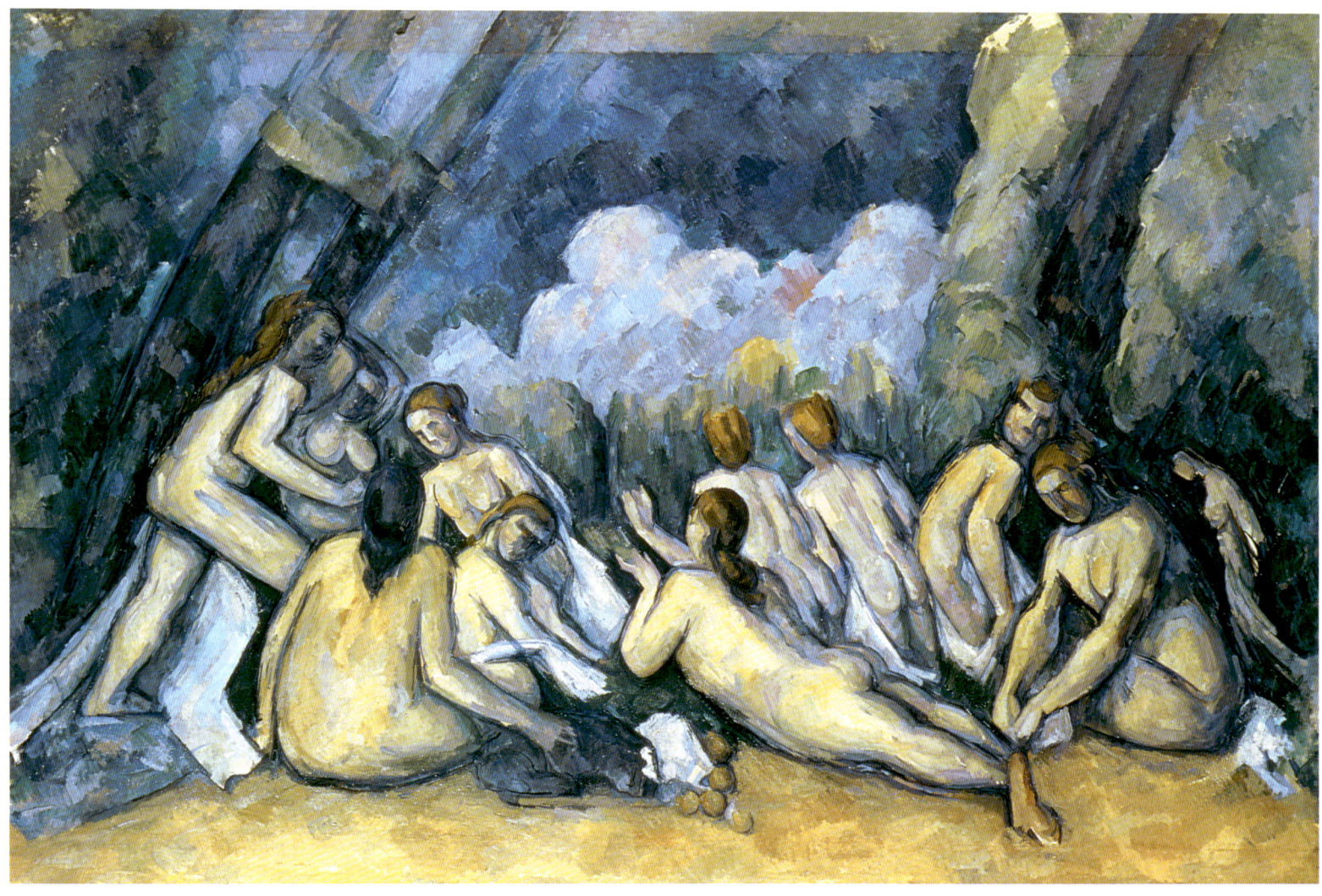

Paul Cézanne (1839–1906)

The Large Bathers

Les Grandes Baigneuses

Die Großen Badenden

Los bañistas

Le grandi bagnanti

Les Grandes Baigneuses

c. 1894–1905, Oil on canvas/Huile sur toile, 127,2 × 196,1 cm, National Gallery, London

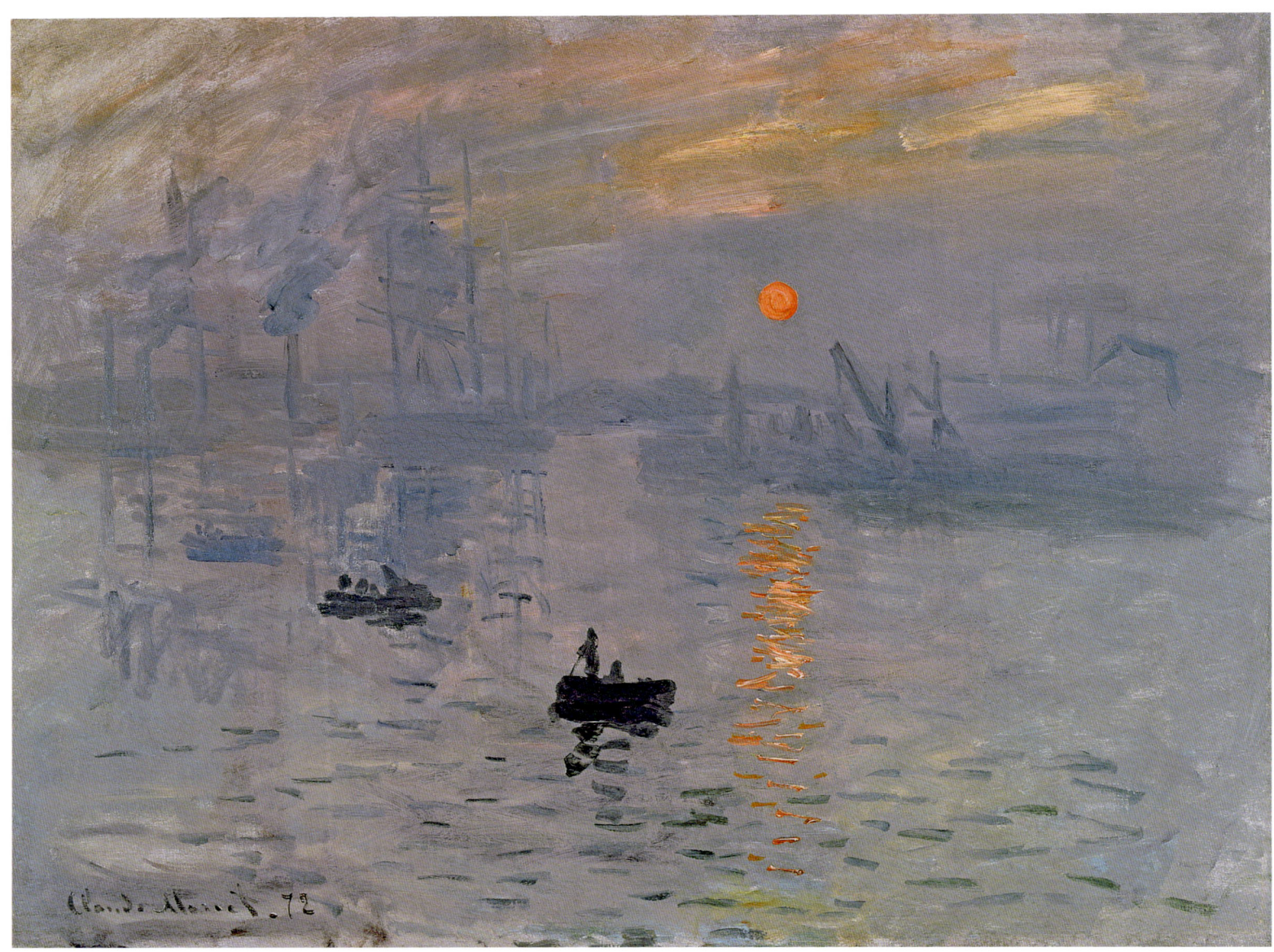

Claude Monet (1840–1926)

Impression: Sunrise

Impression, soleil levant

Impression: Aufgehende Sonne

Impresión, sol naciente

Impressioni: alba

Impressie: zonsopgang

1872, Oil on canvas/Huile sur toile, 48 × 63 cm, Musée Marmottan, Paris

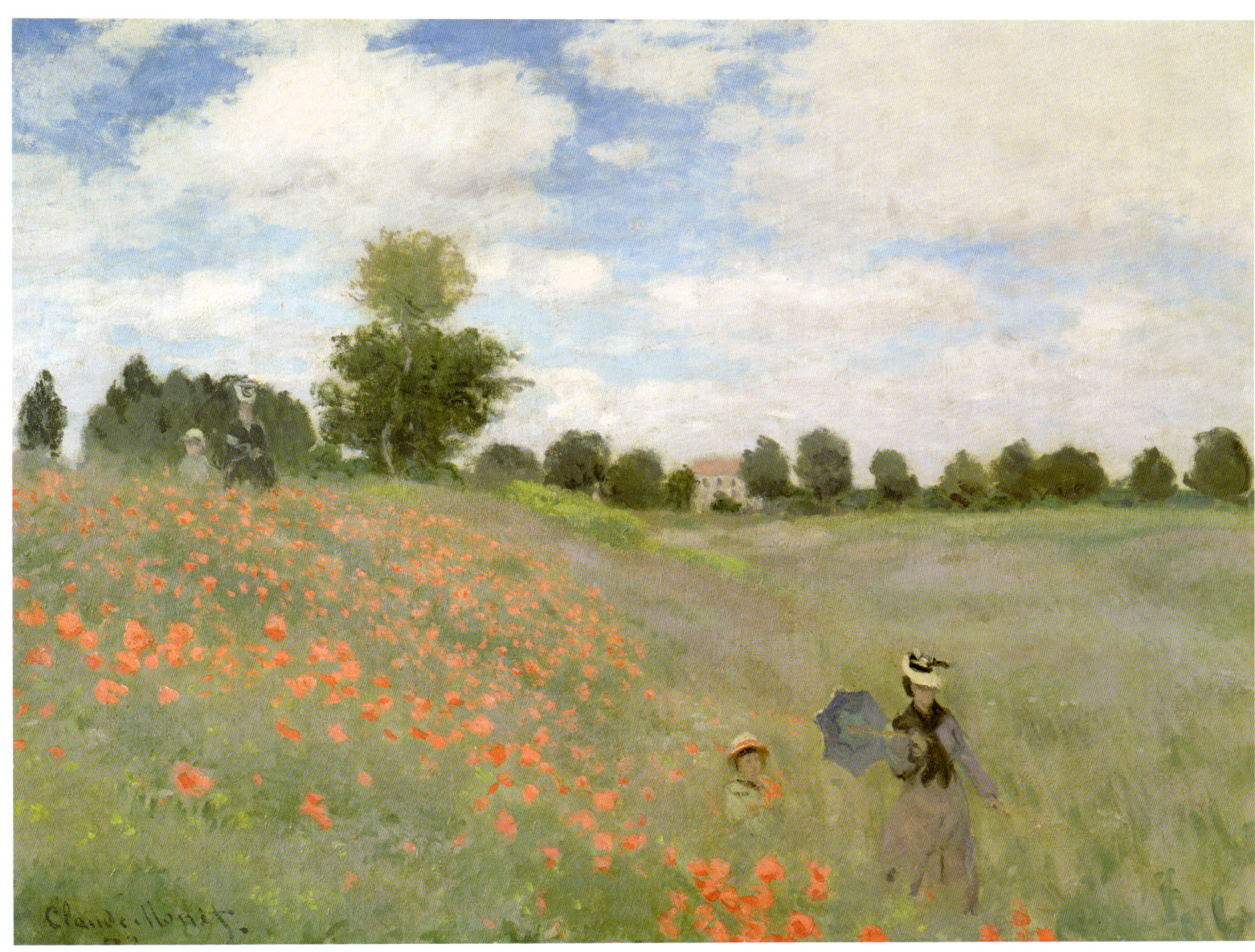

Claude Monet (1840–1926)

Wild Poppies, near Argenteuil

Coquelicots

Mohnfeld bei Argenteuil

Campo de amapolas en Argenteuil

Campo di papaveri vicino Argenteuil

Papaverveld bij Argenteuil

1873, Oil on canvas/Huile sur toile, 50 × 65,3 cm, Musée d'Orsay, Paris

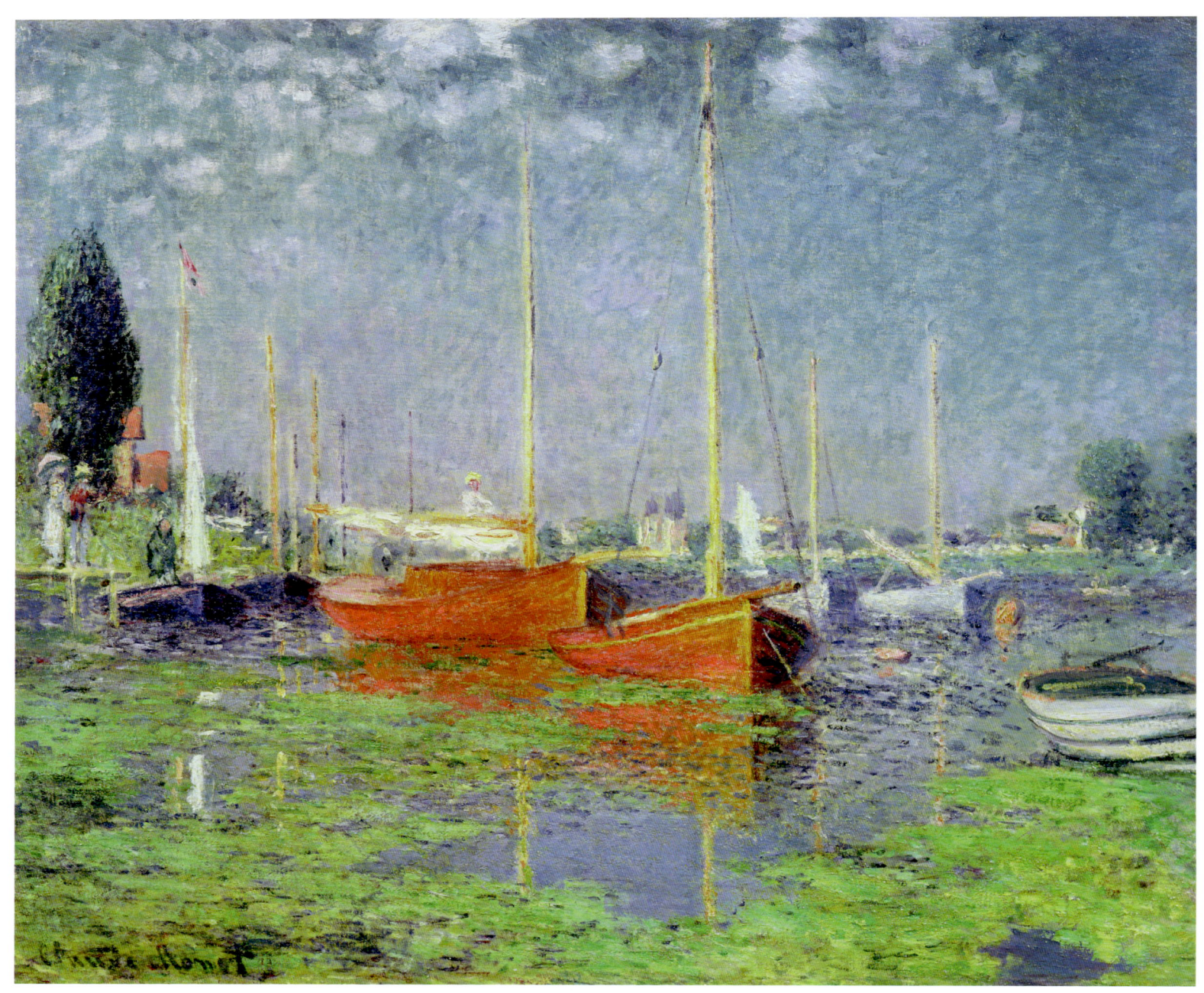

Claude Monet (1840–1926)

Argenteuil

1875, Oil on canvas/Huile sur toile, 56 × 67 cm, Musée de l'Orangerie, Paris

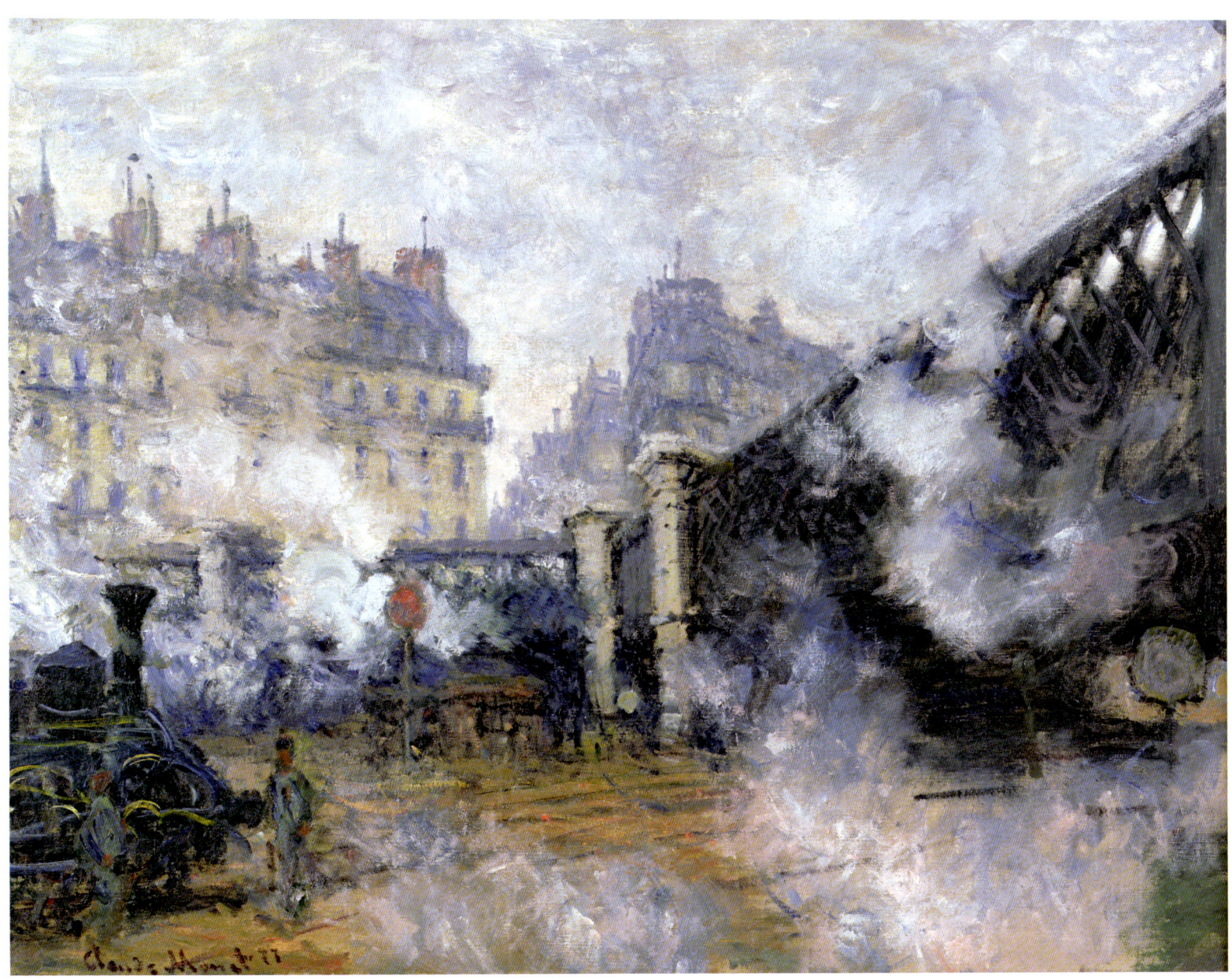

Claude Monet (1840–1926)

The Pont de l'Europe, Gare Saint-Lazare

Le Pont de l'Europe, gare Saint-Lazare

Die Europabrücke am Gare St Lazare

El puente de Europa en la estación de St. Lazare

Il ponte Europa alla Gare Saint Lazare

De Europabrug bij het Gare Saint-Lazare

1877, Oil on canvas/Huile sur toile, 64 × 81 cm, Musée Marmottan Monet, Paris

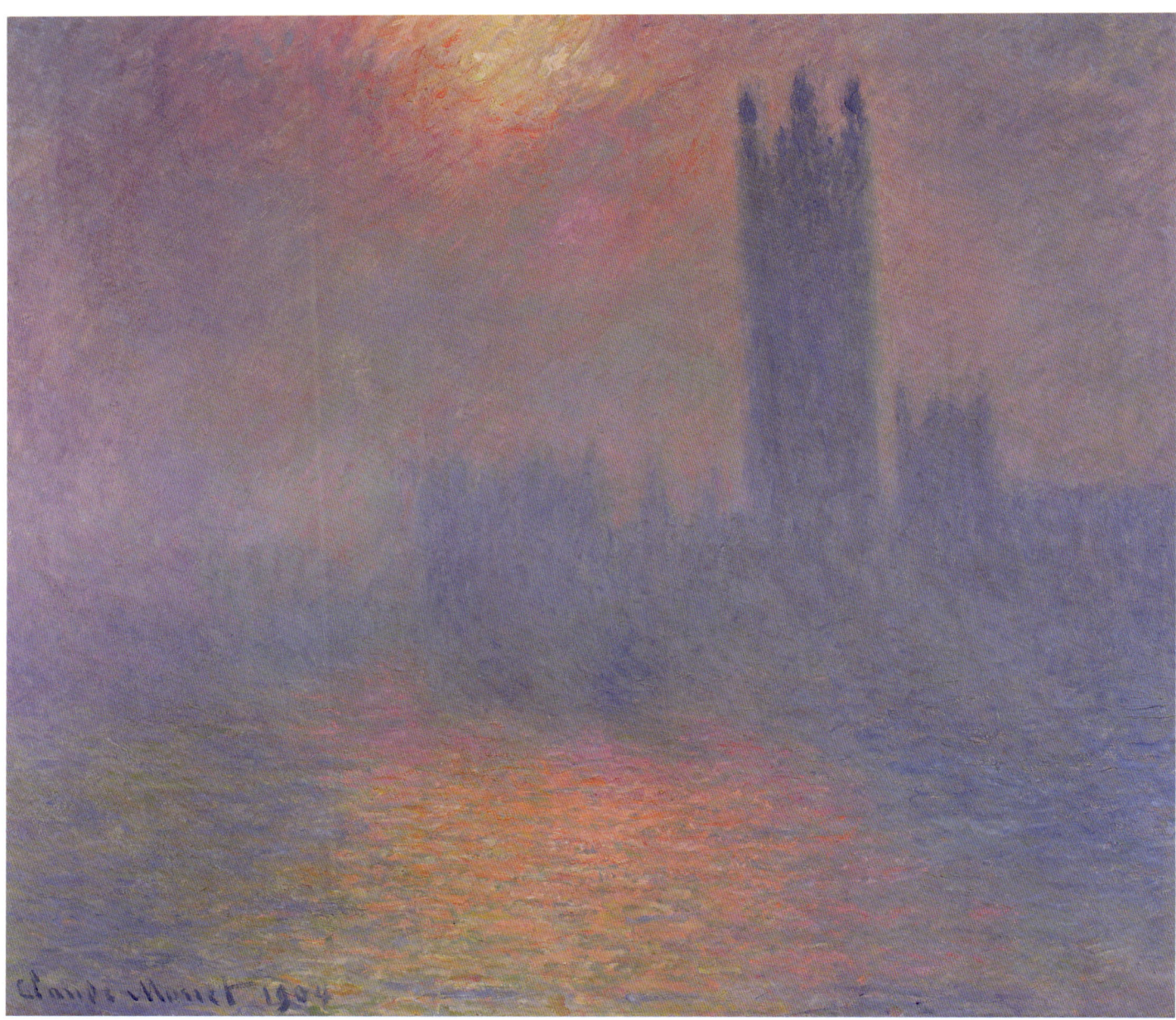

Claude Monet (1840–1926)

The Houses of Parliament, London, with the sun breaking through the fog

Londres, le Parlement. Trouée de soleil dans le brouillard

Die Houses of Parliament in London. Die Sonne bricht durch den Nebel

El Parlamento, Londres. El sol se abre paso entre la niebla

Il Parlamento di Londra, effetto di sole nella nebbia

De Houses of Parliament in Londen. De zon breekt door de mist.

1904, Oil on canvas/Huile sur toile, 81,5 × 92,5 cm, Musée d'Orsay, Paris

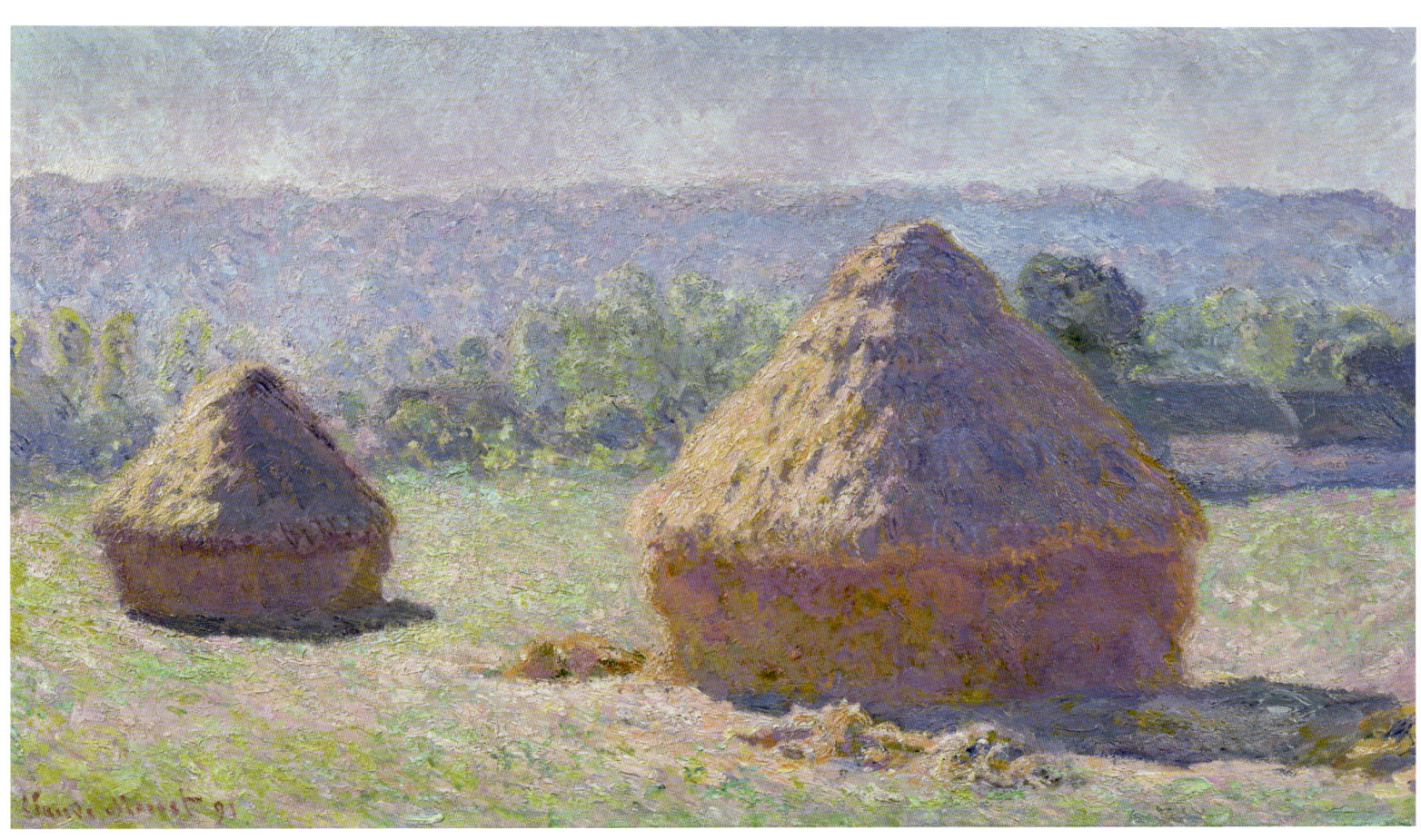

Claude Monet (1840–1926)

Grainstacks at the end of the Summer, Morning effect

Meules, fin de l'été

Heuschober am Ende des Sommers. Effekt der Morgensonne

Montones de heno al final del verano. Efecto del sol matutino.

Covoni di fieno alla fine dell'estate, effetto del sole del mattino

Hooibergen aan het einde van de zomer. Ochtendeffect

1891, Oil on canvas/Huile sur toile, 60 × 100 cm, Musée d'Orsay, Paris

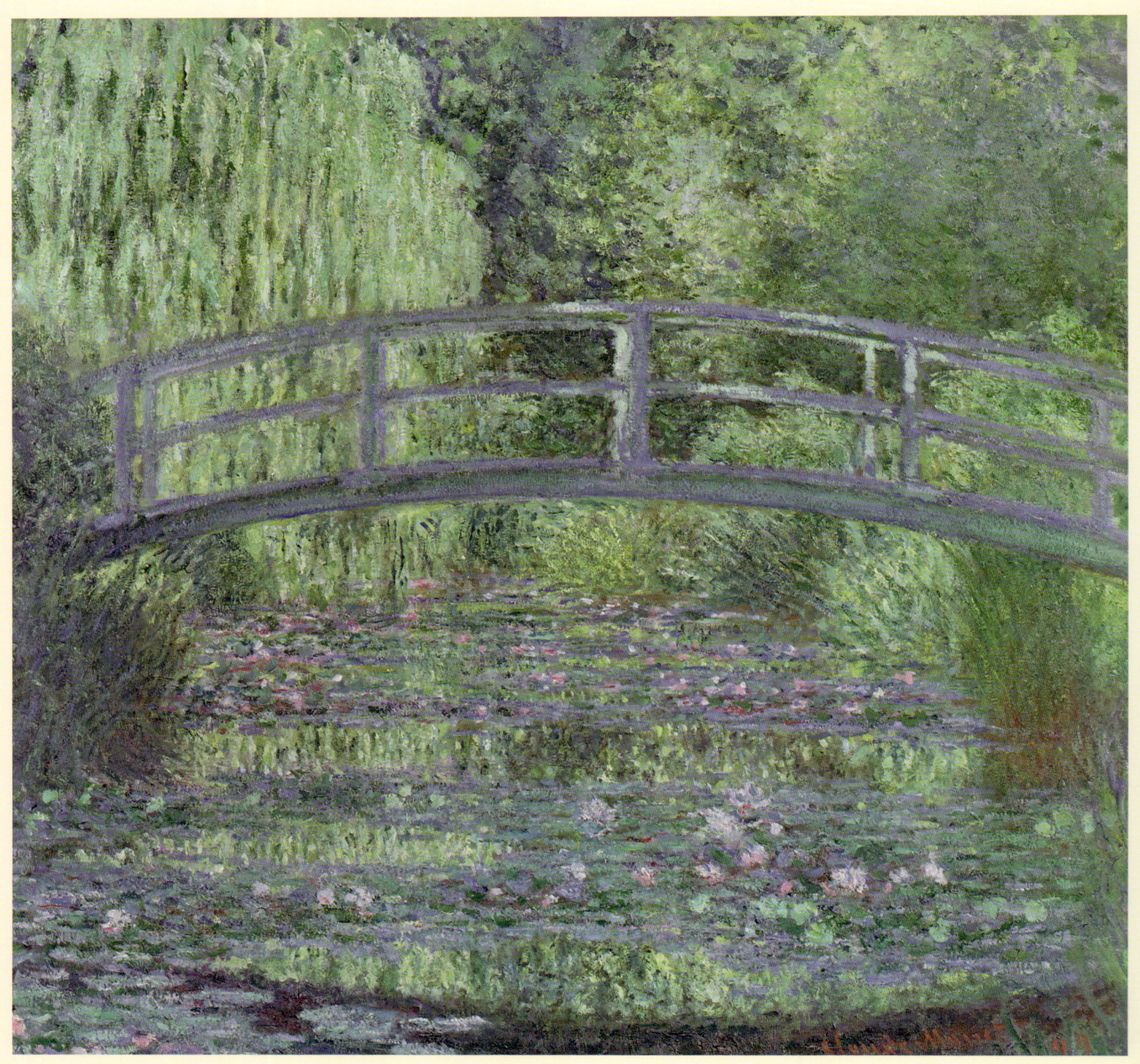

Claude Monet (1840–1926)

The Waterlily Pond: Green Harmony

Le Bassin aux nymphéas, harmonie verte

Der Seerosenteich: Grüne Harmonie

El estanque de nenúfares: Armonía verde

Lo stagno delle ninfee: armonia verde

De waterlelievijver: groene harmonie

1899, Oil on canvas/Huile sur toile, 89 × 93,5 cm, Musée d'Orsay, Paris

With the Water Lilies, Monet created a new kind of painting whose influence reached well into the 20th century and in which the depiction of the subject matters less than the colored nuances which merge into a dense informal tissue. Color and abstraction had become a new theme in painting.

Mit den Seerosenbildern schuf Monet eine neuartige, weit ins 20. Jahrhundert reichende Malerei, die weniger den Gegenstand abbildet sondern die farbigen Nuancen zu einem dichten informellen Gewebe verschmelzen lässt. Farbe und Abstraktion werden zu einem neuen Thema in der Malerei.

Con i quadri delle ninfee Monet creò una pittura innovativa che tendeva al XX secolo, che rappresentava meno l'oggetto ma fondeva le sfumature cromatiche in un tessuto denso e informale. Il colore e l'astrazione divennero un nuovo tema della pittura.

Avec ses tableaux de nymphéas, Monet crée une peinture novatrice, poussée fort en avant dans le xxe siècle. Elle représente moins l'objet qu'elle n'en fusionne les nuances colorées dans un tissu informel et dense. Couleur et abstraction deviennent ainsi un nouveau sujet dans la peinture.

Con sus cuadros de nenúfares Monet creó un nuevo tipo de pintura que extendería su influencia hasta bien entrado el XX, y que se dedica menos a la representación pictórica del objeto y más a la fusión de matices cromáticos en un denso tejido informal. El color y la abstracción se convierten en el nuevo tema en la pintura.

Met zijn schilderijen van waterlelies creëerde Monet een geheel nieuwe schilderkunst waarvan de invloed tot ver in de twintigste eeuw zou reiken, een schilderkunst waarin niet zozeer objecten worden uitgebeeld, maar waarin kleurnuances in een dicht, informeel en abstract weefsel zijn samengebracht en zo een nieuwe artistieke wereld scheppen.

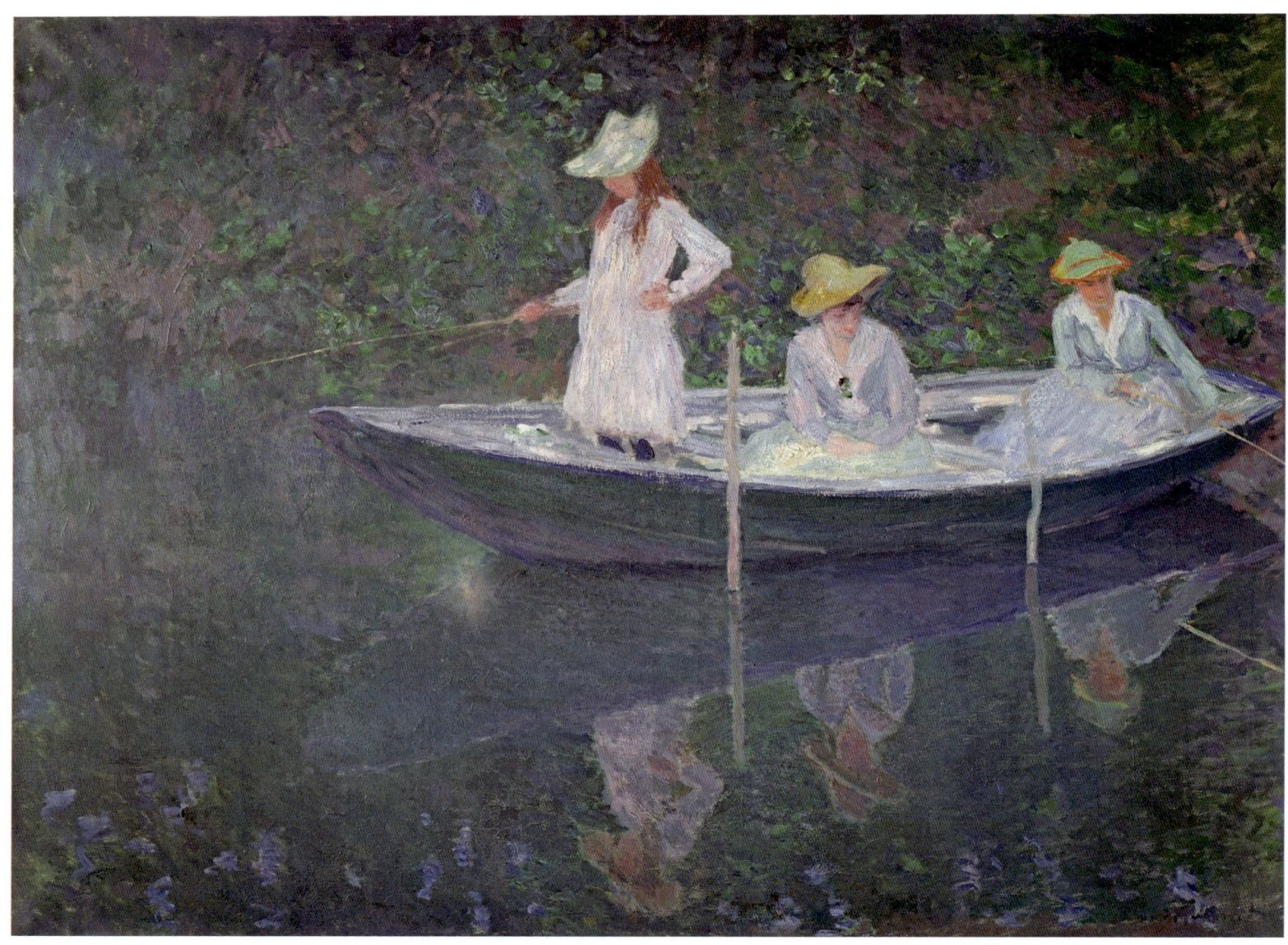

Claude Monet (1840–1926)

The Boat at Giverny

En Norvégienne *ou* La Barque à Giverny

Das Boot in Giverny

El bote en Giverny

La barca a Giverny

De boot in Giverny

c. 1887, Oil on canvas/Huile sur toile, 98 × 131 cm, Musée d'Orsay, Paris

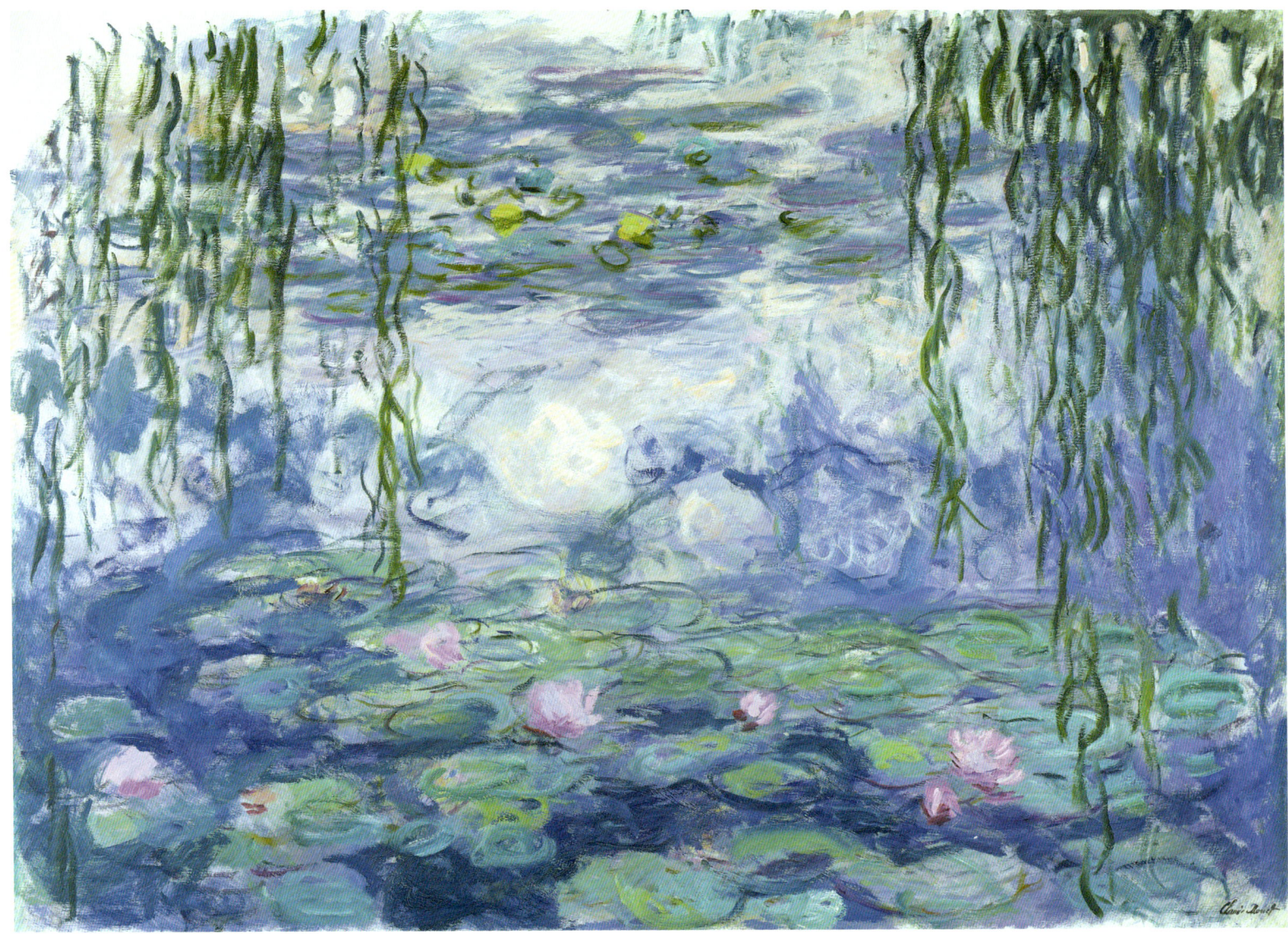

Claude Monet (1840–1926)

Waterlilies

Nymphéas

Seerosen

Nenúfares

Le ninfee

Waterlelies

1916–1919, Oil on canvas/Huile sur toile, 150 × 197 cm, Musée Marmottan Monet, Paris

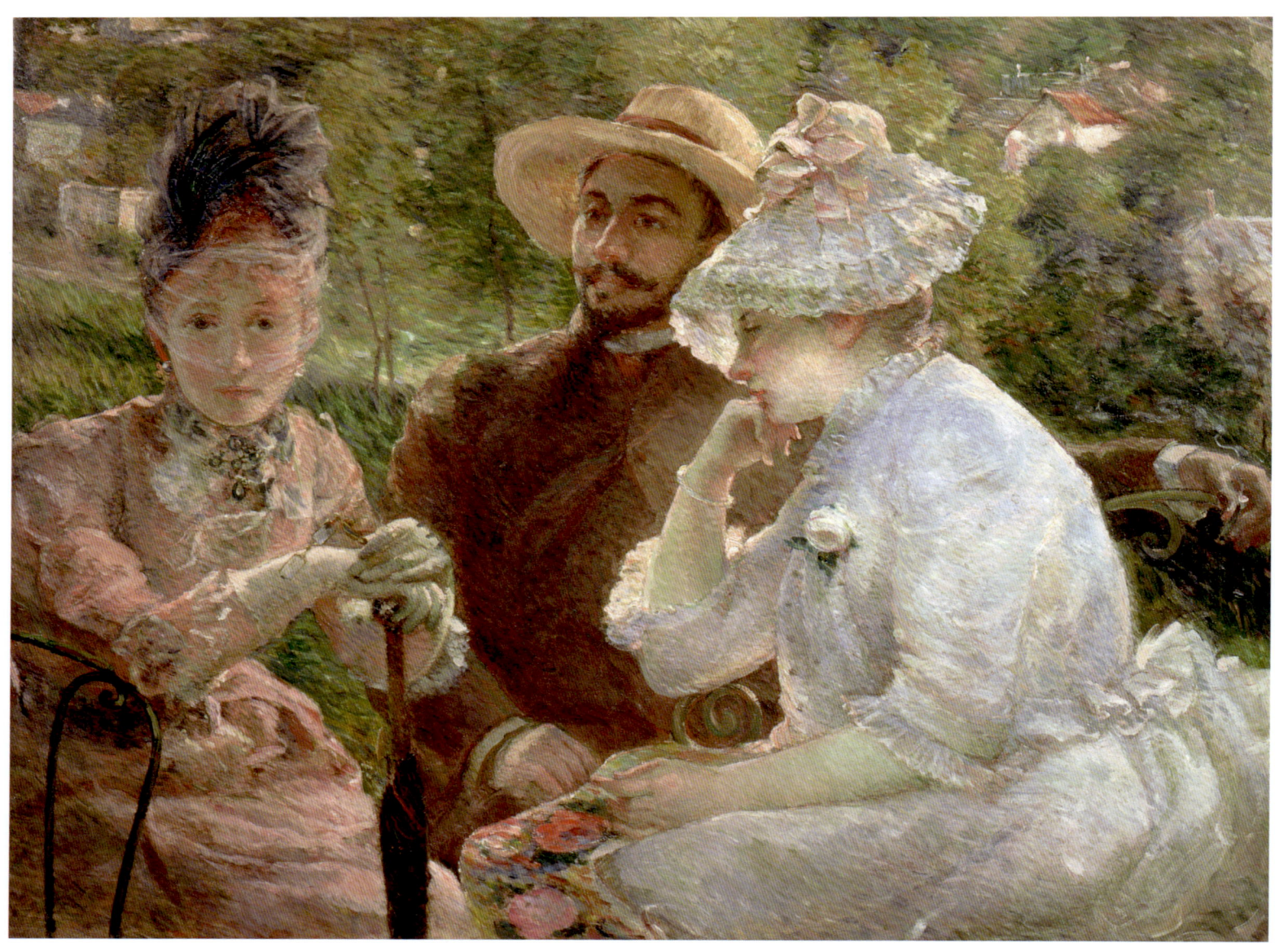

Marie Bracquemond (1840–1916)

On the Terrace at Sèvres

Sur la terrasse à Sèvres

Auf der Terrasse in Sèvres

En la terraza en Sèvres

Sulla terrazza a Sèvres

Op het terras in Sèvres

1880, Oil on canvas/Huile sur toile, 88 × 115 cm, Musée du Petit Palais, Genève

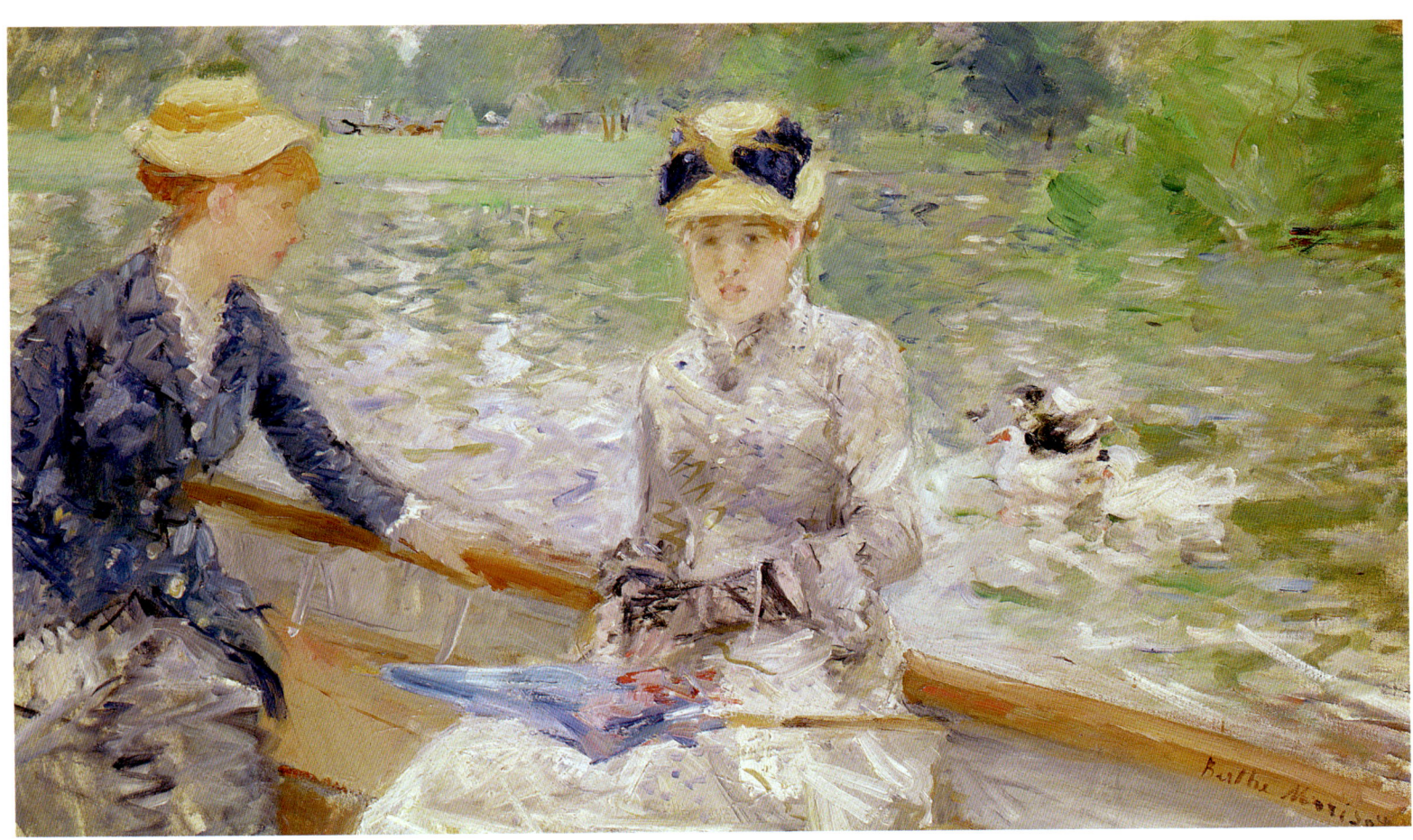

Berthe Morisot (1841–1895)

Summer's Day

Un Jour d'été

Ein Sommertag

Un día de verano

Un giorno d'estate

Een zomerdag

1879, Oil on canvas/Huile sur toile, 45,7 × 75,2 cm, National Gallery, London

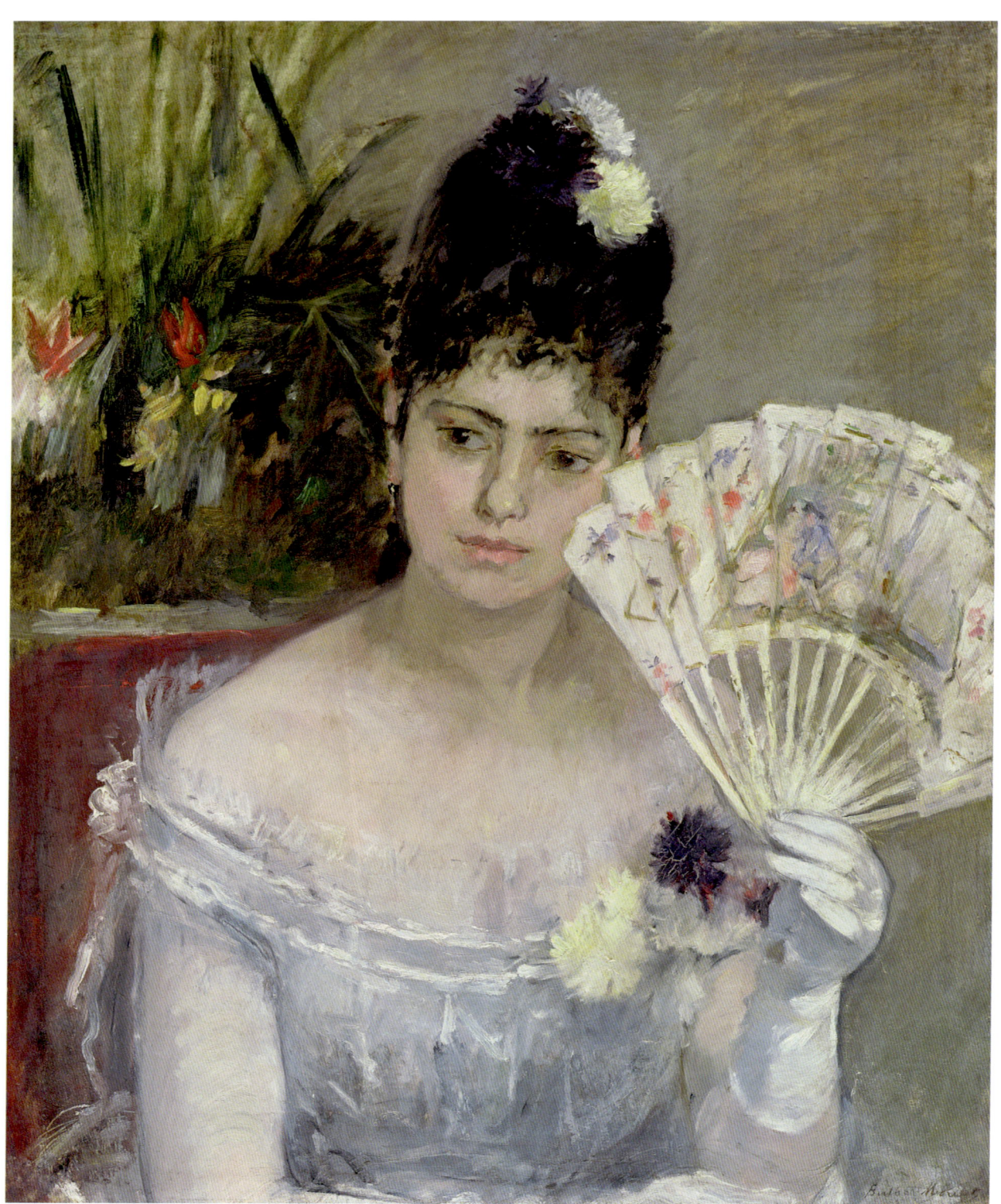

Berthe Morisot (1841–1895)

At the Ball

Au Bal

Auf dem Ball

En el baile

Al ballo

Op het bal

1875, Oil on canvas/Huile
sur toile, 62 × 52 cm, Musée
Marmottan Monet, Paris

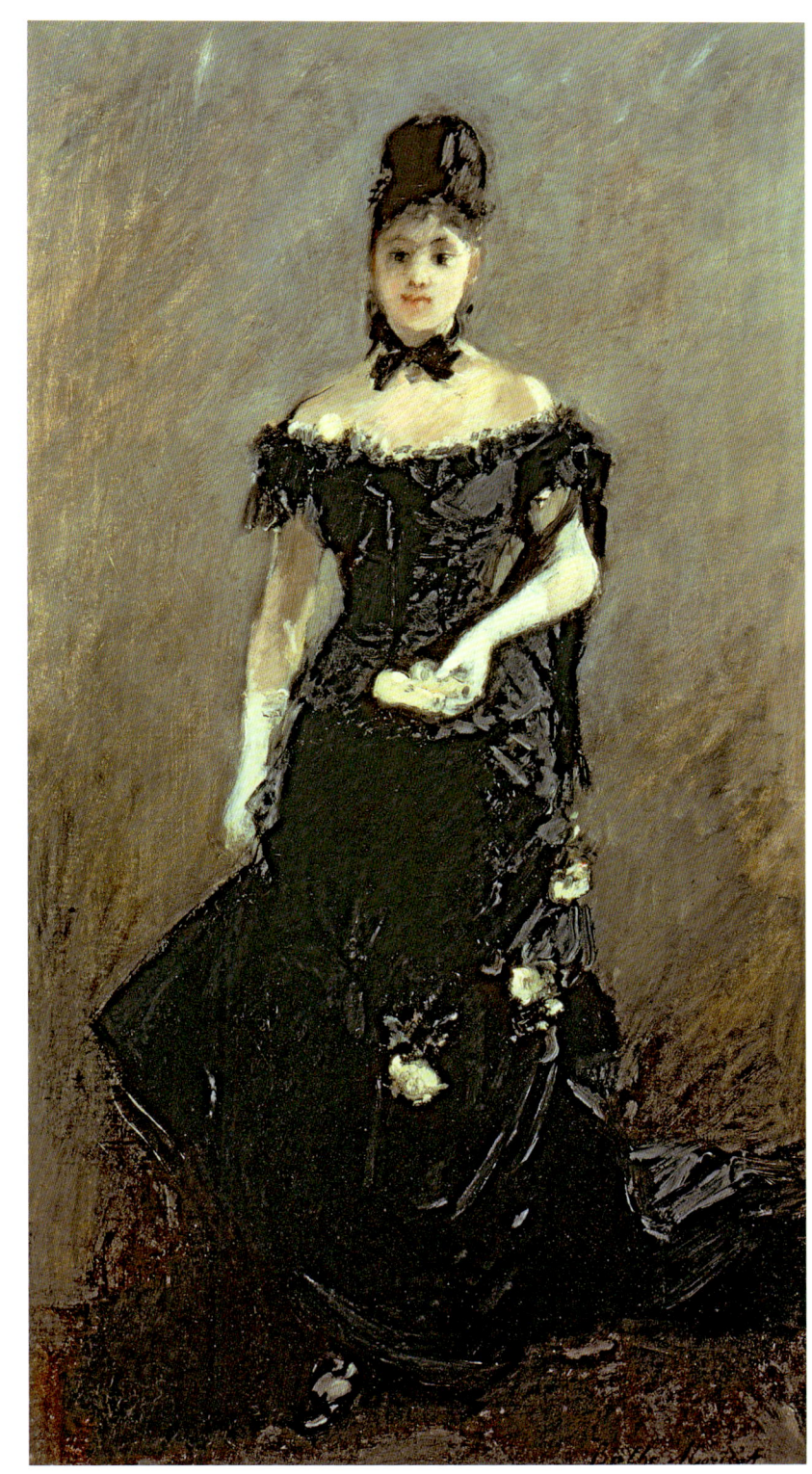

Berthe Morisot (1841–1895)

Before the Theatre

Avant le théâtre

Vor dem Theater

Antes del teatro

Davanti al teatro

Voor het theater

c. 1875, Oil on canvas/Huile sur toile, 57 × 31 cm, Private collection

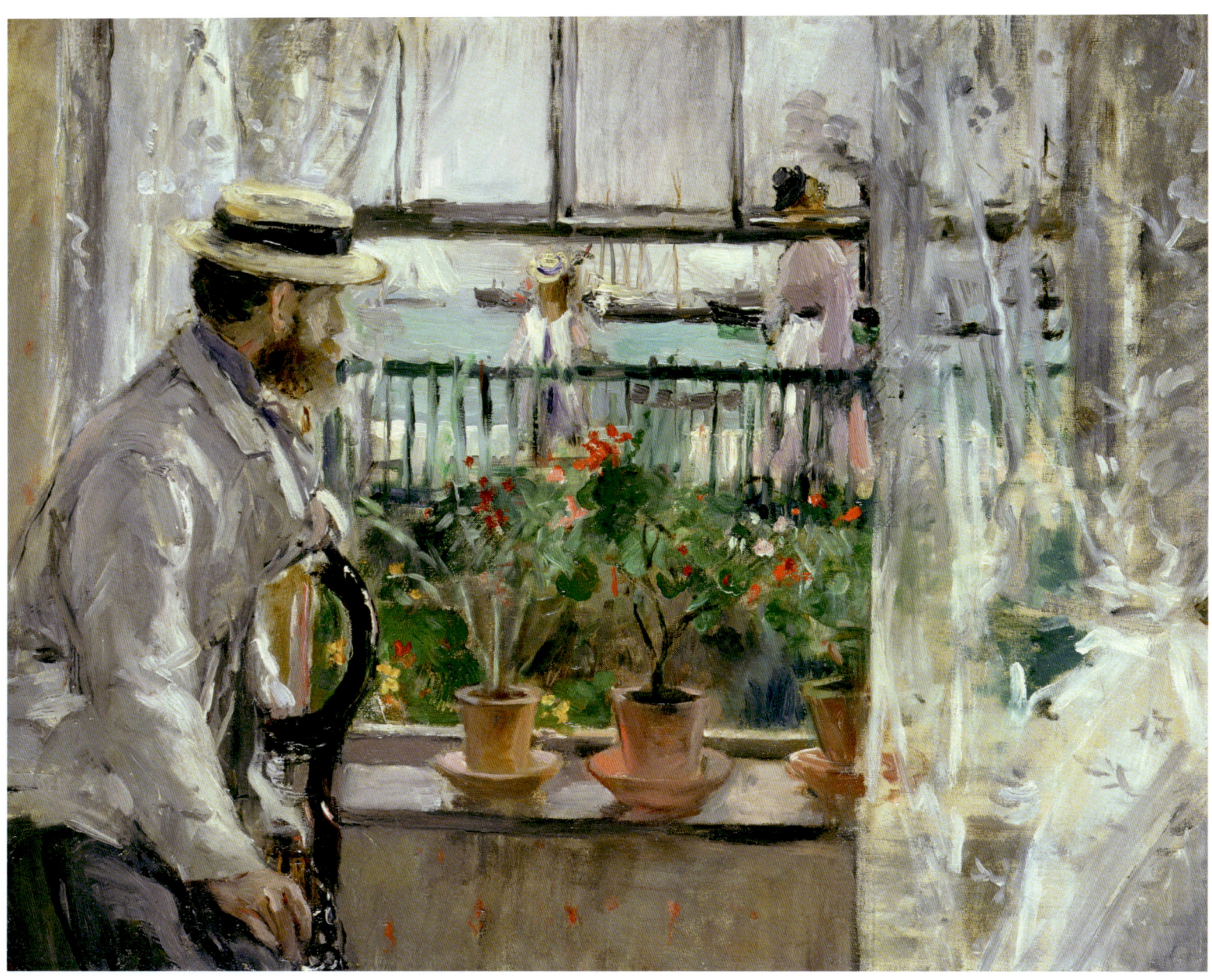

Berthe Morisot (1841–1895)

Eugene Manet on the Isle of Wight   Eugène Manet auf der Ilse of Wight   Eugène Manet sull'isola di Wight

Eugène Manet à l'île de Wight   Eugène Manet en la Isla de Wight   Eugène Manet op het eiland Wight

1875, Oil on canvas/Huile sur toile, 36 × 46 cm, Musée Marmottan Monet, Paris

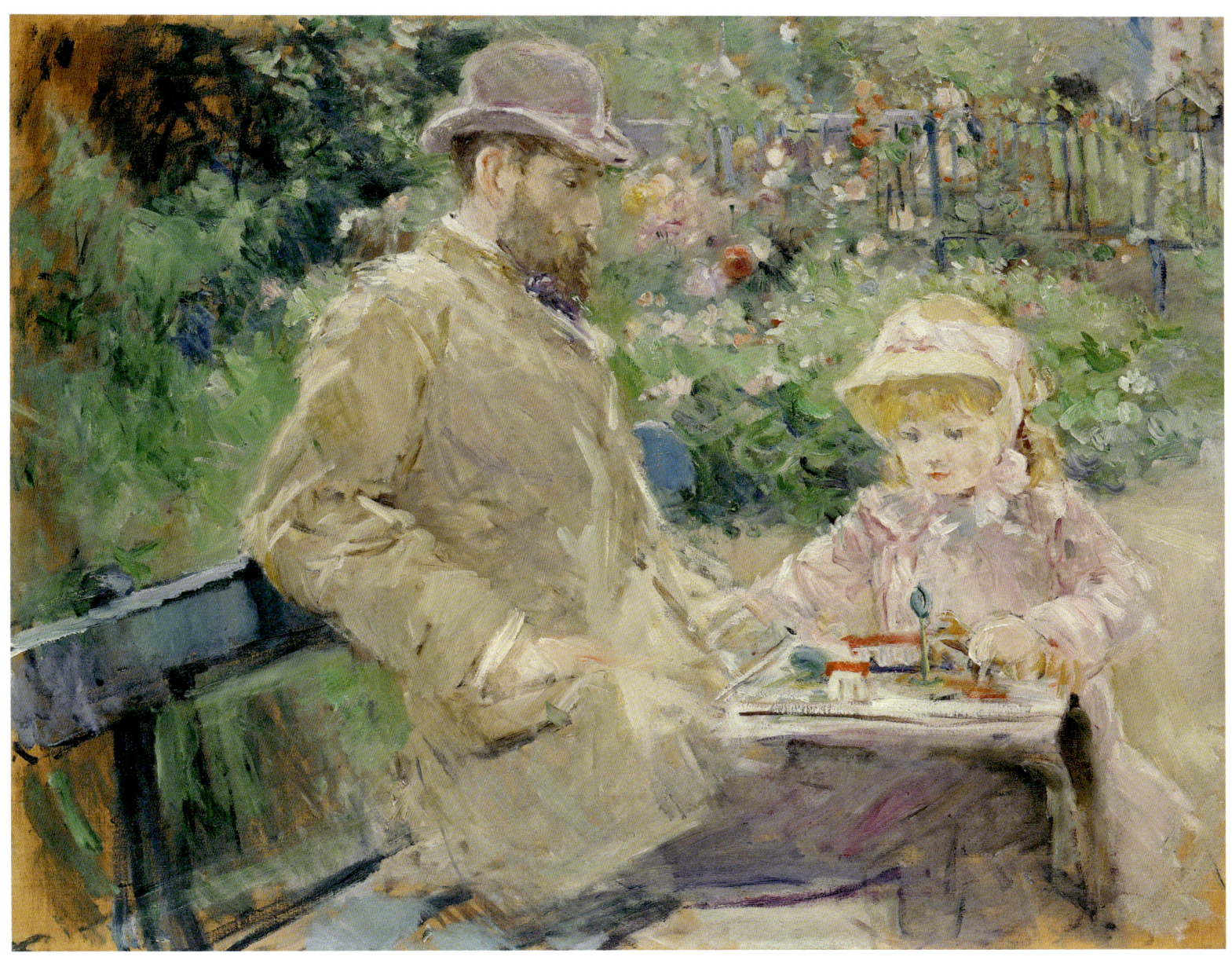

Berthe Morisot (1841–1895)

Eugene Manet with his daughter at Bougival

Eugène Manet et sa fille dans le jardin de Bougival

Eugène Manet mit seiner Tochter in Bougival

Eugene Manet con su hija en Bougival

Eugène Manet con sua figlia a Bougival

Eugène Manet met zijn dochter in Bougival

c. 1881, Oil on canvas/Huile sur toile, 73 × 92 cm, Musée Marmottan Monet, Paris

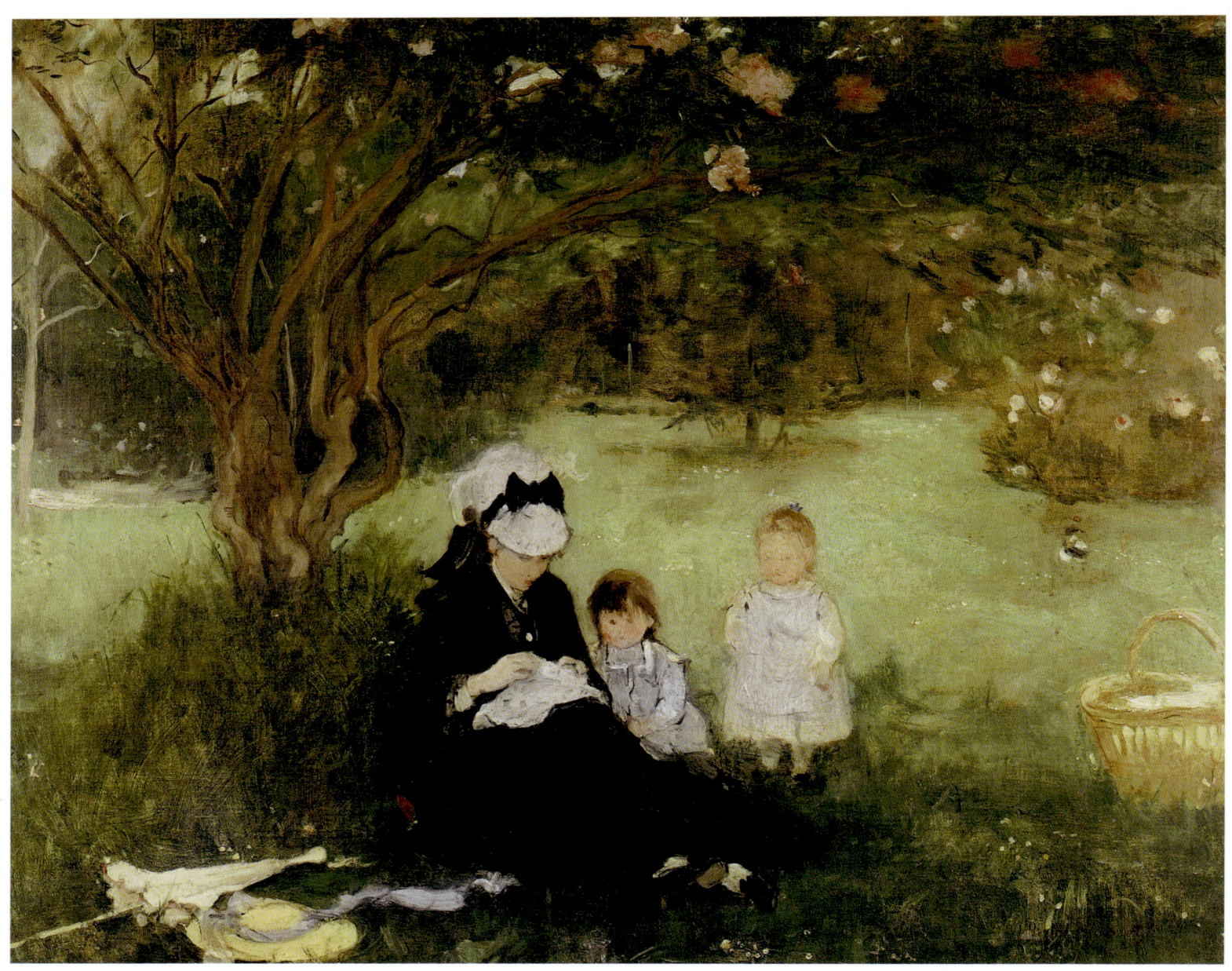

Berthe Morisot (1841–1895)

Beneath the Lilac at Maurecourt	Unter dem Fliederbaum in Maurecourt	Sotto il lillà a Maurecourt
Sous le lilas à Maurecourt	Bajo el árbol de lilas en Maurecourt	Onder de sering in Maurecourt

1874, Oil on canvas/Huile sur toile, 50 × 61 cm, Private collection

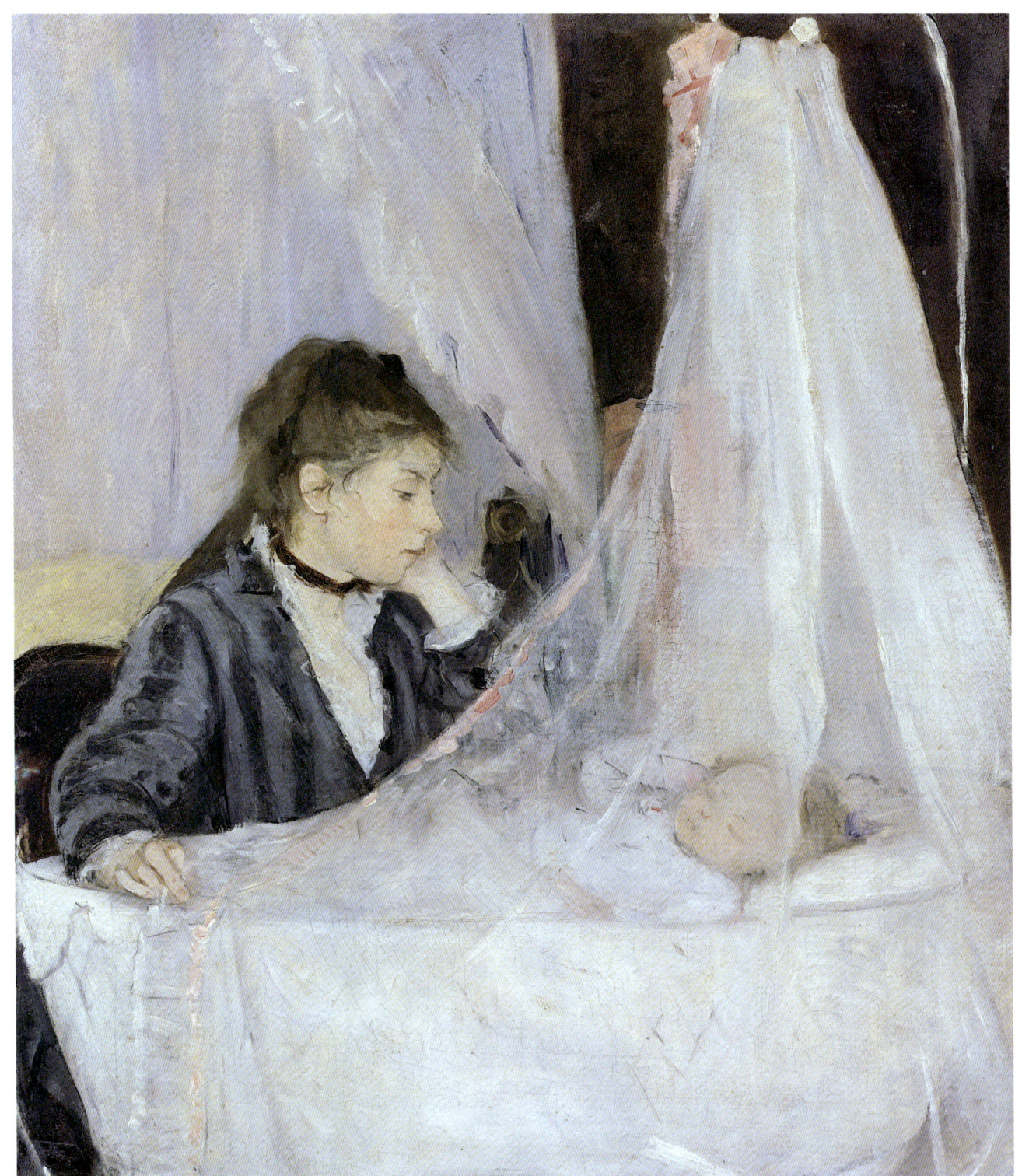

**Berthe Morisot
(1841–1895)**

The Cradle

Le Berceau

Die Wiege

La cuna

La culla

De wieg

1872, Oil on canvas/Huile
sur toile, 56 × 46,5 cm,
Musée d'Orsay, Paris

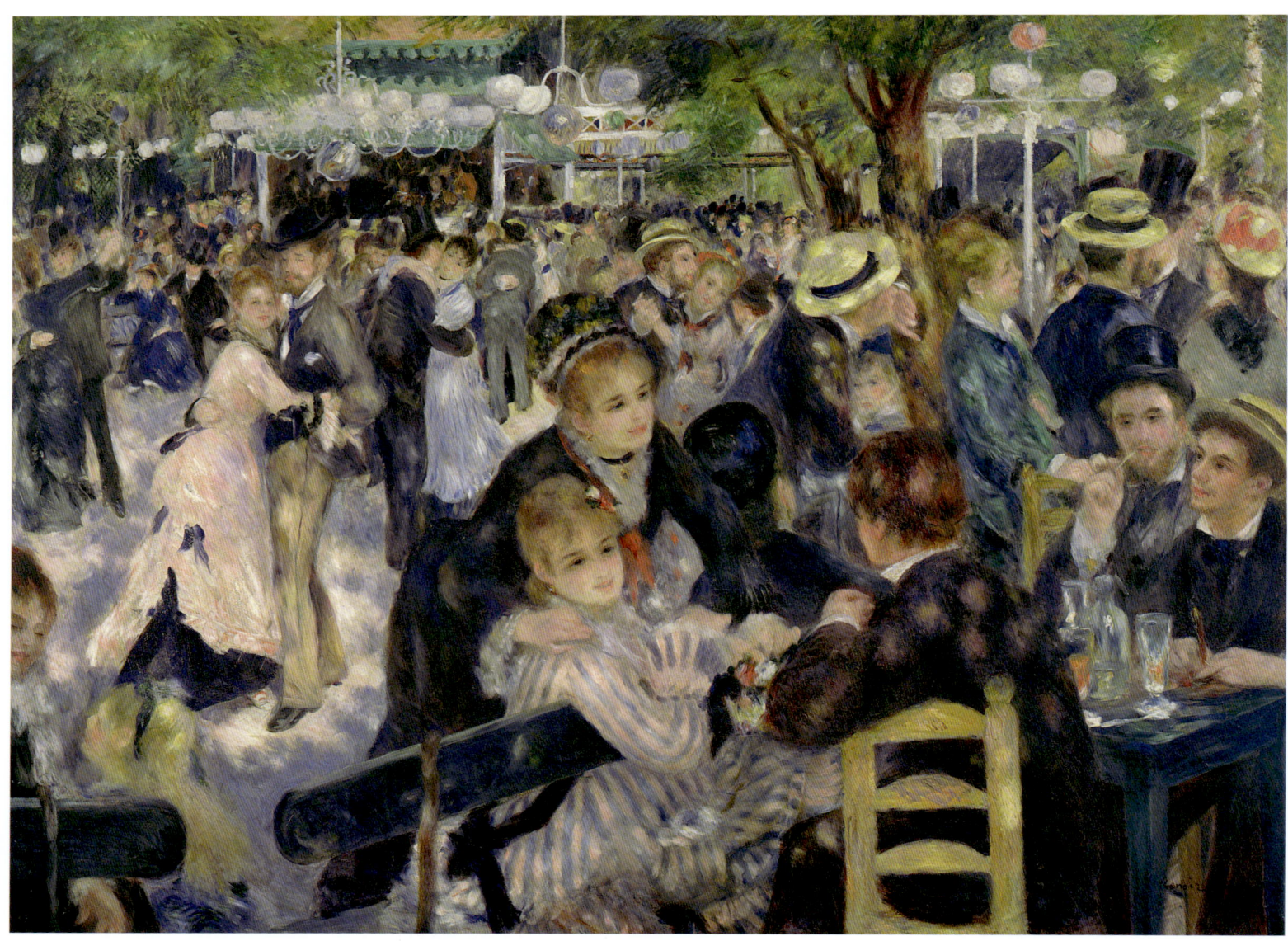

Auguste Renoir (1841–1919)

Ball at the Moulin de la Galette

Le Bal du Moulin de la Galette

Der Ball im Moulin de la Galette

El baile en el Moulin de la Galette

Il ballo al Moulin de la Galette

Het bal in de de Moulin de la Galette

1876, Oil on canvas/Huile sur toile, 131,5 × 176,5 cm, Musée d'Orsay, Paris

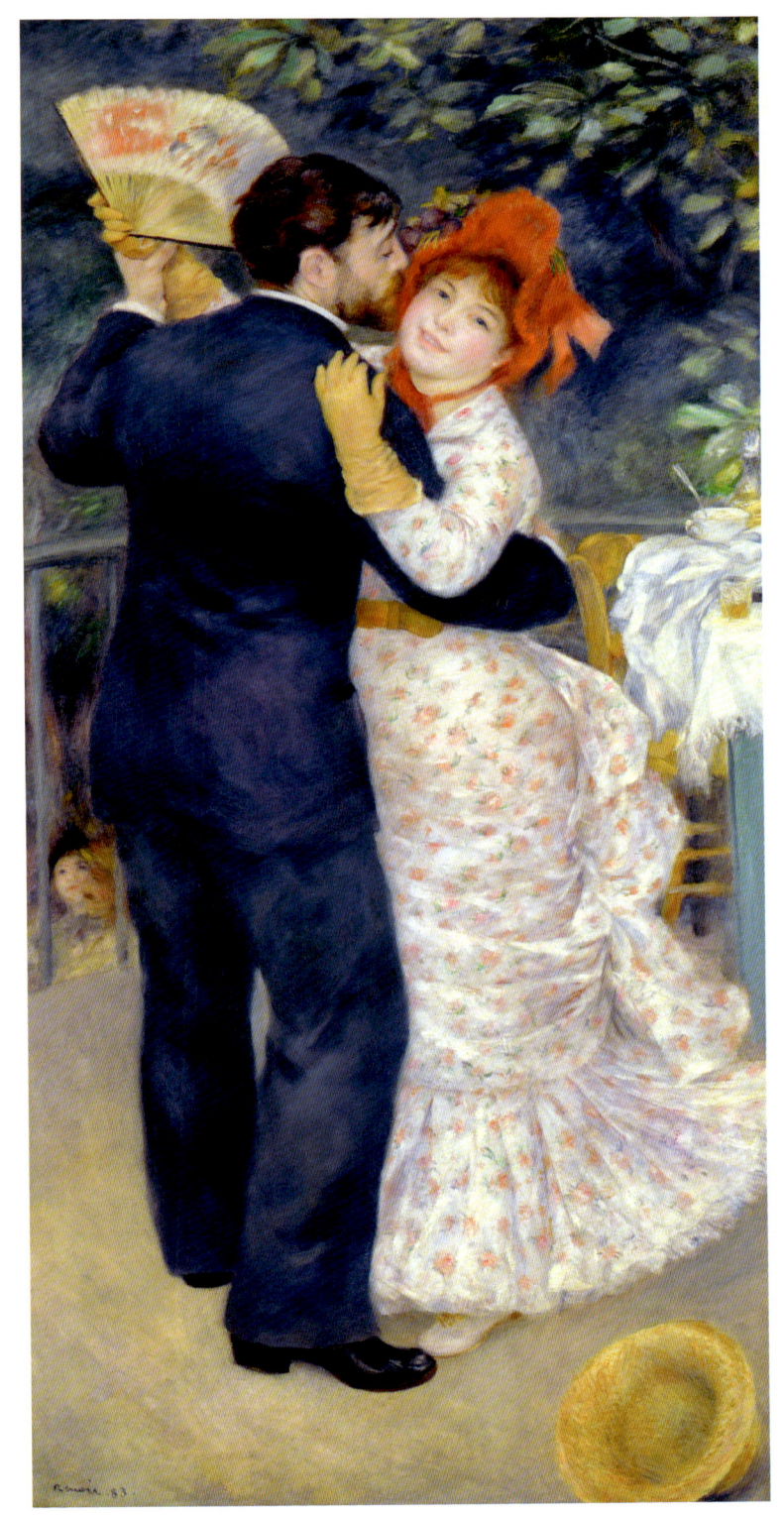

Auguste Renoir (1841–1919)

A Dance in the Country

Danse à la campagne

Ein Tanz auf dem Lande

Baile en el campo

Ballo in campagna

Een dans op het platteland

1883, Oil on canvas/Huile sur toile, 180,3 × 90 cm, Musée d'Orsay, Paris

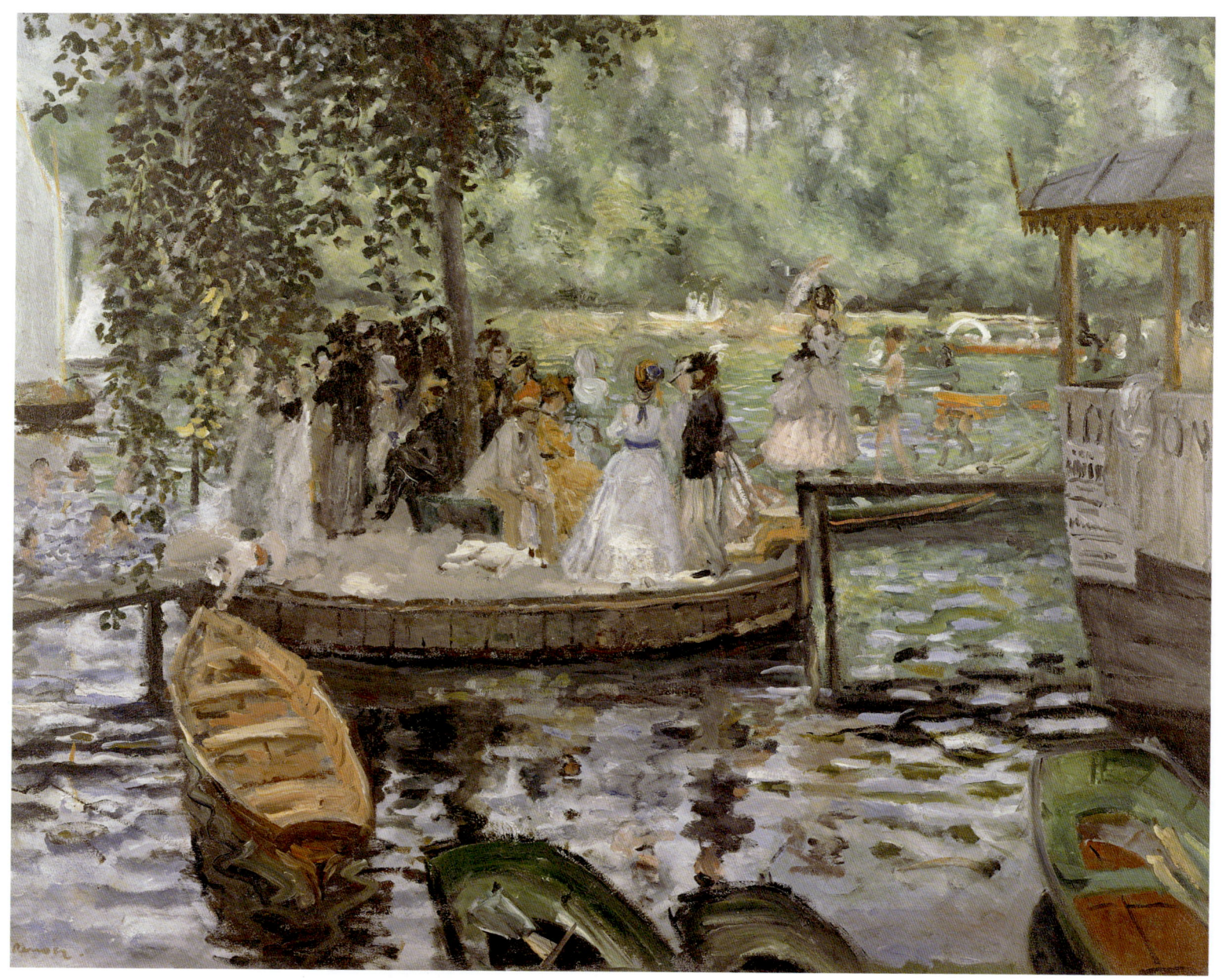

Auguste Renoir (1841–1919)

La Grenouillère

1869, Oil on canvas/Huile sur toile, 66,5 × 81 cm, Nationalmuseum, Stockholm

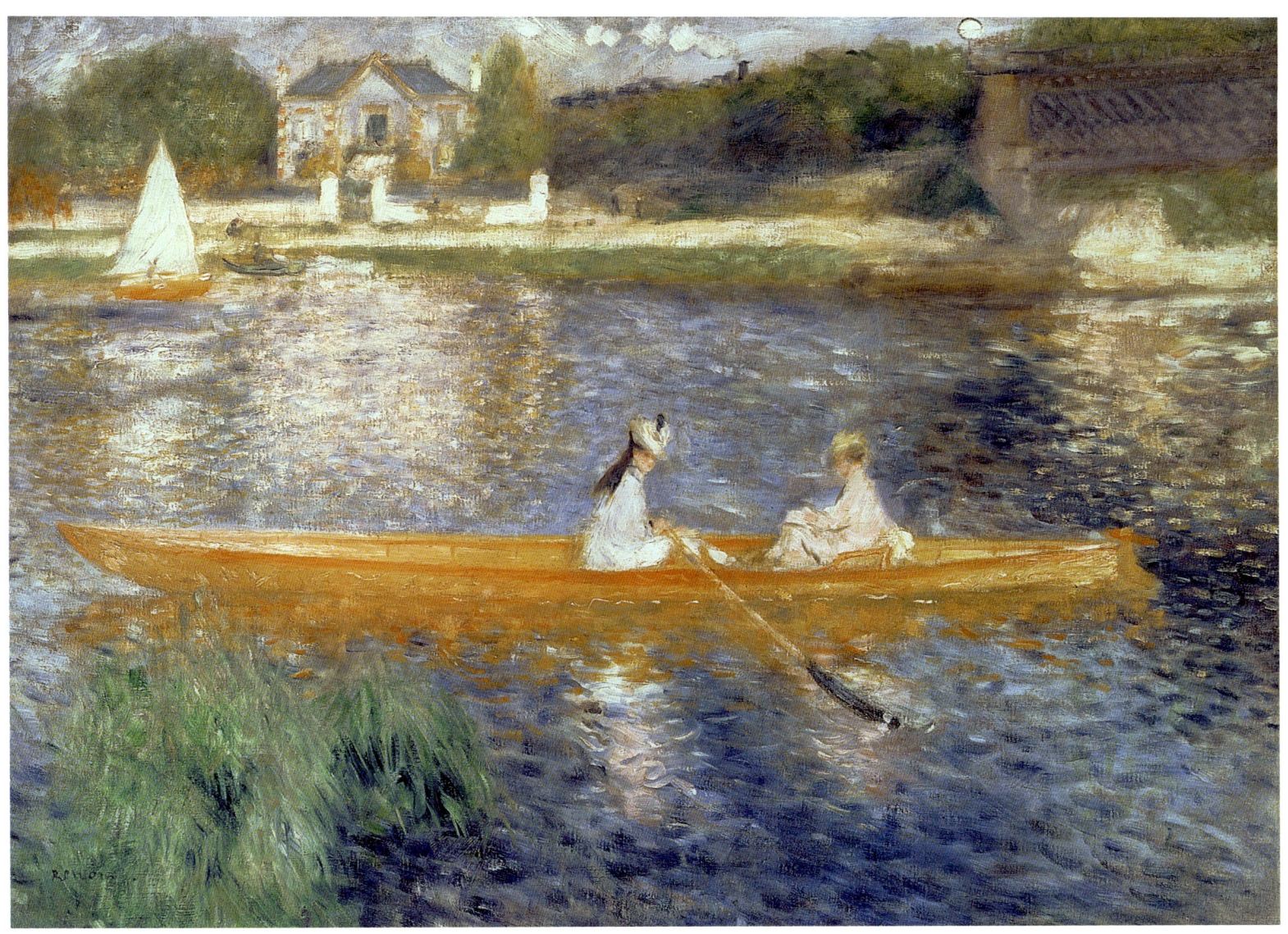

Auguste Renoir (1841–1919)

Boating on the Seine   Rudern auf der Seine   Remando sulla Senna

La Yole   Remando en el Sena   Roeien op de Seine

1875, Oil on canvas/Huile sur toile, 71 × 92 cm, National Gallery, London

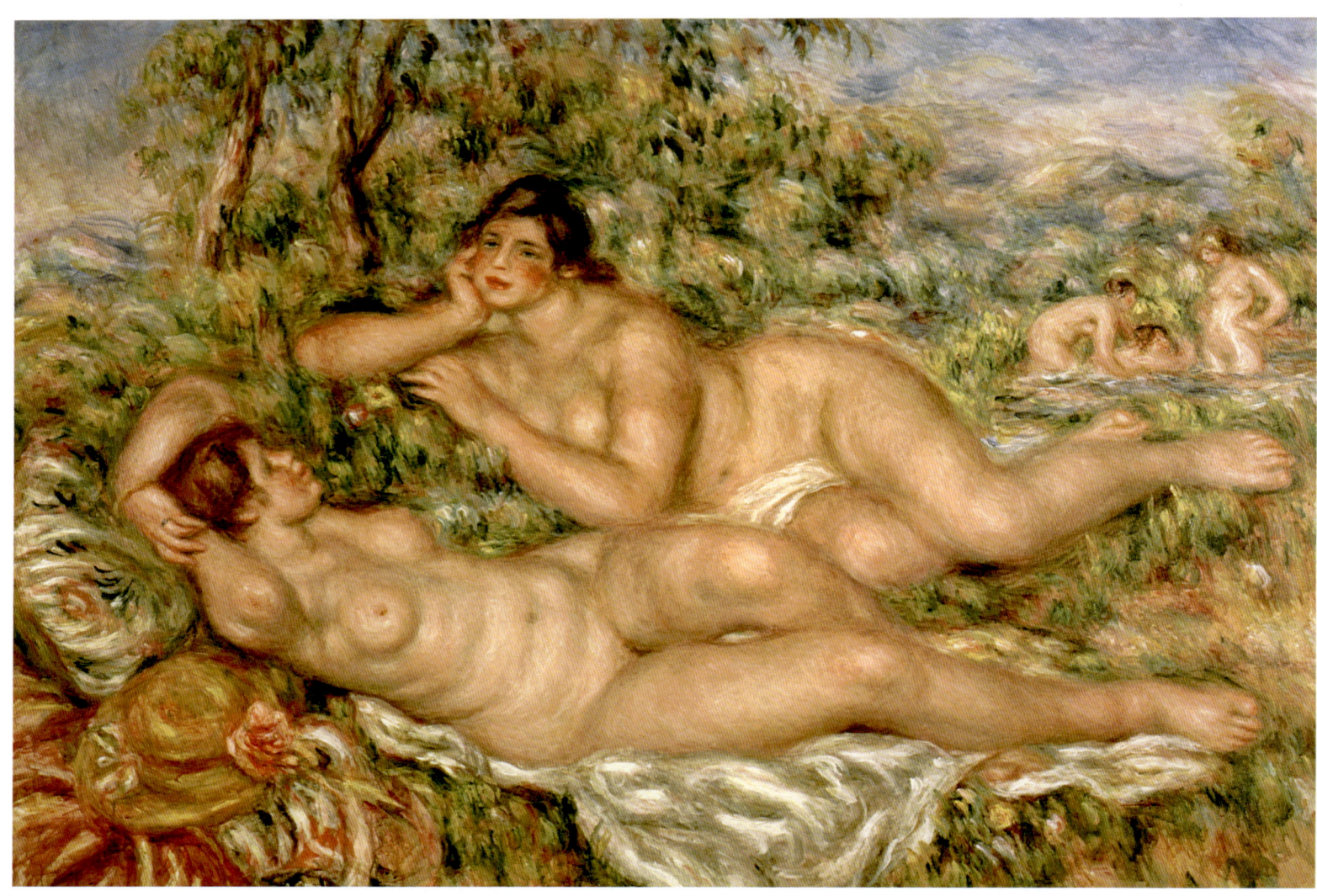

Auguste Renoir (1841–1919)

The Bathers

Les Baigneuses

Die Badenden

Las bañistas

I bagnanti

De baadsters

c. 1918–1919, Oil on canvas/Huile sur toile, 110 × 160 cm, Musée d'Orsay, Paris

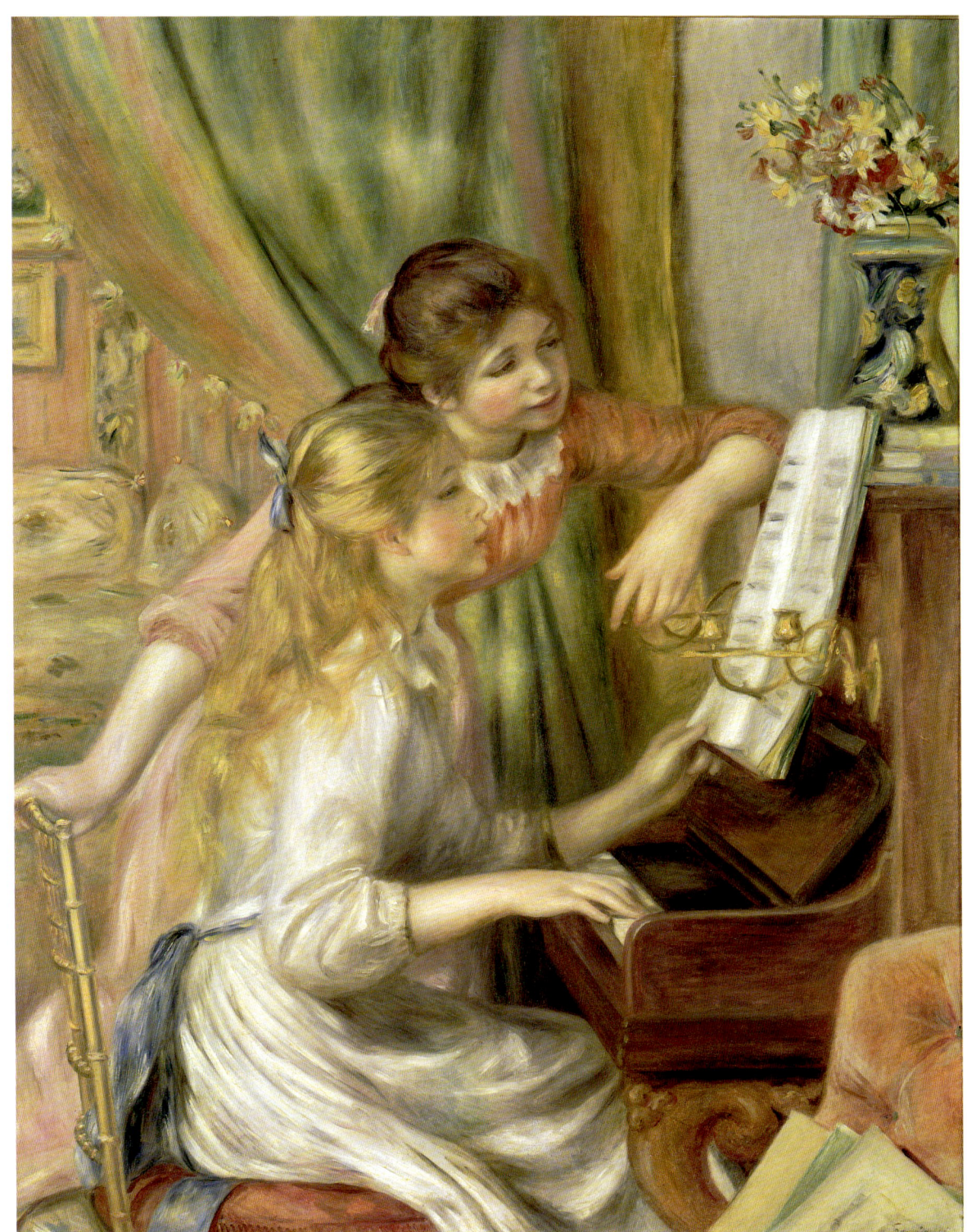

Auguste Renoir (1841–1919)

Young Girls at the Piano

Jeunes filles au piano

Junge Mädchen am Klavier

Jovencitas al piano

Ragazze al pianoforte

Jong meisje aan de piano

1892, Oil on canvas/Huile sur toile,
116 × 90 cm, Musée d'Orsay, Paris

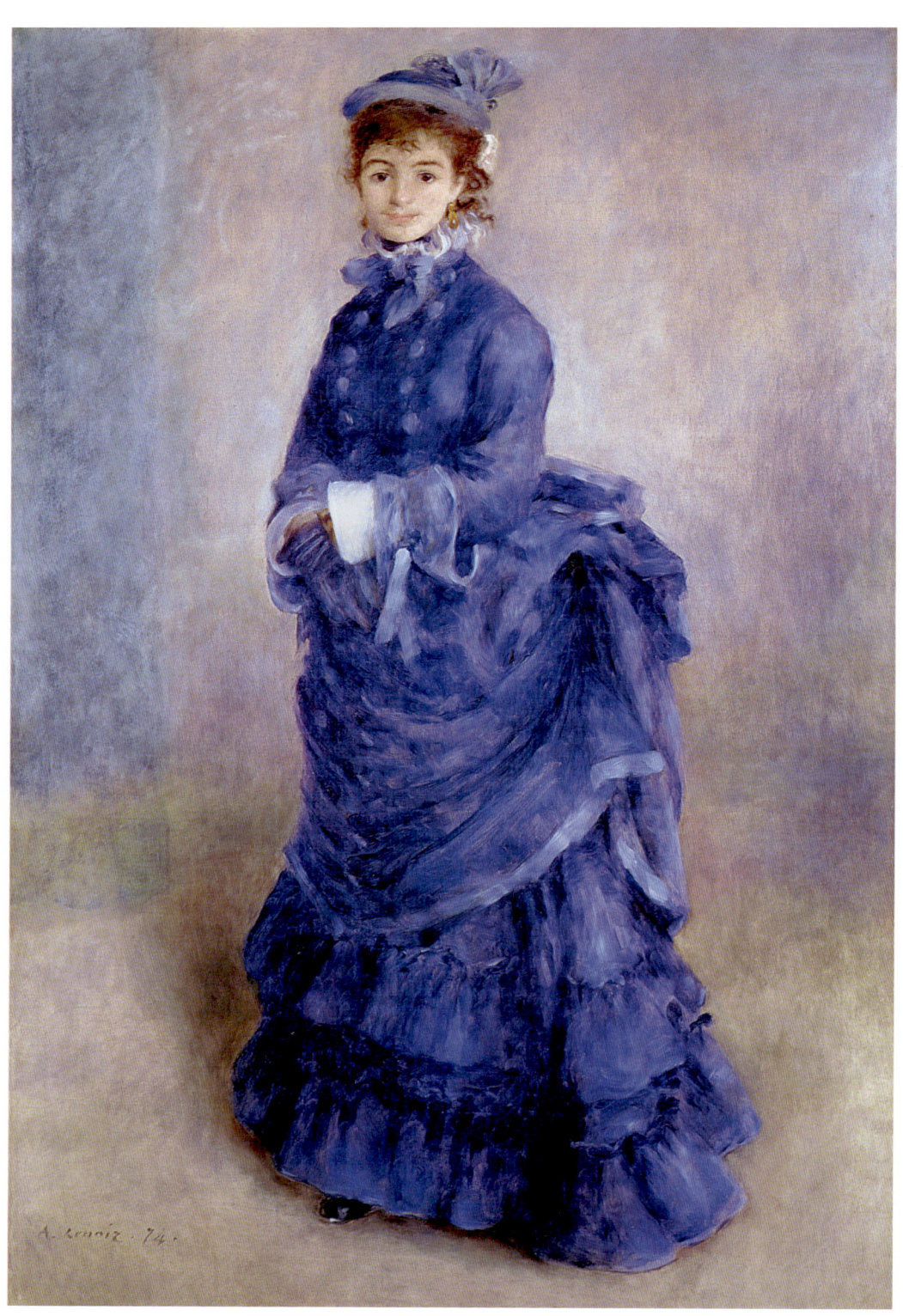

Auguste Renoir (1841–1919)

La Parisienne, The Blue Lady

La Parisienne (la dame en bleu)

Die Pariserin, Die blaue Dame

La parisina, la dama de azul

La parigina, la donna in blu

De Parisienne; De blauwe dame

1874, Oil on canvas/Huile sur toile, 163,2 × 108,3 cm,
National Museum, Cardiff

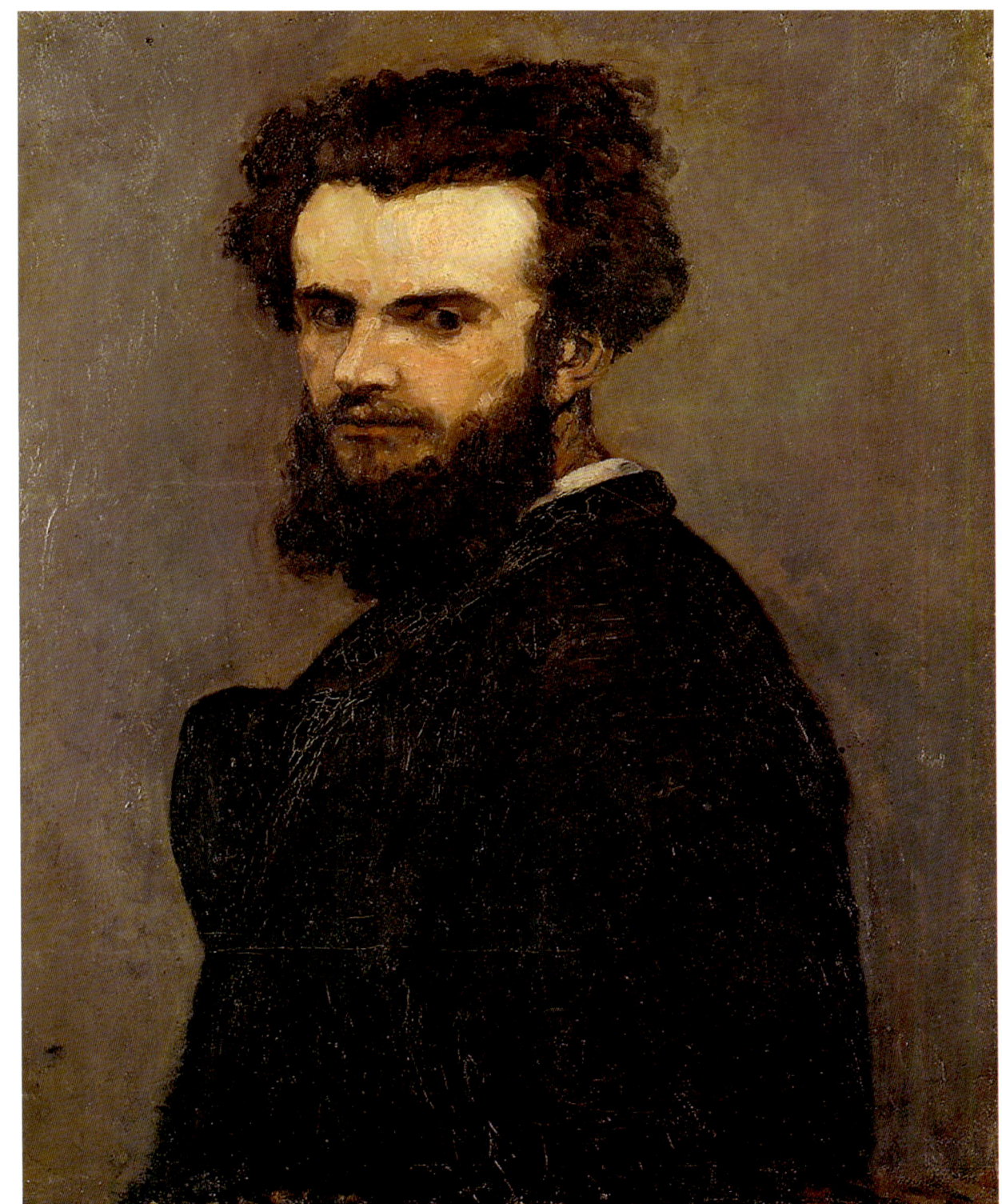

**Armand Guillaumin
(1841–1927)**

Self-portrait

Portrait de l'artiste

Selbstporträt

Autorretrato

Autoritratto

Zelfportret

c. 1875, Oil on canvas/Huile sur
toile, 73 × 60 cm, Musée d'Orsay,
Paris

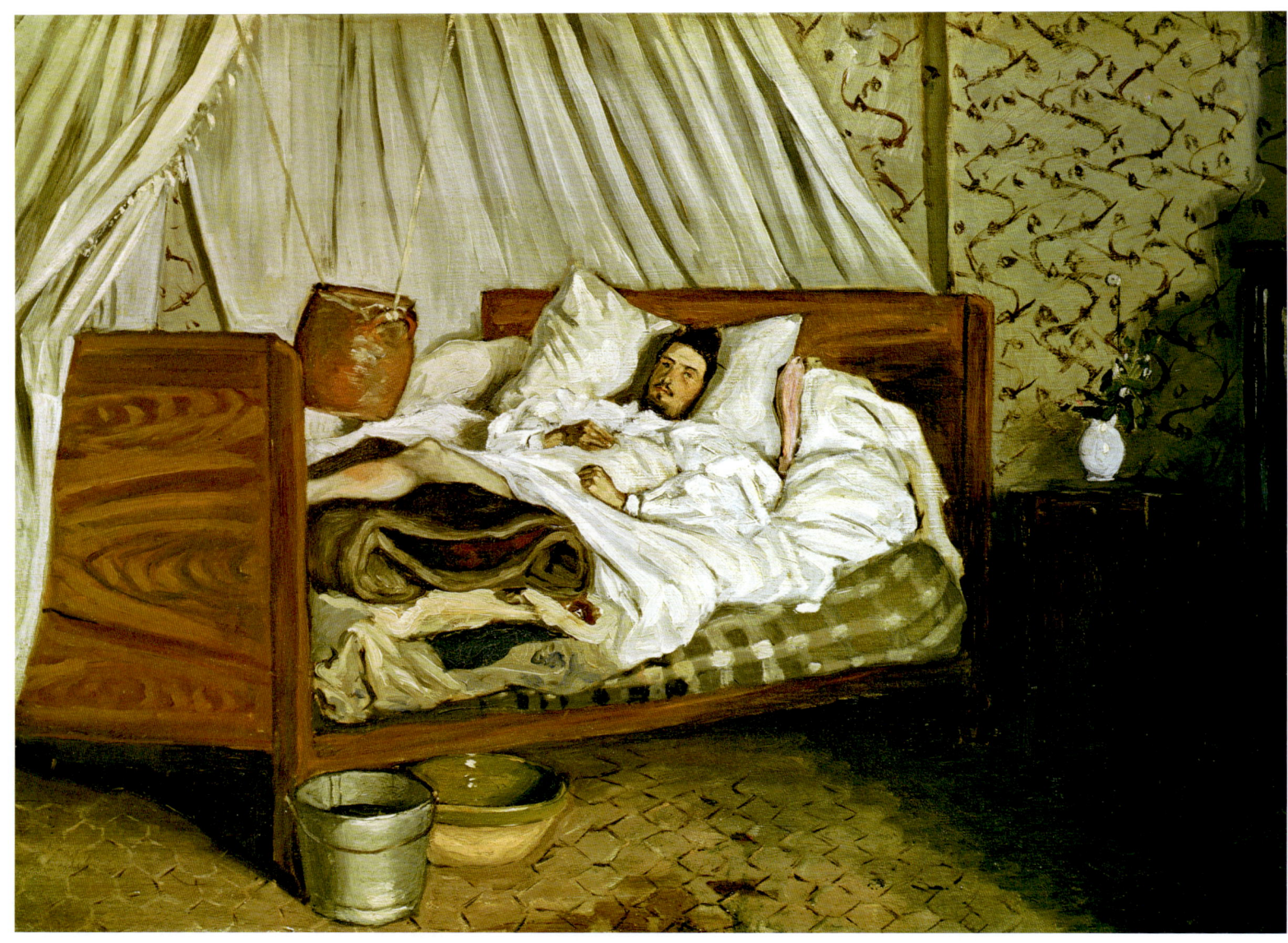

Fréderic Bazille (1841−1870)

The Improvised Ambulance, The Painter Monet Wounded at Chailly-en-Biere

L'Ambulance improvisée

Das improvisierte Krankenzimmer, der verwundete Maler Monet in Chailly-en-Biere

La habitación de hospital improvisada, el pintor convalenciente Monet en Chailly-en-Biere

L'ospedale da campo improvvisato, il pittore Monet ferito a Chailly-en-Biere

De geïmproviseerde ziekenkamer. de gewonde schilder Monet in Chailly-en-Bière

1865, Oil on canvas/Huile sur toile, 48 × 65 cm, Musée d'Orsay, Paris

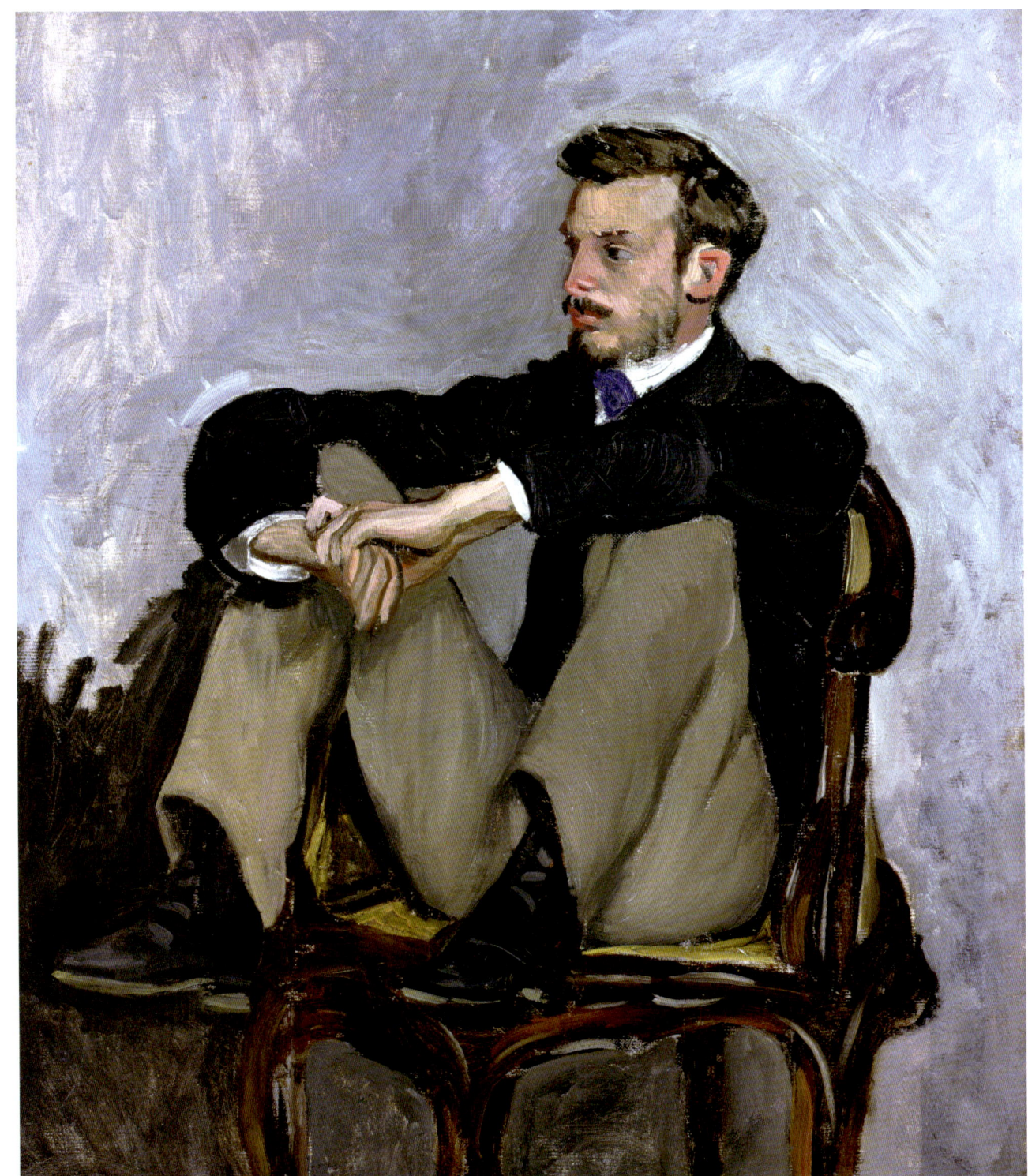

Fréderic Bazille
(1841–1870)

Portrait of Auguste
Renoir

Portrait d'Auguste
Renoir

Bildnis Auguste Renoir

Retrato de Auguste
Renoir

Ritratto di Auguste
Renoir

Portret van Auguste
Renoir

1867, Oil on canvas/Huile
sur toile, 61,2 × 51 cm,
Musée d'Orsay, Paris

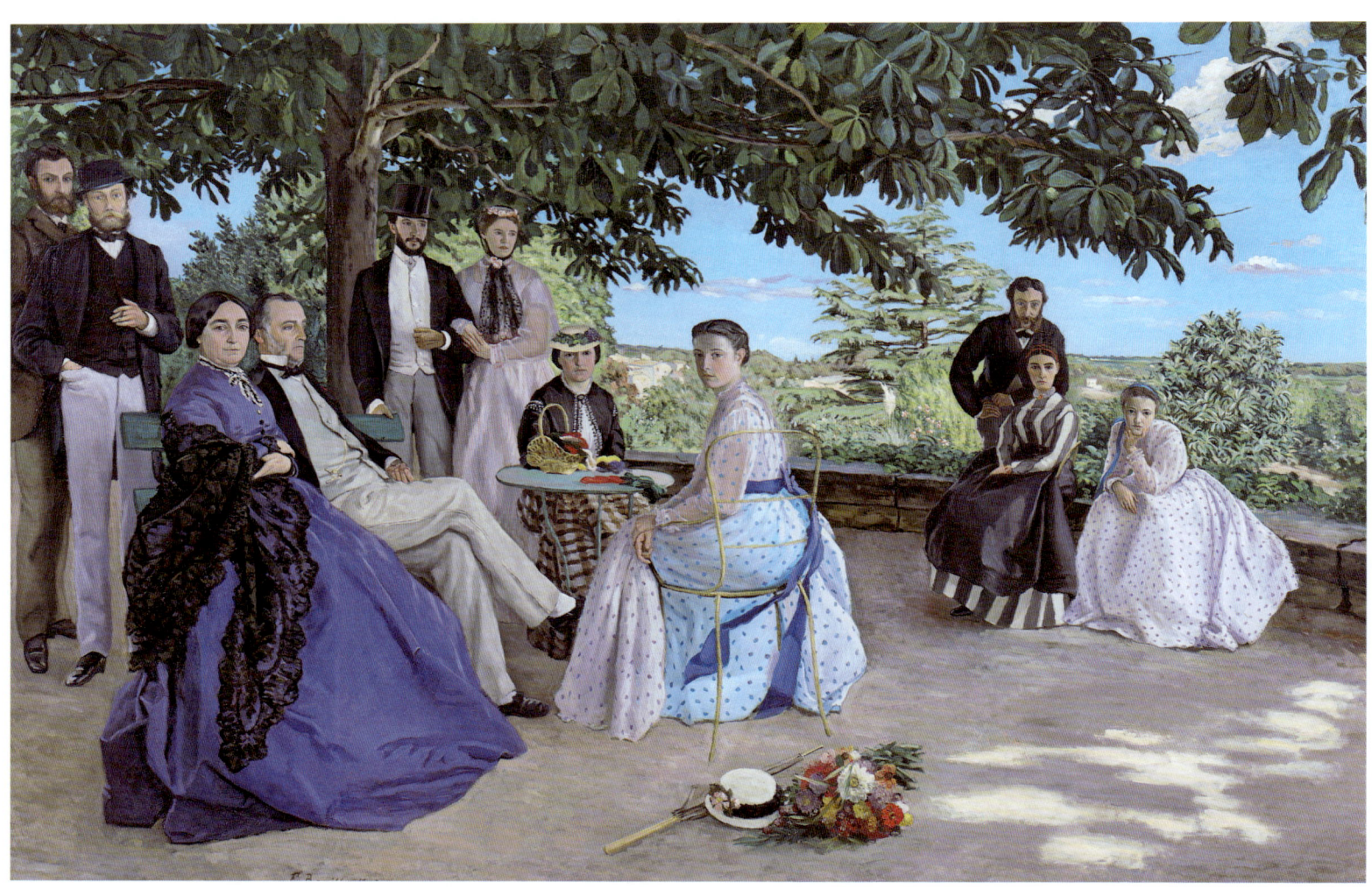

Fréderic Bazille (1841–1870)

Family reunion

Réunion de famille, *dit aussi* Portraits de famille

Familientreffen

Encuentro familiar

Riunione di famiglia

Familiereünie

1867, Oil on canvas/Huile sur toile, 152 × 230 cm, Musée d'Orsay, Paris

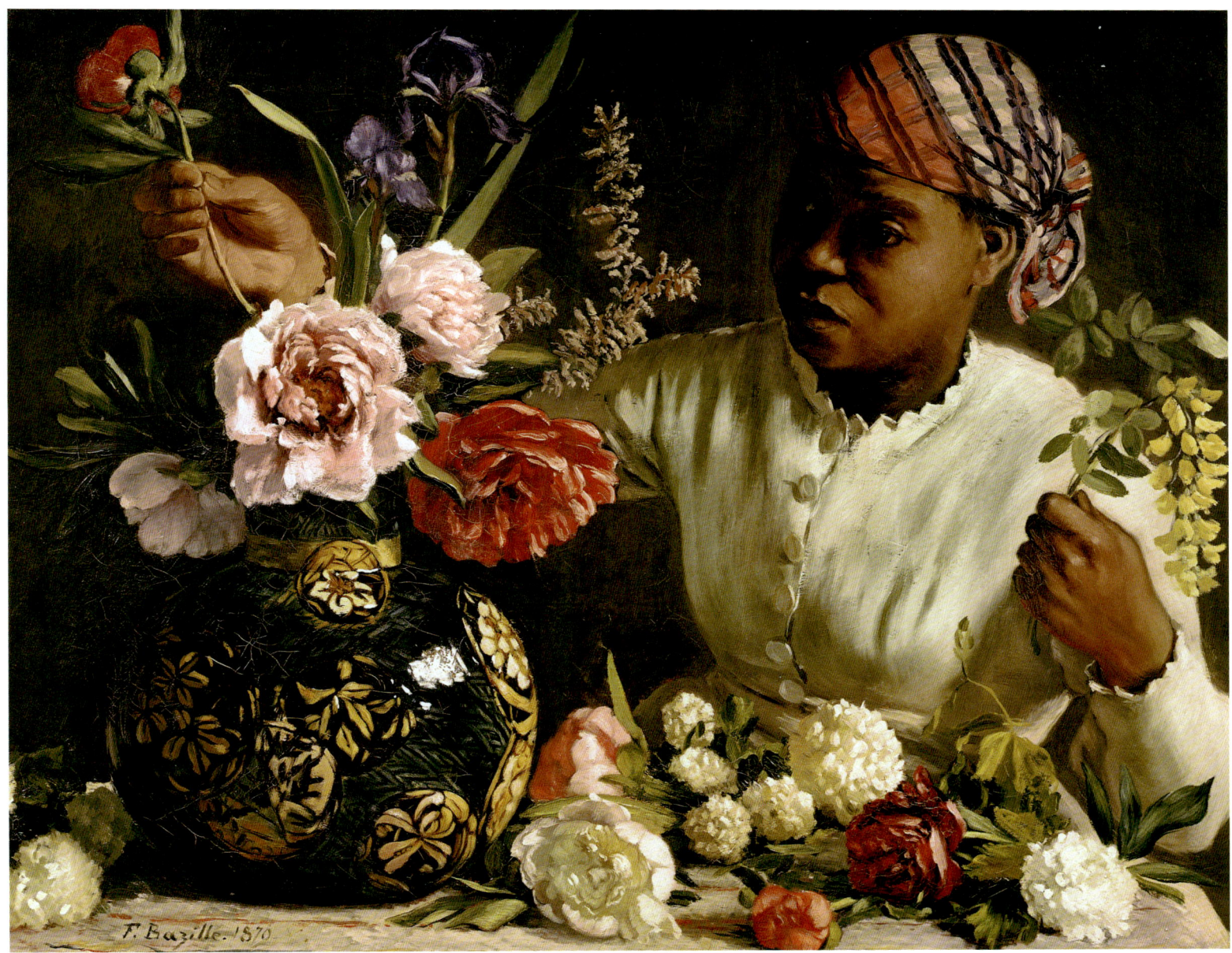

Fréderic Bazille (1841–1870)

Negress with Peonies

La Négresse aux pivoines

Negerin mit Pfingstrosen

Negra con peonías

Negra con peonie

Negerin met pioenrozen

1870, Oil on canvas/Huile sur toile, 60 × 75 cm, Musée Fabre, Montpellier

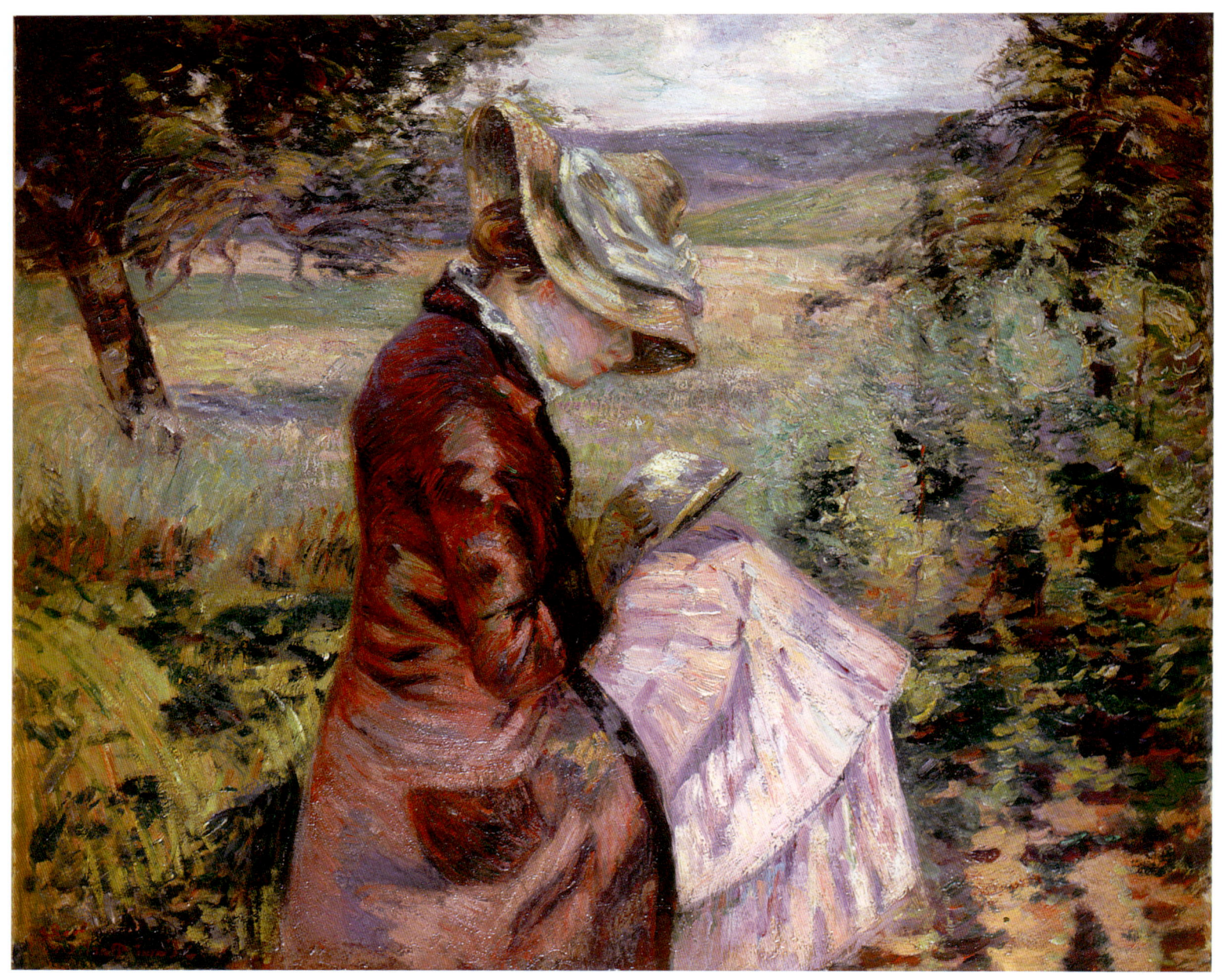

Armand Guillaumin (1841–1927)

Madame Guillaumin reading   Madame Guillaumin lesend   Madame Guillamin che legge

Madame Guillaumin lisant   Madame Guillaumin leyendo   Madame Guillaumin, lezend

c. 1887, Oil on canvas/Huile sur toile, 46,5 × 55 cm, Private collection

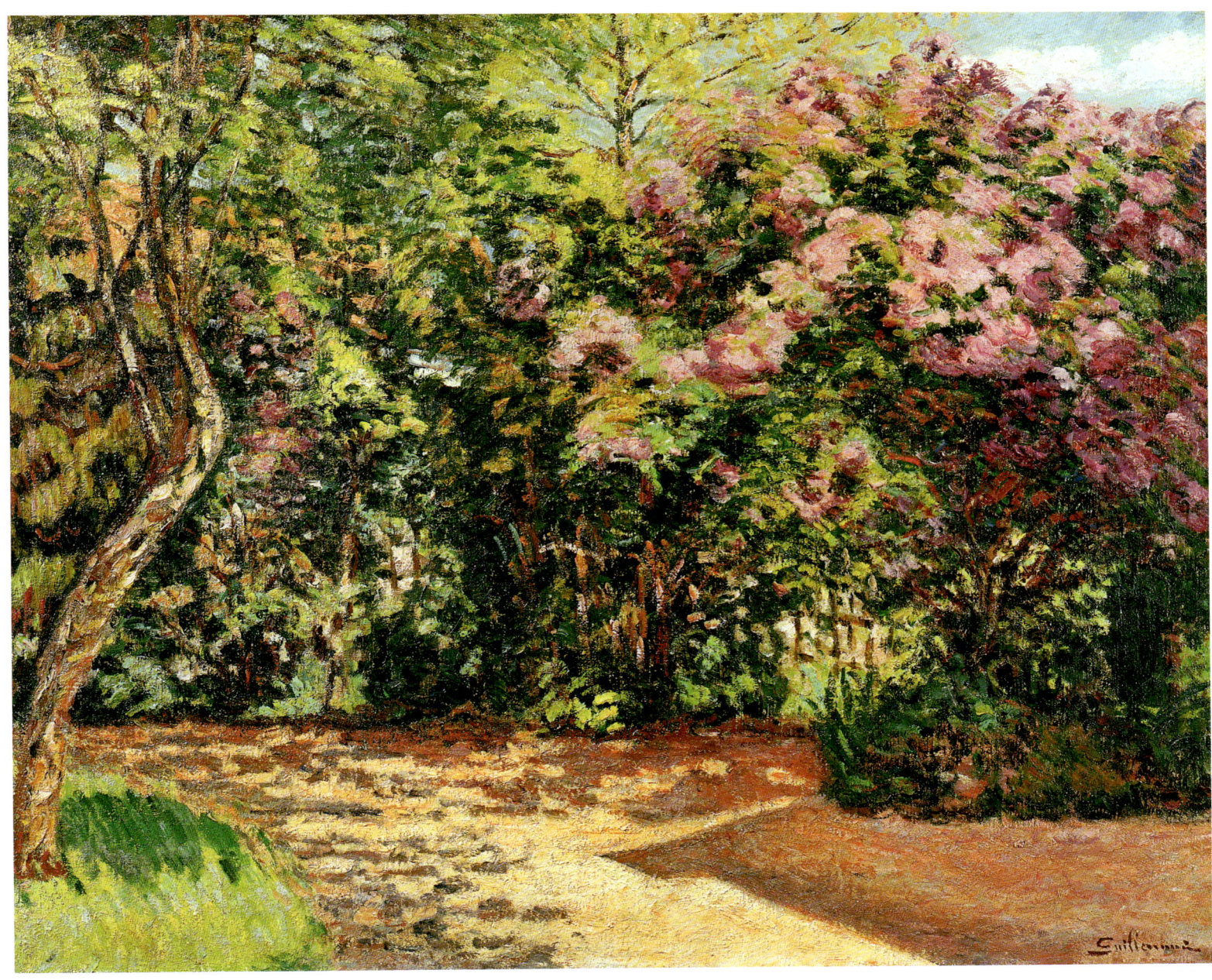

Armand Guillaumin (1841–1927)

Lilac, the Artist's Garden   Flieder im Garten des Künstlers   Lillà nel giardino dell'artista

Les Lilas, jardin de l'artiste   Lilas en el jardín del artista   Seringen in de tuin van de kunstenaar

n. d., Oil on canvas/Huile sur toile, 64 × 80 cm, Musée Bonnat-Helleu, Bayonne

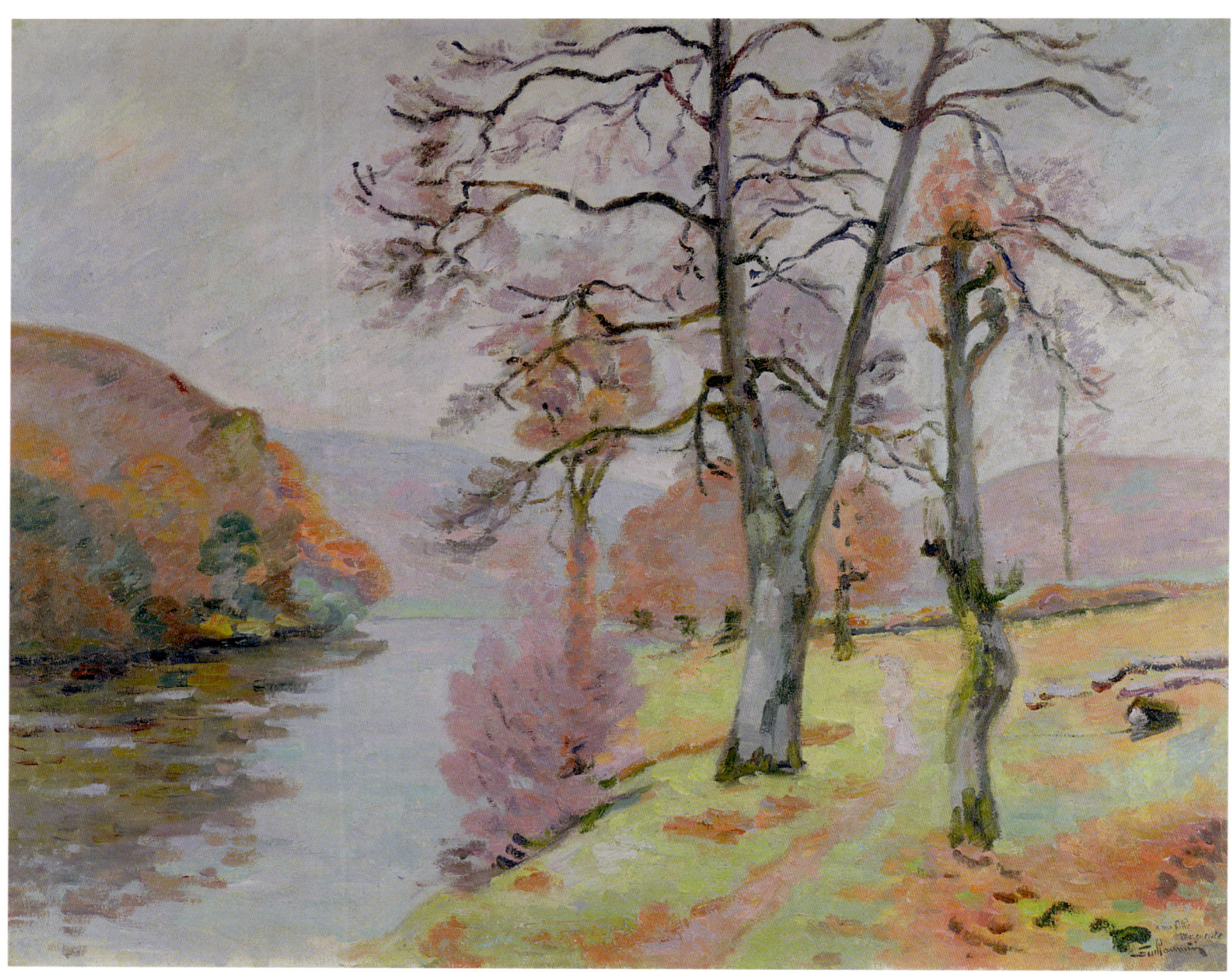

Armand Guillaumin (1841–1927)

Crozant

1912, Oil on canvas/Huile sur toile, 73,5 × 92 cm, Private collection

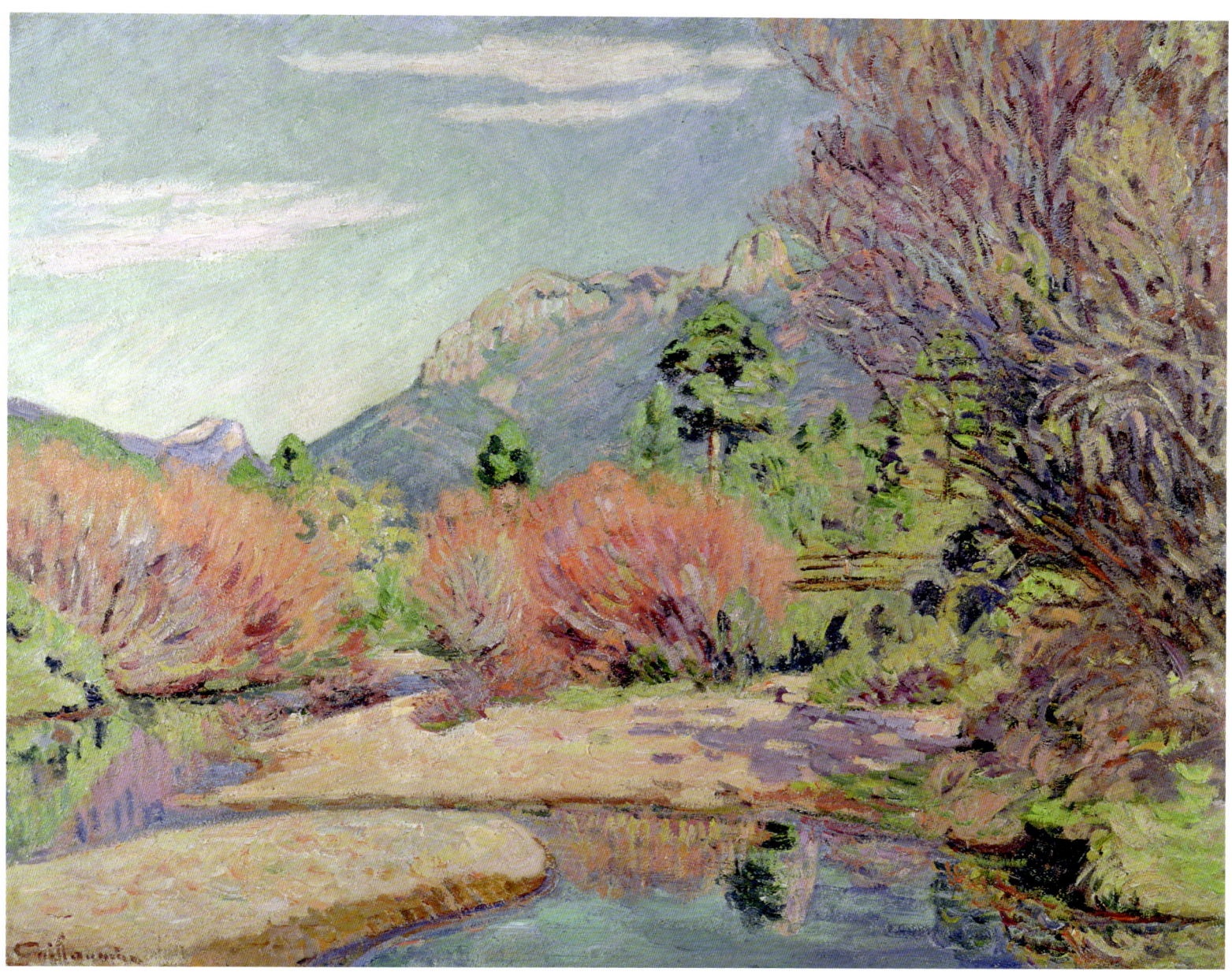

Armand Guillaumin (1841–1927)

The Banks of the Sedelle at Crozant	Die Ufer der Sedelle bei Crozant	Le rive del Sedelle a Crozant
Crozant, les bords de la Sédelle	La orilla del Sedelle en Crozant	De oever van de Sédelle bij Crozant

1895, Oil on canvas/Huile sur toile, 65,5 × 81,2 cm, Musée Bonnat-Helleu, Bayonne

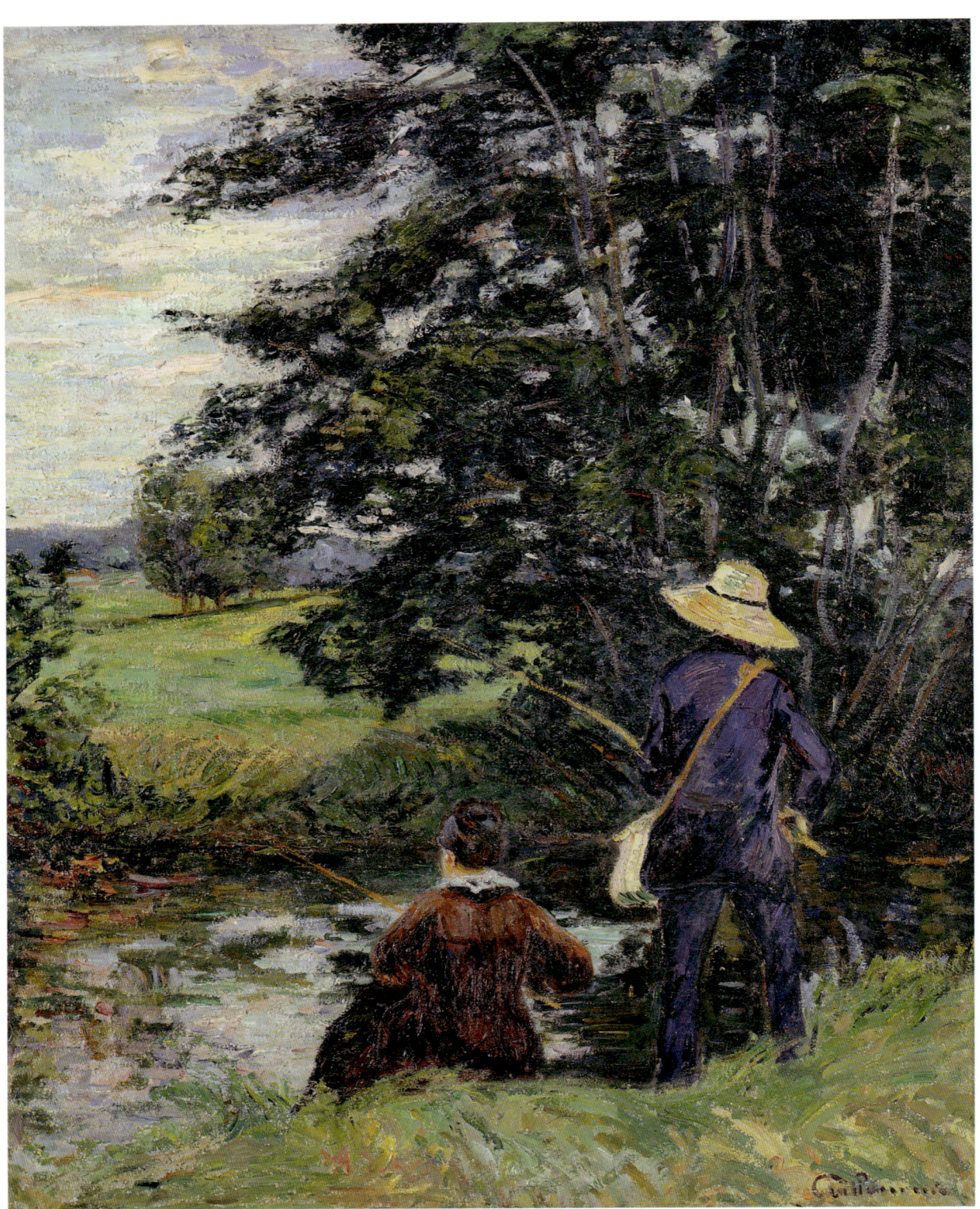

Armand Guillaumin (1841–1927)

The Anglers

Les Pêcheurs

Die Angler

Los pescadores

I pescatori

De vissers

c. 1885, Oil on canvas/Huile sur toile, 81 × 66 cm, Musée d'Orsay, Paris

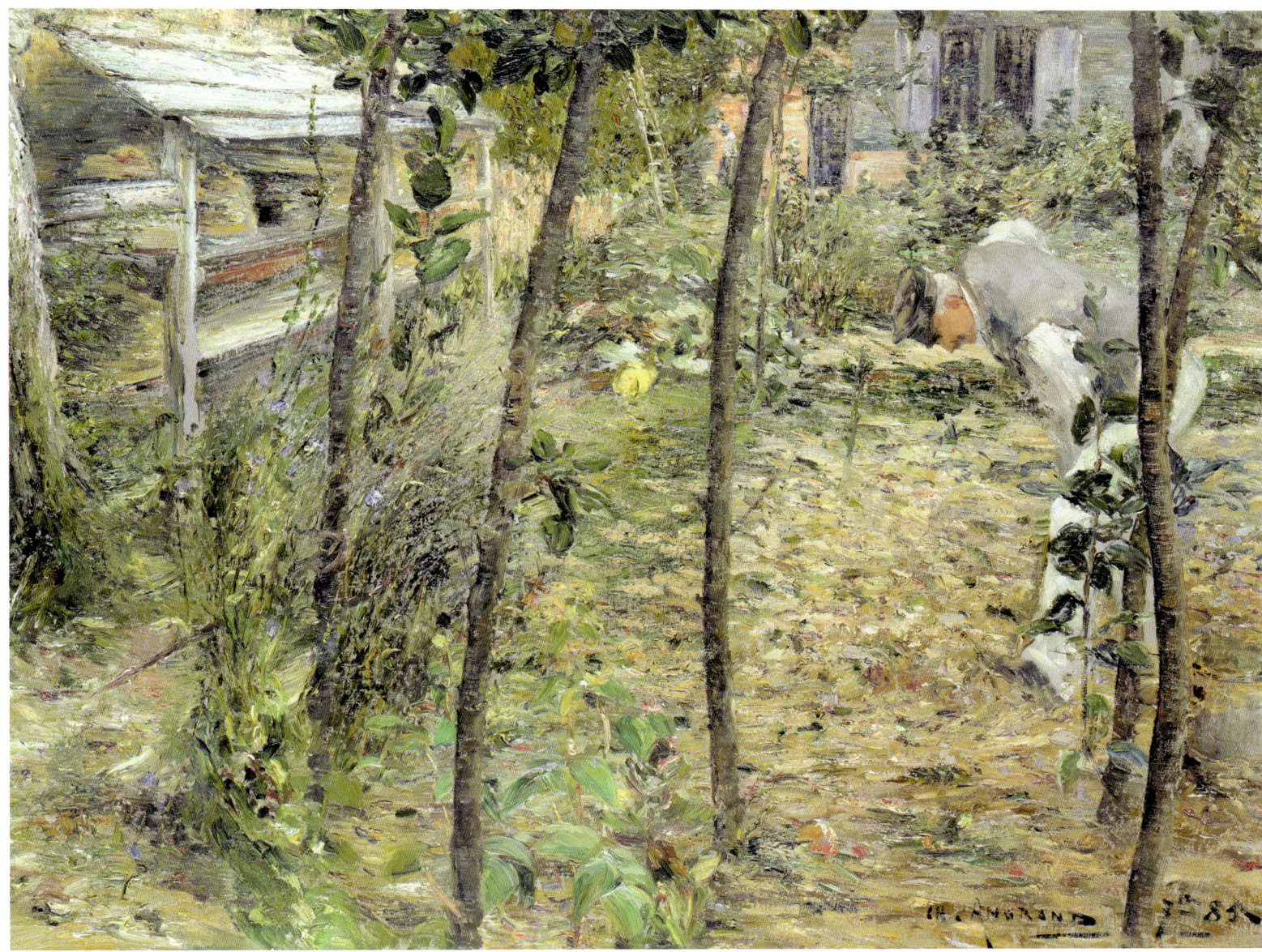

Charles Angrand (1854–1926)

In the Garden

Dans le jardin

Im Garten

En el jardín

In giardino

In de tuin

1885, Oil on canvas/Huile sur toile, 73 × 92 cm, Musée des Beaux-Arts, Rouen

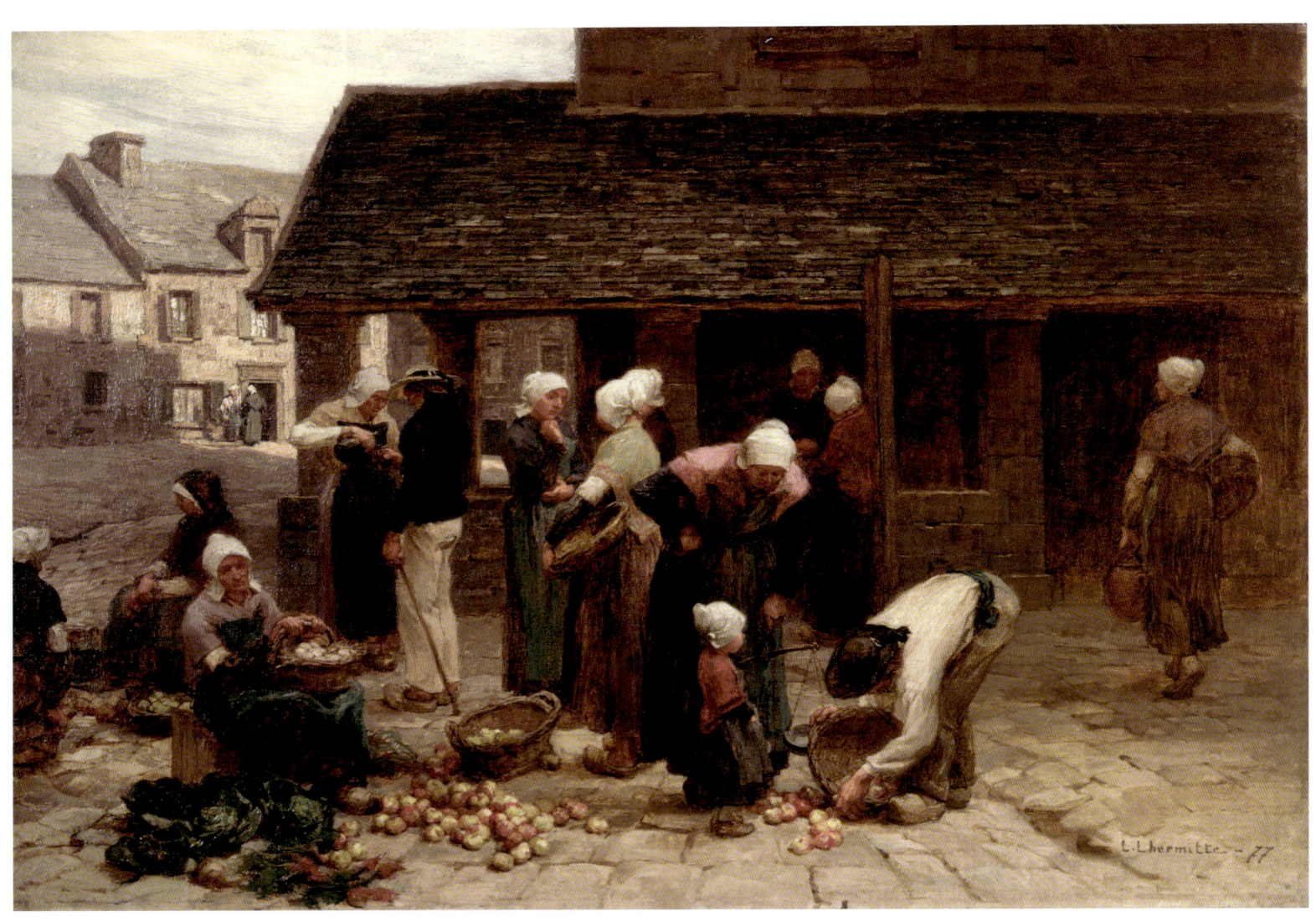

Léon-Augustin Lhermitte (1844–1925)

The Market Place of Ploudalmezeau, Brittany

Le Marché de Ploudalmezeau, en Bretagne

Der Marktplatz von Ploudalmezeau, Bretagne

La plaza del mercado de Ploudalmezeau, Bretaña

La piazza del mercato a Ploudalmezeau, Bretagna

De markt van Ploudalmézeau, Bretagne

1877, Oil on canvas/Huile sur toile, 40 × 57,2 cm, Victoria & Albert Museum, London

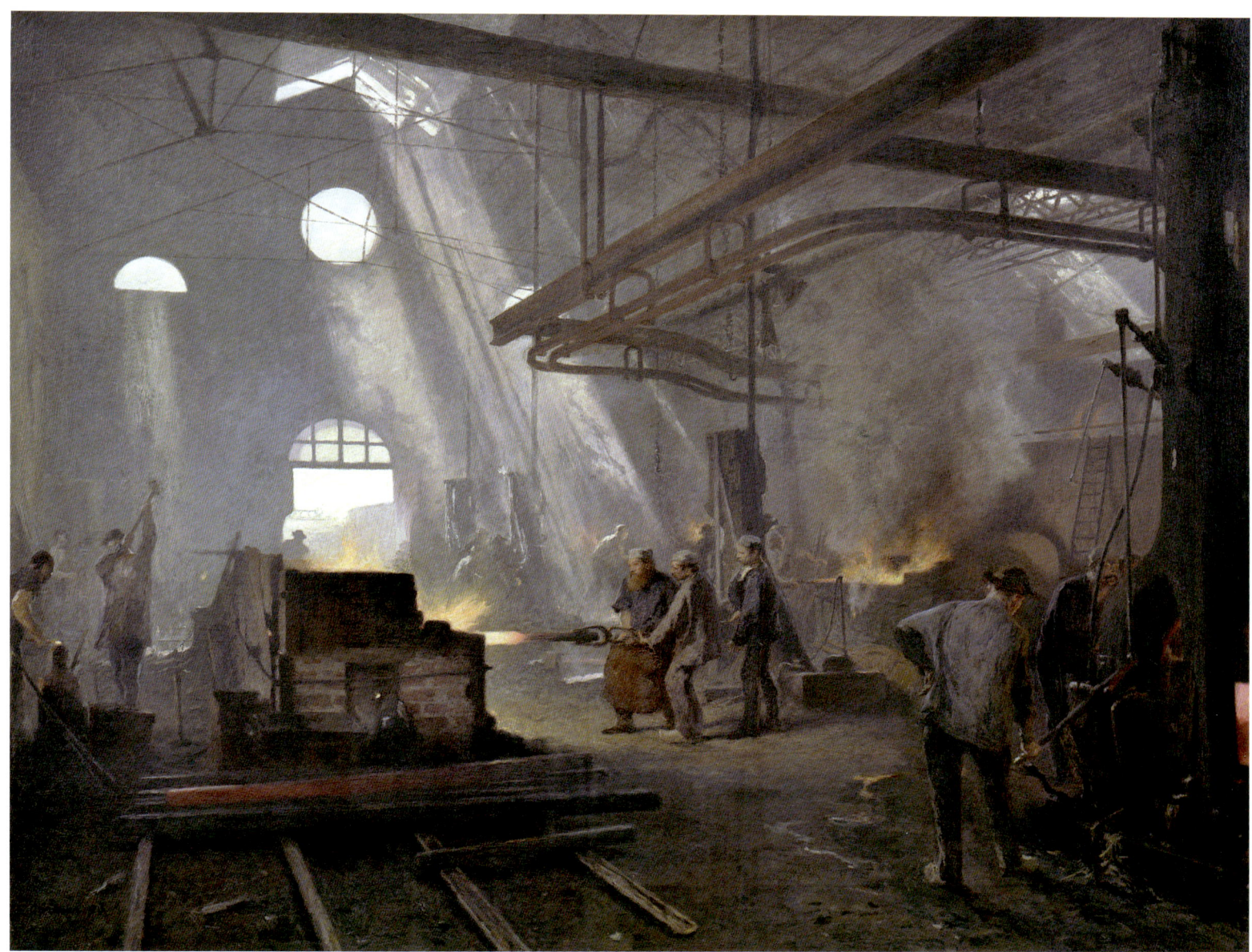

Fernand Cormon (1845–1924)

A Forge

Une Forge

Eine Schmiede

Una fragua

Una fucina

Een smidse

1893, Oil on canvas/Huile sur toile, 72 × 90 cm, Musée d'Orsay, Paris

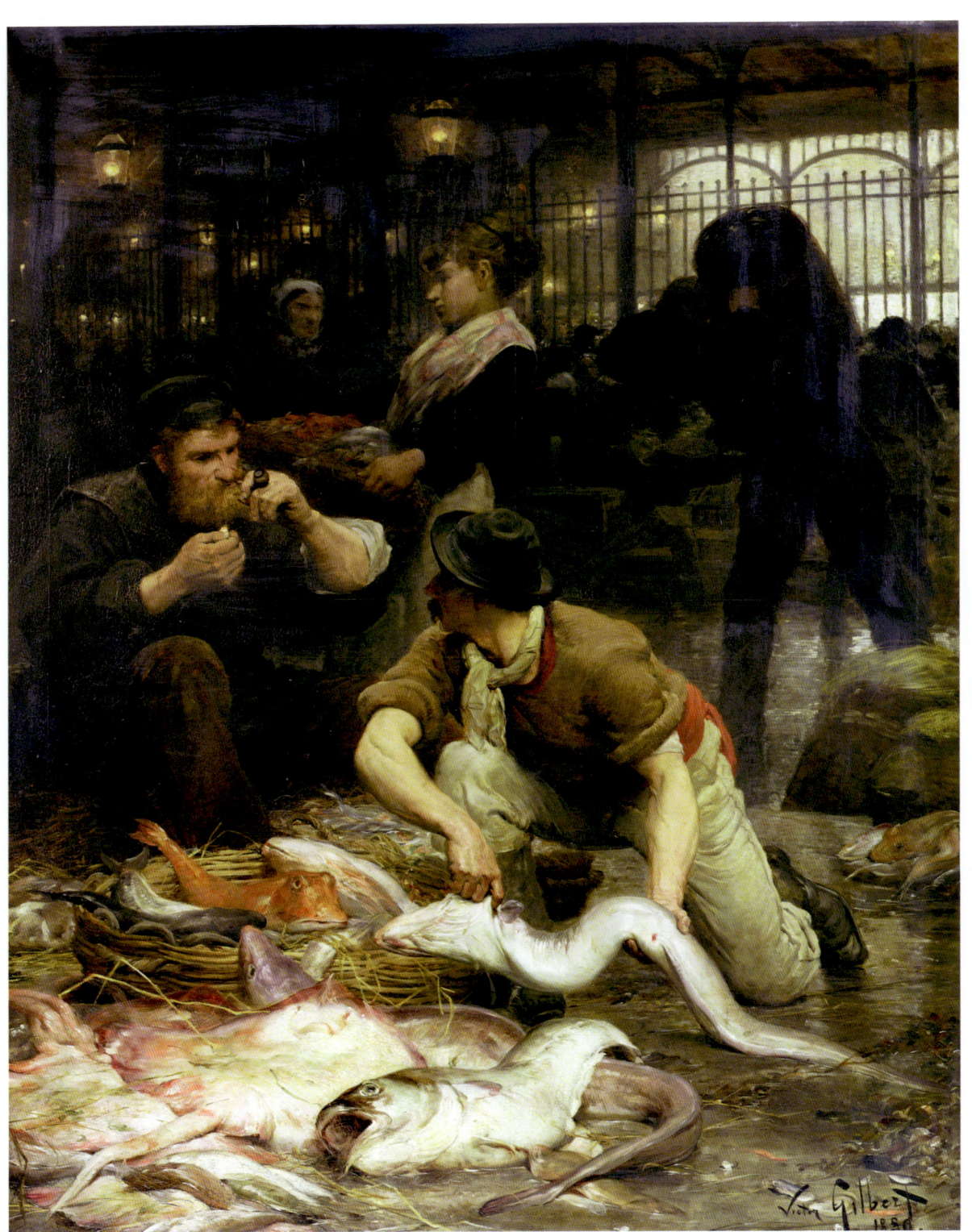

Victor Gilbert (1847–1933)

The Fish Market in the Morning

La Halle aux Poissons, le matin

Der Fischmarkt am Morgen

El mercado del pescado por la mañana

Mercato del pesce al mattino

De vismarkt in de ochtend

1880, Oil on canvas/Huile sur toile, 181 × 140 cm, Palais des Beaux-Arts, Lille

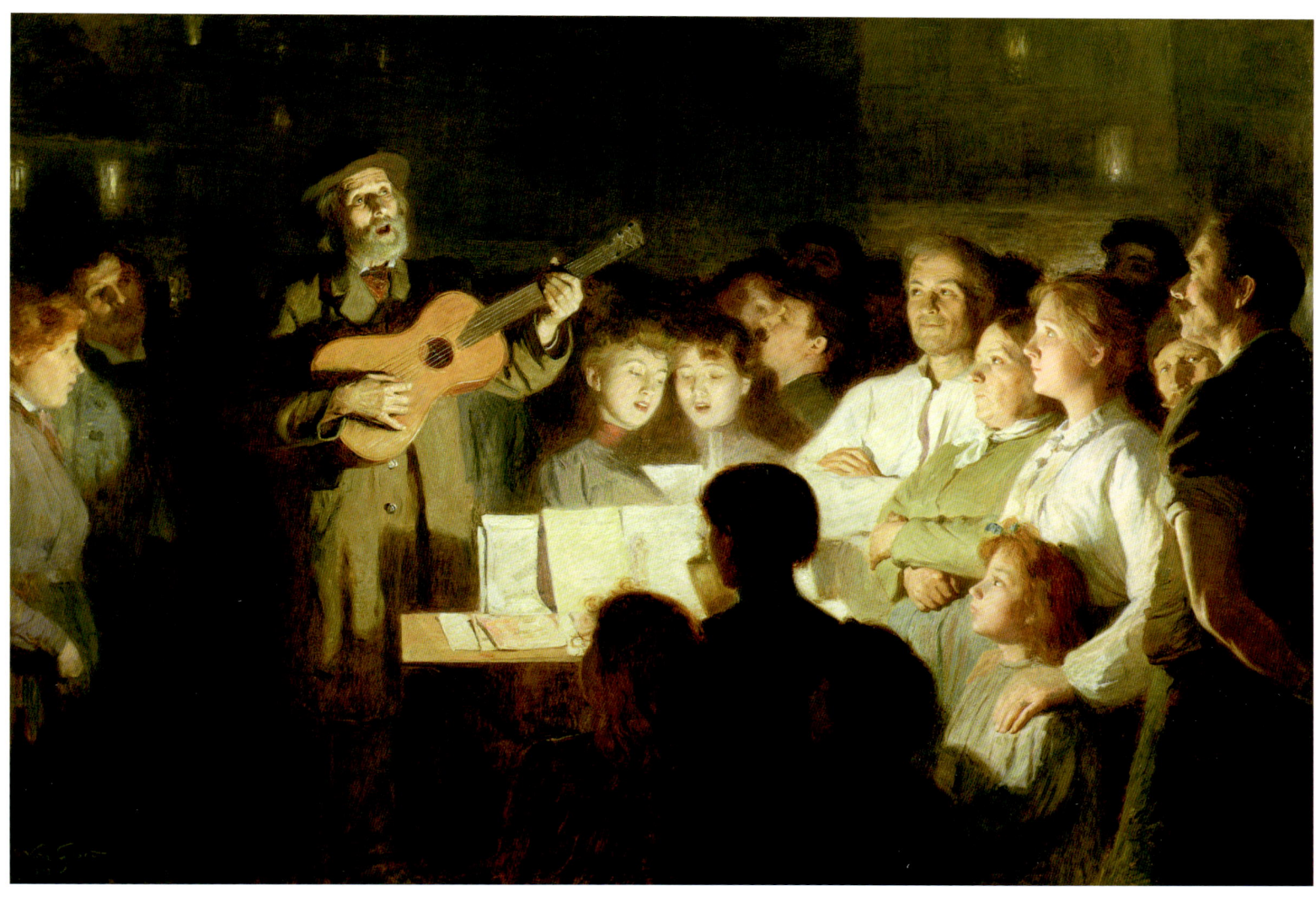

Victor Gilbert (1847–1933)

The Song Seller

Le Marchand de chansons

Der Liedverkäufer

El vendedor de canciones

Il suonatore

De liedjesverkoper

1908, Oil on canvas/Huile sur toile, 108,5 × 157,5 cm, Musée du Petit Palais, Paris

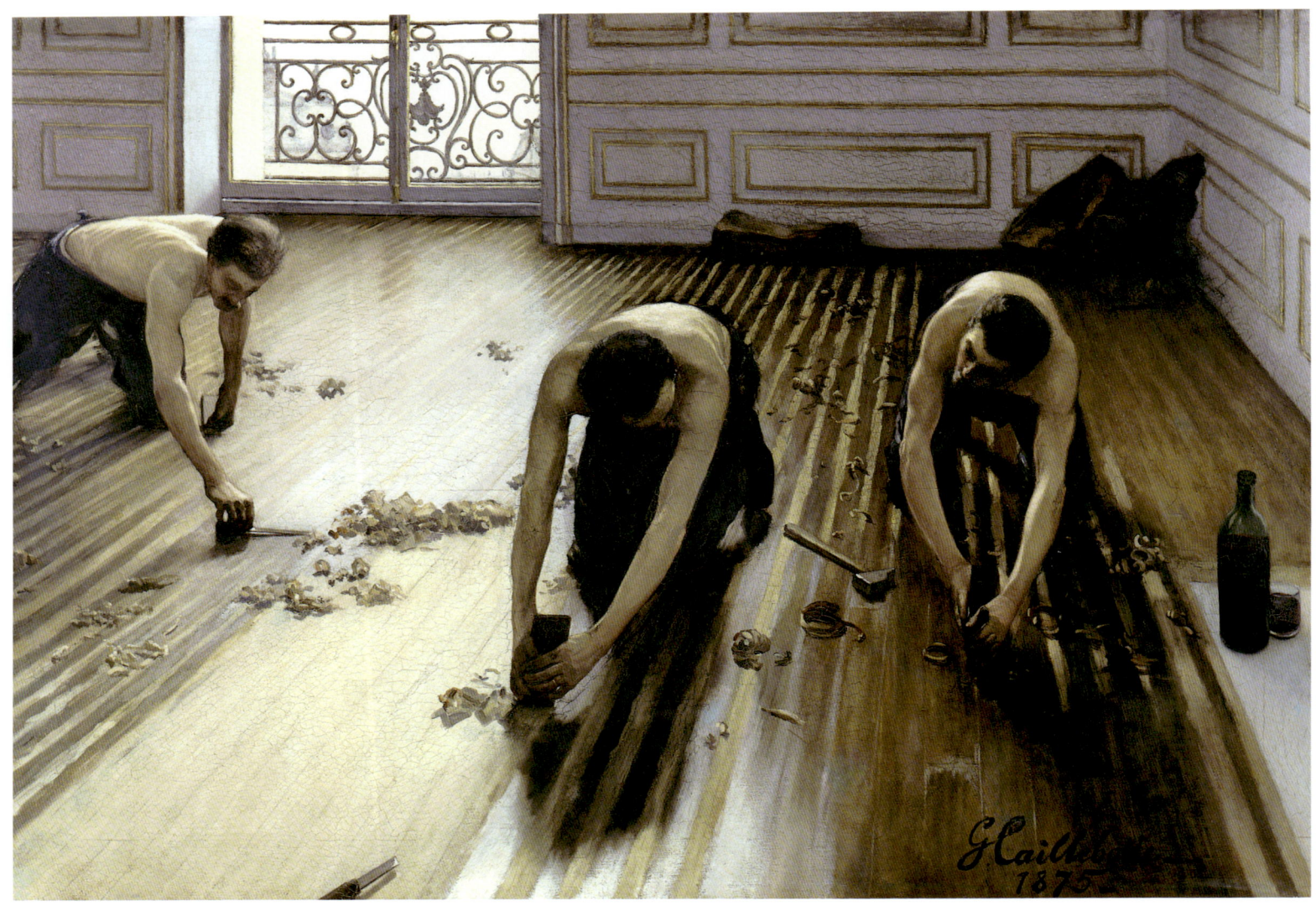

Gustave Caillebotte (1848–1894)

The Parquet Planers

Les Raboteurs de parquet

Die Parkettschleifer

El lijador de suelos

I piallatori di parquet

De parketschuurders

1875, Oil on canvas/Huile sur toile, 102 × 147 cm, Musée d'Orsay, Paris

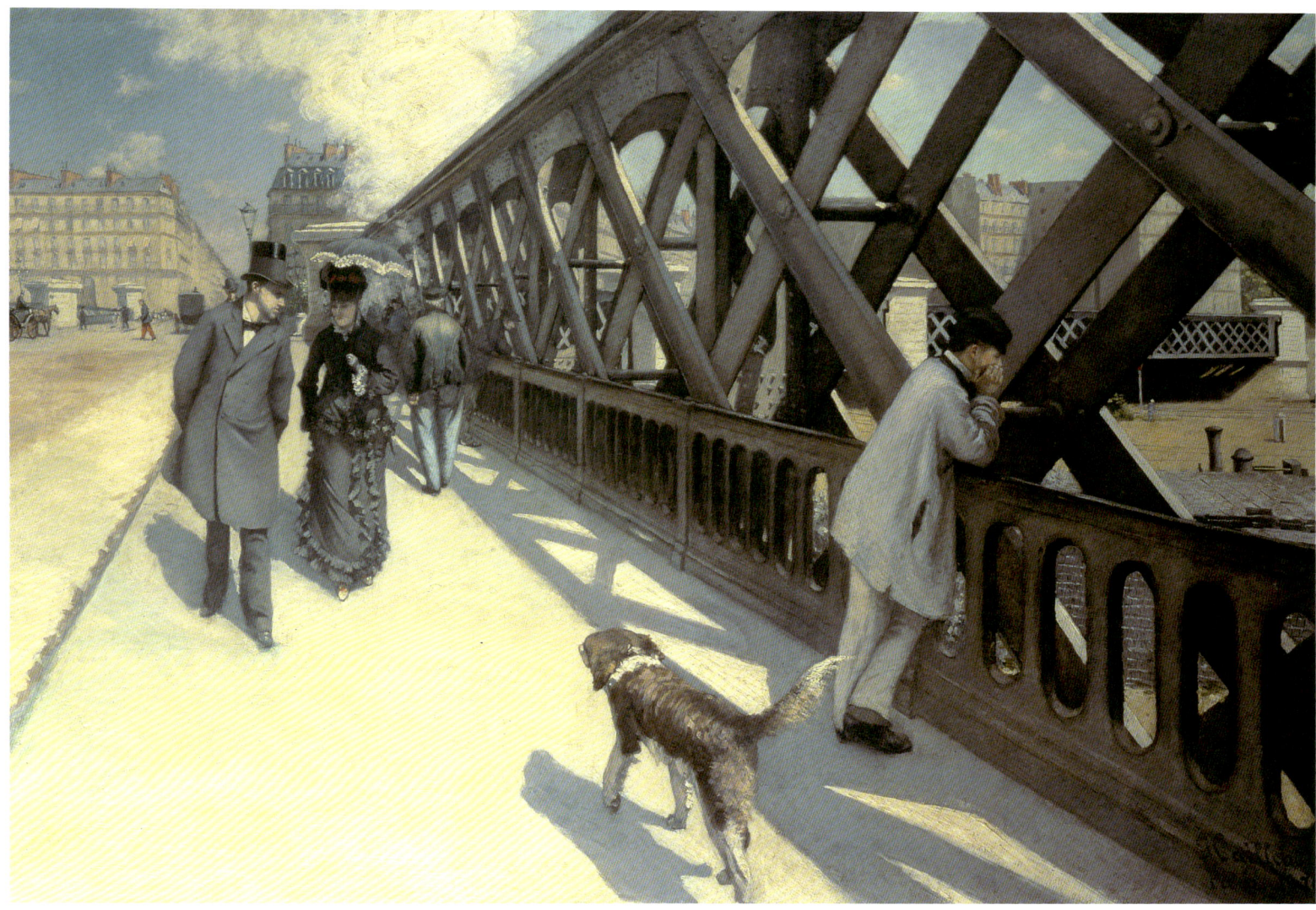

Gustave Caillebotte (1848–1894)

Le Pont de L'Europe

Le Pont de l'Europe

Die Europabrücke

El puente de Europa

Il ponte Europa

De Europabrug

1876, Oil on canvas/Huile sur toile, 125 × 181 cm, Musée du Petit Palais, Genève

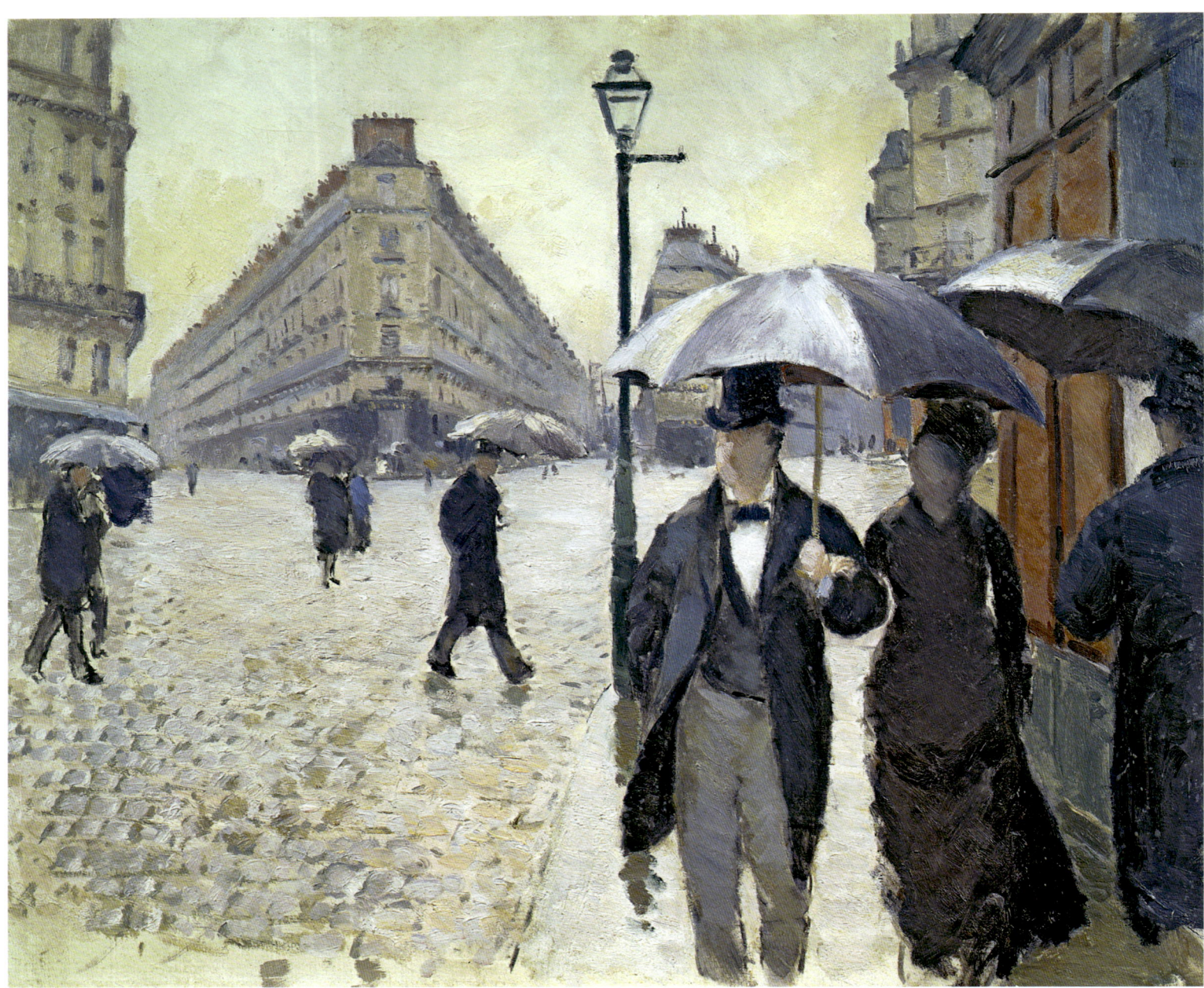

Gustave Caillebotte (1848–1894)

Sketch for Paris, a Rainy Day

Rue de Paris, temps de pluie

Skizze für Paris, Place de
l'Europe, ein Regentag

Boceto para París, Place de
l'Europe, un día de lluvia

Schizzo per Parigi, Place de
l'Europe, un giorno di pioggia

Schets voor Parijs, Place de
l'Europe, een regenachtige dag'

1877, Oil on canvas/Huile sur toile, 54 × 65 cm, Musée Marmottan Monet, Paris

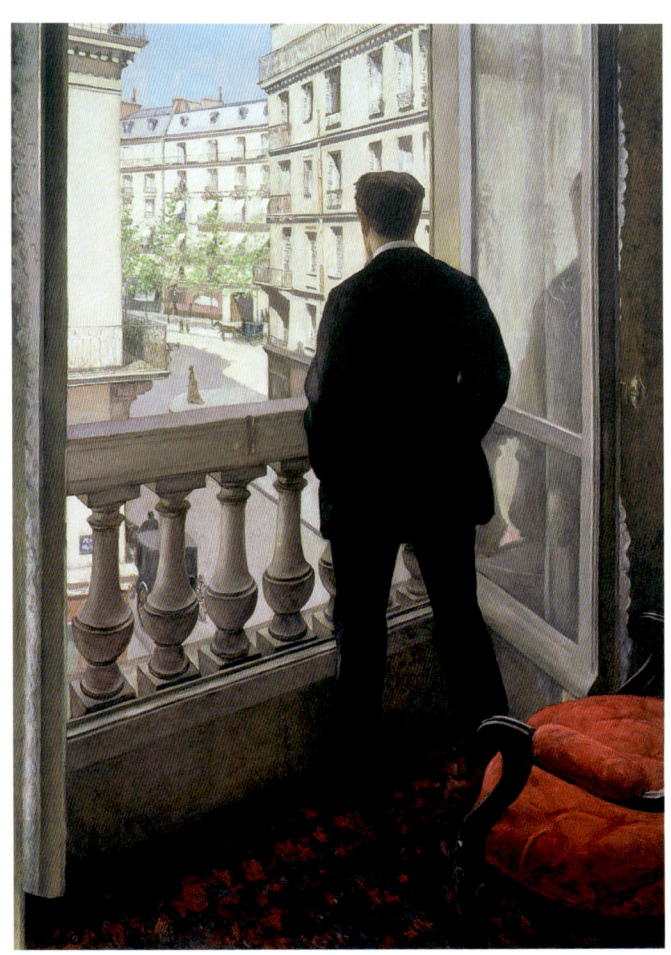

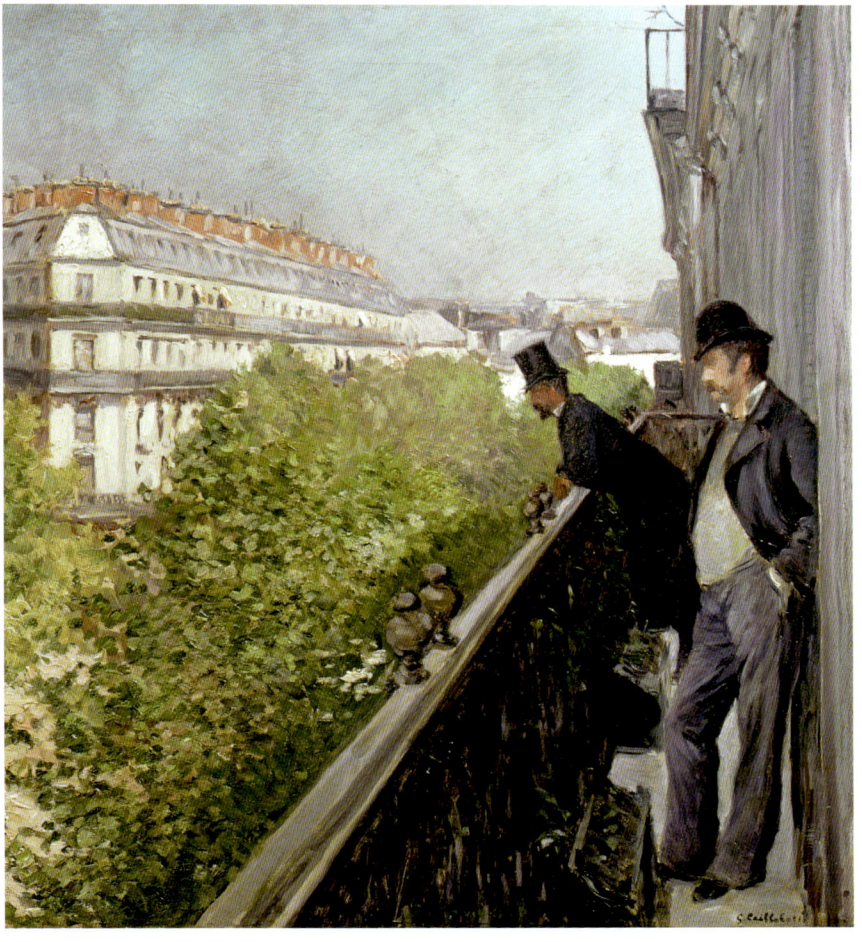

Gustave Caillebotte (1848–1894)

Man at the Window

Homme nu-tête vu de dos à la fenêtre

Mann am Fenster

Hombre en la ventana

Uomo alla finestra

Man aan het raam

1875, Oil on canvas/Huile sur toile, 117 × 83 cm, Private collection

Gustave Caillebotte (1848–1894)

A Balcony, Boulevard Haussmann

Un Balcon, boulevard Haussmann

Ein Balkon, Boulevard Haussmann

Un balcón en el Boulevard Haussmann

Un balcone di Boulevard Haussmann

Een balkon, Boulevard Haussmann

1880, Oil on canvas/Huile sur toile, 69 × 62 cm, Private collection

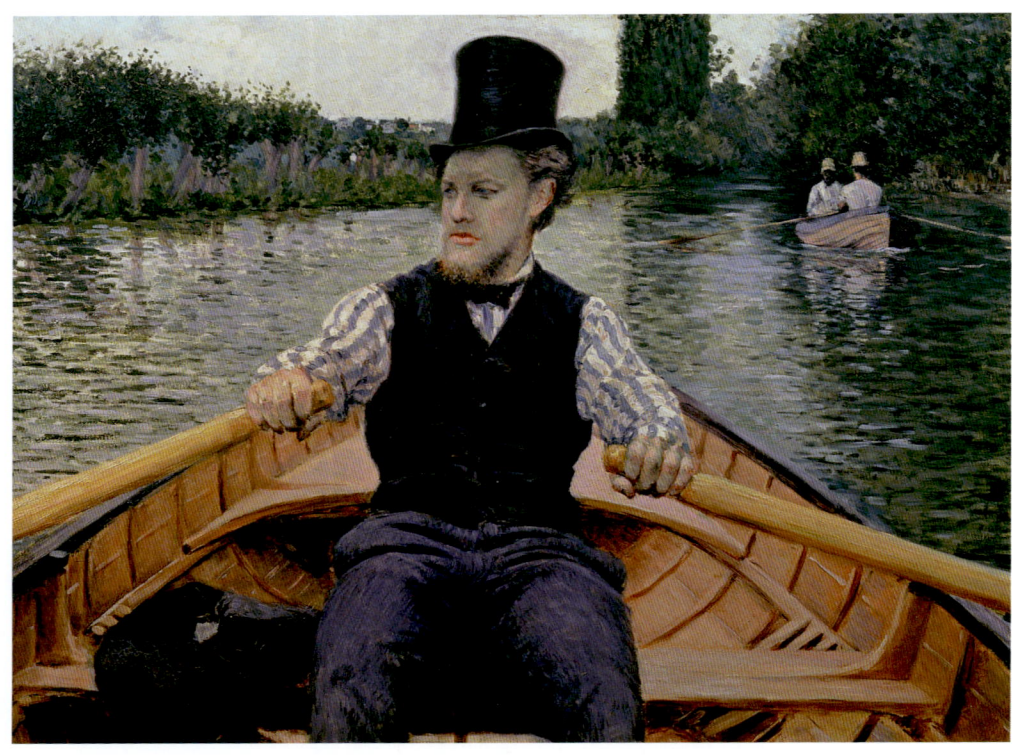

Gustave Caillebotte (1848–1894)

Rower in a Top Hat

Canotier au chapeau haut-de-forme

Ruderer mit Zylinder

Remero con sombrero de copa

Rematore con cappello a cilindro

Roeier met hoge hoed

c. 1877–1878, Oil on canvas/Huile sur toile,
90 × 117 cm, Private collection

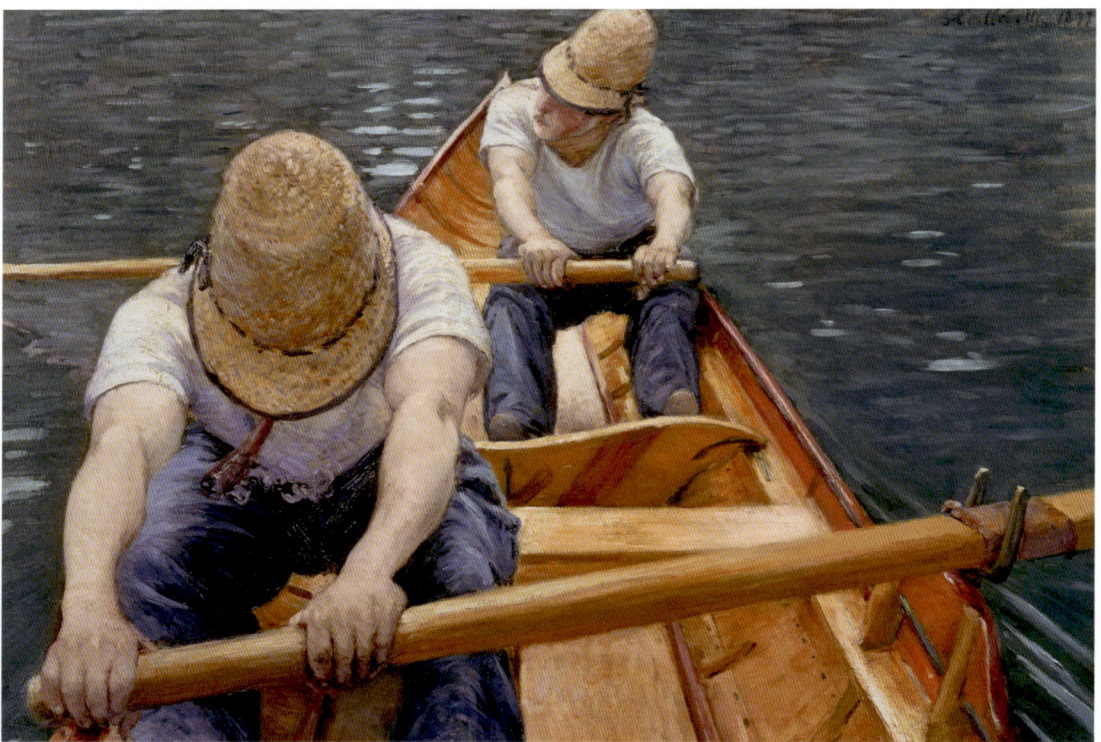

Gustave Caillebotte (1848–1894)

Boaters Rowing on the Yerres

Canotier sur l'Yerres

Ruderer auf der Yerres

Remeros en el Yerres

Canottieri sullo Yerres

Roeiers op de rivier de Yerres

1877–1879, Oil on canvas/Huile sur toile,
81 × 116 cm, Private collection

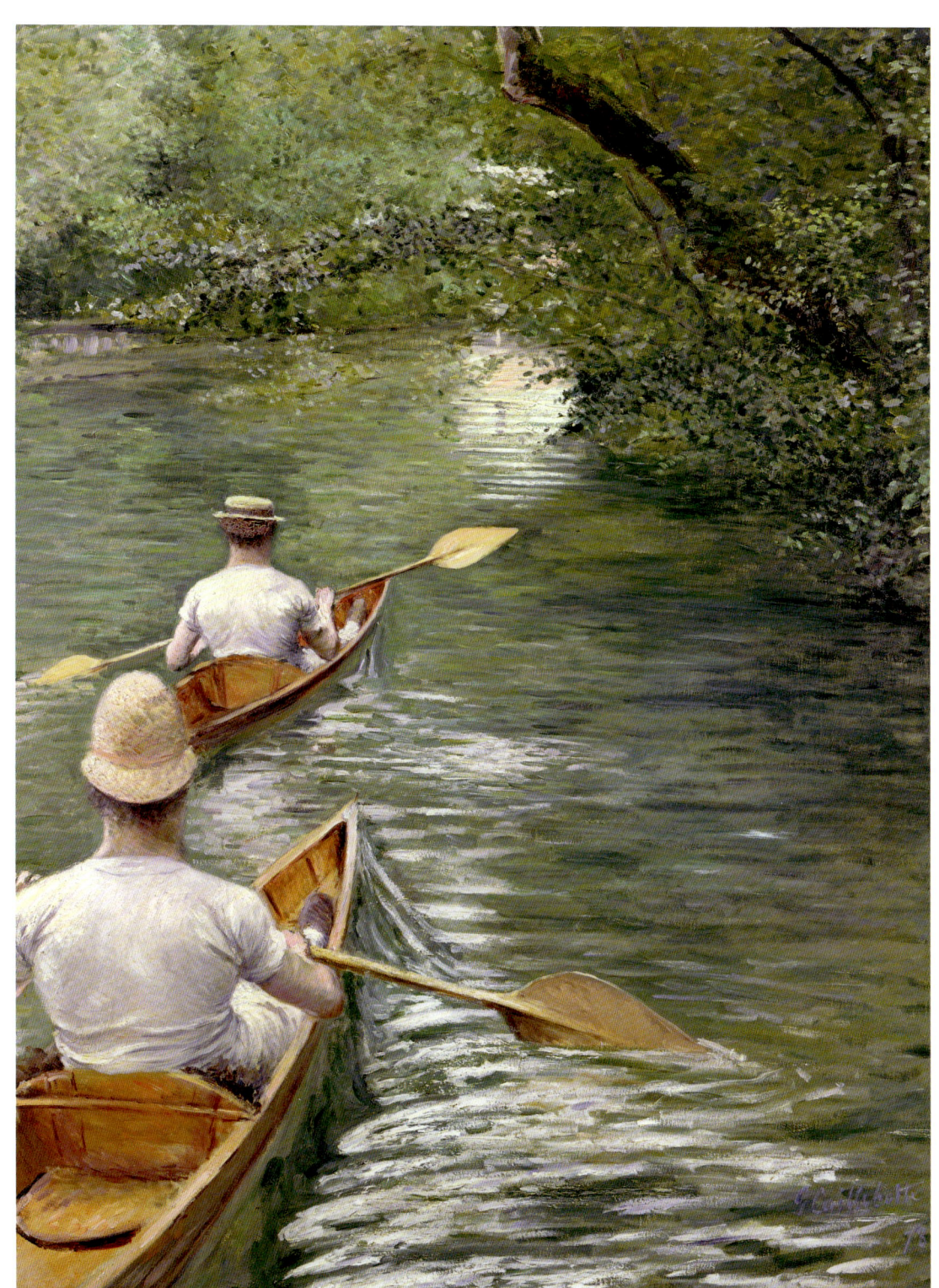

Gustave Caillebotte (1848–1894)

The Canoes

Les Périssoires

Die Kanufahrer

Los piragüistas

I canottieri

De kanovaarders

1878, Oil on canvas/Huile sur toile,
155 × 108,5 cm, Musée des Beaux-Arts, Rennes

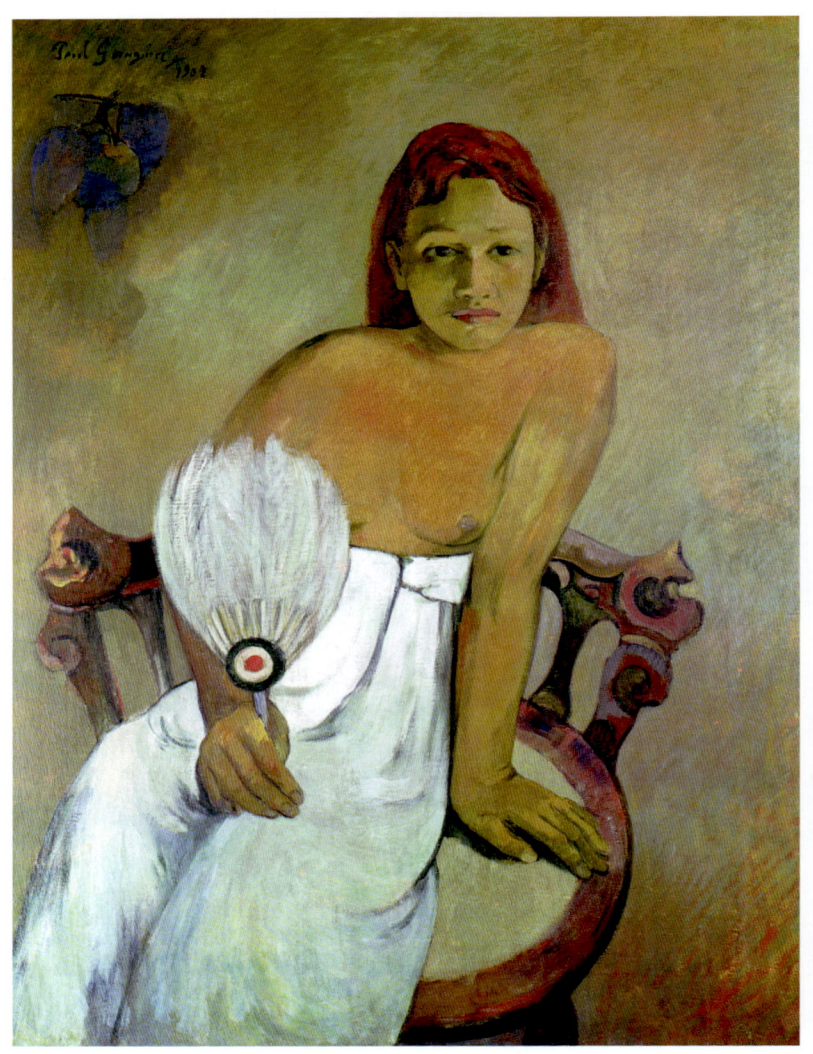

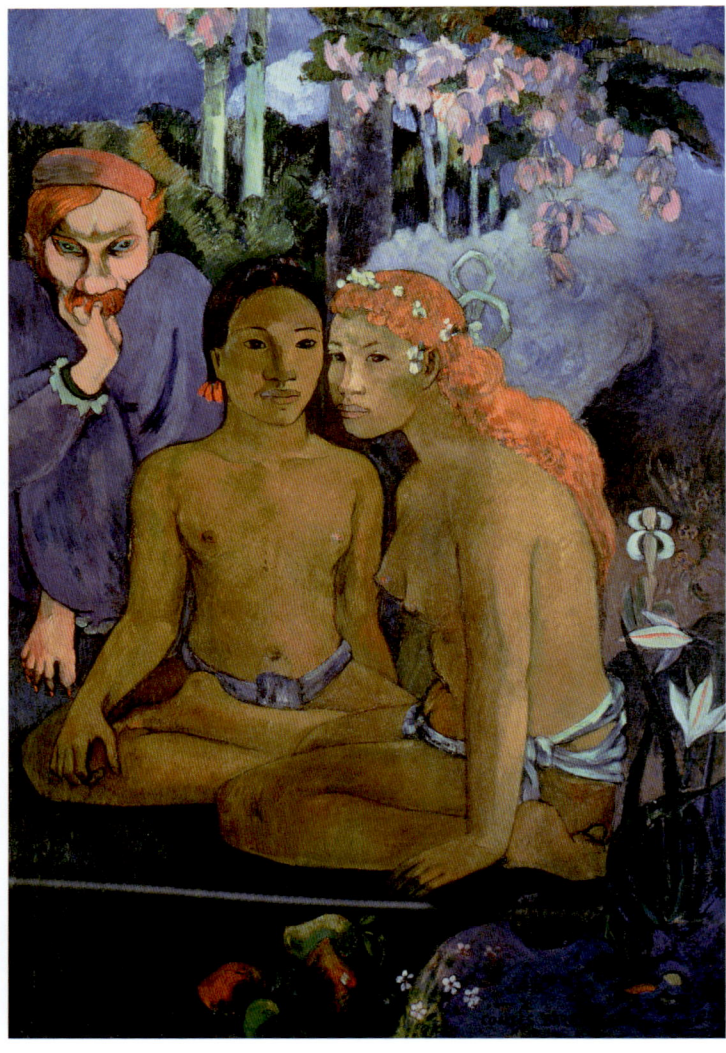

Paul Gauguin (1848–1903)

Girl with Fan

Jeune fille

Mädchen mit Fächer

Niña con abanico

Ragazza con ventaglio

Meisje met waaier

1902, Oil on canvas/Huile sur toile, 92 × 73 cm, Museum Folkwang, Essen

Paul Gauguin (1848–1903)

Contes Barbares

Contes Barbares

Barbarische Erzählungen

Cuentos salvajes

Racconti barbari

Barbaarse vertellingen

1902, Oil on canvas/Huile sur toile, 131 × 90,5 cm, Museum Folkwang, Essen

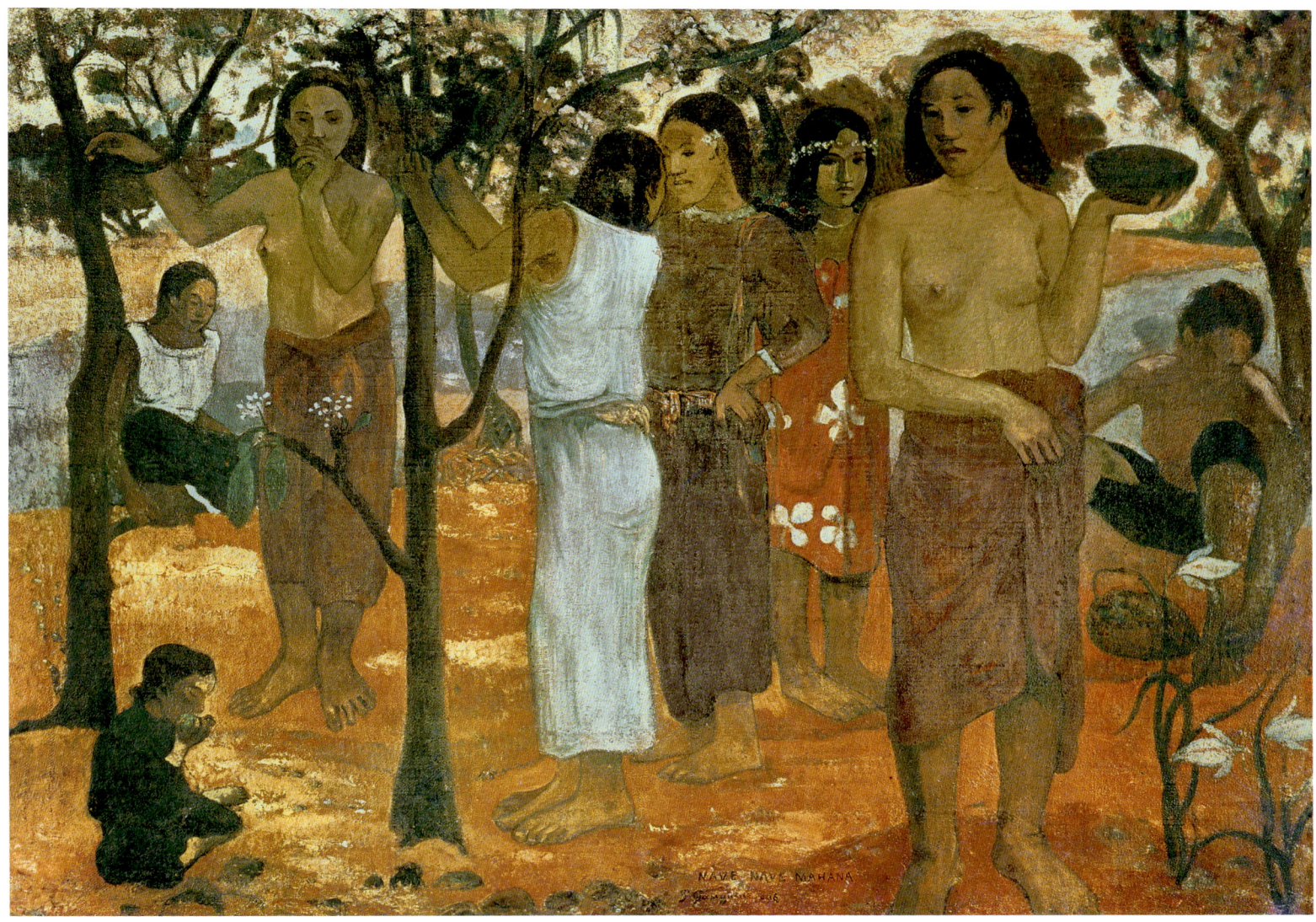

Paul Gauguin (1848–1903)

Nave Nave Mahana (Delightful Days)

Nave Nave Mahana (Jours délicieux)

Nave Nave Mahana (Schöne Tage)

Nave Nave Mahana (Días hermosos)

Nave Nave Mahana (giorni deliziosi)

Nave Nave Mahana' (Heerlijke dagen)

1896, Oil on canvas/Huile sur toile, 95 × 130 cm, Musée des Beaux-Arts, Lyon

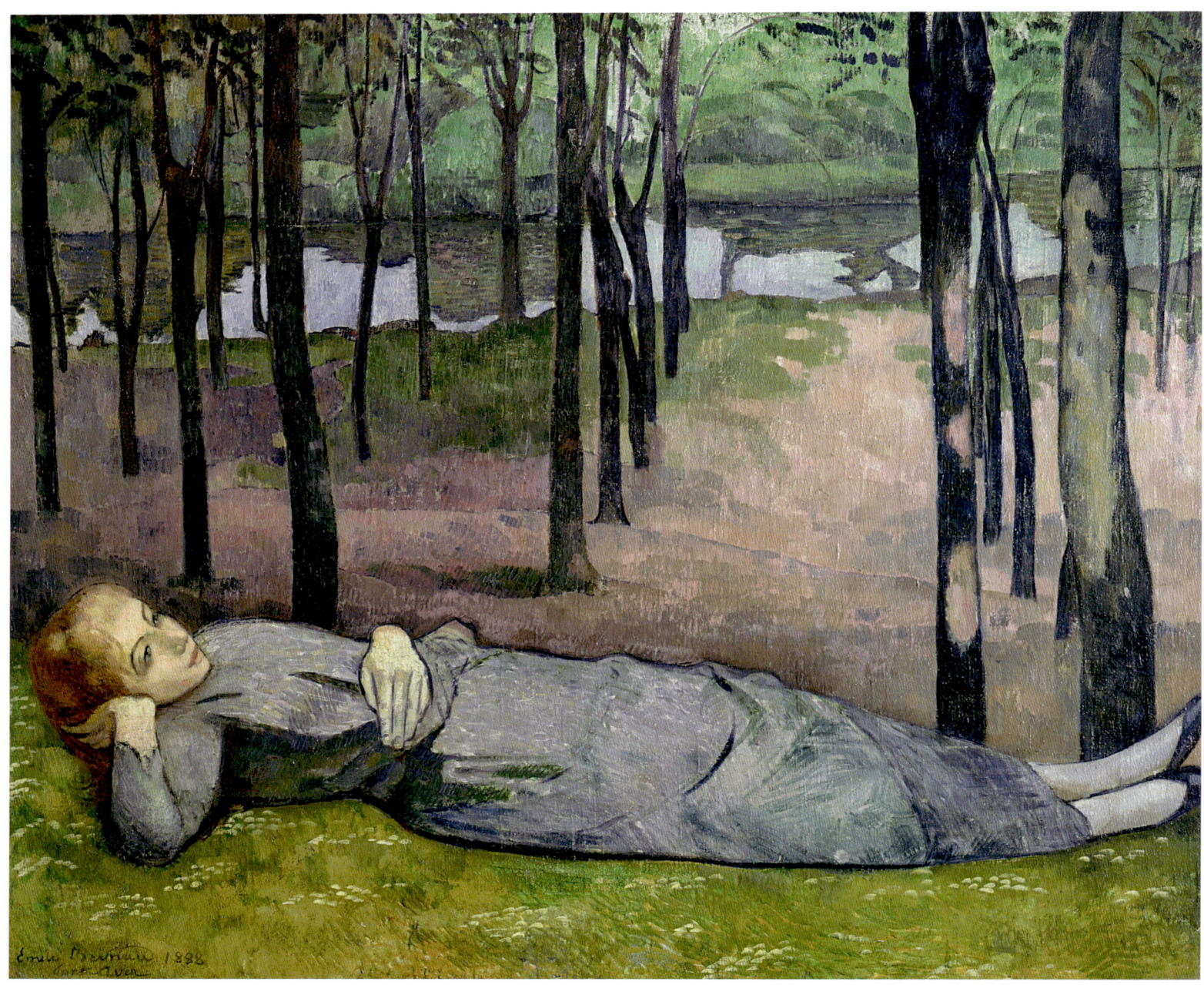

Émile Bernard (1868–1941)

Madeleine in the Bois d'Amour	Madeleine im Bois d'Amour	Madeleine nel Bois d'Amour
Madeleine au Bois d'Amour	Magdalena en el bosque del amor	Madeleine in het bos der liefde

1888, Oil on canvas/Huile sur toile, 138 × 163 cm, Musée d'Orsay, Paris

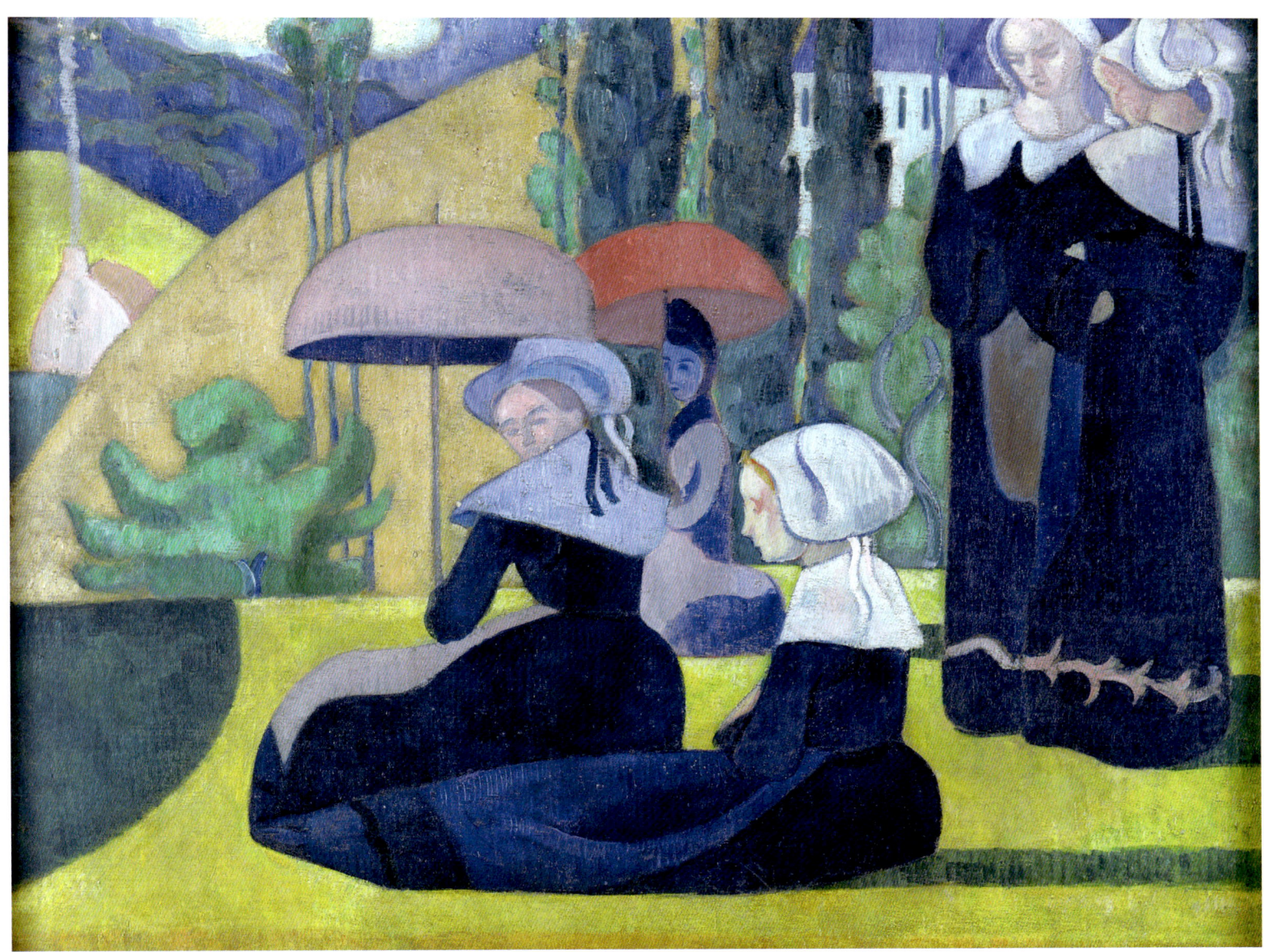

Émile Bernard (1868–1941)

Women with Umbrellas

Les Bretonnes aux ombrelles

Bretonische Frauen mit Sonnenschirmen

Bretonas con sombrillas

Donne bretoni con ombrelli

Bretonse vrouwen met parasols

1892, Oil on canvas/Huile sur toile, 81,3 × 100 cm, Musée d'Orsay, Paris

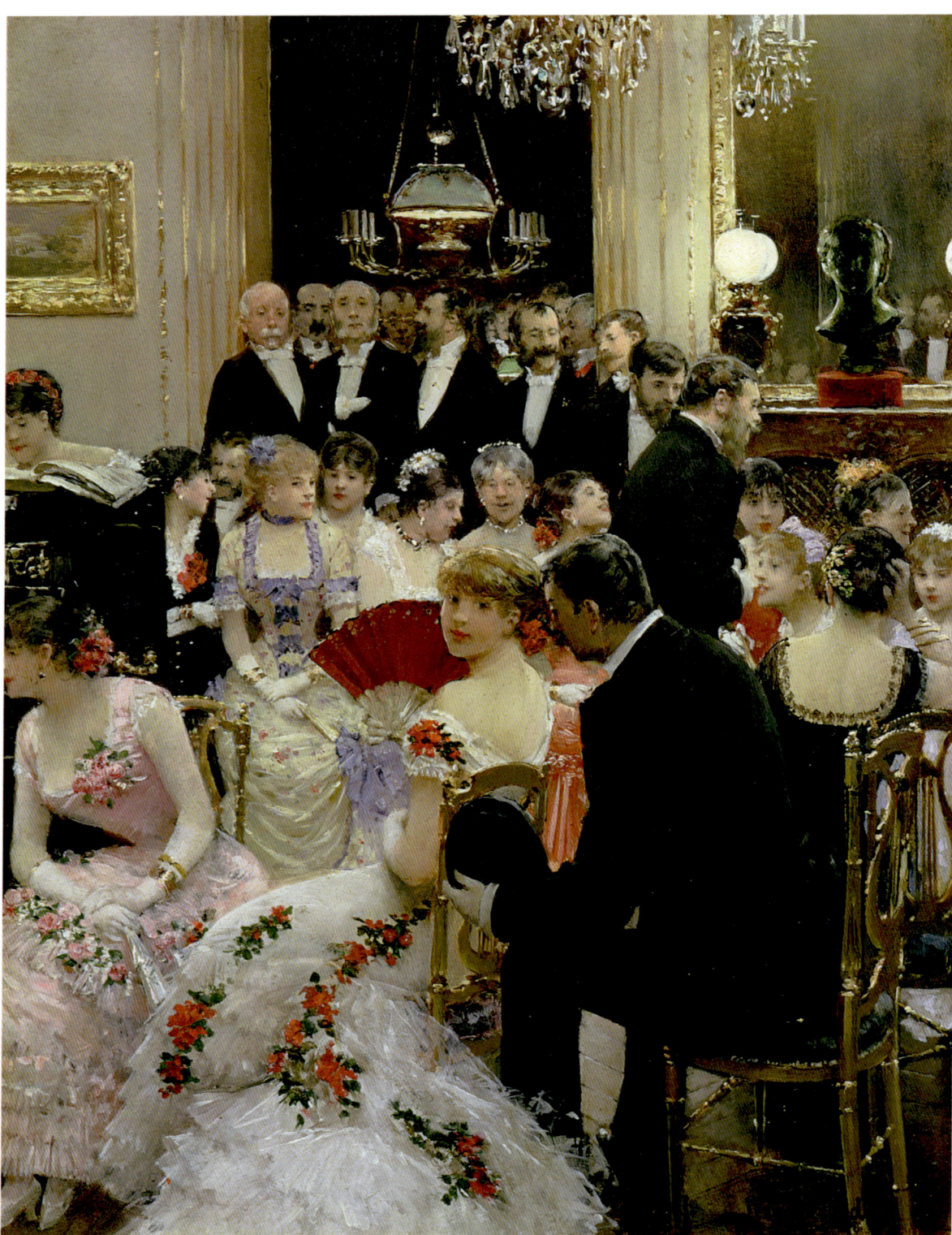

Jean Béraud (1849–1935)

The Soirée

La Soirée

Die Soirée

La Soirée

La soirée

De soirée

c. 1880, Oil on canvas/Huile sur toile,
35 × 27 cm, Musée Carnavalet, Paris

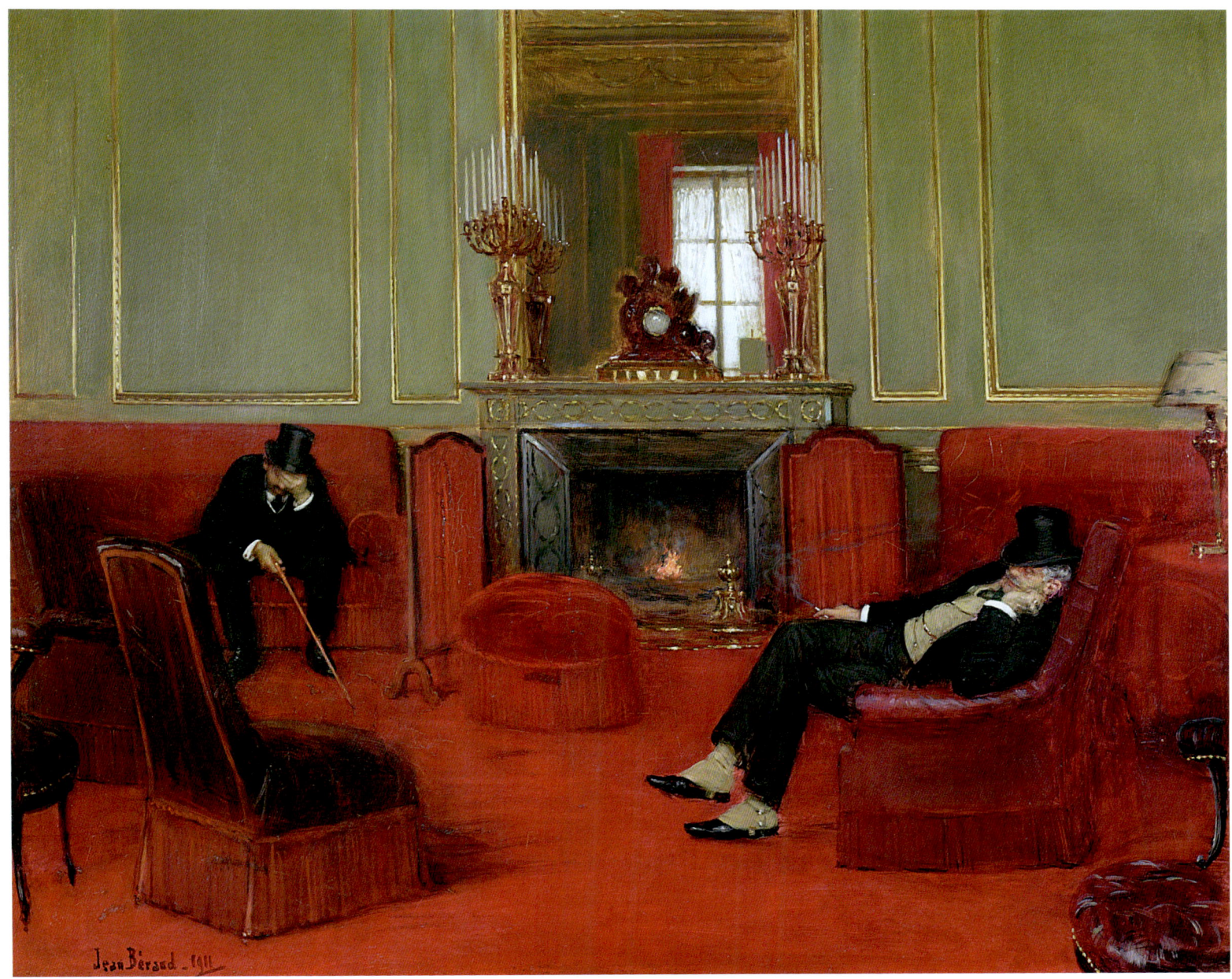

Jean Béraud (1849–1935)

The Club	Im Club	Il club
Le Cercle	En el club	In de club

1911, Oil on canvas/Huile sur toile, 61 × 73,5 cm, Musée d'Orsay, Paris

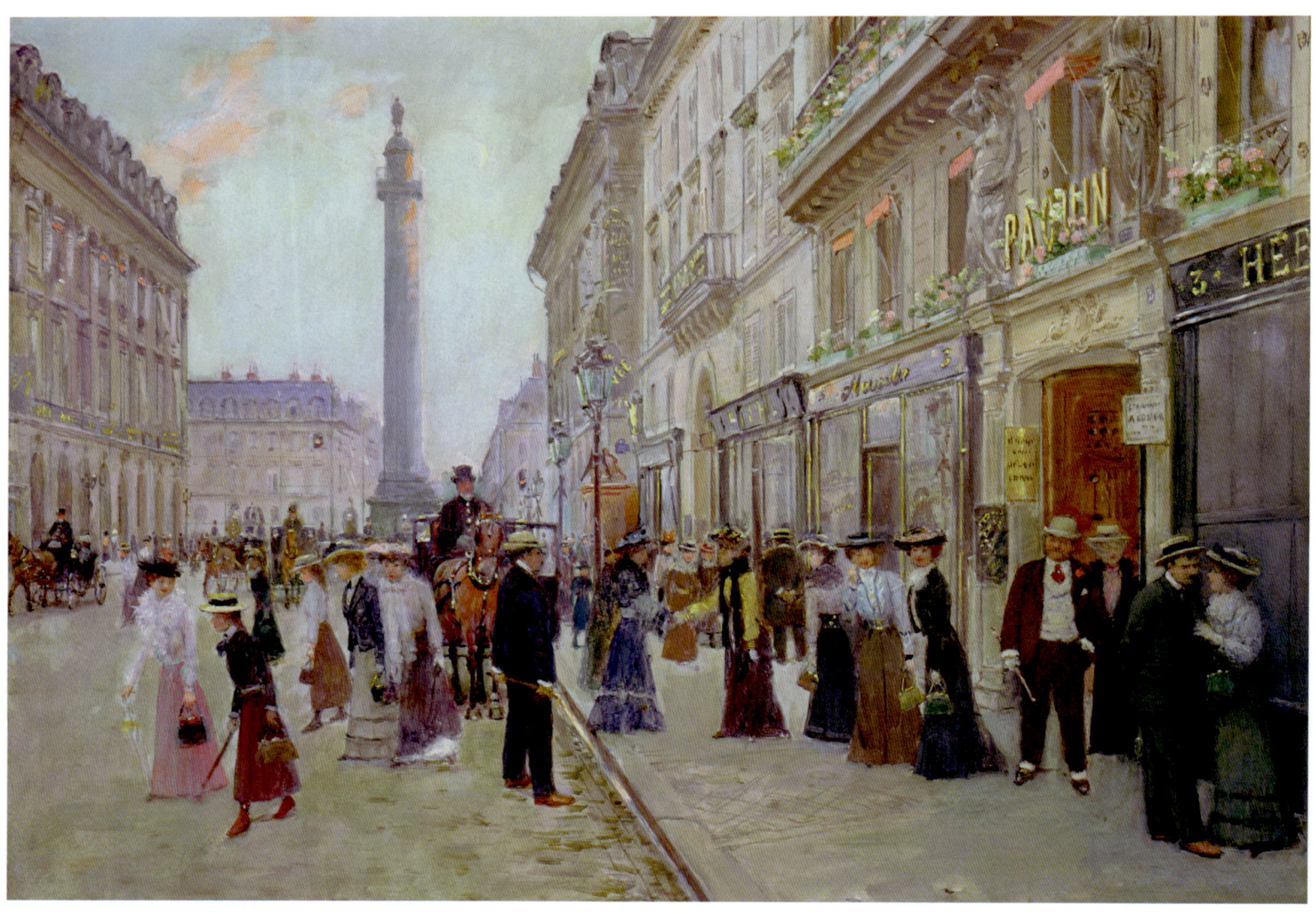

Jean Béraud (1849–1935)

Workers leaving the Maison Paquin, in the Rue de la Paix

La Sortie des ouvrières de la Maison Paquin

Arbeiter beim Verlassen des Maison Paquin in der Rue de la Paix

Trabajadores abandonando la Maison Paquin en la Rue de la Paix

Lavoratori lasciano la Maison Paquin in Rue de la Paix

Arbeiders verlaten het Maison Paquin in de Rue de la Paix

c. 1902, Oil on wood/Huile sur bois, 42 × 55 cm, Musée Carnavalet, Paris

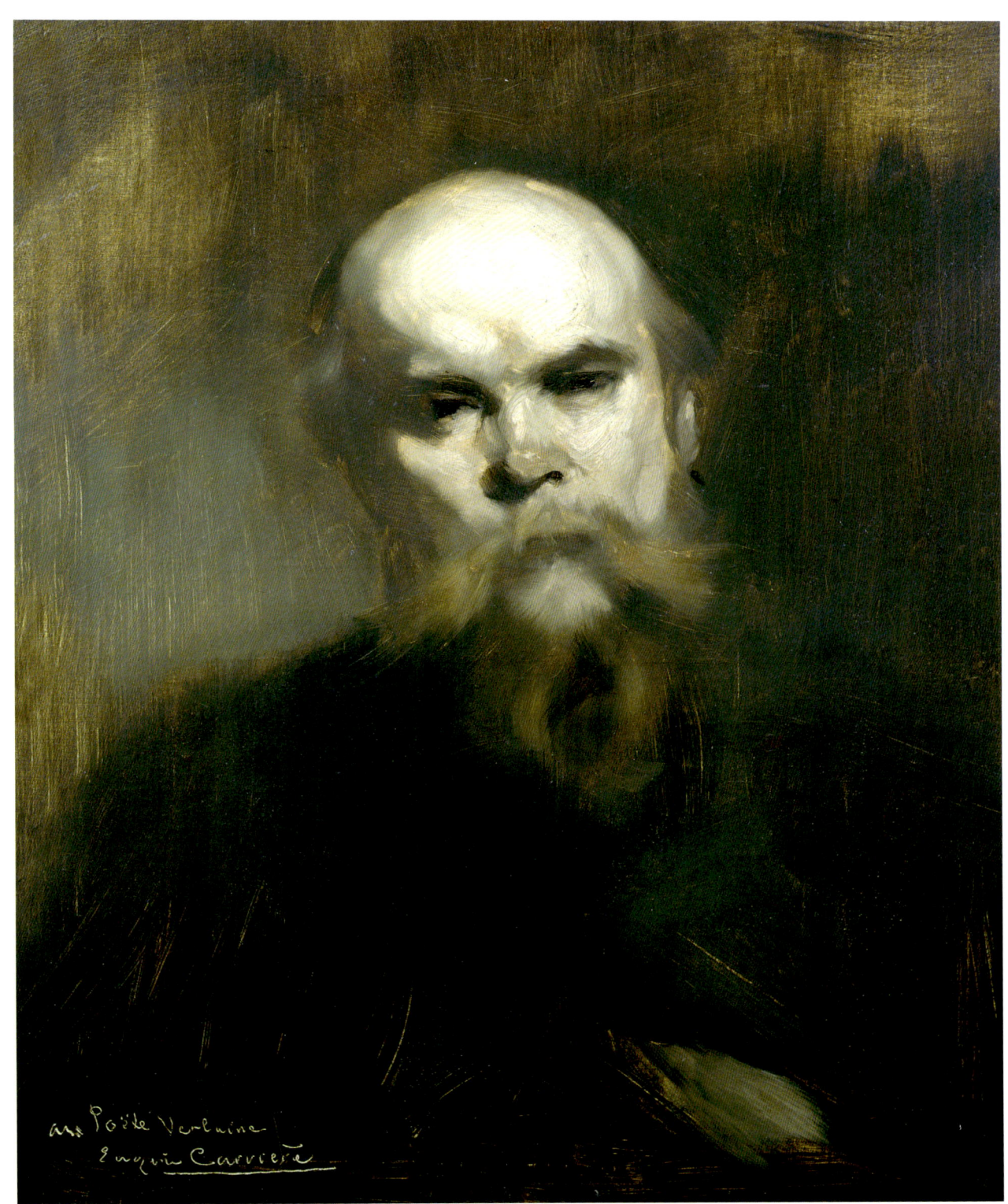

**Eugène Carrière
(1849–1906)**

Paul Verlaine

1890, Oil on canvas/Huile
sur toile, 61,2 × 51 cm, Musée
d'Orsay, Paris

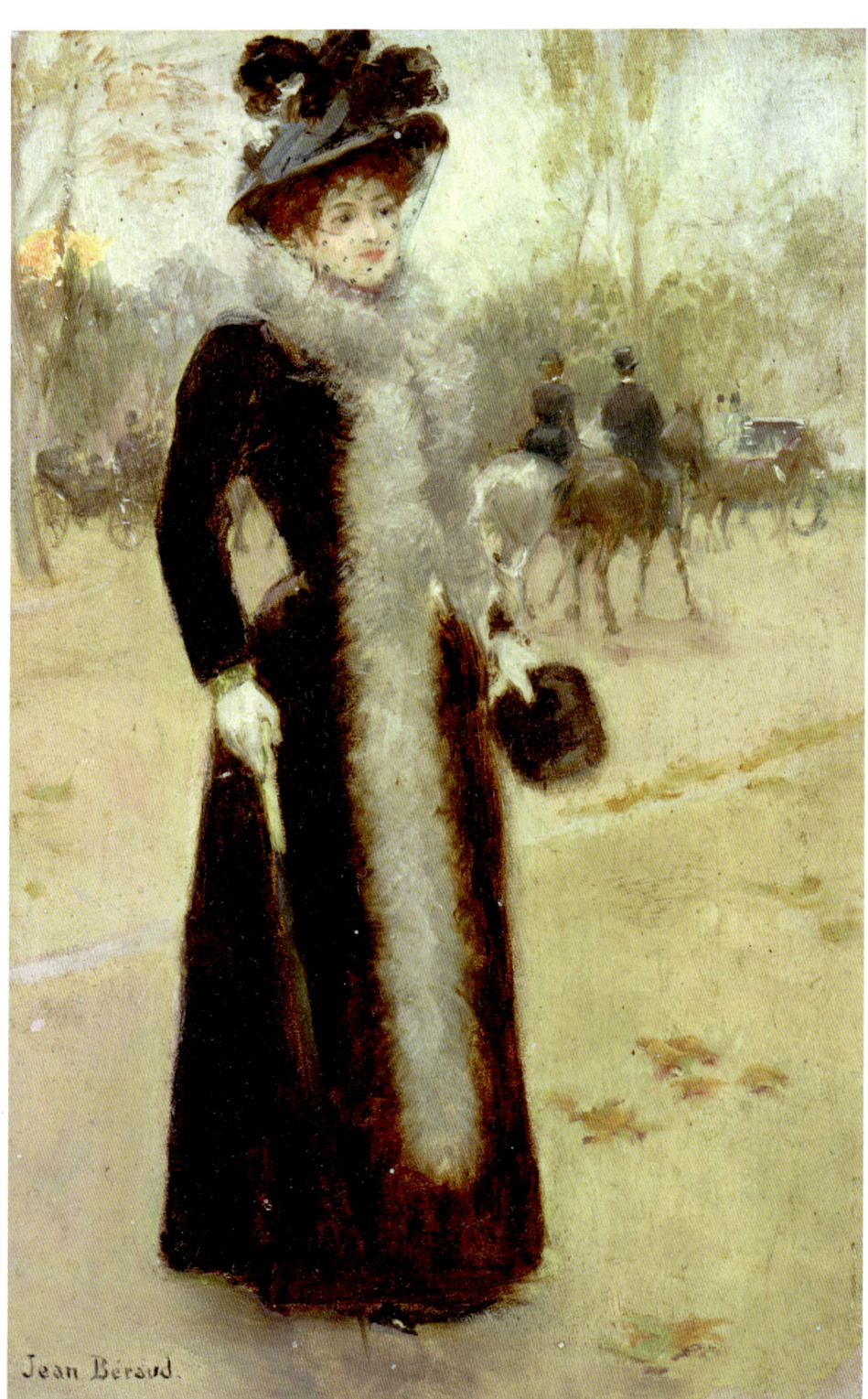

Jean Béraud.

Jean Béraud (1849−1935)

A Parisian Woman in the Bois de Boulogne

Une Parisienne au bois de Boulogne

Eine Pariserin im Bois de Boulogne

Una parisina en el Bois de Boulogne

Una parigina nel Bois de Boulogne

Een Parisienne in het Bois de Boulogne

c. 1899, Oil on canvas/Huile sur toile, 25 × 16 cm, Musée Carnavalet, Paris

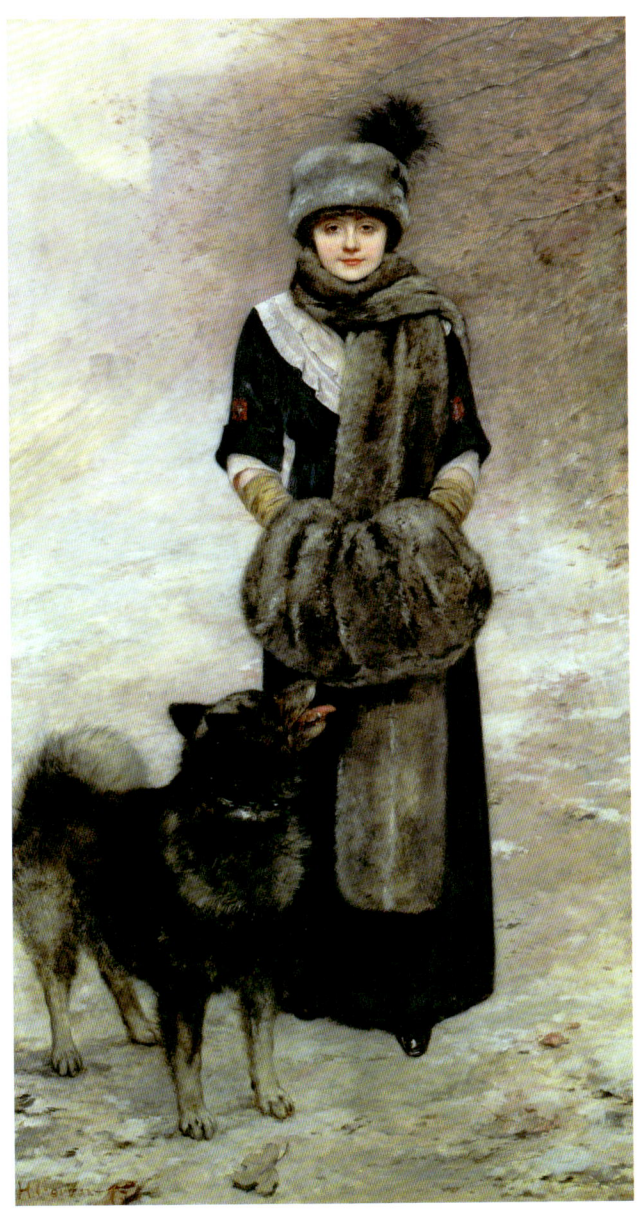

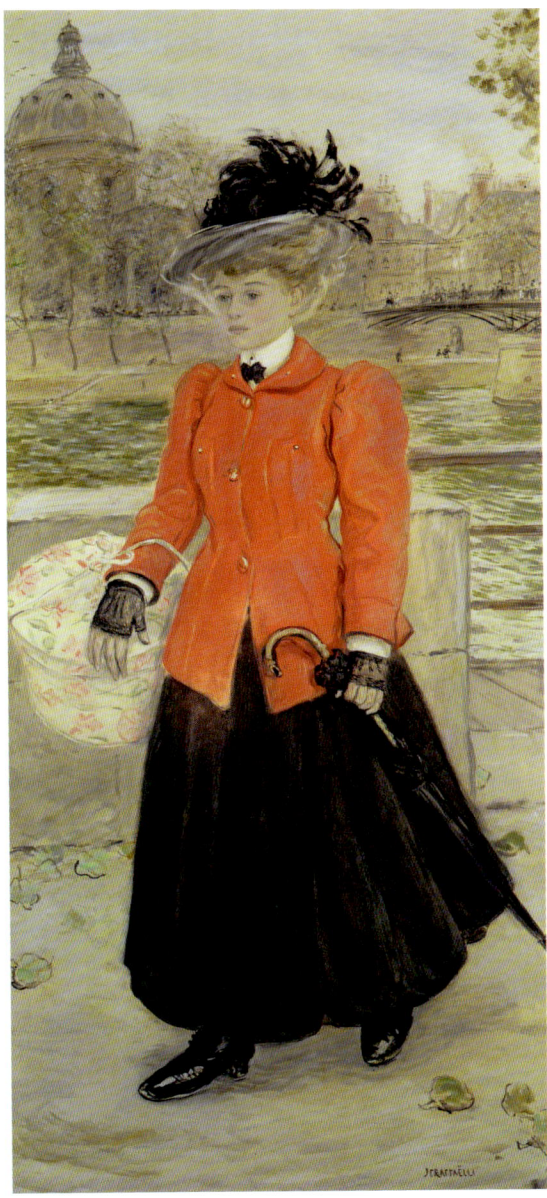

Henri Gervex (1852–1929)

Portrait of Colette Gervex, Daughter of the Artist

Portrait de Colette Gervex

Porträt von Colette Gervex

Retrato de Colette Gervex

Ritratto di Colette Gervex

Portret van Colette Gervex

1910, Oil on canvas/Huile sur toile, 211 × 110 cm, Musée des Beaux-Arts, Nancy

Jean-François Raffaëlli (1850–1924)

The Apprentice

L'Apprentie

Das Lehrmädchen

La aprendiz

L'apprendista

De leerlinge

1908, Oil on canvas/Huile sur toile, 225 × 103 cm, Musée des Beaux-Arts, Pau

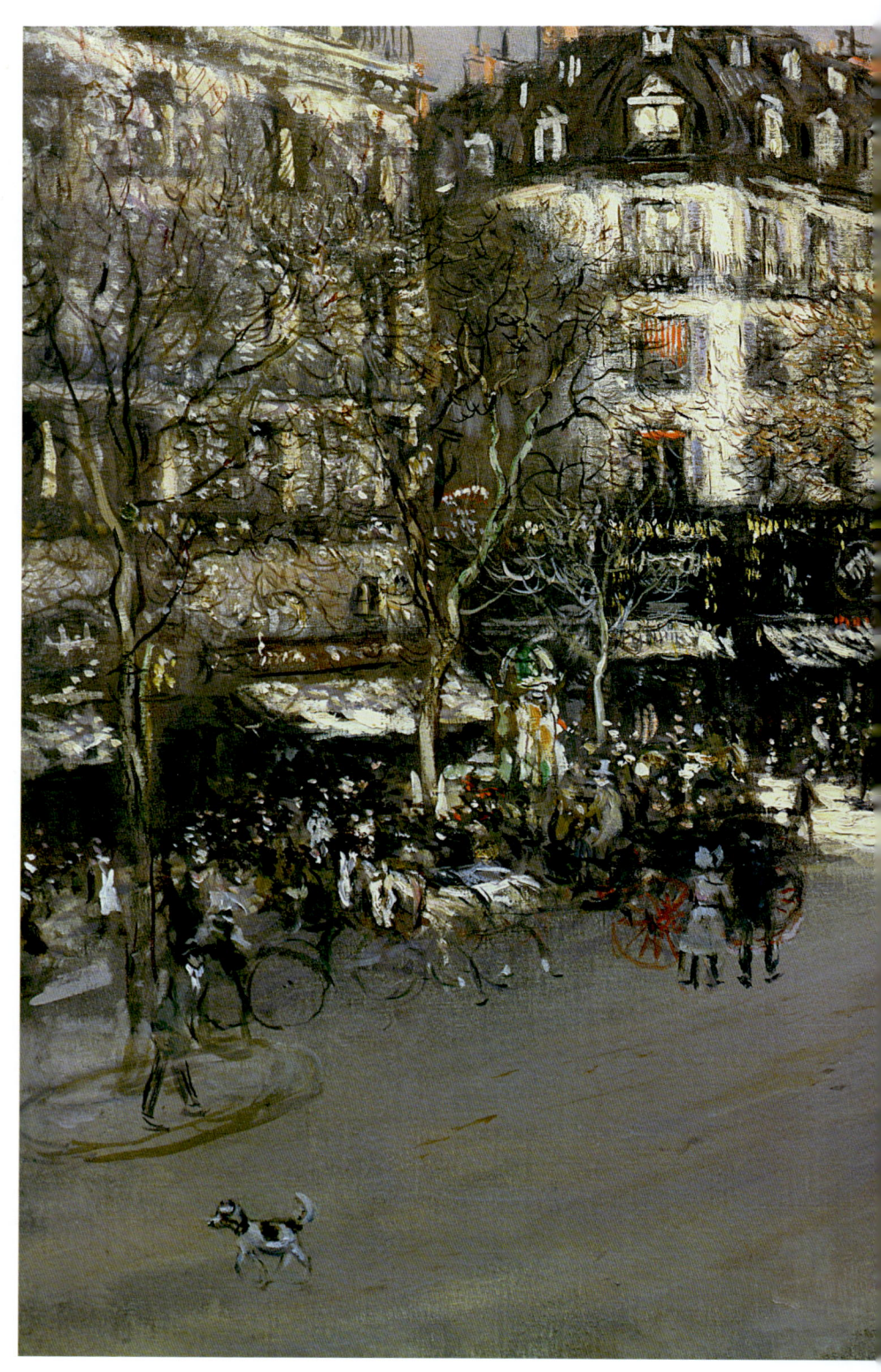

Jean-François Raffaëlli (1850–1924)

Le Boulevard des Italiens

c. 1900, Oil on canvas/Huile sur toile, 63,5 × 108,5 cm, Private collection

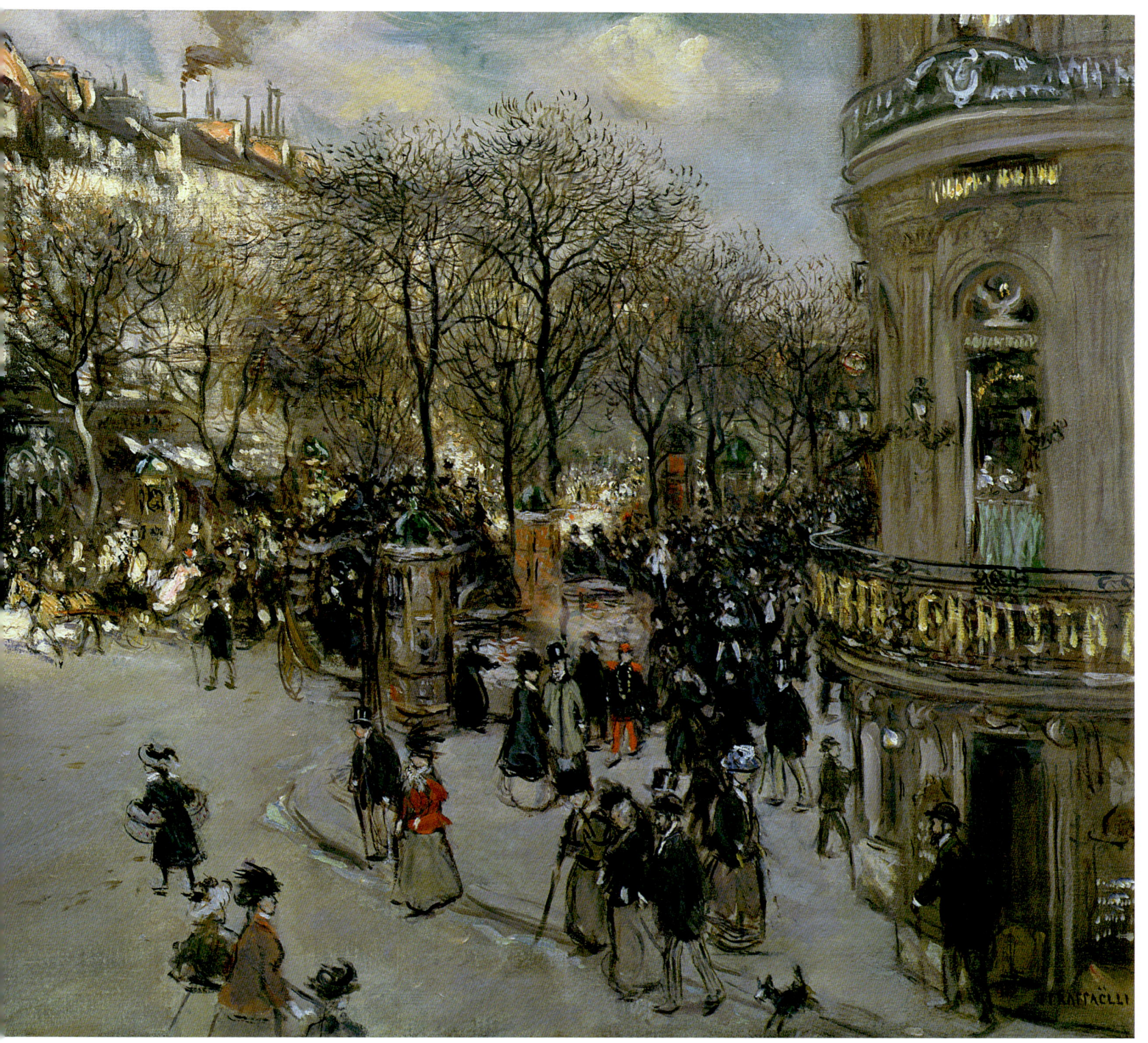

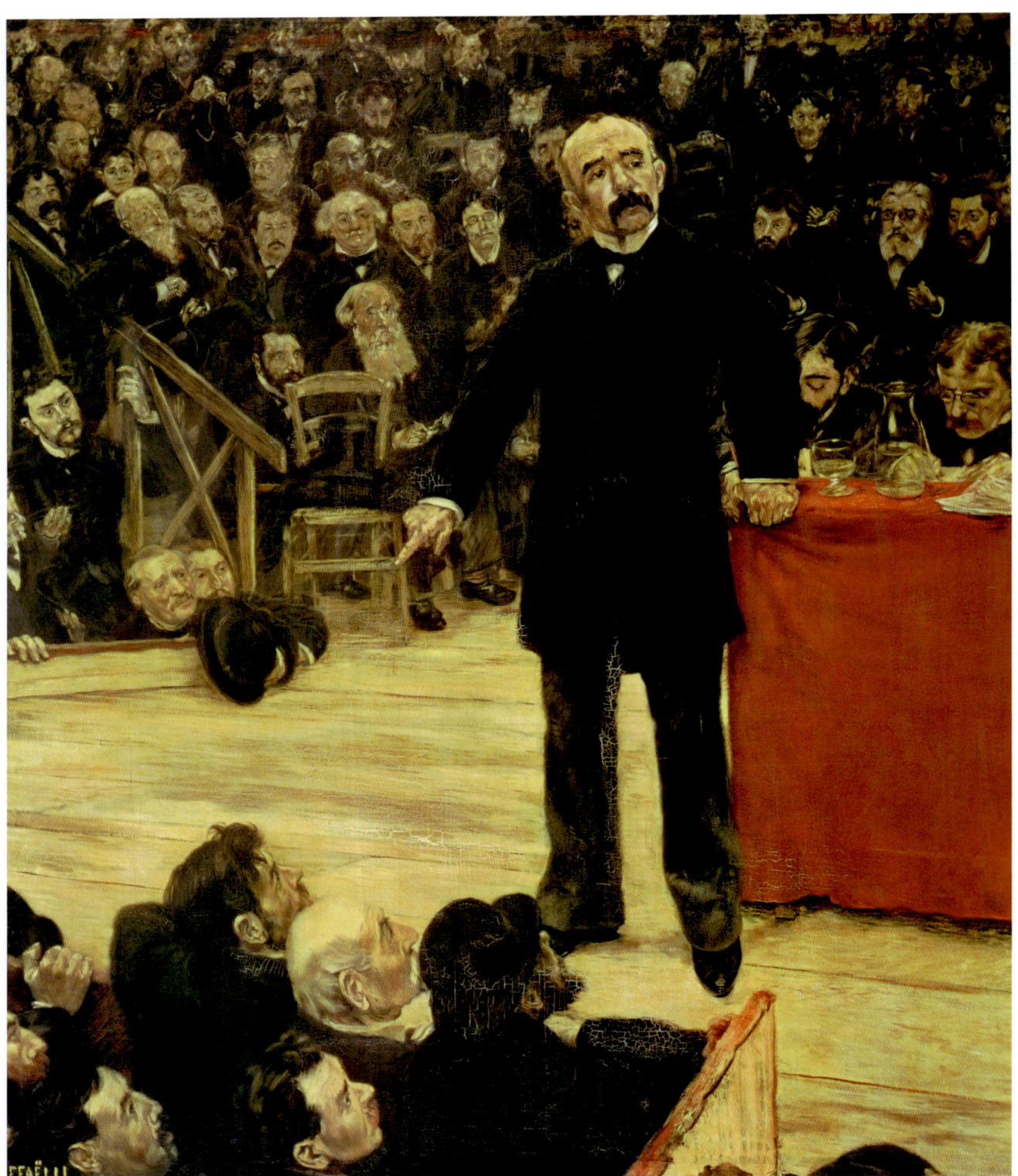

Jean-François Raffaëlli (1850–1924)

Georges Clemenceau Making a Speech at the Cirque Fernando

Georges Clémenceau prononçant un discours pendant une réunion électorale au Cirque Fernando en 1883

Georges Clemenceau hält eine Rede im Zirkus Fernando

Georges Clemenceau da un discurso en el circo Fernando

Georges Clemenceau tiene un discorso al circo Fernando

Georges Clemenceau houdt een rede in het Cirque Fernando

1883, Oil on canvas/ Huile sur toile, 243 × 205,5 cm, Château de Versailles, Versailles

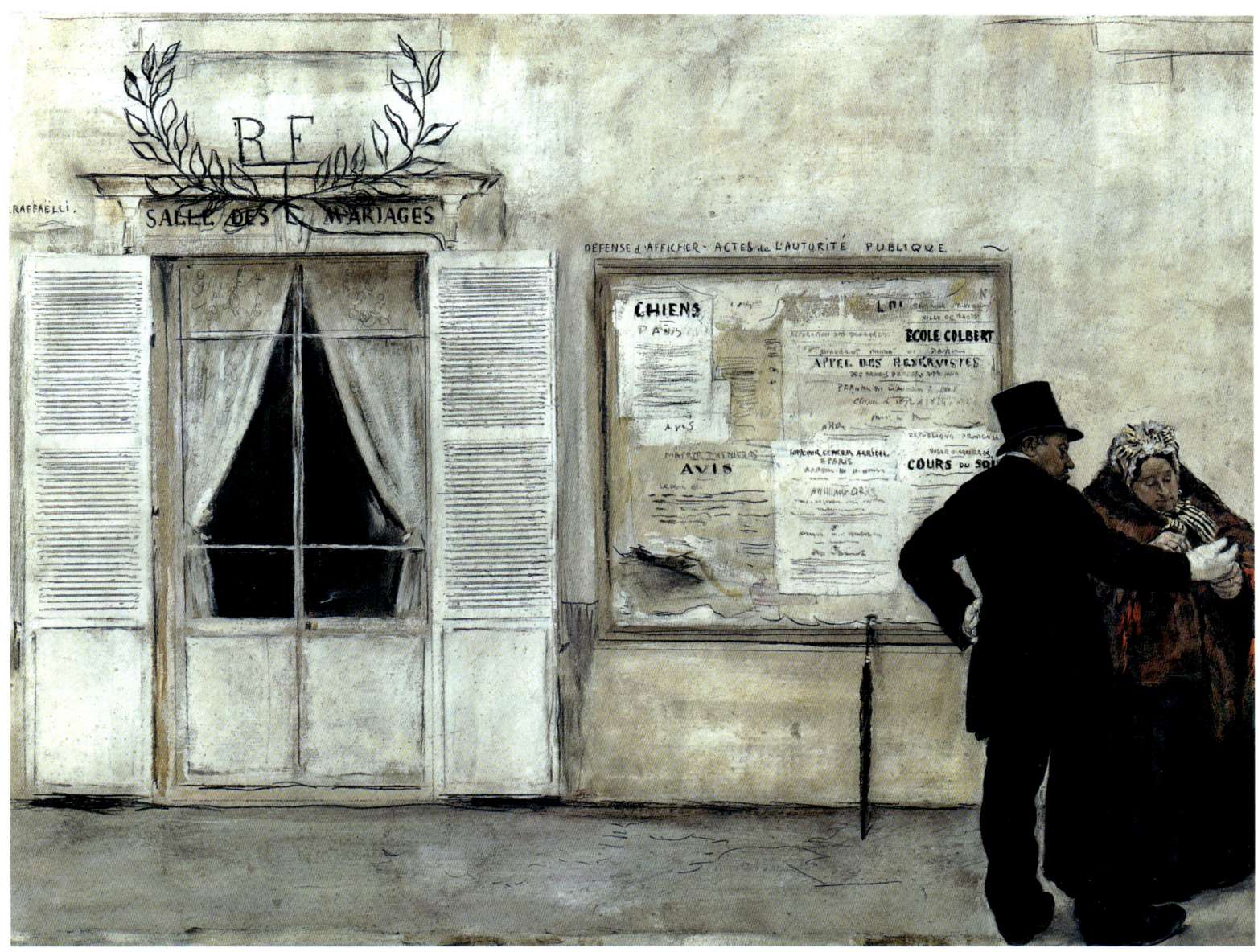

Jean-François Raffaëlli (1850–1924)

Guests Waiting for the Wedding Ceremony

Les Invités attendant la noce

Die Gäste warten auf die Hochzeitsfeier

Los invitados esperan al banquete nupcial

Gli invitati aspettano gli sposi

De gasten wachten op de huwelijksceremonie

c. 1884, Oil on wood/Huile sur bois, 52,5 × 68,5 cm, Musée d'Orsay, Paris

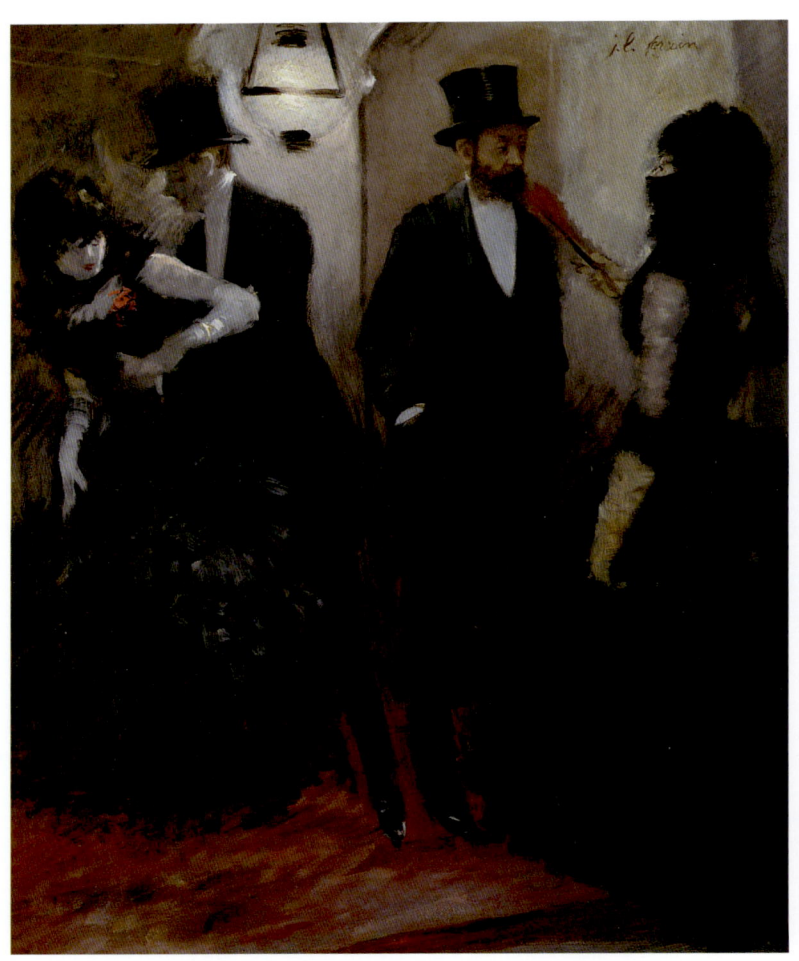

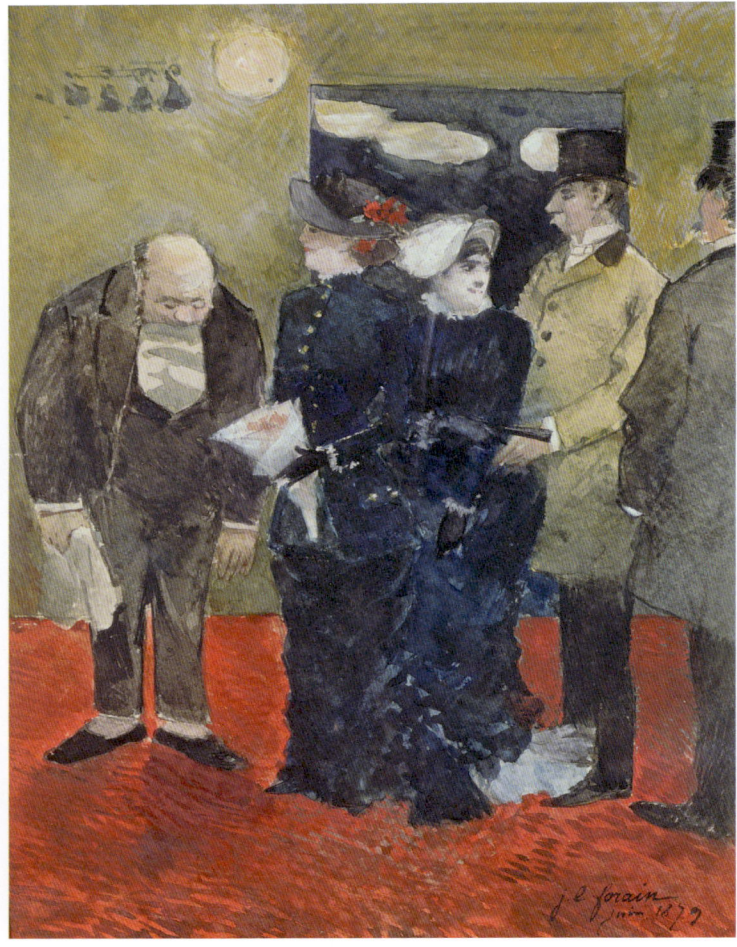

Jean-Louis Forain (1852–1931)

The Corridors at the Opera

Les Couloirs de l'Opéra

Die Flure in der Oper

Los pasillos de la Ópera

I corridoi dell'Opera

De gang van de Opéra

1885, Oil on canvas/Huile sur toile, 57 × 48 cm, Private collection

Jean-Louis Forain (1852–1931)

Entering the Restaurant

L'Arrivée au restaurant

Beim Betreten des Restaurants

A la entrada del restaurante

Entrando al ristorante

Bij het betreden van het restaurant

1879, Oil on canvas/Huile sur toile, 43 × 26 cm, Private collection

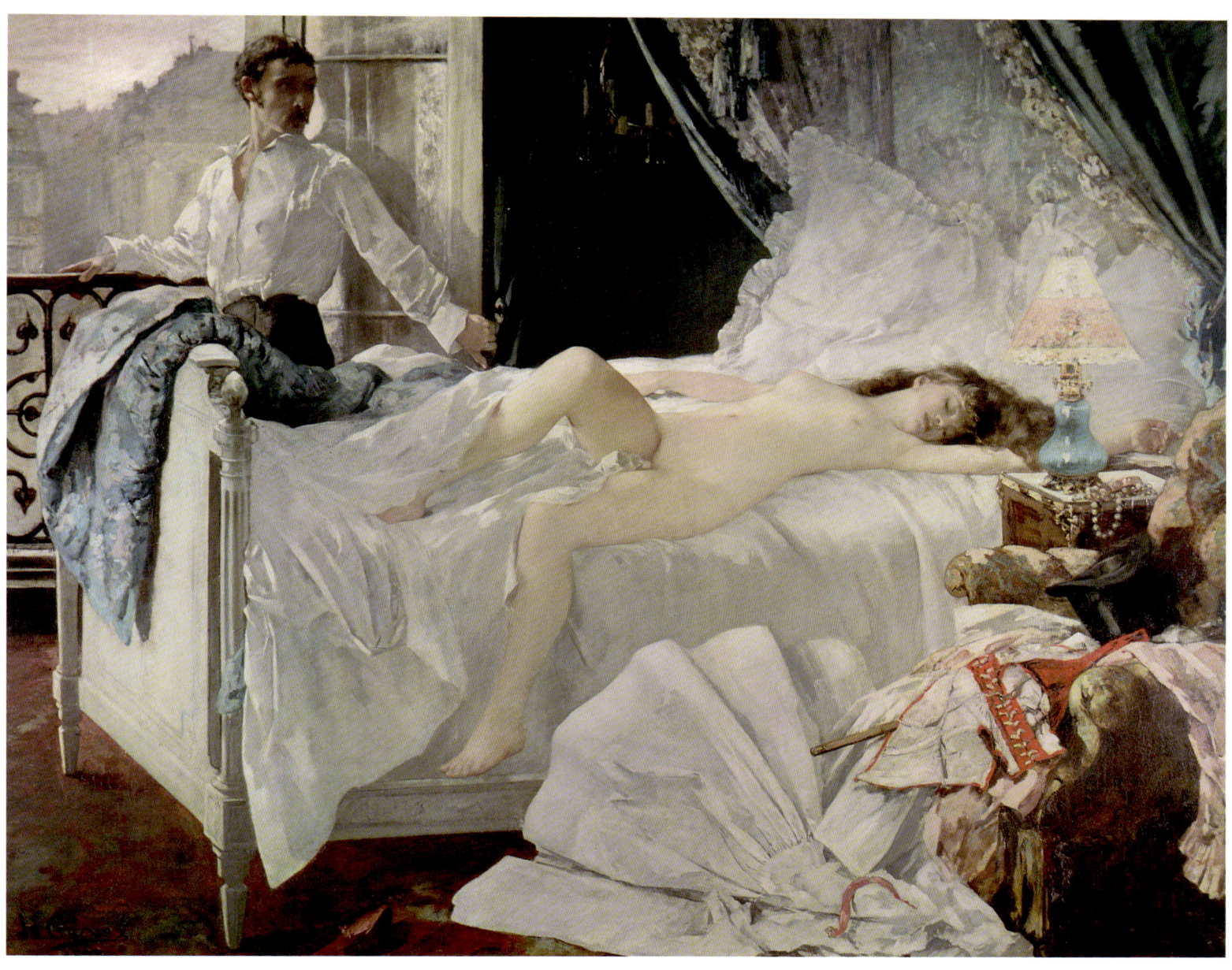

Henri Gervex (1852–1929)

Rolla

1878, Oil on canvas/Huile sur toile, 175 × 220 cm, Musée des Beaux-Arts, Bordeaux

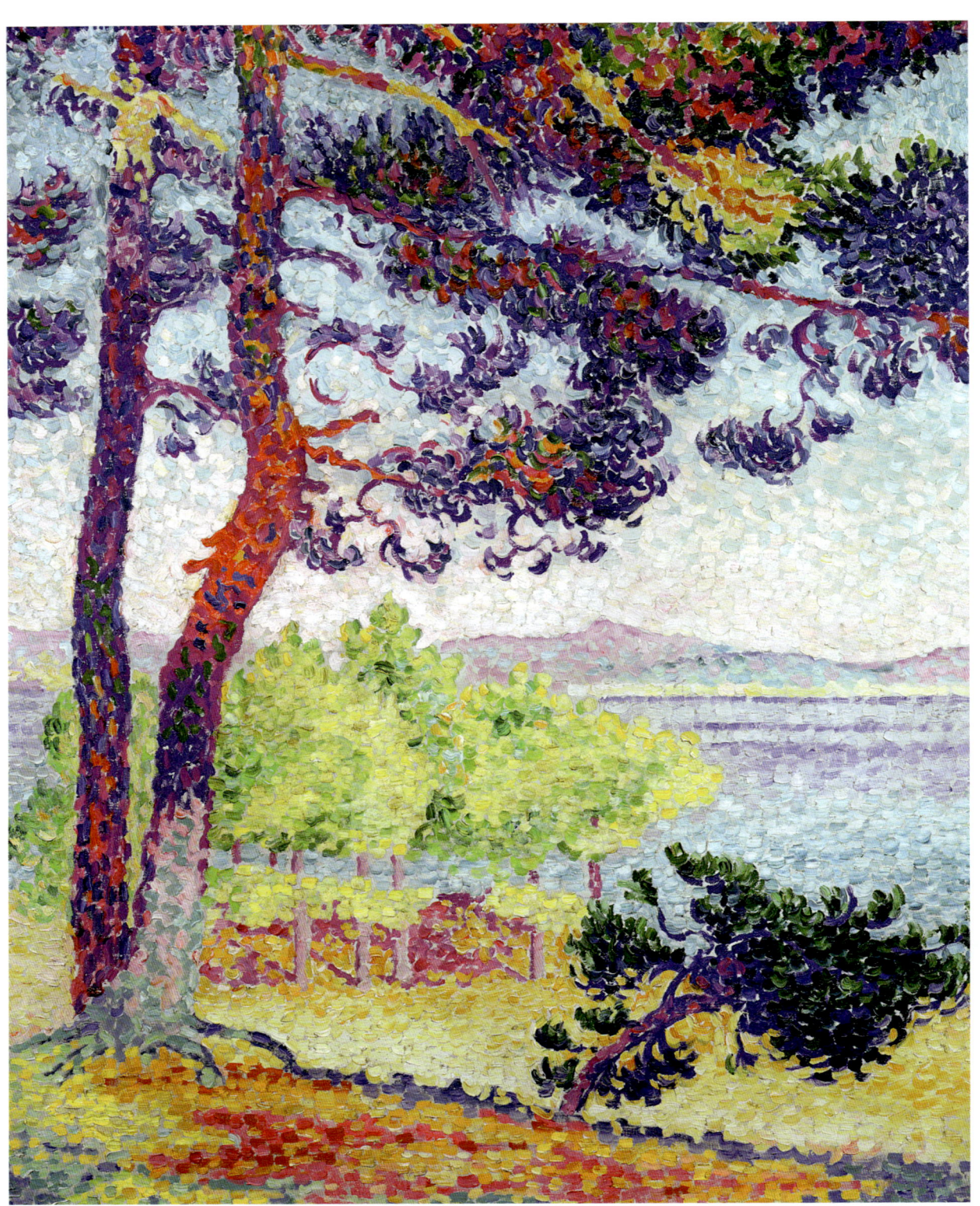

Henri-Edmond Cross (1856–1910)

Afternoon at Pardigon

Après-midi à Pardigon

Nachmittag in Pardigon

Tarde en Pardigon

Pomeriggio a Pardigon

Namiddag in Pardigon

1907, Oil on canvas/Huile sur toile, 80,7 × 65 cm, Musée d'Orsay, Paris

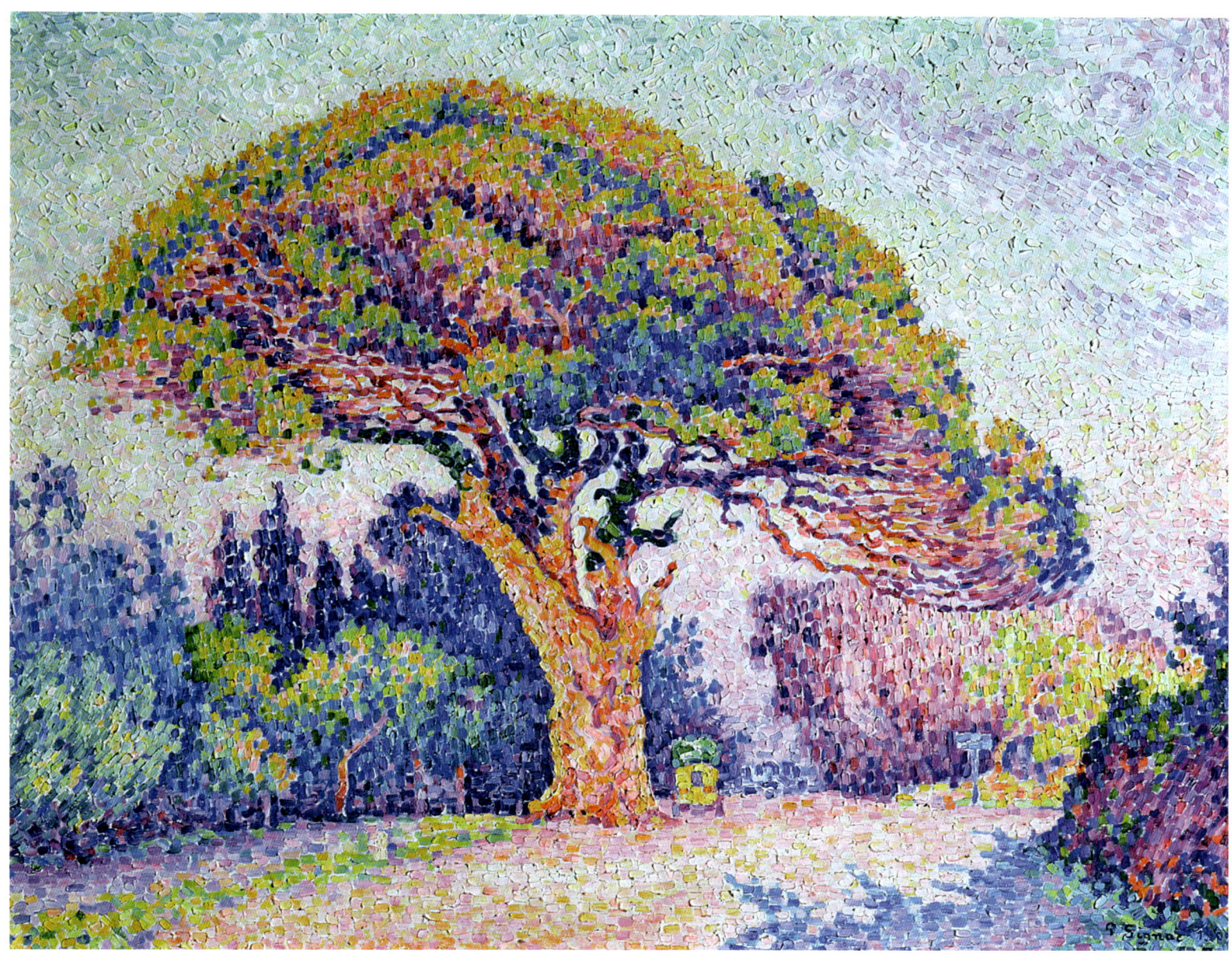

Paul Signac (1863–1935)

The Pine Tree at St. Tropez

Le Pin à Saint-Tropez

Die Pinie in St. Tropez

Los pinos en St. Tropez

Il pino a Saint Tropez

De pijnboom in Saint-Tropez

1909, Oil on canvas/Huile sur toile, 72 × 92 cm, Pushkin State Museum of Fine Arts, Moscow

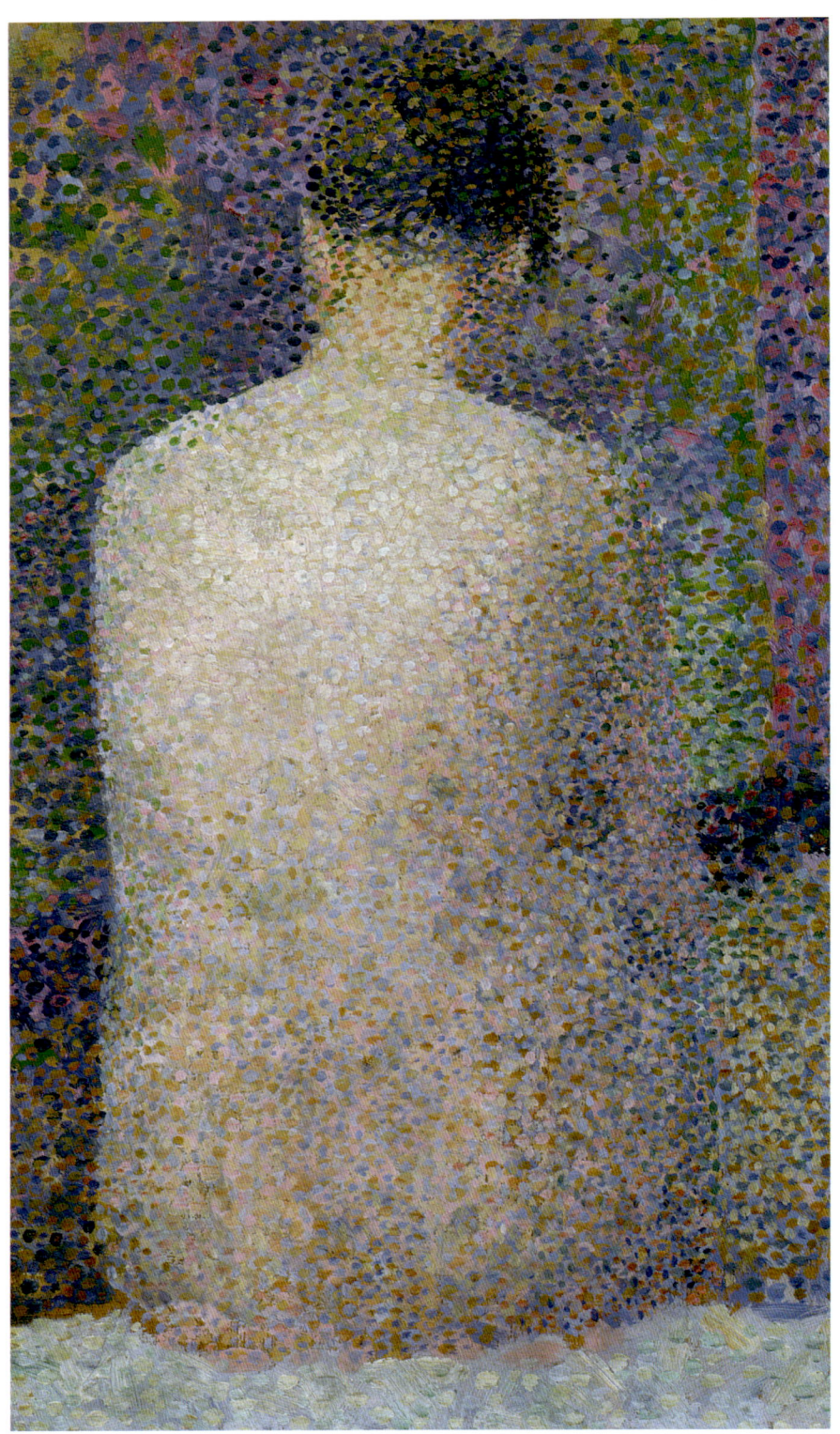

Georges Seurat (1859–1891)

Model from the Back

Poseuse de dos

Modell von hinten

Modelo de espaldas

Modella di spalle

Model op de rug gezien

1887, Oil on wood/Huile sur bois,
24,3 × 15,3 cm, Musée d'Orsay, Paris

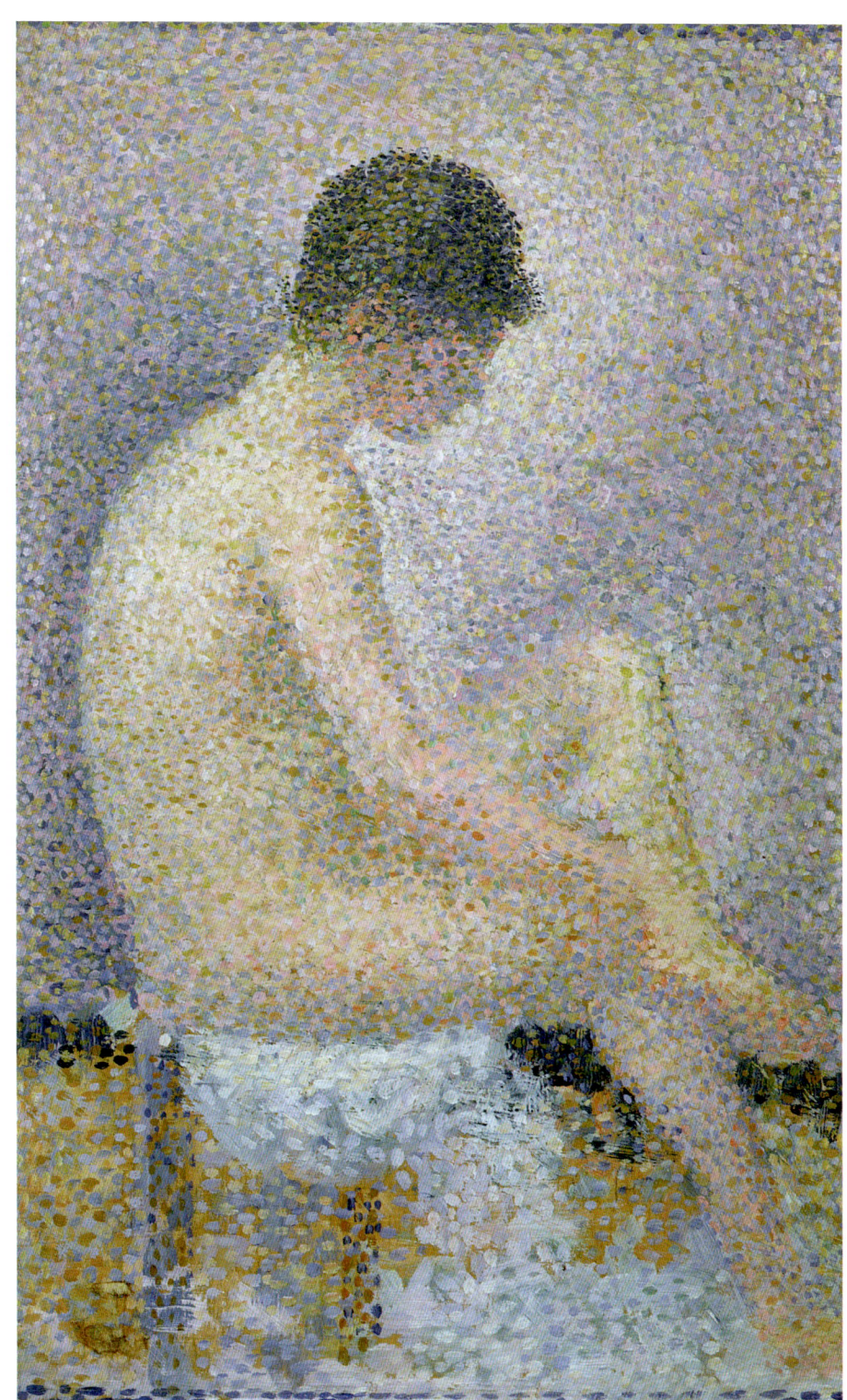

Georges Seurat (1859–1891)

Model in Profile

Poseuse de profil

Modell im Profil

Modelo de perfil

Modella di profilo

Model en profil

1887, Oil on canvas/Huile sur toile,
25 × 16 cm, Musée d'Orsay, Paris

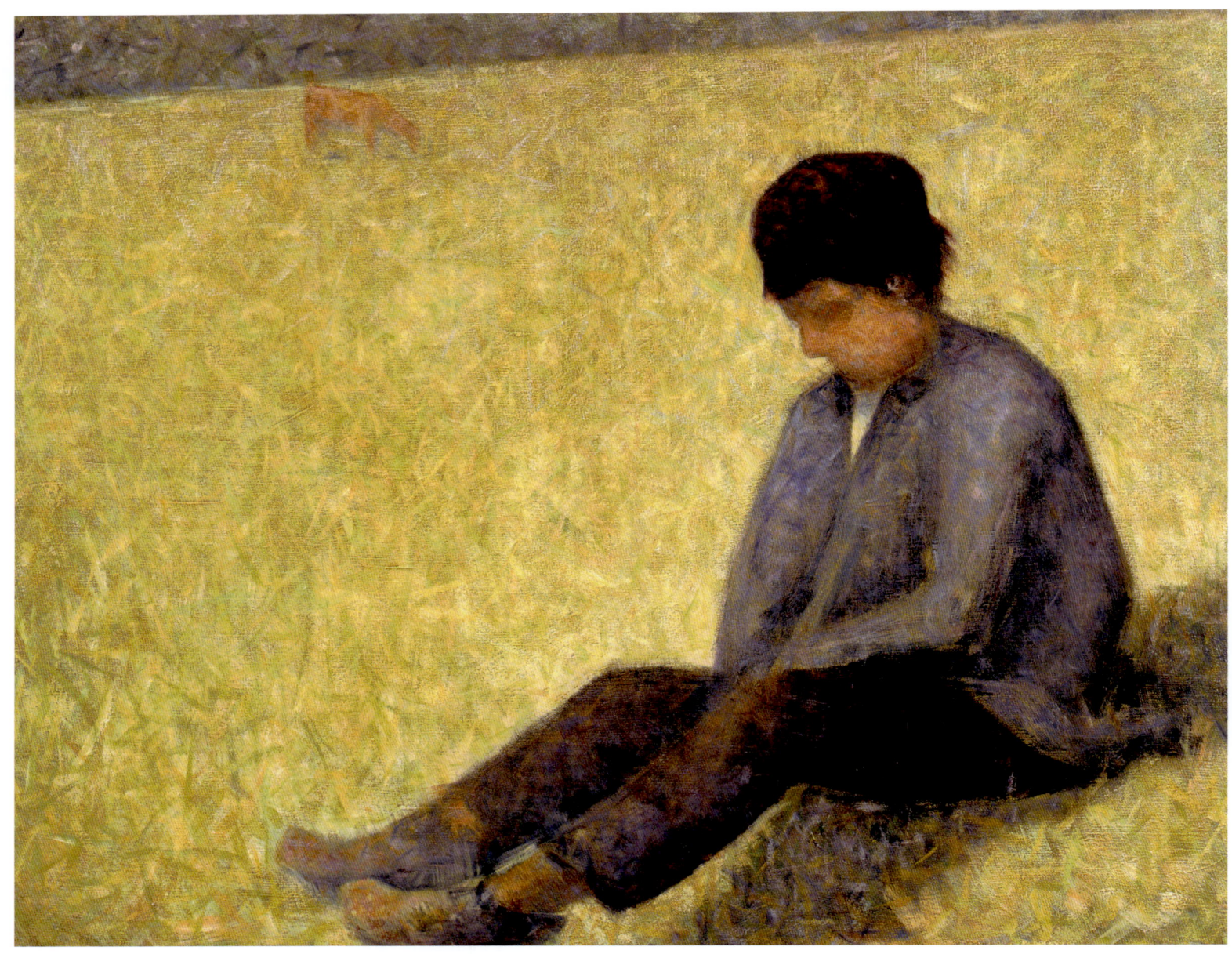

Georges Seurat (1859–1891)

Boy Sitting on the Grass

Petit paysan assis dans un pré

Auf dem Gras sitzender Junge

Joven sentado sobre la hierba

Giovane seduto sull'erba

In het gras zittende jongen

c. 1882, Oil on canvas/Huile sur toile, 63,5 × 79,6 cm, Kelvingrove Art Gallery and Museum, Glasgow

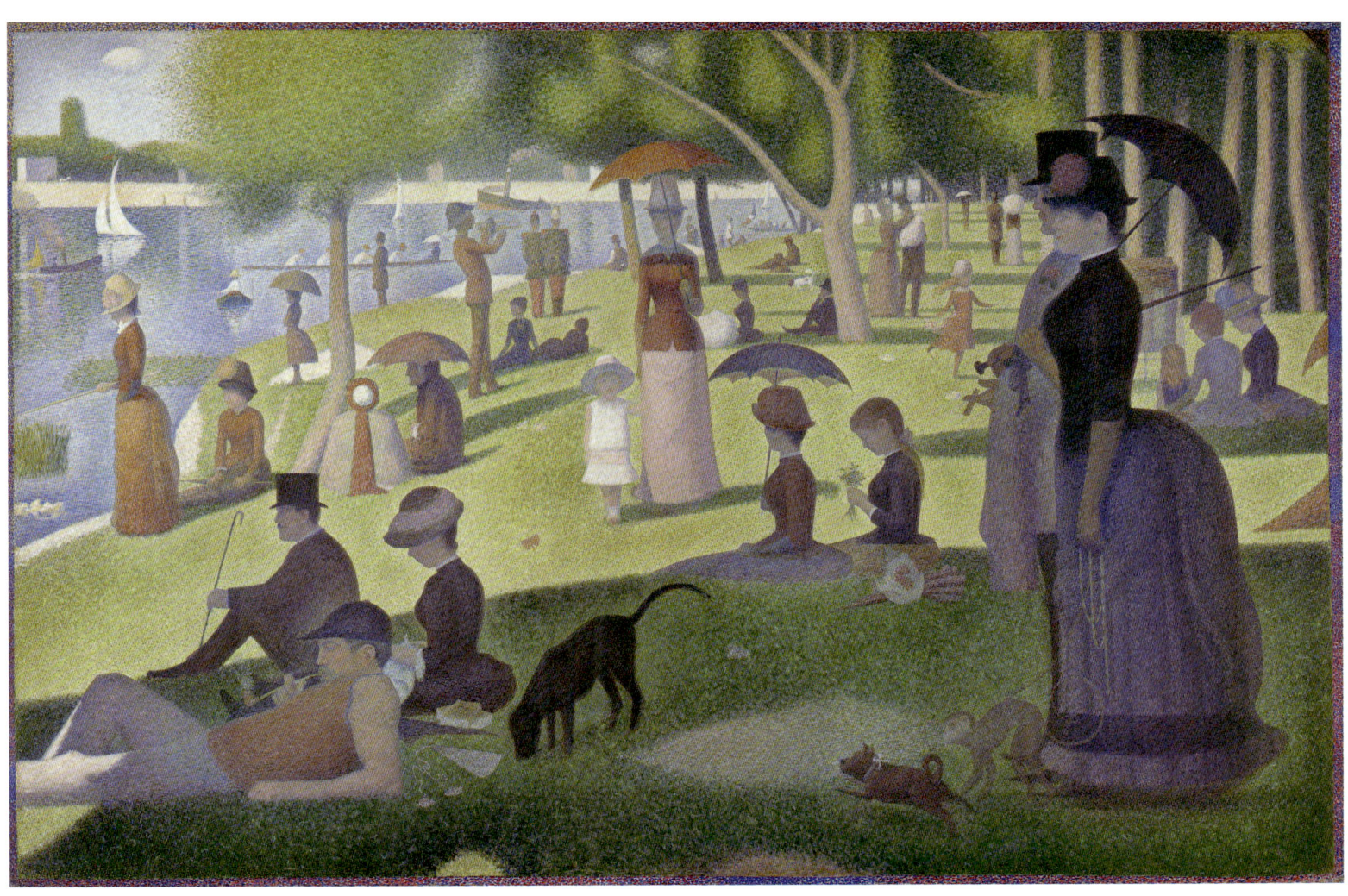

Georges Seurat (1859–1891)

Sunday Afternoon on the Island of La Grand Jatte

Une dimanche après-midi à l'île de la Grande Jatte

Ein Sonntagnachmittag auf der Insel La Grande Jatte

Tarde de domingo en la isla de la Grande Jatte

Una domenica pomeriggio sull'isola della Grande-Jatte

Een zondagmiddag op het eiland la Grande Jatte

1884–1886, Oil on canvas/Huile sur toile, 205,7 × 305,7 cm, The Art Institute, Chicago

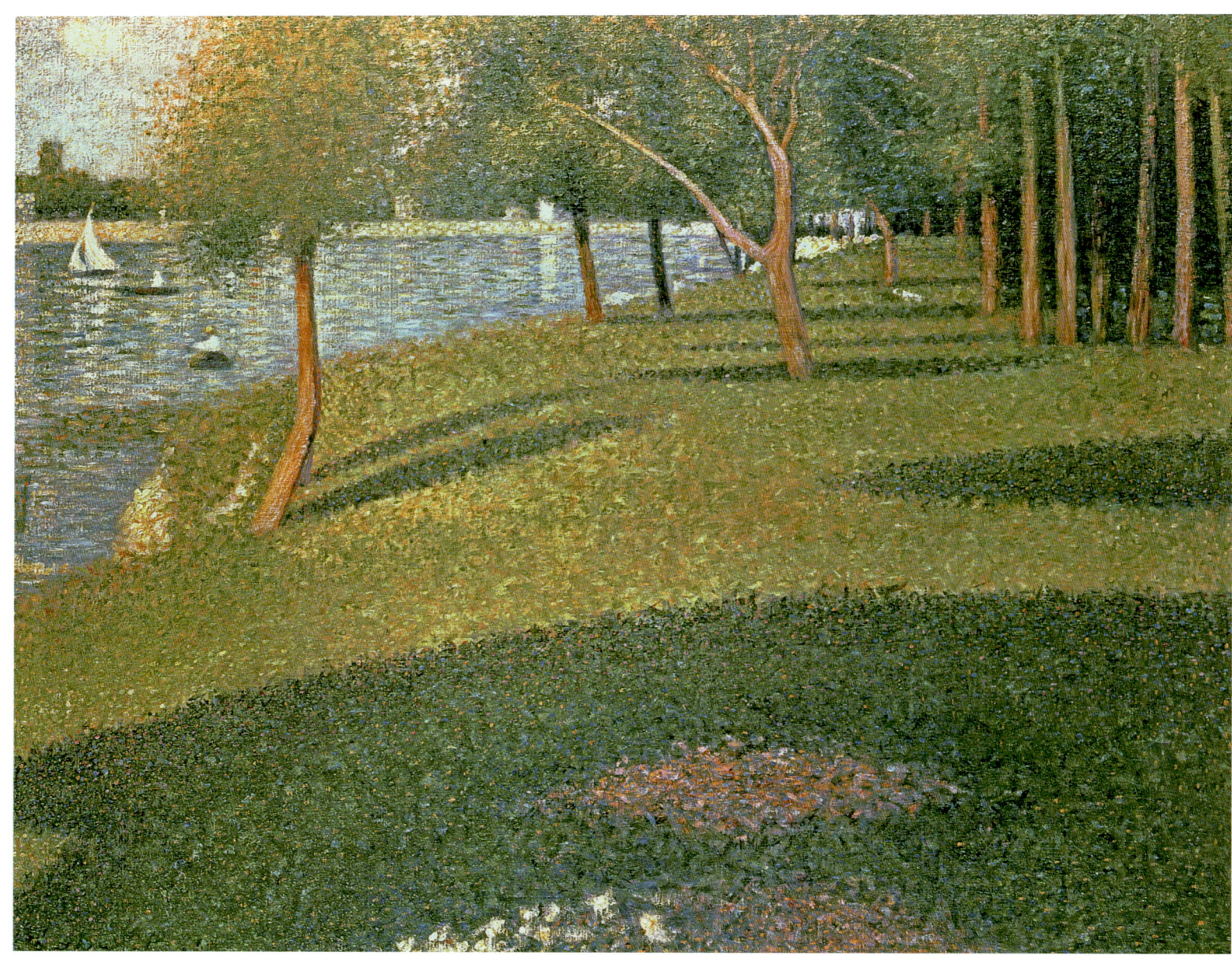

Georges Seurat (1859–1891)

La Grande Jatte

Paysage, l'île de la Grande Jatte

La Grande Jatte

La Grande Jatte

La Grande Jatte

La Grande Jatte

1884, Oil on canvas/Huile sur toile, 65,5 × 79,1 cm, Private collection

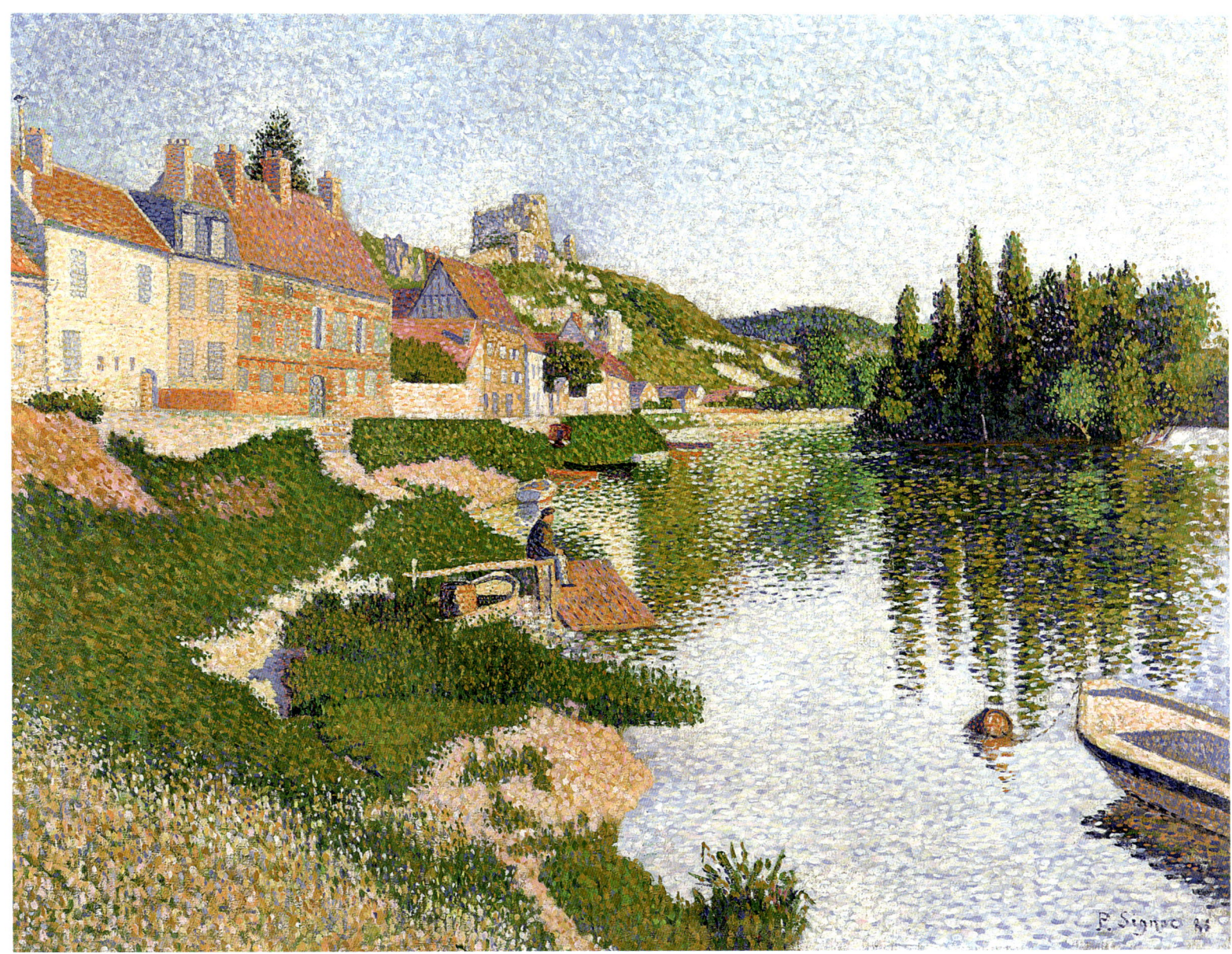

Paul Signac (1863–1935)

The River Bank, Petit-Andely

Les Andelys, la berge

Das Ufer von Petit-Andely

La orilla de Petit-Andely

La riva di Petit-Andely

Rivieroever in Petit-Andely

1886, Oil on canvas/Huile sur toile, 65 × 81 cm, Musée d'Orsay, Paris

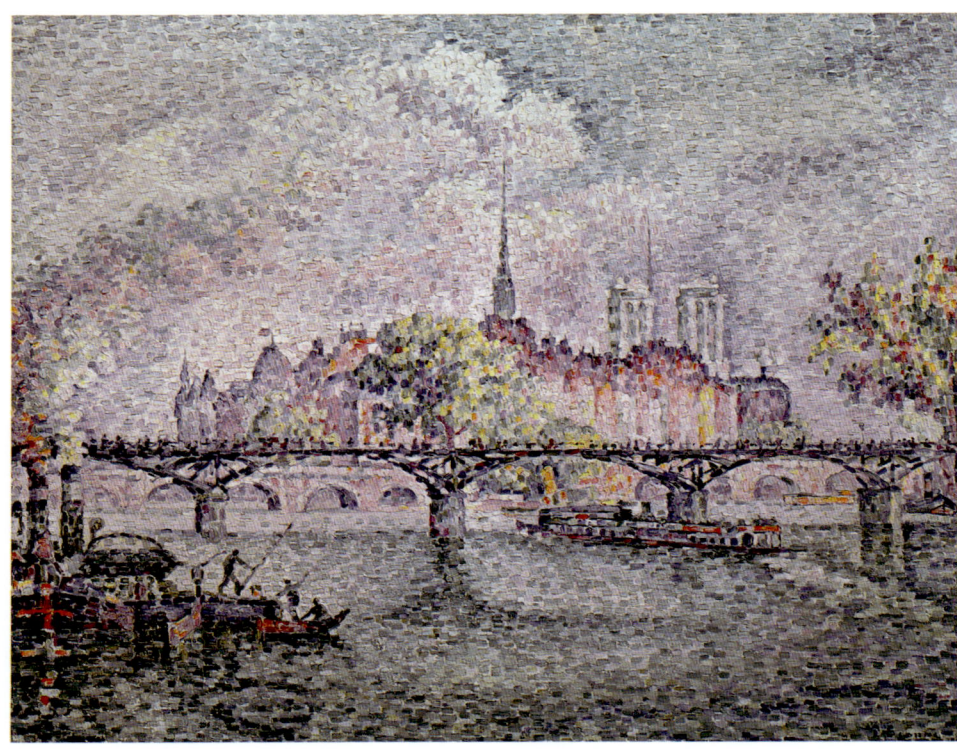

Paul Signac (1863–1935)

Ile de la Cité, Paris

Île de la Cité, Paris

Ile de la Cité, Paris

Ile de la Cité, París

Ile de la Cité, Parigi

Île de la Cité, Parijs

1912, Oil on canvas/Huile sur toile, 81 × 100 cm,
Museum Folkwang, Essen

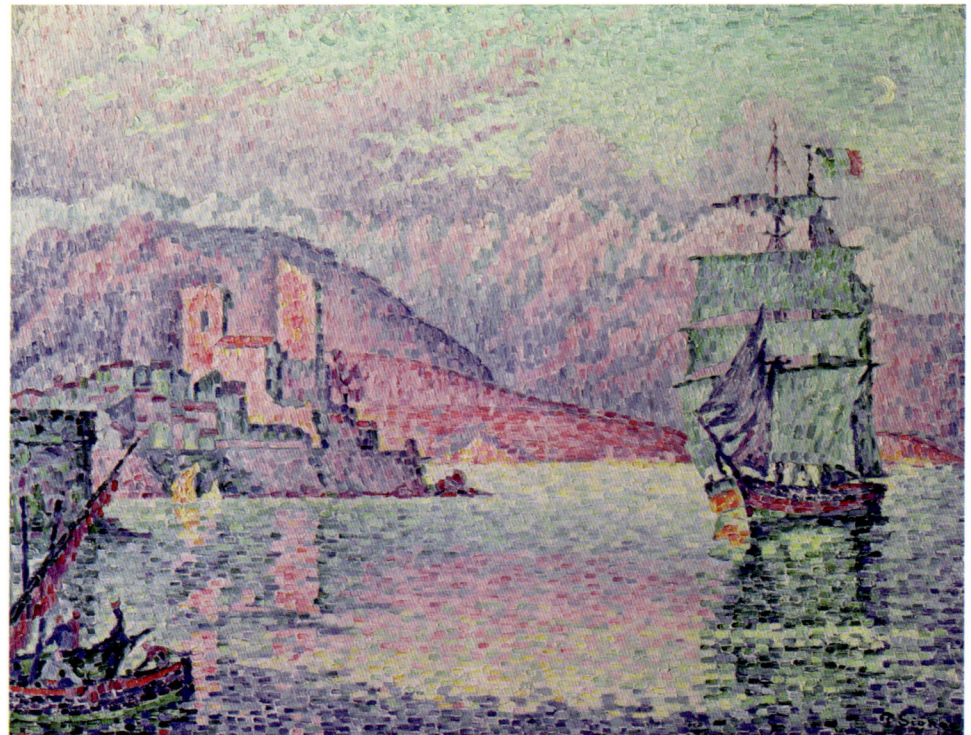

Paul Signac (1863–1935)

Antibes, Evening

Antibes le soir

Antibes am Abend

Antibes por la noche

Antibes di sera

Antibes bij avond

1914, Oil on canvas/Huile sur toile, 73 × 92 cm,
Musée des Beaux-Arts, Strasbourg

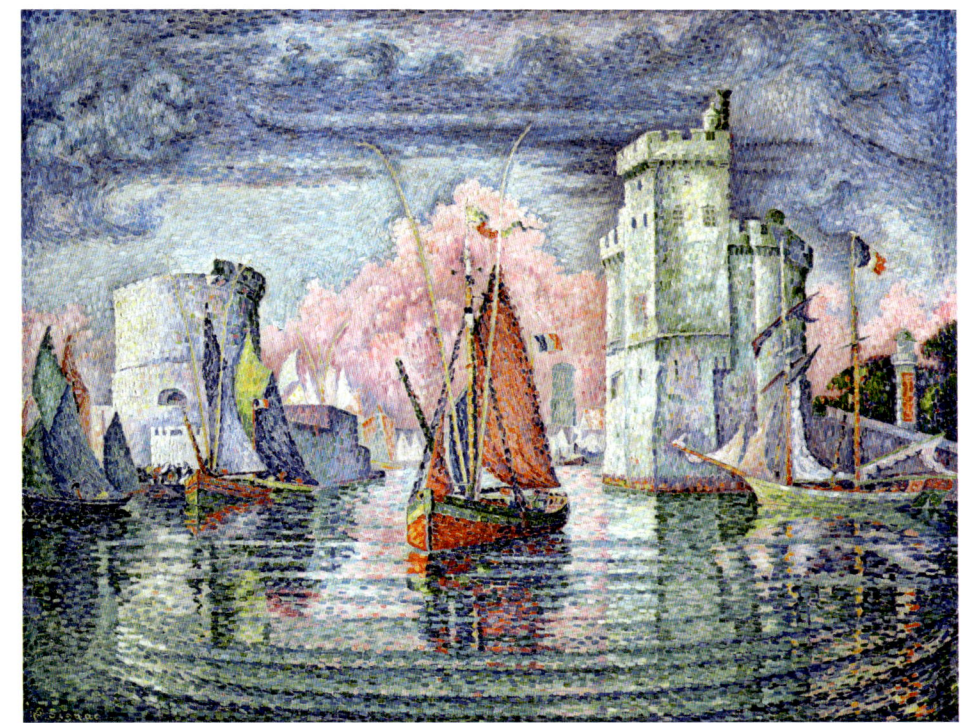

Paul Signac (1863–1935)

The Port at La Rochelle

Entrée du port de la Rochelle

Der Hafen von La Rochelle

Puerto de La Rochelle

Il porto di La Rochelle

De haven van La Rochelle

1921, Oil on canvas/Huile sur toile, 130,5 × 162 cm,
Musée d'Orsay, Paris

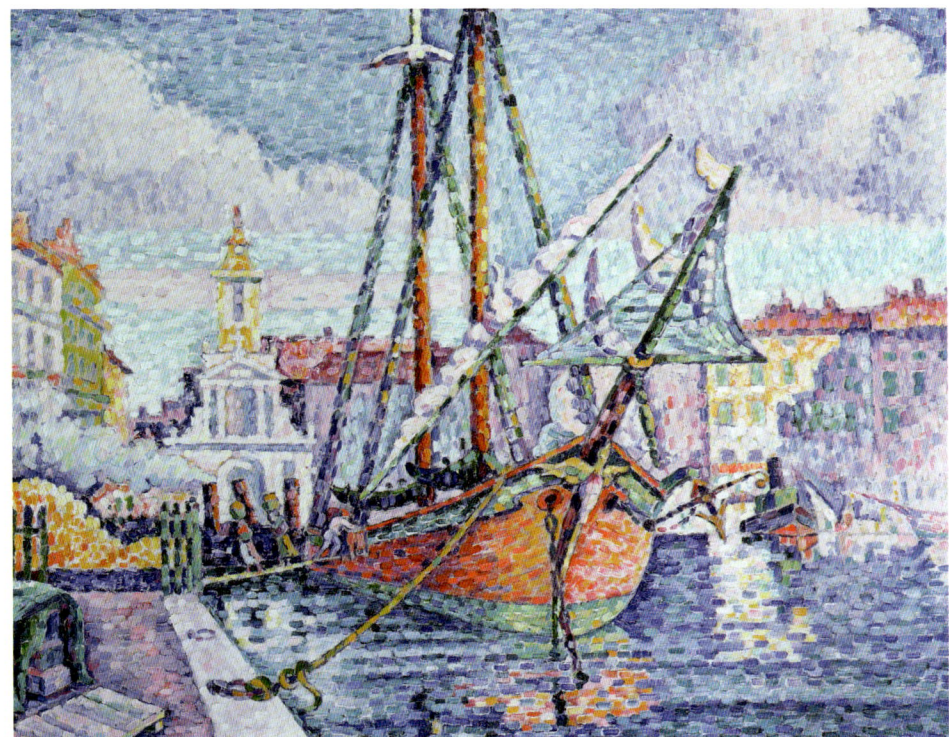

Paul Signac (1863–1935)

The Port

Le Port

Der Hafen

El puerto

Il porto

De haven

1923, Oil on canvas/Huile sur toile, 59,5 × 73,5 cm,
Private collection

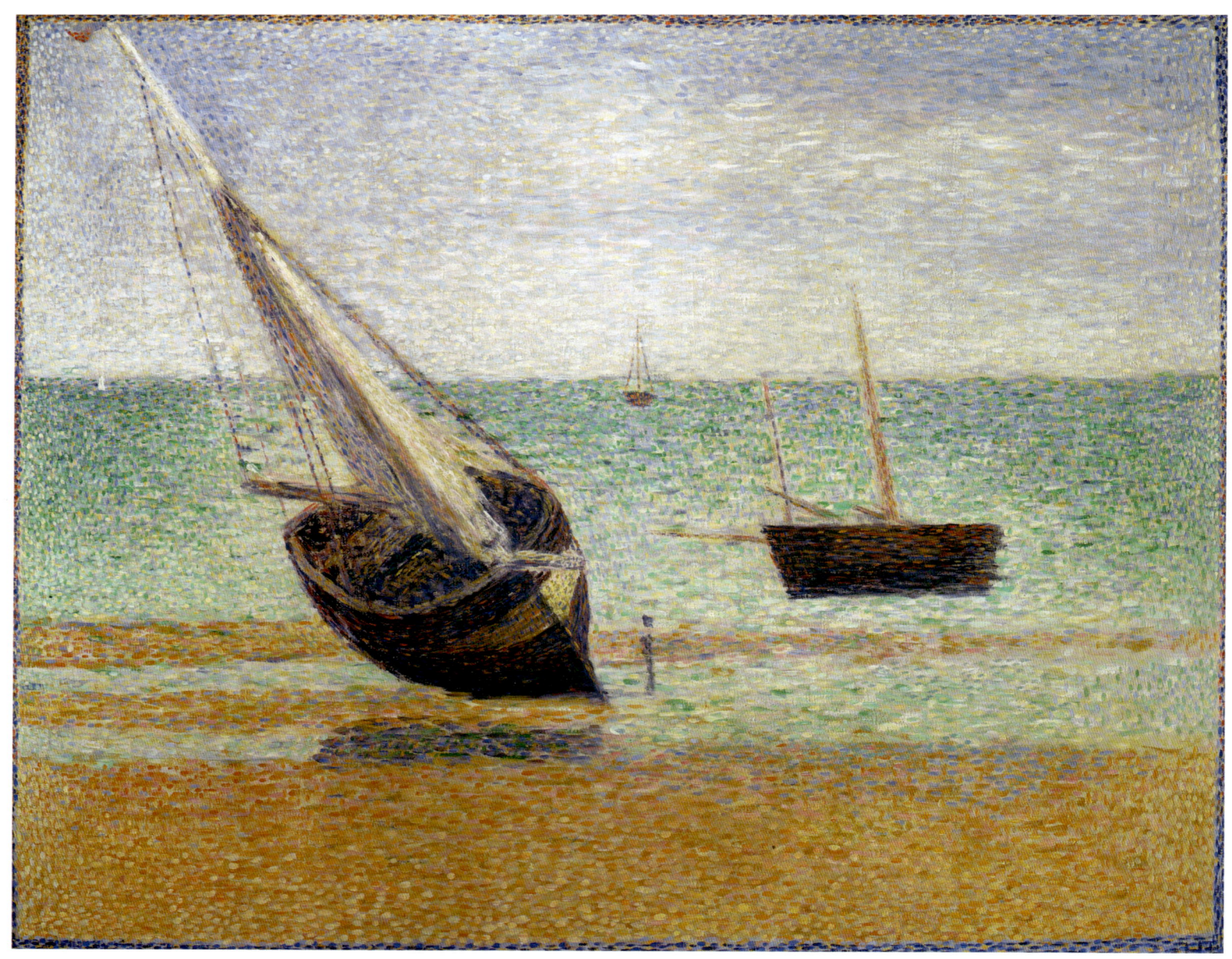

Georges Seurat (1859–1891)

Low Tide at Grandcamp

La Marée basse à Grandcamp

Ebbe bei Grandcamp

Marea baja en Grandcamp

Bassa marea a Grandcamp

Laagtij bij Grandcamp

1885, Oil on canvas/Huile sur toile, 65,5 × 81,5 cm, Private collection

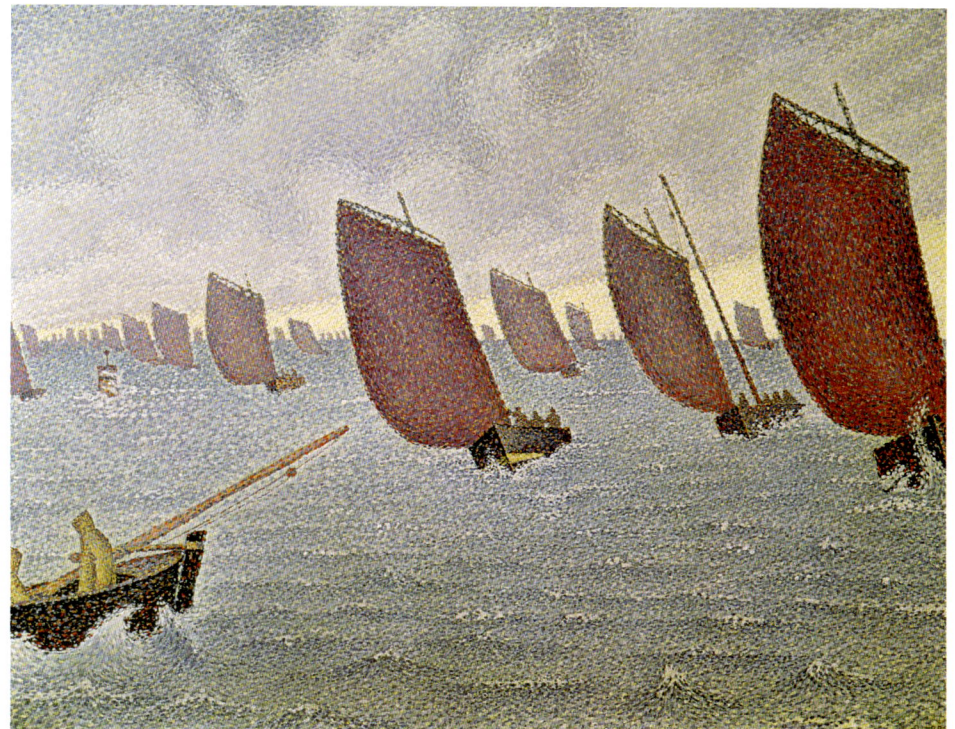

Paul Signac (1863–1935)

Breeze, Concarneau

Brise, Concarneau

Aufkommende Brise in Concarneau

La brisa se levanta en Concarneau

Brezza a Concarneau

Opkomende bries in Concarneau

1891, Oil on canvas/Huile sur toile, 66,5 × 82 cm, Private collection

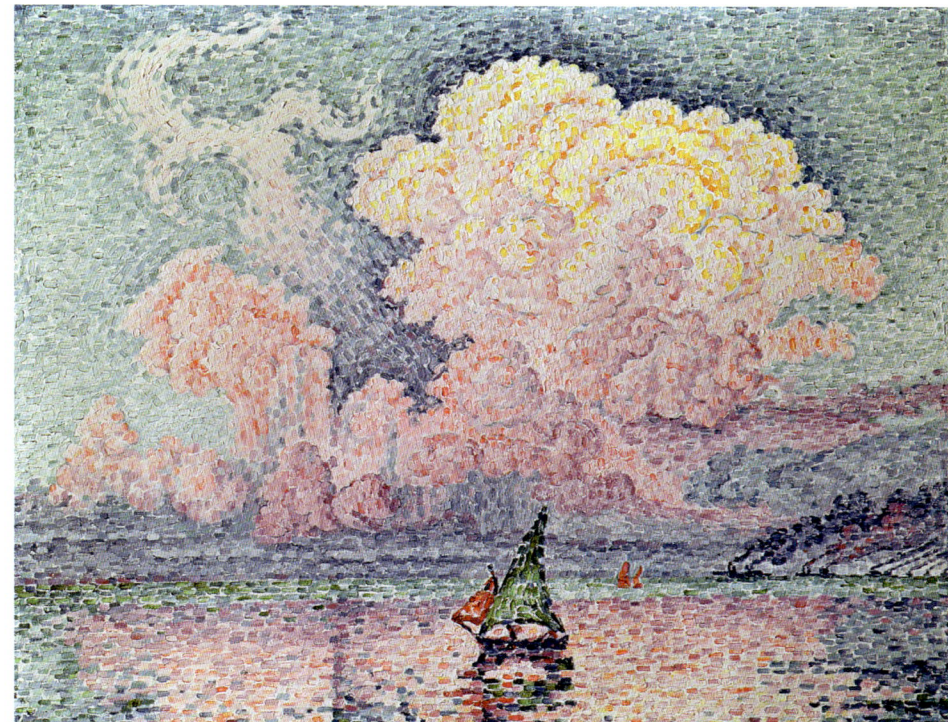

Paul Signac (1863–1935)

Antibes, the Pink Cloud

Antibes, le nuage rose

Antibes, die rosa Wolke

Antibes, la nube rosa

Antibes, la nuvola rosa

Antibes, de roze wolk

1916, Oil on canvas/Huile sur toile, 73 × 92 cm, Private collection

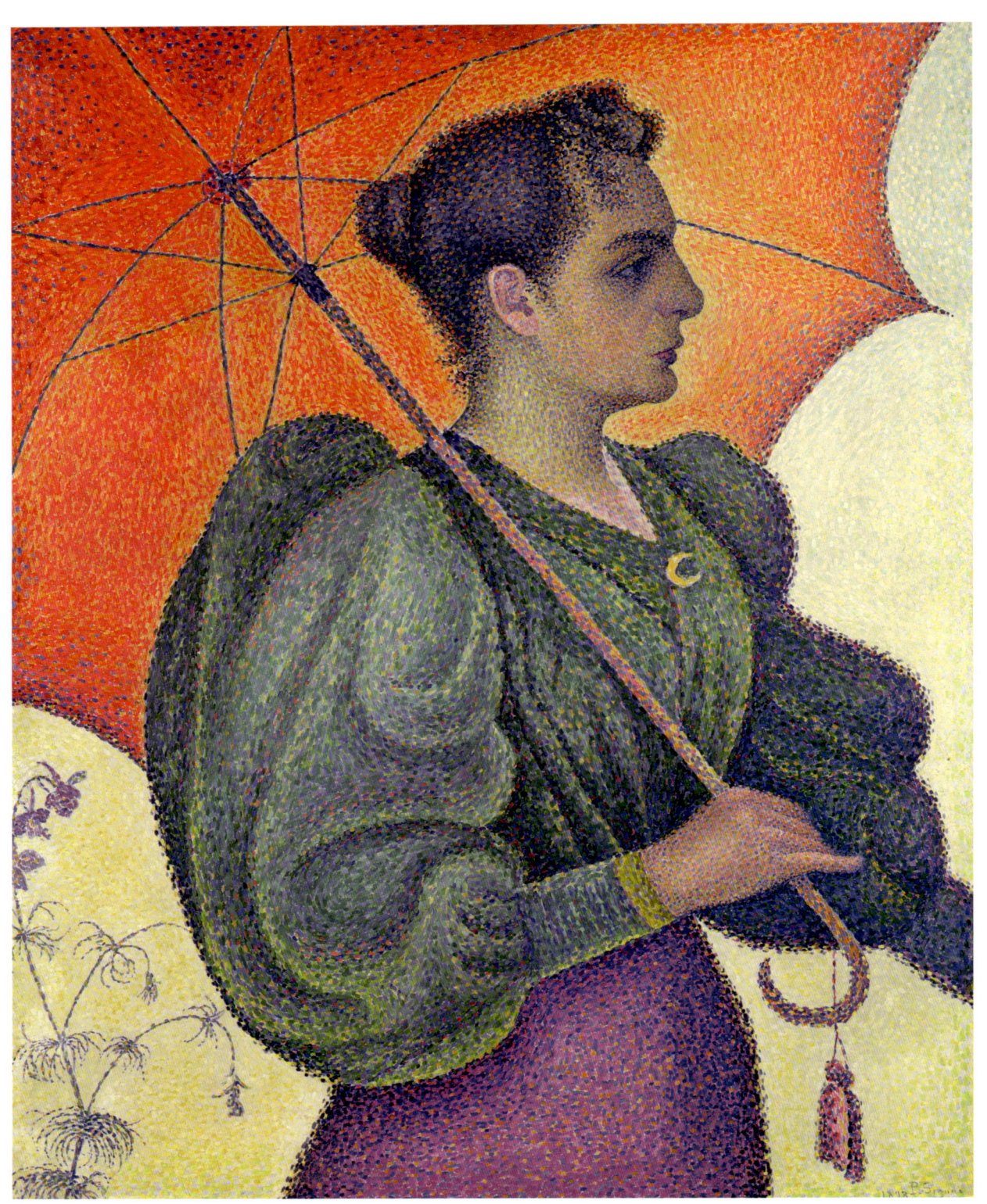

Paul Signac (1863–1935)

Woman with a Parasol

Femme à l'ombrelle

Frau mit Sonnenschirm

Mujer con sombrilla

Donna con parasole

Vrouw met parasol

1893, Oil on canvas/Huile sur toile, 81 × 65 cm, Musée d'Orsay, Paris

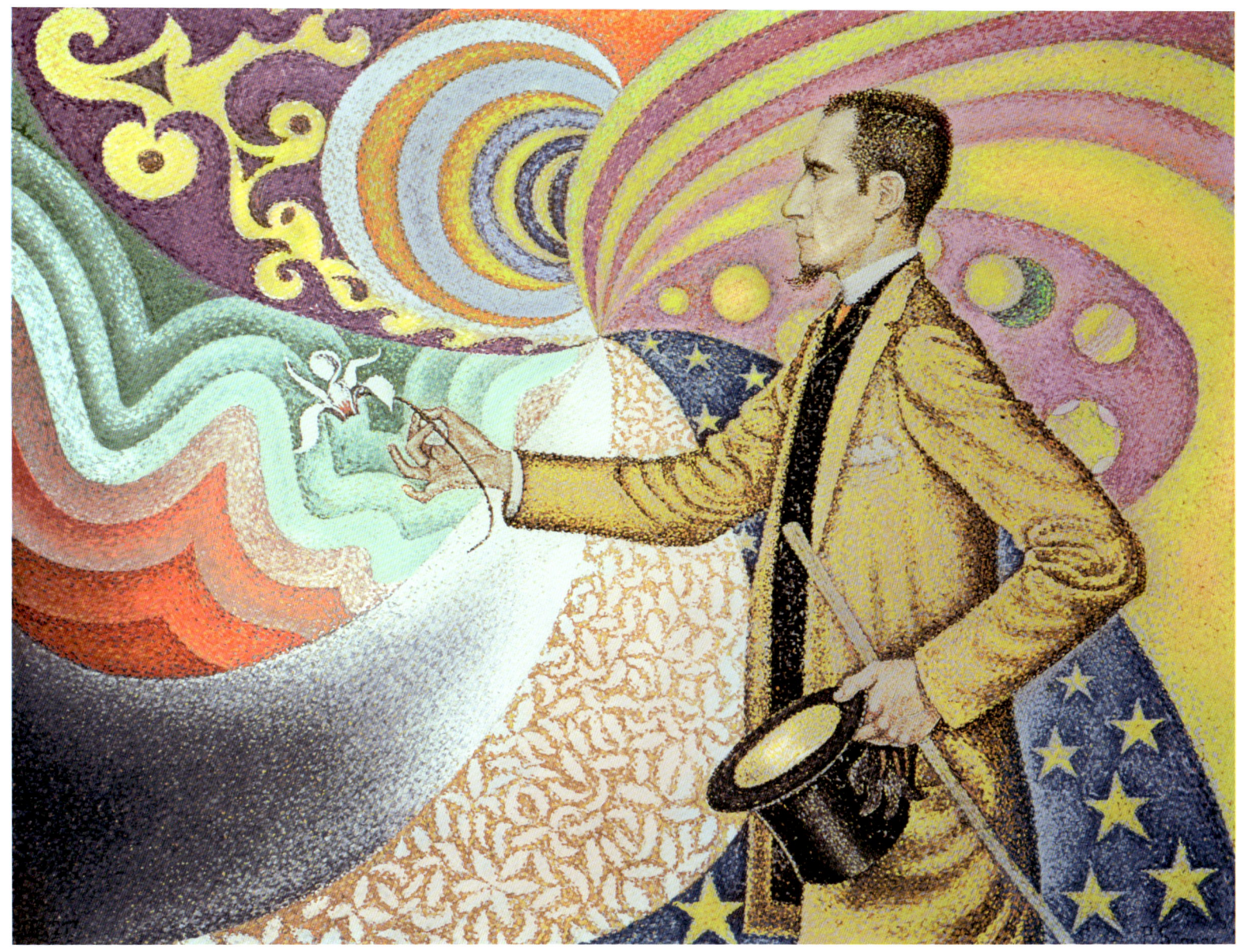

Paul Signac (1863–1935)

Opus 217. Against the Enamel of a Background Rhythmic with Beats and Angles, Tones and Tints, Portrait of Félix Fénéon in 1890

Sur l'émail d'un fond rythmique de mesures et d'angles, de tons et de teintes, Portrait de M. Félix Fénéon en 1890, Opus 217

Opus 217, auf einem nach Maßen, Winkeln, Farben und Helldunkelwerten rhythmisierten Hintergrund, Porträt von Félix Fénéon

Opus 217 sobre un fondo ritmificado con medidas, ángulos, colores y claroscuros, Retrato de Félix Fénéon

Opus 217, contro smalto di uno sfondo ritmico con beats e angoli, toni e tinte, ritratto di Félix Fénéon

Opus 217, op een ritmische ondergrond van maten en toon- en lichtwaarden. Portret van Félix Fénéon

1890, Oil on canvas/Huile sur toile, 73,5 × 92,5 cm, Museum of Modern Art, New York

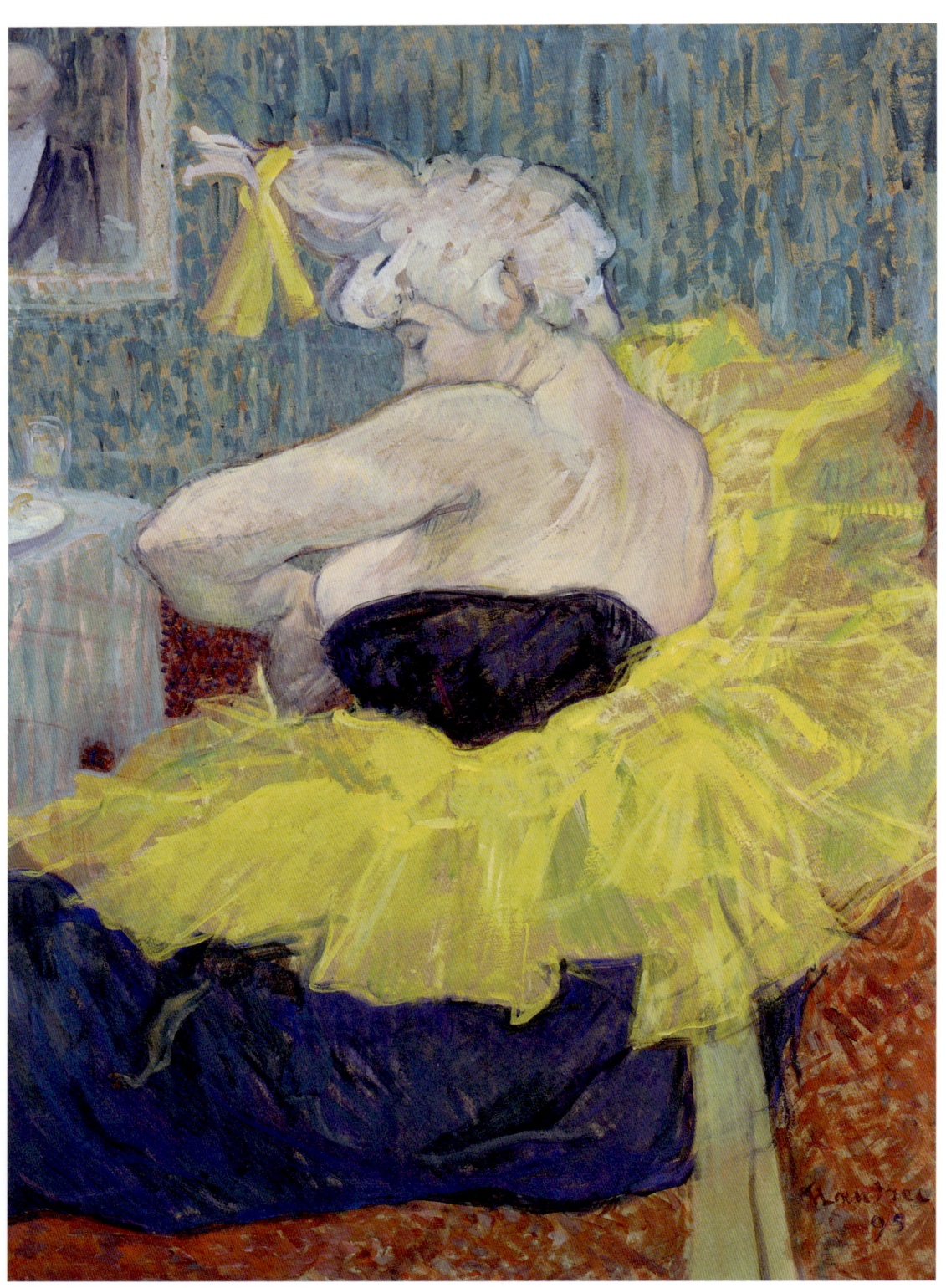

Henri de Toulouse-Lautrec (1864–1901)

The Clowness Cha-U-Kao in a Tutu

La Clownesse Cha-U-Kao

Die Clownin Cha-U-Kao im Tutu

La clown Cha-U-Kao en un tutú

La pagliaccia Cha-U-Kao in tutù

De vrouwelijke clown Cha-U-Kao in een tutu

1895, Oil on cardboard/Huile sur carton,
58 × 43 cm, Musée d'Orsay, Paris

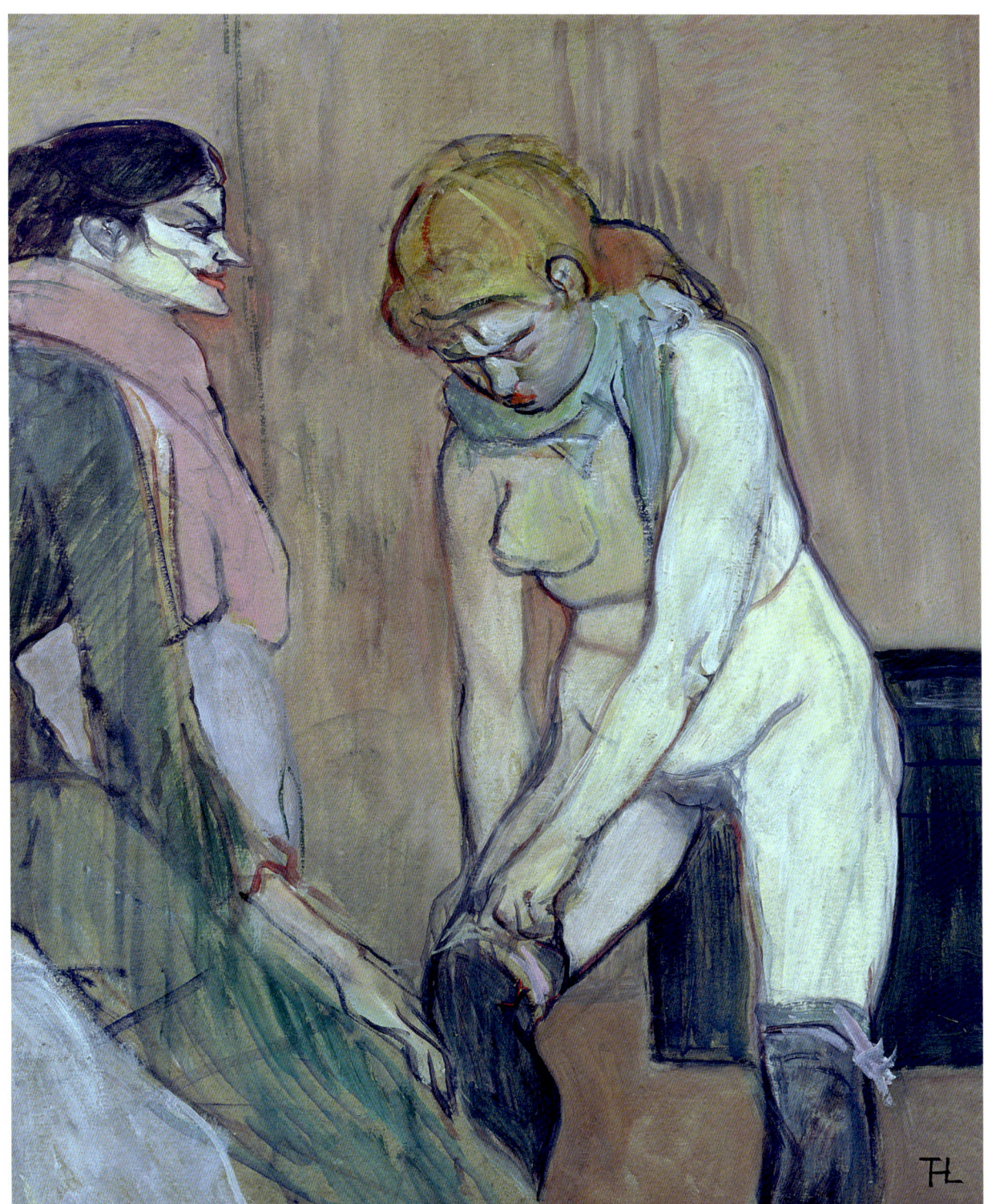

Henri de Toulouse-Lautrec (1864–1901)

Woman Putting on her Stocking, *or* Woman of the House

Femme tirant son bas *ou* femme de maison

Frau beim Strümpfeanziehen *oder* Die Frau des Hauses

Mujer poniéndose las medias *o* La mujer de la casa

Donna che si infila una calza *o* Donna della casa

Vrouw bij het aantrekken van kousen, *of*: De vrouw des huizes

c. 1894, Oil on cardboard/Huile sur carton, 58 × 46 cm, Musée d'Orsay, Paris

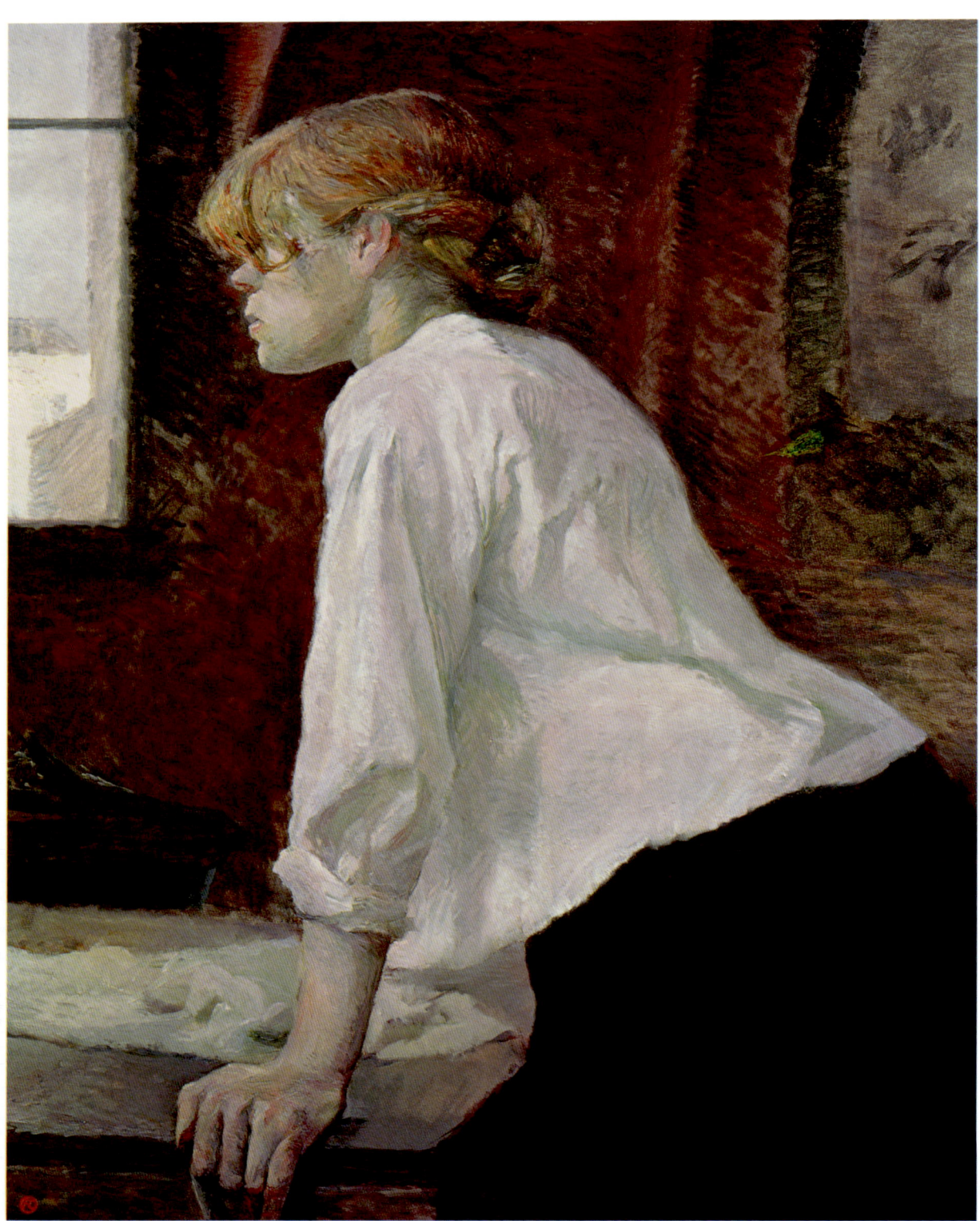

**Henri de Toulouse-Lautrec
(1864–1901)**

The Laundress

La Blanchisseuse

Die Wäscherin

La lavandera

La lavandaia

De wasvrouw

1889, Oil on canvas/Huile sur toile,
93 × 75 cm, Private collection

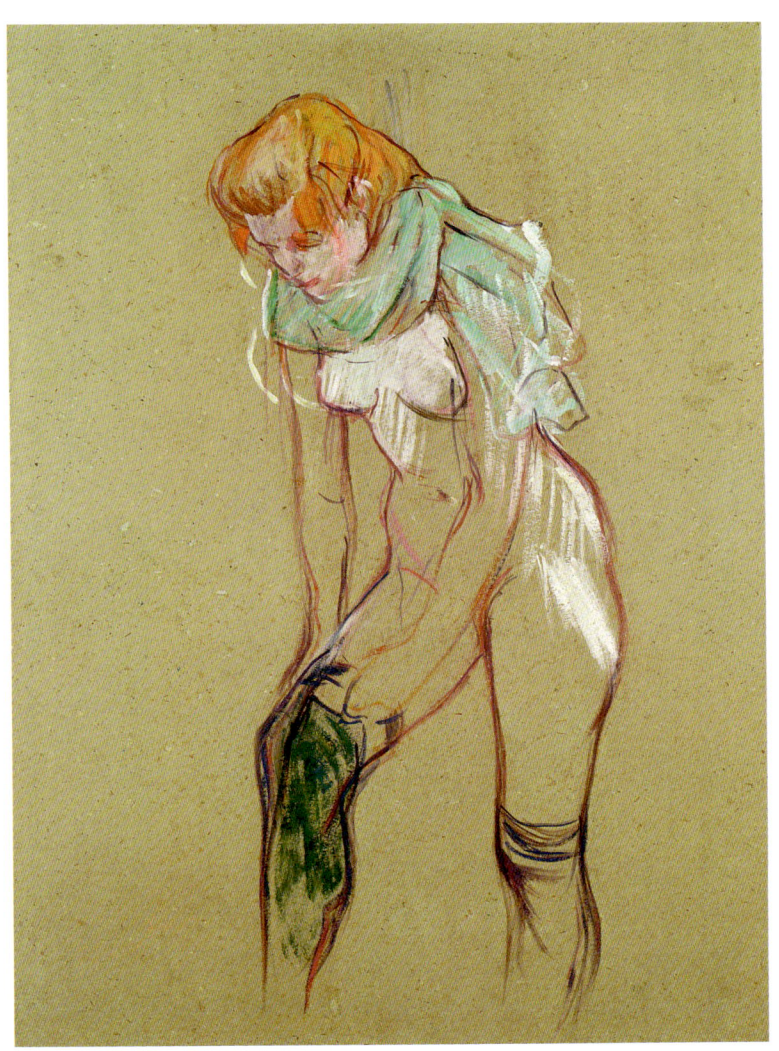

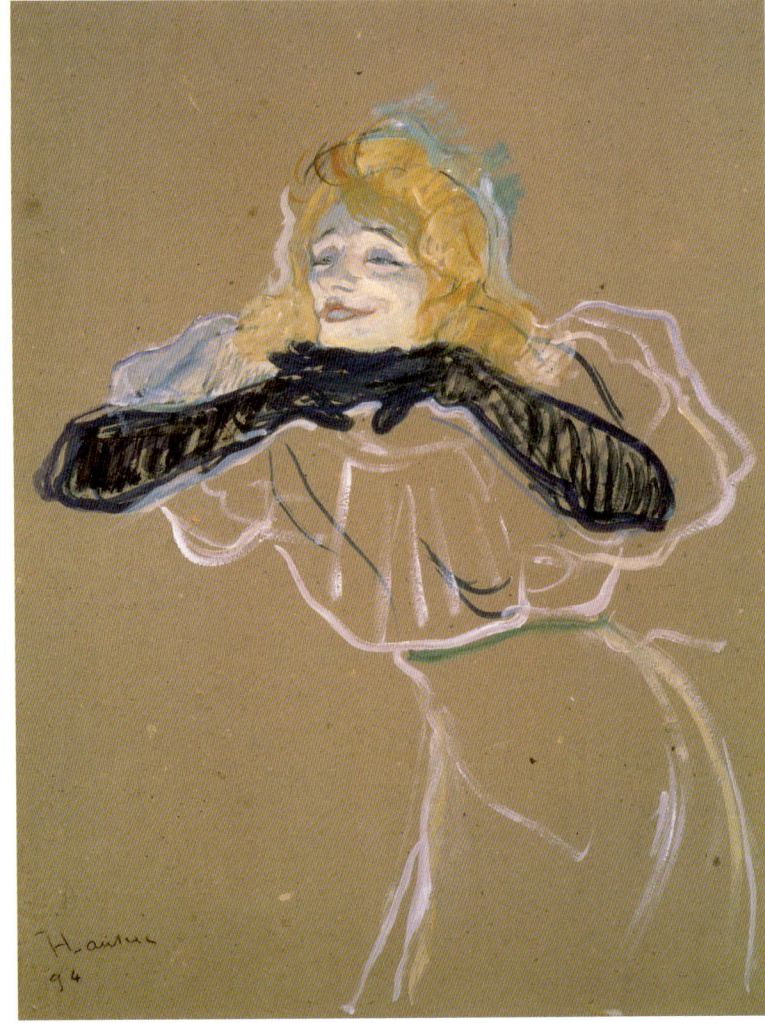

Henri de Toulouse-Lautrec (1864–1901)

Woman Pulling Up her Stocking

Femme qui tire son bas

Frau, sich die Strümpfe hochziehend

Mujer subiéndose las medias

Donna che si infila una calza

Vrouw die haar kousen optrekt

1894, Oil on cardboard/Huile sur carton, 61,5 × 44,5 cm,
Musée Toulouse-Lautrec, Albi

Henri de Toulouse-Lautrec (1864–1901)

Yvette Guilbert

1894, Oil on cardboard/Huile sur carton, 57 × 42 cm,
Pushkin State Museum of Fine Arts, Moscow

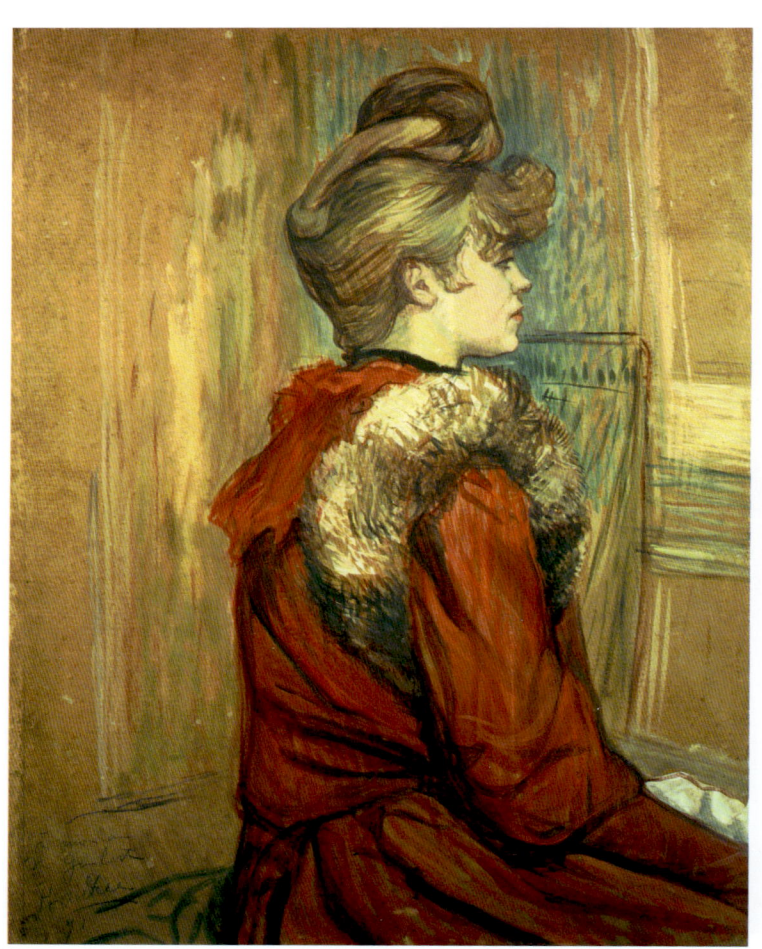

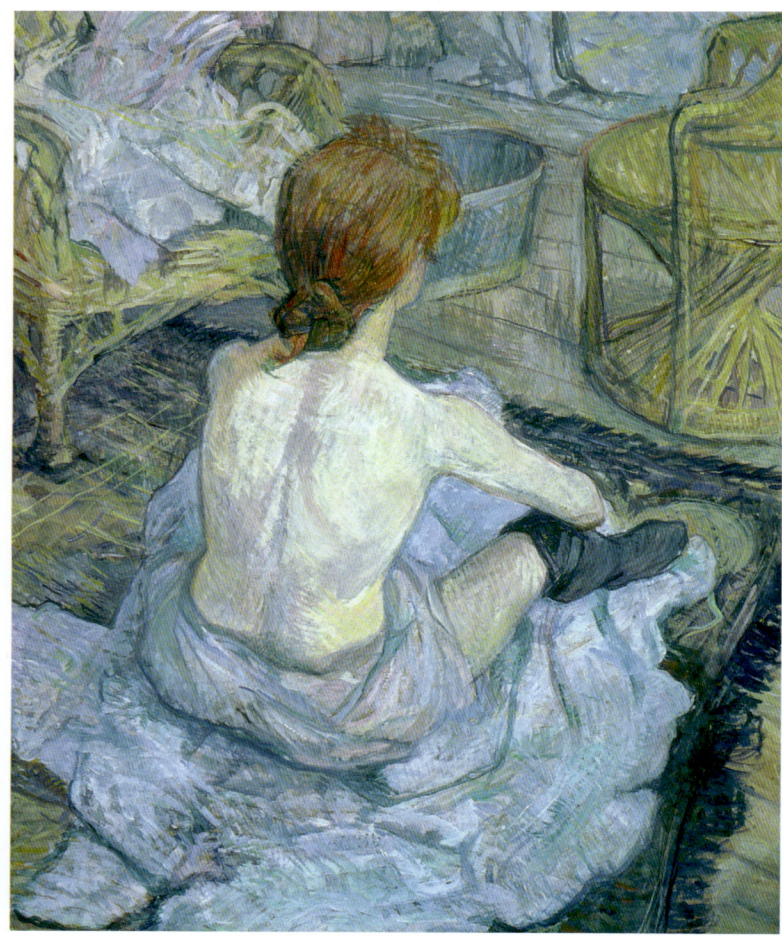

Henri de Toulouse-Lautrec (1864–1901)

Girl with a Fur Stole

Mademoiselle Jeanne Fontaine

Mädchen mit Pelzstola, Mademoiselle Jeanne Fontaine

Joven con estola de pelo, Mademoiselle Jeanne Fontaine

Ragazza con stola di pelliccia, Mademoiselle Jeanne Fontaine

Meisje met bontstola, mademoiselle Jeanne Fontaine

1891, Oil pastel on board/Pastel à l'huile sur carton, 67,5 × 52,8 cm, Private collection

Henri de Toulouse-Lautrec (1864–1901)

Woman at her Toilet

La Toilette

Frau bei der Toilette

Mujer en el baño

Donna alla toeletta

Vrouw bij het toilet

1898, Oil on canvas/Huile sur toile, 67 × 54 cm, Musée d'Orsay, Paris

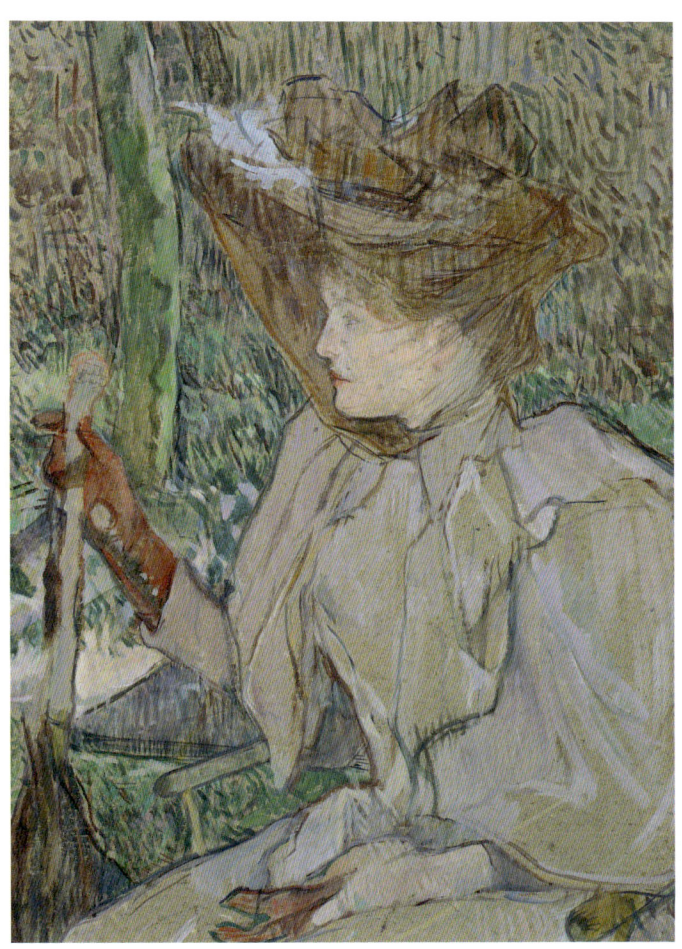

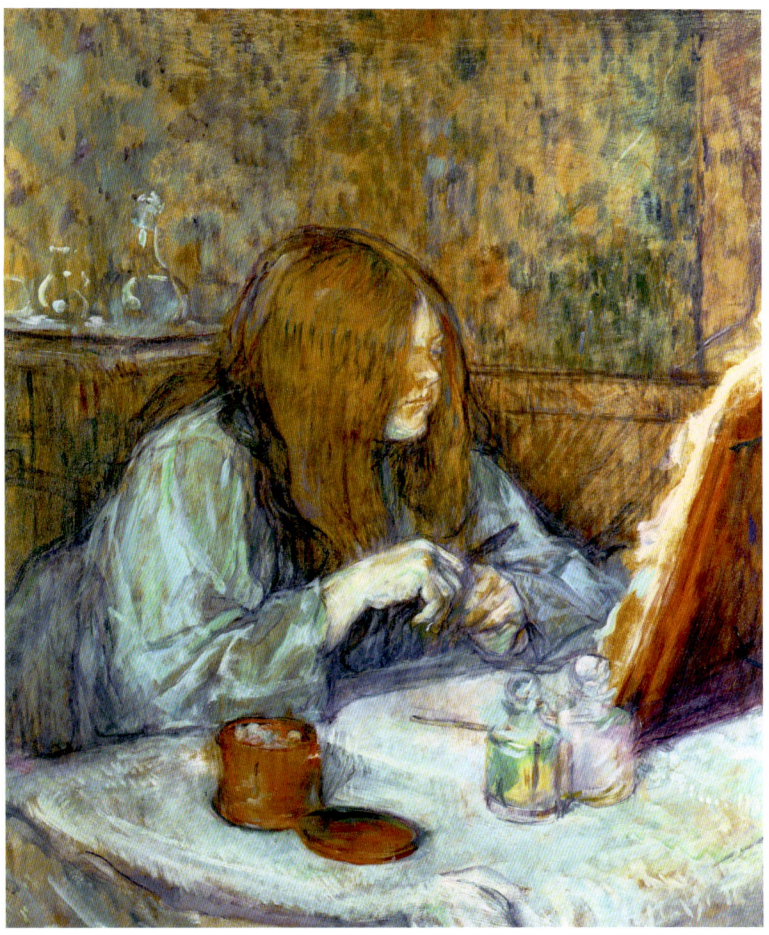

Henri de Toulouse-Lautrec (1864–1901)

Woman with Gloves

La Femme aux gants

Frau mit Handschuhen

Mujer con guantes

Donna con i guanti

Vrouw met handschoenen

1890, Oil on cardboard/Huile sur carton, 54 × 40 cm, Musée d'Orsay, Paris

Henri de Toulouse-Lautrec (1864–1901)

Madame Poupoule at her Toilet

Madame Poupoule à sa toilette

Madame Poupoule bei ihrer Toilette

Madame Poupoule en su baño

Madame Poupoule alla toeletta

Madame Poupoule bij het toilet

1898, Oil on wood/Huile sur bois, 60,8 × 49,6 cm, Musée Toulouse-Lautrec, Albi

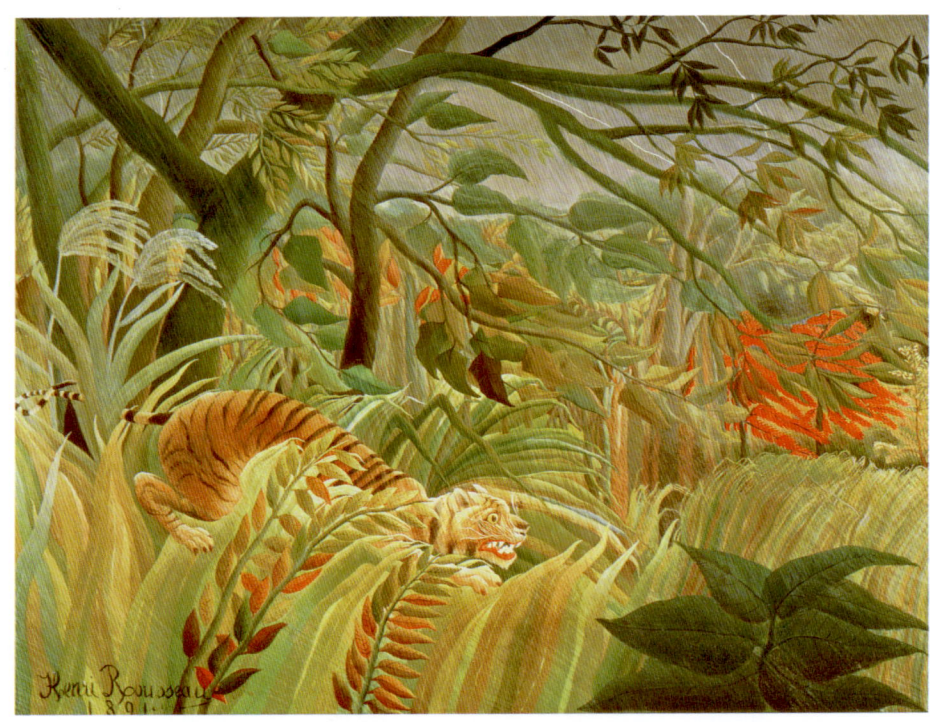

Henri Rousseau (1844–1910)

Tiger in a Tropical Storm (Surprised!)

Tigre dans une tempête tropicale

Tiger im tropischen Sturm

Tigre en una tormenta tropical

Tigre nella giungla in tempesta

Tijger in tropische storm

1891, Oil on canvas/Huile sur toile, 129,8 × 161,9 cm,
National Gallery, London

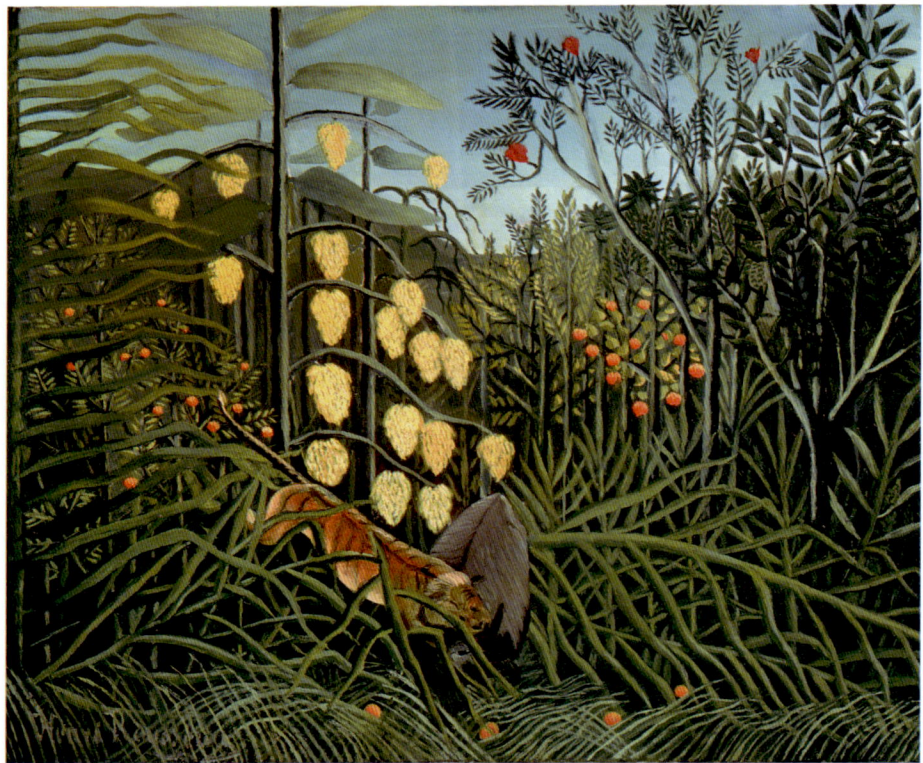

Henri Rousseau (1844–1910)

Tropical Forest: Battling Tiger and Buffalo

Dans la forêt tropicale, combat du tigre et du buffle

Tropischer Urwald: Tiger und Büffel im Kampf

La selva tropical: tigres y búfalos peleando

Foresta tropicale: la lotta tra una tigre e un bufalo

Tropisch oerwoud: vechtende tijger en buffel

c. 1908, Oil on canvas/Huile sur toile, 46 × 55 cm,
State Hermitage Museum, St Petersburg

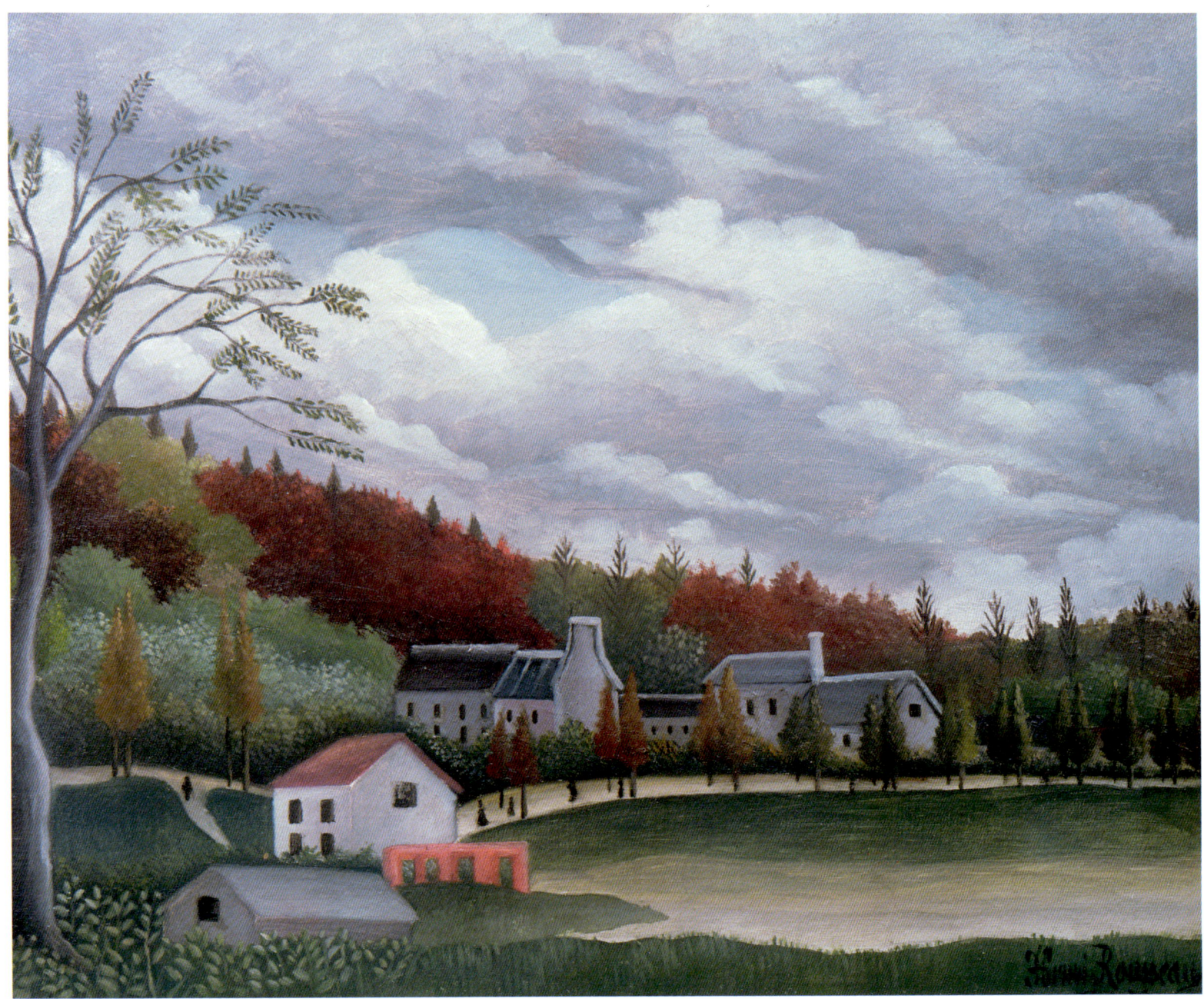

Henri Rousseau (1844–1910)

The Bievre at Gentilly Der Bièvre in Gentilly La Bièvre a Gentilly

La Bièvre à Gentilly El Bièvre en Gentilly De Bièvre in Gentilly

c. 1895, Oil on canvas/Huile sur toile, 38 × 46 cm, Private collection

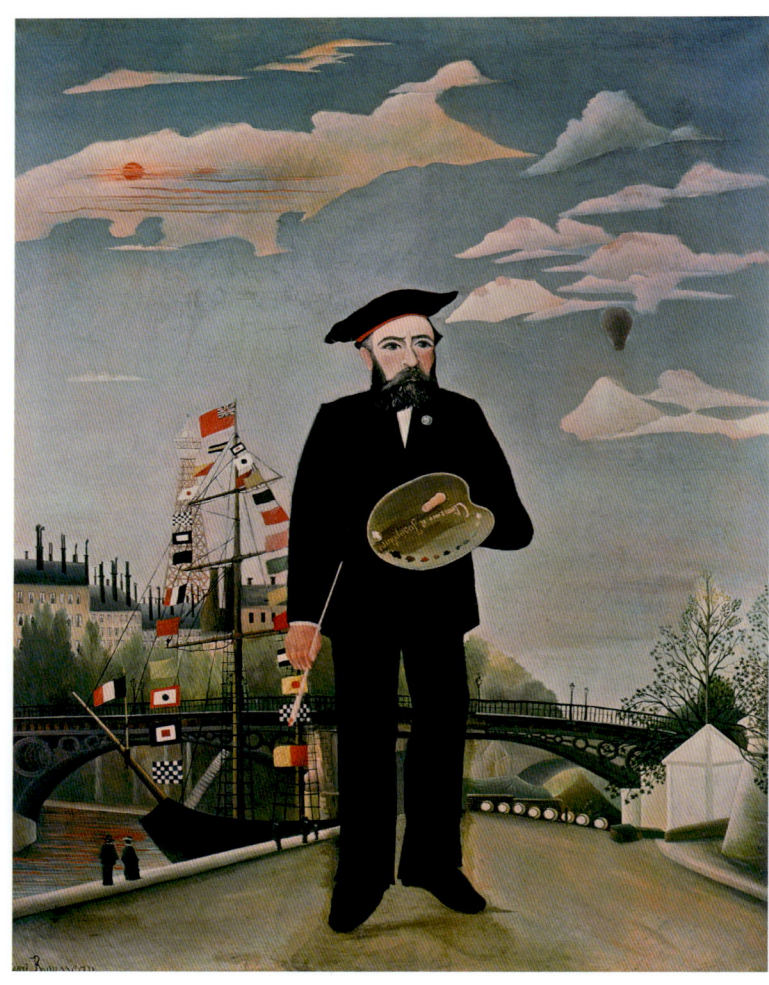

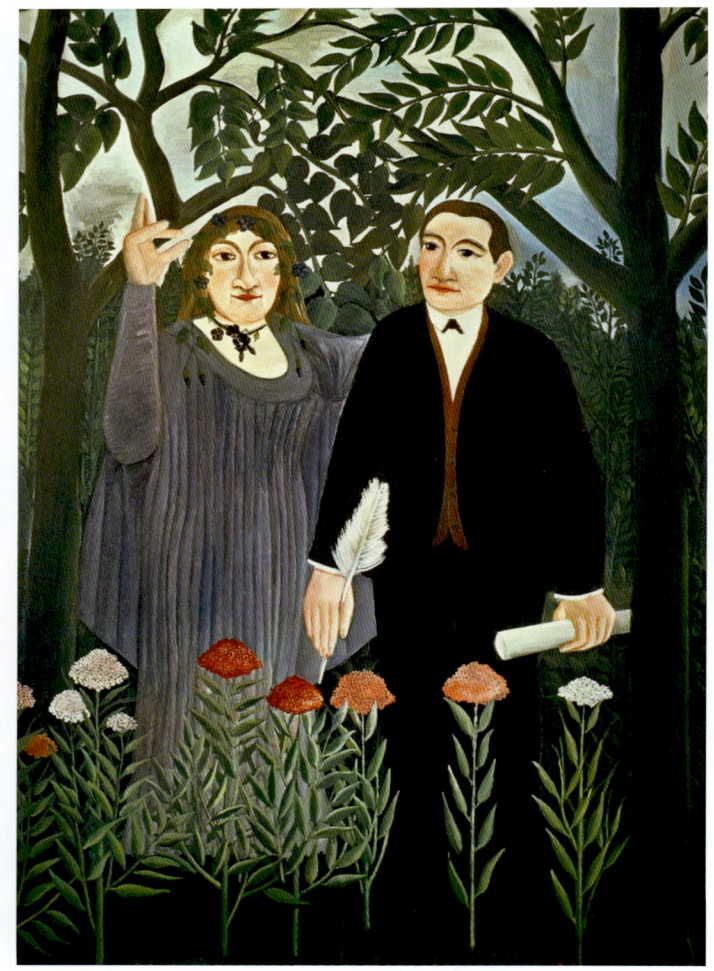

Henri Rousseau (1844–1910)

Self Portrait, from L'île Saint-Louis

Moi-même

Selbstporträt, von der L'île Saint-Louis aus

Autorretrato, visto desde la isla de Saint-Louis

Autoritratto dall'île Saint-Louis

Zelfportret, gezien vanaf het Île Saint-Louis

1890, Oil on canvas/Huile sur toile, 146 × 113 cm, Národní galerie, Praha

Henri Rousseau (1844–1910)

The Muse Inspiring the Poet

La Muse inspirant le poète

Die Muse inspiriert den Dichter

Las musas inspiran al poeta

La musa ispira il poeta

De muze inspireert de dichter

1909, Oil on canvas/Huile sur toile, 146,2 × 96,9 cm, Kunstmuseum, Basel

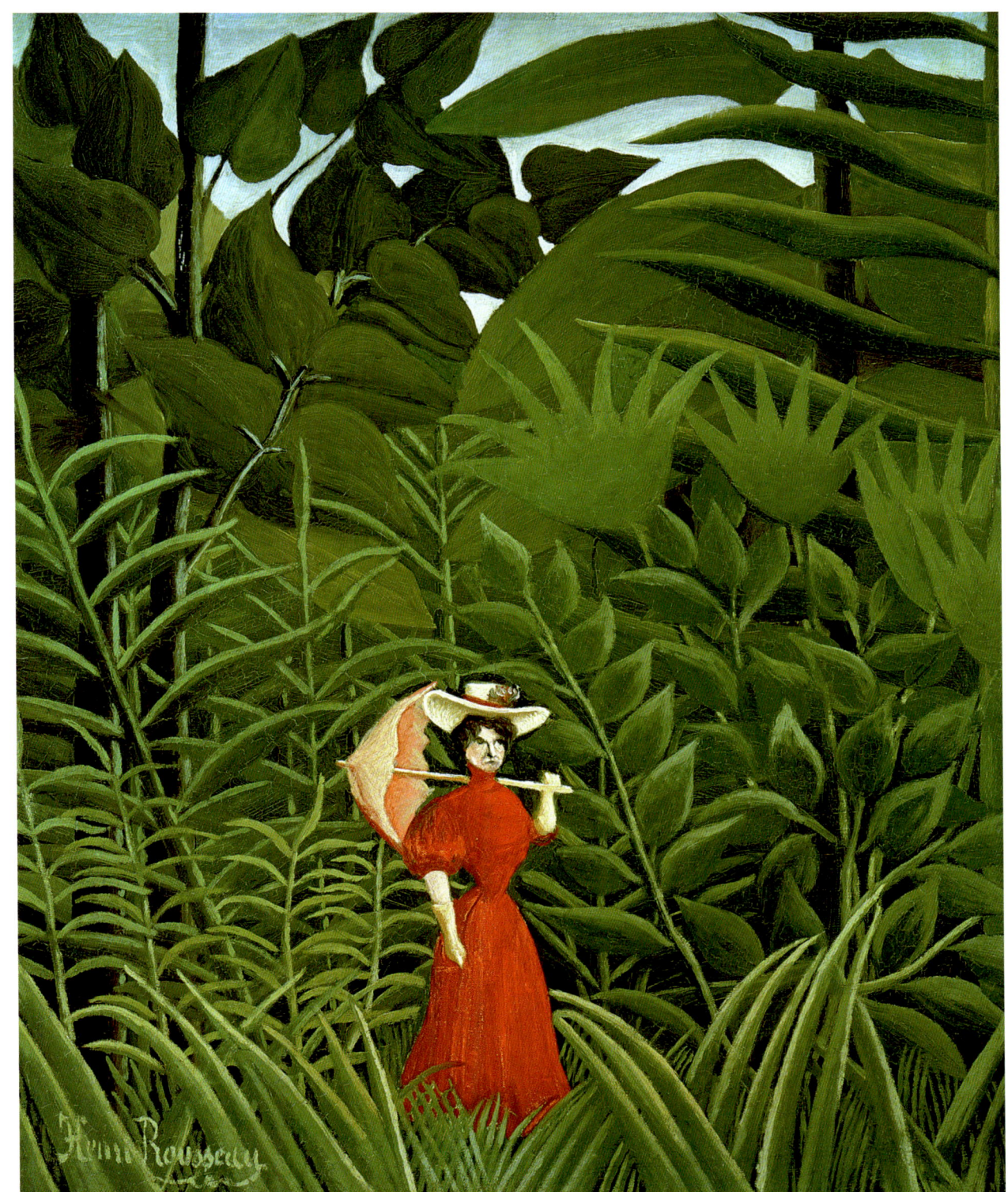

**Henri Rousseau
(1844–1910)**

Woman in Red in the Forest

Femme en rouge
dans la forêt

Frau in Rot im Wald

Mujer de rojo en el bosque

Donna in rosso nel bosco

Vrouw in het rood
in het bos

c. 1907, Oil on canvas/Huile
sur toile, Private collection

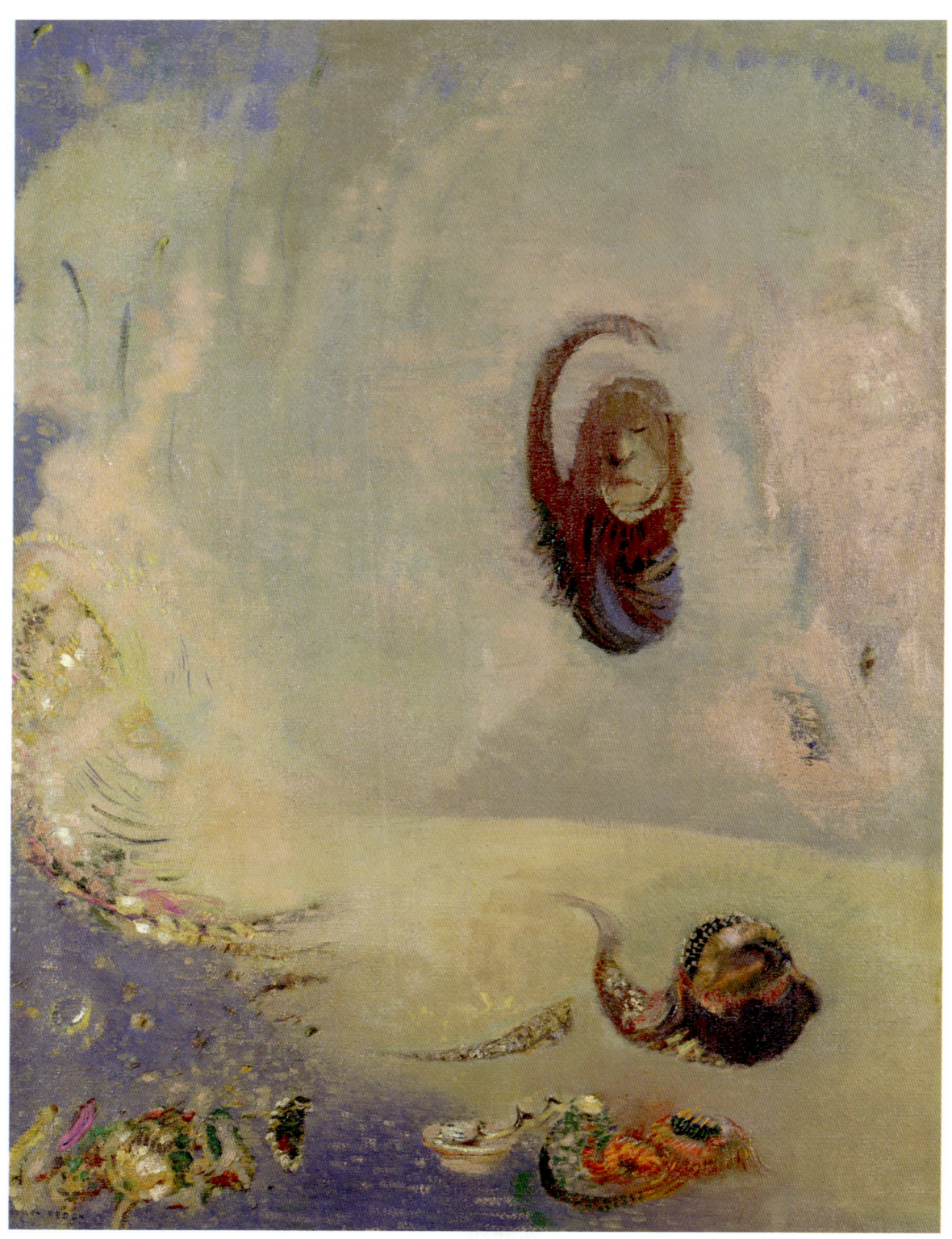

Odilon Redon (1840–1916)

Oannès

c. 1910, Oil on canvas/Huile sur toile,
66 × 51,3 cm, Kröller-Müller Museum,
Otterlo

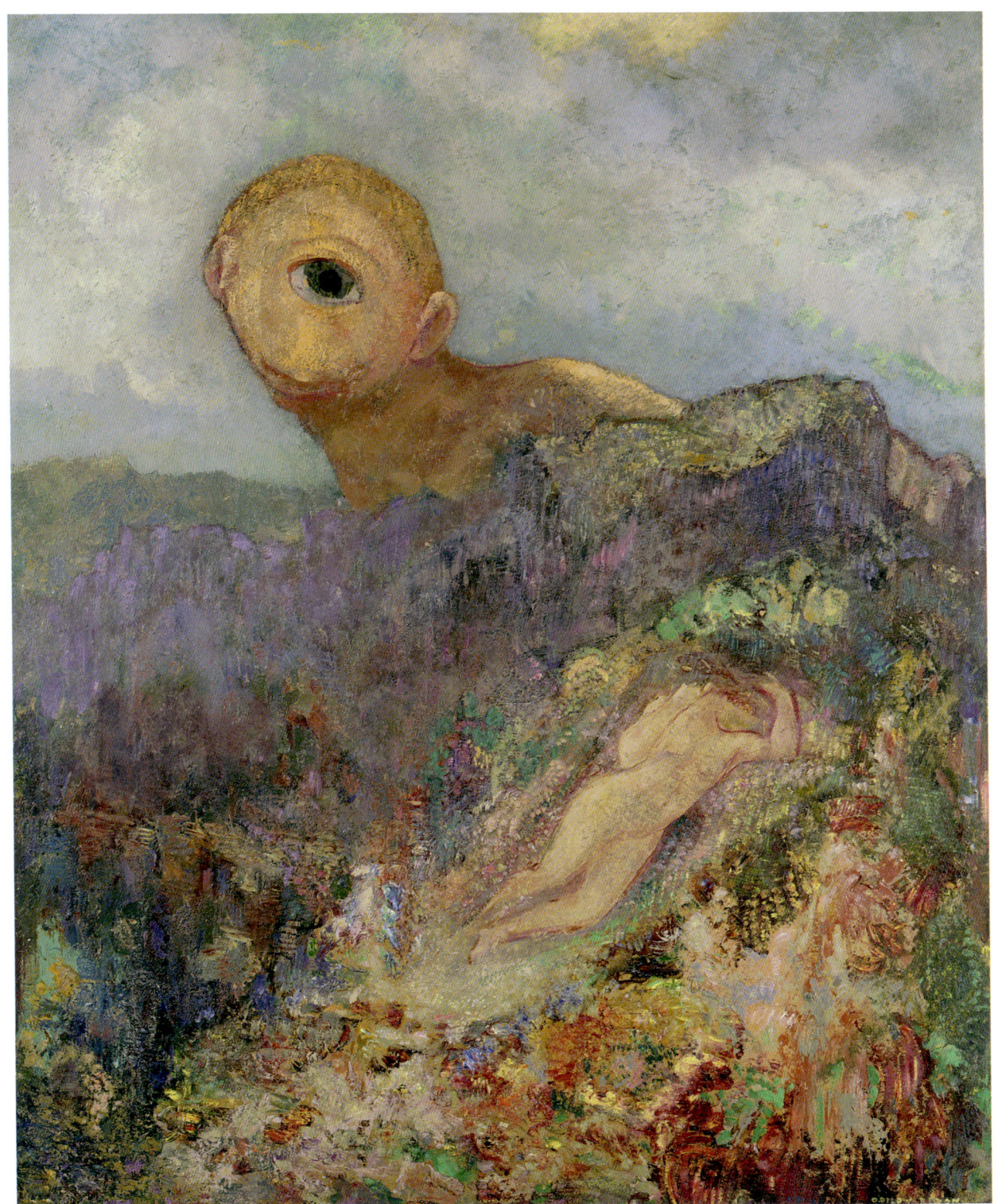

Odilon Redon (1840–1916)

The Cyclops

Le Cyclope

Der Zyklop

El cíclope

Il ciclope

De cycloop

c. 1914, Oil on cardboard
mounted on wood/Huile sur
carton marouflé sur bois,
64 × 51 cm, Kröller-Müller
Museum, Otterlo

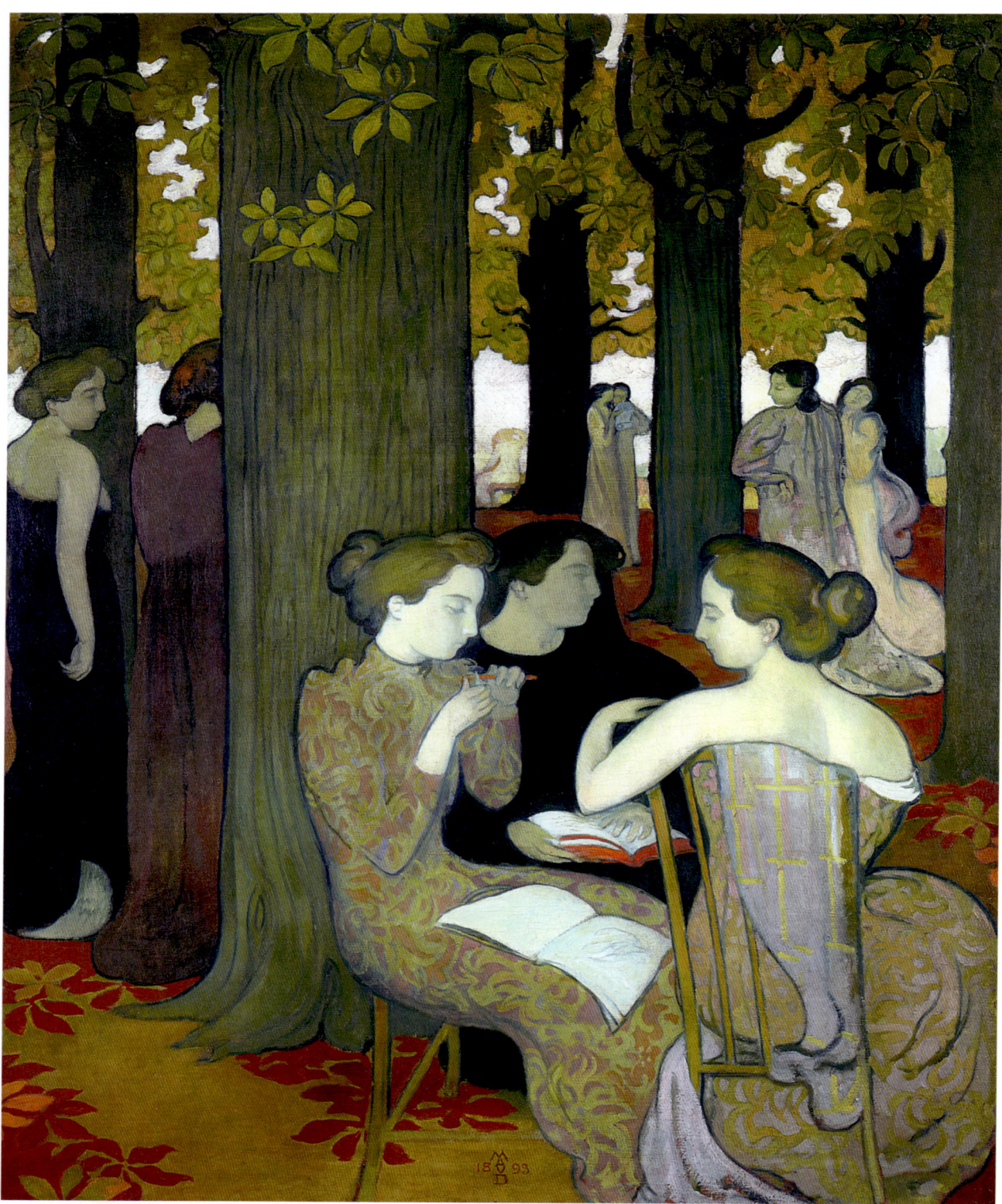

**Maurice Denis
(1870−1943)**

The Muses

Les Muses

Die Musen

Las musas

Le Muse

De muzes

1893, Oil on canvas/Huile sur
toile, 171 × 137,5 cm, Musée
d'Orsay, Paris

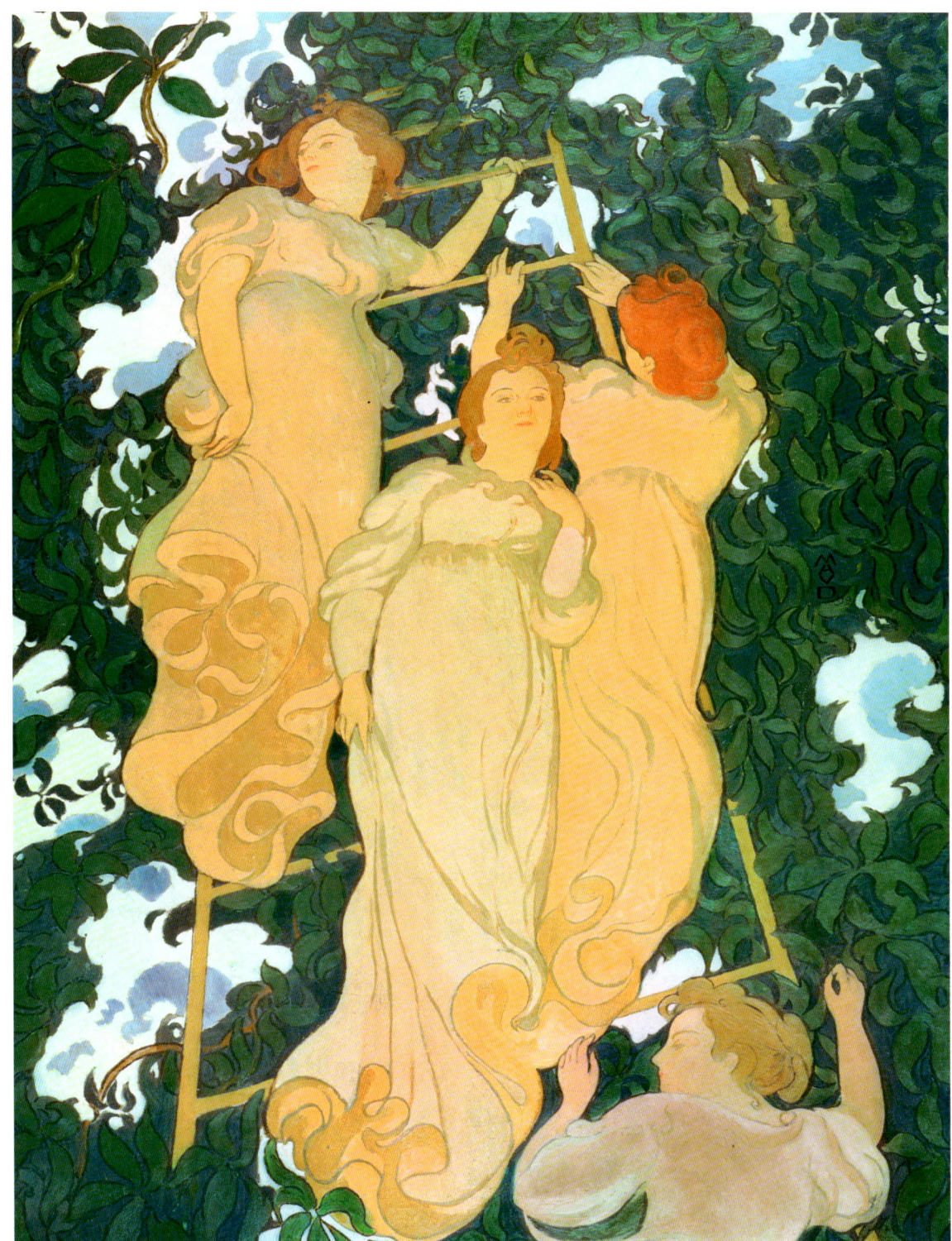

Maurice Denis (1870–1943)

Poetic Arabesques

L'Échelle dans le feuillage *ou* Arabesques poétiques

Die Leiter im Laub *oder* poetische Arabesken

Arabescos poéticos

La scala tra il fogliame *o* Arabeschi poetici

Ladder in het gebladerte *of:* Poëtische arabesken

1892, Oil on canvas/Huile sur toile, 235 × 1725 cm, Musée Maurice Denis, Saint-Germain-en-Laye

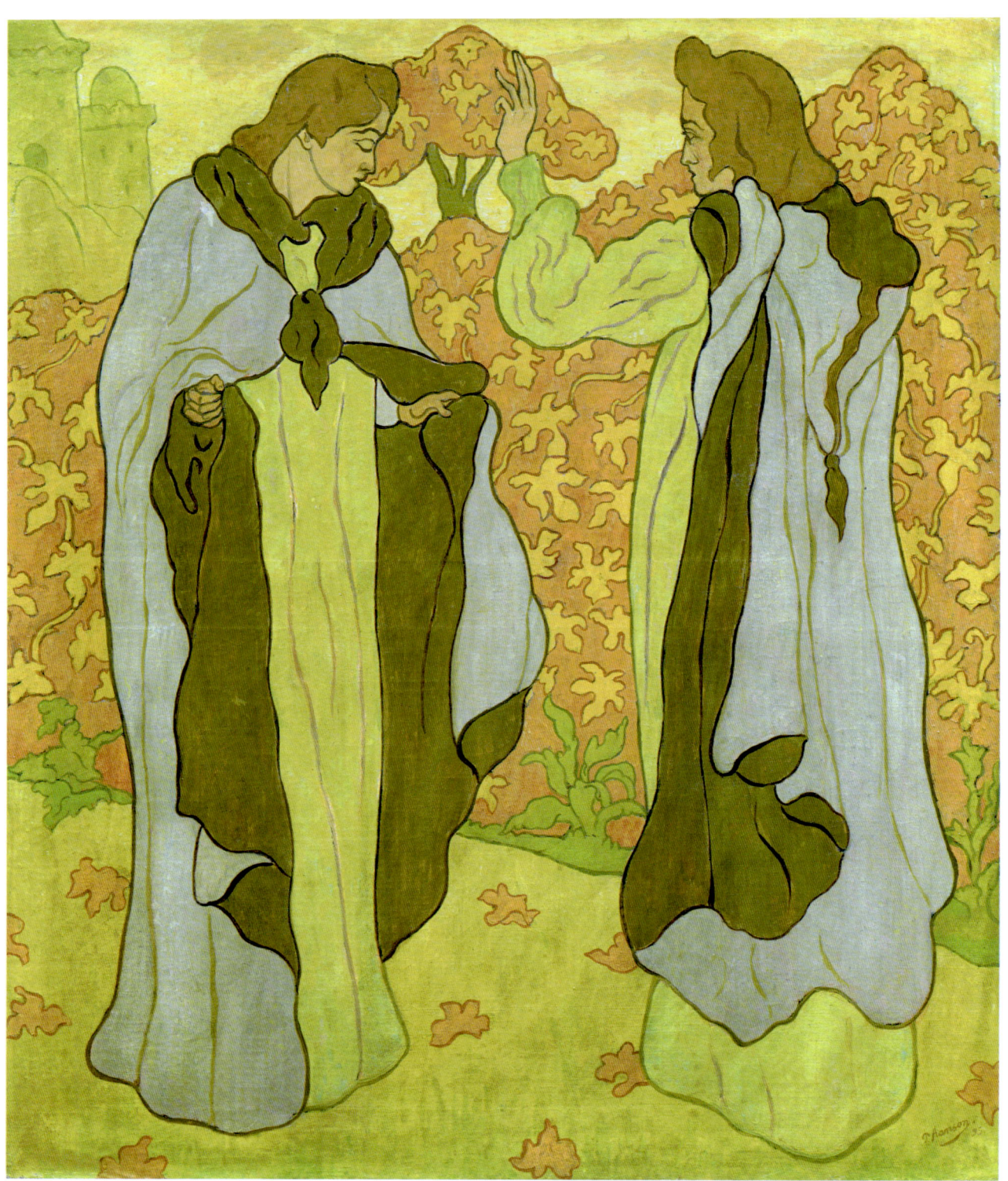

Paul Ranson
(1861–1909)

The Two Graces

Les Deux Grâces

Die zwei Grazien

Las dos Gracias

Le due Grazie

De Twee Gratiën

1895, Oil on canvas/Huile
sur toile, 85 × 70,5 cm,
Private collection

Index